DISMEMBERING THE WHOLE

ANCIENT ISRAEL AND ITS LITERATURE

Thomas C. Römer, General Editor

Editorial Board:
Mark G. Brett
Marc Brettler
Corrine L. Carvalho
Cynthia Edenburg
Konrad Schmid
Gale A. Yee

Number 24

DISMEMBERING THE WHOLE

Composition and Purpose of Judges 19–21

Cynthia Edenburg

SBL PRESS

Atlanta

Copyright © 2016 by SBL Press

All rights reserved. No part of this work may be reproduced or transmitted in any form or by any means, electronic or mechanical, including photocopying and recording, or by means of any information storage or retrieval system, except as may be expressly permitted by the 1976 Copyright Act or in writing from the publisher. Requests for permission should be addressed in writing to the Rights and Permissions Office, SBL Press, 825 Houston Mill Road, Atlanta, GA 30329 USA.

Library of Congress Cataloging-in-Publication Data

Edenburg, Cynthia, author.
 Dismembering the whole : composition and purpose of Judges 19–21 / by Cynthia Edenburg.
   p. cm. — (Ancient Israel and its literature ; number 24)
   Includes bibliographical references and index.
  ISBN 978-1-62837-124-6 (pbk. : alk. paper) – ISBN 978-1-62837-126-0 (hardcover : alk. paper) – ISBN 978-1-62837-125-3 (ebook)
  1. Bible. Judges, XIX–XXI—Criticism, interpretation, etc. I. Title.
 BS1305.52 .E345
 222'.3206—dc23   2015048970

Printed on acid-free paper.

Contents

Preface vii
Abbreviations ix
Introduction 1

1. Textual Artifact and Literary Stratification in Judges 19–21 9
   1.1. Delineation of the Narrative and Its Main Parts   12
   1.2. The Story of the Concubine (19:1–30)   14
   1.3. The Battle at Gibeah (20:1–48)   20
   1.4. The Aftermath of the War (21:1–24)   58
   1.5. Conclusions   75

2. Virtual Space and Real Geography 79
   2.1. Spatial Passage in the Narrative   80
   2.2. Gibeah in Historical Reality and Biblical Tradition   84
   2.3. Mizpah in Historical Reality and Biblical Tradition   96
   2.4. Bethel in Historical Reality and Biblical Tradition   100
   2.5. Bethlehem   102
   2.6. The Rock of Rimmon   104
   2.7. Jabesh-gilead   105
   2.8. Shiloh   107
   2.9. Summary and Conclusions   109

3. Language and Style: Diachronic and Synchronic Aspects 115
   3.1. Morphology   123
   3.2. Syntax   126
   3.3. Lexica   134
   3.4. Conclusions   155

4. Text, Subtext, and Intertextual Mosaic 161
   4.1. Theory and Method in Analyzing Intertextual Relations   161

	4.2. Abraham and Lot (Gen 18–19)	174
	4.3. The Battle at Ai (Josh 7–8)	195
	4.4. The Saul Narratives	221
	4.5. The Laws of Deuteronomy	230
	4.6. The Rape of Tamar (2 Sam 13:11–17)	248
	4.7. The War against Midian (Num 31)	255
	4.8. The Transjordan Altar (Josh 22:9–34)	263
	4.9. Isolated Parallels	274
	4.10. The Prologue and Appendix of Judges	284
	4.11. Summary and Conclusions	312
5.	Context and Purpose of the Story of the Outrage at Gibeah	321

Bibliography 335
Index of Ancient Sources 377
Index of Modern Authors 419

Preface

My work on the bizarre story of the Outrage at Gibeah began long ago and produced its firstfruits in the form of the doctoral dissertation I submitted to the University of Tel Aviv in the spring of 2003. That seminal study provided the springboard for my understanding of the central role the scroll played as the scribal medium and its impact upon book composition and the forms of revisions that were available to biblical scribes. The present book is more than an updated, translated, and edited version of my Hebrew dissertation. I have incorporated my understanding of the growth of the Judges scroll, its place in the Deuteronomistic History, and the role of the Outrage of Gibeah as an overriding revision of the Deuteronomistic account of the role Benjamin and Gibeah played in the early history of the monarchy. Parts of this study have informed papers that I published before this book came to fruition, particularly my work on intertextuality and the nature of Deuteronomism and what is *not* Deuteronomistic. Readers who are adept at redaction criticism undoubtedly will uncover telltale signs of the lengthy textual history of this book, despite my efforts to impart uniformity while revising and updating the discussion.

    I owe much to my teachers and mentors. Professor Yairah Amit and Professor Sara Japhet provided me with role models to emulate as uncompromising scholars who are equally devoted to family and to their careers. The late Professor Moshe Greenberg taught me how to read a biblical text and, possibly more importantly, that no text cannot be improved by shortening. Professor Nadav Na'aman raised my standards of reasoning in ways that are transparent in my methods and conclusions and led me to realize that all our work, theses, and conclusions are provisional and subject to change. Professor Ehud Ben Zvi, Professor Marc Brettler, and Professor Thomas Römer have played a significant role in encouraging me to persist in my research despite the crisis in biblical studies at Israeli academic institutions. I am also indebted to the Open University research authority for support that facilitated the preparation of this book. Special thanks are due to Ms. Anat Shapiro and Mr. Matan Norani for their diligent work in proofing the myriad biblical references throughout the work. Any errors that remain are solely my responsibility.

The initial research for this book was carried out during the childhood and adolescence of Asaf, Daphna, and Avishai, who grew up with a mother who always had a sheaf of papers to edit while waiting to meet with the teachers at parents' night. More valuable than all is the support I have received from my beloved husband, Shlomo, who has encouraged me to achieve all my aspirations.

Abbreviations

ה'	YHWH
AASOR	Annual of the American Schools of Oriental Research
AB	Anchor Bible
ABR	*Australian Biblical Review*
AbrNSup	Abr-Nahrain Supplements
ABS	Archaeology and Biblical Studies
ABRL	Anchor Bible Reference Library
ADPV	Abhandlungen des deutschen Palästinavereins
AIL	Ancient Israel and Its Literature
AnBib	Analecta biblica
ANEM	Ancient Near Eastern Monographs
Ant.	*Jewish Antiquities*
AOAT	Alter Orient und Altes Testament
ATANT	Abhandlungen zur Theologie des Alten und Neuen Testaments
ATD	Das Alte Testament Deutsch
ATSAT	Arbeiten zu Text und Sprache im Alten Testament
b.	Babylonian Talmud
B. Bat.	Baba Batra
B. Meṣ.	Baba Meṣiʿa
B. Qam.	Baba Qamma
BA	*Biblical Archaeologist*
BAIAS	*Bulletin of the Anglo-Israel Archaeological Society*
BAR	*Biblical Archaeology Review*
BASOR	*Bulletin of the American Schools of Oriental Research*
BBB	Bonner Biblische Beiträge
BBR	*Bulletin for Biblical Research*
BDB	Brown, F., S. R. Driver, and C. A. Briggs. *Hebrew and English Lexicon of the Old Testament.* Oxford: Clarendon, 1907.

BEATAJ	Beiträge zur Erforschung des Alten Testaments und des antiken Judentum
BETL	Bibliotheca ephemeridum theologicarum lovaniensium
BH	Biblical Hebrew
BHS	*Biblia hebraica stuttgartensia*
Bib	*Biblica*
Bib. Ant.	*Biblical Antiquities*
BibInt	*Biblical Interpretation*
BibInt	Biblical Interpretation Series
BibOr	Biblica et Orientalia
BibSem	Biblical Seminar
Bek.	Bekhorot
Bik.	Bikkurim
BLS	Bible and Literature Series
BTB	*Biblical Theology Bulletin*
BWANT	Beiträge zur Wissenschaft vom Alten und Neuen Testament
BZ	*Biblische Zeitschrift*
BZABR	Beihefte zur Zeitschrift für altorientalische und biblische Rechtsgeschichte
BZAW	Beihefte zur Zeitschrift für die alttestamentliche Wissenschaft
CAD	*The Assyrian Dictionary of the Oriental Institute of the University of Chicago.* Edited by I. J. Gelb et al. Chicago: Oriental Institute of the University of Chicago, 1956–.
CahRB	Cahiers de la Revue biblique
CBQ	*Catholic Biblical Quarterly*
CC	Continental Commentaries
CH	Code of Hammurabi
CurBS	*Currents in Research: Biblical Studies*
DDD	*Dictionary of Deities and Demons in the Bible.* Edited by Karel van der Toorn, Bob Becking, and Pieter W. van der Horst. 2nd ed. Leiden: Brill; Grand Rapids: Eerdmans, 1999.
ErIsr	*Eretz-Israel*
ETL	*Ephemerides theologicae lovanienses*
ExpTim	*Expository Times*
FAT	Forschungen zum Alten Testament
FCB	Feminist Companion to the Bible

FOTL	Forms of the Old Testament Literature
FRLANT	Forschungen zur Religion und Literatur des Alten und Neuen Testaments
GKC	*Gesenius' Hebrew Grammar*. Edited by E. Kautzsch. Translated by A. E. Cowley. Oxford: Clarendon, 1910.
Glassner	Glassner, Jean-Jacques. *Mesopotamian Chronicles*. WAW 19. Atlanta: Society of Biblical Literature, 2004.
HALOT	Koehler, L., W. Baumgartner, and J. J. Stamm. *The Hebrew and Aramaic Lexicon of the Old Testament*. Translated and edited under the supervision of M. E. J. Richardson. Study edition. 2 vols. Leiden: Brill, 2001.
HAR	*Hebrew Annual Review*
HAT	Handbuch zum Alten Testament
HBAI	*Hebrew Bible and Ancient Israel*
HKAT	Handkommentar zum Alten Testament
HS	*Hebrew Studies*
HSM	Harvard Semitic Monographs
HSS	Harvard Semitic Studies
HTKAT	Herders theologischer Kommentar zum Alten Testament
HTR	*Harvard Theological Review*
HUCA	*Hebrew Union College Annual*
IBHS	Waltke, B. K., and M. O'Connor. *An Introduction to Biblical Hebrew Syntax*. Winona Lake, IN: Eisenbrauns, 1990.
ICC	International Critical Commentary
IEJ	*Israel Exploration Journal*
Int	*Interpretation*
JAJ	*Journal of Ancient Judaism*
JANER	*Journal of Ancient Near Eastern Religions*
JANES	*Journal of the Ancient Near Eastern Society of Columbia University*
Jastrow	Jastrow, M. A. *Dictionary of the Targumim, the Talmud Babli and Yerushalmi, and the Midrashic Literature*. 2nd ed. New York: Putnam, 1903.
JBL	*Journal of Biblical Literature*
JBS	*Jerusalem Biblical Studies*
JCS	*Journal of Cuneiform Studies*
JHS	*Journal of Hebrew Scriptures*
JJS	*Journal of Jewish Studies*
JNES	*Journal of Near Eastern Studies*

JNSL	*Journal of Northwest Semitic Languages*
Joüon	Joüon, P. *A Grammar of Biblical Hebrew*. Translated and revised by T. Muraoka. 2 vols. Subsidia biblica 14.1–2. Rome: Pontifical Biblical Institute, 1991.
JSJSup	Supplements to the Journal of the Study of Judaism
JQR	*Jewish Quarterly Review*
JSOT	*Journal for the Study of the Old Testament*
JSOTSup	Journal for the Study of the Old Testament Supplement Series
KAI	Donner, H., and W. Röllig. *Kanaanäische und aramäische Inschriften*. 2nd ed. Wiesbaden: Harrassowitz, 1966–1969.
KAT	Kommentar zum Alten Testament
Ketub.	Ketubbot
KHAT	Kurzer Hand-commentar zum Alten Testament
KTU	*Die keilalphabetischen Texte aus Ugarit*. Edited by M. Dietrich, O. Loretz, and J. Sanmartín. AOAT 24.1. Neukirchen-Vluyn: Neurkirchener Verlag, 1976.
LBH	Late Biblical Hebrew
LSAWS	Linguistic Studies in Ancient West Semitic
LXX	Septuagint
m.	Mishnah
MAL	Middle Assyrian Laws
Meg.	Megillah
Mek.	Mekhilta
MGWJ	*Monatschrift für Geschichte und Wissenschaft des Judentums*
MH	Mishnaic Hebrew
MT	Masoretic Text
N[1]	primary narrative
NAC	The New American Commentary
NCB	New Century Bible
NICOT	New International Commentary on the Old Testament
OBO	Orbis biblicus et orientalis
ÖBS	Österreichische biblische Studien
Onom.	Onomasticon
OrAnt	*Oriens antiquus*
OTL	Old Testament Library
OtSt	*Oudtestamentische Studien*
PEQ	*Palestine Exploration Quarterly*

Pesaḥ.	Pesaḥim
PHSC	Perspectives on Hebrew Scriptures and Its Contexts
PLT	*PTL: A Journal for Descriptive Poetics and Theory of Literature*
PN	personal name
Qidd.	Qiddushin
R²	expanded narrative
RA	*Revue d'assyriologie et d'archéologie orientale*
Rab.	Rabbah
RB	*Revue biblique*
RBL	*Review of Biblical Literature*
RBS	Resources for Biblical Studies
Roš Haš.	Roš Haššanah
RS	Ras Shamra
Šabb.	Šabbat
Sanh.	Sanhedrin
SBH	Standard Biblical Hebrew
SBLDS	Society of Biblical Literature Dissertation Series
SBLMS	Society of Biblical Literature Monograph Series
SBT	Studies in Biblical Theology
ScrHier	Scripta Hierosolymitana
Šebu.	Šebuʿot
Shnaton	*Shnaton: An Annual for Biblical and Ancient Near Eastern Studies*
SJOT	*Scandinavian Journal of the Old Testament*
SSN	Studia semitica neerlandica
STDJ	Studies on the Texts of the Desert of Judah
SymS	Symposium Series
TA	*Tel Aviv*
TAD	*Textbook of Aramaic Documents from Ancient Egypt*. Copied and translated by B. Porten and A. Yardeni. 4 vols. Jerusalem: Hebrew University Press, 1986–99
TDOT	*Theological Dictionary of the Old Testament*. Edited by G. J. Botterweck, H. Ringgren, and H.-J. Fabry. Translated by J. T. Willis et al. 16 vols. Grand Rapids: Eerdmans, 1974–
Tem.	Temurah
TN	toponym (place name)
TSK	*Theologische Studien und Kritiken*
TZ	*Theologische Zeitschrift*

UF	*Ugarit-Forschungen*
UMI	University Microfilms
VT	*Vetus Testamentum*
VTSup	Supplements to Vetus Testamentum
WBC	Word Biblical Commentary
WMANT	Wissenschaftliche Monographien zum Alten und Neuen Testament
y.	Jerusalem Talmud
Yebam.	Yevamot
ZABR	*Zeitschrift für altorientalische und biblische Rechtsgeschichte*
ZAH	*Zeitschrift für Althebraistik*
ZAW	*Zeitschrift für die alttestamentliche Wissenschaft*
ZBK	Zürcher Bibelkommentare
ZDPV	*Zeitschrift des deutschen Palästina-Vereins*
ZTK	*Zeitschrift für Theologie und Kirche*
ZWT	*Zeitschrift für wissenschaftliche Theologie*

Introduction

The story known as "the Outrage at Gibeah" (Judg 19–21) provokes widely differing responses from its readers, ranging between shock, bewilderment, and comic reaction. The graphic violence that runs throughout the narrative produces a visceral effect in readers who find that it tells a tale of terror. Others point to the many incongruities in the story and the ludicrous behavior of its characters and find it a tale of the absurd.[1] Regardless of the differences in response to the story, critical readers do agree that many elements in the story do not adhere to a consistent narrative logic.

Thus it is surprising that the concubine's husband should wait four months before undertaking to retrieve his recalcitrant wife and then bother to journey as far as Bethlehem to win her back, only to precipitously dispose of her when faced with danger. We might also wonder why he thought that his concubine's body could provide the means to divert the hostile crowd at Gibeah from their original intention to sexually assault him, when they already had refused his host's offer to provide them with women.

Surprising developments also abound when the tribes decide to attack Gibeah in order to avenge the brutal death of the concubine. Although the Israelites' force is fifteen times greater than the Benjaminites', they suffer two disastrous defeats with casualties greater than the entire size of the Benjaminite troops. It is true that this is not inconceivable in terms of biblical thought, since YHWH was thought to be capable of delivering the mighty into the hands of the few (e.g., Judg 7:2; 1 Sam 14:6). However, defeat was generally understood as a sign of divine anger, but in this case the Israelites go to war in order to serve justice and enforce the divine stricture to expunge evil from Israel (Judg 20:13). Furthermore, the Israelites diligently consult the oracle prior to each battle, and each time YHWH

---

1. Feminist interpretation tends to view the story as a tale of terror; see, e.g., Trible 1984; Bal 1988; and Bach 1999; though Lasine 1984 views it as a tale of the absurd.

instructs them to take to the field. Notwithstanding, YHWH delivers the Israelites twice into the hands of the Benjaminites, even though they—the Benjaminites—defend the offenders at Gibeah, who are to be eradicated from the community. Ancient interpreters who attempted to make sense of this perplexing state of affairs concluded that YHWH deliberately misled the Israelites by means of the oracle so they would take to the field and there suffer disastrous setbacks.[2]

The conclusion to the story is no less bewildering. In their zealousness to eradicate the evil exemplified by the Benjaminites' behavior, the Israelites wipe out all Benjaminite men, women, and children with the exception of six hundred fighting men who fled from the battle. Only afterward do the Israelites realize that the near extermination of Benjamin ruptures the integrity of the pantribal structure. However, the restoration of Benjamin is hampered by a precipitous oath that the Israelites swore before the battle to refrain from connubium with the Benjaminites. In the end, the future procreation of the Benjaminites is ensured only through an additional cycle of warfare, abduction, and rape. Thus, ironically, the very actions that provided the justification for the war against Benjamin are now condoned in the name of ensuring the future integrity of the pantribal ideal.

These examples of narrative dissonance in the story of the Outrage at Gibeah create the general impression of a defect in the chain of causality regulating the movement of the plot.[3] We may well wonder whether such discrepancies and convoluted logic are inherent to the plot and figure in the story's message or are an accidental result of composite composition or incomplete editing.

In addition, the story of the Outrage at Gibeah stands out from the rest of the book of Judges. The main body of the book is cast in a cyclical pattern in which the Israelites worship other gods and YHWH counters by relinquishing them to foreign oppressors; only after the Israelites return to YHWH does he deliver them from foreign servitude by means of a savior (מושיע) or inspired leader (Judg 2:6–16:31). The cycle of savior stories is supplied with a chronological framework that details the periods of servitude and alternating years of peace under the leadership of the savior. All these characteristics are absent from the story of the Outrage at Gibeah (Judg 19–21), as well as from the preceding story of Micah's cult image

---

2. See Pseudo-Philo, *Bib. Ant.* 46.1–47.8; b. Sanh. 103b; see also 1 Kgs 22:20 and b. Šebu. 35b; see also Hentschel and Niessen 2008, 23–25.

3. See Gunn 2005, 243–75.

(Judg 17–18). Neither of the stories mentions foreign threats or military leaders who deliver the people from servitude, and both stand outside the chronological scheme of the saviors. Indeed, there is no indication that the events in these two narratives occur after those in the preceding savior stories. On the contrary, both stories mention priests belonging to the third generation of descendants of Moses and Aaron (18:30; 20:28), which should place the events after the notice of Joshua's death at the beginning of the book of Judges.[4]

The stories of the Outrage at Gibeah and Micah's image also share some motifs and formulations, the most notable of which is the recurring phrase, "In those days there was no king in Israel; each man did what he deemed right" (17:6; 21:25; and only the first clause in 18:1 and 19:1). Both also have similar openings, "There was a man from (who lived in) Mount Ephraim" (17:1; 19:1b), and both tell about wayfarers on the road between Bethlehem and Mount Ephraim who stop at the house of an Ephraimite (17:7–10; 19:1, 3, 17–21). In light of these similarities, many scholars thought that the two stories derive either from a common source or from the hand of the same editor. Their placement at the end of the book of Judges helped explain their divergence from the structure, themes, and chronology uniting the savior stories, for they were widely viewed as an intrusive appendix, stemming from a different compositional or editorial layer than the body of the Deuteronomistic book of Judges.[5]

However, the similarities between the two stories may be more apparent than real. The story of Micah's image shares several themes with the Deuteronomistic edition of the savior stories, such as the concern with cultic wrongdoing (17:3–5; 18:14–20, 30–31) and the inefficiency of the supposed premonarchic pantribal organization that fails to secure its aims (17:8–9; 18:1, 19–26). But on these points the story of the Outrage at Gibeah differs from the rest of the book of Judges. Throughout the Gibeah

---

4. Thus in *Ant.* 5.2.1.–5.3.2 §§120–181, Josephus placed the two narratives prior to the savior stories. See also the comment by Isaiah di Trani at 20:28: "This occurred before the judges, but the arranger first set the judges in order, and then wrote these two narratives." Some of the moderns also thought that the original context of these narratives was at the beginning of the book; see Auberlen 1860, 539; Budde 1897, xv; Talmon 1986, 42–47.

5. See Auberlen 1860; Budde 1888; Moore 1895, xxiv–xxxi; Burney 1970, xxxvii, 443–58; Noth 1966, 168; 1991, 77 n. 2; Gray 1967, 242; O'Brien 1989, 98; Becker 1990, 295–96; Römer and de Pury 2000, 122–23.

story, there is no indication of cultic wrongdoing, and only in this story do we find the pantribal organization efficiently convoking and operating "as one man, from Dan to Beer-sheba and the Gilead" (20:1–2; cf., e.g., 19:29; 20:8–11; 21:5–8). Moreover, the other intertribal conflicts in the book of Judges (8:1–3; 12:6–7) relate to local power struggles between neighboring tribes and thus emphasize the disintegration of pantribal unity, while the story of the battle at Gibeah presents an attempt to uphold the ideal of pantribal unity. The story's conclusion also revolves around this ideal, by relating efforts to mend the rift in the pantribal superstructure (21:3, 6–7, 15–17). These aspects set the story of the Outrage at Gibeah apart from the themes and interests of both the savior stories and the story of Micah's image, thus presenting a serious challenge to claims of editorial unity for Judg 17–21 and all the more so for the book of Judges as a whole.[6]

The story of the Outrage at Gibeah is also at odds with the representations of Benjamin, Gibeah, and Jabesh-gilead in the account of the establishment of the monarchy in 1 Sam 8–12. According to Judg 19–21, the towns of Gibeah and Jabesh-gilead were wiped out and the tribe of Benjamin was nearly annihilated in a premonarchic civil war, but shortly afterward these towns play a central role in the account of the establishment of the monarchy, and there Benjamin's standing is strong enough to produce the first king.

Despite these divergences in theme, outlook, chronology, and detail from the main body of the Deuteronomistic History, several scholars hold that the story of the Outrage at Gibeah was composed and set into its context by one or more Deuteronomistic scribes.[7] Although stylistic and structural markers provide the surest means for identifying Deuteronomistic composition, several recent scholars have questioned whether the scribes of the Deuteronomistic school necessarily adhered to a particular idiom and style. As a result, criteria for identifying Deuteronomistic composition have become more relaxed, with a greater emphasis placed on themes and ideologies attributed to different groups of Deuteronomistic scribes.[8]

---

6. Contra Wong 2006, who argues for the compositional unity of the entire book of Judges, which he thinks derives from the hand of a single author. Wong seems to confuse possible synchronic reading with literary-historical analysis.

7. See, e.g., Schunck 1963, 60–68; Veijola 1977, 15–29; 1982, 186–200; Boling 1975, 36–37; Peckham 1985, 35–38; Mayes 2001, 256–58.

8. For discussion of these issues, see Wilson 1999; Lohfink 1999.

INTRODUCTION   5

For the most part, this approach has produced limited agreement regarding the extent of Deuteronomistic composition and editing in the story of the Outrage at Gibeah. This debate has focused on the judgment refrain, "In those days there was no king in Israel; every man did as he saw fit" (17:6; 21:25; cf. 18:1; 19:1). This refrain is presumed to state the purpose of the story, namely, to illustrate the deplorable state of anarchy that held sway in premonarchic Israel, thereby justifying the establishment of central rule through the agency of a king.[9] According to this approach, the story derives from the early preexilic and promonarchic edition of the Deuteronomistic History. However, while this refrain employs the familiar Deuteronomistic idiom "to do as *x* saw fit" (עשה הישר בעיניו), it needs yet to be demonstrated that this refrain also bears affinities with Deuteronomic thought and usage. In addition, the relation between the refrain and the story is questionable. If it can be shown that the refrain is a secondary accretion rather than an integral part of the composition, then its contribution to the purpose of the narrative may be negligible. In this case, the refrain would be irrelevant to the question of Deuteronomistic editing in Judg 19–21.

The approach represented by scholars such as K.-D. Schunck, Timo Veijola, Brian Peckham, and others also raises a methodological issue: Can we classify a composition as Deuteronomistic solely on the basis of theme and ideology? Where does this lead us when we find Deuteronomistic themes and ideologies in patently late works? Would this not indicate that Deuteronomism continued to influence Judean literary production, long after the composition of the Deuteronomistic History?[10] In short, the marked shift in consensus regarding the place of the story of the Outrage at Gibeah in relation to the Deuteronomistic History requires reevaluation. This matter is of crucial importance, since it influences how we define the structure and purpose of the Deuteronomistic History and how we

---

9. See, e.g., Buber 1967, 77–84; Veijola 1977, 15–16; Crüsemann 1978, 162.

10. The long-lasting influence of Deuteronomism is indeed evident in the library of Qumran, as can be seen in works such as Dibrei Moshe (1Q22) and the Temple Scroll (11Q19), as well as in the remains of twenty-seven different copies of Deuteronomy, which is surpassed only by the number of Psalms manuscripts. However, one of the hallmarks of such late works is the juxtaposition of Dtr themes and expressions alongside Priestly idiom and ideology; this tendency is already apparent in biblical books such as Ezekiel and Chronicles.

characterize the compositional techniques of the Deuteronomistic circle of scribes.

Additional issues that need to be examined include the historical context of the narrative, its relation to the literature of the priestly circles, and its ultimate purpose. Throughout most of the twentieth century, scholars thought it possible to isolate a historical kernel in the narrative, which could be of value relating to the history of the premonarchic period. For the most part, such reconstructions built upon the idea of a premonarchic tribal league. Today most hold that such a view of prestate society is untenable, and the question of historical background is ignored or addressed with severe reservations. However, it is possible that later historical events or circumstances may have been retrojected into a fictional or idealized narrative about the distant past. This line of investigation might uncover traces of an event that engendered the kernel of the narrative and may shed light on the historical circumstances in which the text was composed and edited. In a similar vein, questions arise regarding the historical context of the tendentious representation of Benjamin in the story, particularly since this region ultimately became a province of the kingdom of Judah.

Throughout the nineteenth and twentieth centuries, most scholars held that the bulk of the composition in Judg 19–21 is of preexilic origin. To be sure, some Priestly idioms are found in limited passages of the story, but these passages were considered to reflect light reworking at the latest editorial stage.[11] This view was challenged by Uwe Becker, who proposes that the postexilic Priestly editor did not just revise the story but was responsible for the composition of the present narrative.[12] Thus, before we can consider the purpose of this unusual composition, it is necessary to determine whether the Priestly scribe did in fact compose the story or whether he only added easily identifiable material that reflects his particular style and interests.

Much of the recent discussion of the purpose of the story of the Outrage at Gibeah has been dependent upon a priori assumptions regarding its place and role in the final form of the Former Prophets. In other cases, the purpose of the narrative is postulated and its relevance to a particular historical context is used to date the composition. This frequently results

---

11. For example, see Budde 1897, 126–27; Burney 1970, 453–58; Gray 1986, 227. The argument for an early date is most recently revived by Stipp 2006, who proposes that composition stems from the time of the united monarchy.

12. Becker 1990, 298–303.

in circular reasoning in which purpose helps to date the composition, while at the same time the author's historical circumstances help to clarify the composition's purpose. However, purpose is a very tenuous indication of date, since a particular message or *Tendenz* may be relevant to different audiences in different times.

In the following chapters I shall examine indications in the narrative that are independent of purpose and that point to the period of composition. In chapter 1 I undertake an analysis of the structure and compositional history of Judg 19–21, since these provide a necessary basis for the subsequent discussion of the narrative's date and purpose. In chapter 2 I examine the geographical background of the story in order to determine its relation to known historical reality as well as to biblical tradition. By considering the material evidence uncovered from archaeological excavations and surveys, one can evaluate the historical setting of the story's geographical background and how it might reflect the times of the its author. The biblical tradition history of the story's various locales can also shed light on the concerns that shaped the narrative's setting. Chapter 3 examines the language of Judg 19–21 in order to see whether there is sufficient evidence of Late Biblical Hebrew (LBH) to warrant a postexilic date of composition. Even though scholars are divided on the question whether Classical or Standard Biblical Hebrew (SBH) necessarily indicates preexilic composition, all agree that the usage characteristic of LBH provides significant evidence for late dating. In chapter 4 I discuss the intertextual relations between Judg 19–21 and other biblical texts. The story of the Outrage at Gibeah engages a number of other biblical texts, and the nature of such literary echoes and their purpose need to be understood. Do these echoes result from free association between texts and common motifs, or do they derive from literary borrowing? If the last possibility should prove true, then the intertexts might give an indication of the extent of the body of literature that attained authoritative standing by the author's time. Furthermore, the ways the author employed the intertexts could shed light on his purpose and concerns. Chapter 5 presents my conclusions regarding the composition and purpose of the story of the Outrage at Gibeah and investigates implications of this study for understanding the growth of the book of Judges and its place within a Deuteronomistic History. Finally, although the story of the Outrage at Gibeah is patently a literary composition dealing with a distant, fictive past, I propose that it reflects geopolitical concerns that were current during the times of its authors.

1
TEXTUAL ARTIFACT AND LITERARY STRATIFICATION
IN JUDGES 19–21

One of the few points on which modern critical readers of the Outrage at Gibeah (Judg 19–21) agree is that the present narrative is not all of one piece. Even holistic literary readings of the narrative only disregard the narrative breaks and inconsistencies and do not overturn this verdict.[1] At this point the consensus ends, and critics differ not only on details of the analysis but on the criteria for literary criticism as well. Increasing appreciation of stylistics has led to the realization that the use of interchangeable terms is not a reliable key for unraveling sources, since a single author may choose to employ synonymous terms for the sake of stylistic variation.[2] Nonetheless, many based their analysis of Judg 19–21 upon the interchange of terms: בני ישראל versus איש ישראל and בני בנימין versus בנימין.[3] However, analyses that were based upon terminological interchange have failed to produce two independent narrative strands or even one consistent strand that underwent secondary expansion. Furthermore,

---

1. See, e.g., Trible 1984; Webb 1987; L. Klein 1988; Exum 1990; O'Connell 1996, 242–64, 424–32; see also Lasine 1984; Revell 1985; Satterthwaite 1992, who treated only individual sections of the narrative.
2. See Jüngling 1981, 50; Gross 2009, 866–67; against those like Moore 1895, 410; Budde 1897, 128; Burney 1970, 442–43; and Eissfeldt 1925, 98–99, who identified parallel strands in Judg 19 on the basis of interchanging terms, such as אשה/נערה/פילגש and חותן/אבי הנערה.
3. See, e.g., Bertheau 1883, 265–66; Burney 1970, 449; Schunck 1963, 61–63; Besters 1965, 31–38; Crüsemann 1978, 159; Gray 1986, 228–29; Hentschel and Niessen 2008. But see criticism by Budde 1888, 296; Moore 1895, 407; Mayes 1974, 210 n. 99; Joosten 1996, 30–33. Becker (1990, 273, 279) is noteworthy in insisting that literary criteria, such as narrative continuity and consistency, are the only valid standards for literary analysis. Nevertheless, his analysis of the different editorial layers coincides with that achieved by differentiating strands according to the interchange of terms.

in several cases one of the sides—Israel or Benjamin—is referred to with a בני term, while the other side is indicated by the alternate mode of designation (20:21, 25, 31, 35, 36, 48; 21:6, 18). These instances lead me to conclude that stylistic concerns dictated the interchange of terms for the sides in Judg 19–21 and that the alternate designations have no significance for compositional analysis.

As a control against the tendency of critics to multiply compositional layers on the basis of dubious criteria, I find it necessary to affirm the a priori assumption of textual unity. This assumption provides a valid starting point for literary criticism and should be upheld as long as the text displays narrative continuity and unity of content, purpose, and style. Admittedly, it is conceivable that complex editing may produce the appearance of textual unity, particularly if the various editors adhered to the same editorial principles.[4] But this alternative defeats the object of literary criticism from the outset, since critical tools could not validate or falsify either the unity of the text or the proposition of multistage editing. For this reason, I prefer to be guided by the rule of parsimony and grant priority to the simplest explanation for the evolution of the text.

In any case, breaks in the narrative, as well as inconsistencies in content, purpose, and style, present grounds for overturning the assumption of unity. But how do we judge the degree of integration or tension between the different components in the text? According to Gérard Genette, texts are literary palimpsests, for they result from "overwriting" previous texts of the same genre, content, or formulation. These previous texts, which underlie the finished composition, Genette terms *hypotext*, while the complete composition visible to the eye is the *hypertext*.[5] Frequently, the underlying materials (hypotexts) are transformed as they are integrated into their new context. Thus the concept of the "palimpsest" hypertext emphasizes the creative aspect inherent in revision, rewriting, and literary borrowing, for even a redactor or reviser contributes to the composition of the hypertext.[6] According to Genette's approach, there is no fundamental difference between the textual layering resulting from editing and that instilled in the composition by means of allusion or assimilation of another text (e.g., literary borrowing and quotation). However, even though both result in a hypertext, the processes themselves are quite dif-

---

4. Amit 1999, 15–19.
5. Genette 1982, 11–12, 14.
6. See Polak 1994, 358–65.

ferent. Editorial layering may be compared to the structural changes in a preexisting building carried out during renovation and/or expansion with the addition of floors or wings. In such cases, the different stages of construction may be characterized by different architectural styles, as with the dissimilar spires of the Chartres Cathedral. By contrast, compositional layering is akin to construction through reuse of materials, such as blocks or columns, taken from another building or architectural context. Here too the earlier material incorporated into the new building may be distinguished by its difference in form or style, as with the crusader fort at Sepphoris, which has recycled a Hellenistic sarcophagus as a building block.

In the examples detailed above, external data shed light on the relation between the complete structure and its parts, such as documentation of the building stages or other contemporaneous structures whose style is characteristic of the period. However, most biblical texts lack external evidence relating to the underlying foundations or materials.[7] Therefore, the distinction between compositional and redactional layers depends upon internal criteria, such as breaks in the narrative, inconsistencies, repetition, and change in terminology. These criteria can be problematic, because in different cases gaps and breaks, repetition, and varied terms can play a part in the poetics of the narrative.[8] It is therefore desirable to consider the nature of the various phenomena and their relative significance before concluding that they indicate the existence of redactional layers. Narrative breaks and internal contradictions may present strong evidence of editorial stratification, especially when it is possible to reconstruct a supposed original continuity within the text and explain the motives for editorial interference. Repetitions, variation of terms, or the sudden use of Priestly terminology, as well as incidence of late language use, can only assist in basing the hypothesis of editorial stratification.

---

7. Notable exceptions are cases of parallel texts in which one text provided material incorporated into the other (e.g., Obad 1-9 // Jer 49:7-10, 14-16), or when two editions of a text provide evidence of editing, as with the synoptic material in Samuel-Kings // Chronicles.

8. See, e.g., Talmon 1978; Whybray 1987, 56-58; Sternberg 1987, 186-90, 365-440; Polak 1994, 77-80.

1.1. Delineation of the Narrative and Its Main Parts

The story of the Outrage at Gibeah opens with the exposition in 19:1b–2, which presents a new set of different characters and circumstances. The first clause of this exposition ("There was a Levite who lived at the far end of the highlands of Ephraim") is based upon a common formula that presents the character who figures at the outset of the narrative, along with his lineage and his place of origin.[9] The story concludes in 21:24 with a common type of ending in which the characters disperse and return to their homes.[10]

The entire story is framed by editorial comment: "In those days there was no king in Israel" (19:1; 21:25), which also appears twice in the story of Micah's image (17:6; 18:1). The formulation in 19:1 opens in the narrative tense with the verb ויהי, while the other instances of the comment are cast as nominal clauses. In Hans-Winfried Jüngling's opinion, the use of the narrative tense here indicates that the formulation is rooted in the story of the Outrage at Gibeah.[11] However, this seems unlikely, since there is no justification for opening the narrative with double formulas (vv. 1a, b). Indeed, it is more likely that the comment in 19:1a was derived from those in Judg 17–18. There the comments occur within the narrative and mark off its major sections. In any event, the formulation in 19:1 does not function as an independent opening but as a chronological link between the Gibeah story and the story of Micah's image.[12] The author or editor who added this chronological notice to the Gibeah story reformulated it as a verbal clause in order to suit the opening of the narrative.[13] The edito-

---

9. Caspari 1911, 231–33, 243; Jüngling 1981, 74; Niditch 2008, 15; Stipp 2006, 135–37; Levin 2011, 136; R. Müller 2013, 211–15. Compare: "There was a man [ויהי איש] from TN of the family of x and his name was PN" (Judg 13:2; cf. 17:7); "There was a man [ויהי איש] from TN and his name was PN son of [lineage]" (1 Sam 1:1; 9:1); cf. also 2 Sam 20:1; Job 1:1; Esth 2:5. By contrast, new characters are introduced in the middle of a story by means of a noun clause: "And PN son of [lineage] from [TN], and the name of his mother/father was PN" (1 Sam 17:12; 1 Kgs 11:26).

10. See, e.g., Gen 32:1; Num 24:25; 1 Sam 15:34; 24:23; 2 Sam 20:22; discussion by Seeligmann 1962, 306–10.

11. Jüngling 1981, 59–64.

12. See the formula ויהי בימים ההם (Exod 2:11, 23; 1 Sam 28:1), which is used to establish chronological links between different stages in a story; see also Sweeney 1997, 525–26.

13. See, e.g., Noth 1962a, 79; Crüsemann 1978, 156–57; Becker 1990, 258–59;

rial nature of all four comments in Judg 17–21 is clear since their point of reference—the period of the monarchy—lies outside the narratives themselves.[14] Moreover, the editorial origin is also apparent from the concentric alternation of notices with the judgment formula ("Every man did as he thought right," 17:6; 21:25) and those without supplementation (18:1; 19:1). Indeed, concentric arrangement is elsewhere recognized as an editorial device for imposing superficial unity on disparate material.[15]

The narrative in Judg 19–21 divides into three parts: (1) the story of the concubine (19:1b–30); (2) the war against Benjamin (20:1–48); and (3) the rehabilitation of Benjamin. Independent material might lie behind the different sections, but any attempt to sever a section from its place in the present narrative results in disrupting the chain of circumstances that advance the plot. For example, quest or journey narratives frequently end with the hero returning to his home,[16] but the narrative tension is not resolved with the Levite's return home since there he initiates a new chain of actions when he dismembers the concubine in order to call attention to the crime at Gibeah.[17] Similarly, it is not possible to sever the battle description from its present narrative context, since the incident with the

---

Amit 1999, 345–47; Mueller 2001, 204. Judges 17–18 opens with the single expository formula, introducing Micah (17:1). The first episode of the story closes in 17:6 with the chronological note and judgment formula, while the second episode opens with a new expository formula introducing the anonymous Levite (17:7). The third episode opens in 18:1 with the chronological note and exposition that present the circumstances for the Danite migration.

14. Contra Mueller 2001, 104.

15. See the concentric arrangement of the materials in 2 Sam 21–24: A. narrative (21:1–14); B. David's warriors (21:15–22); C. poetry (22:1–51); C. poetry (23:1–7); B. David's warriors (23:8–39); A. narrative (24:1–25).

16. See Seeligman 1962, 306–10; Gross 2009, 812–13; see also the endings of other quest stories in Gen 22:19; 33:18–19; 1 Sam 10:10–16; the Gilgamesh Epic 11.313–22; and the story of Sinuhe 240–310.

17. See, e.g., Fokkelman 1992, 42–43; Gross 2009, 820–21; against the view proposed by Jüngling (1981) that 19:1–30a represents an independent story. Stipp has recently taken up Jüngling's view and argues that the Judg 19 was composed to reflect Judean-Benjaminite rivalry during the period prior to David's acclamation by all the tribes. According to Stipp, the lack of closure in the original story derives from its early composition, before the Saulide partisans were finally defeated (2006, 144). This argument is an example of special pleading, in which date and tendency of composition are predetermined and then employed to justify questionable literary criticism. Stipp (2011, 228) further defends the open end provided by Judg 19:30 by appealing

concubine provides the necessary *causus belli*. Nor is it possible to conclude the narrative with the victory over Benjamin without dealing with the ramifications of the victory, which presents a new set of complications to resolve. Indeed, the final episode is necessary to close the narrative cycle, since the preceding episodes result in further complications: the Levite left home in order to bring his concubine back but returned with a dead body;[18] the tribes went to war against Benjamin in order to right that wrong but only created a more serious lack by nearly decimating an entire tribe, and the narrative tension will not be resolved until the new deficiency is filled.

1.2. The Story of the Concubine (19:1–30)

The section in 19:1–30 is a consistent and unified narrative,[19] distinguished by an even chain of cause and effect and by chronological and geographical markers that account for the passage of time and change of place.[20] The various parts of the narrative are united by the journey schema leading south from Mount Ephraim to Bethlehem and then back north bypassing Jerusalem and stopping at Gibeah before returning to the point of origin in Mount Ephraim. Up to the departure from Gibeah, the narrative time stands in inverse relation to the length of narrated time. The long period of four months after the concubine left the Levite is briefly summed up without further comment (19:2b), while the event that occurs in the shortest time—the overnight stay at Gibeah—is detailed in fourteen verses (19:15–28b). The slowing of pace at this point draws attention to the details of the incident at Gibeah, which will play a central part as the plot develops. However, the well-defined representation of time and space

---

to Jonah 4:11 and Gen 34:31, which are undoubtedly postexilic texts. This is ironic, since Stipp's claims that Judg 19 derives from the late tenth or early ninth century BCE.

18. There is no basis for taking the laconic language in 19:28 to indicate that the concubine was still alive following the night assault, contra Polzin 1980, 201–2; Trible 1984, 79–84; Exum 1990, 428.

19. See, e.g., Noth 1966, 165; Jüngling 1981, 104–5; contra classical source critics like Moore 1895, 410; Budde 1897, 128; Burney 1970, 442–43.

20. See time markers in 19:2, 4, 5, 8, 9, 11, 14, 16, 25, 26, 27. Progression in space is marked by mention of Mount Ephraim (v. 1), Bethlehem (vv. 1–2), Jebus (v. 10), Ramah (v. 13), Gibeah (12–16), the town square (vv. 15, 17, 20), the old Ephraimite's house (vv. 21–22), outside the Ephraimite's house (v. 25), the threshold of the Ephraimite's house (vv. 26–27), and the Levite's house (v. 29).

dissipates at the end of the section. Although verse 29 still relates a series of acts placed within a specific place and time ("he arrived at his home … and sent her throughout the whole territory of Israel"), in verse 30 time is transcended by means of the durative expression והיה ואמר,[21] while the place of action is wherever anyone saw (כל הראה) a part of the concubine's dismembered body.

Most of the section revolves around two hospitality scenes: the first at Bethlehem (19:3–10aα) and the second at Gibeah (19:15–28). Both episodes are patterned around elements that are found in different combinations in other hospitality scenes; thus the formulaic nature of elements would appear to derive from a common type-scene.[22]

The first hospitality scene is set in the father-in-law's house in Bethlehem, where the host "rejoices" to see the Levite and presses him to lengthen his stay from day to day. The episode is modeled upon the graded number (x + 1) pattern in which a series of repetitions or recurring events culminates in a significant break from the pattern.[23] Verse 4 summarizes the first three days and sets the pattern for the repeated eating, drinking, and staying the night. The fourth day of the visit anticipates a break in the repeated pattern, when the Levite attempts to depart after the dining and drinking but is forestalled by his father-in-law's insistence that he stay another night (19:6–7). The repetitious pattern is finally broken on the fifth day, when the Levite adamantly refuses to stay another night and departs on the return journey after dining with his host.

The second hospitality scene stands in harsh contrast to the first.[24] Here no one greets the guests upon their arrival in Gibeah, and they remain in the town square after sunset (vv. 14–15) until they are accosted by an old Ephraimite who is himself a resident alien in Gibeah. This section of the episode is patterned upon a type-scene depicting encounters with strangers.[25] The way the details of this meeting are ordered—exposi-

---

21. See GKC §112ee.
22. See Gen 18:3–8; 19:2–7; 24:31–33, 54; 43:24–25, 32; Exod 2:20; as well as Judg 13:15–20; 17:8–11; 1 Sam 28:22, 25. The common elements of the type-scene include: (1) invitation of hospitality; (2) bringing the guest home; (3) feeding the pack animals; (4) washing the guest's feet; (5) serving a meal; (6) eating; (7) drinking; and (8) staying the night. For the concept of "type-scene," see Alter 1978.
23. On the graded number pattern, see Zakovitch 1979, ii–xxxi; Polak 1994, 52–54, 64–69; Bodi 2013.
24. So also Güdemann 1869, 36; Alter 1986, 37; Amit 2000, 183.
25. See Judg 19:17 with Gen 42:7; Josh 9:8; Judg 17:9; Job 1:7; see also Gen 29:4.

tion noting the old man's origin (vv. 16–17), interrogation of the Levite (v. 18), his answer (vv. 18–19), and his offer of hospitality (v. 20)—creates the impression that the offer was made only because of the common Ephraimite origin shared by host and guest. The hospitality during the short stay at Gibeah is interrupted by the violent demands of the townspeople and the attempts of both host and guest to appease them, culminating in the assault on the concubine. Thus, while the visit in Bethlehem represents the pinnacle of hospitality, the stay in Gibeah is characterized by its abrogation. This characterization may lead the reader to suspect that the hospitality scenes are but a means to depict the contrast in social norms represented by the two cities.

CHARACTERS

Apart from the people of Gibeah, who are presented as a corporate personality, the rest of the characters are individuals. Of these, only the Levite reappears in the next section, and even he disappears after presenting his version of the events at Gibeah before the assembly at Mizpah (20:4–7). Afterward, only corporate entities figure in the story (Israelites, Benjaminites, the people of Jabesh and Shiloh). Since the opening section supplies the justification for the pantribal civil war, there is an apparent discrepancy between the focus on local events in the opening section and the far-reaching extent of the war that follows.[26] The considerable gap in the plot between the cause of the war (rape and death of a woman) and its results (decimation of Benjamin) lends a measure of irony to the narrative and hints at the narrator's critical tendency toward his subject.

The only figure in the story to be depicted in an uncritical fashion is the concubine. Even though the concubine's rape and death instigate the following chain of events, the only action attributed to her is leaving her husband (19:2).[27] The reason she left her husband lies in the expression ותזנה עליו, which is best understood as a unique occurrence of a homonym of זנה, meaning "be angry, wroth."[28] Otherwise, she appears to be

---

26. For attempts to rationalize the discrepancy, see, e.g., Bleek 1878, 201; Jüngling 1981, 253; Soggin 1987, 281; see also Eissfeldt 1963, 71; Becker 1990, 271.

27. In 19:3, the reading ויבא found in some versions is preferred to the MT ותביאהו; see Moore 1895, 410. Accordingly, the concubine does not act upon her husband's reappearance.

28. See *HALOT* 1:275; Liverani 2004, 172; Stipp 2006, 137–38; and see also the

a silent, passive figure, upon which all the men in the section exert their force.²⁹ Thus the concubine is characterized as a silent victim with no control over her fate.

By contrast, all the male characters are depicted in an equivocal, or in an outright negative, fashion. For example, the characterization of the concubine's husband as a Levite is surprising, since no hint of the sacral surrounds his person.³⁰ Moreover, his motives in undertaking the journey to Bethlehem are not easy to fathom. Why did he wait four months before attempting to recover the concubine? If he undertook reconciliation with her as implied in verse 3, then how to explain his subsequent behavior toward her?³¹ On the night of the attack, he forcibly evicts her from the lodging and delivers her up to the crowd, with no care for her fate. Throughout the entire story he addresses her but once, on the morning after the rape, and even then all he says is, "Get up. We're going" (v. 28). It is ironic that he then addresses the lifeless body lying on the threshold as though she were asleep, impervious to her condition following the night's abuse. One might wonder how soundly he himself slept that night. On top of it all, after returning home, he continues to abuse her corpse and dismembers her body so that it may serve as a grisly visual message to others. Was there no other means of sending the message and summoning the tribes—for example, by symbolically dismembering an animal (cf. 1 Sam 11:7)?

Targum, which reads ובסרת עלוהי. The usual meaning of זנה, "to whore," is hard to reconcile with the context, since the girl's father and husband do not treat her as an adulteress. Moreover, when זנה expresses infidelity, the accompanying preposition is prefixed with *mem* (זנה מַעַל); see Hos 9:1; cf. Hos 1:2; 4:12.

29. With the exception of the Levite's servant, who is mentioned in vv. 3, 9, 11, 13, 19. However, the sole purpose of the servant is to serve as the Levite's interlocutor on the return trip from Bethlehem. It is likely that the narrator chose a servant to fill this role so that the concubine would remain silent throughout; see Liverani 2004, 171–72.

30. The MT of 19:18 represents his destination as the temple of YWHW in Mount Ephraim, but this does not necessary imply that he functioned there as Levite. It is equally likely that he simply dwelt in the town where the temple was located, or that he intended a visit similar to that undertaken by Elkanah and his family in 1 Sam 1. However, the LXX reading ביתי for MT בית יהוה may be preferable; see, e.g., Burney 1970, 466–67; Tov 1992, 256–57; and further discussion by Stipp 2006, 138.

31. It is expected that the husband would have paid the girl's father her brideprice. The purpose of his trip may have been to demand the return of the bride-price or to assert his claim to the girl's dowry and only as a last measure to take the girl back; see CH §§141–143; MAL A §38.

The husband's actions also cast doubt on his judgment and credibility. Had he insisted on departing Bethlehem in the morning, as planned, he could have returned to Mount Ephraim by nightfall. Once upon the road, he refuses the servant's suggestion to stay the night in Jerusalem, implying that he thought it safer to stay in any other city as long as it was Israelite (v. 12). In either case, had he acted with better judgment, the catastrophe at Gibeah might have been averted. Finally, in his last appearance in the story (20:4–7), he is shown to be an unreliable witness. In his statement before the Mizpah assembly, he conceals that he handed the concubine over to the mob, and rather than admit that he did so in order to save himself from sexual assault (cf. 19:22), he claims that the men of Gibeah had murderous designs from the outset.[32]

The Ephraimite host also appears to be an equivocal character. He meets the sojourners with suspicion and invites them only after the Levite states his business and adds that they have their own supplies and only want lodging. The Ephraimite's invitation sounds forced, for his words, "Just don't stay in the square" (19:20), seem to imply that he would not have issued the invitation if there were any alternative to their sleeping outside. His insistence on hosting them at his own expense does not represent him as a generous host, since this is a counteroffer, designed to save face after the Levite shamed him by proposing to make do with their own provisions. During the crisis, when the men of Gibeah demand that he hand over the man staying with him, he affirms his obligation toward those enjoying the protection of his roof but then immediately offers to hand over his guest's wife as well as his own virgin daughter. Even if the concubine is not accorded the social standing of her husband, she still is *his* dependent, and only *he* has the right to dispose of her. Thus the host's offer seems to encroach upon the Levite's rights over his concubine. Although the host exhorts the men of Gibeah not to "commit an outrage" (נבלה) and assault the Levite,[33] the Ephraimite suggests instead that the

---

32. See also Niditch 2008, 202. By contrast, Stipp (2006, 143–47) argues at length that the narrator depicts the husband in a sympathetic fashion and intends the audience to identify with him. However, it is difficult to understand how the flow of the narrative justifies Stipp's view.

33. נבלה frequently signifies nonnormative sexual relations; see Gen 34:7; Deut 22:21; 2 Sam 13:12; Jer 29:23; but cf. Phillips 1975, 237–42. On the attitude of the law codes toward same-sex relations and the differentiation between consent and assault, see Olyan 1994.

townsmen rape the women (ענו אותם).³⁴ This seems to imply that the Ephraimite does not consider rape of women to be an outrage as long as their menfolk temporarily waive their rights.

The narrator characterizes the people of Gibeah as בני בליעל (19:22; 20:13), which designates people who abrogate social norms.³⁵ The narrator employs this designation in 19:22 even before the assault takes place and thereby predisposes the reader against the people of Gibeah (cf. Gen 13:13). The subsequent events bear out this characterization. The people of Gibeah not only ignore the travelers on their arrival, but also refuse to recognize their right to protection while under their host's roof. Moreover, they intend to sexually assault the Levite, an action the host terms נבלה. Finally, the act of group rape is indicated by the verb התעלל ("abuse");³⁶ the abuse continues all night long (19:25), and when the townsmen are done, they forcibly send their victim away (וַיְשַׁלְּחוּהָ).³⁷

Of the male figures in the story, only the concubine's father, who lives in Bethlehem, has the appearance of a positive character. He "rejoices" to see his son-in-law (v. 3, וישמח לקראתו), hosts him generously, and even presses him daily to lengthen his stay. Even so, his favorable depiction may be more apparent than real. Could he have been glad to see his daughter's husband, because her reappearance at the paternal house was a source of embarrassment? The father would have received his daughter's bride-price when she joined the Levite's household, and he might have feared that the Levite would now demand restitution of the bride-price if the girl did not return to her husband. Moreover, he undoubtedly was glad at the prospect to be free of her upkeep. Finally, the narrator does not explain whether the concubine returned to her husband of her own free will or because her father threatened to withdraw his protection from her.³⁸

It would appear, then, that the narrator displays at best a reserved attitude toward all the active characters in this section of the story. The

---

34. See Gordon and Washington 1995, 313; Gravett 2004; and Shemesh 2007. Bechtel (1994), Frymer-Kensky (1998), van Wolde (2002), and others have argued that ענה does not necessarily imply rape. However, rape indeed seems to be the plain meaning of ענה here and in Gen 34:2; Deut 21:14; 22:24, 29; 2 Sam 13:12, 14, 22, 32; Ezek 22:10–11; Lam 5:11.
35. See Otzen 1975, 133–36; see, e.g., 1 Sam 10:27; 25:17, 25; 1 Kgs 21:10, 13.
36. See Num 22:29; 1 Sam 31:4; Jer 38:19; see also Sam 6:6.
37. For the causative use of *piel*, see Joüon §52d.
38. See Bohmbach 1999, 94; Gross 2009, 829.

outright negative characterization of the men of Gibeah is essential for justifying the tribes' subsequent action against them. However, the treatment the concubine received at their hands does not stand in marked contrast to that she received from the other characters. All the characters in the story treat the concubine as an object, and it seems that all are shown to be actual or implied partners in the affair that culminated in her rape and death. Thus all the characters seem to work together in order to "punish" the concubine with violent rape for daring to leave her husband.[39]

In spite of this, the narrator's stance with regard to his subject seems more ironic than tragic. Irony results from the discrepancy between the content value of information and the message it relays.[40] Accordingly, there is irony in the character of a Levite whose actions are utterly divorced from the sacral sphere, who goes to considerable trouble to retrieve a wayward wife only to discard her as a worthless object, and who addresses her only after she has become a lifeless corpse. So too the figure of the concubine's father: as a father, his role is to succor his children, but he seems all too glad to return her to her husband. Moreover, his concern with appearing to be the perfect host caused the Levite's late departure, which led to the overnight stop at Gibeah resulting in the demise of the concubine. A touch of irony is also evident in the figure of the reluctant Ephraimite host, who thinks that the obligation of protection concomitant with hospitality is due only to certain of his guests. The ironic stance regarding the characters should be remembered when dealing with the final purpose of the story.

1.3. The Battle at Gibeah

In this section of the story, the scope of the narrative broadens to the national sphere. According to the sequence of events in 19:29–20:2, all the men of Israel assembled at Mizpah after viewing the concubine's

---

39. Similarly, the story of Dinah seems to insinuate that she was raped because she wandered from home to visit the girls of the neighborhood (Gen 34:1). See Sipre Deut. 242 on 22:23, "Had she not gone out about the town, he would not have assaulted her. But *he happened upon her in the town and lay with her*, just as a breach tempts a thief"; so also Rashi.

40. Polak 1994, 338. According to Lasine, "the narrator condemns the Levite by means of the subtle use of irony and absurd humor" (1984, 39), and other characters are depicted in an "absurd," "grotesque," and "ludicrous" fashion (44–50).

dismembered body.⁴¹ This pantribal assembly marks a new stage in the story. Private individuals no longer appear, with the exception of a brief reappearance of the Levite at the Mizpah assembly (20:4–7) and the solitary mention of Phinehas ben Eleazar in 20:28. The actors are now corporate bodies, such as tribes (e.g., "the men/tribes of Israel," "the congregation," "the Benjaminites") or cities (e.g., Jabesh-gilead). This change in horizon occurs at the point in which the injury inflicted upon the Levite's family honor is represented as a matter of national significance (20:6, 10, 13), thus justifying the pantribal war against Benjamin. The transition between the preliminary stages and the outbreak of hostilities is sharp and dramatic, and once the sides mobilize for war there is no more mention of the concubine or the Gibeahites' transgression. This may indicate that the war at Gibeah and the rape of the concubine have been artificially linked together.

According to 20:1–2, a force of four hundred thousand fighting men mobilized at the Mizpah assembly and were deployed at Gibeah (v. 11) even before communicating the assembly's decisions to the people of Benjamin (vv. 12–13). However, the war does not break out until the Benjaminites refuse to comply with the demand to hand over the men of Gibeah (v. 13). The usual elements of battle descriptions immediately follow: mustering and numbering the troops, encampment, oracular consultation, mobilization, battle, flight, statement of defeat, and number of casualties.⁴² Some of the elements recur more than once, since this section of the narrative is also structured according to the graded number pattern in which two separate battles end in defeat and the victory is not achieved until the third and final battle. Nearly half the chapter deals with the decisive battle on the third day (20:26–48), while the fighting on the two previous days is briefly summarized (vv. 18–25). By contrast, there is no indication of the

---

41. Thus according to the sequence in the MT; see Liverani 2004, 162–63. LXX^A has the Levite commissioning the messengers to deliver an oral message as they display the pieces of the body, and this message is nearly identical to 19:30aβ. Many propose emending the MT to agree with LXX^A, e.g., Moore 1895, 421; Wallis 1952, 57; Gray 1986, 352–53; Stipp 2006, 133–34. However, as Burney (1970, 470–71) demonstrated, the version in LXX^A is really a conflation of two different readings; cf. Jüngling 1981, 248–50; Becker 1990, 261; and Gross 2009, 847, who uphold the MT as the preferred reading. In favor of the MT is the additional consideration that throughout the narrative the men of Israel take concerted action without directives from any individual.

42. For the pattern of battle descriptions, see Campbell 1975, 68–70; see also Richter 1963, 182–84, 263.

amount of time that passed from the initial mustering at Mizpah until the final outbreak of war (vv. 1–18).

JUDGES 20:1–13

According to the series of events related in 19:29–20:13, the war broke out after Benjamin would not accede to the tribes' demand to serve justice upon the men of Gibeah. Therefore, 20:1–13 establishes the causal link between the intertribal war and the incident with the concubine.

The sequence of events in 20:2–3a raises expectations that Benjamin will take action in response to the mustering of four hundred thousand men from all of Israel at Mizpah.[43] Mizpah itself lies in Benjamin, not far from Gibeah; therefore it would be natural for the Benjaminites to view the Israelites' actions as a threat.[44] However, the expectation that Benjamin will respond is not immediately fulfilled. Instead, the comment regarding Benjamin is broken off, and the narrator returns to the assembly at Mizpah, where the Israelites demand an explanation of "this evil" (v. 3b), referring to the dismembered corpse. The Levite relates his story, and the tribes confer about how to respond (vv. 4–10). Immediately afterward the narrator relates that the tribes carried out their decision and mobilized the troops against "the city," namely, Gibeah (v. 11).[45] Even then, they do not attack but instead demand to receive the culprits from Gibeah (vv. 12–13). Only in verse 14 does it become clear that war is imminent, when the Ben-

---

43. Elsewhere, "hearing" about the mustering of the one side (cf. v. 3a) brings about the rallying of troops on the rival side; see 1 Sam 7:7; 2 Sam 10:7; 2 Kgs 3:21; and cf. Num 21:1; Josh 9:1–2; 10:1–5; 11:1–4; Judg 4:12–13; 1 Sam 13:3–5; 2 Sam 5:17–18. So similarly in Assyrian annals; see examples from ancient Near Eastern royal inscriptions in Younger 1990, 200–208. Hentschel and Niessen (2008, 18) find it odd that Benjamin should only "hear" of the mobilization at Mizpah, since Mizpah is in Benjaminite territory. Here it seems that the author is following a literary convention that does not necessarily fit the narrative context.

44. So too Gross 2009, 850. On Mizpah, see the LXX version of Josh 18:25–28 and further discussion in ch. 2.

45. The term *the city* occurs another nine times in the narrative, and always indicates Gibeah (19:15, 17, 22; 20:31, 32, 37, 38, 40 twice). In 20:11 LXX^A reads "from the cities" as against the MT reading "to the city." However, this reading of LXX^A probably stems from an attempt to solve the difficulty in the sequence of the mobilization of the troops in vv. 11, 14. Moreover, this reading also reflects the influence of v. 14, where the expression "from the cities" is also found.

jaminites gather at Gibeah "in order to go to war against the men of Israel." The action on the side of Benjamin—mustering and mobilization—is no different from that related of Israel in verses 1 and 11, and yet the narrator refrains from attributing to Israel any warlike intentions and lays the whole burden for the outbreak of hostilities on the side of Benjamin. Even though the Israelites had assembled as a military body at Mizpah at the outset, the order of events in 20:1–13 creates the impression that they attempted to postpone the war even if it could not be adverted. Thus the disruption of the reader's expectations in 20:3b helps pass the onus for the war from Israel to the side of Benjamin. War does not break out because the Benjaminites "heard" (וישמעו) about the massive force assembled at Mizpah (v. 3a), but because they would "not listen to" (לא אבו לשמוע) the demands of Israel (v. 13).[46]

This reading of the present text may indicate how the hypertext was understood by its early readers, but close reading uncovers stylistic irregularity and discrepancies as well as a narrative break following 20:3a. The formulation of verses 1–2 is uncharacteristically verbose in comparison to the rest of the narrative and contains a large number of comparable terms for designating the side of Israel. Two Priestly terms depict the sacral nature of the assembly (עדה, קהל עם האלהים), while its pantribal aspect is emphasized by the designations "all the men of Israel," "all the tribes of Israel," "the leaders [פנות] of all the people," and "as one man from Dan to Beer-sheba and the Gilead." The number of noun clauses affixed by parataxis to the main clauses in these verses may indicate that they have undergone a process of accretion. As for narrative discrepancy, verses 14–16 place the mobilization of Benjamin's troops *after* Israel's forces had first massed at Mizpah and then encamped at Gibeah (vv. 2, 11). But how could Benjamin's forces cross the enemy lines in order to take up position in Gibeah?[47]

The unevenness of the section in 20:1–13 is undoubtedly the result of editorial intervention. The main issues to resolve are: How did the main narrative continue after verses 2–3a? How many compositional or editorial strands are represented in 20:1–13?[48]

---

46. Note the semantic contrast as well as the chiastic order in vv. 3aα/13bα: וישמעו בני בנימן/לא אבו בנימן לשמע.

47. In the ensuing battle descriptions, Benjamin essays forth to battle *from* Gibeah (20:21, 25, 31).

48. See the previous analyses by Budde 1897, 133–34; Burney 1970, 447–54; Becker 1990, 266–72.

In response to the first question, many have excised 20:3b–13 as an interpolation and have found that verse 14 provides the original continuation of verse 3a.[49] In this reconstruction, the purpose of the Mizpah assembly is wholly military. However, this view does not take into consideration the transition between 19:29b and 20:1. According to the flow of the narrative, the assembly at Mizpah convened in order to uncover the circumstances behind the dispatch of the concubine's body parts and to take counsel how to respond.[50] Yet this purpose is left unrealized if the main strand continues directly from verse 3a to verse 14. Readers who assume a primary link between the war and the incident of the concubine must somehow fill the gap between the call to take counsel (19:30) and the outbreak of hostilities (20:14).[51] An additional difficulty with this reading arises from the *Wiederaufnahme* in 20:17, which repeats the details of the Israelite mustering related previously in verse 2. If verses 14–17 directly followed verses 1–3a, then there was no narrative digression that would necessitate a repetitive resumption. Therefore, this approach must also eliminate either verse 2b or verse 17 as an editorial addition.[52]

These difficulties can be avoided if verses 12–13 are added to the scope of the primary narrative (henceforth: N^1). It is true that verse 12 does not directly continue the narrative thread interrupted in verse 3a. However, verse 3a may be a parenthetical comment, which alerts the reader to impending (but not immediate) developments. Thus it relates that the Benjaminites were aware of the Mizpah assembly, although they did not participate. It is possible that the narrator choose to insert the parenthetical comment at this point in order to thwart expectations arising from the common pattern (side x assembles; side y hears and reacts). This narrative strategy is also reflected in a subtle change in wording in the repetitive resumption in verse 17, which reminds the reader that the Israelite forces had *already* assembled, but only now—after the men of Benjamin gathered

---

49. See, e.g., Budde 1897, 133–34; Burney 1970, 447, 453–54; Eissfeldt 1925, 101; Gray 1986, 228.

50. See Jüngling 1981, 246–51.

51. Creative yet plausible solutions might assume one of the following: (1) the representatives deliberated on the course of action *prior* to the convocation at Mizpah; (2) the assembly did meet to consult, but the narrator chose to omit the details; and (3) the Benjaminites responded to the mustering at Mizpah *before* the assembly had time to deliberate.

52. See, e.g., Moore 1895, 424; Budde 1897, 133; Gray 1986, 228–29.

"to go to war" (v. 14, לצאת למלחמה)—are the Israelite forces characterized as "fighting men" (v. 17, כל זה איש מלחמה). The reconstructed narrative strand in 20:1–3a and 12–17 represents a continuous and tight-knit sequence of events that establishes an adequate causal link between the incident of the concubine and the outbreak of war. According to N¹, it appears that the Israelites gathered an armed force at Mizpah in order to "convince" Benjamin to comply with their demand to hand over the men of Gibeah, but the Benjaminites adhered to tribal solidarity and responded defensively by preparing to go to war. At this point the Israelite forces are finally called "men of war."

The reconstructed strand displays an even style in verses 3a and 12–14 that is characterized by simple syntax. However, verses 1–2 are also required by the reconstructed strand, and here the stylistic unevenness noted above seems to indicate that the present text is the result of expansion. The expressions that overload these verses designate different aspects of the pantribal entity, and most of them are found in this section alone or recur only in the last chapter of the narrative.⁵³ Excision of these expressions produces an even and concise text: ויצאו כל בני ישראל [ ] אל המצפה ויתיצבו [ ] ארבע מאות אלף איש רגלי שלף חרב. Thus it is likely that the overloading expressions are editorial accretions.⁵⁴

The expansions seem to represent a single layer (henceforth R²), displaying unity of style and outlook. The style of this layer is marked by the influence of Priestly idiom (v. 1, עדה; v. 2, קהל; v. 6, זמה)⁵⁵ and by a particularly high concentration of rare or atypical usages.⁵⁶ These expansions seem to have been motivated in part by the gap between the

---

53. Unique in the Bible: מדן ועד באר שבע; קהל עם האלהים with the prefixed preposition -ל; single use in Judg 19–21: פנות כל העם (cf. 1 Sam 14:38); recurring in Judg 20: כל בני ישראל (20:26), כל העם (20:8, 16, 26); recurring in Judg 21: עדה (21:10, 13, 16), קהל (21:5, 8), כל שבטי ישראל (21:5). See also Gross 2009, 849–50.

54. These seem to be interpolated in two blocks, each containing three clauses: ותקהל העדה / כאיש אחד / למדן ועד באר שבע וארץ הגלעד and פנות כל העם / כל שבטי ישראל / בקהל עם האלהים.

55. See, e.g., Moore 1895, 422; Burney 1970, 457–58; Becker 1990, 266–69; and further discussion in ch. 3 below. It is possible that Priestly style also influenced v. 9: זה הדבר אשר נעשה, and see similar formulations in Priestly contexts: Gen 6:15; Exod 29:1; cf. זה הדבר אשר followed by other verbs in Exod 16:16; 35:4; Lev 8:5; 9:6; 17:2; Num 30:2; 36:6; Josh 5:4; 2 Kgs 11:5 // 2 Chr 23:4; and in non-Priestly material: Exod 14:12; Jer 38:21.

56. See ch. 3 below.

visual message of the dismembered concubine (19:29–30) and the ultimatum issued to Benjamin (20:12–13). In the new sequence of events, the tribes assemble at Mizpah in order to investigate the circumstances behind the grisly message (20:3b), the Levite testifies to his version of the events (vv. 4–7), and the tribes decide on a course of action, which they hasten to implement (vv. 8–11). Although the formulation of verses 8–10 is uneven, it does not seem to reflect editorial revision, but rather random glossing and transmissional corruption, as demonstrated in the following comments.

Verse 8 appears to be a truncated oath. At the end of the story the people return, each to his own home (21:24), implying that the condition of the oath had been filled. The missing condition may have been transposed by mistake from 20:8 into 20:10bβ. Accordingly, the full oath in verse 8 might have read: לא נלך איש לאהלו ולא נסור איש לביתו עד אשר עשינו לגבעה ככל הנבלה אשר עשה בישראל.

Verse 9b is elliptic, lacking a verb. The wording in the LXX suggests a Hebrew *Vorlage* that reads נעלה עליה בגורל. However, this reading can hardly mean "we shall go against it (in war) by lot," since בגורל does not indicate elsewhere "by lot" but rather refers to the division of land into portions.[57] Thus the LXX does not seem to preserve a preferable reading but probably reflects an attempt to deal with the difficult text as witnessed in the MT. Details of the course of action decided upon should be expected immediately following the announcement: "This is what we shall do."[58] This announcement was probably followed by the decision to go up against Gibeah: נעלה] עליה] (cf. Josh 22:12), and בגורל is likely a gloss influenced by Judg 1:3.[59]

Verse 10bα, לעשות לבואם לגבע בנימן, is senseless. Some prefer the reading reflected in the LXX^A: לבאים לעשות לגבעה.[60] However, this reading also needs emending if it is to flow smoothly from verse 10a: לקחת

---

57. See Num 26:55; 33:54; 34:13; 36:2; Josh 14:2; 19:51; 21:4–8; Judg 1:3; Mic 2:5; 1 Chr 6:46–50; 24:5; cf. Isa 17:14; 57:6. According to the usual usage, the drawing of lots should have been indicated by נפיל עליה גורל (see Ezek 24:6; Jonah 1:7; Neh 10:35; 11:1) or נעלה עליה גורל (see Lev 16:9–10).

58. See similarly Exod 29:1; Judg 21:1; 2 Kgs 11:5 // 2 Chr 23:4.

59. See, e.g., Moore 1895, 426; Becker 1990, 271; and ch. 4 below.

60. See, e.g., Burney 1970, 474; Gray 1986, 354. MT's גבע בנימן is unlikely, since גבע(ת בנימן) refers to a place different from Gibeah (of Saul); see Na'aman 1992, 649–52. LXX^A seems to preserve the correct name.

צדה לעם הבאים לעשות לגבע בנימן ככל הנבלה אשר עשה בישראל (cf. Jer 26:2; 44:14, 28). If, as surmised, this verse has absorbed an interpolation transposed from verse 8, then the original reading was probably akin to: לקחת צדה לעם הבאים [לעשות] לגבעה [בנימן ככל הנבלה אשר עשה בישראל].⁶¹

The course of the expansion by R² is now clear. After the Levite's testimony, the people swear not to return to their homes until they deal with the men of Gibeah in accordance with their just deserts (v. 8). Immediately, they decide to prepare for a lengthy conflict (vv. 9–10), and finally the expansion concludes by noting the mobilization at Gibeah (v. 11).⁶² By advancing the troops' movement to this stage of the narrative, the men of Israel are shown to undertake the execution of their oath without delay. R² simply interpolated his expansion between verses 3a and 12, and either was not aware of or was not troubled by the resulting unevenness of the narrative in which the precipitous movement of the Israelites makes the subsequent mobilization of the Benjaminites at Gibeah implausible.

The unified outlook of the expansions is particularly evident in the ideal unity of "all Israel" in the face of Benjamin's separatism, as can be seen from the expressions: כל העם כאיש; כאיש אחד; כל בני ישראל (v. 1); כל איש ישראל (v. 2); כל שבטי ישראל (vv. 1, 8, 11); כאיש אחד חברים; אחד (v. 11). So too the Priestly terms in vv. 1–2, עדה and קהל, represent the people as a complete entity congregating in order to uphold its self-defining norms.⁶³ "All Israel" is also expressed by its complete and self-contained

---

61. See Trebolle Barrera 2008, 455, who postulates that the Hebrew *Vorlage* behind the LXX and the OL reads לקחת צדה לעם לבואם לגבע בנימן לעשות לה ככל הנבלה.

62. Gross (2009, 854) holds that the unnamed "city" in 20:11 is Mizpah, not Gibeah, and that v. 11 is a *Wiederaufnahme* that refers back to the assembly of the Israelites at Mizpah. Thus vv. 1–10 and 11–13 describe concurrent events rather than successive stages. Gross claims that the collocation אסף אל in conjunction with a PN or TN does not indicate mobilizing for military action, which should be expressed by the preposition על. However, as he admits, interchange between אל and על is frequent (and is considered by some to be an LBH marker). Furthermore, it should be noted that nine of the ten instances of "the city" in Judg 19–20 clearly refer to Gibeah (19:15, 17, 22; 20:31–32, 37–38, 40 twice).

63. On the עדה, see Weinfeld 1983, 75–84; Reviv 1985. The term קהל is reserved in the narrative for the assembly at Mizpah (20:2; 21:5, 8). The corollary of the idea that the assembly is constituted of "all Israel" is presented in 21:5; whoever absented themselves from the assembly in effect excluded themselves from the congregation representing the normative community and were thus subject to sanction. It may be

territory: כל שדה נחלת ישראל (v. 1); למדן ועד באר שבע וארץ הגלעד (v. 6). Together these concepts underline how Benjamin removes itself from the ideal normative community by refusing to comply with the reasonable demands decided upon by the pantribal assembly.

Judges 20:1–13 plays a central role in structuring the narrative in both N¹ and R². Not only does it establish the causal link between the local incident involving the concubine and the subsequent intertribal war, but it also employs stylistic linking, which helps bind together the main parts of the narrative.

Links with the story of the concubine (19:1–30). Both N¹ and R² tightened the transition between the first two parts of the story by employing recurring expressions that are found only in 20:1–13 and 19:1–30 (the asterisks mark expressions not found elsewhere in Judges): N¹: *אנשי(ם) בני בליעל (20:13/19:22); *לא אבו לשמע (20:13/19:25; cf. לא אבה, 19:10); R²: נסור (20:8/19:9); (ו)הלך לאהל (20:3b, 7/19:30); *עצו ודברו ... *נהיתה (20:8/19:12); *עשה נבלה (20:6, 10/19:23, 24). R² also strengthened the ties between the two sections by reintroducing the figure of the concubine's husband (איש לוי, 20:4/19:1), who retells the incident at Gibeah from his point of view (20:4–6).

Links with the war description (20:14–48). In 20:1–13 both N¹ and R² depict preparations for a punitive expedition and thereby build readers' expectations for the war that follows. Thus in N¹ an armed force was mustered from the outset at the Mizpah assembly, while R² adds details of the preparations, which include oath taking, arranging for provisions, and moving against Gibeah. Here too both N¹ and R² utilize expressions that recur only in 20:1–13, 14–48, thereby strengthening the ties between the sections: N¹: שלף חרב (20:2, 17; cf. ארבע מאות אלף איש (רגלי) שלף חרב in 20:25, 35, 46); כל העם (20:2, 8, 26; cf. 20:16); כל בני ישראל (20:1, 26); R²: ויאספו בני בנימן מן הערים (20:11); cf. ויאסף כל איש ישראל אל העיר (20:14).

Links with the outcome of the war (21:1–24). In 20:3a and 13b, Benjamin refrains from participation in the pantribal assembly and refuses to comply with the assembly's demands. By these acts, the narrator presents

---

supposed that only the fighting men and perhaps some of the representative leadership (cf. 21:16) took part in the gatherings at Bethel and the subsequent battles; thus the terms עדה and קהל, which designate the entire congregation, were not appropriate to the narrative 20:14–48. For this reason, it is necessary to consider the likelihood that R² did not limit his intervention to the use of Priestly language.

Benjamin as excluding itself from "all Israel." The final section of the story, 21:1–24, picks up this theme and deals with repairing the breach in the pantribal entity ("all Israel") by restoring Benjamin to its position within the people. In both these sections, Israel is depicted as a collective personality, which consults, deliberates, and speaks with one voice (N[1]: 20:12–13a; R[2]: 20:3b, 8–10; cf. 21:1, 3, 5–8, 10–11, 16–22). The two sections are also connected by means of reference to the assembly at Mizpah and to the oaths sworn there (20:1, 8; 21:1, 5, 7, 18).[64] Once again, the links are strengthened by use of expressions that recur only in these two sections: N[1]: *כל בני ישראל (20:2, 10; 21:5); *לצאת/לעלות אל ה' (20:1; 21:5, 8); R[2]: *עדה (20:1; 21:10, 13, 16); *קהל (20:2; 21:5, 8); *תעשו/נעשה אשר הדבר זה (20:9; 21:11); נחלה (20:6; 21:24).

All of the different sections are additionally bound together with the help of the Leitwort אח (19:23; 20:13, 23, 28; 21:6).[65] The use of this Leitwort in the story conveys the idea that the different constituents of the people are united by ties of brotherhood. The concubine's husband would not stop over in Jebus since it is a foreign city but continue on to the nearest Israelite city, where he expects to be received in a manner commensurate with brotherhood. During the stay in Gibeah, the Ephraimite host calls the Benjaminite men of the town "my brothers" (19:23), which emphasizes that their act of assault violates the concept of ideal brotherhood uniting "all Israel." Just as the men of Gibeah violated the concept of brotherhood by refusing to "hear" the Ephraimite out (19:25, ולא אבו לשמוע לו), so too the Benjaminites refuse to "hearken" to "the voice of their *brothers*, the people of Israel" (20:13), implying that their solidarity with Gibeah flies in the face of true brotherhood. Following each defeat, the men of Israel twice inquire of YWHW: "Shall I continue to go out to war against *my brother*, the Benjaminites?" (20:23, 28), thus displaying hesitation whether to persist in the course of civil war. Finally, the narrator uses the term אח when describing the Israelites' regret over the near annihilation of Benjamin: "The people of Israel relented toward Benjamin, *his brother*, saying: 'A tribe has been cut off today from Israel'" (21:6). Thus the metaphor of brotherhood, signifying the bonds that ideally unite all

---

64. 21:5 relates a different oath from that in 21:1, 7, 18; and both differ from the oath presumed in 20:8.

65. For criteria in identifying the use of *Leitwörter*, see Bar-Efrat 2004, 212–13; Amit 1989; Stadler-Sutskover 2002, 296–97.

of Israel into an inviolable whole, runs throughout each part of the story, stamping the entire narrative with a comprehensive theme.

The compositional analysis of 20:1–17 is as follows (N^1 is in boldface type; R^2 is bracketed in normal type; glosses in superscript).

> ¹ **All the Israelites went out** [and the community congregated as one man from Dan to Beer-sheba and the land of Gilead] **to (the place of) YHWH at Mizpah.** ² **All the tribes of Israel** [the heads of all the people] **presented themselves** [at the assembly of the people of God], **four hundred thousand sword-bearing foot soldiers.** ³ **(The Benjaminites had heard that the Israelites went up to Mizpah.)** [The Israelites said: "Tell how this evil came to pass." ⁴ The Levite, the husband of the murdered woman, answered, saying: "I came to lodge in Gibeah in Benjamin; I and my wife. ⁵ (When it was) night, the people of Gibeah surrounded the house (where) I was; they thought to kill me, and they raped my wife and she died. ⁶ I seized my wife and cut her up and sent her (pieces) throughout all the territory of Israel, for they committed an indecent outrage in Israel. ⁷ Here, all of you are Israelites; confer and take council." ⁸ All the people rose and spoke as one: "Not a man of us will return to his tent and home (¹⁰ᵇ until we deal with Benjamin according to the outrage they committed in Israel). ⁹ This is what we shall to Gibeah: We shall (go up) against it by lot. ¹⁰ᵃ We shall take ten men of every hundred from all the tribes of Israel, and a hundred of every thousand and a thousand of every ten thousand in order to provide for the people coming to Gibeah." ¹¹ All the men of Israel assembled against the city as one man.] ¹² **The tribes of Israel sent men throughout the tribe(s) of Benjamin, saying: "What is this evil that you have done?** ¹³ **Now give us the scoundrels, the men who are in Gibeah, and we will put them to death and eradicate the evil from Israel." But the Benjaminites did not wish to listen to their brothers the Israelites.** ¹⁴ **The Benjaminites gathered from all their cities to Gibeah to go to war against the Israelites.** ¹⁵ **On that day the Benjaminites mustered from their cities twenty-six thousand sword bearers, apart from the people of Gibeah** ᵐᵘˢᵗᵉʳᵉᵈ ˢᵉᵛᵉⁿ ʰᵘⁿᵈʳᵉᵈ ᵖⁱᶜᵏᵉᵈ ᵐᵉⁿ. ¹⁶ [Of all this people, seven hundred picked men were left-handed; all these could sling a stone at a hair and not miss]. ¹⁷ **And the**

TEXTUAL ARTIFACT AND LITERARY STRATIFICATION 31

Israelites mustered—apart from Benjamin—four hundred thousand sword-bearing soldiers.

¹ ויצאו כל בני ישראל [ותקהל העדה כאיש אחד למדן ועד באר שבע וארץ הגלעד] אל ה' המצפה. ² ויתיצבו [פנות כל העם] כל שבטי ישראל [בקהל עם האלהים] ארבע מאות אלף איש רגלי שלף חרב. ³ (וישמעו בני בנימן כי עלו בני ישראל המצפה) [ויאמרו בני ישראל דברו איכה נהיתה הרעה הזאת. ⁴ ויען האיש הלוי איש האשה הנרצחה ויאמר הגבעתה אשר לבנימן באתי אני ופילגשי ללון. ⁵ ויקמו עלי בעלי הגבעה ויסבו עלי את הבית לילה אותי דמו להרג ואת פילגשי ענו ותמת. ⁶ ואחז בפילגשי ואנתחה ואשלחה בכל שדה נחלת ישראל כי עשו זמה ונבלה בישראל. ⁷ הנה כלכם בני ישראל הבו לכם דבר ועצה הלם. ⁸ ויקם כל העם כאיש אחד לאמר לא נלך איש לאהלו ולא נסור איש לביתו. ⁹ ועתה זה הדבר אשר נעשה לגבעה עליה בגורל. ¹⁰ ולקחנו עשרה אנשים למאה לכל שבטי ישראל ומאה לאלף ואלף לרבבה לקחת צדה לעם לעשות לבואם לגבע בנימן ככל הנבלה אשר עשה בישראל. ¹¹ ויאסף כל איש ישראל אל העיר כאיש אחד חברים.] ¹² וישלחו שבטי ישראל אנשים בכל שבטי בנימן לאמר מה הרעה הזאת אשר נהיתה בכם. ¹³ ועתה תנו את האנשים בני בליעל אשר בגבעה ונמיתם ונבערה רעה מישראל ולא אבו בני בנימן לשמע בקול אחיהם בני ישראל. ¹⁴ ויאספו בני בנימן מן הערים הגבעתה לצאת למלחמה עם בני ישראל. ¹⁵ ויתפקדו בני בנימן ביום ההוא מהערים עשרים וששה אלף איש שלף חרב לבד מישבי הגבעה התפקדו שבע מאות איש בחור. ¹⁶ [מכל העם הזה שבע מאות איש בחור אטר יד ימינו כל זה קלע באבן אל השערה ולא יחטא.] ¹⁷ ואיש ישראל התפקדו לבד מבנימן ארבע מאות אלף איש שלף חרב כל זה איש מלחמה.

JUDGES 20:14–48

The war at Gibeah is represented as one campaign played out in a series of three battles, day after day (Judg 20:22, 24, 30). The account of all three battles follows a common pattern: going up to Bethel (20:18, 23, 26), crying before YWHW (20:23, 26), consultation of the oracle (20:18, 23, 27–28), deployment by Israel (20:19–20, 22, 24, 29–30), Benjamin's sortie (20:21, 25, 31a), and summation of defeat (20:21, 25, 35, 44). However, the mobilization of troops is detailed but once, before the first battle (20:14–17), and the decisive outcome is related only at the end of the third day's fighting (20:44–48; cf. v. 35).

The Two Preliminary Battles (20:18–28)

The account of the first two days establishes a clear recurring pattern, but it is not without difficulties. Surprisingly, the first two battles end in defeat, even though the Israelite force is fifteen times greater than the Benjaminites' troops. Moreover, the Israelites are fighting for justice. Not only do they attempt to "eradicate the evil" before going to war, but they diligently consult the oracle on the eve of each battle and take to the field only after receiving what appears to be a positive reply. With everything in their favor, it is hard to understand why they must suffer such disastrous defeats twice in a row, losing 10 percent of their forces in casualties.[66] Thus there is an inherent tension between the motif of oracular consultation on the eve of each battle and the scheme of double defeat followed by victory. This tension may indicate that one of these two elements may have been artificially imposed upon the plot.[67]

There are also irregularities in the sequence of the text: (1) 20:15–16 counts two different groups of "seven hundred picked men"; (2) the question and answer of the oracle in 20:18 are not followed up by the narrative; (3) the sequence of events in 20:22–23 is disrupted; and (4) the third oracular reply in 20:28b is severed from the question in 20:27a. These problems are treated in the following comments.

1. Verses 15b and 16aα initially appear to be variants. LXX^L lacks verse 16aα (מכל העם הזה שבע מאות איש בחור),[68] but the resulting reading for verses 15b–16a is doubtful. With the exception of 1 Kgs 10:15, which is certainly corrupt, לבד מ- always *follows* a listing (e.g., Num 29:39; Deut 3:5; Judg 8:26; 1 Kgs 5:3). Moreover, it is unclear why the left-handed warriors are considered a group apart in relation to the men of Gibeah rather than to Israel. The simplest solution is that the numbering of the men of Gibeah in verse 15b is the result of dittography from verse 16.[69] Thus it is likely that verses 15–16a originally read:

---

66. See also Niditch 2008, 204.
67. According to Josephus *Ant.* 5.2.10 §§156–159, the oracle was consulted only on the eve of the third battle. Josephus has undoubtedly reworked the narrative in order to resolve the theological difficulty presented by the first two oracular consultations. Contra Crüsemann (1978, 159) and Gray (1986, 229), there is no conceivable motivation for a subsequent scribe to add the problematic consultations.
68. See Moore 1895, 430–31.
69. See, e.g., Bertheau 1845, 222; Becker 1990, 274.

TEXTUAL ARTIFACT AND LITERARY STRATIFICATION 33

ויתפקדו בני בנימן ביום ההוא מהערים עשרים וששה אלף איש שלף חרב
לבד מישבי הגבעה. [התפקדו שבע מאות איש בחור] מכל העם הזה שבע
מאות איש בחור אטר יד־ימינו.

2. The question in verse 18, "Who shall lead us into battle?" deviates from the pattern of the questions posed following the defeats (vv. 23, 28), when the Israelites ask whether to wage war against Benjamin (cf. 1 Sam 23:2; 1 Kgs 22:6). It is possible that the Israelites were initially confident that the war was in accord with divine will, and therefore they only inquired how to conduct the battle. But in the wake of the defeats they asked whether to continue the war. However, the spirit of the question and reply in Judg 20:18 (Judah shall lead) deviates from the pantribal tendency of the entire story in which corporate groups receiving special mention are mainly characterized by separatist behavior (e.g., Benjamin, the men of Gibeah and Jabesh). Moreover, Judah receives no further mention in the story. Therefore, the formulation of the question and reply in verse 18 appears foreign to the context.[70] The oracular consultation before the first battle sets the pattern for the subsequent days and must have been part of N[1]'s narrative, but a later reviser (probably R[2]) changed the formulation in order to spotlight Judah.[71] If so, the original formulation of verse 18 might be restored through comparison with verse 23:

MT 20:18

מי יעלה־לנו בתחלה   למלחמה עם־בני בנימן   ויאמר ה' יהודה בתחלה

20:18*

האעלה   למלחמה עם־בני בנימן   ויאמר ה' עלו

MT 20:23

האוסיף לגשת   למלחמה עם־בני בנימן אחי   ויאמר ה' עלו אליו

---

70. See, e.g., Moore 1895, 432; Burney 1970, 448, 454; Noth 1966, 166; Crüsemann 1978, 159; Veijola 1982, 188–86.

71. Contra Noth 1966, 166; Schunck 1963, 61; Rösel 1976, 34–31; Veijola 1977, 22; 1982, 186–88; Gross 2009, 825–26, 853–58, 877, who excise all the scenes at Bethel; see criticism by Becker 1990, 280–81. Surprisingly, Gross (2009, 858) holds that the reviser created the theological problem of repeated defeats following consultation of the oracle, but it is hard to understand why this is preferable to the alternate view, that the discrepancy is inherent to the original composition.

3. Verse 22 appears to have been transposed from its original place *after* verse 23.⁷² Verse 21 reports that the Israelites suffered a disastrous defeat on the first day of fighting, but verse 22 inexplicably reports that the Israelites took heart immediately afterward (ויתחזק; cf. 1 Sam 4:9; 2 Sam 10:12). Moreover, verse 23 breaks the sequence of preparations for battle in verses 22 and 24 (cf. vv. 19–20, 29–30) and transfers the action to the unspecified sanctuary, most likely Bethel,⁷³ where the Israelites weep and again consult the oracle.

4. The notice about the presence of the ark and Phinehas ben Eleazar at the third oracular consultation (vv. 27b–28a) is widely viewed as an interpolation, since it severs the statement וישאלו בני ישראל בה' ("the Israelites inquired of YHWH," v. 27a) from its logical continuation לאמר האוסיף עוד לצאת ("saying, 'Shall I continue to go out,'" v. 28b).⁷⁴ While the notice could be viewed as a parenthetical comment, it is odd that it was not placed earlier in the story, for according to the wording, the ark and Phinehas ben Eleazar were at Bethel "in those days" (בימים ההם).⁷⁵ In addition, neither the ark nor the figure of Phinehas figures further in the narrative. Nor is the ark mentioned elsewhere in Judges, and no other traditions connect it with Bethel. The reference to Phinehas is surprising since all the other characters in the story are anonymous.⁷⁶ Furthermore, the mention of Phinehas son of Eleazar son of Aaron is also inconsistent with the present context of the narrative between the Samson and Samuel stories, for according to the chronological framework of the Deuteron-

---

72. See, e.g., Moore 1895, 431; Burney 1970, 448; Schunck 1963, 61 n. 32. Veijola (1982, 187 n. 37) and Becker (1990, 275) deal with the disrupted sequence by excising sections of vv. 22–24 as late interpolations. However, neither has provided a reasonable motive for the interpolations. Moreover, the graded number (x + 1) pattern is a common narrative device and appears integral to N¹. Any excision destroys the integrity of this pattern.

73. Some, e.g., Eissfeldt 1925, 101–2; Noth 1966, 166; Schunck 1963, 61, take the nonspecification to indicate that the cult site was identified as Bethel only at a secondary stage. This view is based on the incorrect assumption that narrative repetition always reiterates all the necessary details. However, narrative repetition is far more varied; see, e.g., Polak 1994, 59–81.

74. See, e.g., Wellhausen 1957, 237; Moore 1895, 434; Burney 1970, 448; Veijola 1977, 22; Becker 1990, 276.

75. See Bleek 1878, 201; W. Arnold 1917, 115; cf. Pseudo-Philo, *Bib. Ant.* 46.1–4, according to which Phinehas also participated in the previous consultations.

76. See Amit 1999, 348 n. 41; cf. Revell 1996, 191–94.

omistic History, Samson and Samuel belong some four hundred years *after* the time of Phinehas.⁷⁷

What purpose does this interpolation serve, and why was it inserted into verses 27–28? Comparison of each day's report shows that the third detour to Bethel is far more detailed than the previous two and caps the series of graded repetitions in N¹. This time the Israelites not only lament their losses but try to propitiate God with burnt offerings. They also ask the oracle a more explicit question and add the converse option "or shall I desist" (אם אחדל, v. 28aβ), which reflects the Israelites' growing despair in light of their repeated defeats, despite the positive response of the oracle. These additions to the repeated pattern add weight to the scene, hinting that the critical moment has been reached. The imminent change in the course of the war is then signaled as the Israelites receive an unambiguous promise of victory. It seems likely that the interpolation was inserted at the critical juncture, right before the newly phrased question was put to the oracle in order to help justify the promise of victory in the wake of the previous defeats. This positioning of the comment seems to imply that previous consultations were deficient and therefore led to equivocal results.⁷⁸ But if this was the intent of the glossator, he should have specified that the ark and Phinehas were present "on that day" (ביום ההוא; cf. 1 Sam 14:18), which would imply that they were absent from the previous occasions. The glossator appears to have been indifferent to the difficulties resulting from the interpolation and was concerned mainly with loading the final consultation scene with additional factors to ensure that conditions would be ripe for the final promise of victory.⁷⁹

---

77. Cf. the harmonistic placement of the narrative by Josephus in *Ant.* 5.2.8 §136.
78. Cf. b. Šebu. 35b, in which the equivocal outcome results from asking imprecise questions of the oracle.
79. It is possible that the formulation and the placement of the interpolation was influenced by the similar comment in 1 Sam 4:4b: וישם שני בני־עלי עם־ארון ברית האלהים חפני ופינחס; cf. Judg 20:27–28, ושם ארון ברית האלהים בימים ההם ופינחס בן־אלעזר בן־אהרן עמד לפניו בימים ההם. Phinehas and Hophni, sons of Eli, accompany the ark into battle following a defeat with the hope that YHWH will now lead them to victory; however, the outcome is disastrous. The battle is lost, the ark is taken, and Hophni and Phinehas are killed. The glossator in Judg 20:27–28 may have intended to draw a contrasting analogy to 1 Sam 4. In contrast to the conduct of the Israelites at Aphek, the Israelites now inquire of YWHW at a cult site far from the battlefield, in the presence of the ark and a legitimate Aaronite priest named Phinehas.

But why did he add these specific details? The appearance of the ark at Bethel on the eve of the third battle helps present Bethel as an appropriate cult site for the dispensation of the oracular reply. The comment thereby serves to "rewrite" the tradition history of the Bethel cult, which was bound up with the bull images denigrated by the Deuteronomistic scribes (Hos 10:5; 1 Kgs 12:28–32). The glossator thus wishes to imply that Bethel was the home of the legitimate symbol of divine presence prior to the corruption of the cult by Jeroboam.[80]

Additionally, by identifying the priest who presided over the oracle as Phinehas ben Eleazar ben Aaron, the glossator legitimizes the Bethel priesthood by providing them with Aaronide descent.[81] The Deuteronomistic History denigrates the Bethel priesthood as rivals to the Zadokite house presiding in Jerusalem (1 Kgs 12:31), which is viewed as the single legitimate priestly line (1 Kgs 2:26–27, 35; cf. 1 Sam 2:35). While the Aaronide priesthood plays no role in the Deuteronomistic History, it is central to P (Exod 28:1; Num 17:5, 16–24).[82] In P, Phinehas ben Eleazar is promised eternal priesthood (Num 25:13), and his name provides the crucial link to Aaron in the Aaronide genealogies in Ezra 7:5 and 1 Chr 5:30–31.[83] Thus the parenthetical comment in Judg 20:28 draws upon a post-Deuteronomistic view of the Aaronide priesthood in which Phinehas ben Eleazar played a central role in establishing the priestly pedigree. It seems likely that the glossator employed this view in order to sanction the cultic activity of the Israelites at Bethel. Since Phinehas ben Eleazar is rooted in

---

The opposing analogy hints that the final battle at Gibeah must result differently from that at Aphek in the days of Phinehas son of Eli.

80. See Naʾaman 1987, 17–18; Rofé, 2003, 788–89.

81. See, e.g., Burney 1970, 453; Becker 1990, 276–77. Some (e.g., Cross 1973, 198–200; Blenkinsopp 1998, 35–36; 1995, 86) take Exod 32 and 1 Kgs 12:31 as reflecting an historical reality of preexilic Aaronide priesthood at Bethel.

82. See, e.g., Blenkinsopp 1998, 35–36. Deuteronomy regularly refers to the priests as הכהנים הלוים ("Levitical priests"; see Deut 17:9, 18; 18:1; 24:8; 27:9) and mentions Aaron only three times, thereby downplaying his priestly role (Deut 9:20; 10:6; 32:50). Eleazar and Phinehas do figure in Josh 14–24, but this material belongs to the post-Dtr "Priestly" redaction of Joshua; see, e.g., Nelson 1997, 9.

83. The sons of Itamar ben Aaron are relegated to a marginal branch. According to 1 Chr 24:3, the Elides are descended from Ithamar, while Zadok belongs to the line of Eleazar. In the Aaronide genealogy in 1 Chr 5:30 Ithamar is dropped altogether. See also Cody 1969, 171–72; Nelson 1993, 10–11.

Priestly texts, I suggest that the glossator is none other than R², who also displayed Priestly influence in the expansions in 20:1–11.

It is possible that the interpolation in 20:27b–28a was also devised as a counterweight to the scandalous cultic goings-on related in the story of Micah's image in Judg 17–18. The molten image Micah sets up in his private sanctuary (בית אלהים) at his home in Mount Ephraim is later stolen and moved to Dan. It is widely recognized that Micah's molten image alludes to the bull figures Jeroboam established at Bethel and Dan (1 Kgs 12:28–29); therefore it is also probable that the "house of God" established by Micah alludes to the cult site at Bethel (בית־אל).[84] Thus the mention of the ark in the interpolation stands in opposition to Micah's image, while the mention of the legitimate priest, Phinehas son of Eleazar son of Aaron, counters the name of the Levite who officiated before the image: Jonathan son of Gershom son of Moses (מנשה, Judg 18:30).[85] By these means, the interpolation also serves to amend the negative impression of the Bethel cult left by the previous narrative.

The Decisive Battle (20:29–48)

Unlike the schematic accounts of the two previous battles, the description of the third battle is replete with geographical and tactical details. Yet the opening of the third battle description (20:30–31a) still follows the lines of the pattern set by the previous accounts. The routine nature of the initial sortie is emphasized by the expression "as before" (בפעם כפעם, 20:30), but the routine only appears to repeat itself from the Benjaminites' standpoint. The narrator, on his part, alerts the reader of the change in Israelite tactics (v. 29), thus signaling that the course and results of this battle will *not* be "as before."[86]

In spite of some attempts to read the account of the third battle as a continuous narrative,[87] doublets, breaks, and inconsistencies indicate that the narrative is indeed composite.

---

84. See Amit 1990.
85. On the suspended *nun*, see Moore 1895, 401–2.
86. See the similar use of כפעם בפעם at the stage where a recurring pattern is about to be broken in Num 24:1; Judg 16:20; 1 Sam 3:10; 20:25.
87. See Revell 1985; Satterthwaite 1992; and most recently Gross 2009, 855, 860–65. Gross's analysis depends upon his understanding of verbal syntax to represent either flashbacks (*w*-subject + *wəqaṭal*) or repetitive resumptions after depicting

1. According to verse 29, the Israelites set up "ambushes around" (סביב ארבים) Gibeah, but afterward the narrative mentions a single ambush that hid at a specific spot (ארב, vv. 33, 36–38).

2. The narrative relates twice how Benjamin grew confident after inflicting about thirty Israelite casualties (vv. 31–32, 39):

20:31–32

ויצאו בני־בנימן לקראת העם הנתקו מן־העיר ויחלו להכות מהעם
חללים כפעם בפעם ... כשלשים איש בישראל
ויאמרו בני בנימן נגפים הם לפנינו כבראשנה

20:39

ויהפך איש־ישראל במלחמה ובנימן החל להכות חללים באיש־
ישראל כשלשים איש
כי אמרו אך נגוף נגף הוא לפנינו כמלחמה הראשנה

3. Verse 35 summarizes Benjamin's casualties, and in verse 36a the narrator reports that Benjamin realized that they were defeated. This leads the reader to expect that the battle is now over. However, verses 36b–42 return to the midst of the battle, and once more Benjamin strikes Israel and grows confident of victory (v. 39).

4. The ambush springs into action twice, in both verse 33 and verse 37.

5. The results of the battle are summarized twice, in both verse 35 and verses 44–46, but with different figures. Verse 35 reports 25,100 casualties. By contrast, verses 44–45 count 18,000 fallen in battle and another 7,000 struck down in flight, and the final total in verse 46 is short by 100 of the figure in verse 35.

The doublets, and particularly the double summary in verses 35, 44–46, indicate that the account of the third battle is composed of two different descriptions, joined together by verse 36a.[88]

The First Description (20:29–35). The opening note about positioning the ambush (v. 29) breaks the recurring pattern set by the two previous

---

simultaneous events (*wayyiqṭal*). However, serious discrepancies in details relating to the course of the battle impede such a facile solution.

88. See, e.g., Moore 1895, 424–38; Soggin 1987, 293–94.

battle accounts, and the pattern is resumed only in verse 30. Since the ambush is not put into action until verse 33, the notice in verse 29 anticipates later developments. The placement of the notice at the opening of the battle account may have intended to show that the Israelites responded immediately to the oracular reply with a new initiative that will help to realize the divine promise of victory.

The new battle scheme in verses 31b–34 features the ruse of feigned flight, which takes advantage of the enemy's confidence following their previous victories. The feigned flight had a double objective: to create an illusion of defeat and to lure the enemy away from the city in pursuit of the Israelites, who fled along two different routes (מסילות):[89] a northern route toward Bethel and a northeastern route to Geba (vv. 31b–32).[90] The fleeing force regrouped at Baal-tamar,[91] while the ambushers sprang into action on the outskirts of Geba (v. 33).[92] Afterward the narrator relates that a troop of ten thousand men led a frontal attack on Gibeah (v. 34).

It is not clear whether this troop is supposed to be part of the main force, which fled along the two routes, whether it is identical with the ambush, or whether it represents a third group mentioned here for the first

---

89. On the term מסילה, see Dorsey 1991, 228–33; cf. Tidwell 1995.

90. The MT of v. 31 reads "to Gibeah" (גבעתה), but this reading does not fit in with the Israelites' plan to cut the Benjaminites off from the city (v. 32). It seems likely that the text originally read גִּבְעָה ("to Geba"), in which the toponym Geba is followed by the locative case ending (cf. 2 Sam 14:2, תקועה); see also Albright 1924, 34. Others, like Budde 1897, 133; Rösel 1976, 38–39; and Soggin 1987, 296, suggested reading "to Gibeon" (גבעונה), but this is unlikely, since all other geographic references concentrate the fighting north and northeast of Gibeah.

91. Baal-tamar is not otherwise mentioned, and its location is uncertain. Eusebius places it northeast of Gibeah, but he undoubtedly depends upon the details related in v. 33; see Rösel 1976, 44. The toponym most likely represents a location on one of the two flight routes, and it is tempting to identify it with the site of the palm of Deborah (תמר דבורה, Judg 4:5), between Ramah and Bethel, about 5 km. north of Gibeah.

92. MT ממערה גבע is difficult; see Moore 1895, 437–38. Many prefer the reading "west of Gibeah" (ממערב לגבעה), attested to by LXX[L] and other versions; see, e.g., Wellhausen 1899, 232; Moore 1895, 438; Burney 1970, 480. However, it is preferable to retain the MT reading Geba, since placing the ambush west of Geba fits nicely with the route taken by the western flank along the Gibeah-Bethel road; cf. Burney 1970, 480–81. An alternate but unattested reading is ממעבר גבע, "the pass of Geba" (cf. Isa 10:29), running between Geba and Michmash (called the "pass of Michmash" in 1 Sam 13:23; 14:4). From here, the ambush would have acted in coordination with the eastern flank, which fled along the route to Geba.

time.⁹³ The first possibility does not seem likely, since it is hard to imagine how a group from the main force could bypass the Benjaminite troops positioned between them and Gibeah. If a third group is intended, then it could be a second ambush positioned close to the city, but this view runs counter to verse 33, which speaks of a single ambush. Moreover, within the framework of the battle plan in verses 31–34, this ambush would have difficulty finding cover. The access to Gibeah (Tel el-Ful) is from the south, where the slope is moderate, and if the narrator was familiar with the topography of the area, then the main force would have begun its flight south of Gibeah and continued north along the two routes flanking the city on either side.⁹⁴ Thus an ambush positioned by the city could be seen by the pursuing forces. However, it is also conceivable that the account was composed by a scribe with little practical knowledge of the terrain and thus was unaware of the inconsistencies arising from the narrative.

In spite of this reservation, the simplest solution is assuming the placement of a single ambush, which split into two heads after it burst on to the adjacent route. One head closed in on the rear flanks of the Benjaminite force, cutting them off from their path of retreat, and the other head continued south in order to take the city. The only difficulty with this view is that it contradicts the notice in verse 29 that mentions liers-in-wait placed *around* the city. This notice seems to imply that the "ambushers" were to set siege to the city,⁹⁵ but according to verses 33–34, only the force that broke off from the ambush mounted a surprise attack on the city. The tension between verses 33–34 and verse 29 with regard to the position and purpose of the ambush may indicate that the battle description in verses 31b–34 is not the true continuation of verse 29.

The description of the raid on the city is broken off in the middle of verse 34 and is not taken up again before the summation in verse 35. Instead the narrator returns to the battlefield and reports on the action from Benjamin's point of view (v. 34, "the fighting was heavy, but they⁹⁶ did not realize that disaster was upon them"). Since the Benjaminites won

---

93. Cf. Judg 7:16; 9:43; 1 Sam 11:11; 13:17; Job 1:17.
94. On these routes see Gibson and Edelstein 1985, 150–51.
95. This is the only instance of אל x סביב within a military context. However, על x סביב is frequent in the context of siege, e.g., 2 Kgs 25:1, 4; Jer 6:3; 50:14–15; 52:7; Ezek 4:2; 19:8; 23:24; 27:11.
96. The referent of the pronoun is Benjamin, even though the antecedent in the previous clause is the picked force "from all Israel." The tactic of the feigned flight

an easy victory in the previous battles, they were not aware of their dire situation until after the ambush sprang into action. Immediately afterward the account closes in verse 35 with a summation of the Israelite victory.

The Second Description (20:36b–44). The second account (20:36b–44) lacks an independent opening and is joined to the first account by means of verse 36a. The transitional link in verse 36a can read, "the Benjaminites realized that they were routed," which picks up the narrative after the summary in verse 35; or it can represent a new opening anticipating the events related in verse 39 ("the Benjaminites thought that they [the Israelites] were routed").[97] Either way, verse 36a does not create a smooth transition between the two sections and remains an artificial redactional link.

However, it remains to be seen whether verses 36b–44 might originally have been linked to verse 29. The ambush placed at Gibeah is suddenly mentioned as grounds for the Israelites' confidence (v. 36b), which seems to assume a previous exposition such as that in verse 29.[98] Indeed, comparison of the two texts suggests that they are interrelated:

20:29: וישם ישראל <u>ארבים</u> אל־הגבעה סביב
20:36: <u>הארב</u> אשר־<u>שמו</u> אל־הגבעה

Once again, the plural in verse 29 seems to contradict the consistent use of the singular ארב in verses 36–38. The difference in use may be explained if verse 29 had been reworked in accordance with LBH usage, which tends to exchange collectives for simple plurals.[99] Alternately, the plural in verse 29 may be the result of an attempt to harmonize the different depictions of the ambush by presenting them as separate ambushes (vv. 33–34, 36b–44). This may also explain why according to verse 29 the ambushers *surround* the city, since each account locates the ambush in a different place. The original opening of the account in verses 36b–44 might be retrieved by removing the harmonistic elements from verse 29: וישם ישראל ארב[ים] אל־הגבעה [סביב].

---

assumes that the enemy will be surprised to find himself under attack. In v. 41, where the formulation recurs, Benjamin is specified as the referent.

97. See Revell 1985, 430–31.
98. See, e.g., Moore 1895, 439; Soggin 1987, 294.
99. See Polzin 1976, 42–43; Rooker 1990, 46–47, 75–77.

There still remains a narrative gap between this opening and verse 36b, which suddenly skips to the midst of the battle. Therefore, the possibility should be considered that verses 30–31a were also originally connected to the narrative in verses 36b–44 but were reworked in order to introduce the following account in verses 31b–34.

1. The mention of the "the men distanced from the city" (הנתקו מן־העיר, v. 31) anticipates the plan to draw the Benjaminites away from the city (ננוסה ונתקנוהו מן־העיר, v. 32). Neither the verb נתק nor the tactic of feigned flight figures in verses 36b–44. Therefore, the phrase הנתקו מן־העיר may have been inserted into verse 31 in order to adapt it to its new continuation.

2. The clause detailing the two routes (v. 31bβ) severs the main clause ("they began to strike men dead as before") from its conclusion ("about thirty men of Israel"). The two routes play a role in the account following (v. 33) but not in verses 36b–44. Thus the clause detailing the routes may be an anticipatory insertion intended to adapt the opening to the context of the first account.

3. The number of casualties ("about thirty men," v. 31bγ) recurs in verse 39, where it explains the Benjaminites' self-confidence. It is possible that the figure was lifted from verse 39 and inserted into verse 31 in anticipation of the parallel description of Benjamin's confidence in verse 32.

By bracketing the phrases that seem anticipatory or harmonistic, it is possible to recover a continuous text that provides the necessary introductory information between the opening in verse 29 and the account of the battle following in verses 36–44:

29 וישם ישראל ארבים אל־הגבעה [סביב] 30 ויעלו בני־ישראל אל־בני־בנימן ביום השלישי ויערכו אל־הגבעה כפעם בפעם 31 ויצאו בני־בנימן לקראת העם [הנתקו מן־העיר] ויחלו להכות מהעם חללים כפעם בפעם [במסלות אשר אחת עלה בית־אל ואחת גבעתה בשדה כשלשים איש בישראל ...] 36 [ויראו בני־בנימן כי נגפו] ויתנו איש־ישראל מקום לבנימן כי בטחו אל־הארב אשר־שמו אל־הגבעה

The second account of the battle attempts to relate events that occurred simultaneously in two different arenas: among the forces in the field (vv. 36b, 39, 40b–45) and in the city (vv. 37–38, 40a).[100] It begins by report-

---

100. On depiction of simultaneity in biblical narrative, see Talmon 1978.

ing a ploy by the Israelites in the field to divert the enemy's attention and mask the action by the ambushers (v. 36b). Since verse 39 picks up where verse 36b leaves off, it seems that "giving way" (נתן מקום)[101] and "turning in battle" (הפך במלחמה)[102] are two aspects of the same diversion, and involved risking casualties in order to reinforce Benjamin's confidence of an easy victory. In the meantime, the ambush took the city and set it on fire in order to signal the troops in the field to begin the counterattack (vv. 37–38, 40a). Only after a column of smoke rose from the city did the Benjaminites realize what had been going on behind their rear flank (vv. 40b–41).

Battlefield	City
³⁶ᵇ The Israelites *gave way* to Benjamin because they relied on the ambush they set against Gibeah.	
	³⁷ The ambushers hastened to raid Gibeah, then continued to smite the entire city by sword.
³⁹ As the Israelites turned in battle, Benjamin began to smite the Israelites, about thirty casualties; so they thought: "Indeed they are smitten before us, just as in the first battle."	³⁸ (The agreement[103] between the Israelite force and the ambush[104] was for them to send a smoke signal from the city.)
	⁴⁰ᵃ As the signal began to rise in a column of smoke from the city,

---

101. This is the only occurrence of the expression נתן מקום in a battle context. It could indicate yielding ground or retreating, but this could be indicated by more specific expressions, such as נסוג אחור (see Isa 42:17); הפך עורף (see Josh 7:8; cf. Gen 49:8; Exod 23:27; Josh 7:12).

102. The expression is unique. As an intransitive verb, הפך can indicate turning about; cf. 1 Sam 25:12; 2 Chr 9:12. Kimchi took הפך במלחמה to be elliptic for הפך עורף; however, in what follows there is no specific mention of feigned flight, in contrast to the previous account (Judg 20:32b).

103. מועד is employed here in the unique sense of an agreed signal. The usage here might be influenced by texts in which the term indicates an agreed time; cf. Gen 18:14; 1 Sam 13:8; see Burney 1970, 482.

104. The MT adds הרב, which is enigmatic and probably results from partial dittography of the previous word, אורב; see Moore 1895, 442; Burney 1970, 482.

⁴⁰ᵇ Benjamin turned around and there
the whole city went up (in smoke) to
the sky.

⁴¹ When the Israelites turned, the
Benjaminites were alarmed, for they
realized that disaster was upon them.

A new stage in the battle opens in verses 42–43, with Benjamin fleeing eastward by way of the "desert route."¹⁰⁵ These verses stand out with regard to both their distinct style and their irregular syntax. This section contains a large concentration of verbs in the simple perfect *qâṭal* form (הִדְבִּיקָתְהוּ, "to catch up with"; כִּתְּרוּ, "to surround"; הִרְדִּיפָהוּ, "to chase after"; הִדְרִיכָהוּ, "to tread down") and thus deviates from standard narrative style, which prefers the consecutive perfect *wayyiqṭal* form.¹⁰⁶ In addition, the relative clause ואשר מהערים functions as the subject of the main clause in verse 42b, but without any subordination to an antecedent noun or noun clause, in contrast to the regular usage employed throughout the rest of the narrative (19:14, 16; 20:22, 31, 36; 21:12, 13, 14, 23).¹⁰⁷ Furthermore, the identity of the accusative and genitive referents in the phrase משחיתים אותו בתוכו (20:42) is unclear, due to lack of an appropriate antecedent in the immediate context.

From the context in 20:41–43 it is clear that the subject of משחיתים אותו (v. 42) must refer to the Israelites,¹⁰⁸ and the object is undoubtedly Benjamin. The referent implied by the suffix ending of בתוכו in verse 42 is

---

105. Possibly Wadi Farah (cf. Josh 7:2; 8:15) or Wadi Suweinit (cf. 1 Sam 13:16–18); see Mazar et al. 1984; Dorsey 1991, 203–4.

106. On *wayyiqṭal* as "narrative tense," see, e.g., GKC §111; Joüon §118c, k; *IBHS* 457–58, 542. Prose narrative generally limits use of simple perfect *qāṭal* to particular circumstances: (1) When the verb is displaced from the head of the sentence by another word, e.g., a relative pronoun (Judg 20:22, 36, 37, 41; 21:12, 14, 15, 23), exclamation (19:16, 22; 20:40), negative particle (19:25; 20:13, 34; 21:8, 14), or grammatical subject (20:33, 37, 38, 39, 40, 42, 48; 21:1, 15). (2) When two verbs occur in the order *wayyiqṭal-qāṭal*; the change in form of the second verb may be used to indicate synchroneity (20:15, 32), or for stylistic variation. (3) In order to indicate pluperfect.

107. On the syntax of the relative pronoun, see GKC §138e n. 2; *HALOT* 1:98.

108. Contra Bertheau 1845, 226, who took אשר מהערים to be an object clause referring to the Benjaminite cities. This reading is implausible, because the clause lacks the accusative marker את; and if the following accusative pronoun אותו is reiterative, then it is not in agreement with its referent.

TEXTUAL ARTIFACT AND LITERARY STRATIFICATION 45

still enigmatic. The suffix ending agrees in number with the object, Benjamin, but the clause "they destroyed him in his midst" makes little sense. The MT of verse 42 is most likely the product of dittography and wrong word division and should read: ואשר מהער[ים] משחיתים אותו בתוך. כתרו...[109] According to this restored reading, ואשר מהעיר refers to the ambushers who had completed their mission in the city and now return to the field in order to help the main force outflank the fleeing Benjaminites.[110] However, it is odd that the narrator should employ such an enigmatic expression, instead of the term ארב, which indicates the ambushers throughout the rest of the story. These oddities raise the suspicion that foreign material has been incorporated in verse 42. It is possible that the unusual syntax of the clause ואשר מהעיר משחיתים resulted from detaching the clause from its original context. This surmise is supported by the fact that the coordinated form of the relative pronoun ואשר frequently introduces the last element in semantic parallelism, and sometimes introduces explicatory notes.[111]

Attempts have been made in the past to "normalize" the verb tenses in verse 43,[112] but this is unwarranted since overall there are more *qāṭal* verb forms in the third battle description (20:29–48, esp. vv. 36–44) than in the rest of the narrative.[113] Even so, the style in verse 43 is unusual for

---

109. See, e.g., Moore 1895, 440; Burney 1970, 484; Eissfeldt 1925, 104; Soggin 1987, 296. See also Abravanel, who took pl. מהערים to refer to Gibeah alone.

110. So, e.g., the Targum; Abravanel.

111. ואשר occurs 114 times, more than 70 of which follow a previous אשר. Of the remaining 36 instances, more than half introduce the last element in parallel constructions (in both poetry and prose); see Exod 9:20–21; 21:13; Deut 33:29; Isa 44:7; 55:1; Jer 9:11; Ezek 18:17–18; Mic 3:2–3, 5; Qoh 3:15; 10:14; Neh 6:17; cf. Deut 15:3; Isa 17:8; Mic 6:14; Job 3:25; Neh 7:70–71. Even in these cases, when the relative clause acts as subject, the referent of the relative pronoun is usually indicated in the previous member of the parallel construction. Five times ואשר introduces explicatory notes, and some of these are suspected glosses (2 Kgs 18:5; 20:20; Ezek 3:15; Mic 4:6; Esth 7:8). Psalm 41:9 presents the only instance syntactically similar to that in Judg 20:42; there ואשר acts as subject and is only loosely connected to the previous sentence. However, it is been suggested that the text there is corrupt; see G. Driver 1951, 248.

112. See, e.g., Ehrlich 1968, 57; Burney 1970, 484–85; Gray 1986, 388.

113. 20:32–34, three times; 20:36–43, sixteen times; 20:48, once. See 19:1–20:13, four times (19:16, 22, 25; 20:13); 20:14–28, twice (vv. 15, 22); 21:1–23, nine times (vv. 1, 8, 12, 14, 15, 23).

narrative, for there three *qâṭal* verbs open three brief clauses, similar to the usage characteristic of poetry.¹¹⁴

Furthermore, the verbs in verse 43 are rare or employed in an unusual fashion. Thus *hiphil* הִרְדִּיף, "to chase after," here is unique,¹¹⁵ while the form in *qal*, רדף, occurs more than a hundred times. Denominative forms of the root כתר, "surround,"¹¹⁶ occur only five more times in the Bible, and all these other instances are in poetry.¹¹⁷ More usually the act of surrounding is expressed with verbs derived from the roots סבב and נקף.¹¹⁸ הִדְרִיךְ, "tread down," here represents the only instance of the *hiphil* form of דרך in prose,¹¹⁹ and the verb rarely carries this significance.¹²⁰ Such use of rare verbs, like those in verse 43, is consistent with the elevated register of poetic expression.¹²¹ Additionally, the clauses הִרְדִּיפָהוּ מְנוּחָה, "they chase him from Nohah," and הִדְרִיכֻהוּ עַד נֹכַח הַגִּבְעָה, "they trod him down as far as Gibeah," are joined by parataxis, without conjunction or subordina-

---

114. Gross 1996, 96; see, e.g., Exod 15:8, 9, 10, 14, 15; Judg 5:8, 19, 24, 26; Hab 3:6, 13, 14, 15, 16; cf. Gen 40:10 in rhythmic prose. For discussion of the usual narrative syntax with first-place verb forms, see Niccacci 1997.

115. However, some have proposed reading *qal* וַיִּרְדְּפָהוּ or striking the word as a doublet for הדריכהו; cf. Moore 1895, 441; Burney 1970, 484; Gray 1986, 388.

116. The LXX reflects a different reading, either ויכתתו or ויכרתו. Many prefer these readings to the MT; cf. Moore 1895, 442; Budde 1897, 138; Burney 1918, 484; Gray 1986, 388; Soggin 1987, 295. However, it is equally likely that the translator could not make sense of the rare verb and chose to replace it with a more common and graphically similar verb.

117. *Piel*: Judg 20:43; Ps 22:13; Job 36:2; *hiphil*: Hab 1:4; Prov 14:18; Ps 142:8 (but cf. the LXX reading *piel*). The nouns from the root are also infrequent in the Bible: כֶּתֶר, Esth 1:11; 2:17; 6:8; כֹּתֶרֶת, only of the temple columns Yachin and Boaz in 1 Kgs 7:16–42; 2 Chr 4:12–13; and in the list of booty taken by the Babylonians in 2 Kgs 25:17; Jer 52:22. See also Salvesen 1998.

118. See סבב, thirty-six occurrences, e.g., Gen 37:7; Josh 6:15; Judg 16:2; 2 Sam 18:15; 2 Kgs 3:25; 6:15; הקיף, twenty-five occurrences, e.g., Josh 6:3; 2 Kgs 6:14; 11:8; Isa 15:8; Ps 17:9.

119. In poetry, cf., e.g., Isa 11:15; 42:16; 48:17; Jer 9:2; 51:33; Hab 3:19; Pss 25:5, 9; 107:7; 119:35; Prov 4:11; Job 28:8. In addition, only eleven of the thirty cases of *qal* occur in prose: Deut 1:36; 11:24–25; Josh 1:3; 14:9; Judg 9:27; 1 Sam 5:5; Neh 13:15; 1 Chr 5:18; 8:40; 2 Chr 14:7.

120. See elsewhere Isa 11:15; Jer 9:2; 51:33; Job 28:8. Otherwise the verb indicates "to lead, guide."

121. See Watson 1984, 24–27, 49, 233; Polak 1996, 62–63; cf. Cross and Freedman 1997, 18–20, who view poetic use of rare terms and unusual forms as archaisms.

tion, in a manner that is not unusual in poetry but is uncharacteristic of prose narrative.[122] Finally, verse 43 scans neatly into two bicola:

| הִרְדִיפֻהוּ מְנוּחָה | [ו]כִּתְּרוּ אֶת־בִּנְיָמִן |
| מִמִּזְרַח־שָׁמֶשׁ | הִדְרִיכֻהוּ עַד נֹכַח הַגִּבְעָה |

| They surrounded Benjamin | and chased him down from Nohah |
| trod him down as far as Gibeah | facing the sun's rise |

Already in 1963, Isac Leo Seeligmann suggested that verse 43 preserves a poetic fragment, and this opinion was also adopted—but without further development—by his student Talia Rudin-O'Brasky.[123] Other cases of known poetic sources have been shown to generate prose narratives, and the incorporation of independent poetic fragments into narrative is also well known.[124] Of course, the existence of the unknown source cannot be demonstrated, and the narrator may have adopted elevated style at this stage in order to heighten the narrative's climax.[125]

One may judge which of these alternatives is more probable (i.e., use of elevated style by the prose narrator, or reuse of a section lifted from an unknown poetic source) by examining how the details in 20:42b–43 fit in with the overall battle picture. In verse 42a, the Benjaminites flee eastward from the routes north of Gibeah via the desert route, while the main force of the Israelites pursues and attacks from behind. By contrast, according to verses 42b–43, the pursuit of Benjamin started "from Nohah"[126] and continued "as far as Gibeah to the east." It seems then, that the poetic

---

122. See, e.g., Exod 15:5–10; Deut 32: 2, 7a, 8a, 10b, 11b, 20–21, 23, 26; 2 Sam 22:17–20 (//Ps 18:17–20); Isa 1:4, 10, 16–17; 32:9–11a; Ps 77:4–7.

123. Seeligmann 1963, 396–97; Rudin-O'Brasky 1985, 157.

124. For generation of prose narrative from poetic sources such as Exod 14:15–31; 15:1–18; Judg 4, 5, see Halpern 1983, 46–53; Houston 1997. For incorporation of independent poetic fragments in narrative, see, e.g., Num 21:27–30; Josh 10:11b.

125. Cf., e.g., Gen 1:27; 2:23; and see Polak 1994, 43–44.

126. Reading Nohah as a toponym with LXX[B]; see Moore 1895, 443; Burney 1918, 485; Gray 1986, 388; contra Gass 2005, 429. In 1 Chr 8:2, Nohah is named as a Benjaminite clan, and it is possible that the clan took its name from its place of origin, or that the place derived its name from the leading clan that settled there. The Masoretes apparently were no longer familiar with the place name, and therefore read מנוחה as an abstract noun. On spacial merism of the formula מן ... עד, see Wazana 2013, 58–72.

description in verses 42b–43 assumes a line of pursuit from west to east, with Benjamin's flight ending just short of Gibeah, where they were surrounded and cut down by the Israelite forces. In other words, the details of the poetic description in verse 43 do not agree with those of the prose narrative, which details flight and pursuit north of Gibeah (cf. vv. 31, 45) and ends with Benjamin's flight east of Gibeah via the desert route (vv. 42, 45, 47). Accordingly, I conclude that verses 42b–43 represent a fragment from a lost poetic source, which may have preserved a quite different battle description from that in either of the sections in the prose account (20:31–34, 36b–44a).

Additional segments from the poetic source might have been incorporated into the narrative, and these can be identified by the use of rare, unusual, and poetic language, such as, הכה חללים, "to strike dead," which appears only in Judg 20:31, 39;[127] מגיח, "to spring" (v. 33), which is the only instance of the *hiphil* form; נגעה הרעה, "touched by evil" (v. 41);[128] החישו, "to rush" (v. 37), a verbal root that occurs only once more in prose (1 Sam 20:38) while it is frequent in poetry; יְעֹלְלֻהוּ, "glean" (Judg 20:45), a verb that occurs only once more in the sense of gleaning a remnant (Jer 6:9); *niphal* יבהל, "to take fright" (Judg 20:41), which is five times more frequent in poetry than in prose;[129] המלחמה הדביקתהו, "the battle caught him up" (v. 42), which is the only case in which an abstract noun is the subject of the verb הדביק.[130] Most of these segments are now found in 20:37–43, where the bulk of the primary account of the decisive battle is concentrated. That most of the poetic segments are concentrated in this section seems to indicate that the primary narrative (N¹) drew upon this poetic source. It is not impossible that the author of the *Fortschreibung* in verses 30–35 (R²) also drew upon this source, but I think it more likely

---

127. More common is the intransitive expression נפל(ו) חלל(ים), "to fall dead," which occurs more than twenty times in the Bible.

128. Cf. Job 5:19, which represents the only comparable expression.

129. The *niphal* of בהל occurs four times in prose (Gen 45:3; 1 Sam 28:21; 2 Sam 4:1; Qoh 8:3), compared to nineteen instances in poetry (Exod 15:15; Isa 13:8; 21:3; Jer 51:32; Ezek 7:27; 26:18; Zeph 1:18; Pss 6:3–4, 11, 30:8; 48:6; 83:18; 90:7; 104:29; Prov 28:22; Job 4:5; 21:6; 23:15).

130. The root דבק occurs with the meaning "catch up with" six more times in both *qal* and *hiphil* (Gen 19:19; 31:23; Judg 18:22; 1 Sam 14:22; 31:2; 2 Sam 1:6); only here does an abstract noun ("the battle") act as the subject of the verb; elsewhere the subject is a person or group of people.

that the segments in verses 32b and 33b were originally part of the main account and were detached from their context by the later expansions.

Reconstruction of the Underlying Poetic Version

מן העיר אל המסילות	ננוסה ונתקנהו	ויאמרו בני ישראל	32
	החישו ויפשטו על הגבעה	וארב ישראל מגיח מקומו	33, 37
	מן העיר עמוד עשן	והמשאת החלה לעלות	40
	ובנימן החל להכות חללים	ויהפך איש ישראל במלחמה	39
	כי נגעה עליו הרעה	ויפן בנימן ויבהל	40, 41
	ו[ ] משחיתים אותו בתוך	והמלחמה הדביקתהו	42–43
	הרדיפהו מנוחה	[ו]כתרו את בנימין	
	ממזרח שמש	הדריכהו עד נוכח הגבעה	
עד גדעם	וידביקו אחריו	ויעללהו במסלות	45

It now remains to show that the poetic segments in verses 32b and 33b indeed form a cohesive continuity with both the restored opening and the body of the second account (poetic segments marked with underlining):

²⁹ Israel set an ambush[ers] at Gibeah. ³⁰ The Israelites went up against the Benjaminites on the third day, and arrayed for battle at Gibeah as on the previous times. ³¹ The Benjaminites came out toward the people [that were distanced from the town] and began to inflict casualties as on the previous times [along the routes, one of which goes to Bethel and the other to Gibeah—in the field, about thirty Israelite men. 32 The Benjaminites said: They are defeated like the first time] and <u>the Israelites said: Let us flee and cut him off on the routes from the town</u>. ³³ [All the Israelites arose from their positions and regrouped at Baal-tamar] <u>while the Israelite ambush sprang from its place</u> [west of Geba. 34 Ten thousand picked men from all Israel advanced against Gibeah; the battle was heavy, but they did not realize that evil was upon them. 35 YWHW defeated Benjamin before Israel. That day the Israelites destroyed twenty-five thousand one hundred Benjaminites, all wielding swords. 36 Benjamin saw that they were defeated], the men of Israel gave way to Benjamin since they trusted the ambush.

²⁹ וישם ישראל ארב[ים] אל הגבעה [סביב]. ³⁰ ויעלו בני ישראל אל בני בנימן ביום השלישי ויערכו אל הגבעה כפעם בפעם. ³¹ ויצאו בני בנימן לקראת העם [הנתקו מן העיר] ויחלו להכות מהעם חללים כפעם בפעם [במסלות אשר אחת עלה בית אל ואחת גבעתה בשדה כשלשים איש בישראל. 32 ויאמרו

וּבְנֵי יִשְׂרָאֵל אָמְרוּ נָנוּסָה וּנְתַקְּנֻהוּ מִן הָעִיר [בני בנימן נגפים הם לפנינו כבראשנה]
אֶל הַמְסִלּוֹת. 33 [וכל איש ישראל קמו ממקומו ויערכו בבעל תמר] וְאֹרֵב יִשְׂרָאֵל מֵגִיחַ
מִמְּקֹמוֹ [ממערה גבע. 34 ויבאו מנגד לגבעה עשרת אלפים איש בחור מכל ישראל והמלחמה
כבדה והם לא ידעו כי נגעת עליהם הרעה. 35 ויגף ה' את בנימן לפני ישראל וישחיתו בני ישראל בבנימן
ביום ההוא עשרים וחמשה אלף ומאה איש כל אלה שלף חרב. 36 ויראו בני בנימן כי נגפו] וַיִּתְּנוּ
אִישׁ יִשְׂרָאֵל מָקוֹם לְבִנְיָמִן כִּי בָטְחוּ אֶל הָאֹרֵב אֲשֶׁר שָׂמוּ אֶל הַגִּבְעָה.

A final matter needs to be considered: Why did the prose narrator choose to build his narrative around segments lifted from the poetic source? It could be that the story of the battle at Gibeah derives from the poetic source, and the narrator quoted this source in order to lend authority to his narrative.[131] The differences in mode between the narrative context and the embedded poetry would signal the presence of the underlying source, even after the source had been forgotten. Thus, even though the narrator may have provided an entirely new context for story of the battle at Gibeah, his use of the poetic material is a means of declaring that he is only relating the events known, as it were, from the words of his source.

Summation of Battle Outcome (20:45–48). Verses 45–48 sum up the results of battle and close the gap between the two previous summaries (vv. 35, 44). This summary also paves the way for the next section, which will deal with the Benjaminite survivors. Verse 45 repeats the information about Benjamin's flight (v. 42), and this repetitive resumption reinterprets the previous figure of 18,000 dead (v. 44) as a provisional sum. To this interim figure, verse 45 adds another 7,000 who fell in flight, thus resulting in a total of 25,000 Benjaminite casualties (v. 46). The total falls short of the summary in verse 35 by one hundred men, but the deviation may result from rounding off the figure in verse 46.[132] The harmonistic tendency of this section is also evident in the way verse 46 combines the different terms for warriors, as used in the previous summaries:

20:35: עשרים וחמשה אלף ומאה איש כל אלה שֹׁלֵף חֶרֶב
20:44: שמנה עשר אלף איש את כל אלה אַנְשֵׁי חָיִל
20:46: עשרים וחמשה אלף איש שֹׁלֵף חֶרֶב ביום ההוא את כל אלה אַנְשֵׁי חָיִל

---

131. See, e.g., Houston 1997, 546.
132. So Abravanel; Burney 1970, 448, 475. On the harmonistic tendency of vv. 45–46, see also Moore 1895, 441, 443; Besters 1965, 31; Gray 1986, 380–81.

It appears that the figures supplied by the first summary (v. 35), as well as the harmonistic supplement in verses 45–46, are calculated to agree with the number of Benjamin troops in verses 15–16. According to verse 15, the Benjaminite troops numbered 26,000 men total. However, this figure was further expanded by the mention of an additional 700 left-handed warriors in verse 16, thus reflecting a total of 26,700 warriors. In verse 47, the general summary adds that 600 Benjaminites escaped and found refuge at the rock of Rimmon. Calculating the number of casualties by subtracting the 600 survivors from the expanded total of 26,700 warriors produces a discrepancy of 1,000 between the expected result of 26,100 and the figure of 25,100 according to verse 35.[133] This discrepancy may be due to either miscalculation or error in transmission.

By contrast, the figure of 18,000 total casualties in the summary of the second account (v. 44) does not mesh with the other figures in the narrative. It is possible that the author of this account did not think it necessary for the numbers of troops, casualties, and survivors to add up. It is difficult to imagine that the odd figure would have been added to a narrative in which all the other numbers did add up; therefore the 18,000 casualties of verse 44 seems to be an independent datum stemming from N¹. It is likely that the author of the account in verses 29–35 did not tolerate the gap between the figures and thus subtracted the survivors from the number of troops in order to derive the number of casualties, and subsequently added details to verses 45–46 about additional men cut down in flight, in order to recast verse 44 as an interim summary.

It was, however, necessary to integrate the gap-filling figures into the narrative, and this is accomplished by the addition of new information about how and where the additional seven thousand men fell (v. 45). Thus five thousand were picked off in flight on the roads, and an additional two thousand fell when the pursuers caught up with them at Gidom.[134] Verse

---

133. The discrepancy does not exist in LXX^L, which reads 25,000 in v. 15; but this reading is probably harmonistic; see Becker 1990, 274.

134. עד marks the endpoint of pursuit or flight (cf. Josh 7:5; 11:8; Judg 4:16; 7:22; 1 Sam 17:52), thus גדעם should be taken as a toponym; so Bertheau 1845, 227–28; Burney 1970, 486–87; Gray 1986, 389; Soggin 1987, 295. Alternately, Gidom may be a corruption of a well-known toponym, such as Gibeah or Gibeon. Moore (1895, 444) takes עד־גדעם as a parallel expression to the Dtr idiom עד־השמידם. But this is not likely, since the plural accusative suffix ending is not in agreement with the other singular object endings.

45 has a peculiarly poetic flavor in contrast to the summations in verses 35, 44, and 46 and includes colorful imagery ("gleaning" warriors from the roads) and paronomasia (Gidom, גדעם, as the place name where the Benjaminites were "cut down"; see 21:6).[135] These characteristics may indicate that the harmonistic summary was built around segments from the poetic source that were first introduced into the narrative by the author of verses 36b–44 (N¹). Since the harmonistic summary seems to derive from the author of verses 31b–34 (R²), it appears that once again R² has appropriated material that was at home in the primary narrative sequence (N¹). This poetic segment might have originally preceded N¹'s summary in verse 44. R² seems to have reinterpreted this segment. R²'s account of the battle in verses 31b–34 focused on the fighting along the Bethel road, and he might have appropriated the details in verse 45 regarding the causalities incurred in flight on the desert route in order to represent the fighting of the second contingent along the route east to Geba (v. 31). If so, then the reviser apparently intended that the summation in verse 44 would represent only the number of fallen along the route to Bethel.

The final two verses deal with the total destruction of Benjamin (v. 48),[136] excepting the six hundred warriors who found refuge at the rock of Rimmon (v. 47). The main purpose of these verses is to set the stage for the next section of the story, which deals with the aftermath of the war. There the repeated lament over the decimation of Benjamin (21:3, 6, 17), the annihilation of its women (v. 16), and the efforts to provide new wives for the survivors assumes that the six hundred are the only Benjaminite survivors. Some critics have eliminated the final chapter, along with the nar-

---

135. See also Gass 2005, 427.

136. For MT מְעִיר מְתֹם, read מְעִיר מְתָם (cf. Deut 2:34; 3:6; Job 24:12); see Kimchi and nearly all modern critics, e.g., Bertheau 1845, 228; Moore 1895, 444; Ehrlich 1968, 157; Soggin 1987, 296. However, as a construct phrase, מְעִיר מְתָם is unparalleled and pleonastic. The phrase מְעִיר מְתָם עַד בהמה also deviates from the standard use of the formula מ-x עַד y, in which y and x represent two extremes of the same category, such as place (e.g., 1 Sam 6:18; 2 Kgs 18:8), time (e.g., Exod 10:6; 27:21), direction (e.g., Ps 50:1), gender of species (Num 5:3; 1 Sam 15:3), parts of the body (Job 2:7); see Honeyman 1952, 13–14. In the phrase מְעִיר מְתָם עַד בהמה, x is represented by an abstract term (עִיר), while y is concrete (בהמה). The unusual locution here may be the result of allusive revision, influenced by the language in Deut. 2:34; 3:6. If so, the hand of R² may be evident here, while N¹ may have read: ויכום לפי חרב [*מאיש] עד בהמה; see 1 Sam 15:3; 22:19; cf. Josh 6:21; 8:25.

rative link in 20:48, from the primary narrative.[137] However, it is doubtful whether the narrative plot arrives at a suitable resolution at the end of the third day's battle after both sides absorbed heavy losses (30,030 Israelites and 18,000 or 25,000 Benjaminites). Therefore, it seems likely that the primary narrative already related the "rebirth" of Benjamin and thus mended the breach in pantribal unity. Hence both verse 47 and verse 48 are necessary to the narrative, since without verse 48 it difficult to understand what prevented the Benjaminite survivors from marrying women from their own tribe. Nonetheless, verse 48 appears overloaded and may have been expanded by the addition of the clauses emphasizing the totality of Benjamin's destruction (עד כל־הנמצא גם כל־הערים הנמצאות שלחו באש).

Composition of 20:29–48: Literary-Critical Conclusions. The above analysis shows that there can be no doubt that 20:29–48 is a composite narrative. Although past critics have assigned the two accounts of the decisive battle to independent sources or traditions,[138] the detailed examination reveals that most of the material in 20:29–48 can be attributed to the primary narrative strand, which was subsequently expanded and partially modified by a later redactor. Only the second account (20:36b–44) details the part the ambush played in taking the city. There it is said that the ambush was set at Gibeah, and its mission was to capture and torch the city (vv. 36–38). By contrast, in the first account the ambush was located west of Geba (MT: ממערה גבע) and was intended to sever the Benjaminites' line of retreat.[139] Thus the anticipatory notice in verse 29 about setting the ambush at Gibeah is clearly connected to the second account and apparently served as its opening. This opening also included elements of the recurring battle pattern in verses 30–31bα.

The later scribe (R²) interpolated an expansion between the opening in verses 29–31bα and the primary account of the battle in verses 36b–44,

---

137. See e.g., Noth 1966, 168; Schunck 1963, 59–60; Dus 1964, 230–31. Noth thought the primary narrative described a punitive expedition of the amphictyony; therefore material dealing with the rehabilitation of the offender was secondary. Becker (1990, 279) retains parts of ch. 21 but takes 20:48 as secondary; in his opinion v. 47 and v. 48 are mutually exclusive and cannot derive from the same hand.

138. For independent sources, see, e.g., Budde 1897, 132–33; Burney 1970, 449–57; for tradition variants, see, e.g., Besters 1965, 31–41; Rösel 1976, 32–46; but see Becker 1990, 281.

139. See also Hentschel and Niessen 2008, 29–30.

thus severing the main body of the narrative from its exposition. Moreover, the later redactor modified and expanded the introduction in verses 29–31bα in order to adapt it to the battle account that he added. R² or a subsequent scribe may have tried to minimize the discrepancies regarding the number, placement, and purpose of the ambush by revising the proleptic statement in verse 29 so that it would refer to *ambushes* placed *around* Gibeah. In verse 31, the reviser added an anticipatory reference to the tactic of drawing the enemy away from the city. While the narrative of the second day's battle simply reports that Benjamin went out toward the Israelites (v. 25), on the third day the revision states that Benjamin went out toward "the men detached from the city," in anticipation of the plan related in verse 32.

The new account interpolated by R² into verses 31b–34 concentrates on the action in the field but also includes a brief report of the raid on the city (v. 34); this report is broken off, perhaps because the author depended upon the reader to fill in the gaps from the details following in the main narrative (vv. 37–38, 40). The recurring use of the phrase כי נגעה עליו/עליהם הרעה (vv. 34, 41) may also support the conclusion that verses 31b–34 were written to supplement the description of the primary narrative. In verse 41b, Benjamin's cognizance of the situation follows logically after they *saw* that the city was aflame and that the Israelites had initiated a counterattack (vv. 40–41a). By contrast, in verse 34, the Benjaminites are *unaware* that the tide had turned (הם לא ידעו כי נגעת עליהם הרעה), even though they were outflanked and the town was being attacked by ten thousand Israelites (vv. 33–34). The representation of Benjamin's confidence at this juncture is ironic and necessary if verses 31b–34 are to be read as a preliminary stage of the battle.

The motivation for R²'s *Fortschreibung* or "overwriting" might have been to clarify particulars that remained vague in the primary narrative. For example, the geography of N¹ in verses 36b–44 is rather indefinite. The only geographical details mentioned in this account are the desert route (v. 42) and Nohah, opposite Gibeah (43). By contrast, the geographic details in verses 31–34 are considerably more specific, and include the Bethel and Geba routes, Baal-tamar, the Geba pass (v. 33), and the direction against "Gibeah" (v. 34). It is difficult to understand why the narrator in verses 36–44 might choose to represent a vague geographic setting if he were already familiar with an account that was rich in geographical details. Contrariwise, it is easy to comprehend the motives for adding a variant with an explicit geographical background in order to illustrate the less specific description and add credibility to the earlier account.[140] Thus it may be that the Geba road was mentioned, because it provides the approach to the desert route (Wadi Farah or Wadi Suweinit) along which the Benjaminites fled (v. 42), while mention of the Bethel road may explicate the geographic axis for the movements of the main force in the field.

It is also possible that the reviser attempted to explicate some of the vague expressions found in the primary narrative. Thus the details of the feigned flight along the routes (vv. 31–32) might have been added to clarify the vague picture arising from the expression in verse 36, ויתנו איש ישראל מקום לבנימן ("the Israelites gave room to Benjamin"). So too the inexplicit phrase, משחיתים אותו בתוך ("they are destroying him in the midst," v. 42), is rephrased by the redactor with more precision in verse 35: וישחיתו בני ישראל בבנימין ("the Israelites massacred Benjamin"). Moreover, the description in verse 34, ויבאו מנגד לגבעה עשרת אלפים איש בחור מכל־ישראל, may be intended to clarify the poetic segment in verse 43, הדריכהו עד נכח הגבעה. R² also reinterpreted the purpose of the ambush, whose task in N¹ was to take the city and send a smoke signal. The poetic hypotext subsumed by the primary narrative mentions outflanking and encircling the Benjaminites, but N¹ did not explain how this was achieved. R² seems to have assigned to the ambushers a major part of this maneuver by relocating their hiding place west of Geba whence they burst onto the road and severed the Benjaminites' line of retreat.

R² not only supplemented the primary narrative but also revised the casualty figures given in verse 44 by adding a new total derived from subtracting the number of survivors (v. 47) from the total number of troops mobilized for the war (vv. 15–16). The discrepancy between the two summaries in verses 35 and 44 was then masked by means of an expansion added to the end of the main account, according to which an additional seven thousand Benjaminites fell in flight.

Bracketing R²'s expansions and revisions restores a continuous narrative that ties in smoothly with the account in verses 36b–44. The material that I have assigned here to R² (mainly vv. 31b–36a, 45–46, and additional revisions in vv. 29, 31a, 48) displays similar expansionist, explicative, and harmonistic tendencies that were evident in the redactional layer in verses 1–28. The remaining account of the battle in verses 36b–44 along with the

---

140. On the functions of toponyms in endowing credibility to historiographic narrative; see Amit 2001, 118–20.

restored narrative strand in verses 29–31a and 47–48 derives from N¹, who composed the primary narrative throughout chapters 19–21. The account of the decisive battle in N¹ appears to have been built around segments from a poetic source (vv. 37a, 39a–bα, 40a–bα, 41aβ–b, 42b–43). Phrases in verses 32–33 and 45, which deviate from usual prose style, might also derive from this poetic source, and they too might have originally been part of the primary narrative, but they were subsequently appropriated by R² and subsumed into his overwriting. It is not possible to reconstruct the content of the poetic source beyond the surviving fragments, but they do include many of the elements that were incorporated into the prose narrative, such as the mention of Israel and Benjamin; the toponyms Gibeah and Gidom; feigned flight along the routes; raid and conquest of Gibeah by the ambushers; signaling the troops in the field by setting fire to the town; Benjamin's awareness that the tide had changed; and the pursuit, encirclement, and cutting down of Benjamin. Nevertheless, since it is not possible to estimate the extent of the poetic source, there is no way of reconstructing the circumstances that led up to the battle or the consequences resulting from its outcome. Thus there is no certainty that the events described in the poetic source were originally connected to the context presumed by the story of the concubine in Judg 19.

The following is a compositional analysis of 20:29–48 (N¹ is in bold type; R² is bracketed in roman type; poetic segments are underlined):

²⁹ The Israelites set ambusher[s round] **at Gibeah. ³⁰ The Israelites went up against the Benjaminites on the third day and drew up at Gibeah as before. ³¹ The Benjaminites went out toward the people** [distanced from the city] **and began to smite men dead as before** [on the roads, one of which went up to Bethel, and the other to *Geba, in the field, about thirty men from Israel. ³² The Benjaminites said, "They are smitten before us just as at first."] <u>The Israelites said, "Let us flee and draw him out from the city to the roads."</u> ³³ [All the men of Israel arose from their place and drew up at Baal-tamar while] <u>the Israelite ambush sprang from its place</u> [from *west (or: the pass) of Geba. ³⁴ Ten thousand picked men from all Israel came opposite Gibeah and the fighting was heavy, but they did not realize that disaster was upon them. ³⁵ YHWH smote Benjamin before Israel, and the Israelites cut down twenty-five thousand and one hundred from Benjamin on that day; all these wielded swords. ³⁶ The Benjaminites saw that they were smitten] **and the men of Israel gave way to Benjamin because they relied on the ambush they set against Gibeah.** [37] The ambushers hastened and raided Gibeah, then continued to smite the entire city by the sword. [38] The agreement had been made between the Israelite force and the ambush to send a smoke signal from the city. [39] As the men of Israel turned in battle, Benjamin began to smite dead men of Israel—about thirty men; so they thought: "Indeed they are smitten before us, just as in the first battle." [40] As the signal began to rise from the city in a column of smoke, Benjamin turned around and there the whole city went up (in smoke) to the sky. [41] When the men of Israel turned, the men of Benjamin (and) took fright, for they realized that disaster was upon them. [42] They turned from the men of Israel toward the desert road, but the battle caught up with him; they are cutting him down in the midst. [43] They surrounded Benjamin, and chased him down from Nohah, trod him down as far as Gibeah, facing the sun's rising. [44] **Eighteen thousand from Benjamin fell, all these fighting men.** [45] [As they turned and fled to the rock of Rimmon, by way of the desert,] they gleaned on the roads five thousand men, stuck with him as far as Gidom, [and smote two thousand more. [46] In all, twenty-five thousand sword-wielding men fell from Benjamin on that day, all these were fighting men.] [47] **Six hundred men turned and fled to the rock of Rimmon, by way of the desert, and they remained four months at the rock of Rimmon.** [48] The men of Israel returned to *the towns of Benjamin[ites] and put them to sword: (everything) from *man [towns, people] **to beast** [and all that was to be found. All the towns to be found they also set on fire.]

[29] וישם ישראל ארב[ים] אל הגבעה [סביב]. [30] ויעלו בני ישראל אל בני בנימן ביום השלישי ויערכו אל הגבעה כפעם בפעם. [31] ויצאו בני בנימן לקראת העם [הנתקו מן העיר] ויחלו להכות מהעם חללים כפעם בפעם [במסלות אשר אחת עלה בית אל ואחת גבעתה בשדה כשלשים איש בישראל. [32] ויאמרו בני בנימן נגפים הם לפנינו כבראשנה] ובני ישראל אמרו ננוסה ונתקנהו מן העיר אל המסלות. [33] [וכל איש ישראל קמו ממקומו ויערכו בבעל תמר] וארב ישראל מגיח ממקמו [ממערה גבע. [34] ויבאו מנגד לגבעה עשרת אלפים איש בחור מכל ישראל והמלחמה כבדה והם לא ידעו כי

נגעת עליהם הרעה. 35 ויגף ה' את בנימן לפני ישראל וישחיתו בני ישראל בבנימן ביום ההוא עשרים וחמשה אלף ומאה איש כל אלה שלף חרב. 36 ויראו בני בנימן כי נגפו[ויתנו איש ישראל מקום לבנימן כי בטחו אל הארב אשר שמו אל הגבעה. 37 והארב החישו ויפשטו אל הגבעה וימשך הארב ויך את כל העיר לפי חרב. 38 והמועד היה לאיש ישראל עם הארב הרב להעלותם משאת העשן מן העיר. 39 ויהפך איש ישראל במלחמה ובנימן החל להכות חללים באיש ישראל כשלשים איש כי אמרו אך נגוף הוא לפנינו כמלחמה הראשנה. 40 והמשאת החלה לעלות מן העיר עמוד עשן ויפן בנימן אחריו והנה עלה כליל העיר השמימה. 41 ואיש ישראל הפך ויבהל איש בנימן כי ראה כי נגעה עליו הרעה. 42 ויפנו לפני איש ישראל אל דרך המדבר והמלחמה הדביקתהו ואשר מהערים משחיתים אותו בתוכו. 43 כתרו את בנימן הרדיפהו מנוחה הדריכהו עד נכח הגבעה ממזרח שמש. 44 ויפלו מבנימן שמנה עשר אלף איש את כל אלה אנשי חיל. [45]ויפנו וינסו המדברה אל סלע הרמון ויעללהו במסלות חמשת אלפים איש וידביקו אחריו עד גדעם ויכו ממנו אלפים איש. 46 ויהי כל הנפלים מבנימן עשרים וחמשה אלף איש שלף חרב ביום ההוא את כל אלה אנשי חיל. [47 ויפנו וינסו המדברה אל סלע הרמון שש מאות איש וישבו בסלע רמון ארבעה חדשים. 48 ואיש ישראל שבו אל [*ערי] [בני] בנימן ויכום לפי חרב [*מאיש] [מעיר מתם] עד בהמה [עד כל הנמצא גם כל הערים הנמצאות שלחו באש].

1.4. The Aftermath of the War (21:1–24)

The final chapter of the story (21:1–25) centers on a new complication arising from the outcome of the war at Gibeah, which ended with the total destruction of Benjamin, except for six hundred men who found refuge at the rock of Rimmon. Two interrelated themes are woven throughout the chapter: (1) concern for the pan-Israelite unity, which was ruptured by the loss of one of the tribes (21:3, 6, 15, 17); (2) concern over the ability of the Benjaminites to find wives for rebuilding their tribe (21:7, 16, 18). The problem of rehabilitating Benjamin is resolved in two consecutive stages. The first solution provided wives for only four hundred of the men; therefore a separate solution was necessary to find wives for the remaining two hundred. Even though these parts of the narrative are set in a logical causal framework, there are gaps and breaks in the narration.

The chapter opens with a retrospective comment about an oath sworn at Mizpah *before* the battle, when the Israelites foreswore connubium with

TEXTUAL ARTIFACT AND LITERARY STRATIFICATION   59

Benjamin (v. 1).[141] Following this flashback, the scene moves to Bethel, where the people have congregated to lament the outcome of the war (vv. 2–4). Afterward, the oath taken at Mizpah is mentioned again in verse 5b, but its subject is considerably different. This version of the oath deals with the penalty to be suffered by those absent from the Mizpah assembly (v. 5b). This thread is interrupted by a lament over Benjamin's sad fate (v. 6) and a reprise of the first oath to refrain from connubium with Benjamin (v. 7). Verses 8–12 finally pick up where verse 5 left off with the required investigation and punitive expedition against the offending town of Jabesh-Gilead. In the end, it turns out that the expedition had an additional purpose: to provide Benjamin with wives who were not forbidden by the terms of the oath (vv. 13–14).[142] Since this provided only a partial solution to Benjamin's problem, the people again lament Benjamin's bitter fate (vv. 14–15). Once again, they ask, "What shall we do to provide wives for the survivors?" (v. 16; see also v. 7), as if no steps had yet been taken in this regard. From this, the reader might conclude that verses 15–23 are not aware of the previous section of narrative in verses 5–14.[143] Due to the numerous narrative breaks and repetitions, nearly all critics have found chapter 21 to be composite.[144]

---

141. On the retrospective aspect of the note, cf. Josephus, *Ant.* 5.2.12 §169; and Gersonides; in contrast to Veijola 1982, 188 n. 44; Gray 1986, 230, who understand the oath to have been sworn *after* the war.

142. See also Niditch 2008, 209.

143. See, e.g., Böhme 1885, 30; Burney 1970, 449. Josephus (*Ant.* 5.2.11 §164) deletes the fourth scene at Bethel (21:2–4) and places the expedition against Jabesh immediately after the end of the war at Gibeah; the expedition was a complete success and provided wives for *all* the remaining Benjaminites. In this fashion, Josephus simplifies the narrative and eliminates both the double solution to Benjamin's quandary and the superfluous detour to Bethel.

144. Bertheau (1845, 230) and Boling (1975, 294) relegate the material to two independent narratives. Böhme (1885, 81) and Budde (1897, 139) identify three sources. Noth (1966, 162–64) isolates independent accounts stemming from etiological traditions. Moore (1895, 445), Veijola (1982, 188–89), and Becker (1990, 287–91) separate a primary narrative from editorial accretions. Niditch (2008, 209) attempts a holistic reading, which glosses over the inconsistencies.

Redactional Analysis

First of all, the purpose of the retrospective comment in 21:1 is not made clear until 21:6–7, when the tribes express concern for pantribal unity in the aftermath of the war and convene to deliberate how to reestablish Benjamin without abrogating the oath to refrain from connubial ties with Benjamin. Thus it is necessary to examine the purpose of the digression about the weeping at Bethel (vv. 2–4), which is linked to the main narrative by means of 21:5. In itself, this detour to Bethel is no more problematic than the three previous instances (20:18, 23, 26). Even so, in this case certain irregularities raise the suspicion that 21:2–4 is a secondary addition.[145] In the previous instances, the purpose of the detour to Bethel was to consult the oracle. Following the two initial defeats, elements associated with lamentation were added to the account of the second and third visits, but no complaint was voiced by the people, even though it would have been justified by the circumstances (see Josh 7:7–9; 1 Sam 4:3). But now, in the aftermath of the war, the people do complain—surprisingly—of the extent of their victory. This time they do not inquire of the oracle, even though it might have been appropriate to inquire who was absent from the Mizpah assembly, or alternately, whether YHWH might yet sanction connubium with Benjamin. This scene ends with construction of an altar on which offerings (עלות ושלמים) are made (v. 4), but similar offerings were made previously in 20:26 without the necessity of constructing a new altar.[146] These irregularities may indicate that the fourth scene at Bethel was developed separately from the previous scenes that took place there on the eve of each battle. The three previous scenes are built along the lines of a graded pattern that leads up to the climactic victory on the third day. The fourth scene at Bethel following the war diminishes the importance of the third scene that heralds the climactic change in the course of the war and obscures the gradual change in the scenes preceding each battle. In my opinion, the graded number pattern of two + one is rooted in the primary narrative and was based upon a framework of double defeat followed by victory. Hence the fourth scene at Bethel is a secondary addition, which replaces the graduated pattern with a progressive concentric structure of A, AB, AB, B:[147]

---

145. So also Gross 2009, 870–71.
146. See also ibid., 824–25.
147. Contra Becker 1990, 287–88, who retains all four Bethel scenes in the primary narrative.

A   oracular consultation (20:18)
AB weeping + oracular consultation (20:23)
AB weeping + oracular consultation (20:26–28)
B   weeping (21:2–4)

The suspicions regarding the late origin of the fourth scene at Bethel are further supported by the style of its language, particularly in use of the epithet ה' אלהי ישראל ("YHWH the God of Israel") and the collocation היתה זאת. ה' אלהי ישראל (21:3) occurs nowhere else in Judg 19–21. The epithet is sometimes employed in other texts in conjunction with oracular consultation (1 Sam 14:41; 23:10–11). If the same author penned all four of the Bethel scenes, it is surprising that he did not employ the epithet previously in the oracular scenes. The epithet is particularly widespread in postexilic literature,[148] and, although it is frequent in the Deuteronomistic History (particularly in Samuel–Kings[149]), it occurs in Joshua only in the later redactional layers.[150] Thus the use of the epithet in 21:3 may stem from the hand of a scribe who was associated with, or influenced by, the circles responsible for the later redactional layers of Joshua. היתה זאת (21:3) is used indicate an unspecified occurrence in postexilic compositions, while the standard idiom appears to be היה כדבר הזה.[151]

If the first three scenes are original to the primary narrative, then it is reasonable to conclude that the addition of the fourth scene derives from R². The addition of the scene revises the stance of the narrative toward the war. In the previous episodes, the Israelites lamented their losses and made offerings in order to propitiate their God (20:23, 26–28). Following the victory, it might be expected that they would sacrifice thanksgiving offerings. Instead, they offer sacrifice after lamenting the outcome of the war, which is thus represented as a pyrrhic victory.

---

148. For example, in Chronicles' *Sondergut* 1 Chr 22:6; 23:25; 24:19; 28:4; 29:10; 2 Chr 11:16; 13:5; 15:4, 13; 20:19; 30:1, 5; in Ezra 1:3; 4:1, 3; 6:21; 7:6; 9:15; in the Twelve only in Mal 2:16; in Psalms only in doxologies: 41:14; 106:48.

149. Thirty times in Samuel–Kings, including characteristically Dtr contexts, e.g., 1 Sam 2:30; 10:18; 25:32, 34; 1 Kgs 8:15, 17, 20, 23, 25; 11:9; 14:7, 13; 15:30; 16:13, 26, 33; 2 Kgs 21:12.

150. See Josh 7:13, 19–20; 8:30; 9:18–19; 10:40, 42; 13:14, 33; 14:14; 22:24; 24:2, 23. In Judges the epithet is found six more times: 4:6; 5:3, 5; 6:8; 11:21, 23.

151. היתה זאת occurs six more times: 1 Kgs 11:11; Isa 50:11; Joel 1:2; Mal 1:9; Ps 118:23; 2 Chr 1:11. Cf. היה כדבר הזה: Deut 22:20; 2 Kgs 7:19; עשה כדבר הזה: Gen 18:25; 44:7; 2 Sam 15:6; Ezra 10:5; Neh 5:12–13.

Verse 5 presents the redactional link by which the additional Bethel scene is connected to the main narrative. This verse acts as a virtual *Wiederaufnahme*, referring back to the oath taken at Mizpah (כי השבועה הגדולה היתה; cf. v. 1, ואיש ישראל נשבע במצפה), except that the content of this oath is different and pronounces the death penalty for absentees from the assembly. This oath does not recur in the narrative, in contrast to the oath proscribing connubium with Benjamin, which is repeated three times in varying formulations (vv. 1, 7, 18).

21:1

ואיש ישראל נשבע במצפה לאמר   איש ממנו לא־יתן בתו לבנימן לאשה

21:5b

כי השבועה הגדולה היתה   לאשר לא־עלה אל־ה' המצפה לאמר מות יומת

21:7

ואנחנו נשבענו בה'   לבלתי תת־להם מבנותינו לנשים

21:18

ארור   נתן אשה לבנימן

In actuality, verse 5 does not present a true oath formula, but rather a pronouncement of judgment (אשר לא־עלה ... מות יומת)[152] that justifies the expedition against Jabesh. However, the punishment of Jabesh is not really the subject of the section in verses 6–14. If the purpose of the expedition to Jabesh was to execute the punitive measures prescribed by the oath in verse 5, then it is difficult to understand why all the inhabitants—including women and children—were put to death, with the exception of the marriageable virgins.[153] From this it is clear that the main purpose of

---

152. Cf. the explicit oath in 21:18. For formulations parallel to 21:5b (i.e., with the relative clause rather than the participle), see Lev 20:2, 9–10, 15, 20; 27:29. On oath formulas see Kottsieper 2004, 314–16.

153. See Rudin-O'Brasky 1985, 163. According to Josephus, *Ant.* 5.2.11 §§164–167, the Israelites undertook the expedition before they began to regret the decimation of Benjamin and decided to spare the virgin girls of Jabesh out of sympathy with the fate of the dead concubine. Only after the fact did they take pity on the Benjaminites and decide to give them the girls of Jabesh to wed.

TEXTUAL ARTIFACT AND LITERARY STRATIFICATION   63

the section is to provide brides for the remaining Benjaminites within the strictures of the proscription the Israelites had taken upon themselves. This purpose could have been realized, without recourse to a military expedition, simply by investigating who had not participated in the assembly; since the absentees were not partner to the proscription, their daughters would be permitted in marriage to the Benjaminites.

That the oath proscribing connubium with Benjamin recurs throughout the narrative and provides the central theme for the two main sections in verses 6–14 and 16–23 seems to indicate that it is rooted in the primary narrative. The second "oath" pronouncing death for the absentees from the assembly appears to be a secondary accretion added by R² in order to recast the first solution in verses 6–14 as a punitive military expedition. This means that the absentee death oath in verse 5 assumes the connubium oath of verses 1 and 7 but not vice versa.[154] Thus R² seems to have maintained that the Israelites swore three different oaths at Mizpah: the connubium oath (21:1, 7, 18), the absentee oath (21:5), and an oath not to disperse until meting out justice on Gibeah (20:8).

Stylistic considerations support the conclusion that verse 5 belongs to the secondary stratum. The syntax of the verse is tortuous, and it appears to contain an interrogative clause (v. 5a, מי אשר ... אל־ה׳) combined with a circumstantial clause (v. 5b, כי השבועה הגדולה ... מות יומת). However, elsewhere the collocation מי אשר does not open interrogative clauses but stands at the head of the prostasis of conditional clauses.[155] Here the connection between the conditional clause, "He who has" (v. 5aβ), and the apodosis, "shall surely die" (v. 5bγ), has been obscured by the intervening circumstantial clause, "for the solemn oath had been" (v. 5baβ).[156] The unusual syntax in verse 5a may have resulted from the attempt to derive a variant repetition based on verse 8:

---

154. So also Noth 1966, 163–64; Schunck 1963, 59; cf. Bertheau 1845, 229. Others take the two oaths to derive from independent traditions, with the connubium oath belonging to the section about the girls of Shiloh (vv. 16–23), and the absentee oath rooted in the Jabesh narrative (vv. 6–14); see, e.g., Budde 1897, 139; Veijola 1982, 189 n. 46; Becker 1990, 289.

155. Cf., e.g., Exod 32:33; 2 Sam 20:11; Qoh 9:4.

156. For this reason, the circumstantial clause is frequently excised as a gloss; see, e.g., Budde 1897, 139; Burney 1970, 454–55; Eissfeldt 1925, 105; Veijola 1982, 189 n. 46; cf. Becker 1990, 288. In contrast, Moore (1895, 446) views all of vv. 4–5 as an expansion interpolated between vv. 3 and 6.

21:5a

מִי אֲשֶׁר לֹא־עָלָה בקהל מִכָּל־שִׁבְטֵי יִשְׂרָאֵל אֶל־ה' כי השבועה הגדולה היתה

21:8

מִי אֶחָד מִשִּׁבְטֵי יִשְׂרָאֵל אֲשֶׁר לֹא־עָלָה אֶל־ה' הַמִּצְפָּה

Verse 8 is formulated according to the usual syntax and thus appears original, while in verse 5a the unusual use of the collocation מי אשר seems to result from reversing the order of the two middle elements of the clause (ABCD // ACBD).[157] The purpose of the repetition in verse 5a may have been to recast the inquiry in verse 8 as a "solemn oath," so that it would justify the punitive expedition against Jabesh. The editorial technique employed here is characteristic of R², who, as seen before in chapter 20, appended revisions to the narrative in front of the material to be revised.

Thus the continuation of verse 1 in the primary narrative is found in the lament of the Israelites (v. 6) who were bound by the oath against connubium (v. 7) and who then undertook to discover who might not be bound by its strictures (vv. 8–9).[158] However, in verses 8–9 the narrative is repetitive:

21:8

ויאמרו מי ... לא־עלה ... וְהִנֵּה לֹא בָא־אִישׁ אֶל־הַמַּחֲנֶה מִיָּבֵישׁ גִּלְעָד אֶל־הַקָּהָל

21:9

ויתפקד העם   והנה אין־שם איש   מיושבי יבש גלעד

Verse 8b likewise has a double reading: בָּא אֶל־הַמַּחֲנֶה מִיָּבֵישׁ גִּלְעָד / בָּא מִיָּבֵישׁ גִּלְעָד אֶל־הַקָּהָל, and neither variant appears to be at home in N¹.[159] According to verse 9, the Israelites counted those present in order

---

157. Contra Dus 1964, 232, who takes vv. 6–7 to be a later interpretive gloss and views v. 8a as a necessary *Wiederaufnahme* following the parenthetical comment in v. 5b; cf. Becker 1990, 288. While Ehrlich (1968, 157–58) agrees that vv. 6–7 are parenthetical, he reads them as a retrospective comment, not a secondary interpolation.

158. See also Gross 2009, 872.

159. Both have syntactic parallels. For בא אל x מ-y see 2 Kgs 5:22; Ezek 33:21; for בא מ-x אל y, see 1 Kgs 13:1; cf. Jer 3:18 with על for אל. The "assembly" (קהל) at Mizpah was mentioned earlier by R² in 20:2, while the "camp" (מחנה) is not mentioned until 21:12, and there it is located at Shiloh, not at Mizpah. It is likely that one of the variants is a gloss of the other. Of the two terms, only מחנה figures elsewhere as

TEXTUAL ARTIFACT AND LITERARY STRATIFICATION   65

to ascertain who absented themselves from the assembly *before* the war. Such a procedure is illogical. More than thirty thousand Israelites fell in the war, and one cannot expect that a head count at the end of the war would reflect the composition of the troops at the outset. Verse 8b appears to reflect a collective interior monologue,[160] according to which the people recalled that none from Jabesh had been present at the Mizpah assembly. Thus verse 8b bridges the gap between verses 8a and 9 and presents the head count following the war as a means to validate their recollection.[161] It seems likely, then, that verse 8b is a secondary expansion that was interpolated into the narrative in order to smooth the transition from the query to the head count.[162] Once again, the editorial technique of R² is evident in use of interpolation in order to revise and fill gaps in the narrative.

N¹ continues in verses 9, 12–14 and relates that the Israelites found among the people of Jabesh—who were not bound by the oath—four hundred eligible brides, and these girls were handed over to the survivors. R² has interpolated verses 10–11 and added expansions in verses 12b, 13aα, 14aγ. N¹ in verses 9–14 may be reconstructed thus:

9 ויתפקד העם והנה אין־שם איש מיושבי יבש גלעד [10 וישלחו־שם העדה
שנים־עשר אלף איש מבני החיל ויצוו אותם לאמר לכו והכיתם את־יושבי יבש גלעד לפי־חרב והנשים
והטף: 11 וזה הדבר אשר תעשו כל־זכר וכל־אשה ידעת משכב־זכר תחרימו] 12 וימצאו מיושבי
יביש גלעד ארבע מאות נערה בתולה אשר לא־ידעה איש [למשכב זכר
ויבאו אותם אל־המחנה שלה אשר בארץ כנען] 13 וישלחו [כל־העדה וידברו] אל־בני בנימן
אשר בסלע רמון ויקראו להם שלום. 14 וישב בנימן בעת ההיא ויתנו
להם הנשים [אשר חיו מנשי יבש גלעד] ולא־מצאו להם כן:

Verses 10–11 describe the punitive expedition against Jabesh, which is dependent upon the version of the oath in verse 5. These verses also bear marks of R²'s language in chapter 20, such as (1) וזה הדבר אשר תעשו (v.

---

the object of the preposition אל (e.g., Gen 32:9; Exod 32:19; Lev 14:8; 16:26, 28; Num 11:30; 31:12; Josh 9:6; 10:6; Judg 7:15). Moore (1895, 446) and Budde (1897, 140) take אל הקהל to be the gloss, but it is also possible that the more regular expression was intended to "correct" the unusual locution.

160. On interior monologue in biblical narrative, see Weiss 1963, 460–71.
161. See Schunck 1963, 61 n. 30; Becker 1990, 288; cf. Burney 1970, 448–49; Dus 1964, 232.
162. See Becker 1990, 288, who assigns 21:5b–8 to the secondary stratum; contra Böhme 1885, 33, who ruled v. 9 to be secondary.

11; cf. 20:9); (2) the Priestly term עדה (v. 10; cf. 20:1); and (3) additional Priestly vocabulary: משכב, זכר (vv. 11–12).[163]

Verse 12b assumes a military expedition and relates returning with the girls to the Israelite *camp*. Thus it appears to belong with verses 10–11. The camp at Shiloh does not figure elsewhere in the story, but it is explicitly mentioned in Josh 18:9 and is implicit in Josh 22:12. The precise expression שלה אשר בארץ כנען recurs in Josh 22:9. Only in Priestly writings does the relative clause אשר בארץ כנען occur in conjunction with a place name, and each place is so glossed only once, with the exception of Shiloh (Josh 22:9; Judg 21:12).[164] Thus the explicatory comment here seems unnecessary and uncharacteristic.[165] That the formulation of verse 12b shows the influence of the later stratum of Joshua may aid in establishing the relative dating of R².

On the face of it, the affair ends with delivery of the girls to the Benjaminites, but immediately afterward the narrator adds, "but they did not suffice" (ולא־מצאו להם כן, v. 14b). All agree that this comment is a transparent link whose purpose is to justify the necessity of a second solution for the remaining survivors. Many believe that the double solutions represent tradition variants and view verse 14b as a secondary redactional link.[166] However, even if both "solutions" originated as local traditions or if one represents an early tradition while the other is a literary fabrication,[167] it still is possible that both, from the start, were part of the main narrative (N¹). In other words, the author of N¹ may have intended, from the outset, to solve the problem of the Benjaminite survivors in two separate stages, with brides from both Jabesh and Shiloh. If so, then verse 14b would belong to the main narrative strand.[168]

---

163. On Priestly terminology, see below, ch. 3.

164. See Gen 33:18; 35:6; Josh 22:9–10; see also Gen 23:2, without the relative pronoun. These passages are ascribed to P by Westermann 1985, 371, 528; 1986, 197; Budd 1984, 352; Kloppenborg 1981, 355–62.

165. See Moore 1895, 230; Besters 1965, 33 n. 54. Bertheau (1845, 230) and Kaufmann (1961, 301) attempted to justify the comment in light of the movement in the narrative from Transjordan back to Cisjordan. However, there is no similar use elsewhere in Judges–Kings.

166. See, e.g., Bertheau 1845, 230; Böhme 1885, 30; Budde 1897, 139–40; Eissfeldt 1925, 105; Schunck 1963, 58; Becker 1990, 289–90.

167. Most take the Shiloh passage to be "original" and the Jabesh incident to be secondary, e.g., Moore 1895, 445–49; Besters 1965, 33; Veijola 1982, 189 n. 46; Liverani 2004, 179. See Becker 1990, 289–92, for the opposite view.

168. See also Gross 2009, 825.

In the present form of the text, a lengthy section separates the second solution from the narrative link. This intrusive section in verses 15–18 reiterates and embroiders on the motifs and expressions incorporated in the introduction to the first solution (vv. 6–7). Both verse 7 and verse 16–18 present the same question and reservation (... מה־נעשה לנותרים לנשים ואנחנו נשבענו) following the statement that the Israelites regretted what had happened to Benjamin (vv. 6, 15). A comparison of the parallel sections indicates that the order in verses 15–18 has been disrupted.

In verse 7 the reservation (ואנחנו נשבענו) immediately follows the question (מה נעשה) and highlights the predicament: how to rehabilitate Benjamin while upholding the constraints of the oath. In verses 16–18, the link between question and constraint is weakened by the intervening exclamation in verse 17.[169] Moreover, verse 16 and verse 17 have separate speech introductions (ואמרו), even though there is no apparent change of speakers, while verses 6b–7 are presented as a single speech act introduced at the beginning of verse 6b. Thus the possibility should be entertained that a scribe accidentally miscopied the section and that verse 17 was originally placed *before* verse 16.

⁶ª וינחמו בני ישראל אל־בנימן אחיו	¹⁵ והעם נחם לבנימן
	כי־עשה ה' פרץ בשבטי ישראל
ויאמרו נגדע היום שבט אחד מישראל	¹⁷ ויאמרו ירשת פליטה לבנימן ולא־ימחה שבט מישראל
⁷ מה־נעשה להם לנותרים לנשים	¹⁶ ויאמרו זקני העדה מה־נעשה לנותרים לנשים
	כי־נשמדה מבנימן אשה
ואנחנו נשבענו בה' לבלתי תת־להם מבנו־תינו לנשים	¹⁸ ואנחנו לא נוכל לתת־להם נשים מבנותינו
כי־נשבעו בני־ישראל לאמר ארור נתן אשה לבנימן	

---

169. According to Becker 1990, 290, v. 17 is a secondary expansion of v. 16. However, this does not seem likely, since each verse has a different focus; v. 16 spotlights the women, while v. 17 centers on Benjamin, and its survival as a tribe. For the textual difficulties of v. 17 see, e.g., Moore 1895, 450–51, 453; Budde 1897, 141; Ehrlich 1968, 158–59.

According to this postulated sequence, each speech introduction is tied to a different speaker. The exclamation in verse 17 is spoken by the people who regretted the results of the war (v. 15), while the question and reservation in verses 16 and 18 are spoken by the elders. It is possible that the new speaker (זקני העדה) was introduced in verse 16 in order to justify reiterating the words spoken earlier by the Israelites in verses 6–7.

It is evident from the comparison of the parallel sections that verses 15–18 expand upon the motifs and formulations of verses 6–7. For example, verses 16 and 18 add motive clauses (כי נשבעו; כי נשמדה) to the simple formulation in verse 7. In verse 7 the Israelites report the substance of the oath ("we swore by YWHW not to give …"; cf. v. 1), while the narrator in verse 18 adds what he supposed to be the precise version of the self-imprecation ("cursed be he who gives …"). The sudden appearance of the elders in verse 16 appears artificial, for neither they nor any other leaders figured previously in the story. The collocation זקני העדה is an atypical combination of Priestly and non-Priestly terms,[170] similar to that found in 20:2 (קהל עם האלהים). This expansionistic "overwriting," accompanied by use of Priestly language, indicate the hand of R². It is possible that the reviser added this repetitive expansion in order to further develop the themes that he found central to the story, namely, regret over the depletion of the pantribal body that could be restored only with the rehabilitation of Benjamin.

Thus N¹ continued directly from the new complication in plot (v. 14) on to the second solution for the remaining survivors (vv. 19–23). According to the logic of the narrative, the Israelites found no way to alleviate the problem of the remaining survivors after they had handed over the only brides not prohibited by the oath. Instead, they proposed that the remaining survivors take matters into their own hands and abduct their brides without intervention of a third party. The Israelites, on their side, promised to settle with the fathers of the abducted girls, so as to prevent the outbreak of another civil war. In this section the course of the main narrative strand continues fairly smoothly, and editorial revision is limited to single phrases.

Verse 22 has two different circumstantial clauses, כי לא לקחנו איש אשתו במלחמה (22aγ) and כי לא אתם נתתם להם כעת תאשמו (22b),[171]

---

170. See below, ch. 3.
171. Verse 22b has suffered in transmission and should probably read: כִּי לָא אתם

TEXTUAL ARTIFACT AND LITERARY STRATIFICATION 69

neither of which is assumed by the other. The first circumstantial clause, which mentions taking women in war, assumes verses 10–11 and is probably an interpolation. If so, the original continuity probably read: חנונ‍ו
אוֹתָם כִּי לֹא [ ] נתתם להם *כי עתה תאשמו. This restored reading fits the context better because the dispute (ריב) should be with the abductors of the girls, and they are the logical object of the verb חנו. However, in the final form of the text, the object of חנו is the corporate body that failed to supply enough captives to meet the needs of the survivors. It is possible that the revision was initially a supralinear gloss that was later conflated with the original text, thus resulting in the confused reading of the MT:[172]

MT

כי־יבאו ... לריב אלינו ואמרנו אליהם   חנונו אותם כי לא לקחנו איש אשתו

Revision

כי־יבאו ... לריב <u>אלינו ואמרנו</u> אליהם   <u>חנונו</u> כי לא לקחנו איש אשתו

N¹

ואמרתם אליהם אליכם כי־יבאו ... לריב   חנו אותם כי לא לקחו איש אשת

The double concluding formulas in verse 24 may indicate editorial expansion (24a: ויתהלכו איש לשבטו ולמשפחתו; 24b: ויצאו משם איש לנחלתו). The formula in verse 24b is reminiscent of the editorial links in Josh 24:28 and Judg 2:6, which also speak of "sending/going" איש לנחלתו, and may have been patterned upon them. If so, they may derive from R².[173] R² also probably inserted the phrase אל־נחלתם into verse 23, which would previously have read וישובו [אל־נחלתם] ויבנו את־הערים.[174]

THE RELATIONSHIP BETWEEN THE TWO SOLUTIONS (21:8–14, 19–23)

The episode regarding the abduction of the girls of Shiloh (21:19–23) is commonly thought to derive from an earlier layer of tradition than the

---

נתתם להם כי עתה תאשמו; cf., e.g., Gen 31:42; 43:10; 1 Sam 13:13; 14:30; see Moore 1895, 451–54.
    172. For this reading see Moore 1895, 453.
    173. Cf. Böhme 1885, 34; Eissfeldt 1925, 105; Becker 1990, 291.
    174. For שוב ובנה following destruction, see also 2 Kgs 21:3 // 2 Chr 33:3; Mal 1:4.

Jabesh episode and is thus believed to represent the original (and sole) solution to the plight of the Benjaminites.¹⁷⁵ However, even if this episode indeed stems from popular revelries that accompany agricultural festivities, there are no means for judging the antiquity of the tradition, and, at best, one may estimate age of the literary context. Actually, there are several indications that the literary context is late.¹⁷⁶

1. Several usages characteristic of post-Classical Hebrew are concentrated in verses 21-23, namely, the terms חטף (v. 21) and נשא אשה (v. 23) and the use of masculine pronominal endings in reference to feminine objects (vv. 21-22).¹⁷⁷

2. The mention of the annual festival of YWHW at Shiloh (v. 19: 'חג־ה בשלו מימים ימימה) creates an associative link with 1 Sam 1:3, which tells of Elkanah's yearly (מימים ימימה) pilgrimage to Shiloh.¹⁷⁸ The mention of the festival at Shiloh in 1 Sam 1:3 is firmly rooted in its context, for it is the means for tying Samuel's birth narrative in with the story of the decline of the house of Eli. In Judg 21:19-22, however, Shiloh has no far-reaching importance and only serves as the site for a local festivity, which could have been held elsewhere as well. Thus it is possible that the mention of the Shiloh festivities in Judg 21:19-22 was influenced by 1 Sam 1:3-28. If so, the narrator seems to have composed the story for its present context and used the associative link he planted in order to anchor the Gibeah story in its place, preceding Samuel's birth narrative. This would indicate that the tradition of dancing in vineyards at festivities held in Shiloh is only a derivative literary tradition.¹⁷⁹

3. Even if a kernel of tradition lies behind the section, it has undergone extensive literary reworking. Nearly all the information in this section is transmitted in direct speech by an unspecified corporative entity, while

---

175. See, e.g., Moore 1895, 448-50; S. Driver 1972, 170; Budde 1897, 139; Nowack 1902, 179; Gray 1986, 231-32; Soggin 1987, 304. Many mention m. Taʿan. 4:8 as an independent source for this tradition; however, it is very likely that this Mishnah text was influenced by Judg 21:19-21.

176. For the suggestion that the Shiloh passage draws upon an early version of the late Hellenistic story of the rape of the Sabine women, see Gnuse 2007.

177. For discussion, see below, ch. 3.

178. See Zakovitch 1983, 173, 174.

179. 1 Sam 1-4 appear to provide the first mention of Shiloh in DtrH. The references to Shiloh in Josh 18:1, 8-10; 19:51; 21:2; 22:9, 12, belong to the Priestly editorial stratum; see, e.g., Nelson 1997, 208-9. The additional mention of Shiloh in Judg 18:31 is probably a secondary gloss; see Zakovitch 1983, 179; Amit 1999, 317-18.

narration is limited to verse 23 and the speech introductions in verses 19, 20 (וַיְצַו; וַיֹּאמְרוּ). Thus the unspecified speakers in the section are the main means for transmitting the tradition.

In conclusion, there is no firm foundation for assuming the relative priority of the Shiloh episode. Even though it is evident that R² has been particularly active in expanding this chapter, he does not appear to have introduced new material but reinterpreted and elaborated on the themes he found in the preexisting narrative. It seems likely that the narrator (N¹) incorporated a two-stage solution to the plight of the Benjaminite survivors in order to establish a tie between Benjamin's future and the two places of Jabesh and Shiloh. Both places are featured in the opening chapters of Samuel (1 Sam 1–11), and they may have been mentioned in the closing episodes of the Gibeah story to help anchor the narrative in place, directly preceding the transition to the establishment of monarchy. As a result, readers of the final narrative sequence are likely to interpret Judg 19–21 as foreshadowing the "later" events related in 1 Sam 1–11. I find it reasonable to surmise, then, that the entire Gibeah story (Judg 19–21) was composed for its present context. However, this does not necessarily mean that the narrative was originally part of the Deuteronomistic History; it only indicates that the author took care to create links with the surrounding blocks of narrative.

The compositional analysis of 21:1–24 is as follows (N¹ is in boldface type; R² is bracketed in normal type; glosses are in superscript):

¹ The men of Israel swore at Mizpah, saying: "No one of us shall give his daughter in marriage to Benjamin." ² [The people came to Bethel and sat there before God until evening, and cried aloud, weeping bitterly, ³ Saying: "Why, O YHWH, God of Israel, has it come to pass in Israel that a tribe is now missing from Israel?" ⁴ Early the next day, the people built an altar there and made burnt and peace offerings. ⁵ The Israelites said: "Who, of all the tribes of Israel, did not assemble before YHWH?" for the solemn oath applied to any who did not appear before YHWH at Mizpah, saying: "He shall be put to death."] **⁶ The Israelites relented toward Benjamin, their brother, and said: "Today a tribe has been cut down from Israel. ⁷ What shall we do for the survivors (to provide) them with wives, for we have sworn by YHWH not to give them wives from our daughters." ⁸ They inquired: "Are there any of the tribes of Israel who did not appear before**

YHWH at Mizpah?" [They recalled that none from Jabesh-gilead came to the ᶜᵃᵐᵖ assembly.] ⁹ **When the people took count, they found that none from Jabesh-gilead were present.** ¹⁰ [Then the congregation sent there a force of twelve thousand fighting men, and thus instructed them: "Go and put to the sword the people of Jabesh-gilead, (including) the women and children. ¹¹ This is what you shall do: exterminate all the males and all the women who have experienced intercourse."] ¹² **Of the people of Jabesh-gilead they found four hundred virgin girls who did not have experience with men** [intercourse, and they brought them to the camp at Shiloh, which is in the land of Canaan.] ¹³ **They** [all the congregation] **sent** [and spoke] **to the Benjaminites at the rock of Rimmon, and offered to make peace with them.** ¹⁴ **Thereupon, Benjamin returned, and they gave them the women** [that they spared of the women of Jabesh-gilead], **but there were not enough for all.** ¹⁵ [The people relented toward Benjamin, for YHWH had made a breach in the tribes of Israel. ¹⁶ The elders of the congregation said: "What shall we do for the survivors (to provide) them with wives, for all the women of Benjamin have been wiped out." ¹⁷ They said: "A remnant must be left of Benjamin, so that a tribe will not be obliterated from Israel. ¹⁸ But we cannot give them wives from our daughters," for the Israelites swore, saying: "Cursed is he who gives a wife to Benjamin."] ¹⁹ **They said: "The annual festival of YHWH is now being held at Shiloh, which is north of Bethel, east of the road that goes from Bethel to Shechem, and south of Lebonah." ²⁰ They instructed the Benjaminites, saying: "Go and lie in wait in the vineyards ²¹ and watch. If any of the girls of Shiloh go out to dance, then come out from the vineyards and each of you seize a wife from the girls of Shiloh, and go off to the land of Benjamin. ²² If their fathers or brothers come to complain to us, then we will say to them: 'Be generous** ᵗᵒ ᵘˢ **to them** [for we did not take wives for them in the war], **for if you had (freely) given to them, then you would have incurred guilt.'" ²³ The Benjaminites did so, and took wives according to their number from the dancers whom they had abducted, and went and returned** [to their allotment] **and rebuilt the towns and settled in them. ²⁴ Thereupon the Israelites dispersed, each to his own tribe and clan** [and each departed to his allotment].

¹ ואיש ישראל נשבע במצפה לאמר איש ממנו לא יתן בתו לבנימן לאשה. ² [ויבא העם בית אל וישבו שם עד הערב לפני האלהים וישאו קולם ויבכו בכי גדול. ³ ויאמרו למה ה' אלהי ישראל היתה זאת בישראל להפקד היום מישראל שבט אחד. ⁴ ויהי ממחרת וישכימו העם ויבנו שם מזבח ויעלו עלות ושלמים. ⁵ ויאמרו בני ישראל מי אשר לא עלה בקהל מכל שבטי ישראל אל ה' כי השבועה הגדולה היתה לאשר לא עלה אל ה' המצפה לאמר מות יומת.] ⁶ וינחמו בני ישראל אל בנימן אחיו ויאמרו נגדע היום שבט אחד מישראל. ⁷ מה נעשה להם לנותרים לנשים ואנחנו נשבענו בה' לבלתי תת להם מבנותינו לנשים. ⁸ ויאמרו מי אחד משבטי ישראל אשר לא עלה אל ה' המצפה [והנה לא בא איש אל המחנה מיביש גלעד אל הקהל.] ⁹ ויתפקד העם והנה אין שם איש מיושבי יבש גלעד. ¹⁰ [וישלחו שם העדה שנים עשר אלף איש מבני החיל ויצוו אותם לאמר לכו והכיתם את יושבי יבש גלעד לפי חרב והנשים והטף. ¹¹ וזה הדבר אשר תעשו כל זכר וכל אשה ידעת משכב זכר תחרימו.] ¹² וימצאו מיושבי יביש גלעד ארבע מאות נערה בתולה אשר לא ידעה איש [למשכב זכר ויביאו אותם אל המחנה שלה אשר בארץ כנען]. ¹³ וישלחו [כל העדה וידברו] אל בני בנימן אשר בסלע רמון ויקראו להם שלום. ¹⁴ וישב בנימן בעת ההיא ויתנו להם הנשים [אשר חיו מנשי יבש גלעד] ולא מצאו להם כן. ¹⁵ [והעם נחם לבנימן כי עשה ה' פרץ בשבטי ישראל. ¹⁶ ויאמרו זקני העדה מה נעשה לנותרים לנשים כי נשמדה מבנימן אשה. ¹⁷ ויאמרו ירשת פליטה לבנימן ולא ימחה שבט מישראל. ¹⁸ ואנחנו לא נוכל לתת להם נשים מבנותינו כי נשבעו בני ישראל לאמר ארור נתן אשה לבנימן.] ¹⁹ ויאמרו הנה חג ה' בשלו מימים ימימה אשר מצפונה לבית אל מזרחה השמש למסלה העלה מבית אל שכמה ומנגב ללבונה. ²⁰ ויצו את בני בנימן לאמר לכו וארבתם בכרמים. ²¹ וראיתם והנה אם יצאו בנות שילו לחול במחלות ויצאתם מן הכרמים וחטפתם לכם איש אשתו מבנות שילו והלכתם ארץ בנימן. ²² והיה כי יבאו אבותם או אחיהם לרוב אלינו ואמרנו אליהם חנו[נו] אותם [כי לא לקחנו איש אשתו במלחמה] כי לא אתם נתתם להם *כי עתָ* תאשמו. ²³ ויעשו כן בני בנימן וישאו נשים למספרם מן המחללות אשר גזלו וילכו וישובו [אל נחלתם] ויבנו את הערים וישבו בהם. ²⁴ ויתהלכו משם בני ישראל בעת ההיא איש לשבטו ולמשפחתו [ויצאו משם איש לנחלתו].

Repetitions, Links, and Editorial Coherence

Different types of repetition can be employed as a means for imparting a measure of coherence to a composite text.[180] Repeated use of *Leitwörter*, expressions, or motifs impart to the text a semblance of unity, and the repetitions help blur the borders between literary strata. In chapter 21 the repeated elements are found in both N¹ and R²; hence it seems that the final editing took advantage of repetition to achieve two ends: to reiterate and emphasize the themes and motifs embedded in the primary narrative and to smooth the seams between the primary narrative and the expansions.

Leitwort. The term שבט[181] occurs seven times throughout the chapter, denoting a specific tribe, Benjamin (vv. 5, 8, 15); the national entity, "the tribes of Israel" (vv. 5, 8, 15); or the individual's social unit, "each to his tribe and clan" (v. 24). In N¹ the term occurs once in each of the three usages (vv. 6, 8, 24), while R² repeated the use in his presentation of Benjamin (vv. 3, 17) and the pantribal entity (vv. 5, 15). The change in reference—from singular to plural—marks the contrast between the single tribe and the pantribal entity and stresses the supreme importance attached to the unity of body called "the tribes of Israel."

Reiterated motif. The idea that the loss of a tribe mars the unity of "the tribes of Israel" is reiterated four times in different formulations:

21:3	שבט אחד	להפקד היום מישראל
21:6	שבט אחד מישראל	נגדע היום שבט אחד
21:15	בשבטי ישראל	כי־עשה ה' פרץ
21:17	שבט מישראל	ולא־ימחה

Despite the varied formulation, the reiterations (particularly vv. 3, 6, 17) have been cast in a similar mold, opening with a verb in *niphal*, followed by שבט מישראל as the passive subject. The four reiterations have been introduced into each of the three main parts of the chapter: the weeping at Bethel (v. 3), the prologue to the Jabesh solution (v. 6), and the prologue to the Shiloh solution (vv. 15, 17). According to the previous analysis, N¹ referred to this motif just once in verse 6, and R²

---

180. See Polak 1994, 91–106.

181. Surprisingly, the term is not frequent elsewhere in Judges. With the exception of 5:14, all the other occurrences are concentrated in 18:1, 19, 30; 20:2, 10, 12.

added reiterations to his expansions in verses 1–5, 15–18. The added reiterations thus created the effect of a refrain, which helped bind the expansions to the primary narrative and emphasize the concern for the integrity of "all Israel."

Links with previous chapters. A net of thematic links and recurring expressions connect the final chapter to the previous sections. This compositional technique is already evident in N^1, and R^2 strengthened existing links through reiteration and added links of his own. The main theme of the chapter—the concern over the rehabilitation of Benjamin—is directly tied to the outcome of the war as presented in the summation in 20:48 (N^1 and R^2). Throughout chapter 21 and in 20:1–13, the Israelites are represented as a corporate personality that responds to the events, deliberates, and acts as one person. Links include the mention of Mizpah (N^1 20:1; 21:1, 8; R^2 21:5), the detours to Bethel and mourning rites there (N^1 20:23, 26–28; cf. v. 18; R^2 21:2–4), the six hundred Benjaminite survivors (N^1 20:47; 21:12, 14), and the rock of Rimmon (N^1 20:47; 21:13). Recurring expressions include: התפקד^{182} (N^1 20:15, 17; 21:9); [TN] ישבי (N^1 20:15, ישבי גבעה; 21:9–12, יבשי יבש גלעד); תעשו/נעשה אשר הדבר זה (R^2 20:9; 21:11); מזרח השמש (N^1 20:43; 21:19); see also נגדע/עד גדעם (N^1 20:45; 21:6). It is possible that the infrequent collocation נערה בתולה^{183} (N^1 21:12) was intentionally used to evoke the memory of the concubine, who is called נערה six times in 19:3–9. An inverse analogy may be created by word association in the instructions to Benjaminites to "lie in wait" (N^1 21:20, וארבתם), which evokes the memory of the Israelite "ambush" (N^1 20:29, 33, 37, ארב).^{184} Previously the Benjaminites were defeated by means of an ambush, and now they are advised to save themselves by lying in ambush for the girls of Shiloh.

1.5. Conclusions

The analysis has shown that a continuous narrative strand runs throughout Judg 19–21 and that the intrusive materials are sufficiently similar in outlook and style to be attributed to a single revision. The primary narrative (N^1) encompassed all the major plot elements of the text in its final

---

182. The *hithpael* is found only in Judg 20–21.
183. The collocation is found elsewhere only in Deut 22:23, 28; 1 Kgs 1:2; Esth 2:2–3.
184. See also Liverani 2004, 185.

form: the entire incident of the concubine (19:1b–30); the Mizpah assembly (20:1*, 2*, 3a); the ultimatum to hand over the men of Gibeah and Benjamin's refusal (20:12–13); the mobilization of the sides (20:14–17); three detours to Bethel to consult the oracle and three consecutive battles patterned according to a graduated scheme of double defeat followed by victory (20:18*–29*, 30*, 31*, 32*–33*, 36b–45*, 47–48*); retrospective mention of the oath sworn at Mizpah (21:1); regret over the outcome of the war and desire for Benjamin's rehabilitation (21:6–7); delivery to survivors of four hundred virgins from Jabesh (21:8a, 9, 12*, 13*, 14*); advice for the remaining survivors to abduct brides from the girls of Shiloh (21:19–22); and rehabilitation of Benjamin and dispersion of all the Israelites (21:23*–24*).[185] At this stage, it is possible to identify the poetic segments underlying the description of the third battle as a hypotext around which N^1 constructed his composition. The poetic segments may have been lifted from an old source about a war against Benjamin at Gibeah in which all the main tactics of the battle figured. To resume the architectural analogy, the segments of the poetic source have been reused as building material to construct a new prose narrative. Thus the hypertext of N^1 represents a new context in which the remnants of the poetic source are now embedded.

N^1 was subsequently revised in limited sections (20:1–2, 18, 29–31, 48; 21:12–13, 23–24) and expanded by interpolation of 20:3b–11, 27b–28a, 31b–35, 45bβ–46; 21:2–5, 8b, 10–11, 15–18. The revisions and interpolations are stylistically characterized by affinity for Priestly idiom (see 20:1–2, 6; 21:6, 8, 10–13, 16) and complex noun chains (e.g., 20:2, פנות כל־העם ;האיש הלוי איש האשה הנרצחה ;20:4, כל שבטי ישראל בקהל עם האלהים ;20:6, מכל העם הזה שבע מאות איש בחור ;20:16, בכל־שדה נחלת ישראל אטר יד־ימינו כל־זה קלע באבן אל־השערה ולא יחטא). That Priestly terminology was occasionally employed in atypical fashion may indicate that the redactor was influenced by Priestly writings but was not a member of the circles that produced the Priestly corpora.

The secondary redaction (R^2) is distinguished by an expansionist tendency, aimed at highlighting particular themes and closing gaps in the narrative. The expansions throw into relief the central theme: the concern for the ideal unity of all Israel (e.g., 20:1b, 8, 11, "as one man"; 20:11, "all the men of Israel"; 20:1b, "from Dan to Beer-sheba and the Gilead"; 20:6,

---

185. In a similar vein see Gross 2009, 825, but with some difference in details of the analysis.

"all the territory of Israel's possession"; 21:3, "a tribe is missing today from Israel"; 21:15, "YWHW has made a breach in Israel"; 21:17, "a tribe shall not be wiped out from Israel"). Here R² elaborates on a theme already present in the primary narrative (see 20:13, 23, 28; 21:6).

The methods used by R² in filling gaps are midrashic in nature. For example, the expansions inserted into the account of the Mizpah assembly (20:3b–11) reinterpret the nature of the gathering, which N¹ had basically represented as troop mobilization. R² explicates how the tribes were made aware of the nature of the crime against the concubine by means of a quasi-judicial hearing at this gathering. In the hypertext of R², the gathering is now represented as an assembly of the pantribal sacral congregation (עדה), which acts to uphold the integrity of "all Israel" as a united and normative entity.

2

VIRTUAL SPACE AND REAL GEOGRAPHY

All stories attempt to represent a real world existing in time and space. Indeed, no plot development is conceivable outside the dimensions of time and space. Even if the specific time and place of the story are only loosely defined by formulas such as "once upon a time, in a faraway land," they still provide the necessary axis for locating the happenings related in the story. In the Gibeah story, time is indicated by many markers: four months until the Levite departed to bring the concubine home (19:2); five days of feasting in the father-in-law's home (19:4–5, 8); expressions marking the waning of the fifth day (19:8–9, 11, 14); all night long when the men rape the concubine until sending her away at sunrise (19:25); the time she lay on the doorstep of the house "toward morning," until her husband opened the doors in broad daylight (19:26–27); three days of battle at Gibeah (20:22, 24, 30) interspersed with weeping at Bethel until evening (20:23, 26; 21:2). In spite of this, the main narrative (N^1 19:1b–21:24) does not indicate when the story is supposed to occur within the framework of the history of Israel. The chronological context of the narrative can only be inferred from details, which seem to imply the conditions of the premonarchic period. First, the narrative assumes that the tribes already dwell, each in its own territory (19:1b, 16; 21:24); second, there is no indication of centralized political power. The later editor(s) of the narrative attempted to make this context plain by adding the mention of Phinehas ben Eleazar as well as the framing formula: "In those days there was no king in Israel."

The virtual space of the story is delineated with the aid of familiar toponyms, such as Bethlehem, Gibeah, Mizpah, Bethel, Jabesh-gilead and Shiloh, as well as less familiar or otherwise unknown places (e.g., Baal-tamar, Nohah, rock of Rimmon, Gidom). The detailed geographical background helps build the mimetic dimension of the narrative and establish its claim to represent an image of external reality, so that readers will tend to accept its geographical details as basic historical data.¹ Even though the geographical details of some narratives appear to stem from external sources or records (e.g., 2 Kgs 15:29; 18:14), it is still possible that the narrator might extract geographical data from one historical context and reapply the details to a narrative about a different period for which authentic data was lacking.² A narrator might also choose to incorporate references to particular places due to their standing in his own times or in prior tradition or literature. This means that the geographical sphere of the narrative may be artfully constructed in order to evoke values or attack judgments related by tradition to particular places.³ Thus it is necessary to examine the spatial sphere in light of the relationship between the virtual geography of the narrative and that of historical reality.

2.1. Spatial Passage in the Narrative

Each of the main sections of the narrative is organized along a different spatial axis. The story of the concubine and the battle description each runs along a north-south axis: chapter 19 moves along the route from Mount Ephraim to Bethlehem and back again through Gibeah, and the action in chapter 20 moves between Mizpah, Bethel, and Gibeah. By contrast, the description of the rehabilitation of Benjamin (ch. 21) moves in several different directions: the Israelites go up to Bethel, then campaign eastward to Jabesh-gilead, return to their Cisjordan camp at Shiloh, and from there send a delegation to the Benjaminites at the rock of Rimmon; and afterward, the remaining two hundred Benjaminites to up to Shiloh, after which all finally disperse to their homes.

The departure point of the entire narrative is the Levite's home "at the far end of Mount Ephraim" (בירכתי הר אפרים). Neither the narrator nor the Levite specifies where he lives in Mount Ephraim.⁴ Nonetheless, the mention of Mount Ephraim might hint that the Levite hails from Bethel, since Gibeah is located exactly halfway on the route between Bethlehem

---

1. See Amit 2001, 121.
2. See, e.g., Na'aman 1994, 255–56, with regard to the geographical background of Josh 10:29–39.
3. See Amit 2001, 121–25.
4. See similar designations of origin from Mount Ephraim in Judg 17:1, 8; 18:2, 13; 2 Kgs 5:22; see also 2 Sam 20:21.

and Bethel.⁵ Moreover, verse 18 may hint that the Levite's home was at the same place where the sanctuary of YHWH was located (MT: ואת בית ה' אני הלך).⁶

The Levite thus departs from Bethel and journeys to his father-in-law's house in Bethlehem in Judah, where he is warmly received. The identification of his destination as Bethlehem is significant, for the contrasting hospitality scenes at Bethlehem and Gibeah lead readers to associate the two cities with polar value judgments. On his trip home, the Levite passes Jebus/Jerusalem without stopping, so as not to stay in a foreign town. Although Jerusalem is located on the road from Bethlehem to Bethel, it appears to have been mentioned only in order to cast an ironic light on the Levite's calculations. He preferred Israelite Gibeah over Jebusite Jerusalem; but as it turned out, the behavior of the people of the Israelite city evokes that of the men of Sodom.⁷ Thus Gibeah might also stand in contrast to Jebus/Jerusalem, which throughout biblical tradition is tied to positive values as the seat of the Davidic dynasty and of the royal sanctuary.⁸

Nearly half the chapter is centered on the events at Gibeah (vv. 14–28), compared to six verses for Bethlehem (vv. 4–9) and four verses for the trip between the two cities (vv. 10–13). Gibeah is mentioned by name five

---

5. See similar allusions in Jer 4:15; Judg 17:1, 8; 18:2, 13; and see Amit 1990, 13.

6. Many prefer the LXX: ואל ביתי אני הלך, e.g., Moore 1895, 466–67; Jüngling 1981, 186; Gray 1986, 351; Soggin 1987, 287; Tov 1992, 256–57. It has been proposed that the MT reading derived from a scribal error, when the final *yod* of ביתי was mistaken for an abbreviation of the divine name. However, it is equally possible that the LXX reading is a revision of the MT בית ה', since nowhere else in Judges is a sanctuary of YHWH mentioned; see Kaufmann 1961, 286; Becker 1990, 260. If the MT reading is retained, then it is likely that the sanctuary intended is that of Bethel, since that is where all the cultic activity in the story is located (oracular consultation, weeping before YHWH, and sacrifice). Although biblical scribes refrained from using the term בית ה' in conjunction with the Bethel sanctuary, the expression is semantically parallel to the name Bethel; see Besters 1965, 27. Alternatively, it could be that the sanctuary at Shiloh is intended, since it is also called בית ה' in 1 Sam 1:7, 24; 3:15; see Rashi, Kimchi, and Abravanel. According to this alternative, בית ה' was mentioned here to create an associative link with 1 Sam 1–3.

7. See, e.g., Güdemann 1869, 364; and ch. 4 below.

8. By contrast, Avioz (2007, 88–89) thinks that Jebus is intended to show how a gentile city could be so unlike the "Sodom-like" Gibeah in order "to criticize the inhospitable behavior of the Israelite cities." However, this conclusion does not hold, since the first scene of the story has the Levite enjoying excessive hospitality in Israelite Hebron.

times (vv. 12–16) and another three times by the designation "the city" (vv. 16–17, 22), and the repeated designations spotlight this particular city as the main (collective) character of the story.[9] Indeed, the figure of the concubine will soon be forgotten in the next chapter, while "the worthless fellows of Gibeah" and the "evil" and "outrage" they committed will provide the justification for the following war (N¹ 19:23–24; 20:12–13; R² 20:3, 6). The narrator repeatedly emphasizes that Gibeah belongs to Benjamin (19:14, 16; 20:4), thereby establishing Benjamin's responsibility *for* the actions of the men of Gibeah (cf. 20:12–13), as well as their responsibility *toward* the people of the town, expressed in their refusal to comply with the demand to deliver the culprits into the hands of the pantribal assembly (20:13–14).

The axis in Judg 20, Mizpah–Bethel–Gibeah, creates a link with each of the other two chapters. In N¹ Gibeah is mentioned in Judg 19–20, and Mizpah figures in Judg 20–21, while Bethel plays a role only in the middle chapter, Judg 20.[10] However, the movement between the three sites raises questions. According to the battle description in Judg 20, the Israelites first congregated at Mizpah, and then the Israelite forces moved back and forth between Bethel and Gibeah, via Mizpah, before and following each battle. A reader who is familiar with the geography of the region is likely to wonder at the unnecessary movement of troops.[11] The shuttling of troops back and forth could have been avoided by placing the oracular consultation in the Israelite camp by Gibeah, since field consultation of the oracle is known from other stories. Indeed, consultation in the field reflects conditions during battle, when it was not convenient to seek out a sanctuary (e.g., Judg 6:36–40; 1 Sam 14:8–10, 36b–37; 23:2, 6; 30:7–8).[12] Alternatively, it could have been possible to locate all the oracular consultations at Mizpah, which is closer to Gibeah than Bethel.

Both Mizpah and Bethel are designated as cult sites by means of the expressions "to/before YHWH" (אל/לפני ה'),[13] although both sites fill

---

9. See Amit 2001, 125.
10. The mention of Bethel in 21:2–5 derives from R²; see ch. 1 above.
11. See Muilenburg 1947b, 24; Veijola 1982, 187 n. 35; Amit 1999, 356.
12. See also Gross 2009, 856.
13. Of Mizpah: 20:2; 21:5, 8. Of Bethel: 20:26; 21:2 (לפני האלהים); cf. 20:18, 23. For these expressions as designations of cult sites, see Haran 1978, 26; Fowler 1987. It should be noted that אל ה' as a place designation occurs mainly with regard to Mizpah

different functions in the story.[14] Mizpah serves as a place of assembly (20:1), where the tribes swore solemn oaths *before* going out to war (21:1, 5, 8). By contrast, Bethel serves primarily as a cult site where the oracle is consulted prior to each battle (20:18, 23, 26–28), and where the Israelites lament defeat and appease YHWH with burnt offerings.[15]

It is possible that the narrator separated the oracular consultation from the initial assembly at Mizpah in order to build gradually toward the outbreak of war. Biblical battle descriptions generally place oracular consultations or divine assurance of victory immediately before the sides go out to battle.[16] In Judg 20 the Israelites already assembled an armed force at Mizpah (20:2) in the midst of Benjaminite territory, and this act undoubtedly would be considered a threat to Benjaminite autonomy.[17] However, rather than consulting the oracle and attacking Gibeah at this point, the tribes attempted to extradite the culprits without use of force (20:12–13), but Benjamin responded to the ultimatum by preparing for war (20:14). Only then did the Israelites consult YHWH at Bethel (20:17–18), and immediately following, the battle commences (20:20). By deferring the oracular consultation until the failure of negotiations with Benjamin, the narrator delays the outbreak of the war until the Israelites exhausted all possible options to resolve the conflict peaceably. Thus the passage from Mizpah (v. 1) to Bethel (v. 18) and only finally to Gibeah (v. 19) helps build a gradual progression toward the outbreak of war.

Still, the location of the oracular consultation at Bethel seems puzzling, since Mizpah is also represented as a cult site and is closer to the battlefield. For this reason, many attempted to assign the sites to different sources, redactional layers, or streams of tradition.[18] This approach assumes that there is "doubling" in the mention of both Mizpah and Bethel

---

(Judg 20:1; 21:5, 8; 1 Sam 10:17), and otherwise of Mount Sinai (Exod 19:24; 24:1, 2; 32:30) and Zion (Jer 31:6).

14. See Gray 1986, 230; Soggin 1987, 302; Blenkinsopp 1998, 30.

15. See Blenkinsopp 2003, 99. The swearing of the solemn oath does not require cultic personnel or paraphernalia and is an activity frequently undertaken without any connection to cult sites, e.g., 1 Sam 14:26–28; 19:6; 20:42; 24:23; 28:10; 2 Sam 14:11; 19:24; 21:17; 1 Kgs 1:17, 29; 21:3.

16. See, e.g., Judg 4:14–15; 7:9; 1 Sam 7:9–11; 30:7–10.

17. See Hentschel and Niessen 2008, 18.

18. See, e.g., Budde 1888, 296–97; Schunck 1963, 63–68; Dus 1964, 227–35; Besters 1965, 39–40; Gray 1967, 241, 381–79; Mayes 1974, 44–6; De Vries 1975, 90; Crüsemann 1978, 159; Veijola 1982, 186–200; Becker 1990, 279–89.

and that cult sites not only generate their own traditions but also serve as repositories of tradition and centers for literary production. However, the validity of these assumptions is questionable, since neither site doubles the function of the other within the context of the narrative in Judg 20–21.[19] Instead, we might ask whether the description in 20:1 of assembling "before YHWH" at Mizpah does not derive from another literary tradition, namely, 1 Sam 10:17. Thus it is necessary to consider the possibility that the different nature of the activities at each site reflects their standing at the time the narrator composed the story.[20]

In Judg 21 the double solution to the plight of the remaining Benjaminites is also tied to two different places, Jabesh and Shiloh, and many think this indicates a fusion of local traditions or an augmentation of an authentic early tradition with a later literary invention.[21] However, there is no evidence that either is a preliterary tradition, and the compositional analysis shows that the double solution is firmly grounded in N^1. It is likely, then, that the author of N^1 made use of the double solution in order to establish literary blood ties (or to explain existing blood ties) between the rehabilitated Benjamin and both Jabesh and Shiloh.

2.2. Gibeah in Historical Reality and Biblical Tradition

Gibeah is mentioned forty-six times in the Bible, nearly half of which occur in Judg 19–20 (twenty-two times), with an additional ten instances in the stories relating to Saul.[22] The town is also designated Gibeah of Elohim (גבעת האלהים, 1 Sam 10:5) and Gibeah of Saul (גבעת שאול, 1 Sam 11:4; 15:34; 2 Sam 21:6; Isa 10:29).[23] The site of Gibeah is commonly identified with Tel el-Ful, which is located on the main watershed route, approximately 6 kilometers north of Jerusalem and 3 kilometers south of Ramah (er-Ram).[24] This location nicely fits the route taken by the Levite in Judg

---

19. See Soggin 1987, 302; Blenkinsopp 1998, 30–31; Schulte 1972, 97.
20. So also according to Guillaume 2004, 206–7.
21. See, e.g., Noth 1966, 162–64; Veijola 1982, 188–89; Becker 1990, 287–91.
22. 1 Sam 10:5, 10, 26; 11:4; 14:2; 15:34; 22:6; 23:19; 26:1; 2 Sam 21:6.
23. See Na'aman 1992, 650.
24. See Albright 1922; 1924, 28–43; Graham 1981, 1–5, 16; Na'aman 1992, 649–52.

19:8–14[25] and seems to be indicated by Josephus and Jerome as well.[26] According to an alternative proposal advanced by J. Maxwell Miller and Patrick Arnold, Gibeah is a variant of the toponym Geba, and both toponyms indicate the place known today as Jebaʿ.[27] However, this proposal is not convincing, for Gibeah and Geba are mentioned as separate toponyms in Isa 10:28–29. It is true that scribes occasionally erred and exchanged one name for the other, but an examination of the geographical data in each case uncovers the error.[28]

The narrator in Judg 19–20 depicts Gibeah as a premonarchic urban settlement. Urban settlements are distinguished by population density, planned development, communal buildings, and fortifications.[29] Gibeah is not only located on the main watershed highway (19:10–13) but is also connected to Geba and Rimmon by branch roads (20:31, 42, 45). These roads are designated מסילות, "beaten paths" (20:31), which might indicate public works.[30] While there is no mention of a city wall or gate, it is possible that these details are assumed by the narrator when he states that the Benjaminites went out from the city on each day of battle (20:21, 25, 31). According to 19:15, 20, Gibeah had a central plaza (רחוב העיר), which in other contexts is located in front of an important public building, such as a governor's palace or sanctuary (cf. Job 29:7; Esth 4:6; 6:9, 11; Ezra 10:9; Neh 8:1, 3, 16; 2 Chr 29:4). The urban character of Gibeah is also hinted at by the term בעלי גבעה (20:5), since elsewhere the designation בעלי + *city*

---

25. See also 1 Sam 10:2–5 for the route beginning in the north and ending at Gibeah to the south.

26. Josephus, *J.W.* 5.2.1 §§50–51; Jerome, *Epist.* 108.8; see also Albright 1924, 41–42.

27. See Miller 1974b, 162–64; 1975; P. Arnold 1990; Finkelstein 2011a, 361 n. 76; 2011b, 114–15. For criticism of this view, see Naʾaman 1995. Alternate proposals include Gibeon (el-Jib) (van der Born 1954), and Perath/Parah/Phirathon (Finkelstein 2011b, 115–16).

28. E.g., LXX[AL] Gibeah for MT Geba in Judg 20:33; 1 Sam 13:3; Gibeah for MT Geba of Benjamin in Judg 20:10; Geba for MT Gibeah in Judg 20:31; cf. Moore 1895, 436. Only Gibeath Benjamin appears to be a variant for Geba Benjamin (1 Sam 13:2, 15; 14:16; 2 Sam 23:29 // 1 Chr 11:31; see 1 Sam 13:16; 1 Kgs 15:22); see Naʾaman 1992, 652; contra Demsky 1973; and Gass 2005, 405–6.

29. See, e.g., Fritz 1995, 17–19. While cities and towns are regularly designated עיר, rural settlements are designated כפר, חצר, שדה (e.g., Gen 14:7; 25:16; Deut 2:23; Judg 20:6; 1 Chr 27:25). These are mainly differentiated from cities by lack of fortifications.

30. Dorsey 1991, 229–33.

name indicates the body representing the inhabitants of a town, similar to the city elders (זקני העיר).[31]

The Archaeology of Tel el-Ful

The earliest architectural remains at Tel el-Ful were dated by the excavators (Albright, Sinclair, P. and N. Lapp) to Iron I, and they concluded that this phase was destroyed by conflagration.[32] Architectural remains, which the excavators took to represent a fortress and casemate wall, were attributed to different periods of the Iron Age. The first phase of the fortress was dated to the end of the eleventh century and was believed by the excavators to represent Saul's stronghold. This phase ended in conflagration, and shortly afterward phase two of the fortress began. According to the excavators, the reconstructed fortress was abandoned with no signs of destruction in the middle of the tenth century BCE.[33] The third stage of the fortress was dated to the seventh-sixth centuries BCE.[34] Fourteen *lmlk* impressions were found within the fortress and on top of the tell. Previously, all *lmlk* impressions were assigned to the end of the eighth century BCE, and those found at Tel el-Ful were thought to establish the date of the fortress. However, more recently Oded Lipschits, Omer Sergi, and Ido Koch showed that certain types of *lmlk* impressions were produced in the seventh century BCE, and according to Lipschits all the *lmlk* impressions from Tel el-Ful (Gibeah) belong to these types.[35] Stone fragments,

---

31. See בעלי שכם (fifteen times in Judg 9); בעלי יריחו (Josh 24:11); בעלי קעילה (1 Sam 23:11–12); בעלי יבש גלעד (2 Sam 21:12); זקני יביש (1 Sam 11:3); זקני העיר (of Succoth, Judg 8:16; Bethlehem, 1 Sam 16:4; Ruth 4:2; Gebal, Ezek 27:9; and ten times in Deuteronomy as a general term). See also J. McKenzie 1959; de Geus 1976, 139–40; Reviv 1989, 51–70.

32. Albright 1924; N. Lapp 1981.

33. P. Lapp 1965, 2–4; Graham 1981, 7–10, 16.

34. On this stage see also Finkelstein 2011b, 111–13.

35. On the locus of the *lmlk* jar handles, see N. Lapp 1981, 111. The *lmlk* impressions are dated to the times of Hezekiah (ca. 705 BCE) by Aharoni (1979, 394–400) and Na'aman (1979, 1986a, 11–17). Lipschits et al. (2010, 10–16) mention only four impressions from Tel el-Ful belonging to the seventh-century types; however, according to Finkelstein (2010, 5), Lipschits reported privately that all fourteen of the impressions belong to the late types. The fourteen impressions found at Gibeah are not a large quantity compared to the numbers found at places like Mizpah (86), Gibeon (83), Ramat Raḥel (147), Lachish (314), or even compared to the more modest numbers

burned sherds, and ash were found within the fortress, and ash deposits were also found in some of the buildings attributed to this phase. These conflagrations were taken as evidence that the fortress was destroyed by Nebuchadnezzar.[36] However, the destruction at this time was limited mainly to the area of the fortress, and quantities of late-sixth-century pottery uncovered in other areas of the site attest to continuity of settlement. Nancy Lapp, who headed the third expedition to Tel el-Ful, even proposed that the population of Gibeah grew following the destruction of Jerusalem.[37] In Lapp's opinion, the lack of Attic ware or other ceramic forms typical of the Persian period indicates that the site was abandoned before the Persian period.[38]

The reconstruction of the history of the site—particularly by W. F. Albright—has drawn sharp criticism.[39] The focus on architectural remains colored the interpretation of the finds and fed the view that most of these remains belonged to the fortress or other fortifications. The phases of the fortress were determined by supposing changes in its architecture, and the dating of the different phases was dependent upon the biblical traditions regarding Gibeah.[40] The first phase of building was taken to represent Saul's fortress, according to the mention of Gibeah in 1 Sam 14:2, 16.[41] However, the notion that the remains represent a fortress depends upon

---

from Tell el-Judeideh (37) and Beth-shemesh (28) (figures according to Welten 1969). Even so, fifteen impressions from a single site is more than a chance find, and may represent supplies sent to troops which manned the fortress.

36. P. Lapp 1965, 4–6; Graham 1981, 12–14; N. Lapp 1981, 39–41.

37. N. Lapp 1981, 39, 43–44; cf. P. Lapp 1965, 6.

38. P. Lapp 1965, 6–7; N. Lapp 1981, 39–40.

39. For a recent survey of the difficulties related to the site and its finds see Finkelstein 2011b, 108–9.

40. Finkelstein 1988, 57; 2011b, 109.

41. See Albright 1924, 51: "Gibeah played an important role in the Philistine war, when it served as Saul's headquarters for a time, and its commanding watch-tower enabled him to follow military operations at a distance. The fortress of the second period, which we excavated, also served in all probability as Saul's residence." Later P. Lapp (1965, 3), who headed the third expedition to Tel el-Ful, found it necessary to justify Albright's confident statement, "While it is therefore not categorically proved that the fortress belonged to Saul, the identification rests on evidence about as strong as archaeology is ever able to provide—especially in light of the comparably strong case for the identification of Tell el-Ful with Gibeah of Saul." Both Albright and Lapp ignore the possibility that the story might be fictitious, even if its geographical background appears reliable.

the assumption that they represent one corner of a structure that could be reconstructed according to a symmetrical plan. In the report of the third expedition, John Graham questioned whether the architectural remains indeed represent a fortress and whether they can be tied to Saul; but in the end he reiterated the conclusions of his predecessors. Lately, these conclusions have come under attack, since no other architectural remains connected to the corner of the "fortress" have been uncovered, and even this corner cannot be properly dated since its stratigraphy is unclear.[42] Amihai Mazar pointed out that the paucity of Iron I and early Iron II findings does not accord with the biblical descriptions of Gibeah as an established city in premonarchic and early monarchic times. Thus he raised the following possibilities: either the identification of Gibeah with Tel el-Ful is erroneous, or late biblical redactors described Gibeah in an anachronistic fashion, or the narratives about Gibeah (particularly Judg 19–21) are without historical foundation.[43] Since the location of Tel el-Ful best fits the biblical topographic data regarding Gibeah/Gibeah of Saul, it seems that Mazar's last two suggestions should be considered.

Israel Finkelstein (2011b) recently proposed a revised history for the site during the Iron IIC period, according to which this phase began in the first half of the seventh century BCE, possibly as the result of population shifts following the fall of Samaria in 720 or following the campaign of Sennacherib in 701. In his opinion, the "fortress" is but a tower typical of Assyrian military and administrative construction in the area. In his opinion, this stage at the site was initiated by the Assyrians as part of a system of forts and administrative centers around Jerusalem.

Until lately, the question of Gibeah's standing in the later periods has been largely neglected. Although the Lapps briefly remarked that the site appears to have expanded under Babylonian rule, they thought that this stage ended with abandonment of the site at the beginning of Persian rule.[44] While it is true that the classic ceramic forms of the Persian period are absent from the assemblages at Gibeah, a number of scholars stress that these forms did not appear until well into the period of Persian rule, in the middle of the fifth century. As a result, it is sometimes difficult to distinguish between pottery from the end of the Iron Age (seventh–sixth

---

42. Finkelstein 1988, 57–59; 2011b, 109–10; Mazar 1994, 77–78.
43. Mazar 1994, 78; contra Gass 2005, 409–10. This problem is ignored by Avioz, who dates the composition to the premonarchic period (2007, 90).
44. P. Lapp 1965, 6–7; N. Lapp 1981, 39–46, 63–69.

centuries) and the ceramic ware from the early Persian period (early fifth century).[45] Lipschits even suggests that Tel el-Ful produced the most significant pottery assemblage of the Babylonian and early Persian periods.[46] These new views regarding the material culture of the early Persian period justify a reevaluation of the length of settlement at Gibeah following the Babylonian conquest. Thus we should entertain the possibility that Gibeah was not abandoned at the end of the sixth century but continued to be inhabited until the middle of the fifth century under Persian rule.[47]

GIBEAH IN BIBLICAL TRADITION

Nearly all references to Gibeah in the Bible deal with the premonarchic and early monarchic periods, while no mention is made of the town in relation to the Babylonian and Persian periods.[48] References that appear to cast light on Gibeah's standing in the period of the monarchy are 2 Chr 13:2, Isa 10:29, Hos 5:8, and Josh 18:28.

According to 2 Chr 13:2, the mother of Abijah, king of Judah, was from Gibeah, and some think this information derives from a source that was available to the Chronicler. If this datum does not derive from an attempt to resolve the problem arising from 1 Kgs 15:2, 10, which has

---

45. Milevski 1996–97, 11; Lipschits 1999, 179 n. 46; 2005, 190–97; see Faust 2003, 37, 45. The material culture of the Persian period in the land of Israel is in evidence only from 450 BCE onward. Accordingly, sites with continuity of settlement from the sixth century through the early fifth century may display the characteristics of late Iron II material culture; cf. Stern 1982, 229; 2001, 342–44. However, Faust (2003, 38) points out that evidence of Iron II and Persian period occupation at an urban site does not necessarily imply continuity throughout the sixth century, particularly since no "characteristic material culture" is associated with this period.

46. Lipschits 2005, 204–5, 241; see Finkelstein 2011b, 113.

47. See Stern 2001, 576; Lipschits 2005, 195–97, 241, 246; but see Finkelstein 2011b, 113.

48. The negative data is surprising in light of the finds at Tel el-Ful, which indicate expansion of the settled area in the sixth century. The silence of Persian period sources with regard to Gibeah (particularly Ezra-Nehemiah) might strengthen the claim of the Lapps that the site was abandoned at the end of the sixth century; see P. Lapp 1965, 6; N. Lapp 1981, 39–40. But it also is possible that the sources are silent either by chance or by purpose. Moreover, Geba and Gibeon are mentioned a number of times in Persian period sources, and it is possible that in some of these cases transmission errors mask an intended reference to Gibeah; cf. Geba, Zech 14:10; Ezra 2:26 // Neh 7:30; 11:31; 12:29; Gibeon, Neh 3:7; 7:25.

Abijah and Asa sharing the same mother (Maacah daughter of Abishalom), then 2 Chr 13:2 might attest to the habitation of Gibeah during the second half of the tenth century.[49]

Isaiah 10:29 mentions Gibeah as a station on the route of a military campaign directed against Judah from the north (Isa 10:27–32). This campaign followed an eastern route, bypassing the watershed highway that runs through Mizpah and Ramah. The route itself is reasonable, but the description of the campaign in Isa 10:27–32 does not necessarily reflect a historical event from the time of Isaiah, since the opening in verse 27 (והיה ביום ההוא) clearly marks the eschatological nature of this passage.[50] In any event, this passage provides the only independent attestation of the designation "Gibeah of Saul" and indicates that the ties between Gibeah and Saul are rooted in tradition, not only in the literary context of 1 Samuel. This designation was in use at least until the time that Isa 10:27–32 was composed, probably at the end of the eighth or the beginning of the seventh century.[51]

Most think that Hos 5:8–14 reflects a historical event. There Gibeah, Ramah, and Beth-aven are mentioned in conjunction with an invasion of Israel by Judah (v. 10, היו שרי יהודה כמסיגי גבול). According to verse 13, Ephraim reacted by turning to Assyria for help. Although many relate this passage to the Syro-Ephraimite war, it should be noted that several points contradict other accounts of the Syro-Ephraimite war (2 Kgs 16:5–9; Isa 7). Therefore it is more likely that the reference reflects a long-forgotten event.[52] In any event, Gibeah appears in this context as

---

49. On the problems regarding the identity of Abijah's mother, see Williamson 1982, 245; Japhet 1993, 670–71.

50. For the itinerary of the campaign described, see, e.g., Christensen 1976; Oswalt 1986, 273–75; P. Arnold 1990, 119–22; Na'aman 1992, 649–50. Since the itinerary is set within the context of the prophecies against Assyria, one might expect that it describes Sennacherib's campaign against Judah in 701. However, the itinerary of Isa 10:27–32 (north to south on an eastern branch road) does not match the route known from Assyrian sources; see, e.g., Na'aman 1977, 173–77. P. Arnold and others suggested that the itinerary reflects the Syro-Ephraimite war, while Blenkinsopp (2000, 260–61) proposed that the context of the passage is Sargon's campaign of 720. Christiansen and Oswalt pointed to the eschatological nature of the prophecy, which they thought had no real historical context.

51. See, e.g., Blenkinsopp 2000, 171–73, 260–61.

52. On the Syro-Ephraimite war context see, e.g., Wolff 1974, 111–13; Jeremias 1983, 80–81; Stuart 1987, 100–103; P. Arnold 1989, 454–60; Macintosh 1997, 194–98;

a fortified outpost along the northern border of Judah during the second half of the eighth century.

Gibeah is also mentioned in the Benjamin city list in Josh 18:21–28, according to the reading of LXX[A], which is preferable to that of the MT.[53] The list is commonly thought to derive from an administrative document listing the cities of Judah according to their districts in the time of Josiah.[54] Accordingly, Gibeah was among the cities in the western part of the district of Benjamin during Josiah's reign.

Gibeah is mentioned in several different contexts with regard to the history of the house of Saul. It appears to be the hometown of Saul and the seat from which he reigned (1 Sam 10:10, 26; 11:4; 15:34; 22:6; 23:19; 26:1). Prior to the battle of Michmash, it figures as the seat of the Philistine governor(s) (1 Sam 10:5; 13:3[55]). It also appears as a cult site (גבעת האלהים) that had a high place where ecstatic prophets operated (1 Sam 10:5, 10) and where the Gibeonites impaled Saul's sons "before YHWH" (2 Sam 21:6, 9).[56]

Na'aman 2009b, 220–22. The contradictions touch upon the identity of the aggressor, the direction of invasion, and the identity of the side that appealed to Assyria. Those who favor the Syro-Ephraimite war context harmonize the contradictions by textual emendation or gap filling; see criticism by Andersen and Freedman 1980, 402–3; and Jeremias 1983, 80–81. Garrett (1997, 149–50) suggested that the passage does not refer to a specific event, but rather to the general state of affairs during the second half of the eighth century. Others proposed that the reference is to events during the early years of Tiglath-pileser III; see Andersen and Freedman 1980, 404. More recently, Utzschneider (2002, 80–105) suggested that Hos 5:8–6:6 does not reflect a set of historical circumstances, but rather literary motifs. Finally, the possibility of textual corruption should perhaps be considered. Hos 5:8 may have originally read Geba for Gibeah, since in 1 Kgs 15:22 both Ramah and Geba are mentioned as border fortresses along the demarcation line between Judah and Israel. If so, then the added *he* of גבע(ה) may have been influenced by the following initial *khet* of חצצרה.

53. So, e.g., Aharoni 1979, 355–56; Na'aman 2005b, 335; Nelson 1997, 212. The MT of Josh 18:28 reads גבעת קרית following Jerusalem, and then sums up "fourteen towns with their villages"; however, the enumeration of towns in vv. 25–28 does not add up to the sum given. LXX[A] reads instead, "Gibeah *and* Kiriath-jearim," and sums up *thirteen* towns, etc.

54. See Alt 1953; Na'aman 2005b, 331–61. On the shift of Benjamin to the sphere of Judean rule in the seventh century see also Guillaume 2004, 110–12, 200–201; Knauf 2006, 297.

55. The LXX reading *bounō*, "the hill," reflects the toponym Gibeah and is preferable to the MT reading Geba; see McCarter 1980, 225–27.

56. LXX[BA] of 2 Sam 21:6 reads "Gibeon" (בגבעון לה' בהר ה' והוקענום), and most

Gibeah figures in both positive and negative traditions about Saul. On the positive side, Gibeah is where Saul was transformed into "another man," a metamorphosis symbolizing God's "being with" Saul (1 Sam 10:5-7, 10-11). Similarly, the divine spirit gripped Saul at Gibeah, instilling in him the charismatic authority to deliver the people of Jabesh (11:3-6). On the negative side, Gibeah was the seat to which Saul returns after Samuel announced that God had torn the kingdom from him (15:34), and from which he continues to rule although he is no longer God's chosen (22:6). From Gibeah he also sets out in pursuit of David (23:19; 26:1). Thus biblical tradition has imparted to Gibeah the ambivalent attitude shown toward the figure of Saul.

All mention of the town in the story of the Outrage at Gibeah occurs in the first two chapters (Judg 19-20). Until the outbreak of war, the city and its inhabitants are characterized in the most negative fashion, which provides the basis for the town's collective guilt, thereby justifying "exterminating evil from Israel" through civil war (20:12-13). However, after the war begins (20:14-48), Gibeah figures only as an objective to conquer and destroy. The single allusion to a value statement regarding Gibeah at this stage of the narrative is in 20:40, עלה כליל־העיר השמימה, which evokes the language of the law regarding the apostate city, which is to be entirely burned for YHWH (כליל לה', Deut 13:17). Once the Israelites have achieved their objective, the city is no longer mentioned in the narrative. This is probably because its complete destruction (Judg 20:37, 40) was considered just punishment for the heinous acts of its inhabitants (20:13). If extermination of the offending city is the means for "exterminating evil from Israel," then there is no reason to deal with its rehabilitation afterward, and instead all efforts of renewal are directed toward Benjamin in

---

prefer this reading over the MT, which reads בגבעת שאול בחיר ה'; see, e.g., H. Smith 1898, 375; Hertzberg 1964, 380; Blenkinsopp 1972, 92-93; McCarter 1984, 438, 442. However, the LXX reading is not without problems. It is odd that the high place at Gibeon should be termed "mount of YHWH," since this term is elsewhere reserved for Mount Sinai, Mount Moriah, and Mount Zion (Gen 22:14; Num 10:33; Isa 2:3; 30:29; Mic 4:2; Zech 8:3; Ps 24:3); see Edenburg 2014, 171. The narrator may have chosen to locate the impaling of Saul's sons at "Gibeah of Saul," the former royal seat, in order to demonstrate that everything connected with Saul's kingship had been superseded. In addition, it is possible that the designation בחיר ה' may have been used for irony; Saul was YHWH's chosen until superseded by David, and now his line is brought to an end in a shameful fashion.

order to ensure the integrity of the twelve-tribe framework (21:6; cf. vv. 3, 15, 17).

Much has been made of the mention of Gibeah in Hos 9:9 and 10:9, which is commonly taken as an independent witness to the historicity and early composition of the story of the Outrage at Gibeah.[57] In both passages, "the days of Gibeah" figure as a sinister episode in the history of Israel, connected with corruption (שחת, 9:9), iniquity (עון, 9:9), sin (חטא, 9:9; 10:9), and treachery or wrongdoing (עלוה, 10:9).[58] That "the days of Gibeah" served as a byword for iniquity and corruption suggests that the allusion was transparent to the target audience of Hos 9:9 and 10:9. However, the historical context of both passages is unclear, and neither provides specific details that can clarify the background of the allusion. Few attempts have been made to verify whether the narrative of Judg 19–20 indeed fits the context of the accusations in Hos 9:9 and 10:9. For example, the subject of the accusation in Hos 9:9 is Israel/Ephraim (vv. 7–8), who will be required to requite for their sins, just as happened with the corrupt ones from "the days of Gibeah." Thus Israel/Ephraim should be analogous to Benjamin/Gibeah in Judg 19–20. However, this analogy is problematic, because from the time of the monarchy Benjamin lay within the political territory of Judah.[59] Even more difficult is the attempt to uncover in Hos 10:9 an allusion to Judg 19–21.[60] According to the simple sense of the passage, Israel is accused of sinning continuously "from the days of Gibeah." However, in Judg 19–20 Israel is not the side that sins, but rather the side that metes out

---

57. So already Rashi, Ibn Ezra, and Kimchi on Hos 9:9 and 10:9; see, e.g., Moore 1895, 406; Roth 1963, 298–99; Rudolph 1966, 179–80; Mays 1969, 131; Wolff 1974, 158, 184; Andersen and Freedman 1980, 534, 562–67; Emmerson 1984, 105–13; Stuart 1987, 146–47, 168; P. Arnold 1989, 452–54; Macintosh 1997, 357–58.

58. The MT of Hos 10:9 reads עלוה, which is a *hapax*. Some manuscripts do read עולה. It is possible that the form resulted from metathesis in oral speech; see Kimchi; Andersen and Freedman 1980, 565; Macintosh 1997, 412; and see זעוה/זועה (e.g., Deut 28:25); כבש/כשב (e.g., Lev 3:7); שלמה/שמלה (e.g., Ps 104:2).

59. See Na'aman 2009b, with further literature there. Others, such as P. Davies 2007 and Finkelstein 2011a, contest this view and argue that Benjamin was originally part of the territory of the kingdom of Israel and was annexed to Judah sometime at the end of the ninth or during the eighth century BCE.

60. The change in person and number in the inflected verbs (חטאת, עמדו, תשיגם) and the question of the proper reading of the MT לא (לא, לָא, or הֲלֹא) impede understanding of the references within Hos 10:9; see Andersen and Freedman 1980, 561–62; Macintosh 1997, 411–13.

justice upon sinful Gibeah and Benjamin.[61] Some have tried to circumvent these difficulties by emending the text in Hos 10:9 or by postulating that the blame for the intertribal war fell upon Ephraim in the version of the story known to the author of Hosea.[62] Admittedly, Hosea refers elsewhere to divergent variants of pentateuchal traditions (e.g., Hos 11:1–2; 12:4–5), but this does not mask the circular reasoning behind the assumption that Hosea refers to the story of the Outrage at Gibeah. This argument assumes that the phrase "the days of Gibeah" alludes to an event mentioned in the Bible and that the Outrage at Gibeah fits the spirit of Hosea's accusations better than other references to Gibeah;[63] hence it follows that the allusion to "the days of Gibeah" provides independent evidence that the story in Judg 19–20 was well known in Hosea's day. However, there is no firm basis for the assumption that the story of the Outrage at Gibeah was known in any form to the target audience of Hosea. By the same token, it is possible that the vague memory of an event at Gibeah independently generated both the references in Hosea to "the days of Gibeah," as well as the narrative in Judg 19–20. In this context, we should consider the suggestion raised in chapter 1 that the poetic fragments integrated into Judg 20:32–45 provided the source for the story of the war at Gibeah.[64] This poetic source may have commemorated a long-forgotten battle fought in Benjamin at Gibeah, perhaps during the border skirmishes in the days of Asa and Baasha,[65] or during the Syro-Ephraimite war. Hosea 9:9 and 10:9 might

---

61. See, e.g., Harper 1905, 351; Gray 1986, 225; Na'aman 2009b, 222–23.

62. For the view that the author in Hosea was familiar with a different version of the story, see, e.g., Jüngling 1981, 280–84; Rudolph 1966, 179–80, 199–200; Gray 1986, 225; P. Arnold 1989, 452–54; 1990, 116–18; G. Davies, 1992, 223; Macintosh 1997, 411–13.

63. According to an alternate suggestion, "the days of Gibeah" allude to the establishment of the monarchy under Saul; see, e.g., the Targum; Wellhausen 1963, 125–26; Moore 1895, 406; Becker 1990, 263–64; and Blenkinsopp 2006, 639. However, this view is refuted by many, e.g., Moore 1895, 406; Rudolph 1966, 179–80; Wolff 1974, 158, 184; Emmerson 1984, 105–13; G. Davies 1992, 223; Macintosh 1997, 358; Irvine 1998, 651 n. 28. G. Davies and Irvine have suggested that Hosea may be alluding to a forgotten event of tradition that was not preserved in biblical literature.

64. See above, ch. 1.

65. According to Finkelstein (2011a, 357–61; 2012, 26–27), the skirmishes and fortification of the border at Ramah, Geba, and Mizpah (1 Kgs 15:22) reflect the historical reality of the time of Joash king of Judah in the second half of the ninth century BCE rather than the time of Asa about fifty years earlier.

be referring to this event and might even stem from familiarity with the commemorative song itself.[66] If so, this song could have independently inspired both Hos 9:9 and 10:9 as well as Judg 20:29–48, without Hosea knowing anything about the story in which the rape and death of the concubine provide justification for intertribal war.

In summary, some of the biblical references to Gibeah reflect the situation that existed during the eighth-seventh centuries, and according to the archaeological evidence, this period also represents the stage when Gibeah began to develop from a military outpost into a town. The information about the origin of Abijah's mother in 2 Chr 13:2 apparently supplies literary evidence for a settlement at Gibeah already in the ninth century, but this is not supported by the archaeological finds, and the Chronicler may have supplied details reflecting the situation in his days in order to resolve a difficulty in the source text before him. The references to Gibeah during the pre- and early monarchic periods do not agree with the state of the site according to the archaeological evidence for the twelfth-tenth centuries. No private houses or public buildings date to this period, and the only remains are an installation of unknown purpose. Thus it seems that the authors of the story of Saul and the story of the Outrage at Gibeah based their descriptions of Gibeah on later reality, when the site was a thriving community. In the pre-Deuteronomistic story of Saul, Gibeah primarily figures in conjunction with positive traditions regarding Saul (1 Sam 10:5, 10a; 11:4–7; 13:3), while in material deriving from the Deuteronomistic strata, Gibeah occurs mainly with reference to negative episodes (1 Sam 15:34; 22:6; 23:19; 26:1). Although Hos 9:9 and 10:9 represent Gibeah as an exemplar of primal sin, the alluded event remains obscure. In any event, the allusion in Hosea is not dependent upon the representation of Gibeah in the Deuteronomistic History. In Judg 19–21 the urban character of Gibeah was emphasized, as well as its relation to Benjamin; but in reality Gibeah was sparsely populated until the eighth century. Since the description of Gibeah in Judg 19–20 does not accord with the historical reality as reflected by the archaeological remains from the twelfth-tenth centuries, it is necessary to consider the possibility that the references to Gibeah in the narrative are based on, or respond to, the representation of Gibeah in other strata of biblical literature.

---

66. In a similar vein see Na'aman 2009b, 222–23.

2.3. Mizpah in Historical Reality and Biblical Tradition

There is near unanimous consensus that Mizpah is to be identified with Tell en-Naṣbeh.[67] Accordingly, Mizpah is located approximately 7 kilometers north of Gibeah on the main watershed highway.

Tell en-Naṣbeh was excavated in 1926–1935, and the findings were published in 1947. More recently, Jeffrey Zorn (1993) reappraised the findings and uncovered evidence for a Babylonian stratum that had not been identified earlier by the excavators.

Mizpah was first settled in the Early Bronze period but was abandoned at the end of the third millennium, and remained unoccupied until Iron I.[68] From Iron I down to the Persian period, the site is marked by continuity, with no signs of destruction. Israel Finkelstein thought that the site plan underwent few changes throughout the settlement's history, and that Tell e-Naṣbeh provided a unique example of a large "Israelite" town in Iron I.[69] However, in Zorn's opinion, the builders of the Iron II settlement did not make use of earlier construction, but leveled nearly everything in order to make way from new buildings.[70] Accordingly, the Iron I phase may have been of more limited size than the later settlement.

Iron II at Mizpah is marked by continuity of settlement throughout the entire period.[71] The town of this period was enclosed by a peripheral wall and densely built up with small houses usually featuring earth-packed floors.[72] About half the buildings had stone drum pillars. Zorn emphasized the fact that no destruction layer—either ash or sherd-embedded floors—was in evidence for the end of the Iron II settlement. Thus Zorn concluded that the inhabitants left the site in an orderly fashion with their belongings, and only afterward was the site leveled in preparation for new

---

67. See, e.g., Muilenburg 1947b; McCown 1947b; Zorn 1993, 34–46. Magen and Dadon (1999) tried to revive a previous suggestion by Albright that Mizpah should be identified with Nebi Samwil, but this identification was adequately refuted by Muilenburg, McCown, and Zorn. For other identifications, see Gass 2005, 418–19.
68. Zorn 1993, 103, 114.
69. Finkelstein 1988, 63; see also 2011a, 17–19; 2012, 17–19.
70. Zorn 1993, 112.
71. Ibid., 114; Finkelstein 2011a, 17–19.
72. For discussion of dating the "Great Wall," see Finkelstein 2012 with additional literature there.

construction. The historical context for the end of the Iron II settlement was the Babylonian conquest.[73]

The next phase of settlement lasted from the Babylonian conquest down to the middle of the Persian period (587–450/400 BCE). The end of this phase is dated according to the latest type of Attic ware found at the site. Zorn proposed that this phase ended in the conquest of Mizpah, since pottery was found embedded in the floors of some of the rooms.[74] However, there are no signs of conflagration, and the historical context for this presumed conquest is uncertain.[75] This phase, which had been ignored previously, was identified by Zorn after he noticed that three large structures with monolith columns and stone floors were located *across* the path of the Iron II inner peripheral wall and gate. He concluded that these buildings were built *after* the Iron II city was leveled. Other large buildings were subsequently identified within the site area and were attributed to this period.[76] Zorn, and later Oded Lipschits, also identified buildings of the Mesopotamian open-courtyard type, which was in vogue from the Neo-Assyrian to the Persian period. These Mesopotamian-style structures seem to represent public buildings.[77] From the small number of buildings attributed to the phase, it appears that the site was less densely settled in this period than it was during Iron II. A number of small finds belong to this phase as well, including thirty *m(w)ṣh* impressions,[78] twenty-four *yh(w)d* (יהד) impressions, remains of Mesopotamian-style ceramic coffins, and a bronze circlet with a Babylonian inscription. The large number of *m(w)ṣh* and *yh(w)d* impressions point to the likelihood that Tell en-Naṣbeh was the site of an administrative center during the Babylonian and Persian periods.[79] The larger size and the superior quality of both the private houses and the public buildings associated with this phase, as well as the larger amounts of open space, seem to indicate that the site was inhabited mainly by those who had dealings with the administrative center.[80] These

---

73. Zorn 2003, 418–19.
74. Ibid., 428.
75. Zorn 1997; 2003, 443–44.
76. Zorn 1997, 34; 2003, 419–28.
77. Zorn 1993, 173–74; Lipschits 1999, 168–70.
78. On the chronological context of the *m(w)ṣh* impressions, see Stern 1982, 107–9; Zorn et al. 1994; Lipschits 1998, 475; 2005, 149–52.
79. Zorn 1997, 37–38, 66; 2003, 433–38.
80. Lipschits 1999, 168–70.

findings tally well with the biblical descriptions of Mizpah following the conquest of Jerusalem.

The town of Mizpah in Benjamin is mentioned in the Bible twenty-eight times, and more than half of these refer to the periods of Babylonian and Persian rule. According to 2 Kgs 25:22–25 and Jer 40–41, the Babylonians established their administrative center at Mizpah after the destruction of Jerusalem and appointed Gedaliah as a local governor there. Even after the rehabilitation of Jerusalem in the Persian period, Mizpah still remained an administrative center and was counted as one of the five districts of Yehud (Neh 3:7–17). Its high standing in this period is indicated by the fact that it served as the residence of the governor (פחה) of Transeuphrates (עבר הנהר) on his visits in Yehud.[81]

The only direct reference to Mizpah during the monarchic period deals with the border conflict between Israel and Judah in the time of Baasha and Asa. After Baasha was forced to withdraw from Ramah in Judah, Asa fortified Judah's northern border at Geba and Mizpah (1 Kgs 15:17–22; cf. 2 Chr 16:1–6).[82] The standing of the town in the time of Josiah is attested by its place in the Benjaminite city list (Josh 18:21–28), which places it in the center of the northern district of Judah.[83]

Mizpah is also mentioned in Hos 5:1–2, along with Tabor and Shittim. The context is unclear, and it is not certain whether the allusion refers to an ancient tradition regarding these places or to a situation in the times of the author.[84]

---

81. Neh 3:7; see Williamson 1985, 205.

82. According to Finkelstein (2012), the biblical description of Asa's fortifications actually reflects conditions about fifty years later (late Iron IIA) in the time of Joash king of Judah.

83. For the districts of Judah, see Jer 17:26; 32:44; 33:13; and Na'aman 2005b, 345–48.

84. The passage condemns Mizpah, Shittim, and Tabor. Wellhausen (1963, 113), Wolff (1974, 98), and Neef (1987, 225) thought the rebuke was based on other biblical traditions (e.g., 1 Sam 10:17–25; Num 25:1–5); however, there is no negative tradition known regarding Tabor. Alternatively, the passage may be condemning existing cult sites (cf. Hos 4:15; 5:8; 9:15; 10:5; 12:12); see, e.g., Jeremias 1983, 75; Neef 1987, 224. Since Mount Tabor does not appear as a cult site in the Bible, the reference may be to the sacred precinct surrounding the terebinth of Tabor (אלון תבור, 1 Sam 10:2–5; see also Hos 4:13), located in Benjamin, between Rachel's tomb and the cult site at Gibeah. If this is the intent of the passage, then it appears that Mizpah was a known cult site at the time the passage was composed; see also Zorn 2003, 442–43.

All the other references to Mizpah are divided between the story of the war at Gibeah (Judg 20:1, 3; 21:1, 5, 8), and the stories involving Samuel (1 Sam 7:5–7, 11–12, 16; 10:17). In these passages, Mizpah is frequently mentioned in conjunction with verbs of assembly, such as נקהל (Judg 20:1), עלה אל (Judg 20:3; 21:5, 8), קבץ/התקבץ (1 Sam 7:5, 6, 7), and הצעק[85] (1 Sam 10:17). Moreover, in each of these stories Mizpah is characterized as a cult site by means of the expression "to YHWH," אל ה' (Judg 20:1; 21:5, 8; 1 Sam 10:17), or "before YHWH," לפני ה' (1 Sam 7:6). Thus the biblical authors of these passages represent Mizpah as a premonarchic cult site around which the tribes assembled.

Many have followed Martin Noth in viewing these descriptions of Mizpah in the premonarchic period as a reflection of an authentic early local tradition.[86] However, this view is challenged by the fact that all the references to Mizpah in Samuel are found in Deuteronomistic passages. Noth's inclination to locate the Deuteronomist in the Babylonian period at Mizpah should have made him suspect that the biblical "premonarchic" descriptions of the town were influenced by the later historical reality.[87] Thus it is likely that Mizpah was inserted into the narratives in Judg 19–21 and 1 Sam 7–10 due to its standing in the times of the authors or redactors.[88] The archaeological findings and the late biblical literature present evidence for Mizpah's central position throughout the Babylonian and early Persian periods, which declined only after the full restoration of Jerusalem. No remains of a cult site at Mizpah have yet been found;[89] however, cult sites are frequently located outside the area of settlement, and this makes it all the more difficult to identify and uncover their location. Moreover, since Mizpah was an administrative center in the Babylonian and Persian periods, it is possible that a cult site was established there (or in its

---

85. See the use of *niphal* צעק to indicate military mobilization (Judg 7:23–24; 10:17; 12:1; 1 Sam 13:4; 2 Kgs 3:21), similar to זעק in *niphal* (Josh 8:16; Judg 6:34–35; 18:22–23; 1 Sam 14:20) and *hiphil* (Judg 4:10, 13; 2 Sam 20:4–5).

86. See, e.g., Noth 1991, 79, 130; Dus 1964, 235; Hertzberg 1965, 250; de Vaux 1965, 304; Weiser 1962, 10–15; Gray 1967, 240–41; Haran 1978, 32.

87. See Noth 1991, 130 n. 5, 145 n. 1; Veijola 1982, 177–79, 206–10.

88. See, e.g., Muilenburg 1947b, 24–25; Schunck 1963, 59–60, 67–68, 93; Blenkinsopp 1972, 78; Veijola 1982, 176–209; Gray 1986, 230; McCarter 1994, 278–80; Ben Zvi 1997, 203; S. McKenzie 1998, 153–54; Blenkinsopp 1998, 29–31; Lipschits 2005, 110; Blenkinsopp 2006, 642.

89. While cultic artifacts have been found, no remains of a sanctuary have yet been uncovered; see Zorn 2003, 443.

vicinity), since one of the expressions of rule is cult patronage.[90] Thus the representation of Mizpah as a cult site might have been influenced by the late historical reality.

2.4. BETHEL IN HISTORICAL REALITY AND BIBLICAL TRADITION

Bethel is identified with Bēitīn, located about 2 kilometers northwest of et-Tell (Ai) on the main watershed highway (cf. Gen 12:8; Josh 8:9). It is mentioned by name in the Bible more than seventy times, and more than half of the instances refer to the cult site at Bethel.[91]

According to the excavation report, the Iron I site at Bethel was destroyed twice by conflagration within a short period of time.[92] According to James Kelso, Iron II Bethel is characterized by continuity of settlement, although the site underwent three distinct phases of development.[93] Iron II Bethel was destroyed by a conflagration, which the excavators dated to the second half of the sixth century on the basis of the latest ceramic assemblage in the Iron II stratum. Kelso thought that the historical context of the destruction might be related to one of two events, either the widespread rebellion that broke out in the third year of Nabonidus (553 BCE) or the rebellions on the occasion of Cambyses's death (523/521 BCE).[94] However, more recent archaeologists argue that the destruction

---

90. Cf. Zorn 2003, 443, who rejects this view.

91. Some of the references are doubtful. In 1 Sam 30:27 the LXX reads Beth-zur, but the preferred reading is Bethul or Bethuel (cf. Josh 19:4; 1 Chr 4:30); see, e.g., H. Smith 1898, 250; Naʾaman 2005b, 349. Bethel is also a divine name; see Ribichini 1999, 157–59; Röllig 1999, 173–75. Thus it is possible that some of the instances represent this divine name rather than the toponym; see, e.g., Jer 48:13; Zech 7:2. The cult site is additionally mentioned by the name of Beth-aven (Josh 7:2; 18:12; 1 Sam 13:5; 14:23; Hos 4:15; 5:8; 10:5); see Naʾaman 1987.

92. Kelso 1968, 32–35, 45–48; Finkelstein 1988, 72–73; Magen and Finkelstein 1993, 21*.

93. Most recently, Finkelstein and Avitz have reevaluated the excavation findings and propose a more nuanced picture the history of settlement of Iron II Bethel. According to them, Iron II occupation at Bethel is mainly limited to the eighth and early seventh centuries BCE; see Finkelstein and Avitz 2009, 38–43.

94. Kelso 1968, 37. Finkelstein and Avitz (2009, 42–43) argue against Kelso's conclusions and claim that most of the pottery that was assigned by the excavators to the mid- or late sixth century BCE actually belongs to the eight century. They suggest that the site might not have occupied at all during the Babylonian period.

layer should be dated later, circa 500–480 BCE.⁹⁵ Although the excavators did not uncover architectural remains dating to the Persian period, they believed the settlement continued to be inhabited and suggested that the Persian period site may be located in the vicinity of the slope that had not been excavated.⁹⁶ Significantly, the excavations failed to uncover any evidence of a cult site; however, it is likely that the cult site lay on the outskirts of the town, outside the inhabited area that was excavated.⁹⁷

More than half the references to Bethel in the Bible deal with the monarchic and the postexilic periods.⁹⁸ In the books of Kings, Amos, and Hosea, Bethel figures as the site of the royal sanctuary of the kingdom of Israel, and as such it also served as a center for prophetic activity.⁹⁹ Etiological traditions attribute the establishment of the cult site to the patriarchal period (Gen 12:8; 28:19; 31:13; 35:3–7; Hos 12:5), but their purpose is to provide an ancient past for the cult site, founded in the days of the monarchy. Reference to the cult site at Bethel in stories dealing with premonarchic period (Judg 20:18, 26, 32; 21:2, 19; 1 Sam 7:16; 10:3) most likely stem from familiarity with the position of the Bethel sanctuary in the time of the monarchy.

According to the boundary lists in Josh 16:1–2 and 18:12–13, Bethel lay north of the border separating Ephraim from Benjamin.¹⁰⁰ The Benjamin-Ephraim boundary description represents the border separating the kingdom of Judah from Israel (and later, the province of Samaria). In Josiah's time, Judah's border appears to have expanded northward, for the

---

95. See, e.g., Milevski 1996–97, 12; Lipschits 1999, 171–72; 2005, 242–43; Knauf 2006, 307–8. However, Faust's methodological reservation could apply here too (2003, 38; see n. 45 above).

96. Kelso 1968, 38. According to Finkelstein and Avitz (2009, 42–43), there is slight evidence for a very weak Persian period presence at Bethel. They claim that if a Persian period settlement was located in the unexcavated area, it still should have left "a clear ceramic imprint on the site." See also Finkelstein 2011a, 364.

97. See North 1954, 193–94; Kelso 1968, 37, 50–51; Na'aman 1987, 19–21; 2009b, 340–41; Blenkinsopp 1998, 34; 2003, 93–94. Here too Finkelstein and Avitz (2009, 43 n. 122) demur, noting that the intensive surveys "did not reveal the slightest clue for an Iron Age II site, let alone cult site, in this area."

98. For a full discussion, see most recently Köhlmoos 2006.

99. See 1 Kgs 12:29–33; 13:1, 4, 10–11, 32; 2 Kgs 2:2–3, 23; 10:29; 17:28; 23:4, 15–19; Hos 4:15; 5:8; 10:5; Amos 3:14; 4:4; 5:5–6; 7:10.

100. For the historical context of the boundary lists, see Lissovsky and Na'aman 2003 with discussion of previous literature there.

Benjaminite city list (Josh 18:21–28) includes Bethel in the district of Benjamin (v. 22).[101] In Persian period literature, Bethel figures as an inhabited site (Ezra 2:28 // Neh 7:32; 11:31).[102]

In a number of traditions, mourning rites are specifically tied to Bethel. For example, Gen 35:8 tells that an "oak of weeping" (אלון בכות) by Bethel marked the burial site of Rachel's nurse, Deborah. It is possible that this tree and the adjacent tomb lay within the sacred precinct at Bethel.[103] In addition, the LXX identifies the unique toponym Bochim, "weepers" (בכים), in Judg 2:5 with Bethel. Although the LXX reading may have been motivated by the tendency to identify an unfamiliar toponym with a well-known site, this reading is rooted in an early interpretive tradition, and many think it accurately reflects the intent of the MT of Judg 2:1–5.[104] Finally, Hos 12:5 mentions weeping in a variant tradition that locates Jacob's wrestling match at Bethel (cf. Penuel in Gen 32:25–31). In summary, it is not unlikely that the author of the Gibeah story chose to locate all the sacral activities in the narrative at Bethel, due to its standing in his days and its association with mourning rites.

2.5. Bethlehem

Modern-day Bethlehem is densely populated, and therefore only limited excavations and surveys have been conducted there. These have uncovered ceramic remains from the Early through the Late Bronze Age, as well as from Iron II (eighth–sixth centuries BCE).[105] Given the limited investigation of the area, the lack of material finds from the premonarchic period

---

101. See Na'aman 2005b, 350–52, 360.

102. See Williamson 1985, 28–34, 349–50. North (1954), Veijola (1982, 194–96), Blenkinsopp (1998, 32–33, 2003, 100–101), and Knauf (2006, 305–6) have argued that Zech 7:2 provides evidence that the cult site at Bethel was active prior to the restoration of Jerusalem. The view that the Bethel cult site enjoyed renewed popularity following the sack of the Jerusalem temple has much to commend it, but it must be verified by means of other evidence. Reading Bethel as a toponym in Zech 7:2 is problematic; see, e.g., Beuken 1967, 143–44. The most likely reading is to take ביתאל־שראצר as a personal name; see Wellhausen 1963, 186; Hyatt 1937, 387–94.

103. See other trees within the sacred precincts at Shechem (Gen 12:6–7; 35:4; Josh 24:26) and Hebron (Gen 13:18); see Na'aman 1987, 18–21.

104. See, e.g., Moore 1895, 58; Veijola 1982, 186; Na'aman 1987, 18; Gray 1986, 242–43; Amit 2000, 119–29.

105. See Prag 2002, 170.

VIRTUAL SPACE AND REAL GEOGRAPHY 103

(Iron I) may well be coincidental. However, it should be noted that the area of Judah, in general, was sparsely inhabited in Iron I.[106]
The Bible mentions Bethlehem thirty-seven times.[107] Even though it is clear in most contexts that a Judean town is intended,[108] the designation *Judah* is frequently added to the town's name (בית־לחם יהודה, 17:7–9; 19:1–2, 18; 1 Sam 17:12; Ruth 1:1–2). An additional designation that occurs in connection with Bethlehem is (אפרת(ה/י), which apparently derives from the name of a clan that settled in Bethlehem. Some have suggested that the term preserves the memory of the migration of an Ephraimite clan to Bethlehem.[109] Since there is no early evidence for this move, the possibility should be considered that Bethlehem (and possibly other sites in Judah) absorbed Ephraimite refugees following the fall of Samaria. In this case, the marriage ties between the Ephraimite Levite and the Bethlehemite concubine in Judg 19 is not only a device to place the action along the route between Mount Ephraim and Bethlehem, but might also reflect the memory of an old association of Bethlehemite families with Mount Ephraim.
Nearly half the references to Bethlehem deal with David and his lineage (1 Sam 16:4; 17:12–15; 20:6, 28; 2 Sam 2:32; Ruth 1:1–2, 19, 22; 2:4; 4:11; cf. 2 Sam 23:24; Mic 5:1). According to the LXX reading of Josh 15:59b, Bethlehem was included in one of the districts of Judah in the time of Josiah.[110] Some postmonarchic sources also refer to Bethlehem. In the narrative in Jer 41:17, Bethlehem is mentioned as a point of reference for the location of the little-known place Geruth Chimham (גרות כמהם), indicating the standing of the better-known town in generations following the Babylonian conquest. The town is also included the list of

---

106. See Ofer 1994, 106–9.
107. Not including synoptic passages in Chronicles or the designation בית הלחמי, which is found four times in Samuel.
108. Cf. Bethlehem in Zebulon (Josh 19:15), which may also represent the town of the judge Ibzan (Judg 12:8–10); see, e.g., Moore 1895, 310; Soggin 1987, 222; contra Josephus, *Ant*. 5.8.13 §271.
109. Ephrathah is identified with Bethlehem (Gen 35:19; 48:7; see also Mic 5:1; Ruth 4:11) and the gentilicon Ephrati is applied to residents of Bethlehem (1 Sam 17:12; Ruth 1:2; see also 1 Chr 4:4). For the suggestion of an Ephraimite migration to Bethlehem, see, e.g., Na'aman 1984, 2014b; Ofer 1994, 120. For an alternate view, see Blenkinsopp 2006, 630–33.
110. For the district missing from the MT of Josh 15:59b, see Aharoni 1979, 355; Nelson 1997, 185 n. 4.

returnees in Ezra 2:21 // Neh 7:26, indicating either inhabitation in the Persian period or the tenacity with which clans adhered to local origin traditions throughout the exile.[111] In addition, the lists in 1 Chr 2:51, 54, and 4:4 present two "genealogies" for Bethlehem. These genealogies may stem from other literary traditions (e.g., 1 Sam 17:12; Mic 5:1; the LXX reading of Josh 15:59b), but the fact that they were included in the genealogies of Judah indicates interest in traditions dealing with Bethlehem in the times of the Chronicler.

In Judg 19:1–2, 18, Bethlehem figures as the place where the Levite enjoyed the warm hospitality of his father-in-law. Thus the town sets the standard against which hostile Gibeah is to be measured. Since the tradition history of Bethlehem is tied mainly to David, the negative analogy between the two towns might also allude to their standing in the origin traditions of the rival royal houses, Saul of Gibeah and David of Bethlehem.[112]

2.6. The Rock of Rimmon

Several places in the Bible bear the name Rimmon, but most of them are located far from the arena of action in Judg 20–21.[113] The place name, as vocalized by the MT, seems to derive from a pomegranate tree (רמון) that marked the site. But since Rammānu is an epithet of the god Hadad, the masoretic vocalization may have been intended to mask the possibility that the site was named for the god and was dedicated to his cult.[114]

The narrative in Judg 20–21 does not provide details regarding the location of the rock of Rimmon/Rammūn, although the refugees probably would have reached it on their flight via the "desert road."[115] Eusebius

---

111. See Williamson 1985, 33–34; see also Lipschits 2005, 152–68. It should be noted that only two towns south of Jerusalem appear in the list, Bethlehem and Netophah. Perhaps greater representation of towns south of Jerusalem should be expected if the list indeed reflects hometowns of the returnees.

112. See, e.g., Auberlen 1860, 550–58; Güdemann 1869, 365–68; Bleek 1878, 203; Brettler 1989a, 412–15; Amit 1994, 35; 2000, 184–88; de Hoop 2004, 25–26.

113. E.g., Rimmon-perez (Num 33:19–20), Ain-Rimmon (Josh 15:32; 19:7; Neh 11:29; 1 Chr 4:32), Gath-rimmon (Josh 19:45; 21:24–25; 1 Chr 6:54), Rimmon in Zebulon (Josh 19:13), Rimmon south of Jerusalem (Zech 14:10).

114. 2 Kgs 5:18; Zech 12:11; see also the theophoric element in the name Tabrimmon (1 Kgs 15:18); see Greenfield 1999, 379; Avigad and Sass 1997, 531; Gass 2005, 424.

115. See, e.g., Josephus, *Ant.* 5.2.12 §166.

locates Rimmon/Rammān about fifteen milestones north of Jerusalem,[116] but it does not seem reasonable that the Benjaminites fled so far north into the region of Ephraim, when they could have found refuge closer on the desert fringe of Benjamin. Thus it might be preferable to assume that the location of the rock of Rimmon/Rammān has yet to be identified. A likely location might be east of Geba, perhaps in Wadi es-Suweinit, which would provide good cover. Such a location would fit well with the Benjaminites' flight via the "desert road," since Wadi es-Suweinit descends through the desert eastward toward Jericho.[117]

2.7. Jabesh-Gilead

Jabesh is mentioned eighteen times in the Bible (nearly half the instances compounded with *Gilead*). About a third of the references are found in Judg 21, and nearly all the rest in Samuel and synoptic passages in Chronicles.[118] The toponym is preserved in the name of Wadi el-Yabis, which transects northern Gilead from east to west, passing south of Pella. Jabesh has been identified with various locations in the wadi, but the primary candidates are Tell el-Maqlūb and Tell Abu al-Kharaz. The argument in favor of Tell el-Maqlūb rests mainly on the testimony of Eusebius, who located Jabesh six milestones from Pella, on the way to Jerash.[119] Excavations at Tell Abu al-Kharaz have uncovered findings from Iron I–II, which include fortified towers and residences and perhaps also an administrative structure.[120]

Nearly all the references to the town deal with its relations with Benjamin, Saul, and David (Judg 21; 1 Sam 11, 21; 2 Sam 2, 21). On the face of it, these passages assume existing blood ties between Jabesh and Ben-

---

116. See Eusebius, *Onom.* 144.11–12; Moore 1895, 444; Albright 1924, 35; Rösel 1976, 41.

117. See Arnold 1990, 59; Gass 2005, 426–27.

118. See Judg 21:8–10, 12, 14; 1 Sam 11: 1, 3, 5, 9–10; 31:11–13 (// 1 Chr 10:11–12); 2 Sam 2:4–5; 21:12. It is possible that the town figures as the home of Shallum ben Jabesh (2 Kgs 15:10–14) or, alternatively, that the town was named after the eponymous father whose clan settled there; see Montgomery 1951, 455; Cogan and Tadmor 1988, 170.

119. See Eusebius, *Onom.* 110.11–13; Edelman 1992, 594; Hübner 1992, 169; MacDonald 2000, 202–4; Na'aman 2014a, 492.

120. Gass 2005, 506–7.

jamin.¹²¹ Accordingly, the men of Jabesh absented themselves from the Mizpah assembly out of a sense of solidarity with their Benjaminite brethren. The blood tie is also supposed to explain why the people of Jabesh sent to Gibeah of Saul for aid (1 Sam 11:4) and why they undertook a daring mission to Beth-shean in order to retrieve the corpses of Saul and his sons from Philistine hands (1 Sam 31:11–13; 2 Sam 21:12). However, Diana Edelman expressed doubt regarding the ancient blood ties between Jabesh and Benjamin. According to her reading of 2 Sam 2:4–7, Jabesh was included in Saul's kingdom by virtue of a political treaty between the two sides. Thus she concludes that the relations outlined in Judg 21 and 1 Sam 11 are a literary fiction.¹²²

Indeed, the references to Jabesh in Judg 21 and in Samuel appear to be wholly literary, but this does not imply that they stem from one hand or one early tradition. It seems that the Jabesh episode in Judg 21 assumes the story in 1 Sam 11, not vice versa.¹²³ According to the sense of the narrative in 1 Sam 11:3–4, the messengers from Jabesh arrived at Gibeah of Saul after they had made the rounds of "all the territory of Israel" (בכל גבול ישראל). Thus, neither Gibeah nor all Benjamin was the initial addressee of the Jabeshites' call for aid. Only after no response was forthcoming elsewhere did the messagers come to Gibeah. Hence, it is doubtful that the narrative in 1 Sam 11 assumes early blood ties between Jabesh and Benjamin. In contrast, it is reasonable that the narrator in Judg 21 chose to provide the Benjaminite refugees with brides from Jabesh in order to create fictive blood ties between the two groups. The resulting blood ties are intimated only here, but anyone who reads 1 Sam 11 following Judg 21 would be likely to conclude that the relations between Jabesh and Saul are based on the blood ties formed at the conclusion of the war at Gibeah. If so, then the Jabesh episode in Judg 21 seems to have been written as a kind of commentary on the relationship between Jabesh and Saul as described in the book of Samuel.

---

121. See, e.g., Hertzberg 1964, 91–92. Most recently, Na'aman (2014a, 492–94) proposed that Jabesh was a clan name and that the clan split in the early Iron Age, when one group settled in the south of Benjamin while the other group migrated to the western Gilead. Na'aman's view implies that an ancient memory of blood ties between "Benjaminite" Jabeshites and eastern Jabeshites was tenaciously preserved for hundreds of years until the pre-Deuteronomistic history of Saul was written.

122. See Edelman 1992, 594–95. The expressions עשה חסד/טובה indicate the covenant relation between the patron kings, Saul and David, and the town.

123. Noth (1966, 163–64) raises the question but leaves it unsettled.

In other words, it appears that the account in Judg 21 was written for its present context in order to serve as an "introduction" to the story of Saul.[124]

2.8. Shiloh

Shiloh is mentioned four times in the story, and all the instances are in Judg 21: three times in connection with the abduction of the girls of Shiloh (21:19–21) and once as the location of the camp to which the Israelites returned after their campaign against Jabesh (21:12).[125] According to 21:19, Shiloh is located on the road leading to Shechem, between Lebonah in the north and Bethel in the south, and this description fits the site of Khirbet Seilun.[126]

The excavations at Shiloh indicate continuous activity at the site from Middle Bronze III until its destruction toward the end of Iron I in the eleventh century.[127] The site remained uninhabited until the final third of Iron II, when a small settlement was founded (ca. eighth or seventh century BCE). The only Persian and Hellenistic period finds were isolated ceramic remains.

More than half of the biblical references to Shiloh are tied to traditions regarding the cult site there.[128] According to Jer 7:12–14 and 26:6–9, the sanctuary at Shiloh was destroyed long before the final days of the kingdom of Judah,[129] and all other biblical references to the cult site of Shiloh relate it to the premonarchic period. Given the lengthy settlement gap between the Iron I and late Iron II levels at Shiloh, the biblical depiction of Shiloh in early monarchic times probably reflects the reality of late

---

124. The traditions regarding Jabesh and Saul may stem from the local tradition regarding Saul's burial at Jabesh (1 Sam 31:13). Since the family burial site was located at Zela in Benjamin (2 Sam 21:14), it would have been necessary to harmonize the traditions, explain why and how the men of Jabesh buried Saul in their city, and how Saul's remains were finally interned in the family tomb.

125. On the secondary nature of mention of the camp at Shiloh, see above, ch. 1.

126. See Finkelstein 1988, 206.

127. See Finkelstein 1993, 371–89.

128. E.g., with regard to the tabernacle (Josh 18:1; 19:51), the ark (1 Sam 4:3–4), the house of God (Judg 18:31), the sanctuary of YHWH (1 Sam 1:9, 24; Jer 7:14; 26:6, 9), "before YHWH" (לפני ה') Josh 18:8, 10; 19:51), the place where YHWH made his name dwell (Jer 7:12), the dynasty of Elide priests (1 Sam 1:3, 9; 2:14; 4:4; 14:3; 1 Kgs 2:27; see also 1 Sam 3:21).

129. See Day 1979.

Iron II.¹³⁰ This anachronism may indicate the context in which the stories about Ahijah the "Shilonite" were composed. According to Jer 41:5, Shiloh is again represented as an inhabited site in the Babylonian period. There Shiloh is mentioned along with Shechem and Samaria as the place of origin of a group bringing offerings to present at the sanctuary of YHWH. However, it is not certain that this passage provides a reliable witness to the existence of a settlement at Shiloh at the time of Gedaliah,¹³¹ and the places of origin could have been chosen for the sake of alliteration.¹³²

Donald Schley and others have suggested that the references to Shiloh in Judg 21 represent the early "Canaanite" kernel of tradition with regard to Shiloh.¹³³ This view is based on mistaken assumptions about the specification of Shiloh's location (21:19), the designation "Shiloh, which is in the land of Canaan" (21:12), and supposed elements of fertility rites in the description of the festivities at Shiloh (21:21). First, there is no basis for the assumption that the specification of Shiloh's location points to the antiquity of the following tradition. The directions are not necessary to the narrative¹³⁴ and appear to be a "scholarly" note that serves to establish the authority of the narrator.¹³⁵ Second, the literary-critical analysis has shown that the comment, "Shiloh, which is in the land of Canaan" (21:12), derives from R² and therefore does not provide authentic information

---

130. See 1 Kgs 14:3–4; and cf. Ahijah's gentilicon "the Shilonite" (1 Kgs 11:29; 12:15; 15:29; 2 Chr 9:29; 10:15). The gentilicon could possibly be explained as a persistent origin tradition that survived even after the family moved elsewhere, but 1 Kgs 14:3–4 definitely represents Shiloh as the place of Ahijah's home.

131. See Naʾaman 2006, 352 n. 26; but cf. Lipschits 2005, 115.

132. Note the recurring clusters of *mem*, *shin*, and *nun*: יבאו אנשים משכם משלו ומשמרון שמנים איש. Another indication of the literary concerns at work in this verse is the alphabetical progression in the order of the three towns, שכם, שלו, שמרון, which is followed by the number שמנים, resulting in the series *kaph, lamed, mem, nun*.

133. See Schley 1989, 135; see also Hertzberg 1965, 250; Gray 1986, 232.

134. See Kimchi: "I wonder why this (note) was necessary, because Shiloh was (well-)known without directions"; see Bertheau 1845, 231; Bleek 1878, 202; Soggin 1987, 299.

135. See Bleek 1878, 202; Böhme 1885, 34; Fishbane 1988, 44–46, 80–81; Amit 2001, 118–20. See also similar "scholarly" geographical notes in Gen 49:30; Num 33:40; Deut 11:30; Josh 4:19; 7:2. Gass (2005, 401, 404) suggests that the directions in 21:19 and the different orthography, שלו (v. 19) and שלה (v. 12), indicate that these are separate toponyms. But this is disproved by 1 Sam 3:21, where both spellings occur with regard to the same place; cf. the alternate spellings with regard to the Shiloh sanctuary in Judg 18:31; 1 Sam 1:3, 9, 24; 4:3; 14:3; Jer 7:12.

about Shiloh's Canaanite past. Finally, there is no reason to assume that the description of the festivities reflects a "Canaanite" fertility cult. Vintage festivals are so widely celebrated that, when lacking specific reference to a divinity, they should not be identified with a particular cult.

However, if the episode about the girls of Shiloh does not stem from ancient tradition, then why did the narrator choose it as the setting for the second solution to the Benjaminites' plight? It is possible that the Shiloh festivities were well known in the narrator's day, but we have no means to verify this. By contrast, the narrator most certainly was familiar with the birth narrative of Samuel, which mentions the yearly (מימים ימימה) pilgrimage of Elkanah and his family to worship and offer sacrifice to YHWH at Shiloh (1 Sam 1:3; cf. Judg 21:19). It is possible that the narrator chose the annual festivity at Shiloh in order to create an associative link to Samuel's birth narrative. On the one hand, the location of this episode at Shiloh helps smooth the transition between the end of the Gibeah story and the beginning of Samuel's story, and this seems to indicate that Judg 19–21 was composed for this context in the Deuteronomistic History. On the other hand, the editorial recourse to such an artificial means for providing transition seems to indicate that Judg 19–21 was inserted into its context and was not originally part of the Deuteronomistic History.

2.9. Summary and Conclusions

Any discussion of the role played by the places mentioned in a narrative needs to consider both the historical reality known to the authors and the complex of tradition upon which they could draw. Are the localities represented according to the historical reality of the period in which the narrative is supposed to take place? Does the representation of the spatial sphere correspond better to the reality of the author's times? Or is the spatial sphere a fictive construct, influenced perhaps by previous literary tradition?

According to the archaeological findings, the three towns Gibeah, Mizpah, and Bethel all existed throughout Iron I until the end of Iron II, even though they seemed to have waxed and waned at different times. At Shiloh a long gap in settlement separates the end of Iron I from renewed habitation in the final third of Iron II. The information regarding the other sites is patchy, whether due to uncertain identification (e.g., Rimmon, Jabesh) or to difficulties in excavating modern urban areas (Bethlehem). Given the absence of a conflagration layer or pottery embedded in floors of strata from the end of Iron II, many scholars think that Gibeah and Bethel were occupied throughout the Babylonian period and at the beginning of the Persian period. Regarding Mizpah, different findings clearly indicate that the site was settled throughout the Babylonian and Persian periods.

The findings from the final stage of Iron II at Gibeah and Mizpah show that the standing of both these towns changed in the Babylonian period. The main phase of growth at Gibeah occurred during this period, and at the same time Mizpah underwent a transition from a village to an administrative center. This change in the standing of the two towns is apparently tied up with the changes that occurred throughout Judah and Benjamin as a result of the Babylonian conquest. On the basis of an evaluation of the excavation and survey results for these areas, Lipschits determined that the impact of the Babylonian conquest was felt mainly in Jerusalem and its immediate environs to the south, and this limited area was severely depleted.[136] By contrast, the area of Benjamin displays a large degree of continuity. Lipschits surmised that the area of Benjamin was saved from the fate of Jerusalem because its towns surrendered to the Babylonians, while Jerusalem and its environs persisted in the policy of rebellion imposed by the royal house.[137] The growth of Gibeah at this time may be due to an influx of refugees from the environs of Jerusalem. From the middle of the fifth century there is a perceptible decline of settlement throughout all of Benjamin. At this time Gibeah was abandoned, as was the previously settled area in Bethel. This decline is commonly explained as a result of the restoration of Jerusalem, which attracted an influx of population from the surrounding areas.[138]

The representation in Judg 20–21 of Bethel as a cult site, at which the Israelites assemble "before YHWH" to consult the oracle, lament their losses, and offer up sacrifices, derives from its standing as the site of the royal sanctuary of the kingdom of Israel. Despite the report that Josiah dismantled and polluted the cult site (2 Kgs 23:15), it is possible that it continued to be active during the period of Babylonian rule, when the prestige of the Jerusalem cult was badly damaged by the destruction of

---

136. Lipschits 2005, 210–18, 258–71.

137. Lipschits 1998, 472–82; 1999, 158–59, 179–85; 2005, 237–49, 245–300, 366–67; Blenkinsopp 2003, 96. It is possible that the Babylonians located the administrative center at Mizpah, because groups in Benjamin collaborated with the Babylonian authorities; see Jer 37:12–15.

138. See N. Lapp 1981, 39–40; Magen and Finkelstein 1993, 27 (Hebrew section); Milevski 1996–97; Lipschits 1999, 181–85; 2005, 267–71.

the temple.[139] It is significant that Bethel appears in Judg 19–21 as a legitimate cult site and that in neither N^1 nor R^2 is there a trace of anti-Bethel polemic.[140] This depiction of Bethel in a Judean-oriented narrative probably reflects the cultic realities of the period prior to the restoration of the Jerusalem temple. Although the Bethel cult site has not yet been uncovered, it was probably located on the outskirts of the town.

The references to Mizpah as a pantribal assembly center in the premonarchic period do not stem from an early tribal league, for the historical evidence indicates that social organization in the premonarchic period did not transcend the local level.[141] Although Mizpah thrived throughout the Iron Age, there is no evidence that it was of any importance until it became an administrative center under Babylonian rule. Thus it is reasonable to assume that the representation of Mizpah in Judg 20–21 as a place for pantribal assembly, deliberation, and mobilization most probably reflects its standing during the Babylonian and early Persian periods, when it served as the administrative center for the province of Yehud. Similarly, the depiction of Gibeah in Judg 19–20 as a premonarchic urban community has no basis in the archaeological record. This description of Gibeah may stem from the narrator's imagination, but it is also possible that it reflects the historical reality of his times. Since the expansion of settlement at Gibeah is most marked in the Babylonian period, it is tempting to set the depiction of the town in Judg 19–20 in this historical context.

The disparity between the representation of the narrative's spatial sphere and the historical reality of the premonarchic period, when the story supposedly occurs, points to the likelihood that the narrator based the geographical background upon later reality, as well as upon other literary descriptions of premonarchic Israel. In my opinion, the combined reference to Bethlehem, Gibeah, Mizpah, and Bethel in Judg 19–21 may best reflect the circumstances existing in Judah during the period of Babylonian occupation and the beginning of the Persian period.[142] With the

---

139. See, e.g., Blenkinsopp 1998; 2003, 95–99; Guillaume 2004, 201–2. Finkelstein and Avitz, however, find no material evidence for a cult site at Bethel, neither in the period of the monarchy nor following (2009, 43 n. 122).

140. So too Gross 2009, 857.

141. See, e.g., de Geus 1976, 120–50; Lemche 1985, 274–90.

142. Köhlmoos (2006, 289–91) prefers to explain the geographical background against the background of the Ptolemaic period, but this might stem from the fact that her study focuses on Bethel. However, there is but little evidence for activity at

exception of the vicinity of Jerusalem, the area from Bethel to Bethlehem represents the extent of continued habitation in Judah during this period.[143] In this context, it is noteworthy that the Levite passes over Jerusalem without stopping on his trip from Bethlehem to his home in Mount Ephraim/ Bethel, because it is beyond the pale of Israelite inhabitation (Judg 19:12).

The conclusion that the spatial dimension in Judg 19–21 reflects the historical reality of the sixth century may explain why both Mizpah and Bethel were fitted into the story alongside Gibeah. Nearly all the activity in the story is concentrated in the region of Benjamin, which indeed was the center of administrative activity in the Babylonian period. Among the Benjaminite towns, the administrative center of Mizpah was best suited to serve as place of mobilization, deliberation, and decision making, while the cult site of Bethel was best suited as the location for cultic ceremonies.

It remains to consider the motives of the narrator in setting most of the events at Gibeah, since it was equally possible to locate the story at any other Benjaminite town, such as Ramah, Michmash, Geba, or Gibeon. That the narrator was familiar with a tradition about a war at Gibeah (Hos 10:9) and could use a preexisting poetic source that commemorated the battle may have influenced the choice to set the plot in Gibeah. An additional consideration may have been the importance of Gibeah in the Saul traditions. Other places may also have been brought into the story due to their prominence in the Saul and David traditions. For example, mention of Jabesh-gilead in Judg 21 provides a basis for blood ties between this town and Benjamin, following which Saul's heroic rally to save Jabesh appears to be motivated more by personal interest than by divine inspiration. Similarly, Bethlehem might have been chosen as the hometown of the concubine, since it evokes the memory of old associations between a Bethlehemite clan and Ephraim. In addition, the visit at the father-in-law's house in Bethlehem stands in contrast to the disastrous visit at Gibeah and might hint at a similar analogy between the two kings who are related to these cities, David and Saul. Thus the narrator could prejudice the reader against Saul and in favor of David even before the reader encounters them.[144] Finally, the mention of Shiloh in reference to yearly festivities and

---

Tel el-Ful and Tel en-Naṣbeh in the early Hellenistic period; see, e.g., Lipschits and Tal 2007, 33–34. Moreover, it is not clear how the anti-Benjamin polemic in the story serves the concerns of Ptolemaic period.

143. Lipschits 2005, 210–71, 373.

144. See, e.g., Güdemann 1869, 364–65; Brettler 1989a, 412–13; Amit 2000, 184–88.

difficulties in producing issue creates an associative link to the opening of the book of Samuel. Moreover, by establishing literary blood ties with Benjamin, the narrator may be setting the stage for the future abandonment of Shiloh by YHWH (1 Sam 4; Jer 7:12, 14). From all this, it becomes clear that the geographical background of the story does not represent early historical reality but reflects the times and interests of the author.

3
LANGUAGE AND STYLE:
DIACHRONIC AND SYNCHRONIC ASPECTS

The discussion in the previous chapter raised the possibility that the representation of the spatial sphere in Judg 19–21 was influenced by the historical reality of the Babylonian and early Persian periods. This understanding may have implications for determining when the story was composed and its place within the context of the history of biblical literature. However, this matter should not be decided solely on the basis of the late historical reality reflected in the story's setting, since the geographic details could have been inserted into an earlier narrative. Thus it is necessary to seek additional evidence that may confirm the hypothesis of Babylonian or early Persian period composition. For the most part, we lack external documentation of events mentioned in biblical texts, and in the few instances that such sources exist, they only provide an earliest possible date for composition (i.e., no earlier than the event related).

Given this situation, many have appealed to historical linguistics in search of an additional criterion for dating texts that is independent of the subject or ideas expressed by the text. The basic assumption is that literary texts reflect the linguistic characteristics current at the time of composition and that comparison of texts composed in periods separated by hundreds of years will reveal changes in usage by which scholars may reconstruct the history of the language. According to this principle, it should be possible to take a text of unknown provenance and characterize its language and then identify its proper context within the framework of the language's development. This chronological linguistic framework must be anchored in verifiable external data in order for the method to provide an alternative to dating on the basis of internal criteria. Such external data are supplied by extrabiblical texts such as Iron Age Hebrew epigraphs, the writings from the Judean desert (second century BCE–second century CE), as well as the Tannaitic literature of the second-third centuries CE.

Since the nineteenth century, scholars have been aware of differences between Mishnaic Hebrew (MH) and Biblical Hebrew (BH) and have found traces of later Hebrew in various parts of the Bible.[1] However, the effort to identify and characterize the different historical strata of BH was mainly undertaken in the latter half of the twentieth century.[2] At first, the endeavor focused on characterizing the language of books whose content provides a definite *terminus a quo* in the postexilic period (e.g., Esther, Daniel, Ezra-Nehemiah, Chronicles), and according to the extent to which these books reflected characteristics of MH or the influence of Imperial Aramaic, they were considered to represent the stratum of Late Biblical Hebrew (LBH). Following this, indubitably late texts were compared to parallel texts that supposedly date to the preexilic period (the classic test case being Samuel–Kings compared with Chronicles), and the differences in formulation that were not motivated by ideology or tendency could be explained as the result of development from Classical or Standard Biblical Hebrew (SBH) to LBH. On the face of it, the historical linguistic method can provide external criteria for dating the composition of biblical texts. However, a number of methodological problems may be detected in studies utilizing the method.

1. The method has limitations and can only help date texts that display late linguistic characteristics shared with MH. This means that the method can only indicate the probability that a text displaying certain characteristics is indeed late. Practitioners like Avi Hurvitz have admitted that there are no linguistic tools for determining whether a text, written in SBH, is indeed a preexilic composition rather than the product of a later period.[3] However, many have stretched the capabilities of the method in

---

1. See, e.g., S. Driver 1972, 473–75, 504–6; Kropat 1909.
2. Kropat (1909) provides a notable exception. Otherwise see Kutscher 1982; Hurvitz 1972; Polzin 1976; Rooker 1990; Eskult 1990, 103–23; Ehrensvärd 1997; see also Qimron 1986 on Qumran Hebrew. Prior to all these is the Hebrew publication of Bendavid (1951, 1967); however, neither edition has been translated and thus has had little impact outside Israel.
3. See Hurvitz 2000, 146–47: "The existence of old elements in a given text cannot always provide us with solid ground for making chronological judgements, since these elements, whose roots stretch back—linguistically—to remote antiquity, may still be circulating, as genuine survivals, within compositions written (or re-worked)—historically—at a relatively late period. Furthermore, in certain cases such elements may

order to establish that a given text is preexilic and have fallen into the trap of circular argument. Thus the lack of typically late linguistic characteristics has been taken to indicate that texts like the books of Samuel and Kings are preexilic compositions, while at the same time the presumption of preexilic date has provided the basis for comparison with the language of postexilic compositions.[4] However, lately scholars have challenged common assumptions regarding the early composition of different literary sources,[5] thus heightening the problem of basing the chronology of linguistic development on assumptions regarding the identity of preexilic compositions.[6] Most recently, the date of the transition to LBH has been called into question,[7] and some suggest that the traditional line of demarcation should be down-dated to the fifth century or later.

2. According to some of the practitioners of the historical linguistic method, a text should be presumed to be preexilic in origin unless it displays a significant quantity of usages characteristic of LBH.[8] This a priori statement is problematic for two reasons. First, some texts of undoubted

---

reflect a deliberate application of antique style, or a literary borrowing from earlier sources, placed in its extant biblical setting as a stylistic device by a later author. Given the present state of research, it is often extremely difficult to tell a genuinely archaic text from one which is merely archaizing." Cf. Knauf 2006, 311.

4. See criticism of the fallacy by Auld 1994, 9–10; Blenkinsopp 1996, 509–10; Rezetko 2003, 239–40. Hurvitz (1972, 34) warns against the circular reasoning: "It is necessary to beware of the 'vicious circle' whereby the characteristic *x* is believed late because it is found in text *y*, and text *y* is late because of characteristic *x*" (my trans.). But his contention that the burden of proof lies on those who argue for late composition of a given text (pp. 20–21) is in itself based on a circular argument: a given characteristic *x* is early because it is found in text *y*; text *y* is early because of characteristic *x*, and because it *lacks known late characteristics*.

5. On Samuel, see, e.g., Auld 1994, 1998b; Hutzli 2010. On the Yahwistic materials, see, e.g., Van Seters 1975, 1992, 1994; Levin 1993; Knauf 2006, 291–349; and Schmid 2006, 29–50. Down-dating the composition or final redaction of these texts reduces the chronological gap between them and the postexilic texts displaying LBH features.

6. See, e.g., Elwolde 1997, 52–53: "Thus for example, the use of preexilic vocabulary in a document that presents itself as a history of the early preexilic period does not mean that the work itself is preexilic …, but it does show how difficult it can be to determine the date of major texts and how precarious is a linguistic chronology built on such dating (particularly when the dating of the texts has to some extent been motivated by the requirements of an assumed linguistic chronology)."

7. Levin 2006.

8. E.g., Hurvitz 1972, 26; Eskhult 1990, 119.

postexilic origin are written, almost entirely, in SBH (e.g., Zech 1–8; Ps 137; Sirach; and the extracanonical Ps 151 in 11QPs^a 28:3–12).⁹ Second, few have attempted to apply statistical analysis in order to define what constitutes a "significant quantity" of linguistic features.¹⁰

3. Historical linguistic studies frequently assume that the texts examined constitute a single literary stratum and that the linguistic phenomena within it may help to determine the period of the entire composition.¹¹ However, literary-critical analysis frequently indicates that the present form of the text is the product of a lengthy process of redaction and revision. This particularly may be the case when the text under discussion is not a single pericope but an entire book.¹² In this regard, the distribution of the late features within the text may be especially significant. For example, a dense cluster of late phenomena may indicate: (1) late revision of the earlier text;¹³ (2) late expansion;¹⁴ or (3) deliberate change in voice by a late narrator, who imbues his composition with the authority of traditional literature by adopting a classical or archaic style but removes his

---

9. See, e.g., Bendavid 1967, 86; Ehrensvärd 2006; Rezetko 2009, 240–41; Young 2009, 258–59; and cf. Hurvitz 1972, 53–4, 171–72, 174 n. 307; 2006, 206. Hurvitz (1967) argued that the late composition of Ps 151 can be established on the basis of seven LBH usages in the psalm. However, he admitted doubts regarding two of the cases (אמרתי אני; נגיד לעמו) and the only undisputed late expressions in the psalm are the term בני ברית and the epithet אדון הכל; cf. Edenburg 2003, 141 n. 9.

10. For recent studies, see, e.g., Young et al. 2008a, 30–39; 2008b, 85–89; Young 2009, 257–59; see also Verheij 1990; Polak 1998, 2012; and Elwolde 1997, 18; however, their findings may point to stylistic characteristics rather than to historical developments in language use. By contrast, see Hurvitz's (1972, 69 n. *) reservations regarding statistical criteria: "This accumulation [of data] is relative. It is doubtful whether we are justified in applying rules of mechanical statistics and precise mathematical formulas with regard to these linguistic matters" (my trans.). Hurvitz indeed displays great leeway in judging what constitutes significant accumulation of data. Two phenomena throughout the eight verses of Ps 124 and four phenomena throughout the fifteen verses of Ps 144 sufficed for establishing their late composition, while two phenomena throughout the nine verses of Ps 137 were considered insufficient; see Hurvitz 1972, 160–69, 174.

11. See, e.g., the critical comments by Rezetko 2009 and Ben Zvi 1992, 541, in a review of Rooker 1990.

12. Levin 2006.

13. See Young 2009, 260–61.

14. Of course, expansion is a justified conclusion only if supported by literary evidence of a break in the narrative or an abrupt change in point of view, subject, or style; see, e.g., Brettler 1997 on 1 Sam 1–2.

"mask" at a critical juncture in order to sound central concerns in his own voice.[15] On the other hand, even distribution of a relatively few number of late phenomena throughout a lengthy text may indicate late composition of the entire text.

4. Scholarly opinion is divided regarding the criteria for identifying LBH usage.[16] For example, Robert Polzin's list of LBH characteristics found in the language of Chronicles and Ezra-Nehemiah has been reduced by other scholars, who have shown that some of the putatively late morphological and syntactical usages are also found in texts considered to be representative of SBH in the Pentateuch and the Former Prophets.[17]

5. Some have argued against diachronic characterization of lexical usage.[18] A study by John Elwolde shows that unique lexical values represent only 3 percent of all the words in the different groups of extrabiblical texts of the Persian through Roman periods. Moreover, the number of extrabiblical lexica shared by two or more groups of texts is negligible and never exceeded three extrabiblical lexica.[19] This study may indicate that the vocabulary of postexilic extrabiblical texts does not represent a chronological linguistic stratum, because in that case we should expect the textual groups to display a significantly higher proportion of shared extrabiblical lexical values. In fact, Elwolde concludes that lexica can provide a useful tool for characterization of literary strata, while their value for distinguishing diachronic language strata is limited. Other studies have indicated that lexical and syntactical differences between texts are not necessarily the product of historical developments in language[20] but may reflect individual style, contemporaneous differences between dialects,[21] or identification with the ideological platform conveyed by a

---

15. See, e.g., M. Smith 1997, 188–200.
16. See, e.g., Qimron 1992, 352 n. 7.
17. See, e.g., Rendsburg 1980, 72–66; Rooker 1990, 35–40; Elwolde 1997, 53–54 n. 102.
18. See, e.g., Blenkinsopp 1996, 510–16; Qimron 1992, 353–54; Rezetko 2003, 245–49.
19. See Elwolde 1997, 30–22; and similarly Young et al. 2008a, 116. The textual groups reviewed by Elwolde were Sirach, four hymnic texts from the Cairo Geniza, 4QMMT, the Copper Scroll, the remaining Qumran texts, Murabbaʿat texts, and Nahal Hever scrolls.
20. See Qimron 1992, 353; Blenkinsopp 1996, 510–16; Elwolde 1997, 48–53; Young 2009.
21. See Rendsburg 1990; Young 1993, 1997; Schniedewind and Sivan 1997; Young

particular idiom.[22] Hence greater weight should be attributed to variation in morphology as a possible indication of diachronic change.[23]

6. The study of postexilic Hebrew has mostly focused on evidence of "mishnaic" elements or Aramaisms in the texts, which are taken as precursors of linguistic developments that reached their peak in MH. The resulting importance attributed to characteristics perceived as "late" overshadows the large degree of continuity and unity of pre-MH.[24] At the same time, there is growing recognition that Aramaic already exerted influence upon Hebrew in the preexilic period.[25] Preexilic Aramaisms might stem from regional dialects or from the growing importance Aramaic assumed as the lingua franca of the Levant already from the late Neo-Assyrian period.[26]

7. It is commonly assumed that SBH represents the Hebrew of the First Temple period,[27] but this assumption should be examined in light of the evidence of Iron Age Hebrew inscriptions.[28] For example, scholars have repeatedly stated that the use of independent accusative pronouns is drastically reduced in LBH in favor of object suffixes directly affixed to verbs.[29] This is borne out by many of the undisputed postexilic biblical

---

et al. 2008a, 168–69; 2008b, 96–99; cf. Qimron 1992, 358–60. Recently, Young (2009, 263–68) has suggested that LBH is a style preferred by scribes related to the eastern diaspora, and SBH/Early BH is the style preferred in the west, while Ben Zvi (2009, 285–88) prefers to relate LBH and SBH to "Judahite" voices and Babylonian returnee voices within the literary world of the texts.

22. See, e.g., Ben Zvi 1992, 542; 1997, 201–6; 2009; Schniedewind 1999, 242–47.
23. See, e.g., Rezetko 2003, 245.
24. See Qimron 1992; Elwolde 1997; Rezetko 2009.
25. See, e.g., Eskult 2003, 14–16; Hurvitz 2003; Young et al. 2008b, 72–77.
26. See Rendsburg 1990; Tadmor 1987; Lemaire 2006.
27. See, e.g., Eherensvärd 1997, 34.
28. Initial comparative studies were undertaken by Knauf 1990; Gogel 1998; Adams 1987; see also Young 2003.
29. See, e.g., Polzin 1976, 28–31; Rendsburg 1980, 64; Qimron 1986, 75–77; Rooker 1990, 35, 45; Eskhult 1990, 107. Rooker (1990, 86) cites findings according to which verbal object suffixes occur with a frequency of 25 percent in SBH, compared to a frequency of 93 percent in LBH. However, my examination of specific texts produced widely divergent results. Two Priestly texts, Gen 1 and Num 31, display no object suffixes, but they also display low frequencies of independent pronouns (four times, Gen 1:17, 27, 28; and three times, Num 31:6, 47, 53). Ratios of 50 percent or less of object suffixes versus independent pronouns are found in Gen 15 (33 percent suffixes), 1 Sam 5–6 (41 percent suffixes), Josh 7–8 and 1 Sam 12 (44 percent suffixes),

texts, but it also is characteristic of the Hebrew of Iron Age inscriptions.[30] Thus alternative use of independent object pronouns and accusative suffixes may characterize SBH,[31] *regardless of the supposed chronological context of the texts.* Ongoing comparative research of SBH, Iron Age inscriptional Hebrew, and the Hebrew of the Judean Desert casts new light on the assumptions regarding the historical context of "Classical Hebrew."[32]

8. The diachronic study of BH has been based almost exclusively upon the MT, while variants in Qumran texts are generally considered to represent late Hebrew developments. However, Robert Rezetko has demonstrated that text-critical tools establish the priority of different readings found in the Qumran Judges fragments. It follows then that the SBH usage in the MT of the same passages does not help establish the date of the MT

---

2 Kgs 24–25 (50 percent suffixes). Ratios between 51 percent and 75 percent of object suffixes are found in 1 Sam 9 (66 percent suffixes) and Gen 19 (70 percent suffixes), while ratios higher than 75 percent are found in 1 Sam 17 (85 percent suffixes), 1 Sam 1 and 2 Kgs 17 (86 percent suffixes) and Josh 2 (89 percent suffixes). These divergent findings may indicate that increased frequencies of verbal object suffixes stem from personal stylistic preferences, coexistent with the opposite preference among different groups of scribes.

30. Most have overlooked this point, with the notable exception of Qimron 1992, 350 n. 4; and Gogel 1998, 162 n. 193. Based upon the texts included in Aḥituv 1992, I found that in 80 percent of the cases where Iron Age scribes used an accusative pronoun, they preferred an accusative pronominal suffix to an independent object pronoun. The pronominal suffix is found nineteen times in the following texts: Lachish 3 (שלחך), אתננהו), Lachish 4 (יעלהו), Arad 16 (ברתיך), Arad 24 (הבקידם), Arad 40 (נתתים), Kuntillet ʿAjrud pithos 2 (ברכתיך, ישמרך), Ḥorvat ʿUza "Edomite" ostracon (והברכתך), Amman Citadel Inscription (אכחדם), Mesha Stela (ויחלפה, הראני), אענו, החרמתה, הלחמה, ואשאה, ואחזה), Deir ʿAlla, second combination (שאלתיך), Ekron (תברכה, וישמרה; see Gitin et al. 1997). Within this corpus, the independent accusative pronoun occurs only five times: Lachish 3 (אתה), Lachish 4 (אתה), Arad 17 (אחה), Arad 24 (אתם), Kuntillet ʿAjrud pithos 1 (אתכם).

31. As a sample test, the frequency of independent pronouns versus object suffixed endings was checked for masc. 3rd-person sg./pl. in Judges–Kings. The independent pronouns אותו and אותם were found 289 times, as opposed to 266 occurrences of the singular suffix forms -הו, -ו, and -נו and 132 occurrences of the plural suffix form -ם. In all, pronominal suffixes were used in 58 percent of the cases, a frequency lower by 22 percent from that found in Iron Age inscriptions; see Gogel 1998, 162 n. 193.

32. See Young 2003; Young et al. 2008a, 138–39, 143–72; 2008b; Rezetko 2009; Kim 2013. Knauf (1990) went so far as to characterize BH in general as a composite literary language that reflects the lengthy period of text production and transmission from the eighth to the fifth century BCE.

but might indicate instead that LBH and SBH coexisted. Moreover, Rezetko's detailed examination of the Qumran Judges variants shows that the presumed LBH usages are not necessarily characteristic of the Qumran manuscripts, which in some cases are more likely to reflect SBH usage. In other words, a diachronic interpretation of SBH/LBH exchanges between biblical manuscripts can frequently be misleading.[33]

9. One of the main criteria for detecting LBH strata is presumed Aramaic influence reflected in the Hebrew of a text. The importance attached to Aramaisms as a diagnostic feature stems from the assumption that in the postexilic period Aramaic gradually replaced Hebrew as the spoken language in the land of Israel.[34] While the epigraphic findings from 200 BCE–200 CE do indicate a significant rise in use of Aramaic for writing, there is no evidence that it replaced Hebrew as the spoken language in Israel during this time. Aramaic may have been reserved for administrative and literary purposes, while Hebrew continued as the popular spoken language.[35] If so, there is no reason to assume that Aramaisms would intrude into every Hebrew literary text composed in this period.

10. Rare or unusual collocations are of little significance to the diachronic discussion due to insufficient data regarding their distribution. However, rare idioms or unusual usages may be very significant from the synchronic standpoint of stylistics. Formulaic expression may have its roots in oral composition, but it is also a well-known characteristic of many biblical literary compositions.[36] The frequency with which a scribe employs formulas may indicate his dependency upon literary tradition, while a marked preference for rare or unusual collocations may indicate a tendency to deviate from formulaic usage in favor of a personal and innovative style.

The discussion below is arranged according to morphology, syntax, and lexica; and the data in each category is presented as typically late, possibly

---

33. Rezektko 2009, 2013.

34. See, e.g., Hurvitz 1972, 27. However, various scholars argue that Aramaic influence is already apparent in the Iron Age northern dialect ("Israelian" or "Israelite" Hebrew); see, e.g., Hurvitz 2003, 30–31; Knauf 2006, 312–16. Thus Aramaisms are not necessarily a chronological indicator and might instead point to the regional provenance of a text.

35. See, e.g., Barr 1987, 38–41; Qimron 1992, 355, 358–61; Knauf 2006, 311; Polak 2006, 122–25; 2012, 319–20.

36. See, e.g., Polak 1998, 100–103; 2006, 158–59.

late, or rare or unusual usage. "Typically late" are those phenomena that are widely regarded as characteristic of LBH, of extrabiblical texts of the second half of the first millennium, and MH as well. "Possibly late" are phenomena that are considered late by some scholars, or that occur primarily in late compositions. "Rare or unusual usage" are those that occur no more than three times in the entire Bible.

3.1. Morphology

Typically Late Phenomena

Interchange of masculine/feminine third-person plural pronominal endings in both independent pronouns and suffixed forms.[37] Throughout Judg 19–21, masculine endings (ם-) occur wherever the plural of the third-person feminine accusative pronoun is required (19:24; 21:12, 21–23).[38] In 19:12 the feminine third-person plural pronoun occurs where the masculine is required: "We shall not turn aside to a town of aliens [עיר נכרי],[39] who are not Israelites [הנה] אשר לא מבני ישראל]."[40] According to the syntax of the sentence, the pronoun הנה in the relative clause should refer to the object of the main clause (עיר נכרי), except that the feminine plural pronoun is not in agreement either with the *nomen regens* (fem.

---

37. See GKC §135o; Joüon §149b; Qimron 1986 §322.12 n. 79; Polzin 1976, 52–54; Rooker 1990, 78–81.

38. 21:12 "They found 400 virgin *girls* ... from Jabesh-gilead and brought *them* [אותם]"; 21:21–22, "Each of you abduct a woman from the *girls* of Shiloh ... and if *their* fathers [אבותם] or *their* brothers [אחיהם] should come"; 21:23, "They built cities [ערים] and settled in them [בהם]." The use in 19:24 is particularly instructive, since the parallel in Gen 19:8 has classical feminine endings (ן-):

Gen 19:8: הנה־נא לי שתי בנות אשר לא־ידעו איש אוציאה־נא אתהן אליכם ועשו להן כטוב בעיניכם

Judg 19:24: הנה בתי הבתולה ופילגשהו אוציאה־נא אותם וענו אותם ועשו להם הטוב בעיניכם

39. עיר נכרי is most likely a construct with נכרי serving as a collective (see Prov 5:10, בית נכרי; 5:20, חק נכריה; 6:24, לשון נכריה). Alternatively, the MT is corrupt and should read עיר נכריה or עיר נכרים; cf. BHS.

40. The "nunation" of pronominal and verbal endings in later Hebrew appears to be influenced by Aramaic; cf. Segal 1958, §§54, 70; Qimron 1986, §200.142. Exchange of the masculine for the feminine form of the 3rd-person pl. pronoun in LBH is evident in 1 Chr 21:10 (see also 2 Sam 24:12); 2 Chr 18:16 (see also 1 Kgs 22:17); see also Lev 5:22.

sg.) or with the *nomen rectum* (masc. sg.), nor with reading the construct as a metonym representing the residents of the town. Parallel expressions referring to the non-Israelite occupants of the land occur in 2 Sam 21:2 and 1 Kgs 9:20; in both cases the masculine plural pronoun המה is used in complete agreement with their plural referents.

Possibly Late Phenomena

Third-person singular genitive ending הו-. The suffix form is not necessarily late, since it is required with ל"ה verbs.[41] However, in some cases it occurs as a variant of the customary genitive suffix ו-, and this variant use occurs most frequently in postexilic biblical texts.[42] It is also found in Qumran Hebrew, where it frequently replaces the common ו- and יו- in biblical texts.[43] In Judg 19–21 the הו- suffix occurs twice (19:16, מעשהו; 19:24, פילגשהו).[44] It is possible that postexilic scribes made use of the

---

41. The long form is considered to represent the ancient ending הֻ prior to its shortening to ו; see Joüon §§7b, 94b, h.

42. For example, פיהו occurs twenty-one times, almost exclusively in late texts, some of which may be corrupt (1 Kgs 7:31; Jer 34:3; Mal 2:6, 7; Pss 5:10; 10:7; Prov 16:23, 26; 19:24; 20:17; 24:7; Job 3:1; 35:16; 40:23; Cant 1:2; Lam 1:18; 3:29; Qoh 6:7; 10:13 [twice]; 1 Chr 16:12), while the common form פיו occurs approximately seventy times throughout the different compositional layers in the Bible. See also fourteen occurrences of מינהו in P-related texts (Gen 1:12 [twice], 21, 25; 6:20 [twice]; 7:14 [twice]; Lev 11:16, 22 [three times], 29; Deut 14:15) as opposed to מינו (Gen 1:11; Lev 11:15, 22; Deut 14:14); אביהו seven times, mostly in late compositional contexts (Judg 14:10, 19; 16:31; 1 Kgs 5:15; Zech 13:3; 1 Chr 26:10; 2 Chr 3:1) as opposed to more than two hundred occurrences of אביו throughout the Bible; אורהו (Job 25:3) against אורו (Isa 13:10; Ezek 32:7; Job 29:3; 36:30; 37:3, 11); אחיהו (Jer 34:9; Mic 7:2; Job 41:9) as opposed to the commonplace אחיו (more than 250 times in the Hebrew Bible). See also the isolated occurrences of הו- with plural nouns: ידיהו, Hab 3:10; עיניהו, Job 24:23; שסהו, 1 Sam 14:48; רעהו, 1 Sam 30:26; מעלתהו, Ezek 43:17; גבריהו, Nah 2:4.

43. See Qimron 1986 §322.142.

44. 19:24 is the only instance of פילגשהו; cf. nine instances of פילגשו (Gen 22:24; Judg 8:31; 19:2, 9, 10, 25, 27, 29; 1 Chr 7:14). מעשהו occurs nineteen times (Exod 28:8; 39:5; Judg 13:12; 19:16; 1 Sam 25:2; 2 Kgs 16:10; Isa 5:19; 10:12; 19:14; 28:21; 54:16; Pss 33:4; 62:13; 64:10; Prov 16:11; Job 4:17; 37:7; 2 Chr 32:30), but see thirteen times מעשיו (Exod 5:4; Deut 11:3; 1 Sam 19:4; Pss 103:22; 104:31; 106:13; 107:22; 111:6; 145:9, 17; Qoh 3:22; Dan 9:14; Neh 6:14). For מעשיו as an apparent plural, see GKC §91d.

long ending alongside the more common short suffix because they felt it imparted an archaic flavor to their texts.

Increased use of accusative verbal suffixes accompanied by reduced use of independent accusative pronouns.[45] In Judg 19–21 independent accusative pronouns occur eight times: אוֹתָם (19:15, 24 [twice]; 21:10, 12, 22), אוֹתָהּ (19:25), and אוֹתוֹ (20:42). Some of these instances may have been influenced by the use of independent pronouns in parallel intertexts.[46] In three cases the independent pronoun seems to be required by the form of the verb.[47] By contrast, there are eighteen instances of accusative suffixed verbs in Judg 19–20.[48] Interestingly, there are no accusative suffixed verbs in Judg 21.[49] This may stem from the prevalence of direct speech in Judg 21, which might tend to specify objects by means of nouns instead of pronouns.

The findings regarding use of accusative pronouns in Judg 19–21 may be summed up as follows: (1) there is a marked preference for accusative suffixed verbs, which occur in 70 percent of the cases requiring some form of an accusative pronoun; (2) the accusative suffixed verbs are distributed throughout Judg 19–20; (3) in two cases accusative suffixed verbs occur where parallel intertexts employ independent pronouns (Judg 19:22 // Gen 19:5; Judg 20:32 // Josh 8:6). These findings might indicate that the scribes of Judg 19–20 preferred to employ a use typical of LBH and might even indicate that they revised the language of the earlier sources in accordance with the style prevailing in their times.

---

45. See n. 28 above.

46. E.g., Judg 19:24 // Gen 19:8; Judg 19:25 // Gen 19:5; Judg 21:12 // Num 31:54.

47. The independent pronoun occurs twice with participles: 19:15, מֹאֵס; 20:42, מַשְׁחִיתִים; and once in 19:24 with cohortative, אוֹצִיאָה־נָּא. According to Joüon §66a, accusative suffixes do not occur with plural participles and are even rare with singular participles; see also Qimron 1986, §400.08; cf. GKC §§61h, 116f. Although the cohortative may receive an accusative suffix (see Joüon §§45a, 61f), in all the cases of verb + נָא accusative suffixes occur only with imperatives or *yiqṭol* forms.

48. 19:3, לְהָשִׁיבוֹ (*qere*: לְהָשִׁיבָה), וַתְּבִיאֵהוּ, וַיִּרְאוּהוּ; 19:21, וַיְבִיאֵהוּ; 19:22, וְנֵדָעֶנּוּ (cf. the independent pronoun in Gen 19:5); 19:25, וַיִּשְׁלְחוּהָ; 19:28, וַיִּקָּחֶהָ; 19:29, וַיְשַׁלְּחֶהָ (cf. the parallel use in 1 Sam 11:7), וַיְנִתְּחֶהָ; 20:6, וָאֲנַתְּחֶהָ, וָאֹחֲזֶה; 20:28, וָאֶתְּנֶנּוּ בְיָדֶךָ (the independent acc. pronoun is infrequent in the idiom; see Josh 24:8, 11; 1 Sam 17:47; 2 Kgs 3:10, 13); 20:32, וּנְתַקְנֻהוּ (cf. the independent pronoun in Josh 8:6); 20:38, יַעֲלֻהוּ; 20:45, הִדְרִיכֻהוּ, הִרְדִּיפֻהוּ; 20:43, הִדְבִּיקֻתְהוּ; 20:42, לְהַעֲלוֹתָם.

49. A possible exception is 21:22, which may preserve a double reading: חֲנוּנוּ/ חַנּוּ אוֹתָם.

3.2. Syntax

Typically Late Phenomena

Predicative use of infinitive.[50] The infinitive להפקד occurs in predicative use in 21:3: למה ה' אלהי ישראל היתה זאת בישראל להפקד היום מישראל שבט אחד.[51] Elsewhere only finite verbs and participles continue queries formulated with למה (זה).[52] Thus we might expect of SBH a phrase such as למה (זה) יהוה אלהי ישראל נפקד היום מישראל שבט אחד[53] or יהוה אלהי ישראל היה הדבר הזה ונפקד היום מישראל שבט אחד.[54] Since predicative use of infinitives occurs mostly in postexilic texts, the use of the infinitive here might indicate the hand of a late scribe.

Possibly Late Phenomena

Pleonastic use of the pronouns המה/הם. The masculine third-person plural pronoun occurs three times in Judg 19–21 in the shortened form הם (19:11; 20:32, 34), and once in the long form המה (19:22).[55] Since the inflected verb forms in Semitic languages indicate gender and number, the use of nominative pronouns is frequently unnecessary, although sometimes they add emphasis.[56] Even so, some books make more frequent use of nominative pronouns than others, raising the question whether increased use is a stylistic preference or a diachronic characteristic.[57] This may be illus-

---

50. See Qimron 1986, §400.02, Eskhult 1990, 107.

51. For similar use of an infinitive with the phrase היתה זאת, see Lev 16:34; and with the phrase הדבר הזה/כ see Gen 18:25; 34:14; 1 Sam 17:27; Jer 26:1; 27:1; 36:1. However, finite verbs are also found with the phrase היתה זאת (1 Kgs 11:11; 2 Chr 1:11), as well as comparable phrases such as היה/עשה הדבר הזה (Exod 1:18; Deut 22:20).

52. For finite verbs, see, e.g., Gen 18:13; Exod 2:20; Num 11:20; Judg 13:18; 1 Sam 20:8; Jer 20:18. For participles, see Num 14:41; Josh 7:10; 1 Sam 26:18; 2 Sam 12:23; 18:22; 1 Kgs 14:6.

53. See, e.g., Exod 2:20; 32:11; Num 14:41; 1 Sam 4:3; 26:18; 2 Sam 3:24.

54. See Deut 22:20; 1 Kgs 1:27.

55. Excluding the demonstrative use of ההם (19:1; 20:27–28; 21:25), see GKC §§34 g, 136 a, b.

56. See Joüon §146 a–c.

57. Note the marked contrast in the frequency of the pronoun המה/הם in selected books compared to Judg 19–21 (total masc. 3rd-person pl. pronouns/total verses/ frequency relative to number of verses): Genesis: 21 pronouns/1,534 verses/1:73;

trated by the uneven distribution of nominative הם/המה within the book of Judges: six times in Judg 17–18; four times in Judg 19–21; three times in Judg 8; four times more elsewhere in the book.⁵⁸

The use of the nominative pronouns in Judg 19–21 is particularly significant in passages that have intertextual parallels elsewhere:

Judg 19:22: הַמָּה מְסִבִּים אֶת־לְבָם וְהִנֵּה אַנְשֵׁי הָעִיר אַנְשֵׁי בְנֵי־בְלִיַּעַל נָסַבּוּ אֶת־הַבַּיִת
Gen 19:4: טֶרֶם יִשְׁכָּבוּ וְאַנְשֵׁי הָעִיר אַנְשֵׁי סְדֹם נָסַבּוּ עַל־הַבַּיִת

Judg 20:32: וַיֹּאמְרוּ בְּנֵי בִנְיָמִן נִגָּפִים הֵם לְפָנֵינוּ כְּבָרִאשֹׁנָה
Josh 8:6: כִּי יֹאמְרוּ נָסִים לְפָנֵינוּ כַּאֲשֶׁר בָּרִאשֹׁנָה

In both cases, the text in Judg 19–20 supplies a pronoun that does not appear in the intertexts. The use of the pronoun here is not dictated by the participles (מְסִבִּים, נִגָּפִים), since a participle occurs in the Josh 8:6 intertext without a pronoun. Moreover, the lack of nominative pronouns in the two intertexts accords with the use in their contexts: the third-person masculine plural pronoun is totally lacking in Gen 19, and it occurs but once in Josh 7–8 (7:3). The increased use of nominative personal pronouns may indicate a tendency to overexplicate the subject. Thus a parallel text may employ pronouns lacking in its counterpart in order to more fully define the subject, and this may be evidence of literary reworking of prior material.⁵⁹

Agreement of number with collective nouns. In Classical Hebrew, collective subjects appear with both singular and plural verbs, while in LBH and the Dead Sea Scrolls (DSS) collectives are overwhelmingly construed

---

Isaiah: 20 pronouns/1,291 verses/1:64; Deuteronomy: 15 pronouns/955 verses/1:63; Exodus: 20 pronouns/1,209 verses/1:60; Joshua: 12 pronouns/656 verses/1:54; Samuel: 29 pronouns/506 verses/1:52; Leviticus: 19 pronouns/859 verses /1:45; Numbers: 30 pronouns/1,299 verses/1:43; Chronicles: 41 pronouns/1,765 verses/1:43 (32 occur in Chronicles' *Sondergut*); Judges: 17 pronouns/618 verses/1:36; Kings: 58 pronouns/1,534 verses/1:20; Jeremiah: 68 pronouns/1,364 verses/1:20; Ezekiel: 63 pronouns/1,273 verses/1:20; cf. Judg 19–21: 4 pronouns/103 verses/1:26.

58. המה—Judg 10:14; 18:3 (twice), 7, 22, 26, 27; 19:22; הם—Judg 1:22; 2:22; 6:5; 8:5; 19, 24; 19:11; 20:32, 34. It is notable that only Judg 19–21 makes use of both shortened and long forms of the pronoun.

59. See the use by Chronicles of the masc. 3rd-person pl. pronoun when it is lacking in the synoptic material in Samuel–Kings (1 Chr 19:15 // 2 Sam 10:14; 2 Chr 9:11 // 1 Kgs 10:12).

as plurals, with the exception of feminine collectives such as עדה, which, according to Elisha Qimron, generally occur with singular verbs in the DSS and MH.[60] However, in BH the term עדה usually occurs with a plural verb (85 percent of the occurrences).[61] Accordingly, the use in Judg 20:1, ותקהל העדה instead of the more usual plural verb ויקהלו העדה (cf. Josh 18:1; 22:12), is more characteristic of DSS Hebrew than it is of either SBH or LBH.

Increased use of nominal forms of verbs. MH is marked both by widespread use of participles in place of inflected verbs employed by SBH[62] and by increased use of infinitives, particularly inflected infinitives with the prefix -ל.[63] The beginnings of this tendency are already apparent in LBH.[64] Arian Verheij found significant differences between Samuel–Kings and Chronicles in their use of nominal verb forms (in percent of total nominal and finite verbs together):[65]

Participles	Samuel–Kings 9.55%	Chronicles 13.6%
Infinitives	Samuel–Kings 9.6%	Chronicles 13.8%
Total nominal verbs	Samuel–Kings 19.2%	Chronicles 27.4%

The figures for finite versus nominal verb forms in Judg 19–21[66] lie between

---

60. See Qimron 1986, §400.18.

61. עדה + plural verb: Exod 12:47; 16:1, 2; 17:1; 35:20; Lev 4:13; 9:5; 24:14, 16; Num 10:3; 14:2, 10, 36; 15:24, 36; 16:3; 17:6; 20:29; 27:20; 35:24, 25 (twice); Josh 9:18; 18:1; 22:12, 16; Judg 21:10, 13. עדה + singular verb: Lev 8:4; Num 14:1; 20:11; 27:17; Judg 20:1; see Young 2001.

62. See Segal 1958, 54; Bendavid 1967, 87–88.

63. See Segal 1958, 165–67; Joüon §124l (1).

64. See, e.g., Qimron 1986, 70–74; Eskhult 1990, 113; Verheij 1990, 57 n. 1.

65. See Verheij 1990, 55–83; see also Polak 1997, 157, who conducted an independent study of 1 Sam 16–30; 2 Sam 7, 11–15, 17–19, with the following totals for nominal verbs: History of David's Rise + Succession Narrative 17.95 percent; Chronicles 30.61 percent. The deviation between Verheij's and Polak's figures may result from difference of opinion regarding which lexemes should be regarded nominal verbs and which should be treated as substantives; see Verheij 1990, 55, 60.

66. The breakdown of nominal verb forms in Judg 19–21 is as follows: Participles: גר, 19:1, 16; מאסף, 19:15, 18; ארח, 19:17; הלך, עברים, 19:18; מיטיבים, מתדפקים, 19:22; נפלת, 19:27; ענה, 19:28; ראה, 19:30; שלף, 20:2, 15, 17, 35, 46; הנרצחה, 20:4; ארבים, 20:28; עמד, 20:25; שלפי, 20:16; קלע, 20:15; ישבי, 20:10; (לבואם MT:) לבאים, 20:29; עלה, 20:31; נגפים, 20:32; מגיח, ארב, 20:33; נגעת, 20:34; הארב, 20:36–8 (four times); משחיתם, 20:42; נפלים, 20:46; הנמצא/ות, 20:48; לנותרים, 21:7, 16; יושבי,

those found by Verheij and those found by Frank Polak for Samuel–Kings and Chronicles:⁶⁷

	Judg 19	Judg 20	Judg 21	Judg 19–21 Total verbs: 423
Finite:	121 (79%)	128 (73.56%)	74 (77%)	323 (76.35%)
Participles:	13 (8.49%)	28 (16%)	11 (11.45%)	52 (12.29%)
Infinitives:	19 (12.41%)	18 (10.34%)	11 (11.45%)	48 (11.32%)
Total Nominatives:	20.9%	26.43%	22.9%	23.64%

Moreover, comparing these findings to the frequencies of nominal verbs in different texts⁶⁸ shows that the frequency of nominal forms in Judg 19–21 approaches that of postexilic texts:

	Josh 7–8	Gen 19	Num 31	Jonah 1
Finite:	209 (86.72%)	134 (85.89%)	75 (80.64%)	54 (80.59%)
Participles:	14 (5.8%)	5 (3.20%)	12 (12.9%)	4 (5.9%)
Infinitives:	18 (7.46%)	17 (10.89%)	6 (6.4%)	9 (13.4%)
Total Nominatives:	13.27%	14.10%	19.35%	19.40%

21:9–10, 12 (three times); ידעת, 21:11; נחם, 21:15; נתן, 21:18; המחללות, 21:23. Passive participles: חבושים, 19:10; בחור, 20:15, 16, 34; ארור, 21:18. Infinitives: לדבר, להשיבה, לקראתו, 19:3; ללכת, 19:5, 7, 8, 9, 27; לערב, 19:9; ללון, 19:10, 15 (twice); 20:4; לבוא, 19:15; לשמוע, 19:25; 20:13; לפנות, 19:26; להרג, 20:5; לאמר, 20:8, 12, 23, 28; 21:1, 5, 10, 18, 20; לקחת, לעשות, 20:10; לצאת, 20:14, 28; לערך, 20:22; לגשת, 20:23; לקראת, 20:25, 31; להכות, 20:31, 39; להעלותם, 20:38; לעלות, 20:40; להפקד, 21:3; לתת, 21:18; לחול, 21:21; לריב (MT: לרוב), 21:22. Infinitives absolute: נטות, 19:8; חנות, 19:9; עלות, 19:25; 30; נגוף, 20:39; מות, 21:5; תת, 21:7.

67. Polak (1997, 157) found 332 finite verbs (79.05%) and 88 nominal verbs (20.10%) in Judg 19–21. The deviation of 3% between his findings and mine is apparently due to my adopting Verheij's approach (n. 65) regarding disputed nominal verbs.

68. For comparison, I chose six narrative texts, two "classical" or preexilic texts: Gen 19 (J) and Josh 7–8 (DtrH), and four postexilic texts representing different degrees of LBH: Num 31 (P), Josh 22, Jonah 1, and Neh 2. For the relative dating of Num 31, see Budd 1984, 327; Levine 2000, 463–74. On the P composition layer in Josh 22, see, e.g., Kloppenborg 1981, 355–62; Goldstein 2002. For LBH in Jonah, see, e.g., Wolff 1986, 76–8; Young et al. 2008b, 43–45.

	Neh 2	Judg 19–21	Josh 22
Finite:	72 (79.12%)	323 (76.35%)	59 (71%)
Participles:	4 (4.4%)	52 (12.29%)	2 (2.5%)
Infinitives:	15 (16.5%)	48 (11.32%)	22 (26.5%)
Total Nominatives:	21.0%	23.64%	28.91%

The increased use of nominal verb forms appears to stem from ongoing changes in formal literary style, which included increased ratios of nouns to verbs.[69] This development may be responsible for the use of participles in place of an abstract noun or a relative clause, as in the following examples.

1. הנמצא(ות) (20:48), לנותרים (21:7, 16)—these stative participles function as abstract nouns and replace circumlocutory relative clauses, such as אשר נותרו[70] ל(הם) or כל אשר הנמצא(ות) or a comparable noun phrase.[71] This use of stative participles seems to be particularly characteristic of late biblical texts.[72]

2. יֹשְׁבֵי + place name or toponym (TN) (20:15; 21:9, 10, 12)—Biblical Hebrew usually indicates the inhabitants of a place by means of a construct with either the substantive אַנְשֵׁי (fifty-four times)[73] or the participle יֹשְׁבֵי (eighty-four times) as *nomen rectum*. A marked preference

---

69. See Polak 1997, 34–38, 41–51, 156–57; 2002.

70. See אשר נמצא(ו), Exod 35:23–24; 2 Sam 17:12; 2 Kgs 20:13 (// Isa 39:2); 25:19 (// Jer 52:25); Jer 41:3; 1 Chr 4:41; 2 Chr 34:21; אשר נותר(ו), 2 Sam 9:1; 1 Kgs 9:21 (// 2 Chr 8:8); cf. אשר נשאר(ו), 1 Kgs 22:47; 2 Kgs 7:13; Jer 38:22; Neh 1:2–3.

71. Cf. ליתר הפלטה, Exod 10:5; יתר העם, Judg 7:6; 1 Sam 13:2; 2 Sam 10:10; 12:28; 1 Kgs 12:23; 2 Kgs 25:11; Jer 39:9; 52:15; Zech 14:2; Neh 4:8, 13; 1 Chr 19:11.

72. For nominal use of נמצא, see 1 Sam 21:4; Isa 13:15; 22:3; Dan 12:1; 1 Chr 29:8; 2 Chr 29:29; 34:32–33; 35:7. 1 Sam 21:4–7 may stem from a Priestly redactor; for the late origin of Isa 13, see, e.g., Blenkinsopp 2000, 277. Of the fifty-three times נותר is used as a nominative, thirty-eight occur in Priestly literature and contexts: Exod 12:10; 28:10; 29:34; Lev 2:3, 10; 6:9; 7:16–17; 8:32; 10:12 (twice), 16; 14:18, 29; 19:6; 27:18; Josh 17:2, 6; 21:5, 20, 26, 34, 40; 1 Kgs 15:18; Jer 27:18, 19, 21; Ezek 34:18; 39:14; 48:15, 18, 21; Zech 14:16; 1 Chr 6:46, 55, 62; 24:20; 2 Chr 31:10. It also occurs in editorial links and expansions, e.g., Judg 8:10 (see Moore 1895, 221), 1 Sam 30:9 (see McCarter 1980, 431), and in the northern prophets story cycle in 1 Kgs 20:30 (twice); 2 Kgs 4:7 (for the late addition of this material, see S. McKenzie 1991, 81–100).

73. The construct with אנשי also occurs twice in Judg 19–21 (19:16, 22) but with a general term as the *nomen regens* (המקום, העיר) instead of a TN. However, 19:22 may have been influenced by the intertextual parallel in Gen 19:4.

for the construct with the participle יֹשְׁבֵי is found in six groups of texts: Josh 13–19; Judg 1, 19–21; Jeremiah; Ezekiel; Chronicles; all of which are either postexilic compositions or have undergone post-Deuteronomistic redaction. Joshua 13–19, Judg 1, 19–21, and Ezekiel use only the participle construct,[74] while in Chronicles it occurs with a frequency of 95.45 percent.[75] The greatest number of entries occurs in Jeremiah, and still the frequency of the participle constructs is greater than 85 percent.[76] In five groups of texts the participle construct occurs with a frequency of *less* than 55 percent: Josh 6–11; Judg 3–12; Samuel; Kings; Ezra-Nehemiah.[77] The likelihood that differences in preference reflect a diachronic change is most apparent when comparing the findings for Samuel–Kings and Chronicles:

	אַנְשֵׁי : יֹשְׁבֵי
Samuel–Kings	4 : 16
Chronicles	26 : 3

---

74. Josh 15:15, 63; 17:7, 11; Judg 1:11, 19, 27, 30–31, 33; 20:15; 21:9–10, 12; Ezek 11:15; 12:19; 15:6; 27:8; 29:6.

75. יֹשְׁבֵי, 1 Chr 2:55; 4:23; 8:6, 13; 11:5; 2 Chr 20:15, 18, 20, 23; 21:11, 13; 22:1; 31:4; 32:22, 26, 33; 33:9; 34:9, 30, 32; 35:18; cf. אַנְשֵׁי, 1 Chr 7:21.

76. יֹשְׁבֵי, Jer 4:4; 8:1; 11:2, 9, 12; 13:13; 17:20, 25; 18:11; 19:3; 25:2; 32:32; 35:13, 17; 36:31; 42:18; 48:28; 49:8, 20, 30; 50:34–35; 51:12, 24, 35; cf. אַנְשֵׁי, Jer 11:21, 23; 48:31, 36.

77. In Josh 6–11 the participle יֹשְׁבֵי occurs with 54.54 percent frequency, all of which are in redactional sections: Josh 8:24, 26; 9:3; 10:1; 11:19; while the substantive אַנְשֵׁי occurs in the body of the narratives: Josh 7:4–5; 8:20–21, 25; 10:6. In the remaining books the frequencies drop drastically. In Kings the participle occurs with 25 percent frequency: יֹשְׁבֵי, 2 Kgs 23:2; cf. אַנְשֵׁי, 1 Kgs 1:9; 2 Kgs 17:30 (three times); in Samuel the participle occurs with 21.42 percent frequency: יֹשְׁבֵי, 1 Sam 6:21; 23:5; 31:11; see also אַנְשֵׁי, 1 Sam 5:7; 6:15, 19–20; 7:1; 11:1, 5, 9–10; 2 Sam 2:4–5; in the so-called *Retterbuch* the participle occurs with 14.28 percent frequency: יֹשְׁבֵי, Judg 10:18; 11:8; cf. אַנְשֵׁי, Judg 8:5, 8 (twice), 9, 14–16; 9:49, 57; 12:4 (twice), 5. In the returnees list in Ezra-Nehemiah, the substantive construct occurs 8 times, while the participle construct is wholly lacking; see Ezra 2:22–23, 27–28 // Neh 7:26–33. However, this may be due to the literary framework of the list, which supposedly enumerates *returnees* according to their place of origin before the exile; thus they could hardly be considered "the inhabitants [יֹשְׁבֵי] of" a certain place. Otherwise in Ezra-Nehemiah the participle appears with 60 percent frequency: יֹשְׁבֵי, Ezra 4:6; Neh 3:13; 7:3; see also אַנְשֵׁי, Neh 3:2, 7.

This tendency may also be reflected in the distribution of the alternate constructs: ישבי/אנשי יבש (גלעד).[78] In this case there are marked, opposing preferences in Samuel and Judg 21:

	ישבי יבש : אשני יבש
Samuel	6 : 1
Judg 21	0 : 3

3. איש בחור, שלף חרב, קלע באבן (20:2, 15–17, 25, 34–35, 46)—the use of participles to categorize types of warriors is typical of late biblical texts,[79] while Deuteronomistic and earlier texts prefer general terms, such as איש/אנשי/בן/בני חיל; איש/אנשי מלחמה.[80]

Rare or Unusual Syntax

אשר x שם (Judg 19:26, אשר־אדוניה שם). The formula אשר x שם occurs elsewhere only in the collocation אשר אתה/אתם שם (Gen 13:14; Exod 12:13; 1 Sam 19:3); the common syntax of the formula is: אשר שם x.[81]

Use of the relative pronoun אשר *as an indefinite subject or object* (20:42, לאשר לא עלה; 21:5, ואשר מהערים).[82] The relative pronoun functions as

---

78. ישבי יבש גלעד, Judg 21:9–10, 12; 1 Sam 31:11; אנשי יבש (גלעד), 1 Sam 11:1, 5, 9–10; 2 Sam 2:4–5.

79. איש בחור appears elsewhere only in 1 Sam 24:3; 2 Chr 13:3 (twice), 17. שלף חרב appears elsewhere only in Judg 8:10; 2 Sam 24:9 (// 1 Chr 21:5); 2 Kgs 3:26. For the late dating of these passages, see Moore 1895, 221; Levine 1994; Edenburg forthcoming a; S. McKenzie 1991, 95–98. קלע באבן is a unique construction, but see 1 Chr 12:2, מימינים ומשמאלים באבנים. Other similar constructions of participle + weapon type occur mostly in late literature, particularly Chronicles: נקשי קשת (1 Chr 12:2; 2 Chr 17:17); תפשי מלחמה/מגן/חרבות (Num 31:27; Jer 46:9; Ezek 38:4); ערכי/נשא צנה ורמח (1 Chr 12:9, 25; 2 Chr 14:7). Also common in Chronicles and Priestly literature are constructions of a participle with צבא/מלחמה/חיל, e.g., יצאי צבא (1 Chr 5:18; 7:11; 12:34, 37; 2 Chr 26:11); ערכי מלחמה (1 Chr 12:34, 36); חלוצי צבא (Num 31:5; 32:27; Josh 4:13; 1 Chr 12:24–25; 2 Chr 17:18); פקודי חיל (Num 31:14; 2 Kgs 11:15; 2 Chr 23:14).

80. See, e.g., Deut 2:14; 3:18; Josh 10:24; Judg 3:29; 18:2; 1 Sam 18:5; 31:12; 2 Sam 11:16; 1 Kgs 9:22; 2 Kgs 24:16.

81. For x אשר שם, see Gen 2:11; Exod 9:26; 20:21; 1 Sam 3:3; 9:10; 10:5; 1 Kgs 8:21; Ezek 8:3; Ps 104:17. Cf. also אשר שם x, which occurs only as an object clause: Num 21:32; 2 Kgs 23:16, 20.

82. This use is rare; see *IBHS* §19.3c n. 13.

an indefinite subject or object when an antecedent is lacking.[83] In Judg 21:5 it is clear that לאשר לא עלה is equivalent to מי אשר לא־עלה, which occurs at the beginning of the verse. It is possible that the laxity in style was caused by the repetition.

Increased use of apposition. Apposition occurs twenty-one times in the seventy-eight verses of Judg 19–20, and most of the sixteen different phrases represent unique constructions.[84] Such a high incidence is unusual in classical biblical narrative.[85]

Syntax as a Stylistic Characteristic

The ratio between the number of verbs to nouns in a text can characterize a style as "simple" (i.e., akin to spoken language) or "complex" literary language. According to Polak,[86] spoken language is marked by a relatively high frequency of verbs in relation to nouns,[87] while in literary language

---

83. See, e.g., instances with the preposition ־ל: Gen 27:8; Exod 16:16; Lev 27:24; Num 5:7; Josh 17:16; 1 Sam 30:27–31; Isa 2:8; Jer 27:5; 50:20; Amos 6:10.

84. בית לחם יהודה (19:1, 27); (ה)אשה פילגש(ו) (19:1, 20:4); (ה)איש (ה)לוי (19:1–2, 18; see also 17:7–9; 1 Sam 17:12; Ruth 1:1–2); ימים ארבעה חדשים (Judg 19:2, double apposition; cf. the similar expression in 1 Sam 27:7 without apposition); חמורים חבושים (Judg 19:10, apposition of subst. and pass. ptc.; see also 2 Sam 16:1); האיש הזקן (19:17); האיש הארח (19:17); see also 1 Sam 28:14); עיר נכרי (Judg 19:12); האיש בעל הבית אנשי העיר אנשי בליעל (Judg 19:22, two constructs in apposition); הזקן (19:22, double apposition; see also v. 23); בתי הבתולה (19:24); פנות כל העם כל (20:2, two constructs in apposition); שבטי ישראל איש רגלי שלף חרב (20:2; cf. v. 15, apposition of subst. and noun clause; see also איש שלף חרב, Judg 8:10; 2 Kgs 3:26; 1 Chr 21:5; איש חיל שלף חרב, 2 Sam 24:9); האשה הנרצחה (Judg 20:4, apposition of subst. and ptc.); שדה נחלת ישראל (20:6, apposition of subst. and construct); האנשים בני בליעל (20:13; cf. Deut 13:14; 1 Kgs 21:10, 13); איש בחור אטר יד ימינו (Judg 20:16; see also 3:15).

85. See the incidence of apposition in the following narrative units: 1 Sam 11:1–13 (none); Gen 19:1–38 (v. 4, אנשי העיר אנשי סדום; v. 14, חתנו לקחי בנתיו); Josh 7–8 (fifty-five verses total; 7:7, איש גבורי החיל; 8:3, ה' אלהי ישראל; 7:13, 20, ה' אלהים; 8:11, כל העם המלחמה; 8:24, בשדה במדבר; 8:28, תל עולם שממה); Judg 3:12–30 (vv. 12, 14–15, 17, עגליון מלך מואב; v. 18, העם נשאי המנחה); 2 Sam 13:1–22 (vv. 2, 4, 6–8, 10, 20, 22, PN + אחי/אחות; v. 17, נערו משרתו). Of all the texts I examined, 1 Chr 12:1–41 was most similar to Judg 19–21 in frequency and complexity of apposition (see 1 Chr 12:1–2, 9, 25–26, 29–31, 33–34, 39, 41).

86. Polak 2002, 2003, 2012.

87. This can even be illustrated in a literary context. For example, in Judg 19–21

the relative number of nouns increases and reaches a peak in "complex" literary style.

In Judg 19–21 the frequency of nouns varies in the different chapters: 60 percent in chapter 19, 73 percent in chapter 20, and 66 percent in chapter 21.[88] This variation may be due to the relation between the amounts of direct speech to narrative in each chapter; for example, 60 percent of chapter 21 is direct speech, compared to only 25 percent of chapter 20.[89] It is also possible that the variable frequency of nouns is influenced by narrative genre, use of traditional formulas, and literary dependency. For example, many have commented upon the literary similarities between Judg 19 and sections of Gen 19 and 2 Sam 13,[90] and all three texts show similar noun frequencies.[91] The noun frequencies for all of Judg 19–21 average at 68 percent, which places this text in the range of the frequencies found in 2 Sam 24; 2 Kgs 17:7–23; and 2 Chr 20:1–30.[92]

3.3. Lexica

Typically Late Lexica

"Priestly" Vocabulary

From the time of Wellhausen, the postexilic date of the Priestly strand in the Pentateuch and the Former Prophets has been a matter of general consensus.[93] Kaufmann's position, that P is preexilic and predates D, is advocated by a minority, while the majority still adheres to the postex-

---

nouns occur with 50–61 percent frequency in relation to verbs in direct speech, while in narrative the noun frequencies rise to 65–70 percent; see Edenburg 2003, 164.

88. See Stadler-Sutskover 2002, 302.

89. Of the twenty-five verses in Judg 21, fifteen represent direct speech: vv. 1b, 3, 5, 6b–8a, 10b–11, 16–22; while only twelve of the fort-eight verses in Judg 20 are direct speech: vv. 4, 5b–7, 8b–10, 12b–13, 18, 23, 28, 32.

90. See, e.g., Burney 1970, 444; Lasine 1984, 37–41, on the parallels to Gen 19; and Keefe 1993 on 2 Sam 13. For detailed evaluation of the parallels, see below, ch. 4.

91. Judg 19: 59.94 percent nouns; 2 Sam 13: 58.00 percent nouns; Gen 19: 60.89 percent nouns.

92. 2 Sam 24: 68.28 percent nouns; 2 Kgs 17:7–23: 68.75 percent nouns; and 2 Chr 20:1–30: 68.87 percent nouns. For more comparative figures, see Edenburg 2003, 163.

93. See, e.g., S. Driver 1972, 135–59; Whybray 1987, 26–28.

ilic date.⁹⁴ The majority position is based on the fact that the cultic ritual detailed in the Priestly literature is not reflected in undisputed preexilic biblical sources but does play a central role in postexilic literature, such as Ezek 40–48, Ezra-Nehemiah, and Chronicles.⁹⁵ In addition, Baruch Levine has demonstrated that some of the usages in the language of the Priestly strand in the Pentateuch are paralleled only in postexilic literature or in Imperial Aramaic.⁹⁶

עדה (Judg 20:1; 21:10, 13, 16)—In the Pentateuch, the term עדה occurs only in the Priestly strand, where it is frequent (over a hundred occurrences). In the Former Prophets, it occurs more than twenty times, mostly in the Priestly redactional strand of Joshua.⁹⁷ Some have argued that the term itself is of premonarchic origin and is related to the Canaanite *m'd*, mentioned in the Report of Wenamun and in Ugaritic texts.⁹⁸ Therefore, they held that the עדה was a premonarchic popular assembly, which functioned as a "primitive democracy."⁹⁹ However, the validity of this assertion is doubtful, since it ignores the fundamental differences between the biblical עדה and the Canaanite *m'd*.¹⁰⁰ That the עדה disappears from biblical

---

94. See Kaufmann 1960, 175–200; Hurvitz 1974; Milgrom 1976; Haran 1981; Zevit 1982. For a postexilic date, see, e.g., Crüsemann 1996, 282–301; Blenkinsopp 1996; Nihan, 2007, 1–68; Schmid 2010, 237–48; Carr 2011, 292–303; Gertz 2012, 293–303.

95. See, e.g., Whybray 1987, 230–32.

96. See, e.g., Levine 1993, 101–8.

97. See Josh 9:15, 18–19, 21, 27; 18:1; 20:6, 9; 22:12, 16–18, 20, 30; 24:27. Apart from Josh and Judg 19–21, the term occurs only twice in the Former Prophets: 1 Kgs 8:5; 12:20. All these passages are generally ascribed to Priestly redaction; see, e.g., S. Driver 1972, 133; Gray 1976, 205–10; Römer and Brettler 2000, 414.

98. See J. Wilson 1945 on Wenamun 2:70–71; and *KTU* 1.2 I 14 for the pleonasm *pḥr m'd*.

99. See Gordis 1950; Hurvitz 1971; Milgrom 1979. This view of the עדה was influenced by Jacobsen's study of the Mesopotamian *puḥrum*, which he viewed as an institution of "primitive democracy" (1970; originally published in 1943).The occurrence of the phrase *pḥr m'd*, indicating the divine assembly in Ugaritic texts, opened the way for ascribing the characteristics of the Mesopotamian *puḥrum* to the Canaanite *m'd* and to the biblical עדה; see Gordis 1950; Cross 1953, 274 n. 1.

100. The main differences: (1) the *m'd* appears as an urban institution in report of Wenamun and the Ugaritic texts, while the biblical עדה figures most in narratives dealing with the presettlement desert wanderings; (2) the Canaanite *m'd* was a representative body composed of the city's notables, while the biblical עדה was a comprehensive body of all adult males; (3) the Canaanite *m'd* existed alongside monarchy,

narrative after 1 Kgs 12 does not mean that this was a historical, premonarchic institution that died with the establishment of the monarchy. In fact, the term occurs several times in the Persian period Elephantine texts and is very frequent in nonbiblical texts at Qumran.[101] Hence the biblical use of the term עדה reflects an ideal view of prestate society and a retrojection of postexilic circumstances into a distant past.

זקני העדה (Judg 21:16)—this construction appears only once more, in Lev 4:15, where it may be an interpolation.[102] The usual expression used to indicate the elders as representatives of the entire people is זקני ישראל, but this construction is infrequent in P, which generally uses the term (נשיא(ים.[103] However, postexilic writers, who were familiar with Priestly vocabulary, also used the term זקני(ם) to indicate the representative body.[104] Thus it is possible that the unusual construction זקני העדה was coined in this period by a scribe influenced by the Priestly writings.[105]

קהל (Judg 20:1, 2; 21:5, 8)—both the noun and the verb occur mostly in texts of Priestly or postexilic origin.[106] In Judg 20–21 the noun is syn-

---

while, excepting 1 Kgs 8:5 and 12:20, the biblical עדה is not mentioned in conjunction with the monarchy.

101. See, e.g., *TAD* B2 6:22, 26; B3 3:7; 8:21; and more than two hundred times in Qumran texts that include the Damascus Document, the Community Rule, Pesher Habakkuk, and more.

102. See Noth 1965, 41; Elliger 1966, 54.

103. זקני ישראל: Exod 3:16, 18; 12:21; 17:5–6; 18:12; 24:9; Lev 9:1 (P); Num 11:16, 30; 16:25; Deut 27:1; 31:9; Josh 7:6; 8:10; 24:1; 1 Sam 4:3; 8:4; 2 Sam 3:17; 5:3; 17:4, 15; 1 Kgs 8:1, 3; Ezek 14:1; 20:1, 3; 1 Chr 15:25. For נשיא(ים) in P, see Lev 4:22, more than fifity times in Num (e.g., 2:3, 5; 3:32; 7:11, 18, 84; 17:21; 27:2; 34:18), and see particularly the constructions נשיאי העדה: Exod 16:22; Num 4:34; 31:13; 32:2; Josh 9:15, 18; 22:30; נשיאי ישראל: Num 1:44; 4:46; 7:2, 84; Ezek 19:1; 21:17, 30; 22:6; 45:9.

104. See, e.g., Ezek 8:1, 11–12; 20:1; Ezra 10:8, 14; 1 Chr 21:16.

105. Young et al. (2008a, 113) view this type of neologism as characteristic of LBH, in which "old" and "new" terms are combined or interchanged.

106. There are approximately 120 instances of the noun in the Bible, of which eighteen occur in P, fifteen in Ezekiel, and forty-four in Ezra-Nehemiah and Chronicles. In comparison, the term occurs in Deuteronomy nine times, mostly in the late redactional layers (Deut 5:22; 9:10; 10:4; 18:16; 23:2–9; 31:30). In Judges there are no instances outside chs. 20–21, and in Joshua–Samuel it occurs only in two post-Dtr sections: Josh 8:35 (see Anbar 1985) and 1 Sam 17:47 (see Tov 1986; McCarter 1980, 306). In Kings it appears six times, in Deuteronomistic contexts that have been reworked by a Priestly editor (1 Kgs 8:14 [twice], 22, 55, 65; 12:3). The partiality of late writers toward the term can be demonstrated by comparing the frequencies in Samuel–Kings (seven times) with those in Chronicles (thirty-two times). The verb

onymous with עדה, and the verb is used to indicate the congregation of the עדה, usages that are typical of the Priestly writings.¹⁰⁷

זמה (Judg 20:6)—here, and in Priestly writings, the term indicates a severe sexual offense. In this sense, it is most frequent in Ezekiel (thirteen times),¹⁰⁸ while in the Pentateuch it occurs solely in Leviticus.¹⁰⁹

זכר, "male" (Judg 21:11–12)—nearly all the occurrences of the term are in the Priestly strata or in postexilic literature.¹¹⁰ Moreover, the construct that appears here, משכב זכר, recurs only in Num 31:17, 18, 35 (P).

Verbs and Verbal Expressions

דבק אחר (Judg 20:45)—an infrequent expression, comparable to the more frequent רדף אחר.¹¹¹ In 1 Chr 10:2 דבק אחר replaces דבק אֶת,¹¹² which occurs in the parallel text in 1 Sam 31:2. Thus the expression with אחר might be a late idiom.

(*niphal* and *hiphil*) occurs approximately forty times: in Exodus–Numbers, solely in P (thirteen times); in Deuteronomy, solely in the Dtr framework (4:10; 31:12, 28); in the Priestly layer of Josh (18:1; 22:12); once in Samuel (2 Sam 20:14); three times alongside the nouns עדה and קהל in Kings (1 Kgs 8:1, 2; 12:21); and another twelve times in the postexilic books: Esther and Chronicles. Against the four instances of the verb in Samuel–Kings, see seven instances in Chronicles.

107. For the synonymous use of the nouns, see Exod 12:6; Lev 4:13; Num 14:5; 16:3. For the verb with עדה as subject or object, see, e.g., Exod 35:1; Lev 8:3–4; Num 1:18; 8:9; 16:3, 19; 17:7; 20:2, 8; Josh 18:1; 22:12.

108. See Ezek 16:27, 43, 58; 22:9, 11; 23:21, 27, 29, 35, 44, 48–49; 24:13; and see also Jer 13:27; Hos 6:9.

109. See Lev 18:17; 19:29; 20:14 (twice). Elsewhere (particularly wisdom contexts) the term is devoid of sexual connotations; see Isa 32:7; Pss 26:10; 119:150; Prov 10:23; 24:9; Job 31:11.

110. The term occurs fifty times in P in the Pentateuch and twice in the Priestly stratum of Josh (5:4; 17:2). Elsewhere in the Pentateuch it occurs in the firstborn legislation (Exod 13:12, 15; Deut 15:19) and in postexilic texts (Gen 34:15, 22, 24–25; Deut 4:16). Otherwise in the Former Prophets, it is found only in 1 Kgs 11:15–16. In the prophetic books, all five instances are arguably postexilic (Isa 66:7; Jer 20:15; 30:6; Ezek 16:17; Mal 1:14). Another eleven occurrences are in Ezra 8:3–14 and three in Chronicles (2 Chr 6:46; 31:16, 19).

111. For דבק אחר, see 1 Sam 14:22; Jer 42:16; 1 Chr 10:2; but see Ps 63:9, where it means "be attached to." In contrast, רדף אחר occurs more than forty times, and is frequent in DtrH.

112. For דבק את, see Gen 31:23; Judg 18:22.

חֲטֹף *abduct* (Judg 21:21)—occurs only once again in the Bible (Ps 10:9) but is frequent in MH and in Aramaic.[113]

נָשָׂא אִשָּׁה (Judg 21:23)—the expression is infrequent and recurs only in postexilic texts[114] but becomes commonplace in MH.[115]

לַעֲרוֹב, "become evening" (Judg 19:9)—a denominative from עֶרֶב, which recurs only twice in the Hebrew Bible.[116] Apparently, due the limited evidence for this form, BDB proposes to read a nominal form here (לָעֶרֶב) as attested by the LXX.[117] However, לָעֶרֶב also occurs only in late texts.[118]

Nouns and Noun Phrases

יְבוּס (Judg 19:10–11)—the toponym *Jebus* recurs only in 1 Chr 11:4–5, and in both instances a gloss identifies it as the pre-Israelite name of Jerusalem. The name is derived from the gentilicon יְבוּסִי, since the Jebusites are taken to be the pre-Israelite inhabitants of Jerusalem (Josh 15:63; 18:28; Judg

---

113. See, e.g., b. Beṣah 21a; b. Qidd. 13a, 52a; b. B. Meṣ. 104a; b. B. Bat. 33b; y. Ketub. 4.28d; Sipre Num. 157; Gen. Rab. 97:27; Tanḥuma, Wayyišlaḥ 19; and additional citations in Jastrow 450a. The verb that usually signifies abduction in BH is גנב; see Gen 40:15; Exod 21:16; Deut 24:7; 2 Kgs 11:2; cf. 2 Sam 19:42; 21:12; Job 21:18. See also the use of לקח in Judg 18:24.

114. See Ruth 1:4; Ezra 10:44; 2 Chr 11:21; 13:21; 24:3; also Polzin 1976, 146; Kutscher 1982, 83. The act of marrying is usually indicated by לקח אשה, which occurs approximately sixty times in different literary strata (e.g., Gen 4:19; 6:2; 11:29; Lev 18:18; 21:7, 13; Num 12:1; Deut 20:7; 22:13–14; 24:3–5; Judg 3:6; 14:2–3; 19:1; 1 Sam 25:39–40; 2 Sam 12:9; 1 Kgs 16:31; Jer 16:2; Ezra 2:61; 2 Chr 11:18). According to S. Driver (1972, 455), Eskult (2003, 16), and Guenther (2005, 399–401), Judg 21:23 does not reflect the late usage, but rather means "abduct, carry off." But if this is so, then אשר גזלו in v. 23 would be redundant; see Budde 1897, 141.

115. For example, there are more than thirty occurrences in the Mishnah (e.g., Bik. 1:5, Yebam. 1:2, 4:10–11, 10:8–9, 11:3–5, 16:7; Ketub. 1:6, 10:1, 12:1, 13:11; Soṭah 4:3; Qidd. 4:4; Bek. 8:1); and approximately twenty occurrences in Gen. Rab. (e.g., 9:7, 17:7, 18:4, 19:10, 45:3).

116. Isa 24:11 (however, some consider the text corrupt; see BDB 788a); 1 Sam 17:16 (MT plus). See also יַעֲרָב in Sir 36:31.

117. See BDB 788a.

118. See 1 Chr 16:40; 23:30; 2 Chr 2:3; Ezra 3:3; Pss 59:7, 15; 90:6; Qoh 11:6; see also Job 4:20; Gen 49:27. Equivalent expressions that are found in both early and late strata are: לְעֵת (ה)עֶרֶב (Gen 8:11; 24:11; 2 Sam 11:2; Isa 17:14; Zech 14:7), and לִפְנוֹת עֶרֶב(ה) (Gen 24:63; Deut 23:12).

1:21; cf. Josh 15:8; 18:16). The explanatory glosses in Judg 19:10 and 1 Chr 11:4 are most likely tendentious comments, designed to emphasize the non-Israelite character of the city.[119] Since all known extrabiblical sources agree that the ancient name of Jerusalem was Urusalim, it appears that these explanatory glosses are not true antiquarian notes based upon genuine knowledge of an ancient place name.[120] Due to the editorial nature of the gloss, it is quite likely that the use of the unusual toponym in Judg 19:10–11 derives from R².[121] Since the equation Jebus = Jerusalem is based upon information in the Deuteronomistic History about the Jebusites, it is probably of post-Deuteronomistic origin.

שבועה (Judg 21:5)—the noun occurs primarily in Priestly or otherwise late literature[122] and is relatively infrequent in Deuteronomistic literature.[123] The preferred term in the Deuteronomistic History and Jeremiah is אלה;[124] however, אלה appears along with שבועה only in Priestly or postexilic texts.[125] It is therefore possible that in some cases שבועה was inserted into Deuteronomistic contexts by later editors.

---

119. The use of the toponym in 1 Chr 11:4–5 is the result of the Chronicler's deduction from the parallel text in 2 Sam 5:6: "the Jebusites (who) inhabit the land." Consequently, he concluded that the Jebusites inhabited Jerusalem and named the town after themselves (cf. Judg 18:12, 29). See Miller 1974a; Fishbane 1988, 45 n. 3; Hübner 2007; Na'aman 2014a, 481.

120. So also Hübner 2007. Nonetheless, some still uphold the view that the gloss preserves authentic ancient tradition; see, e.g., Stipp 2006, 145, 153; 2011, 234–36; Avioz 2007. Both Stipp and Avioz appeal to the "antiquarian" nature of the gloss as evidence for the antiquity of the narrative in Judg 19.

121. Accordingly, v. 10 absorbed an interpolation: "They came as far as [Jebus, that is] Jerusalem"; and v. 11 originally read: "When they were by <Jersualem>," which R² exchanged for Jebus.

122. Thus in nineteen out of twenty-nine total occurrences: Lev 5:4 (P); Num 5:21 (twice) (P); 30:3, 11, 14 (P); Josh 9:20 (Priestly redaction); 2 Sam 21:7; Isa 65:15; Ezek 21:28; Zech 8:17; Ps 105:9; Qoh 8:2; 9:2; Dan 9:11; Neh 6:18; 10:30; 1 Chr 16:16; 2 Chr 15:15.

123. See Deut 7:8; Josh 2:17, 20; 1 Sam 14:26; 1 Kgs 2:43; Jer 11:5.

124. See Deut 29:11, 13, 18–20; 30:7, 1 Kgs 8:31 (twice); Jer 23:10; 29:18; 42:18; 44:12.

125. See Num 5:21 (twice); Dan 9:11; Neh 10:30.

עלות ושלמים (Judg 20:26; 21:4)—the word pair recurs four more times, all in post-Deuteronomistic material and Chronicles.[126] In earlier literature the terms occur separately.[127]

כל זה (Judg 20:16, 17)—the fixed phrase recurs only in Qoh 7:23; 8:9; 9:1 (twice); Esth 5:13; Neh 13:6. By contrast, the more common phrase כל זאת may be found throughout the Bible in nearly all the literary strata.[128] The different distribution of the phrases stems from the fact that SBH uses the feminine demonstrative pronoun in connection with ambiguous referents.[129] By contrast, MH prefers the masculine demonstrative pronoun in such cases.[130]

כל אלה (Judg 20:25, 35, 44, 46)—the expression occurs fifty-nine times, almost exclusively in Priestly and postexilic literature.[131] It is also frequent in MH.[132] By contrast, it is strikingly absent from the preexilic prophetic literature and is infrequent in the non-Priestly strata in the Pentateuch and in the Deuteronomistic History.[133] It is difficult to account for

---

126. See 2 Sam 24:25 (// 1 Chr 21:26); 1 Kgs 9:25; 1 Chr 16:1, and cf. העלה והשלמים in Lev 9:22; 1 Sam 13:9; 2 Sam 6:18 (// 1 Chr 16:2); לעלה ולשלמים in Ezek 45:15; 2 Chr 31:2.

127. See Exod 20:24; 24:5; 32:6; Josh 8:31; 1 Sam 10:8; 1 Kgs 3:15; but also in late strata, e.g., Num 10:10; Josh 22:27; 2 Sam 6:17; Ezek 43:27; 45:17; 46:2; 2 Chr 7:7. The diachronic difference is further evident in a synoptic passage, where Chronicles has combined the two terms that appear separately in 2 Sam 6:17:

2 Sam 6:17: ויבאו את־ארון ה' ויצגו אתו ... ויעל דוד עלות לפני ה' ושלמים
1 Chr 16:1: ויביאו את־ארון האלהים ויציגו אתו ... ויקריבו עלות ושלמים לפני האלהים

128. See, e.g., Gen 41:39; Deut 32:27; Judg 6:13; 1 Sam 22:15; 2 Sam 14:19; Isa 5:25; Hos 7:10; Mic 1:5; Ps 44:18; Neh 10:1; 2 Chr 21:18; 31:1; 35:20.

129. See GKC §136b; *IBHS* §17.4.3.b.

130. See, e.g., כל זה in b. Beṣa 29a; Meg. 15a; מפני מה זה in m. Sanh. 6:4; b. Roš Haš. 18a. No use is made of the feminine demonstrative pronoun in these phases in either the Mishnah or the Talmud.

131. In P strata and Priestly literature: Gen 10:29 (= 1 Chr 1:23); 25:4 (= 1 Chr 1:33); Lev 18:24 (twice), 20:23; 22:25; 1 Kgs 7:9; Ezek 6:13; 16:30, 43; 17:18; 18:11. In postexilic literature: Isa 45:7; 66:2 (twice); Hag 2:13; Zech 8:12, 17; Job 12:9; 33:29; Qoh 7:28; 11:9; Dan 12:7; Ezra 10:44; Chronicles' *Sondergut*: 1 Chr 2:23; 7:8, 11, 40; 8:38, 40; 9:9; 12:39; 25:5–6; 26:8; 27:31; 29:17; 2 Chr 14:7; 21:2; 29:32.

132. See, e.g., b. Ber. 58a; b. Šabb. 63b; b. Yoma 86b; b. Tem. 7a; Mek. R. Yišmael, Jethro 6 (לא תעשה פסל); Mek. R. Šimʿon Bar Yochai 19:5; Exod. Rab. 1:4; Lev. Rab. 9:8; Num. Rab. 9:47; Lam. Rab. 2:3.

133. Outside P, it is found three times in the Tetrateuch: Gen 14:3; 15:10; 49:28; all of which are now regarded as post-Dtr compositions; see Van Seters 1975, 296–306;

these findings, apart from the surmise that they reflect a stylistic preference. This may be supported by the fact that nearly half of the instances occur in summaries of lists and tallies.[134] Deuteronomistic scribes seem to have preferred introductory formulas over summary formulas; hence the use of the formula *x* ואלה.[135]

Possibly Late Lexica

Verbs and Verbal Expressions

כתר, "surround" (Judg 20:43)[136]—there are only six instances of denominative verbs of the root כתר, and with the exception of Judg 20:43, all occur in poetry.[137] The verb forms do not occur in any of the typically preexilic biblical texts. Instead, SBH expresses the act of surrounding with verbs derived from the roots סבב, נקף, and compare also the verb עטר and the noun עטרה.[138]

Anbar 1982; and Macchi 1999. Dtr use is represented in Deut 3:5; 2 Kgs 10:9; Jer 2:34; 3:7; 5:19; 14:22; while Judg 13:23 belongs to the post-Dtr Samson story.

134. See Gen 10:29; 14:3; 25:4; 49:28; Deut 3:5; Judg 20:25, 44, 46; Ezra 10:44; 1 Chr 2:23; 7:8, 11, 40; 8:38, 40; 9:9; 12:39; 25:5–6; 26:8; 27:31; 2 Chr 14:7; 21:2; 29:32; cf. Gen 15:10.

135. See Deut 27:13; Josh 12:1, 7; Judg 3:1; 2 Sam 5:14; 1 Kgs 4:2, 8. This pattern is also very prevalent in P, Ezekiel, Ezra-Nehemiah, and Chronicles (approximately seventy times), and occurs also in post-Dtr material in Joshua–Samuel: Josh 14:1; 17:3; 1 Sam 6:17.

136. The LXX reflects a different reading, either ויכתתו or ויכרתו; see Moore 1895, 442; Budde 1897, 138; Burney 1970, 484; Gray 1986, 388; Soggin 1987, 295.

137. *Piel*, Judg 20:43; Ps 22:13; Job 36:2; *hiphil*, Hab 1:4; Prov 14:18; Ps 142:8 (but see the LXX reading *piel*). The nouns from the root are also infrequent in the Bible: כֶּתֶר, Esth 1:11; 2:17; 6:8; כֹּתֶרֶת, only of the temple columns Yachin and Boaz in 1 Kgs 7:16–42; 2 Chr 4:12–13, and in the list of booty taken by the Babylonians in 2 Kgs 25:17; Jer 52:22. See Salvesen 1998, 67–73.

138. See סבב—thirty-six occurrences, e.g., Gen 37:7; Josh 6:15.; Judg 16:2; 2 Sam 18:15; 2 Kgs 3:25; 6:15; הקיף—twenty-five occurrences, e.g., Josh 6:3; 2 Kgs 6:14; 11:8; Isa 15:8; Ps 17:9; עטר—1 Sam 23:26; Isa 23:8; Pss 5:13; 8:6; 65:12; 103:4; עטרה—e.g., 2 Sam 12:30; Isa 28:1; 62:3; Jer 13:18; Ezek 16:12; Zech 6:11; Ps 21:4; Prov 4:9; Job 19:9; Cant 3:11; Lam 5:16; Esth 8:15.

Nouns, Pronouns, and Noun Phrases

מזרח שמש (Judg 20:43; 21:19)—the early names for the cardinal directions are based upon personal orientation facing the sunrise. Thus east is קדם, "front"; south is ימין/תימן, "right"; north is שמאל, "left"; and west is ים, "sea."[139] Alongside these terms are found alternate terms for "east" and "west," based upon the rising and the setting of the sun: מזרח שמש, "east"; and מבוא שמש, "west."[140] These alternate terms are semantically parallel to the Akkadian terms for "east" and "west,"[141] so it seems likely that they entered Hebrew through Akkadian influence from the period of Assyrian domination and onward.[142]

רחוב העיר, "town square" (Judg 19:15, 17; cf. 19:20)—the construct recurs only seven times, all in late sources.[143] Moreover, the term רחוב itself occurs mostly in postexilic literature.[144] In preexilic literature, the synonymous term חוץ/חוצות seems to have been preferred.[145] However, it should be noted that all the terms for enclosures (שוק, חצר, חוצות, רחוב)

---

139. For a synchronic discussion of the cardinal directions, see O'Connor 1991.

140. מזרח שמש, Num 21:11; Deut 4:41, 47; Josh 1:15; 12:1; 13:5; 19:12, 27, 34; Judg 20:43; 21:19; 2 Kgs 10:33; Isa 41:25; 45:6; 59:19; מבוא שמש, Deut 11:30; Josh 1:4; 23:4; both terms in conjunction: Mal 1:11; Pss 50:1; 113:3; cf. Zech 8:7.

141. I.e., waṣi šamši and erib šamši. The formal parallel to the Akk. waṣi šamši would be צאת שמש, but this occurs in Hebrew only as a proper verb clause; see Judg 5:31; Isa 13:10; cf. Gen 19:23.

142. This is supported by the fact that the term מזרח is frequent in the Dtr strata of Deuteronomy–Joshua (Deut 3:17, 27; 4:41, 47, 49; Josh 1:15; 11:3, 8; 12:1, 3; 13:5, 8), while קדם occurs there only twice (Deut 2:26; Josh 7:2). Similarly, מזרח is found in Isaiah only in Deutero- and Trito-Isaiah (41:2, 25; 43:5; 45:6; 46:11; 59:19), while קדם occurs only in "first" Isaiah (2:6; 9:11; 11:14; 19:11). Moreover, מזרח is totally absent from J in Gen, whereas קדם occurs fifteen times (2:8, 14; 3:24; 4:16; 10:30; 11:2; 12:8 [twice]; 13:11, 14; 25:6 [twice], 15; 28:14; 29:1).

143. In singular, Esth 4:6; 6:9, 11; in plural, Zech 8:4–5; Lam 2:11–12.

144. The term occurs more than forty times; at least twenty-eight times in postexilic literature (Isa 59:14; Jer 5:1; 9:20; 48:38; 49:26; 50:30; Ezek 16:24, 31; Nah 2:5; Zech 8:4–5; Pss 55:12; 144:14; Job 29:7; Cant 3:2; Lam 2:11–12; 4:18; Esth 4:6; 6:9, 11; Dan 9:25; Ezra 10:9; Neh 8:1, 3, 16 [twice]; 2 Chr 29:4; 32:6). It also occurs twice in late- or post-Dtr additions (Deut 13:17 [see Veijola 1995, 304–8; Otto 1996, 4–20]; 2 Sam 21:12). Only two cases may be assigned to the preexilic period with some certainty: Gen 19:2; Amos 5:16.

145. רחוב and חוץ/חוצות occur in parallelism in Isa 15:3; Jer 5:1; 9:20; Amos 5:16; Nah 2:5; Prov 1:20; 7:12; 22:13. חוץ/חוצות is found in preexilic literature in 2 Sam 1:20; 1 Kgs 20:34; Isa 5:25; 10:6; 24:11; Amos 5:16; Mic 7:10.

in preexilic texts.[161] On the basis of other parallels, it seems likely that an SBH scribe would have chosen a different formulation in verse 14b.[162]

Unusual or Rare Lexica

Time Expressions

Judges 19 is replete with expressions indicating the precise passage of time, and alongside commonplace idioms[163] are a number of unique or unusual formulations, such as: ימים x חדשים (v. 2);[164] נטות היום (v. 8); חנות היום;[165] כל הלילה עד הבקר (v. 9);[166] היום רד מאד (v. 11);[167] רפה היום לערוב (v. 25);[168] and עד האור (v. 26).[169]

Verbs and Verbal Expressions

זנה על ‎(ותזנה עליו, Judg 19:2)—only here does the verbal phrase occur with a personal object.[170] Throughout the Bible the verb indicates whoring

---

161. See Gen 25:11; 35:4; Josh 7:2; 19:46; Judg 9:6; 18:3, 22; 19:11; 1 Sam 10:2; 2 Sam 6:7; 13:23; 19:38; 20:8; 24:16 (= 1 Chr 21:15); 1 Kgs 1:9; 1 Chr 13:14; 26:16. Both formulations (אצל/עם + TN) occur in Judg 19:11, 14; and 1 Kgs 1:9.

162. E.g., ותבא להם השמש עם גבעה אשר לבנימן (cf. Judg 9:6; 1 Sam 10:2; 1 Kgs 1:9); השמש באה והמה באו עד גבעה אשר (see 2 Sam 2:24); ויפגעו בגבעה אשר לבנימן ותבא להם השמש (cf. Gen 28:11).

163. E.g., שלשת ימים (v. 4) occurs more than thirty times elsewhere; באה השמש (v. 14) for "sunset" occurs more than twenty times; עלות השחר (v. 25) occurs in Gen 32:25; Josh 6:15; 1 Sam 9:26; Jonah 4:7; Neh 4:15.

164. Recurs only in 1 Sam 27:7.

165. נטות and חנות occur as infinitive constructs only once more each (respectively, Josh 8:19; Num 1:51).

166. Only here does the verb רפה occur with the subject יום, while the most common idiom with the verb is רפה ידים, which is found eight times.

167. יום + ירד recurs in BH only in 1 Kgs 1:25, but see Arad 40.10–11 for extrabiblical usage. See Young 2003, 301.

168. Recurs only in Lev 6:2.

169. Metonymic use of the term האור to indicate "daybreak" is found elsewhere only in Neh 8:3. The usual expression is עד אור הבקר; cf. Judg 16:2; 1 Sam 14:36; 25:34, 36; 2 Sam 17:22; 2 Kgs 7:9.

170. See Ezek 16:15–16a, where the preposition occurs with an inanimate object. Otherwise, in Ezek 16:15b and 23:7–8 the root occurs in nominal form with the preposition, and is governed by the verbs שפך and נתן. See, however, the use of the nomi-

or illicit fornication; however, this meaning seems at odds with the narrative since the Levite's response to his concubine's action is to try to win her back (v. 3). For these reasons, many have adopted the proposal that here is a unique occurrence of a homonym meaning "to be angry with."[171] In either case, the phrase is unique.

קרב ב- (Judg 19:13)—the verbal phrase occurs only once more.[172] The usual locution combines קרב with אל and an object indicating place.[173] Thus in contrast to the unusual phrase here, Deut 20:10 and Josh 8:5 use the common formulation קרב אל in a similar context of "drawing near" a city.

נהיתה (Judg 19:30; 20:3, 12)—the *niphal* of היה is relatively infrequent in the Bible[174] but becomes commonplace in MH.[175] In some of the cases, the *niphal* of היה is reflexive and signifies "becoming,"[176] although this is usually expressed by the construction in *qal*, היה ל-.[177] In other cases, such as those in 19:30, 20:3, 12, the *niphal* of היה signifies "occurrence."[178]

---

nal form with a personal object in Ezek 16:36, בתזנותיך על־מאהביך. See Stipp 2006, 137–38.

171. See the Targum: ובסרת עלוהי. G. R. Driver first proposed that the homonym is cognate with Akk. *zênu*; see G. Driver 1947. Liverani (2004, 172 n. 18) proposed reading ותזנה ותלך here, as parallel to Akk. *zêru u alāku/ezēbu*, "to repudiate and leave."

172. See Ps 91:10; see also Jer 12:2.

173. קרב אל occurs more than fifty times and is particularly frequent in D and DtrH: Deut 1:17, 22; 4:7; 5:23; 13:8; 20:2, 10; 21:3, 6; 22:2, 14; 30:14; Josh 8:5, 23; 9:16; 1 Kgs 5:7; 8:59; and elsewhere in Samuel–Kings: 1 Sam 14:36; 17:41; 2 Sam 19:43; 20:17; 1 Kgs 2:7.

174. היה occurs in the *qal* thousands of times, but the *niphal* occurs only nineteen times. Apart from the three occurrences in Judg 19–21, the *niphal* form is found once in J (Exod 11:6) and four times in DtrH (Deut 4:32; 27:9; 1 Kgs 1:27; 12:24 // 2 Chr 11:4); but it is more prevalent in postexilic literature (Jer 5:30; 48:19; Ezek 21:12; 39:8; Joel 2:2; Zech 8:10; Prov 13:19; Dan 12:1; Neh 6:8). Two more occurrences in Dan 2:1 and 8:27 are probably textual corruptions; see BHS.

175. See, e.g., m. Ber. 6:2, 8; b. Sanh. 98a, 105a; Gen. Rab. 23:4; 57:4; 88:7; Exod. Rab. 1:8; 23:12; Esth. Rab. 1:10; Qoh. Rab. 3:1.

176. See Deut 27:9; and see Zech 8:10; Prov 13:19.

177. E.g., Gen 2:10; 17:4; Exod 9:24; Num 27:11; Deut 4:20; 20:11; 21:13; 28:25; Josh 7:5; 23:13; Judg 2:3; 10:18; 17:10; 1 Sam 4:9; 10:11; 1 Kgs 4:11; 2 Kgs 21:14; Isa 1:21; Jer 15:16; Mic 7:13.

178. See Exod 11:6; Deut 4:32; 1 Kgs 1:27; 12:24 (// 2 Chr 11:4); Jer 5:30; 48:19; Ezek 21:12; 39:8; Joel 2:2; Dan 12:1; Neh 6:8.

נרצח (Judg 20:4)—the appositional phrase האשה הנרצחה occurs only here. Moreover, there is only one more instance of the *niphal* of רצח (Prov 22:13).[179]

קלע באבן (Judg 20:16)—a unique usage for designating a type of warrior, comparable to the expressions in 1 Chr 12:2.

לא יחטיא (Judg 20:16)—only here is *hiphil* חטא used to signify "missing the target."

השחית (Judg 20:21, 25, 35, 42)—the verb functions here as a synonym of הכה, and this usage is also attested in a few instances elsewhere.[180] However, nowhere else does the verb occur in casualty lists, and this use is otherwise reserved for the more common verbs הרג, נפל, הכה.[181] In addition, the root שחת occurs elsewhere with the locution ארצה only once more in an entirely different context (vv. 21, 25; cf. Gen 38:9).[182]

הכה חללים (Judg 20:31, 39)—the construction here is unique.[183] Usually חלל is adverbial and occurs with an intransitive verb.[184] The expression here may have been coined for the sake of alliteration: ויחלו להכות חללים (v. 39).

מגיח (Judg 20:33)—the only instance of the *hiphil* of גיח. The root occurs otherwise in *qal* and solely in poetic passages.[185]

---

179. The *niphal* of רצח is also uncommon in MH and is found only in late sources, such as Deuteronomy Rabbah, Osar Hamidrashim, and Yalqut Šimoni. According to Young et al. (2008a, 113), the uncommon use of an "old" lexeme in a different stem is another characteristic of LBH.

180. As here, in *hiphil*: 2 Sam 11:1; Ezek 9:5–6, 8; 1 Chr 21:12. See also *piel*: Josh 22:33; 2 Sam 1:14; 24:16–17.

181. See, e.g., in the context of battle descriptions: הכה, Josh 12:1, 7; Judg 3:29; 2 Sam 8:5, 13; 1 Kgs 20:29; 2 Kgs 14:7; Ps 60:2; נפל, Josh 8:25; Judg 4:16; 8:10; 12:6; 1 Sam 4:10; 17:52; 2 Chr 13:17; הרג, Num 31:8; Judg 7:25; 2 Sam 10:18. According to Young et al. (2008a, 113), it is characteristic of LBH to employ an "old" lexeme "with a different meaning or referent, in a different literary genre, etc."

182. But see הכה ארצה (2 Sam 2:22; 18:11); שחט ארצה (1 Sam 14:32); נפל דם/ פגרים ארצה (1 Sam 26:20; 2 Chr 20:24).

183. See the more common נפל(ו) חלל(ים), which occurs more than twenty times, e.g., Judg 9:40; 1 Sam 31:1; Jer 51:4, 47; Ezek 6:7; 30:4; 32:22–24; Dan 11:26; 1 Chr 5:22; 10:1; 2 Chr 13:17.

184. See GKC §118 m, q.

185. See Ezek 32:2; Mic 4:10; Job 38:8; 40:23.

נגעה הרעה (Judg 20:34, 41)—the only instance in which the abstract noun רעה serves as the subject of נגע.[186] Elsewhere, the subject is concrete when the verb indicates inflicting harm.[187]

החישו (Judg 20:37)—the root חוש occurs only once more in prose (1 Sam 20:38; but cf. Isa 8:1, 3), while it is relatively frequent in poetry.[188]

הרדיפהו (Judg 20:43)—the only instance of *hiphil* רדף.[189] By way of contrast, the root occurs in *qal* more than a hundred times.

הדריכהו, "tread down" (Judg 20:43)—the only instance of the *hiphil* in prose.[190] Moreover, the verb is used infrequently with this significance.[191]

ויעללהו, "glean" (Judg 20:45)—the denominative verb is rare and occurs only once more in the sense of "gleaning" a remnant.[192]

שלח באש (Judg 20:48)—the idiom is found only three more times, and in all cases, the subject is a human agent.[193] None of the instances of the idiom are found in typically Deuteronomistic passages. By contrast, the more common expression שרף באש is particularly frequent in Deuteronomistic literature.[194]

---

186. See Job 5:19. The abstract noun רעה is infrequent as a nominative (twenty times, compared to 111 instances of the accusative) and occurs with a transitive verb only in Gen 19:19; Deut 31:29 (see also 31:17, 21); Judg 20:34, 41; Jer 44:23; Amos 9:10; Ps 34:22.

187. E.g., Gen 26:11; Josh 9:19; 2 Sam 14:10; Zech 2:12; Ps 105:15; see also Jer 12:14.

188. See Deut 32:35; Isa 5:19; 60:22; Hab 1:8; Pss 22:20; 38:23; 40:14; 55:9; 70:2, 6; 71:12; 90:10; 119:60; 141:1; Job 20:2.

189. However, some have proposed reading *qal* וַיִּרְדְּפֵהוּ, or striking the word as a doublet for הדריכהו; see Moore 1895, 441; Burney 1970, 484; Gray 1986, 388.

190. In poetry, see, e.g., Isa 11:15; 42:16; 48:17; Jer 51:33; Hab 3:19; Pss 25:5, 9; 107:7; 119:35; Prov 4:11; Job 28:8. In addition, only eleven of the thirty cases of *qal* occur in prose: Deut 1:36; 11:24–25; Josh 1:3; 14:9; Judg 9:27; 1 Sam 5:5; Neh 13:15; 1 Chr 5:18; 8:40; 2 Chr 14:7.

191. See elsewhere Isa 11:15; Jer 9:2 (*BHS*); 51:33; Job 28:8. Otherwise, the verb indicates "to lead, guide."

192. See Jer 6:9; otherwise of picking grapes (Lev 19:10; Deut 24:21). But see the subst. עוללות, "gleanings," as a metaphor for "remnant" (Judg 8:2; Isa 17:6; 24:13; Jer 49:9 // Obad 5; Mic 7:1).

193. See Judg 1:8; 2 Kgs 8:12; Ps 74:7. By contrast, the subject of the idiom שלח ב- אש is always a divine agent; see Ezek 39:6; Hos 8:14; Amos 1:4, 7, 10, 12; 2:2, 5; Lam 1:13. On the distinction between the idioms, see Andersen and Freedman 1989, 239.

194. See thirty-six times in DtrH and Jeremiah, e.g., Deut 7:5, 25; 9:21; 12:3; 13:17; Josh 6:24; 7:15, 25; 11:6, 9, 11; Judg 9:52; 12:1; 18:27; 1 Sam 30:1, 3, 14; 1 Kgs

מצא ל-, "suffice" (Judg 21:14)—the phrase ל- + מצא (prepositional phrase) carries this significance in only five more instances.[195]

עשה פרץ ב-, "made a breach in" (Judg 21:15)—the circumlocution is unique. Elsewhere the act is directly represented by the verb פרץ.[196]

נחם ל- (Judg 21:15)—only here does the verb occur with a prepositional phrase prefixed with -ל. Elsewhere, when the verb requires a preposition, the prepositions used are על, אל, or -מ.[197]

נשמד מ(בנימן) (Judg 21:16)—the *niphal* of שמד is common, but the construction נשמד מ- occurs only three more times, with quite different syntax than that here.[198]

התהלך, "go depart" (Judg 21:24)—the use here of *hithpael* הלך seems to be exceptional. All other cases of this form fall into four categories: (1) walk around;[199] (2) walk with/before Yahweh, or in his ways;[200] (3) move about, stroll;[201] (4) walk alongside, in the midst or at the head.[202] The present use, "walking toward a destination," is usually indicated by the form in *qal*.[203]

9:16; 2 Kgs 17:31; 23:11; 25:9; Jer 19:5; 21:10; 34:2, 22; 37:8; 38:17, 18, 23; 39:8; 43:13; 51:32; 52:13.

195. See Num 11:22 (twice); Josh 17:16; Hos 12:9; Zech 10:10. Otherwise, the phrase usually signifies "find for/with" (someone or something), e.g., Gen 8:9; Deut 21:17; 22:14; 1 Sam 13:22; 2 Sam 20:6; Isa 34:14; Jer 29:14; Ps 132:5; 1 Chr 28:9; 2 Chr 15:2.

196. See, e.g., Exod 19:22; 2 Kgs 14:13; Isa 5:5; Mic 2:13; Ps 80:13; Neh 3:35; and the pleonasm פרץ פרץ in Gen 38:29; 2 Sam 6:8; Job 16:14.

197. See twenty-two instances of נחם על and eight of נחם אל. Both are used interchangeably in 2 Sam 10:2 // 1 Chr 19:2; 2 Sam 24:16 // 1 Chr 21:15; and see נחם אל הרעה in Jer 26:3, 13, 19; 42:10 with נחם על הרעה/הטובה in Jer 8:6; 18:8, 10. See also נחם מ- in Gen 5:29; Judg 2:18; Isa 1:24.

198. See נשמד מפני/מלפני, Deut 12:30; Isa 48:19; נשמד מ- + infinitive, 2 Sam 21:5. More common is the *hiphil* with מפני or מעל פני האדמה; see, e.g., Deut 2:21–22; 6:15; Josh 23:15; 24:8; 1 Kgs 13:34; 2 Kgs 21:9; Amos 2:9; 9:8; 2 Chr 33:9.

199. E.g., Gen 13:17; Josh 18:4, 8; 1 Sam 30:31; 2 Sam 7:6; Zech 1:10–11; 6:7; Job 1:7; 2:2; 1 Chr 21:4.

200. E.g., Gen 5:22, 24; 6:9; 17:1; 24:40; 48:15; 2Kgs 20:3; Zech 10:12; Ps 26:3; Prov 20:7.

201. E.g., Gen 3:8; Exod 21:19; 1 Sam 23:13; 2 Sam 11:2; Ezek 1:13; 28:14; Ps 58:8; Prov 6:22; Job 18:8.

202. E.g., Lev 26:12; Deut 23:15; 1 Sam 2:30, 35; 12:2; 25:27; 2 Sam 7:7; Ezek 19:6.

203. See Josh 22:6; 1 Sam 10:25–26; 15:34; 1 Kgs 12:16.

Noun Phrases

בעל הבית (Judg 19:22, 23)—the construction occurs only twice more in the Bible (Exod 22:7; 1 Kgs 17:17) but is very common in MH, with more than a thousand instances in rabbinic literature.[204]

קהל עם האלהים (Judg 20:2)—the sole instance of this double construct.[205] Even the constituent construct עם (ה)אלהים recurs but one time (2 Sam 14:13).

בעלי גבעה (Judg 20:5)—בעלי + TN is not infrequent, but most of the instances occur in a single narrative (Judg 9) with reference to the residents of Shechem.[206] By contrast, the construction אנשי + TN occurs more than fifty times in different contexts and with reference to many different toponyms.[207] In one case, the two constructions seem to be used interchangeably, but even then the construct with אנשי is preferred, while the construct with בעלי is found a late appendix.[208] It is possible that the construction בעלי + TN is an Aramaism, since this use is found in Aramaic inscriptions from the ninth-eighth century BCE.[209]

כל שדה נחלת ישראל (Judg 20:6)—the complex construct is unique, and the individual components do not occur together elsewhere. שדה occurs with designations such as Edom, Moab, Zoan, Ephraim, and Samaria, but not with Israel.[210] נחלה + collective is generally used with a

---

204. E.g., m. Pe'ah 4:1, 10, 11; m. Šabb. 1:1; m. B. Qam. 5:2–3; b. Ber. 16a; 46a; b. Pesaḥ. 6b; 82a; b. Ketub. 98b, 99a, b; Gen. Rab. 22:6; 72:4.

205. See the more common constructions with קהל, i.e., קהל ה', Num 16:3; 20:4; six times in Deut 23:2–4, 9; Mic 2:5; 1 Chr 28:8 (contrast one instance of קהל האלהים in Neh 13:1); also קהל ישראל, Lev 16:17; Deut 31:30; Josh 8:35; 1 Kgs 8:14, 22, 55; 12:3; 1 Chr 13:2.

206. בעלי שכם occurs sixteen times in Judg 9; see also בעלי יריחו (Josh 24:11), בעלי יבש גלעד (2 Sam 21:12), בעלי יבש גלעד (1 Sam 23:11–12), בעלי קעילה.

207. E.g., Sodom (Gen 13:13; 19:4); Ai (Josh 7:4–5); Gibeon (Josh 10:6; Neh 3:7); Sukkoth (Judg 8:5); Penuel (Judg 8:8–9); Shechem (Judg 9:57); Gilead (Judg 12:4–5); Ashdod (1 Sam 5:7); Beth-shemesh (1 Sam 6:15); Kiriath-jearim (1 Sam 7:1; Neh 7:29); Jabesh (1 Sam 11:1); Babylon, Cutha, Hamath (2 Kgs 17:30); Anathoth (Jer 11:21; Ezra 2:23); Kir-heres (Jer 48:31, 36); Nineveh (Jonah 3:5); Netophah (Ezra 2:22); Michmash (Ezra 2:27); Bethel and Ai (Ezra 2:28); Jericho (Neh 3:2); Bethlehem (Neh 7:26); Beth-azmaveth (Neh 7:28); Ramah and Geba (Neh 7:30); Nebo (Neh 7:33).

208. See אנשי יביש, 1 Sam 11:1, 5, 9, 10; בעלי יביש, 2 Sam 21:12. On the late origin of 2 Sam 21, see Edenburg 2014.

209. See Sefire i A 4; iii 23; Panammu 10; see also Gibson 1975, 35.

210. E.g., שדה אדום, Gen 32:4, Judg 5:4; שדה מואב, Gen 36:35; Num 21:20; Ruth

designation on the clan or tribal level and occurs only three more times with a higher ranking unit.[211]

מערה (Judg 20:33)—MT מערה apparently derives from the root ערה, "be bare," and thus designates an open place, bare of vegetation.[212] The form is unique and the postulated meaning fits the context poorly. For these reasons, some have suggested that the text is corrupt and originally read מערב, "west."[213] However, if מערב is the original reading, then it reflects a typically late usage.[214]

כליל העיר (Judg 20:40)—the construction is unique. Usually כליל is used as an adverb meaning "wholly, completely"; however, the syntax of the sentence here does not support this use.[215] In a few other cases, the word is used as a substantive, as it appears to be here; however, then it is used either of ritual offerings or in the idiom כליל(ת) יפי.[216] The usage in the present case seems to represent an original metaphor that was coined in order to compare the burning of the city to a holocaust offering.[217]

משאת העשן, "smoke signal" (Judg 20:38)—another unique construction. משאת usually signifies an offering, and the meaning of signal occurs only once more in the Bible.[218] A similar term occurs in MH but only in the plural מַשּׂוּאוֹת, which derives from מְשׂוּאָה.[219]

1:6, 1 Chr 1:46; שדה צען, Ps 78:12, 43; שדה אפרים, שדה שמרון, Obad 19; cf. שדה פלשתים, 1 Sam 6:1.

211. See נחלת יעקב, Isa 58:14; נחלת בית ישראל, Ezek 35:15; נחלת גוים, Ps 111:6. For the clan level, see נחלת אב/אבות, Num 27:7; 36:3–4, 7–8; 1 Kgs 21:3–4; Prov 19:14. For the tribal level, see, e.g., x נחלת מטה, Num 36:4, 7; Josh 15:20; 16:8; 19:8; [tribe name] נחלת בני, Josh 13:23, 28; 15:20; 16:9; 18:20, 28; 19:1, 9, 16. However, see נחלת יהוה, 1 Sam 26:19; 2 Sam 20:19; 21:3; Ps 127:3.

212. See the Targum: מישר גבעתא; see Gray 1986, 357.

213. See the LXX; see Moore 1895, 437–38.

214. See Hurvitz 1972, 113–16; cf. R. Wright 2003, 142–44, who argues for a pre-exilic, northern origin for the term.

215. See Exod 28:31; 39:22; Lev 6:15–16; Num 4:6; Deut 13:17; 1 Sam 7:9; Isa 2:18; Ezek 16:14. The syntax of the adverbial use is: first the verb, then the object, then כליל. In order to read כליל as an adverb in Judg 20:40, the syntax would have to be different: עלה העיר כליל.

216. Of cult offerings, see Deut 33:10; Ps 51:21; for the idiomatic usage, see Ezek 27:3; 28:12; Lam 2:15.

217. See Gross 2009, 863.

218. For "signal," see Jer 6:1 and also Lachish 4: וידע כי אל משאת לכש נחנו שמרם. For "offering," see, e.g., Gen 43:34; Jer 40:5; Ezek 20:40; Amos 5:11; Ps 141:2; Esth 2:18; 2 Chr 24:6, 9.

Prepositions and Prepositional Phrases

עד נכח (Judg 19:10; 20:43)—the compound preposition occurs only once (Ezek 47:20). In all three instances עד alone would have sufficed.[220]

y עד(ו) x-לְמַ (Judg 19:30; 20:1)—the formulation with the initial double preposition is relatively infrequent, while the common usage lacks the prefixed -לְ.[221] Moreover, only in 20:1 is the preposition -לְ prefixed to the common formula מדן ועד באר שבע.[222] The use of the prepositional compound -לְמַ appears to be primarily characteristic of Deuteronomistic literature, although it is also found in postexilic literature.[223]

Particles

איכה (Judg 20:3)—the form is found with one-third the frequency of the shorter form איך.[224] The distribution of the different forms seems to indicate the stylistic preferences of different books. Thus Deuteronomy has only the long form איכה, while Samuel has only the short form איך.[225] In addition, there are nuanced differences in syntax in the use of the particle. For example, all the examples in Deuteronomy display the syntax: איכה + *yiqtol* and are properly interrogative,[226] while איכה + *qatal* represents

---

219. See m. Roš Haš. 2:2–4; b. Pesaḥ. 2b. The singular form may be represented in Zeph 1:15, where the Masoretes pointed מְשׁוֹאָה.

220. E.g., compare Judg 19:10 with Gen 12:6; Judg 20:43 with 4:16; Ezek 47:20 with Josh 16:3.

221. *y* עד(ו) *x*-לְמַ occurs thirteen times more: Exod 11:7; Deut 4:32; 2 Sam 6:19; 7:6; 13:22; 2 Kgs 23:2; Jer 31:34; 42:8; 51:62; Zech 14:10; Esth 1:5, 20; 2 Chr 15:13. See also *y* עד(ו) *x*-לְמַן: Exod 9:18; Deut 9:7; 2 Sam 19:25; Jer 7:7, 25; 25:5; 32:31; Mic 7:12; 2 Chr 15:13. By contrast, *y* עד(ו) *x*-מ occurs more than eighty times.

222. See 1 Sam 3:20; 2 Sam 3:10; 17:11; 24:2, 15; 1 Kgs 5:5; see also מבאר שבע ועד דן, 1 Chr 21:2; 2 Chr 30:5; and other formulas opening with Beer-sheba but ending with points other than Dan, e.g., Neh 11:30; 2 Chr 19:4.

223. See למיום, 2 Sam 7:6; Isa 7:17; למן היום, Exod 9:18; Deut 4:32; 9:7; 2 Sam 7:11; 19:25; Jer 7:25; 32:31; Hag 2:18. On the use of compound prepositions, see GKC 119c and n. 2; BDB 583b (מן 9b).

224. איכה occurs seventeen times compared to sixty-one occurrences of איך.

225. איכה, Deut 1:12; 7:17; 12:30; 18:21; 32:30; איך, 1 Sam 16:2; 2 Sam 1:5, 14, 19, 25, 27; 2:22; 6:9; 12:18. Kings and Jeremiah have both forms, but display a marked preference for איך (1 Kgs 12:6; 2 Kgs 10:4; 17:28; 18:24; and seventeen times in Jeremiah) over איכה (2 Kgs 6:13, 15; Jer 8:8; 48:17).

226. See 2 Kgs 6:15; Jer 8:8; Cant 1:7.

rhetorical questions and is characteristic of lament.²²⁷ The use in Judg 20 appears to be exceptional, since the context is one of interrogation, while the syntax corresponds to that of lament.

כעת (Judg 21:22)—usually occurs in construct with a designation of time²²⁸ but is found here in the absolute state.²²⁹ The verse, however, is difficult and is probably corrupt.²³⁰ The most plausible reading exchanges the unusual absolute of כעת the more common expression כי עתה.²³¹

Particularly Frequent Expressions

Different expressions relating to Israel as an integral social unit occur in Judg 19–21 with higher frequency than is generally found elsewhere. Many scholars have held that the different expressions—בני ישראל, איש ישראל, שבט (כל) שבטי ישראל, and שבט—belong to separate compositional strata in the Bible and accordingly viewed changes in terminology as evidence for separating sources or editorial strands.²³² However, application of this criterion has not produced a single consistent literary analysis,²³³ and it is possible that while one scribe may prefer consistent use of a particular term, another may prefer to alternate different terms for stylistic variation.

(כל) שבטי ישראל, שבט—the term is found in different constructions eleven times in Judg 20–21, and they are rather evenly distributed between both N¹ and R². Thus כל שבט ישראל—N¹: 20:2; R²: 20:10; 21:5; שבטי ישראל—N¹: 20:12; 21:8; R²: 21:15; שבט (אחד)—N¹: 20:12;²³⁴ 21:6, 24; R²: 21:3, 17. The extensive use of the term here is exceptional when com-

---

227. See Isa 1:21; Jer 48:17; Lam 1:1; 2:1; 4:1–2.
228. Thus in seventeen cases. The most frequent constructions are כעת חיה (Gen 18:10, 14; 2 Kgs 4:16–17) and כעת מחר (Exod 9:18; 1 Sam 9:16; 20:12; 1 Kgs 19:2; 20:6; 2 Kgs 7:1, 18; 10:6). For other constructions see Josh 11:6; 1 Sam 4:20; Isa 8:23; Dan 9:21; 2 Chr 21:19.
229. For comparable use, see Num 23:23; Judg 13:23; Job 39:18.
230. See, e.g., Moore 1895, 454; Soggin 1987, 300.
231. Reading: כִּי לֹא אתם נתתם להם כי עתה תאשמו; see Gen 31:42; 43:10; Num 22:29; 1 Sam 13:13; 14:30; Job 8:6.
232. See, e.g., Bertheau 1883, 265–80; Schunck 1963, 61–63; Besters 1965, 31–38; Becker 1990, 279–80.
233. For criticism of this method, see, e.g., Moore 1895, 407; Jüngling 1981, 35; Gross 2009, 266–67.
234. The MT reads שבטי בנימן, but this undoubtedly is a scribal error influenced by the plural expression שבטי ישראל, which occurs in the same verse; see, e.g.,

pared to its limited frequency elsewhere in Judges (Judg 5:14; 18:1, 19, 30). שבט is particularly characteristic of Deuteronomistic texts, although it is also found in many post-Deuteronomistic and Priestly-influenced texts.[235] Thus the use of the term in Judg 19–21 does not necessarily indicate that it is a Deuteronomistic composition.

איש ישראל—the term is frequent in Judg 20–21 and occurs mostly in the primary strand (N[1]: 20:17, 20, 22, 36, 38–39, 41–42, 48; 21:1; cf. R[2]: 20:11, 33). No other literary unit employs the term with such high frequency.[236] The independent use of the term in Chronicles, as well as in a late gloss to 1 Kgs 8:1-3,[237] shows that postexilic writers did employ it on occasion, either for stylistic diversity or for its perceived archaic flavor. One of the causes for the exceptional high frequency of the term in Judg 20–21 may stem from the tendency, in this text, toward overdesignation of subjects.[238]

בני ישראל—more than one-third of all the instances of the term in Judges[239] occur in chapters 19–21, where they are mainly concentrated in the primary strand (N[1]: 19:12, 30; 20:1, 3, 13–14, 18–19, 23–27, 30; 21:6,

---

Moore 1895, 430; Soggin 1987, 291; and McCarter 1980, 170, on a similar occurrence in 1 Sam 9:21.

235. See eighteen times in Deuteronomy to ten times in Exodus–Numbers (excluding the phrase שבטי ישראל). The preferred term in P is מטה (more than eighty occurrences). However, שבט is frequent in the post-Dtr strand of Joshua, which also has affinities with P, e.g., Josh 3:12; 4:2; 7:14; 13:7; 18:2; 21:16; 22:7; 24:1). The term is also widespread in postexilic literature, e.g., Ezek 37:19; 45:8; 47:13; 48:1; Zech 9:1; Ezra 6:17; 1 Chr 5:18; 12:38; 23:14; 26:32; 27:16; 28:1; 29:6; 2 Chr 11:16 (all Chronicles' *Sondergut*).

236. See Num 25:8 (twice), 14; Deut 27:14; 29:9; Josh 9:6–7; 10:24; Judg 7:8, 14, 23; 8:22; 9:55; 1 Sam 13:6, 14:22, 24; 17:2, 19, 24–25; 2 Sam 15:13; 16:15, 18; 17:14, 24; 19:42–44 (four times); 20:2; 23:9; 1 Kgs 8:2 (= 2 Chr 5:3); 1 Chr 10:1, 7 (cf. 1 Sam 31:1); 16:3 (cf. 2 Sam 6:19).

237. 1 Kgs 8:2aα is lacking in LXX[BL].

238. See, e.g., Judg 20:20, where איש ישראל follows a previous בני ישראל in v. 19; 20:22, where איש ישראל is in apposition to העם; 20:38, 42, in which איש ישראל appears in a superfluous object phrase.

239. Most of the other thirty-nine instances occur in the editorial framework and pragmatic sections of the book: 2:6, 11; 3:2, 5, 7–9 (four times), 12, 14–15 (three times); 4:1, 3 (twice), 23–24; 6:1–2, 6–7; 8:28, 33–34; 10:6, 8 (twice), 10–11, 15; 13:1. No instances of the term are found in the Abimelech story (Judg 9) or in the story of Micah's cult image (Judg 17–18), and only one mention is found at the beginning of the Samson cycle (Judg 13–16).

24; cf. R²: 20:7, 35; 21:5, 8). The high frequency of the term here is remarkable when compared with the usage elsewhere in Genesis–Kings.²⁴⁰ Similar frequencies to those here within a single literary unit are found only within the P strand in Numbers.²⁴¹

From the breakdown detailed above, it appears that the terms בני ישראל/איש ישראל were used synonymously by both N¹ and R². Moreover, that איש ישראל was occasionally used by postexilic writers disproves the assumption that it indicates preexilic composition for N¹.²⁴² In addition, the high frequencies of the terms discussed above should be considered along with other terms that represent the people as a corporate whole in Judg 19–21: כל העם,²⁴³ עדה, קהל.²⁴⁴ It appears that both N¹ and R² display an unusual proclivity for frequent and interchangeable use of different corporate terms. It is possible that this use did not stem solely from stylistic concerns but was purposely employed in order to emphasize one of the main themes running through the narrative—upholding the ideal of national unity.

3.4. Conclusions

Most of the typically late phenomena identified in Judg 19–21 are lexical. I identified fifteen late locutions (including Priestly vocabulary) appearing a total of twenty-seven times throughout the narrative. These are concentrated in Judg 19:9–11; 20:1–6, 16–17, 25, 35, 44–46; 21:4–5, 8, 10–13, 16, 21, 23, with slightly less than half of the instances in N¹. I found only one instance of late syntactical use: the use of an infinitive as a predicate in 21:3. More significantly, I found five instances throughout the narrative of late morphological use, where masculine forms of plural object endings were used in conjunction with feminine referents. All of these instances are found in N¹ (19:12, 24; 21:12, 22–23). Particularly instructive are two cases in which a parallel intertext is formulated according to

---

240. See the number of instances per book/section, in order of descending frequency, following Judges: Judg 19–21 (22), Judg 1–18 (39), Numbers (171), Exodus (123), Joshua (69), Leviticus (54), Kings (32), Deuteronomy (21), Samuel (17).

241. See, e.g., sixteen times in Num 8:6–20 and eleven times in Num 36:1–13.

242. So assumed by Schunck 1963, 61–62; Besters 1965, 30–38; Rösel 1976, 31–32; and others.

243. N¹: 20:26; R²: 20:2, 8, 16.

244. Only R²; see discussion of terms above.

classical usage (Judg 19:24 // Gen 19:8; Judg 19:12 // 2 Sam 21:2; 1 Kgs 9:20); these seem to indicate that the author of Judg 19–21 revised traditional idioms in accordance with the use prevalent in his times. Typically late constructions are found in all three chapters of the text, although they appear in greatest concentration in chapter 21. There they are distributed throughout the chapter and are evident in both N^1 and R^2. The findings are scantiest in chapter 19, where they are concentrated in verses 9–12.

The phenomena that occur *mostly* in late texts and that *might* represent late usage are more evenly divided between lexical, syntactical, and morphological categories. I found seven possibly late lexica appearing ten times in all: three are concentrated in 19:14–17; another three in 20:9, 43; and the remaining four in 21:5, 11, 19, 23. More than half of these occur in N^1. I also discerned three syntactical phenomena, which *might* indicate late usage, the most prominent of which being increased usage of nominal verb forms, particularly of participle forms. These last occur seventeen times and are fairly evenly distributed between N^1 and R^2.[245] Two morphological phenomena, occurring mainly in N^1, *might* indicate late usage: (1) third-person genitive suffix הֹ-[246] and (2) increased usage of accusative pronominal suffixes.[247]

These two sets of data, taken together, show that both typically late and possibly late phenomena are dispersed throughout the entire text, leaving only small "pockets" of wholly classical formulation. These pockets represent only 50 percent of the entire narrative in Judg 19–21. Taken together, the typically late and possibly late phenomena are found in 56 percent of chapter 19, in 39.5 percent of chapter 20, and in 60 percent of chapter 21. The findings for chapter 19 are particularly significant, since the entire chapter is assigned to N^1, and only minimal glosses can be discerned (e.g., 19:10aβ). Thus it seems reasonable to conclude that even this chapter (taken by some to represent the earliest kernel of the story[248]) was

---

245. N^1, 20:2, 15, 17, 25; 21:7, 9, 12; R^2, 20:15bβ, 16, 34–35, 46, 48; 21:10, 16.
246. Only in N^1, 19:16, 24.
247. N^1, 19:3, 21–22, 25, 28–29; 20:32, 38, 42–43, 45; R^2, 20:6.
248. See, e.g., Jüngling 1981, 245, 259–62; Soggin 1987, 281–82, 302–3; Becker 1990, 264–66; Mayes 2001, 254; and more recently Stipp 2006, 2011. Stipp (2011, 226–27) attempts to base his argument on linguistic data, but his interpretation of the minimal data he discusses is problematic, since he does not adequately consider the relative length of the texts, the narrative constraints in the different sections and the distribution of intertextual links that might color the language.

composed under the influence of LBH. By contrast, the findings for chapter 20 are more ambiguous. Here the pockets of classical formulation represent 60.5 percent of the chapter and include blocks of text in both N^1 and R^2.[249] This does not necessarily mean that these sections derive from an older source or represent an early compositional layer. Much of this material is either formulaic (e.g., vv. 19–24) or seems to have been formulated with an eye toward invoking other classical texts.[250] Thus it is natural that the language in such sections should lean toward classical formulation, even if the composition itself is late.

Since a significant amount of late usage is represented in both the primary narrative and the secondary expansions and revisions, it appears that both belong to the same linguistic stratum. This may indicate that a short period of time separates the primary narrative from the secondary redaction (e.g., one generation). The alternative possibility seems less likely, namely, that the late redactor reformulated the entire narrative in the language characteristic of his times. Were this the case, we should expect editorial traces throughout the entire narrative, including chapter 19; however, here R^2 is most notably absent. The linguistic evidence provides only a basis for relative dating of the composition. The authors used allusion and unmarked quotation to evoke literature that they considered classical but do not seem adept at independent use of the classical style, and most of the sections that are free of literary dependency display some degree of late usage. However, it is clear that the amount of LBH usage is quite limited in relation to compositions like Ezra-Nehemiah and Chronicles. Thus the language of the composition should probably be characterized as "transitional LBH" and may be associated with the early postexilic period.

Rare or unusual usage occurs in 38 of the 103 verses in the text, representing 37 percent of the entire narrative. Since traditional literature (whether oral or written) tends to be formulaic, increased proportions of rare usage distances the text from received tradition. The rare or unusual expressions are concentrated mostly in chapter 19 (nineteen instances in thirty verses, all N^1), and chapter 20 (thirty-one instances in forty-eight

---

249. N^1, 20:3a, 12–14, 18–24, 27a, 28b–31a, 36–37, 39–41, 47; R^2, 20:3–5, 7–8, 10–11, 31b, 33.

250. See, e.g., Judg 20:12–13 // Deut 13:13; 1 Sam 10:26–27; 11:12–13; Judg 20:18 // Judg 1:1–2; 20:29–42 // Josh 8:2–24. See ch. 4 for detailed discussion of the literary dependencies.

verses, evenly distributed between N¹ and R² [251]), while chapter 21 displays significantly lower frequencies (seven instances in twenty-five verses, evenly distributed between N¹ and R²).[252] Significantly, most of the pockets that lack late phenomena are marked by concentrations of rare expressions (cf. particularly 19:1–2, 26–27, 30; 20:3–5, 39–41; 21:14–15). If only typically late phenomenon are taken into account, then only twenty-four verses, or 23 percent of the entire text, are devoid of both late language and rare expressions. If *possibly* late phenomena are included, then only fourteen verses, or 13.6 percent of the entire text, are devoid of late usage and rare expression.

These findings indicate that the language of Judg 19–21—both the primary narrative and the later revision—is somewhat distanced from traditional literary expression and even tends to be innovative. If we were dealing with an early composition, which makes use of original expressions, we might expect that the newly cast expressions would leave an impression on the literary tradition and eventually become well-received formulas. Thus we should consider the possibility that the concentration of unique and unusual expressions in the narrative also mark it as a late composition. However, we should perhaps also entertain alternate explanations. For example, the innovative expressions coined by the authors of Judg 19–21 might not have left a mark on subsequent literature because the language took a sharp turn in the direction of LBH shortly thereafter. It is also possible that the narrative was a peripheral composition, which did not enjoy widespread circulation, and for this reason exerted only limited literary influence.

Finally, the study of the language of Judg 19–21 may provide a basis for conclusions regarding the relation between its authors and the scribes that produced and transmitted the Deuteronomistic and Priestly literary corpora. All instances of Priestly vocabulary fall within sections ascribed to R². The author of N¹ may not have been influenced by Priestly literature, either because he was distanced from the Priestly circles within which these works were composed, transmitted, and circulated, or because the Priestly corpora postdated his composition. Although R² was already familiar with Priestly vocabulary, his use of unusual phrases, like קהל עם האלהים and זקני העדה, may indicate that he too stood outside mainstream Priestly tra-

---

251. Sixteen instances in N¹ (20:12, 21, 31, 37, 38–43, 45; 21:14, 22, 24) and fifteen instances in R² (20:1aγ, 2–6, 16, 33–35, 48; 21:5, 15–16).

252. Three instances in N¹ (21:14, 22, 24) and four instances in R² (21:5, 15, 16).

dition. More debated is the relationship between N¹ and Deuteronomistic scribal circles. Over the last forty years, different scholars have argued that N¹ was composed or edited by Deuteronomistic scribes and incorporated into one of the editions of the Deuteronomistic History.[253] Indeed, the narrator occasionally employs phraseology familiar from Deuteronomistic contexts, but this is also true of authors of other works from the postexilic period, such as Ezekiel, Nehemiah, and Chronicles. Only a thorough comparison of the idioms and their contexts can indicate whether the use of the Deuteronomistic language is derivative or whether it might indicate Deuteronomistic composition. This I shall undertake in the course of the next chapter, as I examine the nature of the relations *between* Judg 19–21 and its various biblical intertexts.

---

253. See, e.g., Schunck 1963, 60–68; Veijola 1977, 16–22; Soggin 1987, 280–303; Mayes 2001, 256–58.

4
TEXT, SUBTEXT, AND INTERTEXTUAL MOSAIC

The discussion in the previous chapters raised the possibility that the author(s) of Judg 19–21 drew upon previous sources, such as fragments from a poetic source, and employed some traditional compositional models, such as type-scenes. My examination of the geographical background and the linguistic characteristics of the composition lead me to surmise that the narrative was composed in the Babylonian period or perhaps even at the beginning of the Persian period. The question to be examined now is whether the relative lateness of composition is also evident in the relationship between Judg 19–21 and other biblical texts.

4.1. THEORY AND METHOD IN ANALYZING INTERTEXTUAL RELATIONS

Scholars have long realized that the story of the war against Benjamin in Judg 19–21 has literary connections with other biblical texts, particularly with the story of Lot in Gen 19,[1] the story of the conquest of Ai in Josh 7–8, and the incident in which Saul dismembers two oxen in order to mobilize troops against the Ammonites in 1 Sam 11. Although the interrelatedness of the texts is widely accepted, there has been some dispute whether the similarities between any two texts are evidence that one of the texts was patterned on the other[2] or that both derive from a common

---

1. Josephus already seems sensitive to the interrelation between Judg 19 and Gen 19, since he inserts into the Gibeah story a description that is based upon Gen 19:9; see *Ant.* 5.2.9 §144; see also Pseudo-Philo, *Bib. Ant.* 45.2–3. The analogy is also mentioned by Nachmanides when commenting on Gen 19:8.
2. Thus, e.g., Wellhausen (1957, 235–37), Burney (1970, 444), Lasine (1984, 37–41), and Soggin (1987, 282) found Judg 19 to be dependent upon Gen 19, while the opposite was argued by Westermann (1985, 297–300), Jüngling (1981, 210, 291), and Niditch (1982, 376–78).

source,³ or whether such similarity results from formulaic or stereotypical composition.⁴ Others have adopted a synchronic approach, concentrating on the final form of the biblical texts and reading one text in the light of another without regard for their diachronic relations. In view of the multiplicity of approaches, it seems necessary to examine the validity of their premises and to characterize the nature and types of interrelations between texts in order to distinguish incidental associations from formal, literary relationships. Only then will it be possible to formulate criteria for identifying and characterizing the interrelations between Judg 19–21 and other texts.⁵

Poststructuralism and the Concept of Intertextuality

Associative relation between texts is broadly covered by the now popular term *intertextuality*. The term *intertextuality* was coined by Julia Kristeva in her study of the "dialogic" role of poetic discourse in Bakhtin's literary criticism (1967).⁶ Intertextuality, as conceived by Kristeva, indicates the ongoing dialogue between a text and any other semiotic system and is not limited to the relationships between literary texts.⁷ In response to Kristeva's pioneering work, poststructuralist critics viewed intertextuality as an aspect of the process of reading, rather than as a characteristic inherent to texts. In other words, they rejected the idea that intertextuality is a property instilled by authors into texts, but rather held that *all* texts are potentially intertextual and that this potential is realized by the reader. Every text, according to Derrida, is imprinted with the "traces" of all the texts that preceded it, and even the choice *not* to interact with a text is a recognition of its trace.⁸ Thus all readers read intertextually, for they interpret every new text in the light of all texts they previously read (even if this means reading Homer's *Odyssey* in light of Joyce's *Ulysses*). Hence text

---

3. On Gen 19/Judg 19, see, e.g., Schulte 1972, 98–100; Rudin 1982, 105; on Josh 8/Judg 20, see Rösel 1976, 36.
4. See, e.g., Culley 1976, 56–59, on Gen 19/Judg 19; Mazor 1994, 99–106; and Nelson 1997, 111–12, on Josh 8/Judg 20.
5. See also Mettinger 1993, 257–65.
6. Kristeva 1986a; cf. Tull 2000, 60–61, 68–72.
7. Kristeva 1986b, 111; cf. Biddle 2002, 619.
8. Derrida 1979, 84, 97, 122–23, 136–37; Frow 1990, 45; see Bautch 2007, 31, on material from the DtrH that was excluded from Chronicles.

production is an ongoing process carried out by an infinite succession of readers who instill the text with significance, and the historical author is no more and no less than the first reader of a text. The concept of intertextuality served as one means for appropriating the rights to text production from the author and transferring them to the reader. Thus according to the ideology behind the poststructuralist theory of intertextuality, there is no reason to favor reading a text as its author intended, for that reading is but one of a myriad of possible readings, none of which is more valid than the other.[9] Here it should be noted that the ideology behind poststructural criticism developed within the historical context of New Left Paris in the late 1960s. The concept of intertextuality served to blur the boundaries separating texts, and thus texts came to be viewed as products of a communal cultural effort, rather than as the creation of individual authors.[10] In this light, the literary terms and concepts conceived and furthered by the poststructuralist critics are tied to a far-reaching political-cultural program, which is not amenable to partial adaptation or implementation. Stripped of its ideological trappings, "intertextuality" simply indicates the relationship between any two texts.[11] Within the poststructuralist program, "intertextuality" is irrelevant to, and even at odds with, the study of literary influence, dependence, and authorial intention.[12]

Poststructural criticism, along with concepts of intertextuality and the "death of the author," enjoyed a large amount of popularity in biblical literary studies since the 1990s.[13] But while poststructural criticism may be helpful in reactualizing ancient texts and uncovering new relevance for modern readers, it does not produce fruitful results for the histori-

---

9. Barthes 1979, 76–79; Tull 2000, 63; cf. Childs 2003, 175; Labahn 2003, 55–56.
10. Mai 1991, 37–41.
11. On this point, see criticism by van Wolde 1997, 3.
12. See Barthes 1979, 77. However, Culler (1981, 98, 104–7) showed that some of the post-structuralists (e.g., Jenny, Riffaterre, and even Kristeva) did not completely free themselves from discussion of literary sources and influence; see also Riffaterre 1990, 56–58.
13. The number of studies dealing with biblical intertextuality has tripled at least since my earlier study (Edenburg 1998). The bibliography of Tull's (2000, 86–90) survey lists sixty-six entries, while a keyword search of the ATLAS database produces 186 publications from 2000 to 2008 alone. See also collected essays edited by Fewell 1992; Exum and Clines 1993; Aichele and Phillips 1995; and the essays from the IOSOT session on "Intertextuality and the Pluralism of Methods" in Lemaire and Sæbø 2000, 17–78.

cal inquiry into the growth of a composition or its purpose. Since poststructuralist critics hold that intertextuality is characteristic of the process of reading and not inherent to a composition, their approach does not indicate anything about sources that influenced a work. Indeed, poststructural critics attach little importance to the historical process by which a composition evolved, and instead emphasize the creativity inherent to the process of reading, by which each (re-)reading produces endless variations of the text.[14] Thus the concept of intertextuality, as developed by the poststructuralist critics, is next to useless in advancing historical research, for the historical literary inquiry is based upon uncovering the relationship between text and its compositional context.

Intertextuality has become a fashionable catchword, but most now employ the term to indicate literary influences and sources.[15] In fact, the term is widely used to indicate various different literary phenomena, such as allusion, secondary use or reutilization, literary dependency, and parallel versions. In this state of affairs, the use of the fashionable term, stripped of its ideological charge, only results in obscuring the nature of the specific literary phenomena perceived in the text. If intertextuality is to be a meaningful term, we should understand it and use it as an integral element of the poststructural literary approach, and if our interests are historical rather than interpretive actualization, we should forgo use of the term.[16] In any case, the term has become a prevalent and convenient means for designating textual interrelations, and some have even limited its sense to signify only textual interrelations that may be verified by specific textual signs.

Nature and Types of Textual Interrelations

Before passing on to consider the nature and types of textual interrelations, it is necessary to state what may appear to be obvious: interrelatedness is

---

14. Tull 2000, 63–64.

15. See, e.g., Nogalski 1996, 102, who employs the term to indicate "the interrelationship between two or more texts which *evidence suggests* (1) was deliberately established by ancient authors/editors or (2) was presupposed by those authors/editors"; see also Bergey 2003, 36, 47, who equates intertextuality with borrowing; see also Biddle 2002, 619–20. Kristeva (1986b, 111) protested this appropriation of the term, and finally replaced it for her purposes with the term *transposition*.

16. See also Sommer 1998, 8–10; cf. van Wolde 1997, 4.

not a quality residing in the single text but is perceived by a reader who places the text within a wider context.[17] This statement has far-reaching consequences for understanding the nature and character of textual interrelations, for most texts do not overtly quote, cite, or refer to other texts. Thus interrelationship between texts is a potentiality that is activated when the process of reading triggers a range of associations, leading the reader to other texts. Readers may relate one text to another solely on the basis of free association, but in some cases intertextual association is triggered by specific textual signs, and only such cases admit the possibility of literary interrelation. Yet the presence of textual triggers is not necessarily indicative of authorial intent since unrelated texts frequently share common generic characteristics, such as structure, subject, or type. Thus it is necessary to survey the nature of the various associative phenomena in order to distinguish between incidental textual triggers that are dictated by formal considerations and between signs that may indicate authorial intent.

Common formal structure. Fixed structures derive from literary tradition and are a formal characteristic of genres, type-scenes, and narrative patterns. Since texts that belong to a common genre or literary pattern share a similar structure, readers might perceive an association between them. However, such an association is like that which exists between one contract or business letter and another—all are written according to the same form, even when they stem from different hands, writing about different matters.[18] In such cases readers might perceive connections between texts due to a structural similarity that is imposed by external formal considerations. Sometimes the external formal considerations are circumvented when an author employs a typical structure for a purpose foreign to its original genre, for example, when the structure of a battle report is employed to describe a love tryst. Hence texts that employ a structure foreign to their genre may stimulate readers to associate them with other texts whose common structure actually derives from their particular genre.[19]

Common motifs. A motif constitutes a single image or theme that can be represented by a short phrase or a single idea. Thus both readers and hearers are likely to associate one text with another on the basis of shared motifs. For example, the numerous occurrences of the "younger

---

17. So also Charlesworth 2006, 43.
18. See Gunn 1974a, 1974b; Alter 1978, 1981, 47–62; Nobel 2002, 232–46.
19. Culler 2002, 153–87; Miner 1993, 40.

son preferred" motif in Genesis (Gen 4:1–5; 17:18–21; 21:12–13; 28:1–9; 37:3; 48:13–19) could produce free associations between these stories as they are performed, and their hearers might also associate them with the similar motifs in 1 Sam 9:20–21 and 16:8–12. Indeed, it is possible that this perception hits upon the very intention behind the use of this motif.[20] However, a recurring motif stemming from popular tradition can also trigger associations between texts, regardless of the divergent use of the motif. For example, the motif of YHWH restraining or dividing the waters occurs in diverse narrative and poetic contexts that do not agree in either details or wording (e.g., Exod 14:21–16; 15:3–10; Josh 3:13–17; Isa 27:1; 51:9–10; Pss 74:13–17; 89:10–11; 104:3–10; Job 26:8–13; 38:8–11).[21] In such a case, readers link together texts that independently drew upon the same traditional motif, while the texts themselves are not necessarily "genetically" related to one another.[22]

Brevard Childs draws attention to a related phenomenon by which readers draw analogies between texts on the basis of shared keywords that then are held to represent broader concepts. When these concepts are subsequently read back into the text without regard for semantic differences in context, the reader is liable to construct significance that is not grounded in the text itself.[23]

Doublets. Doublets convey parallel accounts of a single event and awaken a sense of familiarity within readers who read them synchronically in a shared narrative context. Usually, scholars assumed that a single narrator would not relate the same event twice, hence parallel stories were assigned to separate sources that were combined or placed side by side by an editor with antiquarian interests.[24] A more recent approach holds that doublets might derive from an editorial method in which a rewritten version is placed alongside its "parent" in order to revise the outlook, tendencies, ideals, and concepts that are embodied in the previous narrative.[25]

---

20. See Nogalski 1996, 116–18, on intentional use of the locust motif in the Twelve.
21. See, e.g., Cassuto 1973; Day 1985; Rochberg 2008.
22. See Charlesworth 2006, 48–49.
23. Childs 2003, 178–79.
24. So already Spinoza, *Theological-Political Treatise* (1670), ch. 9; see also Van Seters 1975, 154, 161–64. For a recent and full review of the history of scholarship regarding doublets and tradition variants, see Nahkola, 2001.
25. See, e.g., Sandmel 1961, 120–22; Van Seters 1975, 161–68; Edenburg forthcoming b.

The view of doublets as an editorial device for revision explains why doublets are usually provided with differing circumstances or chronological data that allow the recurring accounts to be read synchronically in the same narrative context. Thus although two different stories tell how Hagar left Abraham's house and wandered in the wilderness until she encounters a divine messenger by a well, the different narrative circumstances make it possible for the two stories to abide side by side in harmony within a larger narrative framework. In the first account Hagar, who is pregnant with Abraham's seed, *flees* due to the abuse she suffers at the hands of her mistress and finally is ordered by the saving angel to return to her mistress. In the second account, Hagar is *banished* for good from Abraham's household, along with the child she bore to Abraham. Thus the two stories about the departure of Hagar from Abraham's household (Gen 16; 21) represent different phases in the story of Abraham. Moreover, parallel accounts may function as a poetic device for depicting recurring events or may serve to present a common theme from different viewpoints. Thus it is feasible, in some cases, that a single author could be responsible for both accounts of a doublet.[26]

Variant accounts. Variant accounts describe divergent and sometimes contradictory circumstances relating to a single event, as with the variant accounts regarding Esau's loss of the birthright in Gen 25:19–34 and 27:1–36. In this case, the two accounts do not really conflict, and generations of readers have had no difficulty reading them as successive events in a single narrative progression.[27] Such divergent accounts may derive as variants on a common theme that were woven into a single narrative framework out of antiquarian interests. Nonetheless, variants can also be composed for the purpose of revision or in order to present an event from different points of view.[28]

Text commenting on text. Sometimes readers may find that a text explicates or comments on a subject, concept, or expression found in another text. This phenomenon has sometimes been called "inner-biblical exegesis" or "inner-biblical interpretation" and has had considerable influence

---

26. See, e.g., Whybray 1987, 76–78; Polak 1994, 351–52; Edenburg 1998, 77–81.

27. In Gen 25:27–34 Esau sells his birthright (בכרה) to Jacob, while in 27:35 Jacob takes the *blessing* (ברכה) of the firstborn, and the paronomasia in 27:36 (ברכה/בכרה) hints at the role of the blessing in establishing the rights of the firstborn.

28. E.g., the variants dealing with killing of Goliath in 1 Sam 17:4, 23, 40–51; 2 Sam 21:19; 1 Chr 20:5; see Seeligman 1962, 312–13; 1963, 401–2.

upon biblical studies, particularly since the initial publication of Michael Fishbane's in-depth study, *Biblical Interpretation in Ancient Israel* in 1985.[29] Fishbane identified four major categories of inner-biblical exegesis, which include "haggadic exegesis" of themes, motifs, and even events. The all-embracing use of the term *inner-biblical exegesis* drew criticism, particularly since is often employed when discussing allusion.[30] Truly exegetical concerns are evident in other categories discussed by Fishbane, such as interpretive glosses, explicative expansions, and narrative actualization of law or religious ideology. Thus Jer 28:7–9 might be considered an interpretive actualization of the law regarding the prophet in Deut 18:21–22.[31] However, the interpretive text is not necessarily later than the text that motivated interpretation. This is particularly true with "antiquarian" comments that purport to preserve information about ancient names or practices.[32] These are not necessarily late glosses but may have been included by the author in order to bolster the authority of his narrative.

Allusion. Allusion is a poetic device in which one text constructs a covert level of significance by indirectly invoking another text. For allusion to fulfill its purpose as a means for transmitting significance, it must be accompanied by textual markers that alert the reader to an underlying significance.[33] The marker may be a verbal element, pattern, or structure that is "borrowed" from another text where it is at home and is planted in a new, foreign context. The reader becomes aware of the marker due to its foreignness since it introduces an element that is not fully actualized in the overt layer of the new text. The foreignness of the marker breaks the rules of the text's narrative grammar and hampers the superficial comprehension of the text's overt significance. The perceived "ungrammaticality" signals the presence of the marker and provokes the reader to seek another textual context in which it was originally integrated.[34]

---

29. For the term *inner-biblical exegesis*, see Sarna 1963 and Fishbane 1988, 7–19.

30. For criticism of the use of the term, see Kugel 1987, 280. The necessity to distinguish between inner-biblical exegesis and inner-biblical allusion is discussed by Sommer 1998, 17–18, 23; and Meek 2014, 288–89.

31. See, e.g., Davidson 1964; Carroll 1986, 544.

32. See antiquarian notices about toponyms, e.g., Josh 14:15; 15:15; Judg 1:10, 11, 23; peoples, e.g., Deut 2:10, 12, 20; institutions, e.g., 1 Sam 9:9; Ruth 4:7.

33. Ben-Porat 1976; 1978, 2; cf. Nogalski 1996, 109; Sommer 1998, 10–13.

34. Riffaterre 1978, 2, 136; cf. Ben-Porat 1976, 107–10. Berlin (1984, 10) wondered how many and what type of points of contact must be detected in order to identify use of allusion. This can be answered according to Ben-Porat's definitions,

In this process the reader (re)creates links between the two (or more) texts. Readers may read the texts synchronically to examine the mutual relations between them and find that the newly found text relates to the base text in either a paragonic or polemic fashion. Or readers may discover that the newly found text enriches the first with covert levels of significance.[35] Notwithstanding, there is no guarantee that readers will decode the markers and identify the allusions. The probability of success improves when the alluded text belongs to a recognized literary canon and when the readers' literary competence approaches that of the author, for then they will draw upon approximately the same stock of texts used by the author in formulating the allusion.[36] From all this, it is clear that allusion represents a diachronic literary dependency, since it serves as a device for reactualizing a prior text. Thus use of allusion is significant for determining both the diachronic relations between texts, as well as the authoritative standing of the alluded text.[37]

Quotation. A quotation is a saying extracted from an external source and planted in a new context. As with allusion, quotation also indicates diachronic relations between texts, since the quoting text is recycling previous material. Marked quotation occurs when formal signs attribute part of a text to an external source, as in Ezek 18:2: "What do you mean by repeat-

---

which stress that the quantitative character of the marker is not relevant to determining use of allusion; the significant criterion remains the foreignness of the marker in the context of the alluding text, compared to its natural integration in the alluded text.

35. Hebel 1989, 15; cf. Sommer 1998, 15.

36. See Riffaterre 1978, 5; Ben-Porat 1985, 172, 175; Miner 1993, 39; Tull 2000, 63. Literary competence indicates the sum of literary and cultural associations absorbed by the reader throughout one's life, and which enables one to identify a text even when displaced from its context. The term *literary competence* was coined by Culler, along the lines of the Chomsky's concept of "linguistic competence," which denotes the internal grammar absorbed from infancy by people living in verbal societies; this internal grammar providing the means that enables basic communication among people speaking the same language. However, it should be noted that the two terms are not commensurate. One is not more, or less, linguistically competent, because competence is a condition for verbal communication. By contrast, there is a qualitative aspect to the concept of literary competence. In other words, the stock of texts upon which a person can draw for literary inference and association increases proportionately the more one is exposed to literary texts, thus making one more literarily competent; see Culler 1981, 50–52; Hebel 1989, 8. For an attempt to measure literary competence, see Ben-Porat 1978.

37. Ben-Porat 1985, 172; Hebel 1989, 16; Sommer 1998, 18–19; Floyd 2003, 226.

ing this proverb ... saying [לאמר], 'The fathers have eaten sour grapes, and the children's teeth are set on edge.'" Here the speech marker לאמר sets the proverb apart from its context. The quoted material becomes part of its new context through the dialogue the text holds with the quotation. In this case, the author enters into polemic discourse on the proverb: "As I live, says the Lord YHWH, this proverb shall no longer be used in Israel" (Ezek 18:3), and this dispute is used to lead up to the author's particular doctrine of retribution. Some passages are verbally identical (or nearly identical) to formulations occurring in another context but lack formal markers of citation. Even then, a passage may be perceived as quotation due to tension (or ungrammaticality) that arises in its present context.[38] For example, the Gibeonites' words, "Your servants came from a very distant land for the sake of YHWH your God, for we heard of his fame and all he did in Egypt" (Josh 9:9), interact with Solomon's prayer in 1 Kgs 8:41–42: "Even the foreigner, who is not of your people Israel, who comes from a distant land for your name's sake, for they heard of your great name and your strong hand and outstretched arm, and came to pray at this house." The combination of expressions shared by these two texts is unique and probably indicates unmarked citation. In this case it would be strange if the author of this section of Solomon's prayer should echo the words of the Gibeonites when portraying his pious foreigner, but it does make sense that author of the story of the Gibeonites should have them parrot the words of Solomon's prayer in order to reinforce the irony of their deception.[39] Such transformation of unmarked citation is characteristic of parody, which uses citation in order to satirize either the cited text or the speaker in the quoting text.[40] Unmarked citation can thus be a marker of allusion, used to enhance the text with added authority, or for polemic or parody.[41]

CRITERIA FOR EVALUATING THE LITERARY RELATIONSHIP
BETWEEN TEXTS

This survey shows how various literary phenomena motivate readers to associate texts with one another, even when they are not historically

---

38. Still and Wharton 1990, 11; cf. Gordis 1949, 166; Fox 1980; Sommer 1998, 21–22.
39. Edenburg 2012a, 124.
40. Rose 1979, 25–26, 54–55.
41. Hebel 1989, 7; A. Wright 1966, 446; Hoffman 1988, 77; Sommer 1998, 28–30.

TEXT, SUBTEXT, AND INTERTEXTUAL MOSAIC 171

related. Such may happen with common motifs, fixed structures, doublets, and variant accounts. Hence strict criteria are necessary in order to distinguish between free association of texts and between *author-intended* textual linking. Even if the biblical authors were available to be interrogated about their intentions, literary critics agree that authors are not necessarily faithful witnesses regarding their intents. Hence criteria for establishing direct literary relation between texts must center on textual evidence.

Before proceeding to formulate such criteria, it is necessary to deal with two objections that challenge the investigation of direct literary relationship and literary dependency. The first objection arises from the fact that biblical discourse makes prominent use of formulaic language and closed lexical sets of technical or ideological terms (such as specific "Priestly" terms and wisdom vocabulary). Hence similar formulation of different texts does not necessarily point to literary dependency, since it might derive from formulaic language or literary convention.[42] This objection can be dealt with by basing arguments for direct literary relationship upon points of similarity that go beyond set formulas or literary conventions.

The second objection arises from the possibility that two similar texts are not directly related but developed independently from a no longer extant third source.[43] However, the lost common source theory is not subject to falsification or validation; therefore, it should not detract from weighing the evidence in the texts before us and considering the likelihood that one rewrites the other. A variation on the third source objection raises the possibility that similar texts derive from common tradition. Such a supposition might be justified when texts only share similar motifs, structure, or formulaic language, but the common tradition explanation loses its credibility when the points of contact include a uniquely shared, uncommon idiom, which most likely derived from acquaintance with a written literary composition. Here too the common tradition is just as intangible as the lost third literary source. We may speculate about the nature of a preliterary tradition, but its shape and formulation are no longer accessible to us.

In all, I propose six criteria for discerning literary dependency.

1. *Similarity of formulation.* In order to avoid the pitfalls of casual or incidental similarity, it is necessary to avoid claiming literary interrelationship

---

42. Hurvitz 1982, 14; Fishbane 1988, 13, 288; Nogalski 1996, 109.
43. See Hurvitz (1982, 14) for the objection, and Rösel (1976, 34) for actualization of this claim.

on the basis of formulaic expressions, popular axioms, or vocabulary characteristic to the subject matter or genre.[44] However, the unique recurrence of peculiar formulations may indicate intentional allusion to a previous text. Such peculiar formulations include otherwise unattested forms, words, or phraseology, as well as more common expressions that are employed in an uncharacteristic fashion. Recurrent use of rare but not unique expressions may be viewed as supporting evidence but should not serve as the prime basis for literary interrelationship, since our knowledge of the language of the biblical authors is limited to a closed corpus of texts, and what appears to be rare within the framework of those texts may have had wider actual usage. It is likely that a longer text will display more common formulations than a short text, but in either case the peculiarity or uniqueness of a common formulation should decide the case. The clustering of common formulations would seem to be evidence that the texts are interrelated; however, this is not a necessary condition since an initial point of literary contact between texts may influence the shape an author gives his text by scattering throughout additional points of contact.[45]

2. *Similarity of context and/or structure.* Similar context or structure may cause readers to draw analogies between texts, but analogy is the product of the interpretive process and cannot directly attest to authorial intent. Since such similarity may only be incidental, it should not provide the basis for the claim. However, similarity of context or structure might strengthen a claim to literary interrelation based upon the criterion of formulation.

3. *Transformation and reactualization of a common element.* This criterion focuses on identifying an intentional change in form or actualization of a common element. Such an intentional transformation can be seen in the formulative or functional inversion of a common element[46] or in an atypical actualization of a formulaic or generic element, as frequently occurs in parody.[47]

4. *"Ungrammatical" actualization of a common element.* Ungrammaticality represents an abrogation of the text's inner logic. In this context, ungrammaticality arises not only from disrupting language norms, but also from employing dysfunctional or "blind" motifs. Some have argued

---

44. See, e.g., Floyd 2003, 230.
45. See, e.g., Magonet 1983, 73–74; cf. Nogalski 1996, 109; Floyd 2003, 239.
46. Seidel 1956, 150; Lasine 1984, 39–40; Zakovitch 1985, 1993; Beentjes 1996.
47. Rose 1979, 21–23.

that narrative ungrammaticality is but a by-product of textual corruption.[48] Indeed, this can be the case, particularly when other textual witnesses provide alternate readings and when it is possible to reconstruct the process by which the text became corrupt. Nonetheless, the alternative readings attested in other witnesses may have been produced in an attempt to simplify a difficult text.[49] As indicated above, ungrammaticality can be an intentional marker of allusion. Thus I consider the ungrammaticality of a common element to be a deciding factor in establishing textual interrelations, particularly when accompanied by other indications of possible interrelatedness, such as similarity in formulation or structure.

5. *Interaction between texts*. I distinguish between two types of textual interaction. In the first type, one text reacts to the other with interpretation, supplementation, or polemic. In the second type, one text "reuses" another to construct subtextual levels of significance. Both types indicate intentional textual interaction.

6. *Accumulative evidence*. Since each individual criterion is subjective to some degree, the weight of accumulative evidence will strengthen the claim of interrelatedness. Even so, the weight attached to the various criteria differs. Therefore, literary interrelation should be proposed only when at least one of the following conditions obtains: (1) unique or rare similarity of formulation, along with other evidence for interrelation; (2) transformation or reactulization of a common element (as with allusion), along with similarity in formulation (not necessarily unique or rare); (3) ungrammaticality of a common element, along with similarity in formulation (not necessarily unique or rare). Of course, the force of the claim will be strengthened according to accumulation of different types of evidence to each of the above conditions.

The question of literary dependency and its direction can be considered only after establishing the existence of a literary interrelation between the texts. The possibility of literary dependency obtains in two cases:

First, an element in one text motivates the shape, formulation or topic of the other text. This condition is evident when a particular common element is fully functional in the one text A but is conspicuous in its ungrammaticality in the other text B; the ungrammaticality indicates that text B borrowed the element from a context in which it was functional, in this

---

48. Cf. S. McKenzie 2010, 440–42, on 1 Sam 24:5–8; and my caveats in Edenburg forthcoming b.
49. Albrektson 1981; Tov 1992, 302–5.

case text A.⁵⁰ This leads to the conclusion that text B is literarily dependent upon text A. This criterion comes into play at an early stage, for ungrammaticality is already perceived in the process of reading, and it motivates the search for another interrelated text.

Second, the comprehension of text B is dependent upon knowledge of text A.⁵¹ This criterion comes into play only after textual interrelationship has been established. Only then is it possible to examine whether the texts display a one-way relationship in which text B is dependent upon and makes use of text A or whether they originated independently of one another.

Admittedly, there may be cases of literary dependency that do not display the conditions required by these two criteria. However, it is methodologically preferable to limit the scope of literary dependency by stringent formal criteria than to consider all cases of literary analogy to be products of literary dependency. In the following, I shall examine the relations between Judg 19–21 and different biblical texts in order to determine which parallels indicate literary dependency and whether Judg 19–21 influenced other texts or whether it was patterned upon them.

Finally, it is necessary to consider the scribe's purpose in evoking previous texts. For example, it is possible that the author reused earlier traditional material in order to imbue his narrative with authority. The reuse of parallel material may also enrich the message of the receptive text by evoking the values and ideas of its sources. Consideration of all these factors not only will aid in placing Judg 19–21 within the framework of relative chronology for biblical literature but will also help uncover the purpose of the composition and characterize its author's concerns, style, and literary competency.

4.2. Abraham and Lot (Gen 18–19)

Structure and Motifs in Judg 19:15–25 and Gen 19:1–13

The similarity between the story of the Outrage at Gibeah (Judg 19) and the story of Sodom (Gen 19) is widely known, but opinions vary greatly regarding the nature and origin of the interrelations.⁵² In both stories,

---

50. Van Seters 1975, 163; Lasine 1984, 39; Brettler 1989a, 411.
51. Magonet 1983, 66; Lasine 1984, 38–39.
52. E.g., for Judg 19 being dependent on Gen 19; see Wellhausen 1957, 235–37;

wayfarers arrive in a strange town, but the townspeople offer no hospitality and only a resident alien grants the guests shelter. During their stay, the people of the town threaten the guests, while the host tries to protect them by negotiating with the mob.

The resemblance between the stories in both structure and language is surprising, since the parallel sections are set in quite different contexts. In the story of Sodom, divine messengers arrive at the town in order to test the townsmen's behavior. In Judg 19, by contrast, the wayfarers stop at Gibeah by chance. The Levite intended to complete the trip in one day, but the stopover became necessary since they departed Bethlehem late in the day and feared to stay in Jebus. The random nature of their destination is marked in the Levite's words: "We shall approach one of these places and stay in Gibeah or Ramah" (19:13), and only the lateness of the hour finally determined where to stay. Also, the results of the visit differ in the two stories. In Sodom, the hostile reception of the guests sufficed for them to render judgment on the spot (Gen 19:13) without waiting to see whether the threatened rape would be carried out. On this point Judg 19 differs; the threat is indeed carried out, not upon the intended victim, the Levite, but upon the concubine, and judgment is deferred until the tribes assemble to investigate the circumstances of the Levite's gruesome message. Finally, each story focuses on a different character. The story of Sodom centers on the figure of Lot and his family, while the guests mainly serve as a means for advancing the plot. The story of Gibeah, however, centers on the figures of the guests—the Levite and the concubine—while the host disappears from the story at the height of the confrontation with the people of the town. These differences indicate that whatever the origin of the similarities, neither story is a blind reflection of the other. Each, rather, is an independent and purposeful composition. Thus the question of the literary interrelationships cannot be determined on the basis of the general similarity between the stories, and instead requires in-depth analysis of the parallel motifs and structural elements, as follows.

Moore 1895, 417; Budde 1897, 131; Gunkel 1910, 217; Burney 1970, 444; van den Born 1954, 210–11; Gray 1986, 226; Boling 1975, 279; Lasine 1984, 37–41; Soggin 1987, 282. For Gen 19 being dependent on Judg 19, see Westermann 1985, 297–300; Niditch 1982, 376–78; Jüngling 1981, 210, 291. For Gen 19 and Judg 19 deriving from a common source, tradition, or theme, see von Rad 1972, 218; Schulte 1972, 98, 100; Rudin-O'Brasky 1982, 105; Arnold 1990, 72–76; Niditch 2008, 192.

The encounter between guests and host. In Gen 19 Lot encounters the guests by the city gate, where he has been sitting. The narrator does not explain why Lot was sitting by the gate, but only describes his behavior from the moment he saw the messengers (vv. 1–2). This creates the impression that Lot had no other purpose than to await arriving wayfarers and offer them hospitality. This purpose is heightened when Lot presses the divine messengers to reconsider their refusal and accept his invitation. Lot's figure, then, stands in converse analogy to that of the men of Sodom, who do not honor the practice of hospitality and who refuse to acknowledge Lot's duty to protect his guests.[53] The converse analogy hints that in contrast to the people of Sodom, Lot has successfully passed the messengers' trial.

The figure of the alien host stands in converse analogy to that of the townspeople in the Gibeah story too, but the purpose of this analogy is not realized since the host disappears from the story at its climax. Moreover, some of the shared motifs are employed in a significantly different fashion. So, for example, the visitors at Gibeah (the Levite and his concubine) sit in the square because "no one took them home to lodge" (Judg 19:15), as opposed to Lot who sat waiting for chance wayfarers. The host at Gibeah encountered the visitors by chance on his way home from his day's work in the field, and in contrast to Lot, he extends an invitation only after questioning the Levite regarding his origins and doings (vv. 16–17). In addition, while Gen 19:3 emphasizes the trouble Lot takes in providing for his guests needs, Judg 19 describes the Ephraimite's hospitality in a cursory fashion: "he fed the donkeys and they washed their feet and ate and drank."[54] It appears that these descriptions in the Gibeah story are aimed to create a gloomy atmosphere prefiguring the coming developments. The visitors sit in the square since no one offers them lodging, and even the resident alien expresses reluctance in extending his invitation (v. 20, "Just don't stay in the square").

---

53. According to Matthews 1992, 3–11, only permanent residents had the right to offer hospitality, and since Lot was a resident alien, the people of Sodom did not recognize his obligation toward his guests. However, Matthews's view is not fully supported by the narrative, since the people of Sodom do seem to recognize his rights as a homeowner, and therefore do not initially attempt to forcibly remove the guests from the house.

54. See Gen 24:32–33; 43:24–25; see also Penchansky 1992, 78–80.

The motif of male rape. In both stories the men of the town demand that the host hand over the male guest(s) so they may use them sexually.[55] In both cases, the host counters by offering them women from his house, but the townsmen express their dissatisfaction (Gen 19:9; Judg 19:25). This motif is appropriate to the context of the story of Sodom, where both the guests are male. The breakdown of negotiations at this point intensifies the violent atmosphere and necessitates supernatural intervention on the part of the divine messengers, thus providing the basis for the judgment to destroy the city (Gen 19:9–13). In Judg 19 the situation is different, for there the guests include a woman, and no heavenly beings are at hand to intervene. Since the townsmen insisted on receiving the male guest and refuse the host's offer of women (Judg 19:25), the Levite's attempt to save himself and mollify the crowd by handing over his concubine appears desperate in the extreme. That this measure did indeed suffice requires explanation. One could assume that the townsmen were so aroused that they would satisfy themselves with any available sexual object, male or female, or, alternatively, that their demand for the Levite did not reflect any sexual preference but stemmed from their intention to shame the wayfarer and thus establish their domination over him.[56] However, a literary explanation must also be considered, namely, that the concubine is the axis around which the plot revolves. Her flight to Bethlehem caused the Levite to leave his home in Mount Ephraim in order to take her back, and his delayed departure from her father's house made it necessary for them to stay the night at Gibeah. Finally, the circumstances of her death provide the justification for the following pantribal war. Since the rape and death of the concubine are an integral part of the story in Judg 19, it would have

---

55. Most commentators agree that the verb ונדענו indicates sexual relations in both Gen 19 and Judg 19; see, e.g., Rashi and Kimchi on Judg 19:22; Nachmanides on Gen 19:8; as well as Moore 1895, 417; Westermann 1985, 301; Gray 1986, 352; Wenham 1994, 55. Boling (1975, 276) tried to expunge the sexual element from the townsmen's demand, as did Doyle (2004, 435–36) in discussing Gen 19; but their interpretation is at odds with the sexual nature of the host's counteroffer. Jüngling (1981, 205–10), who was influenced by Josephus's account (*Ant.* 5.2.8 §143), argued that while ידע carries sexual connotations in Gen 19, the verb indicates "to note" or "get to know" in Judg 19:22, 25. However, this significance does not occur elsewhere with the verb in *qal*, and appears to be limited to *niphal* (Ruth 3:3; Jer 28:9) and *hithpael* (Gen 45:1); see also Soggin's (1987, 288) incisive remarks.

56. See, e.g., Kaufmann 1961, 287; Stone 1995, 87–102; Niditch 2008, 193; Gross 2009, 824.

been more appropriate for the hostile townsmen to demand that the host hand *her* over to them, rather than the Levite. Since this is not the case, and since the motif of male rape is not consonant with the plot of Judg 19, it appears that the motif was borrowed from Gen 19 and applied to the men of Gibeah in order to create an analogy with Sodom, the archetype of the sinful city.[57] At the same time, the author of Judg 19 utilized the common motif in which rape of a woman is the postulated cause of a civil war,[58] and the application of the two disparate motifs gave rise to inconsistency in the narrative.

The host's counteroffer (Judg 19:24; Gen 19:8). In Gen 19:5–8 the townsmen's demand to receive the two male guests is symmetrically countered by Lot with his offer to hand over his two daughters. This offer highlights the lengths Lot will go in order to uphold the norms of hospitality and guarantee the safety of his guests, to the extent that he is willing to sacrifice his daughters' virginity. Such symmetry is not present in Judg 19. The men of Gibeah demand to receive only "the man who has come to your house" (v. 22), even though earlier mention was made of the male servant (נער) who accompanied him (vv. 11–13, 19).[59] In opposition to the mob's demand to hand over one man, the host offers two women, one of whom is his virgin daughter, while the other is the concubine of his male guest. It is also odd that the Ephraimite host should emphasize his concern for the welfare of the man staying in his house (v. 23) but would be willing to

---

57. Similarly, see Budde 1897, 131; Soggin 1987, 282; but see Kaufmann 1961, 287; and Jüngling 1981, 205, 290–91, who take a harmonistic approach.

58. For sexual relations as a metaphor for political relations, see, e.g., Eissfeldt 1963, 71–73; Gordon and Washington 1995. The motif is especially prominent in classical literature, and particularly in Livy (*Hist.* 1.9–10, 58–59; 3.44–50); see Joshel 1992, 112–30; and Guillaume 2004, 219–23. Rape or sexual assault is also a common metaphor in prophetic literature for the conquest of a city; see Gordon and Washington 1995, 315–18; Chapman 2004, 86–88, 106–8. Chapman (2004, 160–63) shows that Assyrian reliefs depicting conquest also employ violent sexual imagery of penetration, both of city walls and of male soldiers. These images might suggest that the rape motif in Judg 19–21 is not only intended to serve as a *causus belli*, but might also indicate a talionic relation between the offense and its penalty—the men of the town raped a woman to death, and as a result the Israelites penetrate and devastate their town.

59. Oddly, this point has gone unnoticed. נער does not necessarily designate youth; it can indicate an adult servant (e.g., Exod 33:11; 1 Sam 2:13, 15; 14:6; 2 Sam 9:9; 2 Kgs 5:20). Thus there is no reason to assume that the servant was ignored because he had not yet reached sexual maturity.

sacrifice his guest's concubine, over whom he had no rights.⁶⁰ It seems that this tension perceived in Judg 19 derives from its dependence upon Gen 19. The author of Judg 19 borrowed from Gen 19 the motif of the host who defends his guests by offering two women from his house.⁶¹ In his source, the women belonged to the host's family, thus showing how the ideal host would spare no means of his own in order to safeguard his guests. However, the circumstances of the story in Judg 19 made it necessary to hint at the concubine's fate, and thus the author traded one of the host's daughters for the concubine of the guest. This tactic casts a shadow on the host's character, but in any event he is depicted as a reluctant host who receives guests only after he is shamed by the Levite's mention that he has provisions of his own (v. 19). This characterization of the Levite may have been intended to cast him as an antithesis to Lot.⁶²

Formulation in Judg 19:15–25 and Gen 19:1–13

The formulation of both scenes (Gen 19:1–10; Judg 19:10–25) is closely interrelated, and most of the parallels go beyond common formulas.

Gen 19:1–10	Judg 19:15–25
¹ The two messengers arrived in Sodom in the evening, as Lot was **sitting** *in the gate of Sodom*. When Lot saw them, he rose to meet them, and bowing low with his face to the ground, ² he said: Please, my lords, turn aside to your servant's house to spend the night and **bathe your feet**; then you may be on your way early.	¹⁵ They turned away to come and spend the night at Gibeah. He came and **sat** *in the city square*, but no one took them home to spend the night. ¹⁶ Then appeared an old man....

---

60. See, e.g., Rudin-O'Brasky 1982, 110. Gray (1986, 348) surmised that two variant traditions were fused here, each of which dealt with the offer of a single woman by the man who had claim to her: the virgin daughter by the host (v. 24), and the concubine by the Levite (v. 25b). Budde (1897, 131), Jüngling (1981, 211), and Stipp (2006, 139, 150, 156) emend Judg 19:24 by eliminating mention of the concubine and reading "her" (לה, אותה) for MT "them" (להם, אותם).

61. So, too, Gross 2009, 825, 837, 840–41, although he views Judg 19:24 as a secondary addition to the narrative.

62. So Lasine 1984, 39; Alter 1986, 37; Klein 1988, 167–68; Brettler 1989a, 411.

But they said: No, **we shall spend the night in the square.** ³ But he urged them strongly, so they turned his way and **came to his house** [ויבאו אל ביתו]. He prepared a feast for them and baked flat bread, and **they ate.** ⁴ Before they lay down, **the men of the city—the men of** Sodom—**surrounded the house,** all the people, from young to old, to the last man. ⁵ They called out to Lot, and said to him: Where are **the men who came to your house** tonight? **Bring them out to us, so we may know them (sexually).**

⁶ Then **Lot went out to them** on the doorstep, closing the door after him ⁷ **and said: Please, my brothers, do not commit such evil.** ⁸ **Here,** *I have* two **daughters,** *who have not known a man*; **I shall bring them out to you and you may do to them as you see fit. Just don't do** anything **to these men, for** *they are under the shelter of my roof*.... ¹⁰ Then the men stretched out their hands and p̲u̲l̲l̲e̲d̲ ̲L̲o̲t̲ ̲i̲n̲t̲o̲ ̲t̲h̲e̲ ̲h̲o̲u̲s̲e̲ with them and closed the door....

²⁰ The old man said: Rest easy, all your needs are on me, only do not **stay the night in the square.** ²¹ He **brought them** [ויביאהו לביתו] **into his house** and fed the donkeys and **they bathed their feet** and ate and drank. ²² While they were enjoying themselves, **the men of the city—men of** no good—**surrounded the house** and pounded on the door. They said to the old homeowner, **Bring out the man who has come to your house, so we may know him (sexually).**

²³ The homeowner **went out to them and said** to them: **Don't, my brothers! Please do not commit such evil, for** *this man has entered my house. Do not* commit this outrage! ²⁴ **Here** *are my* **virgin** daughter and this man's concubine. **I shall bring them out** and you may rape them **and do to them as you see fit. Just don't do this** outrageous **thing to this man.** ²⁵ But the men would not listen to him, so the man seized his concubine and t̲h̲r̲u̲s̲t̲ ̲h̲e̲r̲ ̲o̲u̲t̲ to them....

Sleeping in the square (Judg 19:20; Gen 19:2, 8). The comment regarding sleeping in the square is formulated conversely in each story:

> Gen 19:2: לא כי ב̲ר̲ח̲ו̲ב̲ נלין (refusal of an invitation)
> Judg 19:20: רק ב̲ר̲ח̲ו̲ב̲ א̲ל̲ תלן (reluctant invitation)
> Gen 19:8: רק לאנשים האלה א̲ל̲ תעשו דבר

In Gen 19:2 the wayfarers insist they will sleep in the square, and this comment serves to test Lot to see whether he will persist with his invitation after it has been refused.⁶³ Since the trial motif is absent from Judg 19, the comment about sleeping in the square is voiced by the host and highlights the reluctance with of his invitation, which he extends as a last recourse.

---

63. See also Matthews 1992, 8.

TEXT, SUBTEXT, AND INTERTEXTUAL MOSAIC   181

The Ephraimite's words in Judg 19:20 also share with Gen 19:8 the rare formula expressing reservation: רק ... אל.⁶⁴ It is possible that the formulation of the Ephraimite's words in Judg 19:20 was influenced by two separate verses in the Sodom story, or that the formulation of Gen 19:8 is the product of secondary assimilation of Gen 19 to Judg 19.

Encircling the house (Judg 19:22; Gen 19:4):

Gen 19:4: ואנשי העיר אנשי סדם נסבו על־הבית מנער ועד־זקן כל־
העם מקצה
Judg 19:22: אנשי העיר אנשי בני־בליעל נסבו את־הבית מתדפקים
על־הדלת

The shared collocation, *x* אנשי העיר אנשי, is formed by two constructs in apposition. In Gen 19:4 the apposition serves to identify the subject by name and is equivalent to saying: "the men of the town, that is, the men of Sodom."⁶⁵ In Judg 19:22 the apposition serves to characterize the subject.⁶⁶ In both cases the expressions are problematic. In Gen 19:4 the apposition is unnecessary, since the identity of the townsmen is clear from the outset. It is possible that the phrase "the men of Sodom" is an interpretive interpolation,⁶⁷ but it is also possible that it serves to emphasize that all the Sodomites took part in the attack.⁶⁸ The difficulty in Judg 19:22 derives from the double construct אנשי בני־בליעל, which is a unique formulation.⁶⁹ The most economic explanation of this unusual collocation is that it cites and interprets the parallel expression in Gen 19:4. The term אנשי or בני בליעל characterizes people whose behavior runs against social

---

64. The formula occurs only twice more: Exod 8:25; Job 1:12.
65. See GKC §131.2e; see also 1 Chr 12:31; 2 Chr 17:13.
66. See GKC §131.2b; see also Mic 7:6.
67. See, e.g., Gunkel 1910, 208.
68. See, e.g., Westermann 1985, 301; Rudin-O'Brasky 1982, 110–11; Loader 1990, 37.
69. בליעל usually occurs in simple construct: בליעל (י)בנ (1 Sam 2:12; 10:27; 25:17; 1 Kgs 21:10, 13); אנשי/איש בליעל (1 Sam 25:25; 2 Sam 16:7; 20:1; 1 Kgs 21:13; Prov 16:27), or in apposition: אנשים בני בליעל (Deut 13:14; Judg 20:13; 1 Kgs 21:10, 13). According to Moore (1895, 419) and Kaufmann (1961, 286), the double construct is the result of corruption, and the original text read: אנשים בני בליעל. Others explained the double construct as the result of conflation of אנשי בליעל and בני בליעל; see, e.g., Boling 1975, 276; Soggin 1987, 288; Niditch 1982, 372 n. 11.

norms and order.[70] Thus by borrowing the phrase from Gen 19:4 and substituting בְּנֵי־בְלִיַּעַל for Sodom, N¹ in Judg 19:22 associates the base fellows at Gibeah with the men of Sodom.

The exhortation not to harm the guest (Judg 19:23; Gen 19:7). The syntax of the two similar sentences is unusual. Usually נָא + אַל occurs as a bound phrase joined by a *maqqef* in masoretic tradition. Usually the verb follows immediately after אַל־נָא, while the subject (if indicated) is placed after the verb.[71] Only in Judg 19:23 is אַל separated from נא by an intervening verb (אל תרעו נא), and this syntax emphasizes the negation of the verb. Moreover, only Gen 19:7 has the order אַל־נָא + *subject* [אחי] + *verb* [תרעו]. This order emphasizes the subject (אחי) as the target of the exhortation, since it immediately follows the injunctive construction אַל־נָא. In this case, a third passage (2 Sam 13:12) may cast light on the nature of the interrelation:

2 Sam 13:12   אל־אחי אל־תענני
Judg 19:23   אל־אחי אל־תרעו נא
Gen 19:7   אל־נא אחי תרעו

In all three cases the clause opens with אל אחי/אחי, although Gen 19:7 has an additional intervening נא. The double negative in Judg 19:23 and 2 Sam 13:12 (אל + verb + אל + subject) may indicate intentional patterning of one sentence upon the other, since such double use of אל is found only once more (2 Kgs 4:16). Accordingly, it is possible to surmise that the general similarity between the three passages brought about further assimilation of Judg 19:23 toward Gen 19:7 through the addition of נא to the end of the sentence. This unusual final placement of נא in Judg 19:23 might have been intended to highlight the relation to the other two citations.

The exhortation not to do a thing to the guest (Judg 19:23–24; Gen 19:8). Lot exhorts the townsmen not to do a "thing" (דבר) to the guests, while the Ephraimite twice calls to the people not to do "this outrage/outrageous thing" (את [דבר] הנבלה הזאת). Despite the general formulation of Lot's request in Gen 19:8—not to do a "thing"—the context makes clear that his intention is not to do a thing to harm the guests (cf. Gen 19:7). Even so, the chosen expression is of neutral value (אל תעשו דבר). Judges

---

70. See Otzen 1975, 133–36.

71. See Gen 13:8; 1 Sam 25:25; 2 Sam 13:25. Verbless clauses provide the exception to the rule, as in Gen 19:18; 33:10.

19:23, however, uses a loaded term—*outrage* (נבלה)—to define the act that the townsmen intended to commit with the Levite (אל־תעשו את־הנבלה הזאת). The contrast between the neutral formulation in Gen 19:8 and the negatively charged expression in Judg 19:23–24 might indicate that Judg 19:23–24 is a tendentious reworking of Gen 19:8.[72] This possibility is supported by the fact that the deviation in Judg 19:23–24 from the formulation shared with Gen 19:8 creates an associative link with other texts in which נבלה designates nonnormative sexual relations[73] and particularly with Tamar's plea that Amnon refrain from raping her:

Judg 19:23: אל־תעשו את־הנבלה הזאת
2 Sam 13:12: אל־תעשה את־הנבלה הזאת

In both cases the term הנבלה designates a sexual offense that acts as the first link in a chain of events leading up to civil war. Thus by adding the term נבלה to the host's exhortation not to do a "thing" to the guest, the narrator in Judg 19:23–24 highlights the sexual nature of the townsmen's offense.

In contrast to Lot's single exhortation in Gen 19:8, the exhortation is repeated and frames the host's counterproposal in Judg 19:23–24. Comparison of the parallel texts shows that each part of the frame in Judg 19:23–24 includes an element that is not repeated in the other member but is shared with Gen 19:8:

Judg 19:23: אַחֲרֵי אֲשֶׁר־בָּא הָאִישׁ הַזֶּה אֶל־בֵּיתִי אַל־תַּעֲשׂוּ אֶת־הַנְּבָלָה הַזֹּאת
Gen 19:8: רק לאנשים האל אַל־תַּעֲשׂוּ דָבָר כִּי־עַל־כֵּן בָּאוּ בְּצֵל קֹרָתִי
Judg 19:24: ולאיש הזה לֹא תַעֲשׂוּ דְּבַר הַנְּבָלָה הַזֹּאת

The opening, "for this man has entered my house" (Judg 19:23), echoes Lot's words: "for they are under the shelter of my roof" (Gen 19:8), while the ending, "do not do this outrageous thing" (Judg 19:24), is an expanded parallel to Lot's exhortation, "do not do a thing" (Gen 19:8). Thus the framing repetition appears to derive from reworking the simple formula-

---

72. So also Brettler 1989a, 411.
73. See above, ch. 1, n. 33; contra Jüngling 1981, 216–17, who makes an unnecessary distinction between the significance of the term in v. 23 (outrageous violation of hospitality) and v. 24 (outrageous violation of sexuality).

tion of the single exhortation in Gen 19:8. In this case, the converse possibility—that Gen 19:8 derives from Judg 19:23–24—seems less likely since it could be expected that the text in Gen 19:8 would parallel either part of the frame rather than work them together. Moreover, Gen 19:8 makes no mention of the term נבלה even though it would have been appropriate to the context. Finally, the collocation דבר הנבלה is unique and is readily explained as an artificial construct deriving from or influenced by the text of Gen 19:8.

THE RELATIONS BETWEEN JUDG 19:15–25 AND GEN 19:1–13

The examination of the parallels between the two stories showed that they are closely related, both in structure and in language. All the common structural elements and motifs were found to be fully functional in the story of Sodom, while some of them were problematic in the context of the Gibeah story, especially the motif of same-sex intercourse and the inclusion of the concubine in the host's counterproposal of two women. These irregularities may indicate that these elements were grafted on to the Gibeah story in order to create an analogy between the events there and those at Sodom. The close examination of the verbal parallels also uncovered evidence that Judg 19 is dependent upon Gen 19. The peculiar construction אנשי העיר אנשי בני־בליעל (Judg 19:22) was inspired by אנשי העיר אנשי סדם in Gen 19:4. The unique construct דבר הנבלה (Judg 19:24) was influenced by the text in Gen 19:8. Judges 19:23–24 was formulated, in part, by breaking up elements from Gen 19:8 and integrating them into two separate but parallel sentences. Lastly, the third person feminine pronominal suffixes characteristic of SBH (להן, אתהן) were replaced by masculine forms (להם, אותם), as frequently occurs in LBH and Qumran Hebrew.[74] The accumulative weight of the evidence is decisive and leads me to conclude that Judg 19 was patterned upon Gen 19.

Why did the author of Judg 19–21 fashion the description of the visit at Gibeah as a reflection of the story of the divine messengers' visit to Sodom? In other texts Sodom is depicted as the archetype of a sinful city[75] or as a desolate place that had been totally destroyed.[76] This last image

---

74. See above, ch. 3.

75. See, e.g., Isa 3:9; Jer 23:14; Lam 4:6; and especially Ezek 16:44–58, where Jerusalem's wantonness is compared to the abominations of "her sister," Sodom.

76. See, e.g., Isa 13:19; Jer 49:18; 50:40; Amos 4:11; Zeph 2:9; Lam 4:6.

usually represents the severe punishment God metes out upon those who deviate from the ways of YHWH.[77] Thus the view of Sodom as the model of an irredeemable sinful city (or people) is deeply entrenched in biblical literature from the eighth century to the early Persian period.[78]

Classical source criticism assigned the story of Lot in Sodom in Gen 19 to a tenth- or ninth-century Yahwist; however, classical source criticism has undergone a serious upheaval in recent years. Although scribes must have been involved in administrative activity and documentation from the inception of the monarchy, most think that the conditions for the type of literary activity attributed to the "Yahwist" did not take hold until the eighth century. Accordingly, some who still adhere to the view of a preexilic Yahwist now attribute the J source to the eight century at the earliest.[79] Others view J as a supplementary source or redaction that presumes the Deuteronomistic History and serves as its new prologue. According to this approach, J was composed in the Babylonian or Persian periods, although the author or redactor may have incorporated earlier material.[80] Another group eschews the classical view of the pentateuchal sources (or redactions) in favor of independent blocks that underwent a complex tradition history. This group generally views the Abraham narratives as Babylonian or Persian period additions to the developing pentateuchal narrative; however, even within this group there is a noticeable tendency to locate the kernel of the Abraham-Lot complex in Gen 13 and 18–19 to a seventh- or sixth-century Judean setting.[81] Given the lack of consensus regarding the composition of the Abraham-Lot complex, it is best to refrain from specific chronological delineations at this point in the intertextual investigation and limit the conclusions to a relative chronol-

---

77. See Deut 29:21–24; Isa 1:4–9; Amos 4:11; Lam 4:6; cf. Isa 13:9, 19; Jer 49:18; 50:40; Zeph 2:9, where the image describes the punishment of the nations who schemed against Israel.

78. For the eighth century, see, e.g., Amos 4:11; and for the Babylonian–early Persian period, see, e.g., Jer 49:18; 50:40; Ezek 16:44–58; Lam 4:6.

79. E.g., Zenger 2008, 76–77, 100–103.

80. See, e.g., Van Seters 1975, 209–26, 310–11; 1992, 257–60, 331–32; Levin 1993, 23–34, 389–96.

81. See, e.g., Römer 2001, 193–96; Schmid 2010, 95–98; Kratz 2005, 270–73; Finkelstein and Römer 2014, 12–17. Already Gunkel (1997, 159–60) held that the Abraham-Lot stories represent the original core of tradition that was subsequently supplemented; however, Gunkel attributed this core to oral tradition that was redacted by the scribes who produced the early J document.

ogy. Accordingly, the author of the Gibeah story was familiar the literary version of the story of Lot in Sodom (and not only with a vague tradition regarding the destruction of the Sodom due to its sins).

Against this background, it appears that the Gibeah story in Judg 19 was modeled upon the story of Sodom in order to suggest, by means of analogy, that Gibeah is the spiritual "sister" of Sodom.[82] This analogy casts a shadow over the city, its inhabitants, and the Benjaminites as well, since they would not bring the wrongdoers to justice. Furthermore, the analogy leaves a detrimental association in the mind of readers who subsequently encounter Gibeah and Benjamin again, farther on in the Deuteronomistic History. If the author and his audience were familiar with Gibeah and its contemporary inhabitants, then the analogy might also serve to cast suspicion on them as well. It would seem, then, that the analogy between Gibeah and Sodom may be rooted in a polemic directed against Gibeah and Benjamin.

Comparisons within the Wider Context of Judg 19–21 and Gen 18–19

Additional parallels suggest themselves within the broader context of Judg 19–21 and Gen 18–19. It needs to be seen whether these parallels were formed along with those in Gen 19:1–10 and Judg 19:15–25 or whether a later scribe observed the initial similarity between the stories was motivated to enlarge the scope of the allusions.

Structural Analogies

Double antithetic hospitality scenes. Both Judg 19–21 and Gen 18–19 open with hospitality scenes featuring a generous and gracious host (Abraham in Gen 18:1–8 and the father-in-law in Judg 19:3–9). Afterward the guests pay a second visit elsewhere, where they are received with hostility. The placement of the gracious hospitality scene before the description of the disastrous visit creates an antithetical analogy between the places—Sodom as opposed to the oaks of Mamre and Gibeah as opposed to Bethlehem—and helps justify the judgment against the sinful city.[83]

---

82. See the analogy between Jerusalem and Sodom in Ezek 16:48–58.

83. See Van Seters 1975, 215–16; e.g., Rudin-O'Brasky 1982, 103–4; Wenham 1994, 43–44; Stipp 2011, 230–33; see Amit 1994, 35.

The doubling of the hospitality scenes also invites the reader to compare the different hosts, and in both cases the comparison favors the first host (Abraham as against Lot, and the father-in-law as against the old Ephraimite).[84] And yet the double hospitality motif plays a fundamentally different part in the two narratives. In Gen 18–19 the spotlight is fixed upon the hosts, and the guests are means to test and reward them. In Judg 19, however, the narrator displays no particular interest in the hosts' fate and focuses only on their role in providing hospitality to the guests.

Concern for future progeny for the survivors of the disaster. Both narratives center on a disaster that annihilates a complete population; and the few escaping survivors find refuge in a fringe area (Gen 19:30, וישב בהר; Judg 20:45, 47, וינוסו המדברה). In addition, both narratives end with concern for the fate of the survivors in light of obstacles hindering their natural reproduction (Gen 19:31–35; Judg 21:6–22).[85] In both narratives extreme and even reprehensible measures are employed in order to find mates for the survivors. And yet here too there are significant differences. First, the survivors from Sodom are of both sexes (Lot and his two daughters), while the Benjaminite refugees are male only. Second, the problem facing the survivors from Sodom is to provide husbands for Lot's daughters (Gen 19:31), while the problem of the Benjaminites is to provide them with wives (Judg 21:1, 7, 16). Third, Lot's daughters solve their problem on their own (Gen 19:31–35), while a third party (the עדה) is involved in providing wives for the Benjaminites (Judg 21:6–22). Lastly, Lot's two daughters satisfactorily solve their problem by means of a single, common solution—their father (Gen 19:32), while two separate solutions (virgins from Jabesh and girls from Shiloh) are necessary to resolve the Benjaminites' problem (Judg 21:10–14, 19–23).

Some of these differences derive from the differing context of the sections where this shared motif was applied. Genesis 19:30–38 is mainly concerned with the circumstances surrounding the origins of Ammon

---

84. In Gen 18:4–8, the lengthy description of Abraham's hospitality serves to present him as an ideal host, while the description in Lot's hospitality in Gen 19:3 is short and formulaic. The brevity of the description in Gen 19:3 does not necessarily disparage Lot's hospitality, since the narrator may have chosen to highlight instead Lot's efforts to protect his guests; see Rudin-O'Brasky 1982, 108; Wenham 1994, 53; Loader 1990, 36.

85. See also Liverani 2004, 178; Rudin-O'Brasky 1982, 104, 135; 1985, 158–59; Lasine 1984, 40.

and Moab. The origin traditions dealing with the birth of nations relate the birth of the eponymous father, and birth stories focus on the birth mother no less (if not more) than on the figure of the father.[86] This may partly explain why the narrative in Gen 19:30–35 relates the fate of the survivors from the perspective of Lot's daughters. From their point of view, the problem is that there is no man available, apart from Lot, with whom they can mate and bear children (Gen 19:31).[87] The only apparent solution lay in impregnation by their father, despite the taboo of incest. The story implies that Lot would not have accepted this solution, since the daughters take steps to "steal" his seed without his conscious cooperation (vv. 33, 35). Thus the author's choice, to represent the birth of Moab and Ammon as the result of incest, made it necessary for Lot's daughters to solve their problem on their own.

In the Gibeah story, the problem of the refugees arises from the outcome of the war: the refugees are all warriors who fled from the battlefield, while all the Benjaminite women were annihilated by the Israelite forces (Judg 20:48; 21:16). Moreover, the Israelites supposedly foreswore connubium with the Benjaminites before going out to war. Because of this double catch, the Benjaminites are dependent upon the willingness of a third party to help them find a solution. Thus the narrative in Judg 21 presents the problem from the perspective of the Israelites rather than from the side of the survivors. The question of partners for the survivors arises in the narrative when the Israelites regret the "cutting down" (21:6) of Benjamin and wish to restore the tribe in order to preserve the wholeness of "all Israel" (21:3, 6–7, 15–18). Like the incest committed by Lot's daughters, the two solutions in verses 8–14 and 19–23 are extreme and problematic. Although the Israelites regret that they nearly annihilated an entire tribe, they are willing to destroy an entire city (Jabesh) in order to procure women to restore that tribe.[88] Even more surprising is the intercession of

---

86. See, e.g., Gen 16:10–12; 22:20–24; 25:1–4, 21–26; 29:31–30:23.

87. According to Gen. Rab. 51.8, the eldest daughter thought that Lot was the only surviving man in the world; see also, e.g., Rashi; Ibn Ezra; Gunkel 1910, 218–19; Skinner 1930, 313. However, it is also possible that her words אין איש בארץ have local reference; given their situation, in a remote place and under their father's supervision, they would have had no contact with other men.

88. Surprisingly, the girls of Jabesh who are spared are described with the same restrictive relative clause used by Lot when offering his daughters to the Sodomites: "who have not experienced intercourse with a man" (אשר לא ידעו איש); the expression occurs only in Gen 19:8; Judg 21:12.

the Israelites in suggesting the second solution, for if the Benjaminites are to abduct their wives, then why do they need anyone's permission, and why should they limit themselves to girls from Shiloh? These difficulties should be regarded in light of the importance the story attributed to Benjamin's rehabilitation as a means to restoring the wholeness of the people. According to the logic of the narrative, these ends could be achieved only through the intervention of the עדה, which represents the ideal incarnation of Israel, charged with upholding the norms defining the community.[89]

It is difficult to determine whether the shared motif of providing partners for the survivors derives from literary influence, since there are no verbal similarities between the stories about Lot's daughters and the fate of the remaining Benjaminites. On the one hand, the story of Lot's daughters does not appear to be an integral part of the Sodom story but is rather an independent section grafted on the end of the Sodom narrative in order to denigrate Ammon and Moab as the offspring of incestuous relations.[90] On the other hand, I have argued above (ch. 1) that the rehabilitation of Benjamin is an integral and necessary element in the Gibeah narrative. This understanding of the compositional context of the two survivor stories could lead to the conclusion that the redactor, who supplemented the Sodom story with the story of Lot's daughters, was influenced by the structure of Judg 19–21. However, it is also conceivable that the author of Judg 19–21 already was familiar with and influenced by Gen 18–19 in its final form. The criterion of the dysfunctional motif may be employed here in order to decide between these two alternatives. As noted previously, in Gen 19 Lot has two daughters (v. 8, 30) and both need to find a mate, but they have recourse to the same solution—their father Lot (v. 32). The narrative in Judg 21, by contrast, provides for the Benjaminite survivors by means of two separate solutions (Jabesh virgins *and* Shiloh girls), and this double solution appears forced, even though it does not necessarily result

---

89. See Reviv 1985.

90. See, e.g., Gunkel 1910, 217–18; Skinner 1930, 312–14; von Rad 1972, 223–24; Westermann 1985, 311–15; contra Van Seters 1975, 217–21; Rudin-O'Brasky 1982, 117–18, 135; Weisman 1992. However, Gunkel, Skinner, and Westermann thought that the story about Lot's daughters is inherently positive and represents an early Moabite tradition about the restoration of humanity following a universal catastrophe. But this view seems doubtful, since incest taboos are widespread throughout the ancient Near East; see, e.g., CH §154; Hittite Laws §189; see also Weisman 1992; Wenham 1994, 61–62; Polak 1994, 197.

from secondary interpolation.[91] If the conclusion of the Gibeah narrative was patterned on the final structure of Gen 18–19, then the double solution in Judg 21 may have been influenced by the need to provide for the *two* daughters in Gen 19:30–38.

Verbal Analogies

Interrelation between the Hospitality Scenes in Judg 19:3–9 and Gen 18:1–5 and 19:1–3

He saw [x] and [verb] toward [לקראתו/ם] *him/them* (Judg 19:3; Gen 18:2; 19:1)—Although the expression appears to be formulaic, it does not occur outside these three hospitality scenes. Thus the parallel usage here is unique.

He urged [ויפצר] *him/them strongly* (Judg 19:7; Gen 19:3)—The verb פצר is rare,[92] and the context in both instances is similar: a host (the father-in-law in Bethlehem and Lot in Sodom) "presses" a visitor to accept his invitation. Thus it is possible that the parallel use here is the result of one text intentionally invoking the other.

The offer of hospitality (Judg 19:5, 9; Gen 18:5; 19:2)—The Levite's visit in Bethlehem is modeled on the pattern of graded repetition. After a summary account of the first three days (Judg 19:4), the recurring pattern is expanded with two detailed invitations to sup and stay the night (vv. 5–6, 8–9). Comparison shows that the father's invitation to dine on the fourth day (Judg 19:5) is verbally parallel to Abraham's invitation in Gen 18:5, while the invitation on the fifth day (Judg 19:9) parallels Lot's invitation in Gen 19:2.[93]

---

91. See above, ch. 1.

92. The verb occurs six times in the Bible, three of which are in the texts discussed (Gen 19:3, 9; 33:11; Judg 19:7; 2 Kgs 2:17; 5:16).

93. On the basis of the parallel between Judg 19:5 and Gen 18:5, Stipp (2011, 230) concludes that the Bethlehemite father-in-law is patterned upon the figure of Abraham. However, he overlooks the further parallel between Judg 19:9 and Gen 19:2. Thus if one follows his line of reasoning, the father-in-law must be patterned upon an amalgamation of both the figures of Abraham and Lot. But this conclusion hardly furthers Stipp's purpose to demonstrate a Judahite and Davidic tendency in Judg 19.

TEXT, SUBTEXT, AND INTERTEXTUAL MOSAIC

Gen 18:5   ואקחה   פת־לחם   וסעדו לבבכם   אחר תעברו

Judg 19:5   סעד לבך   פת־לחם   ואחר תלכו

Judg 19:9   לין פה וייטב לבבך   והשכמתם מחר לדרככם   והלכת לאהלך

Gen 19:2   ולינו ורחצו רגליכם   והשכמתם   והלכתם לדרככם

In Judg 19 these parallels frame the account of the fourth and fifth days of the Levite's visit. Since the narrator depicts the father-in-law as eager to extend the guests' visit, he could have added the offer to stay the night on the fourth day immediately after the invitation to dine, but instead he chose to separate the two parts of the invitation (Judg 19:5–6). Here he seems to have been influenced by the model he found in Gen 18:5, which did not include the offer of lodging.[94] The parallel between the invitation on the fifth day in Bethlehem (Judg 19:9–10) and Lot's offer in Sodom (Gen 19:2) also includes the negative response of the visitors, although the rationale for refusal is different in each story.[95] The fact that in Judg 19 two contiguous stages of the visit in Bethlehem (the fourth and fifth days) display parallels to separate hospitality accounts at Hebron and Sodom in Gen 18–19, might indicate more than the common use of popular motifs. In this case, it seems likely that the author of Judg 19 consciously drew upon offers of hospitality in Gen 18–19 in order to frame the account of the Levite's lengthened stay in Bethlehem, which led to his late departure and arrival at Gibeah at sundown.

---

94. It is likely that an offer to stay the night was not included in Gen 18, since the wider narrative context in Gen 18–19 required that the messengers continue on their way so as to reach Sodom by evening.

95. The Levite's refusal can be viewed as a reaction to the overbearing urging of his father-in-law to prolong his visit again, beyond his original intention; but it also serves the needs of the wider narrative that requires him and the concubine to arrive by sundown to the town that will serve as an antithesis to Bethlehem. In Gen 19 the messengers' refusal derives from the testing motif, by which Lot is given the chance to prove himself worthy of deliverance from the destruction of Sodom.

Gen 18

[1] YHWH appeared before him by the terebinths of Mamre. He was sitting by the entrance of the tent at the heat of the day, [2] when he looked up and **saw** three men standing before him. Then he *ran* **to meet them** [וירץ לקראתם] from the entrance of the tent, bowed to the ground, [3] and said: "If it please my lords, do not pass by your servant. [4] Let a little water be brought so you may bathe your feet and recline beneath the tree. [5] And I will fetch **a bit of bread so you may refresh yourselves, and then you can** *pass on* [תעברו]."

Judg 19:3–5

[3] Her husband took himself off—with his servant and two donkeys—and went after her to woo her back. When he arrived* at her father's house, the girl's father **saw** him and *was glad* **to meet him** [וישמח לקראתו]. [4] His father-in-law, the girl's father, detained him and he stayed with him three days; they ate, drank, and lodged there. [5] Then, on the fourth day, they rose early in the morning and prepared to go, when the girl's father said to his son-in-law: "**Refresh yourselves with a bit of bread, and then** *go* [תלכו]."

* Reading ויבא with LXX[AL] for MT ותביאהו.

Gen 19

[1] The two messengers arrived in Sodom in the evening, as Lot was sitting in the gate of Sodom. When Lot **saw** them, *he rose* **to meet them** [ויקם לקראתם], and bowing low with his face to the ground,

[2] he said, "**Please** [הנה נא], my lords, **please** *turn aside* [סורו נא] to your servant's house to **spend the night** [ולינו] and bathe your feet; then you may **be on your way early** [והשכמתם והלכתם לדרככם]." But they said, "No, we shall spend the night in the square." [3] But he **urged them strongly** [ויפצר בם], so they turned his way and came to his house. He prepared a feast for them and baked flat bread, and they ate.
[16] But **he lingered** [ויתמהמה], so *the men seized* his hand, and the hands of his wife, and his two daughters—in YHWH's mercy on him—and *took him out* [ויצאהו מחוץ] and led him outside the city.

Judg 19:3–9

[3] Her husband took himself off—with his servant and two donkeys—and went after her to woo her back. When he arrived at her father's house, the girl's father **saw** him and *was glad* **to meet him** [וישמח לקראתו].

[7] The man got up to leave, but his father-in-law **urged him strongly** [ויפצר בו], so he turned back and stayed there. [8] He arose early to leave on the fifth day, but the girl's father said: "Please refresh yourself and **linger** [והתמהמהו] until past noon," and the two of them ate. [9] Then the man got up to leave—he, his concubine, and his servant—but his father-in-law, the girl's father said to him: "**Look** [הנה נא], the day is waning to evening; **please spend the night** [לינו נא]. See, the day is declining, **spend the night** [לין] here and enjoy yourself, then **be on your way** *tomorrow* **early and go** home [והשכמתם לדרככם והלכת]."
[10] But the man would not stay over....

> [25] But the men would not listen to him, *so **the man seized** his concubine and **thrust her out** [ויצא החוץ] to them*....

Interrelation between Gen 19:16 and Judg 19:8, 25

Lingering [התמהמה] *that delays departure* (Judg 19:8; Gen 19:16). The verb התמהמה is uncommon[96] and is used in both contexts to depict unwillingness to leave a place. In Gen 19:15–16, the celestial visitors attempt to hasten the host's departure, but he and his family linger and endanger themselves, until the visitors forcibly intervene to prevent disaster. In Judg 19, the converse situation obtains. There the guest is in a hurry to leave the host's house, but the host presses him to linger, thereby sparking a chain of events that leads to disastrous results. The host's suggestion to linger until past noon (התמהמהו עד נטות היום) is odd[97] and might indicate that the verb was borrowed from its smoother context in Gen 19:16.

Bringing outside (Judg 19:25; Gen 19:16). Similar formulation in both cases is used to describe action of the guests:

Gen 19:16: ויחזיקו האנשים בידו ... ויצאהו וינחהו מחוץ לעיר
Judg 19:25: ויחזק האיש בפילגשו ויצא אליהם החוץ

The parallel formulation in Judg 19:25 is significant, since the action of the Levite could have been expressed differently, for example: ויתפש האיש בפילגשו ויביא/ויוציא אותה אליהם (cf. Deut 21:19; 22:15). Moreover, the word *outside* (החוץ) is overly explicit following "he thrust her *out* to them" and was not used before in verse 23 when the host goes out of the house to address the townsmen. In Gen 19:16, by contrast, the statement that the messengers took Lot and his family *outside* (מחוץ לעיר) the city is necessary, since the city is about to be destroyed; in this context *outside* represents a place of refuge. Since, in Judg 19:25, *outside* is the realm of licentiousness and danger, the emphasis that the Levite brought the concubine *outside* to the men may represent an attempt to

---

96. The verb occurs four more times in narrative (Gen 43:10; Exod 12:39; Judg 3:26; 2 Sam 15:28) and three times in poetry (Isa 29:9; Hab 2:3; Ps 119:60).

97. Others chose to eliminate the oddness of the proposal by emending the verb to narrative tense: ויתמהמה; see, e.g., Moore 1895, 411–12; Burney 1970, 461–62; Soggin 1987, 285.

create an inverse analogy between the two stories. While the divine messengers took hold of Lot and his family and brought them outside the city in as an expression of YHWH's compassion (Gen 19:16), the Levite acts out of selfish motives when he takes hold of concubine and thrusts her outside the house.[98]

In summary, parallel elements that are at home in Gen 19:16 have been incorporated in two separate contexts in Judg 19, both of which stand in inverse relation to the situation depicted in Gen 19:16. In light of the number of points in which Gen 19 exerted influence upon Judg 19, it seems most likely that in this case too a single verse from Gen 19 generated two separate inverse analogies in Judg 19.

NATURE AND ORIGIN OF INTERRELATIONS IN THE WIDER CONTEXT

The interrelations between the wider contexts of Judg 19–21 and Gen 18–19 may derive from three different types of processes: (1) allusions to the Abraham and Lot stories woven into the Gibeah story by N^1; (2) expansion of the scope of parallels by R^2 or a subsequent scribe; (3) secondary assimilation of verbal elements from the Gibeah story into Gen 19.

The endings of the two narratives (Judg 21; Gen 19:30–38) have similar structure and motifs but do not share verbal parallels. The story of Lot's daughters seems to be a secondary accretion to the Sodom story, while the narrative about Benjamin's rehabilitation is necessary for a satisfactory ending to the Gibeah story. However, the linguistic evidence examined in chapter 3 points to the relatively late composition of Judg 21; thus it is reasonable to conclude that the author of Judg 19–21 could have been familiar with the final form of the story of Lot and might have employed the entire scope of Gen 19 as a source of allusion. This conclusion helps explain the motive for solving the Benjaminites' problem in two stages, which may now be seen as a reflection of the two-stage resolution of the problem facing Lot's daughters.

The analogy in structure and the verbal similarities indicates a literary interrelation between the hospitality scenes in Bethlehem (Judg 19:3–10) and Hebron (Gen 18). The scene in Bethlehem evinces parallels to both the Hebron and Sodom stories (Gen 18–19), and they are employed to

---

98. It is implied that the Levite himself remained *inside*, on the safe side of the door; see Niditch 2008, 193.

frame the account of the critical fourth and fifth days' visit, when the Levite's departure is repeatedly delayed. This may indicate authorial intent and provide evidence that the N¹ was familiar with Gen 18–19 as a united literary unit. There is also cause to believe that the description of Lot's departure from Sodom left its mark on the Gibeah story. Two verbal elements from Gen 19:16 (התמהמה; החזק ויצא מ/החוץ) are applied in inverse fashion in the Gibeah story (Judg 19:8, 25), and the cumulative evidence for the direction of dependency (Sodom story influencing the Gibeah story) supports assuming that in this case too the parallels originated in the Sodom story and were borrowed by N¹.

Additional, loose connections may be detected between the two narratives. It is not uncommon for readers who become aware of textual interrelations to expand the scope of the parallels, even when the perceived allusions are not inherent in the compositions themselves. This does not necessarily mean that these parallels derive from loose association since they may derive from independent use of the same motif or expression. However, when the reader is also a scribe responsible for transmitting texts, he may be motivated to intervene and insert additional parallels, thus further enhancing the interrelation between the texts. This seems to be the case with various parallel expressions in Judg 20:40/Gen 19:26 (ויפן/ותבט מ/אחריו ... והנה עלה), Judg 20:41/Gen 19:19 (תדבק/נגעה הרעה), and Judg 20:48/Gen 19:15 (הנמצאת/ות). In these cases, it is not unlikely that independent use was made of the same elements or even that Gen 19 assimilated the expressions from Judg 20 in the course of scribal transmission.

4.3. The Battle at Ai (Josh 7–8)

The accounts of the battles at Gibeah (Judg 20) and Ai (Josh 7–8) are among the most elaborate battle reports in the Bible, and both relate how victory was achieved after a previous defeat thanks to the unique tactic of feigned flight combined with conquest of the town by ambush. The two descriptions of the decisive battle at Ai and Gibeah are also marked by similar phraseology.

The relations between the two stories has been much discussed, but the debate has produced little consensus. Classic literary critics such as Wellhausen and Burney ruled that the story of the war at Gibeah was dependent upon the description of the battle at Ai, but this view changed after the excavations at Ai (et-Tell) indicated that the tradition regarding the conquest of Ai lacks any historical basis.⁹⁹ For example, Wolfgang Roth argued that the story of Ai was a reworking of the battle at Gibeah, and his position assumed that the ahistorical account must be a literary adaptation of the other story, which reflects early historical reality.¹⁰⁰ But this assumption is erroneous since the questions of literary dependency and historical reliability are mutually independent. Other scholars have avoided the question of literary dependency and postulated a preliterary origin for the interrelations, stemming from use of common motifs,¹⁰¹ combination of local traditions,¹⁰² or dependency upon a lost third source.¹⁰³

Development of the Narrative Complex in Josh 7:1–8:29

Narrative breaks as well as changes in style and concept cast doubt on the literary integrity of Josh 7:1–8:29. If the account of the war at Gibeah interacts with the final form of the Ai story, then the compositional history of Josh 7:1–8:29 could have significance in establishing a relative date for the composition of the Gibeah story.

It seems that the account of the conquest in Josh 6–10 was originally designed along the lines of the Deuteronomic rules of war in Deut 20:10–14. The first conquest (Jericho) was conceived as a "firstfruits" offering, followed by a case of a city that resists (Ai; see Deut 20:12–14) and a city

---

99. For the classic view, see Wellhausen 1899, 231; Burney 1970, 455–57; and more recently Gray 1986, 229 (but see earlier Gray 1967, 240–41); Rudin-O'Brasky 1985, 156–57. On Ai, see Albright 1939, 240–41; Callaway 1968, 314–15; Zevit 1983, 24–28; contra Grintz 1961.

100. See Roth 1963, 299–301; as well as de Vaux 1978, 619; Arnold 1990, 83–84; Aḥituv 1995, 140.

101. See, e.g., Moore 1895, 435; Schunck 1963, 65 n. 55; Mazor 1994, 99–106; Nelson 1997, 111–12. Mazor claimed that the MT of Josh 8 is an expansion of the original narrative as preserved in the LXX and that the similarity between Judg 20:29–48 and Josh 8* derives from formulaic language, while the expansions in the MT of Josh 8 are the result of literary assimilation toward Judg 20. However, the categorical claim that the LXX preserves the original version of Josh 8 is debatable; see van der Meer 2004, 434–39. In any event, the parallel formulations between Judg 20:29–48 and the postulated original version of Josh 8 include rare and peculiar expressions.

102. See, e.g., Gray 1967, 240–41.

103. See, e.g., Rösel 1976, 36.

that capitulates (Gibeon; see Deut 20:10–11).¹⁰⁴ After the initial conquest of Jericho, the following conquest accounts open with the kings of Canaan, "hearing" about Joshua's success (Josh 6:27; see also 9:1–2; 11:1–5) and then mobilizing for war against the Israelites. Hence the comment that YHWH was with Joshua and that news of his fame was heard throughout the land (Josh 6:27*) undoubtedly served as the original opening of the story of the conquest of Ai.¹⁰⁵ Like the other kings of Canaan, "hearing" about Joshua's conquests prompted the king of Ai to go to war with the Israelites, which he immediately did upon seeing the Israelite troops massed outside the city gates (Josh 8:10–14). In the final form of the narrative the introduction was rewritten, so that the notice about Achan's violation of the Jericho חרם now obscures the immediate resistance of the king of Ai. In the primary composition, the outcome of the conquest of Ai (Josh 8:24–25*, 27*–29) possibly spared women and children as booty in accordance with Deut 20:14.¹⁰⁶ I concur with those who hold that the conquest account was initially composed in the late seventh century BCE to justify the annexation of southern Samaria by Josiah.¹⁰⁷ Thus the preexilic primary narrative of the conquest of Ai comprised Josh 6:27* and 8:10–29*. In the Babylonian period, the conquest narrative was revised to reflect the utopian Deuteronomistic חרם ideology.¹⁰⁸ In this second stage, the story of the conquest of Ai was revised to reflect the complete proscription of the inhabitants of Ai (Josh 8:2, 25aβ, 26; 10:1).

The most extensive elaboration of the Ai story was the addition of the incident of Achan (Josh 7:1–26),¹⁰⁹ which furthers the historiographic moral that compliance with YHWH's commandments brings victory,

---

104. Edenburg 2012a, 128. The conclusion that the conquest of Ai was designed to illustrate the application of Deut 20:12–14 is supported by the remarks permitting the taking of booty in Josh 8:2aβ, 27, which are remarkably similar to the provision in Deut 20:14.

105. This understanding of the function of Josh 6:27 is further reflected by the MT division into *sederim* in which the verse marks the incipit of the fourth of the *sederim* in the book of Joshua.

106. See Edenburg 2015, 125–27.

107. See, e.g., Römer 2005, 82–90; cf. Knauf, 2008, 17–18.

108. See Edenburg 2012a, 127–29, with additional literature in Edenburg 2015, 126–27.

109. See, e.g., Noth 1935, 23 n. 2; 1971, 43–49; Hertzberg 1965, 50–52, 60; Soggin 1972, 98, 103–4; Boling 1982, 230; Zevit 1983, 23, 32; Gray 1986, 84–86; Nelson 1997, 98–99, 111–12; Dietrich 2007.

while disobedience, even at the level of the individual, is liable to bring disaster upon the entire people. This representation of divine justice, as well as the principle of double causality that combines human and divine causality, are wholly in accordance with the outlook that dictated the structure of the Deuteronomistic History. [110]

Notwithstanding, the Achan narrative builds upon bodies of pentateuchal law that are assigned by many scholars to late exilic or postexilic strata. For example, the idea that the conquest of Jericho was to be a firstfruits offering dedicated wholly to YHWH presents an opportunity to consider the implications of appropriating that which has been devoted to the Deity. The Deuteronomistic laws that mandate the חרם of the towns of Canaan are unconcerned with material booty since they are directed toward the annihilation of a people rather than the sacral devotion of goods. Instead, the matter dealt with in the Achan passage—the misappropriation of dedicated or sacral items—is addressed by late additions to the Deuteronomistic corpus (Deut 7:25–26; 13:13–18),[111] as well as by Priestly legislation (Lev 5:15–26; 27:28–29).

The Achan passage also employs some Priestly idioms (מעל, Josh 7:1; כחש, v. 11; רגם, v. 25)[112] and demonstrates ideas and themes that are at home in Priestly law. For example, the notion that the inviolability of objects that have been devoted for sacral purposes is a source of "contagion" is related to the Priestly concept of the contagion conveyed by sources of defilement.[113] So too Joshua's exhortation that Achan confess his sin is unparalleled in the Deuteronomistic History and might be inspired by the call in texts in the Priestly law corpus to confess transgressions of מעל (Lev 26:40; Num 5:6–7). Since the Achan passage does not illustrate or interpret any specific Priestly law, but draws upon Priestly idiom and concepts in order to interpret and explicate the larger story of the conquest of Ai in

---

110. See, e.g., Begg 1986, 322–26; Seeligmann 1963; Amit 1987.

111. For a late exilic or postexilic origin of Deut 7:25–26 and 13:13–18, see , e.g., Nielsen 1995, 102–3; Dietrich 2007, 64; Otto 1996, 20–24; Pakkala 1999, 49; 2006, 134–37.

112. In biblical law, כחש occurs only in Lev 5:21–22 and 19:11 and only twice more in the Pentateuch (Gen 18:15; Deut 33:29). Apart from Josh 7:11, the term occurs in DtrH only in Persian period additions (Josh 24:27; 1 Kgs 13:18). רגם occurs eight times in P (Lev 20:2; 20:27; 24:14, 16, 23; Num 14:10; 15:35–36), compared to only once in Deut (21:21) and once in DtrH (1 Kgs 12:18). In prophetic literature the verb occurs only in Ezek 16:40; 23:47.

113. See Nelson 1997, 101.

Josh 7-8, it seems that the passage as a whole is an interpretive expansion of the base narrative. The sole purpose of the account of the preliminary defeat (Josh 7:2-5) is to demonstrate the consequences of going to war when YHWH retracts his support due to an unknown infringement of his commands. Hence the preliminary defeat should also be relegated to the stratum comprising the Achan passage.

STRUCTURAL COMPARISON OF THE INITIAL DEFEATS AT AI AND GIBEAH

The descriptions of the preliminary battles at Ai and Gibeah share a unique two-stage structure of defeat in battle followed by propitiatory rites (Josh 7:6; Judg 20:23aα, 26) accompanied by prayer (Josh 7:7-9) or oracular consultation (Judg 20:23aβ, 27-28a), which finally results in a divine promise of victory before the decisive battle (Josh 8:1; Judg 20:28b). Otherwise, the structural elements shared by the narratives are standard to battle descriptions. However, several of the *differences* in structure and details between the two narratives produce difficulties in the Gibeah story. The Ai story features the figure of a commander who leads the forces in battle, and Joshua's role in this capacity is commensurate with the part he plays throughout the conquest stories in Josh 6-11. The Gibeah story, surprisingly, lacks a commanding figure, and in this regard it is set apart from the main body of the book of Judges.[114] Instead, the course of the battle is determined spontaneously and decisions are unanimously made without the intervention of formal leadership. In this particular, it is possible that the author of the story was reflecting the reality of his own period or was taking a stand against the necessity of central leadership.

Similarly, the Ai story lacks a preliminary oracular consultation since its final form was designed to exemplify the causal connection between sin and the fate of the people. The opening of the story already alludes to the cause of the forthcoming defeat: divine wrath due to the secret infringement of the ban by Achan. Had Joshua inquired of God, he undoubtedly would have been informed, either directly or indirectly, of the divine wrath and taken steps to discover the culprit, allay God's anger, and thus avoid defeat. Instead, the purpose of the story is furthered by Joshua's prayer fol-

---

114. See the role of Gideon and Jephtah in intertribal disputes (Judg 8:1-3; 12:1-6).

lowing the defeat, which provides the opportunity for YHWH to instruct Joshua how to eradicate the unknown cause of sin that lead to defeat.

By contrast, no attempt is made to explain either of the defeats at Gibeah, neither by covert or overt sin, nor by divine anger, nor even by bad tactics. The Israelites are on the side or the just. Not only do they attempt to "eradicate the evil" before going to war, but they diligently consult the oracle before each battle, and the oracular replies lead both them and the reader to expect victory, not defeat. Furthermore, their force is sixteen times larger than the Benjaminites'! With everything in their favor, it is hard to understand why they must suffer two disastrous defeats and lose 10 percent of their forces in casualties. It appears that the main purpose of the double defeat is to explain why the Benjaminites fell for the Israelites' ruse of the feigned flight on the third day (see Judg 20:31, 39). Therefore, there is reason to suspect that the defeat and victory schema is not integral to the Gibeah story but was inspired by the final form of the Ai narrative.

An additional element that functions fully in the battle at Ai story but not in the Gibeah story is the feigned flight. Joshua 7:4–5 describes how the Israelites fled and were pursued by the men of Ai. This prepares the way for the tactic of feigned flight, which builds upon the enemy's expectations from the previous battle (see Josh 8:6). The war at Gibeah also employs the feigned flight tactic and builds on the enemy's misplaced confidence (Judg 20:32), but the narrator neglects to mention that the Israelites had fled from the previous encounters. Here too there is reason to suspect that the motif of feigned flight is not firmly rooted in the Gibeah story, but rather was borrowed from the final form of the Ai story.

Structural Comparison of the Decisive Battles at Ai and Gibeah

My compositional analysis of Judg 20 demonstrated that R^2 grafted an expansion onto the opening of the narrative of the decisive battle and thus severed the opening in verses 29–31a from its original continuation in verses 36b–48. While N^1 focused on the role of the ambush in taking the city, R^2 highlighted the tactic of feigned flight and added topographical details, foremost of which were the routes to Geba[115] and Bethel (20:31). It appears that R^2 assumed that the events detailed in verses 31b–34 occurred

---

115. This route is probably identical with the "desert route" mentioned by N^1 (20:42). Wadi es-Suweinit runs close by Geba and from there runs east into Wadi Farah, which descends toward Jericho.

concurrently with those described by N^1 in verses 36–44. In order to determine the extent of the interrelation with the Ai story during the different redactional stages of the Gibeah story, it is necessary to compare each compositional strand separately.

Each of the three descriptions (Josh 8, N^1 and R^2 in Judg 20:29–48) is built upon a three-stage scheme comprising: (1) a diversion tactic by the main force in the field, (2) an ambush by a picked group, and (3) an assault of the enemy by the main force.

In N^1 (Judg 20:36–44), the first-stage diversion comprises a slow retreat of the main force (v. 36, "giving way to Benjamin") accompanied by limited casualties. This narrative strand does not relate that the enemy pursued the retreating force, but it is assumed that the enemy was drawn far enough away from the city so that the ambushers could act unhindered. In the second stage, the ambushers raid and torch the city in order to signal the main force in the field, thus initiating the third stage, in which the main force stops its retreat and turns upon the enemy. The enemy then flees eastward while the main force takes up the pursuit. The narrative flow between the second and third stages is not smooth (vv. 39–41), but this could be due to the fact that the narrator tried to mimic the simultaneous occurrence taking place in two different arenas: in the field and in the city. N^1 includes unique elements not found either in R^2 or in the Ai story. These are the description of the enemy's flight in the third stage and its pursuit by the main force in the field, and these details derive from the old poetic source subsumed into the prose narrative (vv. 42–43). An additional unique element deals with the arrangements for the smoke signal (v. 38). This detail may have been added to fill a gap in the elliptic poetic source.

In R^2 (Judg 20:30–35) the first stage opens with the main force absorbing limited casualties in the field, after which they decide to feign flight toward Bethel. At Baal-tamar the force remobilizes for the counterattack. In this stage, there is an apparent gap in the narrative between the decision to flee and the remobilization, since the flight itself is not reported (vv. 32b–33a). In addition, it is not stated that the enemy pursued the retreating force, although the Israelites' tactic is based upon this assumption (20:32b). In the second stage, the ambush bursts on to the road from its hiding place west of Geba. The objective of the ambush is not clearly indicated by R^2. While the ambushers surprised the Benjaminites, a picked force was sent south to Gibeah (v. 34a). Here too it is not clear whether this picked force is identical with the ambush group or represents a third column. Their mission appears to be to take the city, but once again, this objective is not clearly stated, and R² does not indicate whether this objective was actually achieved. The third stage is reflected by the statement, "the fighting was heavy" (20:34), which seems to depict the counterattack after the enemy was caught between the main force and the ambushers. R² has one unique element that does not occur in either of the other two accounts: the remobilization at Baal-tamar before initiating the counterattack. This element may have been added in order to provide the description with geographical details familiar to the audience.

The story of Ai alludes to Israelite casualties in the first stage of the decisive battle (Josh 8:15, "they were smitten," ויננעו), after which the main force fled and lured the enemy away from the city in pursuit. In the second stage, the ambush sprang into action, took the city, and set it afire. In the third stage, the force in the field noted the smoke from the city, stopped its flight, and began its counterattack. At the same time, the ambushers left the city and joined the force in the field to trap the enemy between the two prongs of the Israelite forces. The only gap in the Ai narrative relates to the lack of arrangements for an agreed signal between the ambush and the force in the field; however, this detail may have been to be assimilated into the flow of the narrative, since the third stage opens when the force in the field notices the smoke rising from the city.

Of the three descriptions, the Ai narrative is smoothest and most detailed. In my opinion, this indicates that the description of the decisive battle at Ai was written independently of the descriptions in the Gibeah story. N¹ of the Gibeah story shares many elements with the story of Ai, including the use of an ambush to take the city and to send a signal to the main force in the field. However, while the Ai story explicitly depicts the feigned flight diversion, this tactic is only vaguely alluded to by N¹ in Judg 20 by "giving way to Benjamin" (v. 36). Thus the element of diversion was only partially adapted by N¹ to the needs of the conquest by ambush narrative.[116] The R² strand shares two elements with the Ai story: the feigned flight and entrapment of the enemy between the main force and the ambushers. In the Ai story both elements are explicitly detailed, while in the Gibeah story R² only partially applied the feigned flight motif, and the entrapment of the enemy is assumed rather than clearly stated.

---

116. Alternatively, this detail may belong to a section of the poetic source subsumed by R² in 20:32b: "The Israelites said / let us flee and draw him out / from the city to the roads." If this section does derive from the poetic source, it might initially have been integrated in N¹ after v. 36a, and placed in its present context by R².

Since all the shared elements are fully functional in the Ai story, it would appear that they are at home there. That different shared elements have not been smoothly integrated into either N¹ or R² strands of the account of the decisive battle at Gibeah seems to indicate that the Ai story influenced the shape of the story of the third battle at Gibeah.

If the early core of the Gibeah story is contained in the reconstructed poetic fragments, then this source fragment shared many elements related by the account of the decisive battle at Ai, including the feigned flight (Judg 20:32b), the raid on the town by ambushers (vv. 33b, 37a), the smoke signal (v. 40a), limited casualties in the field (v. 39a–bα), looking back upon the town realizing the deception (vv. 40b–41), outflanking the enemy (vv. 42b–43aα), and pursuing and felling the enemy (vv. 43aβ–b, 45aβ–bα). The reconstructed poetic fragment actually shares more elements with the Ai story than either the present N¹ or R² threads. Yet the fact that the poetic source and the Ai narrative share the same tactical elements only indicates that they both draw upon a battle scheme known from the art of warfare. However, when the poetic fragment was reworked into a prose narrative, the author of N¹ worked to deepen the general similarity to the final form of the Ai story by borrowing additional motifs from the Ai story, including the scheme of defeat followed by victory. R² subsequently enhanced the similarity by incorporating additional tactics that were not prominent in N¹, such as the feigned flight.

Formulation in Judg 20:23–48 and Josh 7–8

The structural similarity between the stories is accompanied by extensive parallel phraseology. Some scholars hold that the shared language is due to commonplace expressions, which do not indicate literary relations between the narratives.[117] A thorough examination of the language shared

---

117. See Moore 1895, 435; Mazor 1994, 99–100; Nelson 1997, 111. Mazor argues that all the parallel phrasing is secondary to Josh 7–8. Her view is built on the assumption that the *Vorlage* of the LXX in Josh 7–8 is prior to the MT and that the MT plusses are expansions that were influenced by the Gibeah narrative. But Mazor overlooks the fact that the similarity between the Ai and Gibeah stories is already evident in the LXX *Vorlage* to Josh 7–8, e.g., Josh 8:5–6 // Judg 20:31–32, 39; Josh 8:14b–15a // Judg 20:34b–35a; Josh 8:19 // Judg 20:37–38; Josh 8:20–21 // Judg 20:40; Josh 8:21b // Judg 20:48; Josh 8:24 // Judg 20:31, 45, 47. As van der Meer (2004, 436) points out, Mazor's discussion is one-sided and does not falsify the possibility that Josh 8 influenced Judg 20.

by the two stories demonstrates that the literary relations between them are far more complex.

Josh 7–8	Judg 20
7 ⁶ Joshua tore his clothes and lay face down **until evening** [עד הערב] on the ground **before the ark of YHWH** [לפני ארון ה']—he and the elders of Israel—and they threw earth on their heads.	²³ The Israelites went up and wept **before YHWH until evening** [לפני ה' עד הערב]. ²⁶⁻²⁷ All the people … wept and sat there **before YHWH** and fasted … **until evening** … and **the ark** of God's covenant was there.
8 ¹⁴ The men of the town **went out toward** [ויצאו אנשי העיר לקראת] the Israelites.	²⁵ The Benjaminites **went out toward** them from Gibeah [ויצא לקראתם מן הגבעה]. ³¹ The Benjaminites **went** away from the town **toward** the people [ויצאו לקראת העם הנתקו מן העיר].
8 ² "Set an ambush [שים לך ארב] behind the city.	²⁹ The Israelites set ambushers [וישם ארבים] round at Gibeah. ³⁶ The ambush they set [הארב אשר שמו] against Gibeah.
8 ⁵⁻⁶ I and all the men with me will draw near the city, and when they **come out toward** us [יצאו לקראתנו], we shall flee before them **as at first** [כאשר בראשונה]. They shall pursue us until we draw them away from the city [התיקנו אותם מן־העיר], for **they shall say: 'They are fleeing before us as at first** [יאמרו נסים לפנינו כאשר בראשנה]'. Thus we shall flee [ונסנו] before them."	³⁰⁻³² The Israelites went up against the Benjaminites on the third day and drew up at Gibeah **as before** [כפעם בפעם]. The Benjaminites **went out toward** [ויצאו לקראת] the people **distanced from the city** [הנתקו מן העיר] and began to smite men dead *as before*. The Benjaminites **said: "They are** *routed* **before us just as at first** [ויאמרו בני בנימן נגפים הם לפנינו כבראשנה]." The Israelites said: "**Let us flee** and **draw him out from the city** [ננוסה ונתקנוהו מן־העיר]," ³⁹ so **they thought**: "Indeed, **they are** routed **before us, just as in the first** battle [כי אמרו אך נגוף נגף הוא לפנינו כמלחמה הראשנה]."
8 ²⁴ After the Israelites finished killing all the inhabitants of Ai in **the field** [בשדה], in the desert, where they had pursued them, and they all fell by the	³¹ They began to smite men dead as before on the roads, one of which went up to Bethel, and the other to *Geba, **in the field, about thirty men from Israel**

TEXT, SUBTEXT, AND INTERTEXTUAL MOSAIC 205

sword to the last man, then all the Israelites returned to Ai.
7 ⁵ The men of Ai smote some thirty-six men [כשלשים וששה איש] of theirs.

8 ¹⁹ The **ambush** quickly **rose from its place** [והאורב קם מהרה ממקומו] and ran … and came to the city [ויבאו העיר], captured it, and quickly set it on fire.
8 ¹¹ All the fighting men with him **went up against** the city [ויבוא נגד העיר].

8 ¹⁴ **But he did not know** that the ambush lay behind the city. Then Joshua and all Israel let themselves seem to be routed [וינגעו] before them.

8 ¹⁴ [They] went out … he and all his people to the **appointed place** [למועד] facing the Arabah.

8 ²⁰ The men of Ai **turned round** [ויפנו אחריהם] to look and **Lo! The city was going up in smoke to the sky** [והנה עלה עשן העיר השמימה]. They had no room to flee anywhere, for the people who had fled toward the desert **turned** [נהפך] upon the pursuers.

8 ¹⁵ [They] let themselves seem to be routed before them and **fled to the desert road** [וינסו דרך המדבר].
8 ²⁰ The people who had **fled toward the desert** [הנס המדבר] turned upon the pursuers.
8 ²⁴ After the Israelites finished killing all the inhabitants of Ai in the field, **in the desert**, where they had pursued them [במדבר אשר רדפום בו].

8 ²² The others came **out of the city** [מן העיר] toward them, and they were trapped on both sides **between** [בתוך]

[בשדה כשלשים איש בישראל].
³⁹ Benjamin began to smite dead men of Israel—**about thirty men** [כשלשים איש].

³³ All the men of Israel **rose from their place** [קמו ממקומו] and drew up at Baal-tamar while the Israelite **ambush sprang from its place** [וארב ישראל מגיח ממקמו] from *west of Geba. Ten thousand picked men of all of Israel **went against** Gibeah [ויבאו מנגד לגבעה],

³⁴ **but they did not realize** [והם לא ידעו] that disaster was upon them [נגעת עליהם].

³⁸ The **agreement** [המועד] had been made between the Israelite force and the ambush to send a smoke signal from the city.

⁴⁰ As the signal began to rise from the city in a column of smoke, Benjamin **turned around** and **Lo! The whole city was going up [in smoke] to the sky** [ויפן בנימן אחריו והנה עלה כליל־העיר השמימה]. ⁴¹ When the men of Israel **turned** [הפך], the men of Benjamin took fright, for they realized that disaster was upon them.

⁴² They turned from the men of Israel to the **desert road** [דרך המדבר].
⁴⁵ They turned and **fled toward the desert** [וינסו המדברה]
⁴⁷ and **fled toward the desert** [וינסו המדברה].

⁴² The **ones from the city** [ואשר מהעיר[ים]] are cutting him down in the **midst** [בתוך[ם]].

Israel, and they slaughtered them until none remained to escape.

8 ²⁴ Then all **the Israelites returned** to Ai **and put it to the sword** [־וישבו כל ישראל העי ויכו אתה לפי־חרב].

³⁷ The ambushers continued to **put the entire city to the sword** [ויך את־כל־ העיר לפי־חרב].
⁴⁸ **The men of Israel returned** [שבו] **to the towns** of Benjamin[ites] **and put them to the sword** [ויכום לפי חרב].

Mourning before YHWH until evening before the ark (Judg 20:23, 26–27; Josh 7:6). In both cases the mourning rites are held following the defeat and continue until evening (עד הערב) at a cult site and/or in the presence of the ark (Josh 7:6, לפני ארון ה'/Judg 20:27, ושם ארון ברית האלהים). And yet the mourning rites differ in each narrative: weeping and fasting in Judg 20:23, 26–27, as opposed to tearing clothes, falling to the ground, and throwing earth on the head in Josh 7:6.

שים ארב/ים ל[עיר] סביב/מאחריה (Judg 20:29/Josh 8:2). The similar expressions appear in similar contexts and announce a new turn in events at the outset of the decisive battle.¹¹⁸ Outside the Ai and Gibeah stories, the expression שים ארב occurs only once more, in Judg 9:25.¹¹⁹ In both the Ai and Gibeah stories the expression occurs in regard to placing an ambush on a town. A different context obtains in Judg 9:25, where the ambush is stationed on the hilltops above. The likelihood that the similarity in expression in Josh 8:2, 12; Judg 20:29, 36 is intentional and not casual is further enhanced by the fact that alternate collocations could have been employed, such as נתן ה' מארבים (2 Chr 20:22).¹²⁰ In Josh 8:2 שים לך ארב לעיר מאחריה indicates that the ambush was placed opposite the far end of the city, concealed from the line of sight of those going out from the city to battle. This position is twice reiterated in 8:4 and 14 by the prepositional phrase מאחרי העיר. In Judg 20:29 שים ארבים אל־הגבעה סביב seems to

---

118. Moore (1895, 435) and Mazor (1994, 99–100) hold that the similarity derives from independent application of the same tactic in both stories.

119. The collocation is also found in Jer 9:7, but the text may be corrupt, since a better parallel with the previous colon, חיץ שחוט לשונם, is obtained by reading ובקרבו ישים חרבו. For interchange of the gutturals ע, ח, ה, א, see Tov 1992, 251.

120. שים and נתן על are frequently interchangeable; e.g., Ezek 4:2: ונתתה עליה מצור ... ונתתה עליה מחנות ושים־עליה כרים סביב; see also Mic 4:14: מצור שם עלינו. See also Exod 18:25; Deut 1:15 vs. Judg 11:11; see Deut 26:19; 28:1, 48; 1 Sam 17:38; 1 Kgs 5:21; 7:16; 10:9; 14:7; 16:2; 2 Kgs 16:17.

indicate that the ambush was set up around the city, but this is not mentioned elsewhere in the narrative.[121]

The similarity in formulation, placement, and function of the notices in Judg 20:29 and Josh 8:2 is probably not incidental. Since there is no echo in the Ai story of setting an ambush *around* the city as found in Judg 20:29, it would appear that either both notices independently draw upon a common source, or that Judg 20:29 was initially modeled upon Josh 8:2 and subsequently revised to reflect setting an ambush *about* the city.

Judges 20:30–32/Joshua 8:5–6 display an intricate network of connections as mapped out below as well as significant contextual differences that bear consequences for evaluating the logic of each narrative.

First, Josh 8:5–6 is part of Joshua's speech in which he imparts his orders to the ambushers (vv. 4–8). Even the words of the enemy, "they are fleeing before us as at first" (v. 6), are mouthed by Joshua in order to demonstrate the purpose of the planned tactic; he is certain that the men of Ai will pursue them, since they will think that this battle is just like the one before, when the Israelites also fled. By contrast, Judg 20:30–32 is reported by the narrator, and the speech of Benjamin and the Israelites is related by him while reporting on the course of the battle. The Israelites' words, "Let us flee and draw him out from the city," appear to be spoken in spontaneous consultation, in reaction to the confident words of Benjamin. However, Benjamin's words, "They are routed before us just as at first," most likely represent an interior monologue rather than actual speech.[122] Such an attempt by a narrator to display and enter into the thoughts of the sides while reporting on the course of a battle is out of keeping with the genre of battle accounts and indicates literary adaptation.

Second, according to the sequence of narrative in Judg 20:30–32, the plan to simulate flight was conceived in the midst of the battle and only *after* Benjamin had already struck the first blow, inflicting Israelite casualties. By contrast, in Josh 8:5–6 the feigned flight scheme is planned in advance, and announced by Joshua *prior* to going to battle.

Lastly, in Josh 8:6 Joshua explains the rationale behind the tactic; when the men of Ai sally forth from the city, the Israelites will begin to flee in order to draw them away from the city. By contrast, in Judg 20:31 the force

---

121. See 20:36, הארב אשר שמו אל־הגבעה, where סביב is noticeably lacking.
122. On interior monologue, see Weiss 1963, 460–71.

in the field is *already* distanced from the city at the outset of the battle, even before deciding to undertake the feigned flight.

Josh 8:5: "I and all the men with me will draw near the city,
   and when they **come out toward** us *like the first time*...."
Judg 20:30–31: The Israelites ... drew up at Gibeah *as before*.
   The Benjaminites **went out toward** the people.

ואני וכל־העם אשר אתי נקרב אל־העיר	Josh 8:5
והיה כי־יצאו לקראתנו כאשר בראשנה ונסנו לפניהם	
ויעלו בני־ישראל ... ויערכו אל־הגבעה	Judg 20:30–31
כפעם בפעם ויצאו בני־בנימן לקראת העם	

Josh 8:6: "They shall **go** *after us*
   until we **separate** them **from the city**."
Judg 20:31: The Benjaminites **went** *out toward*
   the people **separated from the city**,

ויצאו אחרינו	Josh 8:6
עד התיקנו אותם מן־העיר	
ויצאו בני־בנימן לקראת	Judg 20:31
העם הנתקו מן־העיר	

Josh 8:6: for **they shall say**: 'They are *fleeing* before us like the first time.'
   Thus **we shall flee** before them."
Judg 20:32: The Benjaminites **said**: "They are *routed* before us like the
   first time,"
   and the Israelites said: "**We shall flee**."

כי יאמרו נסים לפנינו כאשר בראשנוה	Josh 8:6
ונסנו לפניהם	
ויאמרו בני בנימן נגפים הם לפנינו	Judg 20:32
כבראשנה ובני ישראל אמרו ננוסה	

Josh 8:6: "They shall go after us until we **separate** them **from the city** for
   they shall say,.... Then **we shall flee** before them."
Judg 20:32: The Israelites said: "**We shall flee** and **separate** him **from
   the city**."

ויצאו אחרינו עד התיקנו אותם מן־העיר כי יאמרו ... ונסנו לפניהם	Josh 8:6
ובני ישראל אמרו ננוסה ונתקנוהו מן־העיר	Judg 20:32

Within this section three parallel formulations are particularly significant for evaluating the literary relations between the texts: "separate from the city" (נתק מן העיר, Judg 20:31–32; Josh 8:6, 16); "like the first time" (כאשר/כבראשנה, Judg 20:32; Josh 8:5, 6; cf. Judg 20:39); and "separate from ... flee" (נתק and נוס, Josh 8:6; Judg 20:32).

1. The expression נתק מן העיר, "separate from the city," occurs only in Judg 20:31–32 and Josh 8:6, 16.[123] In Judg 20:32 and Josh 6:16, the expression indicates detaching the enemy from the city by spurring them to pursue the flight of the Israelite forces. In Judg 20:31 the expression also occurs, but here it is applied to the position of the Israelite forces at the outset of the battle, rather than the position into which the enemy will be lured. The inverse application of the expression in Judg 20:31 is not well suited to the battle description, since the feigned flight tactic is designed to draw the *enemy* away from the town so the ambush will be free to act. If, at the outset, the forces in the field were already distanced from the town, then there would be no need for the feigned flight.[124] It appears then that the inverse reapplication of the expression in Judg 20:31 is artificial, and its "ungrammatical" application may have been intended to signal allusion to another narrative context, that is, the Ai story.

2. There are slight, but significant, differences in the expression of the enemy's confidence that the course of the battle *is as before*: כבראשנה /כאשר בראשנה/כמלחמה הראשנה (Judg 20:32; Josh 8:5, 6; Judg 20:39). At first glance, the difference in idiom seems no more than a common interchange between כ- and כאשר. Although כאשר בראשנה is infrequent, its use in Josh 8:5, 6 is consistent with the usage elsewhere (Josh 8:33; 2 Sam 7:10 // 1 Chr 17:9).[125] By contrast, in Judg 20:32 כבראשנה is employed in an atypical fashion. All the other instances of כבראשנה occur with the verb שוב in *qal* or *hiphil*, and they indicate a reversion to the state that existed *at first*, before a change occurred (1 Kgs 13:6; Isa 1:26; Jer 33:7, 11). In Judg 20:32, however, כבראשנה does not express reversion to a prior state, but rather recurrence. This atypical use of the idiom may stem from

---

123. The verb נתק usually signifies severing, e.g., of thread, rope, thong, bar, string, root, or body part; see, e.g., Lev 22:24; Judg 16:9, 12; Isa 5:27; 58:6: Ezek 17:9; 23:34; Qoh 4:12. The meaning of "detaching" or "drawing away from," as in Josh 8 and Judg 20, is otherwise attested only in Josh 4:18, where it signifies the detaching of feet from the Jordan to dry land.

124. See also Moore 1895, 438; Becker 1990, 227.

125. See also בראשנה [verb] אשר (Gen 13:4; 1 Kgs 20:9; Jer 7:12).

stylistic considerations. Surprisingly, there are no instances of the relative conjunction כאשר in Judg 19–21. Since this relative conjunction is common in biblical prose of all periods, it seems that the author of the Gibeah story avoided its use due to personal preference. It appears that R² was familiar with the context in Josh 8:5–6 where he found the idiom כאשר בראשנה, which he replaced with כבראשנה. Again, the atypical use indicates a marker of allusion. N¹ also avoided the relative conjunction כאשר, and exchanged the expression he found in Josh 8:6 with כמלחמה הראשנה (Judg 20:39). However, N¹'s reading is problematic in its narrative context, since it implies that only *one* defeat preceded the present battle. The exchange here reveals the dependency of N¹ on the final form of the Ai story, since there only a single defeat preceded the decisive battle.¹²⁶ Moreover, N¹ could have employed other expressions that would have been consistent with the multiple defeats, such as כפעם בפעם (cf. vv. 30–31).

3. נסנו/ננוסה, התיק/נתק מן העיר (Josh 8:6; Judg 20:32). These elements occur in inverse order:

ויצאו אחרינו עד התיקנו אותם מן־העיר ... וננסנו לפניהם :Josh 8:6
ננוסה ונתקנוהו מן־העיר אל־המסלות :Judg 20:32

In Josh 8:6 these elements are separated by the words Joshua puts in the mouths of the enemy (... כי אמרו). Since the final words, וננסנו לפניהם, are lacking in the LXX, some think they were copied by mistake from verse 5.¹²⁷ In this case, the inverse parallel noted here may be simply the result of a scribal error. However, it is also possible that R² was already familiar with the MT reading in Josh 8:6 and deliberately inverted the order of the elements in Judg 20:32.¹²⁸

---

126. See Frankenberg 1895, 75, 77; Becker 1990, 283. Following Frankenberg's lead, Rösel (1976, 32–34, 46), Crüsemann (1978, 159), and Gray (1986, 229) concluded that the main narrative strand in Judg 20 dealt with only one defeat before the decisive battle (20:11, 17, 20, 29, 33, 36–46). Becker, by contrast, takes vv. 36–46 to be a secondary expansion of the Gibeah battle account, and rules that only this expansion was influenced by Josh 7–8. However, Becker does not seem to have noticed that the atypical use of כבראשנה in v. 32 is as strange to the context as כמלחמה הראשנה in v. 39.

127. See, e.g., Noth 1971, 44 n. 6a; Fritz 1994, 87; Nelson 1997, 108 n. e. Conversely, the translator may have omitted the phrase since it appeared superfluous.

128. This possibility could indicate the relative lateness of R². If the *Vorlage* of

TEXT, SUBTEXT, AND INTERTEXTUAL MOSAIC   211

In summary, the analysis of the parallels between Judg 20:30–32 and Josh 8:5–6 seem to indicate a one-sided influence that the Ai story exerted upon R²'s version of the decisive battle at Gibeah. These findings have significant diachronic implications, since Josh 8:3–9 is widely regarded as a secondary expansion that disrupts the narrative thread relating to the mobilization at Ai in Josh 8:1–2, 10–14.[129] It appears then that R² was familiar with this late and possibly post-Deuteronomistic revision of the story of the conquest of Ai.

בשדה (Judg 20:31/Josh 8:24). Both stories mention the felling of casualties "in the field" along with the path of flight and pursuit. The two descriptions are also inversely related; in Judg 20:31 the *enemy* (Benjamin) *begins* to strike Israelites dead in the field, while in Josh 8:24 *Israel finishes* killing the enemy (men of Ai) in the field.

Judg 30:31: וַיָּחֵלּוּ לְהַכּוֹת מֵהָעָם חֲלָלִים כְּפַעַם בְּפַעַם כְּפַעַם בַּמְסִלּוֹת אֲשֶׁר
אַחַת עֹלָה בֵּית־אֵל וְאַחַת גִּבְעָתָה בַשָּׂדֶה
Josh 8:24: כְּכַלּוֹת יִשְׂרָאֵל לַהֲרֹג אֶת־כָּל־יֹשְׁבֵי הָעַי בַּמִּדְבָּר בַשָּׂדֶה אֲשֶׁר
רְדָפוּם בּוֹ

The accumulated points of contact here strengthen the case for literary interrelation. The direction of the relationship is indicated by the parallel mention of the field, which has been tacked on to the end of the clause detailing the roads in Judg 30:31.[130] In Josh 8:24, however, the mention of killing *in the field* is appropriate since it stands in opposition to finishing off the people who remained *in Ai* (v. 24b). Thus it is possible that "in the field" was added to Judg 30:31 in order to heighten the interrelation with the story of Ai.

---

the LXX of Josh 8:6 represents the original text, then it would date to the end of the seventh–mid-sixth century BCE, depending upon the approach taken regarding the composition of the conquest account. If the MT of Josh 8:6 is a secondary expansion, then it originated in a period when enough copies of the Joshua scroll existed for variant texts to evolve. In principle, textual errors or variants can be perpetuated in the third generation of copying. If the MT of Josh 8:6 was created in a "third-generation" text, then it should perhaps belong to the sixth–fifth century BCE. Judges 20:32b may then be dependent upon a "third-generation" copy of the Joshua scroll, which would place R² no earlier than the mid-sixth century.

129. See Edenburg 2012c, 56–57, with additional literature there.
130. See Boling 1982, 297, who surmises that במסלות/בשדה are textual variants.

About thirty/thirty-six men (Judg 20:31, 39; Josh 7:5). The collocation כשלשים occurs only in these verses. The figure indicates the number of Israelite casualties felled by the enemy in both stories, but at different stages of the narrative. In the Ai story an exact figure—"thirty-six," (כ)שלשים וששה—is given for the *preliminary defeat*, while in the Gibeah story the approximate number כשלשים is represented in the *final battle*. The figures of Israelite casualties in the final battle at Gibeah are markedly disproportionate in comparison to those given for the previous engagements. On the decisive third day, the Benjaminites are confident that course of the battle has been decided "just as before" after felling only thirty Israelites, but the Israelite casualties were massively greater in the previous engagements (20,000 on the first day and 18,000 on the second, Judg 20:21, 25).[131] The figures for the initial defeats at Gibeah seem to be calculated to indicate a loss of about 10 percent of the troops, which numbered 400,000 at the outset (20:17), and they are consistent with the inner logic of the narrative. Thus the parallel figure "about thirty" in Judg 20:31, 39 might have been influenced by the Ai story. At the same time, it should be noted that the reading בִּשְׁלֹשִׁים וששה is odd, since the *kaph* of approximation is not expected with an exact number.[132] It is possible then, that the initial parallel between the texts caused a subsequent assimilation in Josh 7:5 of the prefix appearing in Judg 20:31, 39.

Swiftly rose/sprung from his place (קם מהרה/מגיח ממקומו, Judg 20:33–34; Josh 8:19; cf. Judg 20:37). Here also the texts interrelate in an intricate fashion. Surprisingly, the collocation קם + ממקום occurs only in Judg 20:33a and Josh 8:19aα. Different parts of the Israelite force are described as "rising from their place" in the two stories: the ambushers in Josh 8:19, as opposed to the main force (כל איש ישראל) in Judg 20:33a. In both instances, the subject is a collective noun. All parts of the sentence in

---

131. The figure "about thirty" in Judg 20:31, 39 is generally considered the number of actual casualties, while casualty figures for the preliminary battles are thought to be inflated or to represent the number of troops (אלף); see, e.g., Noth 1966, 166; Boling 1982, 284–85, 287. Neither of these proposals is necessary if one acknowledges the fictive nature of the story.

132. Aḥituv (1995, 124), citing Kimchi, takes this to be the *kaph veritatis*, meaning here "*precisely* thirty-six." However, according to GKC §118x, the *kaph veritatis* emphasizes comparison rather than identity. *Kaph* is generally prefixed to round numbers (fifteen instances), and only twice more does it occur with an exact number: Ezek 8:16 (see Zimmerli 1979, 221) and 1 Sam 25:13, which seems to be a harmonistic gloss or conflated reading based on the figures in 1 Sam 22:2; 23:13.

Josh 8:19aα are construed in the singular (מקומו, קם, אורב), while in Judg 20:33a the verb is plural while the genitive suffix is singular (קמו ממקומו). Although a scribal error might have produced the awkward text in Judg 20:33a,[133] it is equally possible that the ungrammaticality indicates the literary influence of Josh 8:19aα. If so, R² preferred to construe the verb in Judg 20:33a as a plural, perhaps due to the tendency in LBH to construe collective nouns as plurals,[134] while he left the genitive suffix in the singular (ממקומו), just as he found in Josh 8:19aα.

Judg 20:33a: וכל איש ישראל קמו ממקומו ויערכו בבעל תמר
Josh 8:19: והאורב קם מהרה ממקומו ... ויבאו העי[ר]
Judg 20:33b–34: וארב ישראל מגיח ממקמו ... ויבאו מנגד לגבעה עשרת אלפים איש
Judg 20:37: והארב החישו ויפשטו אל־הגבעה

Although all versions (Josh 8:19; R² in Judg 20:33; and N¹ in Judg 20:37) describe the swiftness of the ambush, the Gibeah story employs poetic expressions (החישו, מגיח Judg 20:33, 37), while the Ai narrative uses prosaic language (מהרה, Josh 8:19).[135] If Judg 20:33b and 37a derive from a prior poetic source, as surmised above,[136] then the description of the speed of the ambush was not influenced by the Ai story. Indeed, it is possible that on this point the Gibeah story exerted its influence on the final form of the story of Ai, causing a late scribe to add the adverb מהרה to Josh 8:19 in order to heighten the similarity between the descriptions.

"Went up against" (בא + נגד) is unique to Josh 8:11 and Judg 20:34. The preposition נגד generally occurs with stative verbs,[137] such as חנה נגד (Exod 19:2; Num 2:2), and indeed in Josh 8:11 בא נגד appears in the

---

133. Moore (1895, 438) found the style "not elegant," but did not suggest emendation; see Kaufmann 1961, 295. Budde (1897, 137) and Ehrlich (1968, 156) suggested instead that ממקומו is out of place in v. 33a and was miscopied from v. 33b, while Burney (1970, 480) prefers emending the text for agreement in number.

134. See Polzin 1976, 42–43; Rooker 1990, 46–47, 75–77.

135. For מגיח, החישו, see above, ch. 3. מהרה occurs twenty-two times in the Bible, fourteen of which are in prose (Num 17:11; Deut 11:17; Josh 8:19; 10:6; 23:16; Judg 9:54; 1 Sam 20:38; 23:27; 2 Sam 17:16, 18, 21; 1 Kgs 22:9; Jer 27:16).

136. See ch. 1.

137. See, e.g., with עמד/התיצב (2 Sam 18:13; 1 Kgs 8:22; Obad 11; Ps 5:6), ישב (1 Kgs 21:3), כרע (2 Kgs 1:13), ראה (2 Kgs 2:15; 3:22; 4:25). An exception is לך מנגד (Prov 14:7), which is probably idiomatic, meaning "stay away from."

context of camping opposite the city. In Judg 20:34, however, בא מנגד describes the action of the force attacking the town. The use of this collocation in Judg 20:34 seems intentional, since the author could have written בא עד־נכח as in 19:10 and 20:43. Again, the unusual usage here may indicate that the expression was borrowed from the more fitting context in Josh 8:11.

They/he did not know that ... be upon/touched them (והם/הוא לא ידע/ו וינגעו ... /כי נגעת, Judg 20:34; Josh 8:14–15). The expression "*x* did not know" (*x* לא ידע) commonly indicates unawareness of events, deception, or secret happenings.[138] And yet Josh 8 and Judg 20 are the only battle descriptions in which the expression occurs. In both stories, the enemy is unaware of the developments. In the Ai story, the enemy *did not know* that an ambush was stationed behind the city, while in the Gibeah story, the enemy *did not know* that the course of the battle had turned to his detriment. Both stories also utilize the root נגע, but in different fashions. Judges 20:34 (R²) employs the collocation נגע + רעה, which recurs only in this narrative (N¹, v. 41). In Josh 8:15, however, the reading וינגעו לפני may be the result of assimilation in the direction of the text of Judg 20:34.

[They] turned round and Lo! the (whole) city was going up in smoke skyward ... and x turned (ויפן אחריו והנה עלה כליל/ עשן העיר השמימה/ ... ו-*x* נ/הפך, Judg 20:40–41; Josh 8:20). In both Judg 20:40–41 and Josh 8:20, the enemy turns about and sees that their city is going up in smoke, and this signals the Israelite main force to begin the counterattack and "turn" upon the enemy.[139] There is an ironic touch to the *turning* of the Israelites upon their enemy in Josh 8:20, since this marks the end of their false flight, while during the first battle at Ai, the Israelites *turned* their backs (הפך ערף) in actual flight (7:8). However, while Josh 8:20 states prosaically that the city was going up in *smoke* (עשן העיר),[140] Judg 20:40 employs the unique construct כליל העיר. From the context, it is clear that the unusual expression indeed represents the smoke of the (burning) city, since earlier it states that the ambush was to send a smoke signal from the town (v. 38) and that the signal began to rise in a column of smoke from the city (v. 40). כליל העיר is an original metaphor that compares the

---

138. See, e.g., Gen 38:16; 42:23; Exod 34:29; Num 22:34; Judg 13:16; 16:20; 1 Kgs 1:11.

139. For this understanding of הפך, see also Josephus, *Ant.* 5.2.11 §161.

140. For עלה עשן, see also Exod 19:18; 2 Sam 22:9 // Ps 18:9; Cant 3:6.

smoke of the burning of the city to a holocaust offering.¹⁴¹ This metaphor is appropriate to the context of the Ai story, which stresses the importance of consecrating the conquered town to YHWH (Josh 8:2, 26–28). Therefore, it might be expected that the author of Josh 7–8 would have borrowed it for his own use, had he been familiar with the Gibeah story. Since this is not the case, it seems likely that the author of Judg 20:40 based himself upon the formulation in Josh 8:20 but exchanged the prosaic construct found there for the metaphor כליל העיר, in order to allude to burning the city *completely* (כליל), as ordered with regard to the apostate city in Deut 13:17.

They fled via the desert (road) (וינסו [דרך] המדבר, Judg 20:42, 45, 47; Josh 8:15, 20; see also v. 24). The motif of flight via the desert route is applied in a converse fashion in the two stories. In the Ai story, the desert route was the path of the Israelites' *false* flight, while in the Gibeah story, this was the route of the enemy's (Benjamin's) *actual* flight. The desert is not mentioned in the Old Greek of Josh 8;¹⁴² however, the three mentions in the MT are integrated into the narrative in different stages and appear independent of one another. Verse 15 represents the false flight *via the desert road*, verse 20 describes the counterattack when those who "fled" *in the direction of the desert* turned upon their pursuers, and verse 24 deals with the final stage in which the Israelites now pursue and pick off the men of Ai *in the desert field* (i.e., the outskirts of the town).¹⁴³ In Judg 20, by contrast, the threefold mention of *the desert (road)* are all dependent upon one another and deal with the same matter, namely, the flight of the enemy who can no longer retreat back into the city. The geographical details of the Ai story also support the mention of the desert in Josh 8:15, 20, since the path of the false flight most likely was identical with flight path the day before, when the Israelites fled southeast from Ai toward Jericho. "Desert Road" is indeed a fitting name for this route, which connected to the Arabah route at Jericho.¹⁴⁴ In Judg 20, the "Desert Road" leads to the rock of Rimmon (vv. 45, 47), which cannot be located with certainty, although tradition attested from Byzantine times placed it south of Beth-

---

141. See above, ch. 3.
142. In Josh 8:24 the OG reads instead במורד, but this reading might reflect a scribal accident that was influenced by the memory of 7:5, וירדפום ... ויכום במורד.
143. Taking בשדה במדבר as hendiadys. For the meaning "outskirts," see Isa 43:20; Joel 1:19–20; see 1 Sam 25:14–15.
144. See Aharoni 1979, 60; Dorsey 1991, 203–4; see also v. 14; 1 Sam 13:17–18.

el.¹⁴⁵ According to this tradition, the Benjaminites' flight led northward, and this also is indicated by the mention of the Bethel and Geba routes in verses 31–32 (cf. v. 45). Thus terming the direction of Benjamin's flight as דרך המדבר or המדברה does not fit well with the topographical details of the battle. It seems likely, then, that this detail was taken over from the Ai story, where it is at home.

The combination of expressions מן העיר ... בתוך is used in both Judg 20:42 and Josh 8:22 to describe the entrapment of the enemy *between* the force in the field and the ambush as it emerged *from the city*.¹⁴⁶ Judges 20:42b stems from the postulated poetic source, although the use of the relative clause *אשר מהעיר* ("those from the city") is difficult both in poetry and in prose.¹⁴⁷ It is possible that the poetic source limited the mission of the ambush to taking the city and sending the smoke signal, while the encirclement of Benjamin was achieved alone by the force in the field (cf. v. 43). If so, N¹ may have exchanged the song's original subject for *אשר מהעיר* in order to heighten the similarity to the Ai narrative. However, if *אשר מהעיר* is original to the poetic source, then the song independently represented a battle picture similar to that in Josh 8, and this initial similarity may have been one of the factors that motivated N¹ to fashion the Gibeah narrative along the lines of the Ai story.

Return ... and cut down by the sword (שוב ... והכה לפי חרב, Judg 20:48; Josh 8:24). "Cut down by the sword" (הכה לפי חרב) is a common expression that occurs more than twenty times in the Bible, and it frequently indicates the conquest of a city (e.g., Josh 10:28, 30; 11:12; Judg 1:25; 20:37; 1 Sam 22:19). In Josh 8:19–22, the ambushers quickly raided the city, set it afire, and rejoined the field in order to cut off the line of retreat. Thus following the victory in the field, it was necessary to return to the city and finish off all those remaining in it, such as the women and children. In Judg 20:48 too, the Israelites *return* to strike the enemy, but they do not return to Gibeah, which already had been finished off by the ambush (v. 37). Instead, their objective this time is all of Benjamin's cities. The object of the war is no longer limited to meting out justice upon Gibeah but is now expanded to include all of Benjamin. Within the larger context,

---

145. See above, ch. 2.

146. Elsewhere, the entrapment of the enemy between the flanks of the army is described by the expression היתה אליו פני המלחמה מפנים ומאחור ("the fighting was in front and behind him/them," 2 Sam 10:9; 1 Chr 19:10; 2 Chr 13:14).

147. See above, ch. 1, n. 111.

this notice sets the stage for the next episode dealing with the fate of the Benjaminite refugees. Even so, it was not necessary to relate that the Israelites "returned" (שבו) to the Benjaminites in order to destroy their cities. Indeed, there is no real "return" here, since the Israelites do not return to their target as in Josh 8 but undertake a new objective. Thus it appears that this formulation was borrowed from its proper context in Josh 8.

SUMMARY AND CONCLUSIONS

The extensive comparison between the narrative of the war at Gibeah and the story of the conquest of Ai produces much evidence for literary interaction between the two texts, including cumulative connections, unique parallels, inverse application of shared elements, and "ungrammatical" application of a shared element. The texts also contain more common parallels that may reflect independent use as well as secondary textual assimilation.

Distribution of cumulative connections. Judges 20 shares language with Josh 7–8 on more than twenty different points, and these are distributed throughout the description of the third battle at Gibeah (Judg 20:29–48), both in N[1] and R[2]. Three sections in Judg 20 display a critical mass of connections with Josh 7–8: Judg 20:31–32 // Josh 8:5–6 (נתק; יצא לקראת; מן העיר; נסים לפנינו כ[אשר] בראשנה/אמר נגפים); Judg 20:34 // Josh 8:11, 14–15 (בא נגד; והם/הוא לא ידע/ו; נגע עליו/נגגע); Judg 20:40–42 // Josh 8:20 (ויפנו/נס; [וראה]; פנה אחריו; והנה עלה כליל/עשן העיר השמימה; [דרך] המדבר). These cumulative connections may point to intentional literary interrelation. The only verses within Judg 20:29–48 that are free of contact with the Ai story are the opening of the third battle description, which is built upon the model of the previous two days (v. 30; cf. vv. 20–21, 22, 24–25); the prearranged signal with the ambush force (v. 38); a section of the song (v. 43); and the casualty figures (vv. 35, 44, 46). Within Josh 8, the distribution of the points of contact are markedly more sporadic. Surprisingly, sections detailing the common tactics share no language with the description of the third battle at Gibeah (vv. 4, 7–8, 17) and instead evince independent formulation. Thus the distribution of contacts seems to indicate that while the description of the final battle at Gibeah displays a consistent interrelation with the Ai story, the Ai story is relatively independent.

Unique points of contact. Three collocations appear only in these two stories: נתק מן העיר (Judg 20:31–32; Josh 8:6, 16); קם ממקומו (Judg 20:33;

Josh 8:19); בא נגד (Judg 20:34; Josh 8:11). In addition, the expression הם הוא לא ידעו/ (Judg 20:34; Josh 8:14) does not occur in other battle narratives. All of these expression are found in Judg 20 only in the R² expansions.

Inverse application. Four shared elements occur in inverse application. Two of them occur in Judg 20 only in R²: נתק מן העיר (Judg 20:31–32; Josh 8:6) and כבלות להרג בשדה/להכות בשדה ויחלו (Judg 20:31; Judg 8:24). The remaining two occur in both N¹ and R²: איש ... כשלשים (Judg 20:31, 39; Josh 7:5) and נגע עליו/נגגע(Judg 20:34, 41; Josh 8:15).

Intentional exchange. I identified two cases of intentional exchange in which sentences in both stories are parallel in vocabulary and syntax but differ in a significant detail that can be explained as an intentional exchange of terms. Both Judg 20:29 and Josh 8:2 employ the expression [name of town] שים ארב אל/ל-עיר, but R² in Judg 20 changed the singular ארב to plural and added the adverbial סביב in order to accommodate the two different descriptions of the ambush in verses 33–34, 37–38. Judges 20:40 and Josh 8:20 also share the description והנה עלה [ ] העיר השמימה. While Josh 8:20 uses the common expression עלה עשן, Judg 20:40 makes metonymic use of the term כליל even though elsewhere the narrative makes reference to smoke (vv. 38, 40, עלה מן העיר משאת עמוד עשן/). Since the term כליל is used of the burnt offering and of the burning of the apostate town (Deut 13:17), the exchange of terms seems to be tendentious.

Ungrammatical application of a shared element. Eleven shared elements were utilized in the Gibeah story without proper adaptation to the context or syntax. Contextually difficult are mention of "the ark" (Judg 20:27), the people "distanced from the city" (20:31, הנתקו מן העיר), killing "in the field" (20:31), "like the first battle" (20:39), about "thirty men" (20:31, 39), flight on the "desert route" (20:42, 45, 47), and "returning" to smite the enemy (20:48). Syntactic difficulties or deviation from common usage characterize the collocation קמו ממקומו (20:33), כבראשנה (20:32), and perhaps also בא נגד(20:34) and *אשר מהעיר (20:42).

Parallels attested elsewhere. Five common expressions occur in other contexts, including other battle descriptions. These include שים ארב (Judg 20:29, 36; Josh 8:2, 12); יצא לקראת (Judg 20:25, 31; Josh 8:5, 14, 22); הכה לפי חרב (Judg 20:37, 48; Josh 8:24); הפך/נהפך (Judg 20:39, 41; Josh 8:20); and [וראה] פנה אחריו (Judg 20:40; Josh 8:20). The recurrence of these expressions by themselves cannot indicate literary interdependence, but they can strengthen the case when additional evidence is at hand.

TEXT, SUBTEXT, AND INTERTEXTUAL MOSAIC   219

Independent use. Three shared elements are found in Judg 20 in sections attributed to the poetic source. The swift action of the ambush is indicated twice by verbs that figure mainly in poetic contexts (מגיח, v. 33; החישו, v. 37), while Josh 8:19 employs the common adverb מהרה. In addition, מועד (Judg 20:38; Josh 8:14) occurs in different contexts and with different meaning in both stories. In all these cases, it is plausible that the usages are independent of one another.[148]

Secondary textual assimilation. The similarity between the two stories appears to have exerted influence on the transmission of the text of the Ai story. Thus the *kaph* of approximation with an exact number in Josh 7:5 (כשלשים וששה) was undoubtedly influenced by the appearance of כשלשים as a round number in Judg 20:31, 39. It is also possible that the unparalleled ויגעו לפני in Josh 8:15 originally read ויגפו לפני but was influenced by the usage of the verb נגע in Judg 20:34, 41.

On the basis of these results, it is possible to evaluate the degree of interaction with the Ai story in both N¹ and R² of the Gibeah story. Parallel usage in N¹ and the Ai story mainly consists of isolated expressions or motifs, such as כשלשים איש, הכה לפי חרב, נגע, הפך, כמלחמה הראשנה, and flight on the "desert route." A more extensive connection is noticeable in three sentences: *city* ויפן אחריו והנה עלה x שים ארב אל העיר; מן העיר ... בתוך; השמימה *x*. By contrast, the parallel usage in R² consists of sentences displaying a network of contacts, sometimes touching upon a number of different verses from the Ai story, as can be seen from the comparisons of Judg 20:31–32 // Josh 8:5–6, 24; Judg 20:33–34 // Josh 8:11, 19; Judg 20:34 // Josh 8:14–15; Judg 20:48 // Josh 8:24, 27–28. Isolated contact is limited to the recurring phraseology of "about thirty men" (Judg 20:31) and flight on the "desert route" (Judg 20:45), as well as the mention of the ark on the eve of the battle (Judg 20:27).

In two instances it is possible to see that R² reuses phrases from N¹ and rephrases them in order to tighten the similarity to the Ai story:

1. N¹ Judg 20:41: כי ראה כי נגעה עליו הרעה
   R² Judg 20:34: והם לא ידעו כי נגעת עליהם הרעה
   Josh 8:14–15: ... והוא לא ידע כי כי־ארב לו מאחרי העיר וינגעו

---

148. See also van der Meer 2004, 437; contra Mazor 1994, 105–6.

2. N¹ Judg 20:37: והארב החישו ויפשטו אל־הגבעה
R² Judg 20:33–34: וארב ישראל מגיח ממקמו *ממערב גבע ויבאו מנגד לגבעה
Josh 8:19: ממקומו קם מהרה והאורב ויבאו העיר

In the second example, the description of the speedy action of the ambushers is original to the poetic source of the Gibeah battle, but the double prepositional phrase in Judg 20:33, *"from its place from *west of Geba"* (ממקומו *ממערב גבע), may be due to the efforts of R² to heighten the parallel with Josh 8:19.

In conclusion, the examination of the parallel phraseology revealed significant evidence of deliberate literary contact between the story of Ai and the story of Gibeah. The structural comparison between the stories shows that the Gibeah story is fraught with narrative gaps and dysfunctional motifs, while the story of Ai is characterized by a smooth flow of narrative. Since it is doubtful that an author would pattern his narrative upon a deficient model, it is most likely that the Ai story is an independent composition. It is possible that an initial general similarity between the story of Ai and the poetic source for the battle at Gibeah motivated N¹ to flesh out the prose narrative with phrases and motifs borrowed from Josh 7–8. During the later revision of the Gibeah story, R² added a complementary battle description and a harmonistic summary, both of which further tighten the interrelation with the Ai story. Finally, the evident similarity between the descriptions influenced the process of textual transmission, in the course of which certain points in the text of the Ai story assimilated toward the text of the Gibeah narrative.

These conclusions have far-reaching consequences for dating the composition of the Gibeah story. The core of the story of the conquest of Ai was composed for the Deuteronomistic account of the conquest.[149] Since the prose version of the battle at Gibeah is dependent upon the story of Ai, it would appear that the whole narrative in Judg 19–21 must derive from a period later than the surmised late-seventh-century composition of the Deuteronomistic conquest account. Moreover, the tendentious use of materials that stem from the Deuteronomistic source as well as the post-Deuteronomistic revision of the combined Ai and Achan

---

149. See, e.g., Naʾaman 1994, 259; Römer 2005, 82–90; contra van der Meer 2004, 445–48, who argues for a pre-Dtr narrative that was later revised by the Dtr.

stories provides support for viewing the story of the Gibeah war as a post-Deuteronomistic composition.

It is likely that additional motives, apart from the initial similarity between the poetic Gibeah source and the Ai story, moved N¹ to model his battle description upon the shape and phraseology of the story of Ai. Previously, it was seen that by weaving borrowed phraseology and allusions to the story of Sodom, N¹ created an analogy between Gibeah and Sodom, which is infamous in tradition as the city of sin. The addition of allusions to Ai may have been intended to draw an analogy between the fate of Ai, which ended as "a mound of ruins for all time, a desolation to this very day" (Josh 8:28), and the fate the author wished upon Gibeah. Perhaps, in his time, Gibeah was already abandoned, and comparable to a "ruin for all time."

4.4. The Saul Narratives

Gibeah is prominent not only in Judg 19–21 but also in the book of Samuel, where it is the place of Saul's residence.[150] The placement of the story of Gibeah, immediately before Samuel's birth and the establishment of the monarchy, suggests an attempt to draw an analogy between the events connected with Gibeah in Judg 19–21 and in the Saul narratives.

1 Samuel 11:7

Judg 19:29–20:1	1 Sam 11:7
19 ²⁹ **He took** [ויקח] the knife and seized his concubine and **cut her** [וינתחה] limb by limb into twelve pieces, and **sent her throughout the territory of Israel** [וישלחה בכל גבול ישראל]. [LXX^A: and instructed the men he sent, saying (ויצו האנשים אשר שלח לאמר): "So you shall say to all the Israelites, 'Has such a thing happened …'."] ³⁰ All who saw it said, "Never has such a thing happened from the day the Israelites came up from the land of Egypt to	⁷ **He took** [ויקח] a pair of oxen and **cut them** into pieces [וינתחהו] and sent them throughout the territory of Israel [וישלח בכל גבול ישראל] by means of messengers, saying [ביד המלאכים לאמר]: "Thus shall be done to the cattle of whoever does not follow Saul and Samuel."

---

150. See 1 Sam 10:5, 26; 11:4; 14:2; 15:34; 22:6; 23:19; 26:1; 2 Sam 21:6.

this day! Take note of this, take counsel and decide." 20 ¹ Then all the Israelites came forth [ויצאו] and the assembly gathered **as one man** [כאיש אחד].

Terror of YHWH fell upon the people, and **they came out as one man** [ויצאו כאיש אחד].

Judges 19:29–20:1 and 1 Sam 11:7 employ similar phraseology to describe the mustering the people by means of body parts sent throughout the territory of Israel.[151] Three striking expressions are shared by both texts. "To go forth as one man" (יצא כאיש אחד) occurs only in Judg 20:1 and 1 Sam 11:7.[152] "Send throughout the borders [= territory] of Israel" (שלח בכל גבול ישראל) occurs only in Judg 19:29 and 1 Sam 11:3, 7, and its double occurrence in 1 Sam 11 suggests that it is firmly rooted in the story of Saul.[153] The final striking verbal parallel is the verb נתח, "to cut up" (Judg 19:29; 1 Sam 11:7). Elsewhere in the Bible this verb is restricted to cultic contexts dealing with sacrificial offerings, and the object of the verb is invariably an animal (Exod 29:17; Lev 1:6, 12; 1 Kgs 18:23, 33), as it also is in 1 Sam 11:7 (oxen).[154] The divinely inspired terror induced by Saul's step indicates that he was performing a cultic act as YHWH's agent. By contrast, the object of the verb נתח in Judg 19:29 is human rather than animal, and there is no indication that the action was performed in the name of YHWH. Instead, the concubine's husband acts on his own initiative as a private agent, and the shock of the people who viewed the dismembered body (Judg 19:30) indicates the extraordinary nature of the act. Thus the use of the cult term נתח to describe cutting up the concubine's body deviates from the standard usage and may indicate that the Levite's actions are patterned upon those of Saul in 1 Sam 11:7, but with a dramatic twist: the concubine takes the place of Saul's oxen as sacrificial victim and without any divine ordinance.[155]

---

151. See, e.g., Bertheau 1845, 219; Bleek 1878, 202; Moore 1895, 420–21; Budde 1897, 132; Burney 1970, 444–45; Schunck 1963, 63–64, 90–91; Gray 1986, 352; Amit 2000, 181; de Hoop 2004, 23–24.

152. But כאיש אחד alone occurs twice more in Judg 20:8, 11, as well as five more times in other contexts: Num 14:15; Judg 6:16; 2 Sam 19:15; Ezra 3:1; Neh 8:1.

153. בכל גבול ישראל alone occurs elsewhere four more times: 1 Sam 27:1; 2 Sam 21:5; 1 Kgs 1:3; 2 Kgs 10:32.

154. See also Gross 2009, 845–46.

155. The collocation used here, וינתחה לעצמיה, is similar to the expression נתח לנתחיו, which is employed in cultic contexts dealing with dismembering the sacrificial victim; see Exod 29:17; Lev 1:6, 12; 8:20; see also Ezek 24:4.

At the same time, there are significant differences between the two contexts that must be considered as well.[156] Thus Judg 19:29 specifies that the Levite cut the concubine into "twelve pieces," which seems to indicate that a piece was sent to each tribe (including Benjamin!).[157] By contrast, 1 Sam 11:7 does not mention the number of pieces or whether the territory of Israel included twelve tribes. Indeed, it is not certain whether the dismembered oxen were sent along with the messengers commissioned by Saul to deliver his message.[158] More significantly, the MT of Judg 19:29–30 makes no mention of messengers or of a verbal message to accompany the body parts, which is in marked contrast to 1 Sam 11:7.[159] There the messengers are commissioned by Saul to deliver a conditioned threat: "Thus shall be done to the cattle of whoever does not follow Saul." Saul's act in cutting up his oxen is construed as a symbolic threat that illustrates the consequences of noncompliance with the call to muster.[160]

In summation, in 1 Sam 11, Saul acts as a figure of authority who uses the pieces of his oxen along with a conditional threat in order to muster the people. This description accords well with the circumstances of the Ammonite threat and with Saul's standing in the narrative. By contrast, the purpose of the Levite's act is not clear in its context. The choice of the Levite to dismember his concubine rather than an ox, donkey, or sheep arouses astonishment, and the MT of Judg 19:29–30 leaves his aims unexplained. It is possible that the grotesque nature of the scene, along with its similarity to

---

156. See, e.g., Miller 1974a, 167–68; Jüngling 1981, 237; Soggin 1987, 289; Becker 1990, 261.

157. So Josephus, *Ant.* 5.2.8 §149; Abravanel. The notion that a piece was also sent to Benjamin is not at odds with the logic of the narrative, since Benjamin was free to ignore the summons; see O'Connell 1996, 260. Most likely, the twelve pieces reflect the ideal totality of the people residing "throughout the territory of Israel," which was subsequently marred by Benjamin's separatism; cf. Liverani 2004, 162–66; Gross 2009, 846–47.

158. Elsewhere, שלח ביד x לאמר only indicates commissioning a messenger to deliver a verbal message; see 2 Kgs 17:13; see also Jer 27:3 (LXX); Zech 7:12; 2 Chr 36:15.

159. LXX[A] fills this gap with instructions that the Levite gave his messengers, but this description comes *after* the people already respond to the sight of the body pieces in 19:30a. Most likely, the reading by LXX[A] reflects and interpretive elaboration by the translator that was influenced by 1 Sam 11:7. See also Gross 2009, 807, 847.

160. Symbolic actions that represent conditional threats are not uncommon to ancient Near Eastern treaties; see, e.g., Sefire i A 39–40; and the treaty between Matiʿilu and Assurnirari VI (I, 10–35); see also Wallis 1952; Polzin 1969, 234–37.

that in 1 Sam 11:7, indicates that the Levite's actions in Judg 19:29 were formulated as a parody of Saul as he appears in 1 Sam 11:7. If so, then N¹ borrowed from 1 Sam 11 the motif of mustering by means of circulating pieces a dismembered body among the people.¹⁶¹ Since the story of Saul's victory over the Ammonites in 1 Sam 11:1–11 is generally considered to belong to the pre-Deuteronomistic source for the history of Saul,¹⁶² the dependency of Judg 19:29–20:1 upon 1 Sam 11:7 is of limited value for establishing a relative date for the composition of the Gibeah story.

1 Samuel 10:26–27; 11:12–13

Judg 20:13	1 Sam 10:26–27; 11:12–13
¹³ "And now **turn over the men** [תנו את האנשים], the **scoundrels** [בני בליעל], in **Gibeah** and **we will put them to death** [ונמיתם] and eradicate evil from Israel." But Benjamin would not comply with the demand of their brothers [ולא אבו בני בנימין לשמע בקול אחיהם], the Israelites.	10 ²⁶ Saul also went home to **Gibeah**, accompanied by men of substance whose hearts God had touched. ²⁷ But **scoundrels** [בני בליעל] said: "How can this one save us? They held him in contempt and brought him no tribute, while he let it pass [ויהי כמחריש]."¹⁶³ 11 ¹² The people said to Samuel: "Who says, 'Shall Saul be king over us?' **Turn over the men and we will put them to death** [תנו האנשים ונמיתם]." ¹³ But Saul said, "No one shall die this day, for today YHWH has brought victory to Israel."

The verbal parallels between Judg 20:13 and the sections framing the story of Saul's victory over the Ammonites include mention of men from Gibeah, the expression בני בליעל, and the demand תנו (את) האנשים ונמיתם.¹⁶⁴ In both contexts (Judg 20:13; 1 Sam 10:27), the term בני בליעל is indefinite. The lack of determination fits the context in 1 Sam 10:27,

---

161. So also Lasine 1984, 41–43; Brettler 1989a, 412–13; Amit 2000, 181; see also Schunck 1963, 63–64.

162. See, e.g., Schunck 1963, 93–91; Veijola 1977, 39–40; McCarter 1980, 206–7; Na'aman 1992, 642–43.

163. 4QSamᵃ reads ויהי כְּמַחֲדֵשׁ, "after a month." Many scholars prefer this reading over the MT; see, e.g., McCarter 1980, 199–200.

164. See also Bleek 1878, 202; Becker 1990, 21–24.

where Saul's detractors are anonymous. However, in Judg 20:13 the lack of determination is grammatically difficult since the indefinite term appears in apposition with the definite noun האנשים.[165] If the narrator wanted to employ standard usage and characterize the men (האנשים) as בני בליעל, he could have used a construct, such as אנשי הבליעל.[166] Thus the irregular usage in Judg 20:13 may result from inserting the characterization בני בליעל into the phrase "turn over the men so we may put them to death" (תנו האנשים ונמיתם), which was borrowed from 1 Sam 10:27. The men of Gibeah were previously characterized as בני בליעל in Judg 19:22, and there too the term was inserted into a phrase borrowed from Gen 19:4.[167] It is true that N[1] may have freely chosen the term in both instances, instead of analogous expressions, such as בני עולה or אנשי און.[168] However, the possibility should also be considered that the term בני בליעל was employed, because it occurred in texts upon which the author drew, such as 1 Sam 10:27.

An additional indication of the literary interrelation between the texts is the inverse relation between the scoundrels (בני בליעל) and the town of Gibeah. In Judg 20:13 the scoundrels are the men of Gibeah, while in 1 Sam 10:26–27 and 11:12–13 the scoundrels are anonymous men who questioned the authority of Saul, the man from Gibeah.

The evidence for evaluating the relations between Judg 20:13 and 1 Sam 10:26–27; 11:12–13 is relatively slim. The sections that frame the story of the battle with the Ammonites present Saul in a favorable light and characterize him as a modest man who waited patiently for recognition until his success in battle removes all doubts that he indeed was YHWH's designated ruler. In this context, his refusal to put the scoundrels to death can be viewed as an act of magnanimity. By contrast, the Benjaminites' refusal to hand over the scoundrels in Gibeah is viewed as an act of rebellion. It is not reasonable that an author would employ phraseology from the Gibeah story when composing a passage designed to legitimize Saul's claim to rule, since Saul's ties to Gibeah would defeat

---

165. See Joüon §138. The collocation האנשים בני בליעל occurs once more in 1 Kgs 21:13, but the reading here may be a conflation of two variants: ויבאו שני האנשים/ויבאו בני בליעל.

166. See 1 Kgs 21:13aγ; see also 1 Sam 25:25; 2 Sam 16:7.

167. See above, 181–82.

168. See Otzen 1975, 134 n. 24; 2 Sam 3:34; 7:10; Isa 55:7; Prov 6:12; see also Isa 31:2; Hos 6:8.

this purpose by raising associations with the heinous acts related to the town. However, it is conceivable that the author of the Gibeah story would borrow language from Saul's history in order to undermine the favorable depiction of Saul and lead the reader to associate him with the scoundrels from Gibeah who caused the intertribal war.

The framing passages, 1 Sam 10:26–27 and 11:12–13, are generally assigned to a Deuteronomistic editor who combined the old story of the Ammonite war with the later compositions regarding Saul's designation by lot and Samuel's farewell speech (1 Sam 10:17–25; 12:1–25).[169] If Judg 20:13 was indeed patterned on 1 Sam 10:26–27 and 11:12–13, and reflects a covert polemic directed against Saul, then it is reasonable to assume that it was composed by a post-Deuteronomistic author.

1 SAMUEL 14

Three brief passages in 1 Sam 14 have parallels in Judg 20. Thus the expression פנות (כל) העם occurs only in Judg 20:2 and 1 Sam 14:38. פנה generally means "corner," but most assume that פנות כל העם represent the heads or leaders of the people.[170] In 1 Sam 14:38, it appears that Saul indeed calls upon a select group of the people to witness the procedure for identifying the guilty party. However, in Judg 20:2, פנות כל העם are the four hundred thousand fighting men who presented themselves (ויתיצבו) in the assembly. There it is not likely that the expression represents the *leaders* of the people. It is possible that R² borrowed the expression from 1 Sam 14:38 and understood it to mean "all Israel,"[171] since in 1 Sam 14:40 lots are drawn to chose between Saul and Jonathan on one side and "all Israel" (i.e., the rest of the fighting force) on the other side. If so, then it seems that the use of the expression פנות כל העם in Judg 20:2 was due to

---

169. See, e.g., Stoebe 1973, 219; Veijola 1977, 39–52; Klein 1983, 97, 104; O'Brien 1989, 119–20; Na'aman 1992, 642–45; Nihan 2013, 249–50, 255, with further literature there. By contrast, McCarter (1980, 20) assigns the passages to a pre-Dtr prophetic editor, while Miller (1974a, 165–67) includes the framing sections in the old story of the Ammonite war. By contrast, Dietrich (2013, 57–58) assigns the designation by lot to a postexilic DtrN, which implies that the framing passages cannot be earlier than this redaction.

170. See Isa 19:13, where פנת שבטיה parallels "the nobles of" (שרי) Zoan and Memphis; see the Targum רישי עמא (Judg 20:2; 1 Sam 14:38). See, e.g., Moore 1895, 423, 425; Budde 1897, 133.

171. See also Gross 2009, 825, 848.

a misinterpretation of its meaning in 1 Sam 14:38–40. First Samuel 14:38–40 is assigned to a tendentious (and possibly post-Dtr) revision of the story of the battle at Michmash.[172] Thus it seems reasonable to conclude that R² was familiar with this revision and was influenced by its language.

"Six hundred men" are associated with the verb ישב, "to sit or stay," and with a site identified as Rimmon (רמון) in both Judg 20:47 and 1 Sam 14:2. In Judg 20:47, "six hundred" Benjaminite survivors find refuge at the rock of Rimmon (רמון), where they "stayed" (וישבו) four months until the tribes convened to discuss their fate. This mention of the number of survivors plays an important role in preparing the reader for the necessity of a two-stage solution of the survivors' predicament in the last chapter of the narrative. Even so, the figure of six hundred men does not fit with the figures given for the total number of Benjaminite warriors and their casualties.[173] For this reason, the figure of six hundred men is suspect and may have been inspired by another source. It is possible that this figure was borrowed from 1 Sam 14:2, where Saul, the Benjaminite king, is depicted as "sitting" (יושב) beneath a "pomegranate tree" (רמון) on the outskirts of Gibeah, accompanied by "six hundred men," who had not yet joined the battle (cf. v. 20).[174] This figure accords with the notice in 13:15–16 regarding the six hundred men that remained with Saul at Geba/Gibeah of Benjamin. The description of the king sitting beneath a tree while his son undertakes a raid on the Philistine camp sets Saul's passivity in ironic opposition to Jonathan's heroic initiative, and subtly undermines the efficacy of Saul as a savior figure. Thus 1 Sam 14:2 probably derives from the late Deuteronomistic or post-Deuteronomistic revision of the story. Judges 20:47 is assigned to N¹, so if the awkward figure there of "six hundred men" indeed derives from 1 Sam 14:2, then we may conclude that N¹ already was familiar with the late revision of the story of the battle of Michmash.

Finally, the final forms of the story of the Michmash battle and the story of the Gibeah war include the parenthetical remark that "the ark was there on that day [in those days]" when a priest presided over the oracle prior to battle (Judg 20:27b–28a; 1 Sam 14:18).[175] Judges 20:27 is an explanatory gloss that was added by R² to justify the promise of victory following the third oracular consultation. The comment about the "ark of

---

172. See, e.g., Na'aman 1992, 646.
173. See above, ch. 1.
174. See also Amit 2000, 181.
175. Hebrew: ושם/היה ארון (ברית) האלהים בימים ההוא/ביום ההוא.

God" in 1 Sam 14:18 is problematic as well. The ark does not figure elsewhere as an apparatus for divination; instead this function is filled by the Urim and Thummim or the ephod (cf. Num 27:19-21; 1 Sam 14:41; 23:6, 9-11; 30:7-8). Indeed, and the LXX reads "ephod" (אפוד) for "ark" (ארון) in this passage. These variant readings probably arose due to graphic similarity between the Hebrew terms along with the fact that priests are variously depicted bearing both the ephod (e.g., 1 Sam 2:28; 14:3) and the ark (e.g., Josh 3:8, 17; 4:10, 16; 6:6, 12; 8:33; cf. 2 Sam 15:24; 1 Kgs 2:26).[176] Regardless of whether the reading of the MT is earlier, later, or synchronic with the version of the LXX *Vorlage*, once the ark was mentioned in the phrase "bring the ark of God" in 1 Sam 14:18, it became necessary to add the explanatory gloss, "for the ark was there on that day," since the last time the ark appeared in the larger narrative context it was housed at the sanctuary in Kiriath-jearim (1 Sam 7:1-2a).

It is possible that the comment that in Judg 20:27, "the ark was there [at Bethel] in those days," was inserted into the narrative in order to interact with 1 Sam 14:18. There Saul, the Benjaminite, intended to consult the oracle through an officiating priest in the presence of the ark, but did not complete the undertaking (vv. 18-19). Further on, in verse 37, he makes another attempt and this time completes his question, but YHWH does not reply.[177] In Judg 20:27-28, by contrast, the Israelites inquire, through a priest and in the presence of the ark, whether to go to war against Benjamin, and they receive an unambiguous and favorable reply. R^2, then, seems to fashion the Israelite's final oracular consultation as a positive counterpart to Saul's blundering attempts. Thus it is likely that R^2 was familiar with and employed the MT of 1 Sam 14:18, and even alluded to 1 Sam 14:36-37, both of which belong to the late revision of the story of the battle at Michmash.

---

176. The MT of v. 18b seems truncated: "for the ark of God was there on that day and the Israelites [ובני ישראל]." The Targum reads instead: "with the Israelites" (עם בני ישראל), while the LXX has an entirely different reading: "for he was bearing the ephod that day before Israel" (cf. v. 3). The LXX reading is preferred by S. Driver 1913, 110; McCarter 1980, 237; Klein 1983, 123; while the *lectio difficilior* of the MT is preferred by, e.g., Arnold 1917, 13-16; Blenkinsopp 1964, 428 n. 21; Stoebe 1973, 260; P. Davies 1977, 15-16; Ahlström 1984, 145.

177. The early version of the story ended with the remark that "YHWH delivered Israel on that day" (1 Sam 14:23), but the later revision limited the victory by having Saul break off his pursuit of the Philistines (v. 46) after a chain of events triggered by the failure of the oracular consultation; see Na'aman 1992, 646.

This review establishes reasonable grounds to conclude that the parallel elements in Judg 20 and 1 Sam 14 are original to the story of the battle of Michmash and were reemployed and transformed by the authors of the Gibeah story. N¹ in Judg 20:47 made use of the late revision of the Michmash story in 1 Sam 14:2. This means that the compositional layer of the Gibeah story was familiar with the Deuteronomistic (or even post-Dtr) redactional layer in Samuel. R² in Judg 20:27 seems to have made use of the MT reading in 1 Sam 14:18. If the MT reading there is secondary, then R² not only knew the Michmash story in its final form but also was familiar with a copy of Samuel that already reflected the MT reading.¹⁷⁸ Once again, R² appears to be aware of the interaction of N¹ with his source texts and attempted to broaden the points of contact. Both N¹ and R² seem to interact with 1 Sam 14 in order to mark the contrast between the sweeping victory of the Israelites over Benjamin following YHWH's favorable response to the oracle on the one hand, and the limited success in battle by Saul, the Benjaminite king, who due to his shortcomings did not receive any response from the oracle.

CONCLUSIONS

My analysis of the points of contact between Judg 19–21 and the different passages from the history of Saul reveal concrete evidence that the Gibeah story was patterned in part on the story of Saul. The narratives that were employed as literary sources deal with the beginning of Saul's rule: the rescue of Jabesh-gilead (including the editorial frame of the story) and the battle of Michmash. While the first narrative bolsters the authority of Saul as a military hero and the divine designate, the second story already begins to highlight his shortcomings. N¹ in Judg 20 interacts with all the different compositional layers, from the pre-Deuteronomistic story in 1 Sam 11:1–11 to the Deuteronomistic editorial sections in 1 Sam 10:27 and 11:12–13, and the post-Deuteronomistic revision of 1 Sam 14. My findings show that R² (Judg 20:2, 27) acted to enhance the contact between the narratives by borrowing from the late revision of the Michmash story (1 Sam 14:18, 38).

---

178. There is no reason to suppose that this hypothetical copy is later than the LXX, since manuscripts with variant readings seem to have been in circulation prior to the Greek translation. In principle, variants or scribal errors may occur already in second-generation copies.

In most of the instances, the borrowed elements were transformed or integrated in inverse fashion, creating an antithesis to the representations in the story of Saul. Thus the Levite's action in cutting up his concubine's corpse in order to muster the tribes is presented as a parodic reflection of Saul's act in mustering the people to go to war against Ammon. Saul's magnanimity in refusing to put to death the scoundrels who mocked his authority is transformed and distorted in the context of the Gibeah story, where the Benjaminites refuse to comply with the demand to hand over the scoundrels of Gibeah so they may be put to death. In these instances, Saul's admirable behavior is cast into a new context where it appears ridiculous or even despicable. Similarly, the authors of the Gibeah story reused elements critical of Saul but applied them to nonjudgmental contexts. Thus the scene in which Saul sits passively beneath the pomegranate tree (הרמון) with six hundred of his men while Jonathan is fighting the Philistines at Michmash is refashioned to represent the stay of the six hundred Benjaminite survivors at Rimmon after they fought for three days. Saul's inability to complete his oracular inquiry in the presence of the ark is contrasted with the Israelites' tenacity in consulting the oracle for the third time, this time in front of the ark, when they are finally rewarded with the promise of victory. In addition to all the above, the very location of the crime and punishment in Judg 19–21 is liable to raise doubts in a reader's mind regarding Saul's suitability to rule, since his lineage relates him with the scoundrels responsible for the concubine's rape and death and with the Benjaminites who shielded them from justice. Thus the authors of Judg 19–21 lifted elements from the history of Saul and reapplied them in a narrative supposedly occurring before there was a king, in order to predispose readers against Saul and subvert any sympathy the narratives in Samuel may raise.

4.5. The Laws of Deuteronomy

Different passages in Judg 20:19–21 appear to interrelate with laws in Deuteronomy, and such interaction could help clarify the relationship of Judg 19–21 to the corpus of Deuteronomistic literature.[179] In this case, evaluating the result of intertextual analysis is complicated by the redactional

---

179. See, e.g., Merendino 1969, 77–78; Seitz 1971, 131–32, 141–49; Jüngling 1981, 266–69; Veijola 1995, 305.

complexity of the Deuteronom(ist)ic law corpus. Current research displays a marked lack of consensus regarding the shape and extent of the original core of Deuteronomy. Some scholars uphold the basic unity of the laws along with the narrative framework and the accompanying paraenesis, comprising at least Deut 1–28.[180] Others adhere to redactional-critical models that are based upon various literary-critical criteria, such as multiple superscriptions; disruption of continuity; change of topic, voice, or number; digression; and resumptive repetitions. Most agree that these tools help uncover the seams and fractures in the text, which provide evidence of editorial intervention; but agreement breaks down on the questions of the diachronic relations between the materials, the extent of the primary Deuteronomic layer (*Urdeuteronomium*), and the number of redactional layers. Continental scholars seem to concur that the literary archaeology of Deuteronomy comprises at least four layers: pre-Deuteronomistic (or pre-Josianic) legal source material; Deuteronomic (Josianic) composition; exilic revisions, additions, and expansions; and finally, a layer of postexilic revisions.[181] The "Josianic" *Urdeuteronomium* is usually thought to comprise the bulk of the law corpus along with its introduction and conclusion (Deut 6:4–28:69).[182] However, scholars differ—sometimes greatly—when it comes to assigning the various materials to the different layers. Although these problems are beyond the scope of the present discussion, different aspects of the redactional history of Deuteronomy must be taken into account in order to determine whether the possible interaction between the Gibeah story and the laws of Deuteronomy derives from late redaction or from the primary stage of composition.

THE LAW OF THE APOSTATE TOWN (DEUT 13:13–18)

The law of the apostate town is the last paragraph of a section dealing with incitement to worship other gods. The first paragraph deals with an inciting prophet (vv. 2–6), the second paragraph centers on incitement by a family member (vv. 7–12), and the final paragraph presents the case in which townsmen incite their neighbors to follow other gods (vv. 13–18). All three laws have been fashioned according to the same model and are

---

180. For example, Weinfeld 1991, 10; Lundbom, 1996; 2013, 9–10, 73–74.
181. See, e.g., Seitz 1971, 13–23; Mayes 1981, 34–55; Römer 1994, 184–94; 2005, 56–65; O'Brien 1995, 95–128; Otto 1996, 1–6; 2012, 231–57; Veijola 2004, 2–5.
182. See, e.g., Veijola 2004, 129–31; Otto 2012, 234–38.

bound together by a framing repetition that exhorts the people to keep YHWH's commandments (vv. 1, 19).[183]

The style and content of the law of the apostate town in verses 13–18 differ on many points from the previous two paragraphs, and these differences might indicate separate origin.[184]

1. In the first two paragraphs, the interdiction is intended to neutralize the influence of the inciting agent (vv. 4, 9, "you shall not listen"), but in the final paragraph the interdiction has nothing to do with the offense, but rather with the execution of judgment (v. 18, "let nothing that has been banned stick to your hand").

2. The first two paragraphs justify the verdict with similar motive clauses (vv. 6, 11), in contrast to the final paragraph, where a different motive clause serves to justify the prohibition against violating the ban and taking proscribed goods (v. 18b).[185]

3. The offense in the first two paragraphs is incitement, and judgment is rendered upon the provocateur, while the final paragraph deals with submission to incitement, and judgment is rendered upon those who strayed from exclusive worship of YHWH.

4. The offender in the first two paragraphs is a single person, and the judgment applies to him alone, while in the final paragraph the offending party is a collective body, and the entire town bears the penalty of the law.

5. The first two paragraphs deal with firsthand evidence of incitement, while the final paragraph deals with a rumor that an entire town was lead astray (v. 13, כי תשמע, "if you should hear").

6. In contrast to the first two cases, the third paragraph orders that an inquiry be held to verify the truth of the accusation before carrying out the verdict.

---

183. See, e.g., Seitz 1971, 144–45; Rofé 1988a, 60. All three laws share: (1) a second person formulation in the apodosis; (2) the same description of the offense (vv. 3, 7, 14: "he/they said, 'Let us go and worship other gods'"); (3) the use of the verb הדיח, "lead astray" (vv. 6, 11, 14); and (4) a verdict of death.

184. Horst 1930, 28; Otto 1996, 20–21.

185. The verses read as follows: (6) "For he spoke rebellious things against YHWH [כי דבר סרה על ה'] your God who brought you out of the land of Egypt and redeemed you from slavery"; (11) "For he sought to turn you away from YHWH [כי בקש להדיחך מעל ה'] your God who brought you out of the land of Egypt, from slavery"; (18b) "So that YWHW turns from his anger [למען ישוב ה' מחרון אפו]."

One could argue that these differences derive from the particularly severe circumstances of the case of the apostate city[186] and that for this reason it was placed at the end of the series as its climax.[187] But this does not necessarily indicate that the chapter is a compositional unity, since a later redactor may have chosen to expand the section by adding a particularly severe case as the final paragraph. Indeed, several of these differences are not required by the change in circumstances, and they provide support for the view that the final paragraph was subsequently added to the first two. In this case, the scribe responsible for the addition shaped it according to the general style of the section, but did not strictly adhere to the structure of the previous laws.

Many of the formulations in Deut 13 have close parallels in Neo-Assyrian loyalty oaths and treaties, particularly with the so-called Vassal Treaties of Esarhaddon (VTE; today generally termed "succession treaties"). Several scholars conclude from this that Deut 13 must derive from the scribal culture of the seventh century BCE.[188] But the pursuit of secure dates for compositions on the basis of cross-cultural parallels is rife with methodological difficulties. Judean scribes might plausibly be familiar with the stipulations of the VTE, since Judah was an Assyrian vassal state. Furthermore, it now seems that copies of the VTE were deposited in national sanctuaries of the vassal states.[189] Hence it is likely that a copy was also deposited in the Jerusalem temple. However, the law of the apostate town (vv. 13–18) has no parallel in the VTE, but is best paralleled by a clause in the Aramaic Sefire treaty (iii 12–13) from the mid-eighth century BCE: an attempt of a vassal city to assassinate the suzerain or his offspring will be avenged by putting the entire town to the sword.[190] This treaty was drawn up to govern the relations between two Aramean kingdoms in northern Syria, KTK and Arpad, and its contents could hardly have been known to scribes in either Judah or Israel. An

---

186. Dion 1991, 163–68; Koch 2008, 124–25.

187. E.g., Seitz 1971, 146; Nelson 2002, 167.

188. See, e.g., Weinfeld 1972, 91–100; Dion 1991, 196–206; Otto 1996, 32–52; 1997, 325–33; 1999, 15–90; Levinson and Stackert 2012. In these publications, Otto went as far as to argue that the author of Deut 13:2–12 was familiar with the VTE and drew upon its language; see also Steymans 2006. Otto concluded that this secures a precise period for the initial composition of Deut 13:2–12 between 672 and 612 BCE.

189. Lauinger 2011, 8–12; Harrison and Osborne 2012, 137–40; Fales 2012; but see Crouch 2014, 148–51.

190. Fitzmyer 1995, 18–19, 135–61.

important point that must govern comparative studies is the realization that literary parallels only provide *attested* evidence for the use of formulations and that relatively early parallels only provide a possible starting point (terminus a quo) for the literary history of the motif or expression. Once a formula or motif enters the scribal repertoire, it may continue to circulate long after its original context was forgotten.[191] Hence the parallels between Neo-Assyrian loyalty oaths and treaties and the stipulations in Deut 13:1–19 may merely derive from the widespread diffusion of legal formulas and literary convention.[192] Christoph Koch's thorough analysis of Deut 13 demonstrated that it comprises a mixture of source materials, which indicate derivative use of a literary tradition by scribes living in a period distant by one or two generations from the political realities of the Neo-Assyrian period.[193]

In my opinion, the law of the apostate town is indeed a late addition to the chapter. Its purpose was to present an extreme case of incitement to rebellion in which an entire town submitted to incitement, and thus the extreme nature of the penalty—destruction by the sword and total burning of the city—stands in direct proportion to the severity of the offense. Framed in this fashion, this law could be employed to explain and justify the fate of Jerusalem to an audience in the exilic period. Thus the law of the apostate town should be assigned to the postmonarchic Deuteronomistic revision of Deuteronomy.[194]

---

191. For example, the reference to "the land of the Hittites" in Josh 1:4 is undoubtedly a reflection of the Akkadian expression *māt Ḫatti*, which indicates that geographical extent of land west of the Euphrates, from Asia Minor to Egypt. The phrase itself in Josh 1:4 appears to gloss the detailed geographical designations for the extent of the land. The roots of the term *māt Ḫatti* lie in the second millennium, but it became prevalent in the Neo-Assyrian period as a designation for the land west of the Euphrates, and afterward remained in the scribal curriculum as a "fossil," as attested by its use in Babylonian Chronicles and chronographic literature from the late seventh century BCE down to the Seluecid period. See Glassner 24 line 16, rev. line 9; 52 iii line 14'; 53 iv lines 50', 57'.

192. See Veijola 1995, 310; Tadmor 2006, 184, 200–207; Rütersworden 2002, 199–203; Pakkala 1999, 41–47; 2006, 129–34; Koch 2008, 266–88; Zehnder 2009.

193. Koch 2008, 266–69.

194. See also Veijola 1995, 308–10; Otto 1996, 20–24; Pakkala 1999, 47–56; 2006, 136–37; in contrast to Dion 1991, 175–96, who attributes all three laws in Deut 13 to a Josianic Deuteronomist (Dtr[1]).

A further question to be considered deals with the literary integrity of the law of the apostate town. Methodological difficulties arise when attempting to separate later editorial layers from the basic layer of Deuteronom(ist)ic composition, although many continental scholars propose complex scenarios of overwriting (*Fortschreibung*).[195] Deuteronom(ist)ic style is exhortatory; it frequently addresses the audience directly in the second person (singular and plural) and seeks to persuade by reinforcing its instructions with multiple motive clauses. For this reason, redactional analysis in Deuteronomy should not solely depend solely upon variation in address or multiple motive clauses.[196] Thus if the criteria for identifying redactional expansions are limited to inconsistency in content or language, then there is good cause to argue for the compositional unity of Deut 13:13–18.[197]

Different scholars have noted interrelations between the law regarding the apostate town in Deut 13:13–18 and the story of Gibeah.[198] However, Judg 19–21 makes no allusion to the offense of the apostate town, and there is no attempt to portray the men of Gibeah or the Benjaminites as breaking faith with YHWH by worshiping other gods. Only a general analogy may be drawn between the crime of the men of Gibeah and the offense of the apostate town, for in both instances a corporate body breaches the norms of the larger community, and the entire community is called upon to eradicate the offending body. Further parallels may be discerned in the phrasing of different passages.

---

195. See the different analyses by Merendino 1969; Veijola 1995, 304–5; 2004, 284; Horst 1930; Seitz 1971; and Koch 2008, 126–29. They agree in viewing vv. 17b–18a as a redactional expansion, but greatly differ in the details of their analyses for the rest of the paragraph. Some of the analyses are based on the notion that Josh 6–8 influenced the formulation of Deut 13:17–18; see, e.g., Merendino 1969, 69–70; Veijola 2004, 284; Otto 1996, 24; cf. Seitz 1971, 149. However, it is more likely that Josh 6–8 was revised to reflect and illustrate changes in the Dtr law corpus; see Edenburg 2015.

196. See, e.g., Römer 2005, 73–74; cf. Veijola 1995, 292; 1996, 244–59; 2004, 282, who holds that free interchange of singular and plural second person address is characteristic of the late Dtr^B redaction.

197. See, e.g., Dion 1991, 174–75; Nielsen 1995; Otto 1996; Rüterswörden 2002, 193–95.

198. See, e.g., Hölscher 1922, 192–93; Seitz 1971, 149; Niditch 1982, 372; Weinfeld 1997, 218–19; Veijola 1995, 305; O'Connell 1996, 243, 252–57.

Deut 13:13–18	Judg 19–20
13 If you should hear about one of your towns that YHWH your God has given you to settle there, that **14 men, men of no good** [אנשים בני בליעל], have gone out from among you and led the inhabitants of their town astray, saying: "Let us go and worship other gods whom you do not know"; **15** then you should investigate and inquire and interrogate thoroughly, and if it is indeed true that the abomination was committed in your midst, **16** you shall **put the inhabitants of that town to the sword** [הכה את ישבי העיר ההוא לפי חרב]. Place it and *all within it* [ואת כל אשר בה] under ban and [put] its **cattle** [בהמתה] to the sword. **17** Gather all its spoil in the square and **burn the town by fire** [ושרפת באש את העיר] and all its spoil **wholly** [כליל] for YHWH your God. It shall be an everlasting ruin, never to be rebuilt.	**19 22** … the men of the city—**men of no good** [אנשי בני בליעל]. **20 13** And now hand over the **men, men of no good** [האנשים בני בליעל], who are in Gibeah, and we will put them to death and exterminate the evil from Israel **20 3** The Israelites said: "How did this evil come to pass? **20 6** for they have committed an outrageous act of depravity in Israel." **20 48** They **put them to the sword**, [everything] from town and people **to beast** [ויכום לפי חרב מעיר מתם עד בהמה] and *all that was to be found* [עד כל הנמצא]. All **the towns** to be found they also **set on fire** [כל הערים הנמצ־ אות שלחו באש]. **20 37** They **put the entire city to the sword** [ויך את כל העיר לפי חרב]. **20 40** And there the **whole** city went up [in smoke] to the sky [והנה עלה כליל העיר השמימה].

The description of the destruction of Gibeah (Judg 20:37, 40) and the towns of Benjamin (20:48) is formulated in a fashion similar to the instructions for the destruction of the apostate town in Deut 13:16–17. Like the apostate town, the destruction of Gibeah and the towns of Benjamin includes two stages: death by the sword (Judg 20:37, 48; Deut 13:16) and burning by fire (Judg 20:40, 48; Deut 13:17). But while the root חרם ("ban, dedicate") is prominent in the law of the apostate town (Deut 13:16, 18), it is markedly absent from the description of the war at Gibeah even though the circumstances of the war and its outcome warrant use of the term.

More particularly, both Judg 20:48 and Deut 13:16 specify putting to the sword all the cattle and other contents of the town along with its inhabitants. Furthermore, both texts share the same four-member structure, opening with a general description, which is subsequently detailed in the following three members. In Deut 13:16, the details are joined by means of coordination, while in Judg 20:48 they are set within the formula "from

TEXT, SUBTEXT, AND INTERTEXTUAL MOSAIC 237

x to *y*," which is a merism that indicates everything from one extreme to the other.[199]

	Deut 13:16		Judg 20:48
A₁	הכה תכה את־יֹשְׁבֵי הָעִיר הַהוּא לְפִי־חָרֶב	B₁	וַיַּכּוּם לְפִי־חֶרֶב
B₁	החרם אֹתָהּ	A₁	מֵעִיר מְתֹם
B₂	וְאֶת־כָּל־אֲשֶׁר־בָּהּ	A₂	עַד־בְּהֵמָה
A₂	וְאֶת־בְּהֶמְתָּהּ לְפִי־חָרֶב	B₂	עד כל־הנמצא

The verbal similarity between the two texts is not remarkable in itself. But the two texts do relate to one another in their choice and arrangement of elements.[200] Deuteronomy 13:16 frames the ban description with the expression "by the sword" (לפי חרב; A1 of the town, A2 of its cattle). The two middle members relate to the town (החרם אתה, "put *it* to the ban") and "all within it." Judges 20:48 also places the expression "put to the sword" in the opening member but only alludes to the object by means of a pronominal suffix (ויכום, "smite *them*"; see above, B1 in Deut 13:16). The closing member in Judg 20:48a—"and all that was to be found" (עד כל הנמצא)—corresponds to Deut 13:16 (B2), "and all within it" (כל אשר בה). Both phrases are semantic equivalents, but while כל אשר ב- is found in all BH strata,[201] the collocation כל הנמצא is typically found in late contexts.[202] Furthermore, the two middle members of the

---

199. See, e.g., Gen 14:23; 19:4; 31:24; 47:21; 1 Sam 3:20; 1 Kgs 6:24; 2 Kgs 24:7; Amos 8:12; Qoh 3:11. See Honeyman 1952.

200. הכה לפי חרב occurs more than twenty-five times in the Bible, mostly in Dtr literature, and several times its grammatical object is עיר, "town" (e.g., Judg 1:8, 25; 18:27; 20:37; 1 Sam 22:19; 2 Sam 15:14). Only in Deut 13:16 and Judg 20:48 are בהמה, "cattle," specifically proscribed, while Deut 2:35, 3:7; 20:14; Josh 8:2, 27; 11:14 specifically exclude them from the ban. Elsewhere the animals listed as subject to ban are oxen (שור), sheep, (camel), and ass; see Josh 6:21; 1 Sam 15:3; 22:19. Only Deut 13:16 and Judg 20:48 specify total destruction by means of the three terms *town, cattle,* and *all within it/all that was to be found.* Deuteronomy 2:34–35 and 3:6–7 do bear remarkable similarity to Judg 20:48 by mentioning "town," "men" (מתם), and "cattle," but these passages differ by excluding the cattle from the ban.

201. See, e.g., Gen 6:17; 19:12; 34:29; 41:56; Exod 20:11; Lev 8:10; 14:36; Num 19:14; Deut 10:14; 20:14; Josh 2:19; 6:21, 24; Judg 9:44; 2 Kgs 15:16; 20:15; Isa 39:4, 6; Ezra 10:14.

202. See above, ch. 3.

parallel text in Judg 20:48 correspond to first and last members in Deut 13:16 (both marked A1, A2 above), since these contain mention of the "cattle" (בהמה) and the semantic parallel regarding the inhabitants of the town (עיר מתם // יֹשְׁבֵי הָעִיר הַהוּא). The choice and inverse arrangement of the elements in Deut 13:16 and Judg 20:48 (ABBA/BAAB) is unique and suggestive of literary patterning.

A further significant connection between the Gibeah story and the law of the apostate town is the use of the term כליל, "wholly," in relation to burning the offending city. The law in Deut 13:17 requires burning the apostate town and all its spoils "wholly for YHWH" (כליל לה'). In this context, כליל is an adverb that imparts a sacral character to the burning of the town;[203] the town that fell away from exclusive worship of YHWH is now burnt as a holocaust sacrifice to YHWH. By contrast, in Judg 20:40, כליל is employed as a substantive in construct with העיר.[204] There it is clear that "the whole of the town" (כליל העיר) going up skyward (v. 40b) is equivalent to the previously mentioned "signal" (משאת) "going up from the city in a column of smoke" (v. 40a). This use of the term כליל as a substantive departs from standard usage and may have resulted from the combination of two different literary allusions into one compact collocation. This unusual construct alludes both to the smoke of the city (עשן העיר) going up from Ai (Josh 8:20) as well as to the complete burning of the apostate town (Deut 13:17). The additional analogy to the apostate town implies that the severity of Gibeah's offense was as great as that of the apostate town and could be remedied only by sanctifying the entire town as a holocaust sacrifice to YHWH.

In my opinion, R² was aware of the analogy that N¹ drew between Gibeah and the apostate town, and it inspired him to broaden the scope of burning to include all the Benjaminite towns. While the other Benjaminite towns did not participate in the crime of Gibeah, they became accomplices when they refused to hand over the culprits. The idea expressed both here and in the law of the apostate town holds that whoever does not take action to exterminate evil becomes an accomplice in crime and shares the fate of the actual culprits. However, the analogy is not perfect; since the apostate town is exterminated not because its inhabitants *tolerated* subversive religious activity, but rather because they themselves submitted to religious

---

203. See Seitz 1971, 149; see similarly Lev 6:15–16; 1 Sam 7:9.
204. See above, ch. 3; see also Seitz 1971, 149 n. 176.

subversion until the entire town was held unfaithful to YHWH. Thus R² takes a more extreme stand than N¹ by applying the verdict of the apostate town upon all of Benjamin's cities, instead of the guilty town alone.²⁰⁵

Finally, the appositional phrase (ה)אנשים בני בליעל is shared by Deut 13:14 and Judg 20:13 (cf. Judg 19:22).²⁰⁶ The phrase in Judg 20:13 is definite, but contrary to regular usage, the definite article was affixed only to the first member of the apposition. This irregularity does not occur in Deut 13:14 since the expression there is indefinite. The irregular usage in Judg 20:13 might reflect an attempt to allude to two separate texts: 1 Sam 11:12, תנו האנשים ונמיתם, and Deut 13:14, יצאו אנשים בני־בליעל מקרבך אנשים בני) "the men, scoundrels" to allusion The .וידיחו את־ישבי עירם בליעל) of the apostate town might indicate that narrator wished to draw an analogy between the severity of that offense and the outrageous treatment of the concubine at Gibeah, since in both cases the offense taints all the men of the town (cf. Gen 19:4). This would explain why the Israelites demanded that the Benjaminites hand over all the men of Gibeah, not just those who were responsible for the concubine's death, so they could be put to death. The allusion also implies that the fate of Gibeah will be analogous to that of the apostate town, that is, to be totally destroyed and never resettled again.

In summary, I have found several points of contact between the Gibeah story and the law in Deut 13:13–18, and these points are distributed in Judg 19:22; 20:13, 37, 40, 48. While it is conceivable that some of the shared elements might derive from common motifs and formulas (e.g., האנשים בני בליעל; הכה לפי חרב; and burning of the town), two significant points show signs of intentional reactualization of borrowed material. The first of these is the unique recurrence of the term כליל in connection with burning a town; this term is employed according to its usual usage in Deut 13:17, while its use in Judg 20:40 is atypical and forced. The second point is the chiastic arrangement of the parallel elements in the descriptions of the destruction of the apostate town (Deut 13:16) and of Benjamin's cities (Judg 20:48). While the description in Deut 13:16 employs formulaic

---

205. Gross (2009, 863) thinks that the analogy between the Gibeah and the apostate town is "cynical," and could only derive from the hand of the "Bethel" reviser. However, it is not clear why the base narrative cannot contain "cynical" elements.

206. This phrase occurs also in 1 Kgs 21:10, 13, where it characterizes the false witnesses against Naboth. The Naboth story as a whole draws upon the laws of Deuteronomy; see Rofé 1988b, 101.

language, the parallel in Judg 20:48 is marked by peculiar idioms (מעיר מתם) and late usage (כל הנמצא). Thus it is reasonable to conclude that R² expanded Judg 20:48 in order to evoke the model in Deut 13:16, but reversed the order of the elements and used language more characteristic of his times.

The literary allusions to the law of the apostate town were most likely woven into the Gibeah story in order to add yet another thread to the web of analogies between Gibeah and other infamous cities in the Bible. Gibeah is "sister" not only to the Canaanite towns of Sodom and Ai, which were destroyed and never resettled, but also to the Israelite town that strays and rebels against YHWH the sovereign god. Accordingly, the allusions to the law of the apostate town serve to compare the fate of Gibeah and the Benjaminite towns with that of the apostate town, and also to compare their crime with the severe offense of deviation from exclusive worship of YHWH.

The literary dependency of Judg 19–21 upon Deut 13:13–18 provides additional evidence for the relative dating of the composition. As I argued above, there is good reason to consider the law of the apostate town to be a late addition to Deut 13. According to many, the law of the apostate town is utopian in scope;[207] therefore it does not necessarily assume enforcement by a centralized governing authority. Indeed, the zealous extremism of the law best fits in with loss of self-government and disruption of the orderly cult. Therefore, Deut 13:13–18 should be dated to the Babylonian period, as suggested by Veijola, Otto, Pakkala, and others. Regardless of whether the law of the apostate town is a compositional unity or whether it has undergone a process of expansion and revision, the Gibeah story interrelates with it at different points, and this seems to indicate that the entire law in its final form was known to N¹. R² also drew upon this late Deuteronomistic stratum in Deut 13:13–18 when he expanded the parallel in Judg 20:48. One way or the other, the law of the apostate town is Deuteronomistic in character, rather than Deuteronomic, and the fact that both layers of the Gibeah story are familiar with the law and were influenced by its language and ideals supports that likelihood that the prose story in Judg 20 is a post-Deuteronomistic composition.

---

207. See, e.g., Hölscher 1922, 192–93; Horst 1930, 17, 22; Veijola 1995, 307; Otto 1996, 24; Pakkala 1999, 40, 47–50; 2006, 136–37; contra, e.g., Dion 1991, 204–5.

TEXT, SUBTEXT, AND INTERTEXTUAL MOSAIC   241

UNIQUE MOTIFS IN THE LAWS OF DEUTERONOMY

You shall investigate (and inquire and interrogate) thoroughly, (and if indeed it is true)—the instruction "to investigate thoroughly" (דרש היטב) occurs in Deut 13:15, 17:4, and 19:18. Within the context of the laws in Deut 17:2–7 and 19:16–20, the verb *investigate* (דרש) clearly indicates a judicial procedure (cf. 17:9), and this meaning may also be inferred in 13:15.[208] The necessity of a judicial inquiry in 13:13–18 and 17:2–7 stems from the fact that the accusation is based upon rumor (13:13, "If you should hear"; 17:4, "You were told and you heard").[209] Although the Gibeah story makes no verbal reference to Deuteronomy's instruction "to investigate thoroughly," Judg 20:3b–13 is fashioned on the model of a judicial inquiry, which opens with the question: "How did this evil come about?" (20:3b), then continues with the Levite's testimony (vv. 4–7), and closes with the demand to execute the culprits (vv. 12–13).[210] It is also possible that the verification in Deut 13:15 and 17:4, "the abomination was committed" (נעשתה התועבה), is echoed in the accusation by the Levite: "they have committed an outrageous act of depravity" (עשו זמה ונבלה, Judg 20:6) "in Israel." The term תועבה, which occurs in Deut 13:15 and 17:4, is frequent in all strata of BH and indicates a wide range of religious abominations.[211] In place of this term, Judg 20:6 employs the unique collocation זמה ונבלה.[212] The expression עשה נבלה frequently signifies transgression of sexual norms,[213] and the expanded phrase עשה נבלה בישראל is characteristic of Deuteronomistic literature.[214] The term זמה, by comparison, occurs mainly with

---

208. See also Nelson 2002, 173.
209. See Hoffmann 1913, 187; Horst 1930, 18–19; Seitz 1971, 145–46; Rofé 1988a, 60; Dion 1991, 164; Nelson 2002, 167, 220.
210. See Jüngling 1981, 264–69; cf. Boecker 1970, 18–41.
211. The term occurs more than one hundred times, and is increasingly frequent in literature of the Babylonian and Persian periods. The offenses indicated by the term include worship of other gods (Deut 13:15; 17:4; Ezek 11:18; 18:12); divination, witchcraft, and inquiring of the dead (Deut 18:9–12), eating impure food (Deut 14:3), and transgressing normative sexual and marital boundaries (Lev 18:22, 26; Deut 24:4; Ezek 22:11).
212. תועבה and זמה appear in parallelism (Ezek 22:11; Prov 21:27; 24:9), and may have been considered interchangeable equivalents.
213. See Gen 34:7; Deut 22:21; Judg 19:23, 24; 20:6, 10; 2 Sam 13:12; Jer 29:23.
214. See Deut 22:21; Josh 7:15; Jer 29:23. The expanded phrase "commit an outrage *in Israel*" is also found in Gen 34:7, but it has recently been suggested that Gen

regard to harlotry and adultery and is chiefly found in Priestly literature.[215] Thus Judg 20:4–6 may have been devised to illustrate the type of judicial inquiry prescribed by the laws of Deuteronomy, except that R² replaced the common phrase עשה תועבה with the unique collocation זמה ונבלה possibly in order to allude to the severity of the sexual offense implied by these terms elsewhere.

The formula "expunge the evil from your midst" or "from Israel" (ובערת הרע מקרבך/מישראל) occurs in a series of laws in Deuteronomy dealing with various capital offenses ranging from apostasy to abrogation of marital rights and abduction with the intent to sell the victim into slavery.[216] The "expunge the evil" formula in these laws serves to justify the death sentence. According to the inner logic of the "expunge the evil" laws, those who violate these injunctions must be executed in order to uproot the evil they committed, which otherwise would contaminate the entire community.[217] Outside the laws of Deuteronomy the expression "expunge the evil" (בער הרע/ה) recurs only in Judg 20:13.[218] While the second person address of the law is voiced by the implied legislator in order to motivate the addressee to implement the law, the call in Judg 20:13 is voiced by the representatives of the ideal pantribal body, who use it to establish their authority and justify the steps they subsequently take. The single use of the expression in narrative, in contrast to its frequency in the laws of Deuteronomy, points to the likelihood that

---

34 is a Persian period text; see, e.g., Na'aman 2006, 355–56; Amit 2000a, 206–11; Rofé 2005, 372–74. Thus the use in Gen 34:7 would reflect post-Dtr use of the Dtr idiom. For other views, see Seitz 1971, 137; Locher 1986, 56.

215. See above, ch. 3.

216. Deut 13:6; 17:7, 12; 19:19; 21:21; 22:21, 22, 24; 24:7; see also "expunge blood-guilt," ובערת/תבער דם נקי מקרבך/מישראל, in Deut 19:13; 21:9. The interchange מקרבך/מישראל undoubtedly occurred only for the sake of varying the idiom in neighboring passages (Deut 17:7, 12; 22:21–22). Other formulas recurring in these laws provided the basis for assigning additional cases to the series, even though they lack the ובערת formula (Deut 13:7–12, 13–18). In contrast to the rest of the series, Deut 19:19 does not specify capital punishment, but the talionic ruling for the perjurous witness was probably intended for capital cases.

217. See Rüterswörden 1996, 236–38.

218. But see the ironic paraphrase in 1 Kgs 21:21, "I will bring evil upon you and exterminate those after you" (הנני מבי אליך רעה ובערתי אחריך). This reformulation identifies Ahab as the evil to be expunged since he is responsible for the false testimony borne against Naboth (cf. Deut 19:17–19). See the discussion by Rüterswörden 1996, 236–38.

N¹ took up the formula familiar to him from Deuteronomy and adapted it for use within the narrative.[219] This conclusion appears more reasonable than the alternative possibilities, such as a single independent use of the formula in Judg 20:13, or influence exerted by Judg 20:13 upon nine different laws in Deuteronomy.[220] By transferring the formula from the theoretical context postulated by the laws to a specific situation related by the narrative, N¹ casts the story as an ideal illustration of how the laws should be enforced.[221]

However, the only offense in Deuteronomy that is punishable by decimation of an entire population is the incitement of a whole city to worship other gods (Deut 13:13–18), while the offenses attributed to Gibeah, namely, sexual assault and homicide, entail individual retribution rather than corporate punishment. It appears then that N¹ employed the "eradication of evil" formula in order to justify the far-reaching steps taken in the narrative, and to excuse the considerable gap in the plot between the cause (rape of a woman) and the result of the war (decimation of Benjamin). Such use of the formula does not further the themes of the Deuteronomistic History, and thus seems more derivative than properly Deuteronomistic.

It is not likely that the "expunge the evil" laws ever constituted an independent collection,[222] although it is not certain whether they should be attributed to the early core of Deuteronomic law or to the Deuteronomistic redaction of Deuteronomy.[223] The derivative use N¹ made of the Deuteronomistic idiom, which he adapted to the narrative context in Judg 20:13, again indicates that the composition is not pre-Deuteronomistic in origin, and may derive from post-Deuteronomistic circles.

---

219. See, e.g., Otto 1995, 16 n. 69.
220. See Merendino 1969, 77–78; Seitz 1971, 131–32, 141, for the view that the narrative in Judg 20 provides the *Sitz im Leben* for the formula in Deuteronomy.
221. See Jüngling 1981, 265–69.
222. See, e.g., Seitz 1971, 131–32; Dion 1980, 321–49; Mayes 1981, 51; Veijola 1995, 297; Nielsen 1995, 145–46, 213; contra L'Hour 1963, 3–26; Merendino 1969, 336–45; Ringgren 1977, 203; Locher 1986, 47–64.
223. Dion (1980, 337–46) attributes the "expunge the evil" laws to preexilic times, since they assume the central authority of monarchic rule, and at least some (Deut 13, 17:2–7) he assigns to a Josianic Dtr; see also Dion 1991; cf. Rofé 1988a, 66–71, 152; Rütersworden 1996, 231–33. For exilic Dtr attribution, see, e.g., Nielsen 1995, 145–45, 215; Veijola 1995, 297.

Deuteronomy 22:13–29

The laws in Deut 22:13–29 deal with various cases of sexual offenses involving women. The section deals first with women whose marriage has been consummated (vv. 13–22) and then with virgin girls, whether betrothed or free (vv. 23–29).[224] The first case (vv. 13–21) deals with the suspicion that a girl who was married off as a virgin actually had intercourse with another man *prior* to her marriage. The second case (v. 22) discusses adultery proper, that is, intercourse of a married woman with a man other than her husband *after* her marriage. The law does not raise the possibility that a married woman might be raped, and it is not at all certain whether the law distinguishes, in the case of a married woman, between consensual intercourse and rape.[225] The following cases all deal with the rape (root ענה) of a virgin girl (בתולה נערה), distinguishing mainly between the girl who is betrothed (מארשה, vv. 23–27) and girls not yet promised in marriage (vv. 28–29).[226] The status of the betrothed girl is comparable to that of the married woman (cf. v. 24aγ), and for this reason the law deals with her more severely than the girl who is not engaged.[227] If she is raped within the precincts of the town, she is held responsible under the presumption that she would have been saved if only she cried out for help; the very fact that she was violated in the town is held as evidence of her tacit consent (vv. 23–24). The law does not entertain the possibility that she resisted without crying out, or that she did cry for help but none was forthcoming. Extenuating circumstances are recognized only in case she is assaulted in the open field, where no others are around to heed her cries

---

224. For further discussion of Deut 22:13–29, see Rothenbusch 2003; Edenburg 2009, with additional literature there.

225. The laws of Hammurabi (§§129–130) also lack this distinction, while the Middle Assyrian laws (A §§12, 16) present differential rulings according to the circumstances that distinguish between assault of a married woman and consensual relations. See Otto 1994, 167–68; Edenburg 2009, 51–53.

226. The use of the term בתולה in Deut 22 designates the girl as a virgin, as can be seen in vv. 14–15, where בתולים signifies evidence of her virginity at marriage. See, e.g., Rofé 1987, 136 n. 11; Locher 1986, 176–92; Pressler 1993, 25–28; Nelson 2002, 265; cf. the dissenting views of Wenham 1972, 326–48; and Frymer-Kensky 1998. מארשה signifies the girl's standing after her future husband has paid her bride price, but prior to his consummation of the marriage; see Pressler 1993, 32; Nielsen 1995, 216.

227. By contrast, in the cuneiform law collections only the man is held liable for deflowering the betrothed girl; see Edenburg 2009, 53–55.

TEXT, SUBTEXT, AND INTERTEXTUAL MOSAIC

(vv. 25–27). The final case (vv. 28–29) deals with the rape of a virgin who is not betrothed; since she is free, it is possible to compel her attacker to marry her.[228]

Although there are grounds to suppose that these laws were originally rooted in an independent collection of family laws,[229] the scribe who composed the section carefully chose the cases and rulings from the well of legal tradition in order to reflect distinctive Deuteronomistic notions regarding the fidelity that clients owe their patrons.[230] Elsewhere I suggested that the laws in Deut 22:13–29 were composed along with the final, late Deuteronomistic editing of the laws of apostasy in Deut 13 and that they reflect the same uncompromising outlook.[231] Thus if it is found that Judg 19–21 evokes the language motifs of Deut 22, then such a literary allusion would provide additional evidence for the lateness of composition and revision of the Gibeah story.

Admittedly, the case of the concubine does not come within the purview of these laws. The concubine is a secondary wife[232] who is forcibly violated in the town, while the laws in Deut 22 do not deal with rape of a married woman nor do they recognize the possibility of rape in the town. Nonetheless, there are apparent verbal parallels between the laws and the Gibeah story, which may point to intentional literary allusion.

Deut 22:13–29	Judg 19–21
[20] If this charge is true and the girl's virginity was not established, [21] then *they shall take* the girl *out to* [והוציאו אל] the *entrance of her father's house* [פתח בית אביה] [where] the people of her town shall stone her until she dies, **for she has committed an outrage in Israel** [כי עשתה נבלה בישראל] by **fornicating** [while living] in **her father's house** [לזנות בית אביה]. **So you shall expunge**	19 [25] The man seized his concubine and took *her outside to them* [ויוצא אליהם; cf. vv. 22, 24] 19 [27] There was the woman, his concubine, lying at the *entrance of the house* [פתח הבית]. 19 [23, 24] "Do not **commit this outrage** [תעשו את הנבלה]." 20 [6] "For they have **committed an outrageous** act of depravity [כי עשו זמה]

---

228. See Exod 22:15–16; Gen 34:12.
229. Merendino 1969, 257–71; Phillips 1973, 353–54; Locher 1986, 48–57; Rofé 1987, 131–35, 143, 156–57; Stulman 1992, 57–61.
230. Edenburg 2009, 56–60; cf. Otto 1993, 259–62, 274–81; 1998.
231. Edenburg 2009, 56–58.
232. See Jüngling 1981, 80–82; Engelkern 1989, 587–89; see Gen 25:1, 6; 35:22; 37:2; 1 Chr 1:32, where Bilhah and Keturah are alternately termed *wife* and *concubine*.

evil from your midst. ²² If a man is found lying with another man's wife, both of them shall die, the man who lay with the woman, and the woman. **So you shall expunge evil from Israel.** ²³ If a virgin girl is betrothed to a man, and another man finds her in the town and lies with her, ²⁴ you shall take the two of them out to the gate of that town and stone them until they are dead, the girl for not crying out in the town, and the man for **violating** [ענה] another man's wife. **So you shall expunge evil from your midst.**

28 If a man finds a **virgin girl** [נער בתולה], who has *not* been betrothed, and seizes here and lies with her, and they are discovered, ²⁹ then the man who lay with her shall give to **the girl's father** [אבי הנער; cf. vv. 15–16, 19] fifty [shekels of] silver and she shall be his wife as restitution for the violation [תחת אשר ענה]; he may never divorce her.

ונבלה בישראל; cf. v. 10]." 19 ² His concubine was angry with him and left him for **her father's house** [ותזנה פילגשו ותלך מאתו אל בית אביה].

20 ⁵ "They **violated** [ענו] my concubine and she died."

20 ¹² "So *we* shall **expunge evil from Israel.**"

21 ¹² **virgin girl[s]** [נערה בתולה] *who have not* experienced intercourse with a man

19 ³⁻⁶, ⁸⁻⁹ **the girl's father** [אבי הנערה]

Unique Parallel Usages

The collocation אבי הנערה occurs in the Bible only in Deut 22:15–16, 19, 29; Judg 19:3–6, 8–9. Since the concubine's father is also referred to as the "father-in-law" of the Levite (Judg 19:4, 7, 9), she clearly is considered a married woman who has already been possessed by her husband. Indeed, the narrator calls her, for the most part, either "concubine" (פלגש, 19:1–2, 9–10, 24–25, 27, 29; 20:4–6) or "woman" (אשה, 19:26–27; 20:4). It is strange, then, that the narrator did not term her father אבי הפלגש or אבי האשה since נערה generally designates a girl's status prior to the consummation of her marriage, when she is still in the custody of her father or brother.²³³ In Deut 22:15–16, 19 the father of the slandered bride is also termed אבי הנערה even though the girl is already married. But there the

---

233. See Gen 24:16, 28–29, 50–51; 34:3, 12; Num 30:17; 2 Kgs 5:2, 4; Esth 2:7; see Ruth 2:5.

expression occurs with reference to her behavior *before* marriage. Thus the possibility should be considered that the usage in Judg 19 was influenced by that found in Deut 22.

The appositional phrase נערה בתולה (Deut 22:23, 28; Judg 21:12) is found in two more texts,[234] but only in Deut 22:28 and Judg 21:12 does it occur with a restrictive relative clause, "who has not [אשר לא]." In both cases, the relative clause serves to exclude a group of girls from the set of women otherwise sentenced to death, and they are spared only to enter into coerced marriage. At any rate, the case of the girls from Jabesh is closer to that of the captive woman (Deut 21:10–13), while the coerced marriage of the violated girl in Deut 22:23 is more similar to that of the girls of Shiloh (Judg 21:21–22).

Unusual Usage

Judges 19:2 presents a unique occurrence of the collocation זנה על, which probably reflects a homonymic root signifying "be angry with."[235] Since the author could have availed himself of a more common alternative, such as רגז על or כעס על, the question arises whether the choice of the rare homonym was influenced by association between the two contexts, both mentioning "her father's house" (אביה בית). The bride in Deut 22:21 is condemned to death since she is guilty of whoring in her father's house (לזנות בית אביה),[236] while the concubine dies for having left her husband in anger to return to her father's house (ותזנה עליו פילגשו ותלך מאתו אל־ בית אביה).

Inverse Application

The expression פתח הבית (Deut 22:21; Judg 19:27) is common throughout all literary strata in the Bible.[237] In both Judg 19:27 and Deut 22:21 (as well as Gen 19:6, 11), the entrance of the house delineates the boundary between the outside, where danger lurks, and the refuge inside the

---

234. 1 Kgs 1:2; Esth 2:2–3.
235. See ch. 3.
236. Taking בית אביה as an accusative of place; see Gen 38:11; see also Nielsen 1995, 210; GKC §118g.
237. See, e.g., Gen 43:19; Lev 14:38; 2 Sam 11:9; Isa 14:17; Prov 5:8; Esth 5:1; Neh 3:20.

house.²³⁸ But in Deut 22:21 the wayward girl is taken *out* from the secure zone within her father's house to the entrance where the people of her town wait to stone her, while in Judg 19:27 the concubine expires at the entrance of the house in an attempt to return to the safety afforded *within*.

In summary, the contextual "ungrammaticality" of the expression אבי הנערה (Judg 19:3–6, 8–9) and the estrangement arising from the unusual use of the root זנה (Judg 19:2), along with the inverse application of the motif פתח הבית, seem to indicate that N¹ intentionally invoked the language of the laws in Deut 22. Moreover, he appears to have applied the allusions not only to the figure of the concubine but also to the virgin girls of Jabesh-gilead (Judg 21:12). Nonetheless, the question arises regarding the purpose of these associative links, since none of the laws in Deut 22 actually applies to the situation of either the concubine or the girls of Jabesh. It is possible that the author planted the associative links in order to demonstrate the range of his literary competency. He may also have intended to present an ironic comparison between the situation of the concubine and that of the betrothed girl who is raped in the town. In contrast to the basic assumption of the law in Deut 22:24, no amount of resistance could save the concubine from the rape, and therefore she can hardly be accused of complicity. Thus within the world of the narrative, proper social norms have been overturned. The section dealing with the girls of Jabesh in the final chapter may have been included in the web of associative links in order to impose a measure of unity upon the entire narrative, for the characterization of the girls there also echoes Lot's description of his daughters, "who have not experienced intercourse with a man" (Judg 21:12; Gen 19:8). The manipulative use of borrowed elements by N¹ and R² seems to indicate their distance from the Deuteronomistic composition of the laws in Deut 13:13–29 and thus might support a post-Deuteronomistic origin for the composition and revision of the Gibeah story in Judg 19–21.

4.6. The Rape of Tamar (2 Sam 13:11–17)

Both the story of the outrage at Gibeah and the story of Amnon and Tamar tell how a woman's rape led men to avenge her by killing the culprits. Moreover, in each case the victim is sent to the scene of the rape by the man who has custody over her; in the Gibeah story the concubine is cast out

---

238. See also Exod 12:22–23; see Trible 1984, 78–79; Doyle 2004, 441–43.

to the mob by her husband, while Tamar is sent to Amnon's house by her father, David (2 Sam 13:7).[239] There are, however, significant differences between the stories: (1) Tamar is raped by her brother, while the concubine is raped by anonymous men in a strange town where she has no kin; (2) Tamar actively resists her rapist, whereas the concubine is depicted as silently passive; (3) Tamar negotiates with her rapist in order to avert her rape, while in the Gibeah story a third party (the old Ephraimite) negotiates to substitute the sex of the intended victim (the Levite), without any attempt to prevent the rape itself; (4) Tamar survives her rape and obtains her brother Absalom's protection, while the concubine lost her husband's protection and dies as a result of the rape; (5) there are no witnesses to Tamar's rape, which occurs in a secluded room, while the concubine is raped outside, in front of all the men of the town; and (6) Tamar's rape is considered a violation of the family honor, to be avenged by her brother, while the concubine's rape becomes a national matter to be avenged by the entire people. These significant differences between the two stories attest to the fact that their plots developed independently of each other. At the same time, the two stories employ similar language, which occasionally is applied in inverse fashion.

2 Sam 13:11–17	Judg 19–21
[11] When she brought [them] to him to eat, he **seized** her [ויחזק בה] and said to her: "Come, lay with me, my sister."	19 [25] The man **seized** his concubine [ויחזק בפילגשו] and thrust her out to them. They had sex with her....
[12] She said to him: "**Don't, my brother! Do not** [אל אחי אל] **rape me** [תענני], for such a thing is not done in Israel. **Do not commit this outrage** [אל תעשה את הנבלה הזאת]!"	19 [23] The homeowner went out to them and said to them: "**Don't, my brothers!** Please **do not** [אל אחי אל] commit such evil, for this man has entered my house. **Do not commit this outrage** [אל תעשו את הנבלה הזאת]! [24] Here are my virgin daughter and this man's concubine. I shall bring them out and you may **rape them** [וענו] and do to them as you see fit. Just **don't do this outrageous thing** [אל תעשו את דבר הנבלה הזאת] to this man." [25] But the men would not listen
[14] But he would not listen to her; he	

---

239. Some of the similarities have been previously noted by Carlson 1964, 165–66; Keefe 1993; more recently by Gross 2009, 839; and Stipp 2011, 229. For the sociological aspects of the rape story, see, e.g., Propp 1993; Dijk-Hemmes 1989.

overpowered her [ולא אבה לשמע בקולה ויחזק ממנה] and lay with her by force.

¹⁵ ... Amnon **said to her: "Get up and go** [ויאמר לה אמנון קומי לכי]!"

¹⁶ Tamar said to him: "Don't! To send me away would be a greater **wrong** [הרעה] than the other you other you committed against me." **But he would not listen to her** [ולא אבה לשמע לה].

¹⁷ He called his servant and said: "Send [שלחו] that woman **out** [החוצה], away from me, and *lock the door* behind her."

to him, so the man seized his concubine [ולא־אבו האנשים לשמע לו ויחזק האיש בפילגשו] and thrust her out to them, and they had sex with her and abused her....

19 ²⁸ He **said to her: "Get up! Let's go** [ויאמר אליה קומי ונלכה]!"

20 ¹³ "So we shall expunge evil [הרעה] from Israel." **But** Benjamin **would not listen to** [ולא אבו לשמע] their brothers the Israelites.

19 ²⁵ The man seized his concubine and thrust her **out** [החוץ] to them, and they had sex with her and abused her all night until morning, then sent her away [וישלחה].... 19 ²⁷ Her husband rose in the morning and *opened the doors* of the house to go on his way; but there was the woman—his concubine—lying at the entrance of the house.

UNIQUE EXPRESSIONS

The plea "Don't my brother(s)! Do not ..." (אל אחי אל, Judg 19:23, 24; 2 Sam 13:12) occurs only in these two passages, and in both cases it is followed by the exhortation not to commit an outrageous act (אל תעשה/ו את הנבלה הזאת).²⁴⁰ In 2 Sam 13:12 the plea is voiced by Tamar, the victim, while in Judg 19:23–24 it is uttered by a third party, the host, who provided shelter for the Levite and his wife. His plea is intended to prevent the rape of the male guest, the Levite, although he has no objection to the rape of his daughter and the wife of his guest. The marked verbal similarity between the two double exhortations in Judg 19:23–24 and 2 Sam 13:12 does not seem to derive from formulaic usage appropriate to a type-scene, since these exhortations are noticeably lacking from the story of Dinah, despite the use there of other shared terms (e.g., Gen 34:2, ענה; 34:7, עשה נבלה). Therefore, it seems most likely that the verbal similarity between

---

240. Elsewhere, עשה נבלה generally occurs in a motive clause; see Gen 34:7; Deut 22:21; Josh 7:15; Jer 29:23; see Judg 20:6.

Judg 19:23-24 and 2 Sam 13:12 derives from literary dependency. In Judg 19 these verbal parallels are woven into the plotline borrowed from the story of Sodom, where a third party, the host, pleads with the excited crowd outside not to harm his male guests. For this reason, it seems that the exhortations are original to Tamar's story and were borrowed by N¹, who reapplied them to the Gibeah story.

Only in Judg 19:28 and 2 Sam 13:15 is a woman commanded to *get up and go* (ויאמר אליה/לה קומי ונלכה/לכי) from the scene of her rape.²⁴¹ Amnon commands Tamar to "get up and go" in order to send her away after he raped her. This behavior fits the story, since the narrator prepared the reader beforehand for Amnon's change of sentiment with regard to Tamar (2 Sam 13:15a). The Levite also addresses the concubine after her rape with the same words, but includes himself in the cohortative, "Let's go!" The Levite aims to leave Gibeah and resume his journey home, but the concubine lying across the entrance to the house impedes him. It is ironic that only here in the entire story does the narrator have the Levite address the concubine, only now he grotesquely addresses a corpse. Amnon's callousness is too plausible to have been modeled upon the Levite's ludicrous behavior, but the narrator in Judg 19 might have had the Levite invoke Amnon's words in order to compare the Levite with Amnon.

RARE OR INFREQUENT SHARED USAGE

In both these texts the verb החזיק indicates the rapist's seizing of the victim (Judg 19:25; 2 Sam 13:11, 14). This verb is also employed in the law regarding rape in the field, which is taken to be a secluded place where no witnesses are present (Deut 22:25). In a similar fashion, Tamar is raped when secluded with Amnon in his room after the only possible witness had left.²⁴² In the story of Tamar, the rapist (Amnon) seizes his victim (cf. Deut 22:25); but in the Gibeah story, a third party (the Levite) takes hold of the victim (the concubine) and hands her over to the rapists.

The expression "would not hear" (ולא אבה/ו לשמוע, Judg 19:25; 20:13; 2 Sam 13:14, 16) occurs twice in each story, although it is not frequent

---

241. The phrase קומי לכי occurs in other contexts in 1 Kgs 14:12; 2 Kgs 8:1; Cant 2:10, 13.
242. In other rape descriptions, the verbs תפש (Deut 22:28; cf. Gen 39:12) and לקח (Gen 34:2) occur.

elsewhere.²⁴³ This suggests that the doubled occurrence in the one story was influenced by the recurrence in the other. The close verbal parallel is especially evident in Judg 19:25 and 2 Sam 13:14, where both Amnon and the men of Gibeah refuse to listen to the pleas to refrain from their acting upon their intent. Twice Amnon does not hearken to Tamar's pleadings. In the first instance, he "would not heed" her "plea" not to rape her (2 Sam 13:14), which is paralleled by Judg 19:25, where the men of Gibeah "would not heed" the host's "plea" not to commit an outrageous act. In the second instance, Tamar pleas with her brother not to increase the wrong (הרעה) by sending her away, but "he would not listen" to her (2 Sam 13:16), while in Judg 20:13 the Benjaminites "would not listen" to their *brothers'* demand to hand over the men of Gibeah and thus eradicate the wrong. If Judg 20:13 indeed derives from N¹, then the double usage in the Gibeah story stems from one hand. In Judg 19:25, the author apparently intended to draw an analogy between the outrage at Gibeah and the rape of Tamar, and he reemployed the parallel phrase in 20:13 in a different context, in order to present all the Benjaminites as partners to the crime at Gibeah. Alternately, if Judg 20:13 derives from R², then the redactor appears to have been aware of the previous analogy to the story of Tamar, which he expanded by reemploying the parallel phrase, but this time with reference to all the men of Benjamin.

INVERSE APPLICATION OF SHARED LANGUAGE

The verb ענה, "rape" (Judg 19:24; 2 Sam 13:12), occurs in inverse contexts in the two stories. In Judg 19:24, the host *offers* his daughter and the concubine so the men of Gibeah may rape them, while in 2 Sam 13:12 Tamar begs Amnon *not* to rape her.

The two descriptions of sending the victim away (... יצא החוץ וישלחוה/שלחו החוצה, Judg 19:25; 2 Sam 13:17) stand in inverse relation. The scene of the rape in the story of Amnon and Tamar is Amnon's house; and following the rape, Amnon demands to send Tamar out, away from him. At Gibeah the concubine is thrust outdoors, where she is raped; after the rapists send her away she returns to the entrance of the house and expires outside on the doorstep.

---

243. The expression occurs only three more times: Deut 23:6; Ezek 3:7; 20:8.

Inversion is also evident in application of the motif of *opening/locking the door* (Judg 19:27; 2 Sam 13:27). Amnon commands his servant to "lock the door" after the rape victim (Tamar) has been turned out. Conversely, the Levite "opens the doors" of the house on the morning after the rape and finds the raped concubine lying at the entrance. The Gibeah story is tantalizingly indeterminate on the question of whether the door was locked throughout the night. Was the door unlocked, but the concubine expired before she could open it, or did she die because she was locked out?

Several points of contact with the Gibeah story were found in the eight verses relating the rape of Tamar, including verbal parallels not directly related to the rape motif, such as the plea "Don't my brother(s)! Do not …"; the expression "would not hear … and siezed her"; and the command, "Get up and (let's) go." A unique parallel was represented by the phrase אל אחי combined with עשה נבלה. Inverse application was observed in use of the verb ענה, in the phrase "Get up! Let's go!" as well as in the motifs of sending outside and opening/locking the door. Such inverse application might indicate intentional transformation of a borrowed element in order to stress ironic differences between a well-known, authoritative narrative and its looking-glass reflection. These findings provide a strong basis for concluding that the two stories are interrelated. However, only one point provides evidence for the direction of literary dependence, namely, the Ephraimite host's exhortation in Judg 19:23–24, which evokes two separate texts (Gen 19:7 and 2 Sam 13:12). In my opinion, this indicates that the Ephraimite's speech has been modeled upon both those sources; this conclusion appears more likely than the alternative, that Judg 19:23–24 inspired separate sets of parallels in two different texts.

The web of links with the story of Tamar may have been intended to augment the characterization of three different figures in the Gibeah story—the Ephraimite host, the Levite, and the Benjaminites—all of who are likened to Amnon. N^1 shaped the character of the concubine as a passive and voiceless victim, whose rape is permitted by those responsible for her protection. For this reason, he does not place Tamar's plea in her mouth and instead has it issue from the mouth of the host, who is responsible for the welfare of his guests. However, the host's plea is not intended to prevent the rape; although it would be outrageous to violate his male guest, he encourages the men to do as they please with the women in the house. The Levite more specifically plays the part of Amnon by "seizing" (ויחזק) the concubine before the rape and then afterward addressing her with Amnon's words, "Get up and go." The analogy with Amnon places the

Levite's callous behavior in a new perspective, for he is now compared to an active participant in the rape. Later on, the analogy with Amnon is further broadened to embrace all the men of Benjamin, since they would not listen (ולא אבו לשמע) to their brothers, just as Amnon would not listen to his sister's plea. By refusing to listen to their brothers' exhortation to eradicate the evil in their midst, the Benjaminites' identify themselves with the actual culprits. This analogy with Amnon may raise expectations in the mind of the reader regarding the results of their refusal to listen, for just as Tamar's brother Absalom avenged his sister's rape by killing the rapist, the Israelites, who are "brothers" to Benjamin, will similarly mete out justice, not only upon the guilty parties at Gibeah but also upon all who identify with them. Although the reader of the Gibeah story is likely to fully comprehend the characters of the host, the Levite, and the Benjaminites even upon a superficial reading of the narrative, the web of links to the story of Tamar contributes to enriching the composition with an additional layer of allusion.

If the story of Amnon and Tamar indeed served as a source of allusion for the Gibeah story, then it indicates that N^1 was familiar with the Succession Narrative of which the story of Tamar is a part. However, there is considerable debate over dating the composition of the Succession Narrative. Leonhard Rost and others held that the Succession Narrative was composed no more than one generation after the events it describes.[244] However, it is unlikely that conditions were ripe in the tenth and ninth centuries BCE for literary activity of the type that produced the Succession Narrative.[245] The chronological distribution of epigraphic finds from Judah and Israel indicates limited scribal activity prior to the eighth century BCE, and literary tradition developed elsewhere throughout the ancient Near East only after at least several generations of administrative scribal activity. Some scholars associate the Succession Narrative with concerns prevalent in the times of Hezekiah or Josiah, while others advance arguments for an exilic or postexilic origin of the composition.[246] However this debate is to be resolved, it seems most likely that N^1 became familiar with the story of

---

244. For the view that the Succession Narrative is either a contemporary composition or based upon contemporary sources, see, e.g., Rost 1982, 103–6; von Rad 1966; Barton 2004; Stipp 2011, 229–30.

245. See, e.g., Na'aman 1996, 170–73; Carr 2005, 111–42; van der Toorn 2007, 9–26; Rollston 2010.

246. For an eighth- or seventh-century BCE context of composition, see Blenkin-

Tamar either as part of the Deuteronomistic History or as part of a formative Samuel scroll. The derivative use N[1] makes of the Tamar story is a sign of his chronological distance from his source material, and provides support from a post-Deuteronomistic provenance for the Gibeah story.

4.7. The War against Midian (Num 31)

In both Num 31 and Judg 19–21, a sexual offense leads to a war that concludes with the burning of the enemy's cities and decimating their people. In both cases, the supposed annihilation of the enemy—Midian and Benjamin, respectively—is irreconcilable with the subsequent status of these groups according to older sources; the Gideon cycle likens the numbers of Midianites to a swarm of locusts (Judg 6:5), while the towns of Gibeah and Jabesh as well as the tribe of Benjamin are well-established entities in the Saul narratives. Notwithstanding, the stories differ greatly in their details. The war against Midian was motivated by the promiscuous behavior of the Midianite women at Peor (Num 31:16; cf. ch. 25) and was waged against a foreign people. The war at Gibeah, by contrast, was a civil war, which broke out following the rape and death of the concubine.[247]

Num 31	Judg 19–21
[4] "You shall send ... a thousand **from each of the tribes of Israel** [לכל מטות ישראל]." [5] A thousand from each tribe was provided: **twelve thousand** *picked for the campaign* [שנים עשר אלף חלוצי צבא]. [6] Moses sent them ... a thousand from each tribe, with **Phinehas ben**	20 [10] "We shall take ten men from a hundred, **from each of the tribes of Israel** [לכל שבטי ישראל], and one hundred from a thousand and a thousand from ten thousand, to bring provisions for the people coming up against Gibeah."

---

sopp 2013, 58; Sweeney 2001, 106–9. For an exilic Dtr origin, see S. McKenzie 2000; and for a postexilic origin, see Van Seters 1983, 277–91; 2000.

247. For parallels between Judg 21:10–12 and Num 31, see , e.g., Bertheau 1845, 229; Böhme 1885, 35; Moore 1895, 445; Snaith 1967, 325; Levine 2000, 455–56, 466; Blenkinsopp 2006, 641. Most assume that the Jabesh incident drew upon Num 31, although Burney (1970, 454, 456 n.*); and Kaufmann (1961, 301) hold that the differences in the context of the parallel material preclude any literary influence.

Eleazar the priest.
⁷ They campaigned against Midian as YHWH ordered Moses, and they killed **every male** [כל זכר].

⁹ The Israelites took the Midianite women and their children captive and took as spoil all their cattle and flocks and all their wealth. ¹⁰ *They burned with fire* [שרפו באש] **all their towns** [כל עריהם] in which they settled.

¹⁵ Moses said to them, "You **spared** *all the women* [החייתם כל נקבה]! ¹⁶ But they are the very ones who, at the bidding of Balaam, incited the Israelites to trespass against YHWH in the matter of Peor, so that YHWH's congregation was struck by plague. ¹⁷ Now, therefore, *kill every male child and kill* **every woman who has experienced sexual intercourse with a man** [הרגו כל זכר בטף וכל אשה ידעת איש למשכב זכר], ¹⁸ while you may keep alive for yourselves all the *young women* [הטף בנשים] **who have not experienced sexual intercourse with a man** [אשר לא ידעו משכב זכר החיו לכם]."

⁴⁹ They said to Moses, "Your servants have counted all the warriors in our charge and *not a man is* **missing** [נפקד]."

21¹⁰ The congregation sent there a force of **twelve thousand** *fighting men* [שנים עשר אלף מבני החיל].
20 ²⁸ **Phinehas ben Eleazar** ben Aaron served [before the ark] in those days.

20 ⁴⁸ The men of Israel returned to the Benjaminites and put them to the sword, from towns [and] people to beast and all that was to be found. **All the towns** [כל עריהם] to be found *they also set* **on fire** [שלחו באש].

21 ¹⁴ They gave them the women which they **spared** from the women of Jabesh-gilead [הנשים אשר חיו].
21 ¹⁰ They instructed them: "Go and put to the sword the people of Jabesh-gilead, [even] *the women and children* [והנשים והטף]. ¹¹ This is what you shall do: *exterminate* **every male** and **every woman who has experienced sexual intercourse** [כל זכר וכל אשה ידעת משכב זכר תחרימו]." ¹² Of the people of Jabesh-gilead they found four hundred *virgin girls* [נערה בתולה] **who did not experience sexual intercourse with a man** [אשר לא ידעה איש למשכב זכר].

21 ³ Saying: "Why, YHWH, God of Israel, has it come to pass in Israel that a tribe is now **missing** [להפקד] from Israel?"

Two motifs shared by both narratives might provide evidence that Num 31 exerted influence on the final shape of Judg 19–21. First, in both Num 31:5 and Judg 21:10 the Israelites employ a force of *twelve thousand* warriors. In Num 31:4–5 the number derives from mustering one thousand from each tribe, disregarding the size or relative strength of the different tribes. Here the number probably reflects an ideal view of the relative standing of the twelve tribes.[248] While the typological number *twelve thousand* is

---

248. See Levine 2000, 465; see Noth 1968, 229; Budd 1984, 330; Knauf 1988, 165.

appropriate to the ideological outlook of Judg 21 regarding the integrity of the tribal league, the force of twelve thousand sent against Jabesh actually comprises representatives from only eleven tribes. Benjamin was not yet rehabilitated and would hardly participate in a punitive campaign directed against an ally. Thus the typological number hardly fits with the details of the narrative in Judg 21 and could have been borrowed from the context in Num 31:5, where it expresses the idea of equal intertribal cooperation.[249]

The second element that appears to be more at home in Num 31 than in the Gibeah story is the figure of Phinehas ben Eleazar. In Num 31:6, Phinehas accompanies the troops in battle against Midian in order to sound the trumpets, as stipulated by the commandment in Num 10:8–9. In this case, Phinehas fits the chronological framework of the story, which is the period of the desert wanderings, when Phinehas appears alongside his father, Eleazar, after Aaron's demise. It is likely that Phinehas was designated to accompany the troops in this story in order to protect the high priest Eleazar from corpse pollution on the battlefield.[250] Phinehas was also previously connected with action against Midian in the Baal of Peor incident (Num 25:6–13). By contrast, in Judg 20:28 Phinehas is mentioned in an intrusive gloss that breaks the natural continuity between 20:27a and 20:28b.[251]

The most striking verbal parallel between the two stories occurs in the instructions to the troops in Num 31:17–18 and Judg 21:10–12:

Num 31:17: וְעַתָּה הִרְגוּ כָל־זָכָר בַּטָּף וְכָל־אִשָּׁה יֹדַעַת אִישׁ לְמִשְׁכַּב זָכָר הֲרֹגוּ

Judg 21:11: זֶה הַדָּבָר אֲשֶׁר תַּעֲשׂוּ כָּל־זָכָר וְכָל־אִשָּׁה יֹדַעַת מִשְׁכַּב־זָכָר תַּחֲרִימוּ

Judg 21:10: לְכוּ וְהִכִּיתֶם אֶת־יוֹשְׁבֵי יָבֵשׁ גִּלְעָד לְפִי־חֶרֶב וְהַנָּשִׁים וְהַטָּף

Num 31:18: וְכֹל הַטַּף בַּנָּשִׁים אֲשֶׁר לֹא־יָדְעוּ מִשְׁכַּב זָכָר הַחֲיוּ לָכֶם

Judg 21:12: וַיִּמְצְאוּ מִיּוֹשְׁבֵי יָבֵישׁ גִּלְעָד אַרְבַּע מֵאוֹת נַעֲרָה בְתוּלָה אֲשֶׁר לֹא־יָדְעָה אִישׁ לְמִשְׁכַּב זָכָר

---

249. The figure 12,000 occurs in other military contexts in the Bible but without reference to the tribal league; see Josh 8:25; 2 Sam 10:6; 17:1; 1 Kgs 5:6; 10:26; Ps 60:2.
250. See, e.g., Licht 1995, 118–19.
251. See ch. 1 1.3.2.1.

The construct משכב זכר occurs only in Num 31:17–18, 35, and Judg 21:11–12.²⁵² The sexually experienced woman is indicated in Num 31:17 by the expression אשה ידעת איש למשכב זכר, which conflates separately attested expressions: אשה ידעת איש and אשה ידעת משכב־זכר,²⁵³ while the parallel reference in Judg 21:11 utilizes the simpler collocation אשה ידעת משכב זכר. Conversely, Judg 21:12 employs the conflated expression in conjunction with the virgin girls who did *not* experience sexual intercourse with a man (אשר לא־ידעה איש למשכב זכר), while the parallel reference in Num 31:18 utilizes the simpler collocation:

Num 31:17: אשה ידעת איש למשכב זכר
Judg 21:11: אשה ידעת משכב־זכר
Num 31:18: הטף בנשים אשר לא־ידעו משכב זכר
Judg 21:12: נערה בתולה אשר לא־ידעה איש למשכב זכר

The inversion in variation between the simple and conflated expressions is a possible indication of literary interrelation. In the context of Num 31, where Moses attempts to rectify the situation arising with regard to the Midianite captives, the narrator has Moses give overly explicit instructions in order to remove any trace of doubt which women exactly must be eliminated, and then he simplifies the formulation with regard to the girls who may be saved. By contrast, there is no obvious rationale behind

---

252. According to Levine (2000, 456), the infinitive משכב displays Aramaic influence through the addition of an initial *mem*. The form occurs in a sexual context in Ezek 23:17; otherwise, see 2 Sam 4:5. According to Olyan (1994, 184–86), משכב זכר indicates penile penetration, and ידע משכב זכר relates to experiencing penetration. In Lev 18:22 and 20:13, the converse expression משכב אשה indicates the part played by the partner being penetrated.

253. For ידעה איש (לא) as an expression of female sexual (in)experience, see Gen 19:8; 24:16; Judg 11:39. Interestingly, CH §130 presents an Akkadian parallel: *aššat awīlim ša zikaram la idûma*, which appears to be the sole Akkadian attestation of the expression; see *CAD* I/J:28b. It is surprising that this circumlocution should be found both in the Old Babylonian law and in biblical literature of a millennium later, particularly since both Akkadian and BH share the simpler cognate term *batultu*/בתולה, "virgin"; see Landsberger 1968, 41–65. The existence of Neo-Assyrian copies of the laws of Hammurabi indicate that they were part of the curriculum in scribal schools. It is tempting, therefore, to surmise that the circumlocution may have found its way into to Hebrew through the agency of Judean scribes who studied the laws of Hammurabi as part of their training, either in the Akkadian original or perhaps in an Aramaic translation; see D. Wright 2003.

the reverse variation in simple and conflate expressions in Judg 21, where first the experienced women are indicated with the simple formulation, following which the virgins are indicated by means of the conflate expression. Furthermore, the formulation in Judg 21:12, "virgin girls who have not experienced sex with a man" (נערה בתולה אשר לא־ידעה איש למשכב זכר), is overly explicit since "virgins" (נערה בתולה) by definition have not experienced sexual intercourse (לא־ידעה איש).²⁵⁴ By contrast, the formulation in Num 31:18 is appropriate to its context. The two sentences in Moses's instructions in Num 31:17–18 are parallel in structure:

Num 31:17: כל־זכר בטף וכל־אשה ידעת איש למשכב זכר הרגו
Num 31:18: וכל הטף בנשים אשר לא־ידעו משכב זכר החיו לכם

In verse 17, Moses orders Moses orders the army to kill all the male children (כל־זכר בטף) who remained in the Midianite camp and all the sexually experienced women. In verse 18, the narrator completes the parallel and reemploys the term טף but in reverse sequence (זכר // הטף בנשים בטף), and it is possible that he found this more aesthetically pleasing than a simpler formulation like וכל אשה אשר לא ידעה משכב זכר. The tautology in Judg 21:12 might be explained as the result of literary borrowing in which the scribe combined more than one intertextual reference. Judges 21:12 retains the composite structure of Num 31:18 in order to define the virgins (nominal collocation + the relative clause אשר לא־ידעה), but the scribe replaced הטף בנשים with the apposition נערה בתולה, which he probably borrowed from Deut 22:23, 28.

Finally, there is a telling discrepancy in the instructions to the punitive force in Judg 21:10–12 that might be the mark of a blind motif and indicate dependency of the passage in Judg 21 upon its parallel in Num 31. The instructions that distinguish between virgin maidens and all other women in Judg 21:10–11 only detail who should be killed, namely, "every male and every woman who experienced sexual intercourse" (v. 11), but they neglect to indicate what should be done with the virgins.²⁵⁵ By con-

---

254. Wenham (1972) argued, on the basis of this apparent tautology, that בתולה does not indicate lack of sexual experience, but rather the girl's having reached marriageable age. But if this meaning is adopted there still remains a tautology in the expression נערה בתולה (see Deut 22:23, 28; 1 Kgs 1:2; Esth 2:3); see also Rofé 1987, 136; Pressler 1993, 25–28.

255. LXX[B] and the Vulgate add at the end of v. 11: "but you are to spare the vir-

trast, the forces sent to war with Midian in Num 31 are not told in advance how to treat the noncombatant Midianites; and accordingly the fighting men did as they saw fit and took Midianite women and children captive. This aroused Moses's anger since the Midianite women incited the Israelites to transgress at Peor (Num 31:14–16). Moses then provided ad hoc instructions that take into account the warriors' sexual passions; they are ordered to kill every male and all the sexually experienced women, leaving only the virgins alive.[256] It is possible, as Moore thought, that the partial instructions in Judg 21:10–11, along with the verbal similarity to Num 31:17–18, indicate that R² quoted the parallel section from Num 31 but mistakenly omitted the main point, namely, that the virgins should be spared.[257] On the other hand, it could be that the instructions were adapted to the context in each story. In Num 31, complete instructions are required for the characterization of Moses as remedying the slipup by the fighting men, while in Judg 21 there is no need to fully detail both the orders and their execution, since they may be reconstructed through complementary reading.

Literary interaction between the stories seems to have left its mark on other passages as well. Thus the rare expression ‎נפקד מ- is shared by Num 31:49 and Judg 21:3.[258] In Num 31:49, a head count is taken of the fighting men, and none is found to be missing (‎ולא־נפקד ממנו איש). The use here is similar to that in 1 Sam 20:18, 25, 27; 2 Sam 2:30; 1 Kgs 20:39; 2 Kgs

---

gins. And they did so." Many, such as Böhme 1885, 33; Burney 1970, 490; Gray 1986, 362, thought that these clauses were accidentally omitted from the MT of v. 11, but it seems more likely that the plus reflects a deductive expansion based on comparison with Num 31:18; see Kaufmann 1961, 301; Amit 1999, 311.

256. Some think the order to kill every woman with sexual experience reflects the rules of war in Deut 20:13–14; 21:11–14; see, e.g., Levine 2000, 468–70. But these laws make no reference to the distinction between virgins and all other women. It could be that the command in Num 31:17–18 stems from the Priestly ideology concerned with purity and separation of things of different orders, which in this case is reflected by the concern to prevent mixing Israelite and Midianite semen in the body of the captive women. Since the virgins were considered to be "new" and "empty" receptacles, they were permitted to the Israelite men. Brown (2015) suggests that Num 31:13–18 belongs to a *post*-Priestly depiction of Moses, in which he (overzealously?) goes beyond Yahweh's initial requirement.

257. Moore 1895, 447.

258. The expression occurs only twice more in 1 Sam 25:21 and 2 Sam 2:30, although the *niphal* of ‎פקד signifies "to be missing, lacking," in eight more instances (1 Sam 20:18, 25, 27; 25:7; 1 Kgs 20:39 [twice]; 2 Kgs 10:19 [twice]).

TEXT, SUBTEXT, AND INTERTEXTUAL MOSAIC 261

10:19. In Judg 21:3, the Israelites lament that a tribe is lacking from Israel (להפקד מישראל שבט אחד) as a result of the annihilation of Benjamin. The use of the verb here is not self-evident, since the narrator could have employed an alternative expression like מ- נכרת,[259] מ- נגרע,[260] or נבלע.[261] It is possible that the *niphal* of פקד was employed in Judg 21:3, rather than an appropriate alternative verb, in order to deepen the verbal interrelation to Num 31.

So too the mention of the elders of the congregation (זקני העדה) in Judg 21:16 might have been influenced by the double appearance of the representatives of the congregation that appear alongside Eleazar the priest in Num 31:13, 26 (v. 13, "chiefs of the congregation," נשיאי העדה; v. 26, "heads of the families of the congregation," ראשי אבות העדה). Both נשיא and ראשי אבות commonly indicate the representative leadership in the Priestly strata of the so-called Hexateuch, and their appearance in Num 31 is in accord with the context of the narrative.[262] By contrast, mention of "the elders of the congregation" (זקני העדה) in Judg 21:16 is wholly unexpected. Up to this point, the narrative makes no mention of any representative or governing body. On the contrary, the Israelites are repeatedly portrayed as acting in concert without the direction of any leadership (e.g., 20:1–2, 3b, 8, 11–12, 17–18; 21:1–3, 5, 8–10). Moreover, the question the elders ask in verse 16 was previously voiced by all the Israelites in verses 6–7. Furthermore, the collocation זקני העדה is unusual. The "elders" frequently figure in the Yahwistic and Deuteronomic strata of the Pentateuch[263] but are rarely mentioned in the Priestly literature, and those cases are generally considered secondary interpolations.[264] Thus there are grounds to suspect that "the elders of the congregation" are a secondary

---

259. See, e.g., Gen 17:14; Exod 30:33; Lev 17:4; Jer 7:28; 11:19; cf. Num 4:18; Ps 37:28, 38.
260. See, e.g., Num 27:4; 36:3; cf. Exod 5:11.
261. See, e.g., Hos 8:8; cf. use of the *piel* in 2 Sam 20:19–20; Job 8:18.
262. For the construct נשיאי העדה, see Exod 16:22; Num 4:34; 16:2; 31:13; 32:2; Josh 9:15, 18; 22:30. For ראשי אבות, see Exod 6:25; Num 32:28; 36:1; Josh 14:1; 21:1; 22:14; cf. Neh 12:22; 1 Chr 7:7; 8:6, 10, 28; 9:9, 33; 24:6.
263. See, e.g., Exod 3:16, 18; 4:29; 12:21; 17:5–6; 18:12; 19:7; 24:1, 9, 14; Num 11:16, 24–25; Deut 19:12; 27:1; 29:9; 31:9, 28.
264. Lev 4:15 suddenly mentions "the elders," זקני העדה, while in the previous verses, vv. 13–14, it is the congregation (קהל) who acts on behalf of the עדה; see Noth 1965, 41; Elliger 1966, 54. Similarly, Lev 9:1 mentions the elders alongside Aaron and his sons, while Moses subsequently addresses Aaron (v. 2), instructing him in v. 3 to

element, artificially introduced into the narrative in 21:16. It is possible, then, that this mention of זקני העדה was influenced by the appearance of ראשי אבות העדה in Num 31:26.

The comparison between Num 31 and Judg 19–21 revealed a unique recurrence of the expression אשה ידעת למשכב זכר (Num 31:17–18 // Judg 21:11–12), and parallel elements that were appropriate to their context in the story of the Midianite war but that proved to be nonfunctional or "ungrammatical" in the Gibeah narrative (the figure "twelve thousand," Phinehas ben Eleazar, and the "elders of the congregation"), as well as close verbal parallels in Judg 21:10–12 and Num 31:5, 17–18. Therefore, it is reasonable to conclude that we are dealing here with literary dependency and that R² drew upon Num 31, rather than vice versa.

The parallels with Num 31 are distributed throughout the R² stratum in Judg 20–21 (20:28, 48; 21:3, 10–12, 16) and help establish a relative date for this revision. R² was not only familiar with the story of the Midianite war in Num 31, but also recycled some of its elements in a fashion foreign to their original use. This seems to indicate that this revision of the Gibeah story was carried out somewhat later than the composition of Num 31. The narrative in Num 31 is replete with Priestly vocabulary and ideology, but at the same time it reinterprets Deuteronomic and Priestly law. Thus it is thought to be of post-Priestly origin.[265] Aramaisms and stylistic affinities with Chronicles further aid in establishing quite a late date for the composition of Num 31, probably sometime in the mid-fourth century BCE.[266] Accordingly, R² may have been contemporary with the Chronicler, or even a generation later.

Finally, we must consider the purpose of the links with the narrative of the Midianite war. Yairah Amit suggested that the author in Judg 21 had a twofold purpose: to "solve" the dilemma regarding the Benjaminite survivors through the agency of women captives of war, as well as to denigrate the relations between Jabesh-gilead and Saul the Benjaminite king (1 Sam

---

command the Israelites (בני ישראל), with no further mention of the elders or any other representatives.

265. See Brown 2015 with further references there.
266. See Levine 2000, 451, 465–66; Snaith 1967, 326; Noth 1968, 229; Niditch 1993, 79–89; cf. Böhme 1885, 35–36; Moore 1895, 445; and additional literature in Budd 1984, 327. Knierim and Coats (2005, 295–97) stress that the narrative lacks connective links to its context, and thus view it as a late addition to P; in a similar vein, see Achenbach 2003, 615–22; Schmidt 2004, 186.

11; 31:11–13; 2 Sam 2:5–7; 21:12).²⁶⁷ However, according to the redaction analysis of Judg 20–21, all the links with Num 31 may be attributed to R², while the critical stance toward Jabesh and the necessity to find brides for the Benjaminite survivors are already evident in N¹ (21:7–9). Thus the purpose of the intertextual links with Num 31 should be reconsidered. Perhaps R² added the allusions to the story of the Midianite war in order to hint at a critical stance toward the story he was revising. In the story of the Midianite war, the command to kill all males and all the sexually experienced women serves to remedy the oversight made by the warriors during the battle. The similar command in the Gibeah story is also presented as a corrective measure after the battle, but its purpose here is to remedy the wrongful annihilation of the opponent. In my opinion, R² employed the elements borrowed from Num 31 with irony in order to emphasize the absurdity of the tribes' attempt to remedy this situation by means of additional mass killing.²⁶⁸

4.8. The Transjordan Altar (Josh 22:9–34)

The stories about the Transjordan altar (Josh 22) and the war with Benjamin (Judg 19–21) relate similar episodes in which the people assemble as a ritual congregation in order to suppress and punish the nonnormative behavior of a particular group within the community. In both stories, the congregation appears to act without prompting and mobilizes for war without the direction of a military leader. Instead, the leaders that do figure in the story are the collective bodies of the elders and tribal heads, along with Phinehas the priest (Josh 22:13–14, 30–32; Judg 20:28a; 21:16). But while the outrage of the community in Judg 19–21 centers on the violation of social norms exemplified by the breach of hospitality and sexual assault, the focus in Josh 22 is on nonnormative cultic practice. There the building of an altar is considered an act of rebellion against YHWH, comparable with the defilement incurred by the community at Peor or the misappropriation by Achan of the items dedicated to YHWH (Josh 22:17, 20).

Two issues require clarification in Josh 22 in order to understand the aim of the narrative and its compositional history. First, the specific nature of the transgression has been obscured by confusion arising from

---

267. Amit 1999, 309–10.
268. See Rudin 1985, 160.

conflicting statements regarding the location of the altar in verses 10–11.[269] Since the force of the argument in Josh 22 is directed against the Transjordanian tribes, who erected the altar in order to sanctify their land east of the Jordan (vv. 24–25), we should locate the altar in the Transjordan in accordance with verse 11. This location is additionally supported by the naming of the altar, which seems to reflect an alternate etiology for Gilead (v. 34).[270] Therefore, it is reasonable to expect that the objection of the western tribes is tied to the eastern location of the altar. Second, in verse 19 two incommensurate complaints are raised against the Transjordanian tribes and their altar: (1) their settlement of the Transjordan—opposite Canaan—brought them to rebel against YHWH, since that region lies outside the precincts sanctified by YHWH;[271] (2) they violated the exclusivity of the tabernacle.[272] The first complaint seems to reject the altar because it was not erected on sanctified land, implying that it would have been acceptable if it were built within the holy precincts of Canaan. However, this implication is then contradicted by the second claim: no altar that competes with the tabernacle can be legitimate. Earlier scholars evaded the basic incommensurability of the two complaints and attempted to resolve the issue by differentiating between a Deuteronomistic source and a Priestly redaction.[273] According to this view, the primary story dealt with an infringement of cult centralization, and this source was later

---

269. V. 10 places the site of the altar in "the foothills of the Jordan, which is in the land of Canaan," while v. 11 locates it "opposite Canaan by the foothills of the Jordan, across from the Israelites." On the basis of v. 10, many opted for a Cisjordan site for the altar at Gilgal; see Möhlenbrink 1938, 248–49; Soggin 1972, 212–14; Snaith 1978, 330–35; Butler 1983, 243, 245; cf. Fritz 1994, 220–22, 227; Aḥituv 1995, 354–56; Nelson 1997, 246, 252, who refrain from identifying the specific Cisjordan locality of the altar. However the plain meaning of אל־מול ארץ כנען אל־גלילות הירדן אל־ עבר בני ישראל in v. 11 clearly indicates a Transjordan location; see Kaufmann 1959, 240–42; Boling 1982, 551; Assis 2004, 217–18. Fritz (1994, 226) unnecessarily thinks that v. 11 is an editorial expansion. It is likely that the conflicting statements regarding the site of the altar—in or opposite Canaan—are due to a transmission error in v. 10, which mistakenly reproduces the phrase "which is in the land of Canaan" from the previous v. 9; see also Levine 2000, 505.

270. See, e.g., Kaufmann 1959, 243.

271. Fritz 1994, 221–24; Nelson 1997, 247.

272. See Lev 17:4; see Levine 2000, 507. The tabernacle mentioned in v. 19 presumably alludes to Shiloh; see 18:1.

273. See Möhlenbrink 1938, 247–49; Soggin 1972, 214; Snaith 1978, 330–31; and Kloppenborg's harmonistic attempt: "Clearly the idea of 'Holy Land' is operative, and

TEXT, SUBTEXT, AND INTERTEXTUAL MOSAIC   265

revised by a Priestly redactor who added the theme of the sanctity of the land. However, the question of the sanctity of the land is intrinsic to this story, not a secondary motif. Hence it seems more likely that the entire story was composed and added to the Deuteronomistic History by a post-Deuteronomistic, Priestly author.[274]

The story of the Transjordan altar and the Gibeah narrative share a similar five-stage structure, as well as some common formulations and motifs.[275] However, the two stories differ greatly in their endings; in Josh 22 the delegation sent to the Transjordanian tribes successfully negotiates and prevents the outbreak of hostilities,[276] while in Judg 20 the Benjaminites refuse the delegation's demands to hand over the offenders from Gibeah, thus leading to an unprecedented civil war.

STRUCTURAL ANALOGIES

Report of a nonnormative act (Josh 22:11; Judg 19:30–20:7). In Josh 22:11 the community learns about the transgression and the identity of its perpetrators by means of an oral report or rumor (וישמעו בני ישראל לאמר, Josh 22:11). Similarly, in Judg 20 the tribes learn the nature of the crime and the perpetrators' identity only after inquiring about the circumstances of the concubine's brutal dismemberment, thus providing the Levite with an opportunity to report the incident (Judg 20:3–6).

In both stories, *the congregation spontaneously assembles as a military body* in response to a suspicion that a nonnormative act has been committed (Josh 22:12; Judg 20:1–2).

Dispatch of a delegation to the offending party (Josh 22:13–15; Judg 20:12a). In Josh 22, the deployment of troops is postponed and the Cisjordanian tribes send a delegation to negotiate with the offending party in hopes of reaching a satisfactory settlement without bloodshed. The theme of negotiation plays a major role throughout Josh 22, while the assembly of

---

indeed a Land of which the Transjordan is not part. What sanctifies the land and makes worship possible is the presence of the tabernacle" (1981, 354).

274. See, e.g., Fritz 1994, 221–24; Aḥituv 1995, 353–54; Nelson 1997, 247–50; Levine 2000, 507; Goldstein 2002, 46–49, 78–81.

275. For various aspects of the similarities between the stories, see Möhlenbrink 1938, 249–50; Boecker 1970, 40; Kloppenborg 1981, 347; Boling 1982, 511–22; Niditch 1982, 374–75; Weinfeld 1983, 79–81; Assis 2004, 219–20; Wong 2006, 71–74.

276. Nelson 1997, 249.

the congregation as a military body is mentioned mainly in order to show that civil war may be averted through successful negotiation. By contrast, military mobilization plays a major role in the narrative of Judg 20, since it deals with the disastrous results of civil war. In Judg 20, R^2 precipitated the deployment of troops before the delegation was sent to negotiate terms with Benjamin (20:11–12a). This results in undermining the purpose of the delegation, since deployment in the heartland of Benjamin would be viewed as an act of hostile aggression. The effect of this revision by R^2 is a more sympathetic portrayal of Benjamin than found in the primary narrative, for according to the revised narrative Benjamin's hostility is not simply the result of stubborn intransigence but rather a reaction to the other tribes' aggression.

Accusatory interrogation (Josh 22:16; Judg 20:12b). In both stories, the delegations open with an accusatory question: "What is this treachery/evil?" Similar questions frequently occur in biblical narrative and provide an opening for the accused to explain and justify his actions.[277] In Josh 22:21–29, the Transjordanian tribes take advantage of the opportunity to justify themselves and refute the accusation. In Judg 20:12b, by contrast, the question, "What is this evil that has occurred among you?" is not directed at those who committed the transgression—the men of Gibeah—but rather toward the larger group to which the people of Gibeah belong, that is, the tribe of Benjamin. It goes without saying that the Benjaminites were not called upon to justify the actions of the men of Gibeah, but rather to comply immediately with the demands by the other tribes. In this context, the interrogatory question, "What is this?" has been turned into an accusation, allowing for no retort or justification, but calling only for immediate execution of judgment.

Demand to remove the offending object or body (Josh 22:19; Judg 20:13). In both stories, the demand follows immediately upon the accusatory question. In Josh 22:19, the delegation demands that the Transjordanian tribes desist from their rebellion against YHWH and abandon the altar they built on desecrated ground. In Judg 20:13, the delegation demands that the Benjaminites hand over the men of Gibeah so they may be put to death and thus "remove the evil from Israel."

---

277. Contra Boecker 1970, 26–31, 34; see Gen 3:13–14; 20:9–12; 29:25–26; 31:26, 31; Exod 14:11–13; Num 23:11–12; Judg 8:1–3; 15:11; 2 Sam 12:21–23.

Verbal Analogies

Josh 22	Judg 20–21
[9] The Reubenites, the Gadites, and the half-tribe of Manasseh departed from the Israelites, from **Shiloh, which is in the land of Canaan** [משלה אשר בארץ כנען], to go to **the land of Gilead** [ארץ הגלעד].	21 [12] They found four hundred virgin girls … among the residents of Jabesh-gilead and brought them to the camp at **Shiloh, which is in the land of Canaan** [שלה אשר בארץ כנען].
[12] When the Israelites heard, the **entire congregation** of Israelites **assembled** [ויקהלו כל־עדת בני־ישראל] at Shiloh to go to war against them [לעלות עליהם לצבא].	20 [1] Thereupon, all the Israelites went out and **the congregation assembled** [ותקהל העדה] as one man from Dan to Beer-sheba and the **land of Gilead** [ארץ הגלעד] before YHWH at Mizpah. 20 [9] "Against them by lot [עליה בגורל (נעלה)]!"
[13] **The Israelites sent** [וישלחו בני ישראל] **Phinehas ben Eleazar** the priest to the Reubenites, the Gadites, and the half-tribe of Manasseh in the land of Gilead	20 [12] **The tribes of Israel sent** [וישלחו שבטי ישראל] men *throughout the tribes* of Benjamin [בכל שבטי בנימן].
[14] accompanied by **ten** *chieftains* [ועשרה נשיאים]; one chieftain for the paternal houses of **each of the tribes of Israel** [לכל מטות ישראל], and each was the head of his paternal house among the **contingents** of Israel [לאלפי ישראל].	20 [10] "We shall take **ten** *men* [עשרה אנשים] from each hundred of **each of the tribes of Israel** [לכל שבטי ישראל], and one hundred from a **thousand** [לאלף], and a thousand from each ten thousand, to bring provisions for the people."
[15] They came to the Reubenites, the Gadites, and the half-tribe of Manasseh in the land of Gilead and spoke to them as follows: [16] "So says the entire congregation of YHWH, '**What is this** *treachery* you have committed against the God of Israel [מה־המעל הזה אשר מעלתם]?'"	20 [12] The tribes of Israel sent men throughout the tribes of Benjamin, saying, "**What is this** *evil* that has occurred among you [מה־הרעה הזה אשר נהיתה בכם]?"

שָׁלֹה אשר בארץ כנען (Josh 22:9; Judg 21:12)—the expression is unique to these two contexts.[278] The relative clause "which is in the land of

---

278. See, however, בשלה בארץ כנען in Josh 21:2.

Canaan" occurs elsewhere in Priestly contexts dealing with periods prior to the Israelite occupation, when the land indeed was considered by the narrator(s) as "the land of Canaan."[279] However, the story of the Benjaminite war takes place after the occupation, when "the land of Canaan" had become "the land of Israel"; thus the comment "in the land of Canaan" is at odds with the chronological context of the Gibeah story. Moreover, excepting the case of Shiloh, the comment "in the land of Canaan" clarifies the locality of each different place only once. In fact, this clarification in Judg 21:12 is superfluous, since an identical comment already appears in Josh 22:9. Thus the clarifying comment, "Shiloh, which is in the land of Canaan," is well fitted to the context of Josh 22 but "ungrammatical" in the context of Judg 20–21.[280] In light of other points of contact between the two stories, it seems likely that the comment was copied by the author of Gibeah story from its original context in Josh 22.

ארץ הגלעד (Josh 22:9; Judg 20:1)—Gilead is mentioned four times in Josh 22 (vv. 9, 13, 15, 32), and each time in the construct phrase: "the land of Gilead." The mention of Gilead is integral to the story of the Transjordan altar, which, according to the narrative, was erected by tribes that settled in the Gilead. However, the mention of the "land of Gilead" is not necessary to the context of Judg 20:1, where it is tacked on to the set formula, "from Dan to Beer-sheba." This formula, which indicates the extent of Israel from north to south, occurs elsewhere without any reference to Transjordan.[281] It is possible that the role of the land of Gilead in Josh 22 influenced R[2] or a subsequent scribe who appended the reference to the extent of land formula.

The Israelites heard/came out and the whole congregation of Israelites assembled at Shiloh/Mizpah (Josh 22:12; Judg 20:1):

Josh 22:12: וישמעו בני ישראל ויקהלו כל־עדת בני־ישראל
Judg 20:1: ויצאו כל־בני ישראל ותקהל העדה ... אל ה' המצפה

Both passages similarly describe the spontaneous assembly of the Israelites in reaction to a transgression committed. In Josh 22, the building

---

279. Gen 23:2, 19; 33:18; 35:6; 49:30; Num 33:40. See also Josh 22:10, which seems to be the result of a transmission error influenced by the occurrence of the phrase in v. 9.

280. On the purpose of the comment in Josh 22:9, see Assis 2004, 215.

281. See 1 Sam 3:20; 2 Sam 3:10; 17:11; 24:2, 15; 1 Kgs 5:5; 2 Chr 30:5.

of the Transjordan altar is considered a transgression that endangers the well-being of the congregation (Josh 22:18). Thus it is natural that the עדה should be mentioned frequently throughout the story (Josh 22:16, 17, 18, 20, 30), since the term indicates Israel as a religious community, responsible for upholding religious and social norms. By contrast, the assembly and intervention of the congregation is not self-evident in the case of the concubine's rape and death in Judg 19–20, since such a matter was generally under local jurisdiction.[282] Nor do the laws associated with the עדה in the Priestly literature provide a precedent for the intervention of the congregation.[283] It is possible that R[2] chose to adapt the formulation of Josh 22:12 in order to magnify the severity of the transgression of the men of Gibeah and to present the Benjaminites as rebels against the authority of the congregation—all of which serves to impart a sacral tone to the war against Benjamin.

לעלות עליהם לצבא (Josh 22:12, 33)/עליה בגורל (Judg 20:9)—The phrase *to go to war against them* (לעלות עליהם לצבא) in Josh 22:12 and 33 explains the congregation's purpose in assembling after learning about the altar erected by the Transjordanian tribes.[284] In Judg 20:9, the rally cry, "Against them by lot!" (בגורל עליה), is part of a decision reached through intertribal consultations ("This is the thing that we shall do with regard to Gibeah," v. 9). The rally cry in the MT is elliptic, and it is quite possible that the verb נעלה dropped from the text through haplography, although it is preserved in the LXX reading. Thus the reading attested to by the LXX creates an apt parallel to Josh 22:12:

Josh 22:12: לעלות עליהם לצבא
Judg 20:9: נעלה עליה בגורל

---

282. See, e.g., Gen 34; Deut 22:22–29; 2 Sam 13. See Willis 2001, 232–33, 307–12.
283. Intervention of the congregation is prescribed in three situations: (1) invoking the name of YHWH in an imprecation (Lev 24:14), (2) gathering wood on the Sabbath (Num 15:35), and (3) the flight of a killer to a city of refuge (Num 35:24–25). In the last case, the congregation litigates between the killer and the blood avenger, in order to determine whether the case is manslaughter or murder. Even if it is assumed that the assault of the concubine at Gibeah is a case of murder, the law does not explain the assembly of the congregation in Judg 20:1, since the circumstances of the concubine's death become known only after the Levite's testimony in Judg 20:4–7.
284. For discussion of this collocation, see Goldstein 2002, 46–47.

However, the end of the phase in Judg 20:9 is problematic in both the MT and LXX readings, since the construction ב + גורל always occurs in contexts dealing with division of territory for the purpose of settlement.[285] If the author of Judg 20:9 intended to call for a deployment against Gibeah, then it is strange that he chose a term belonging to a context of settlement, rather than a military term as in Josh 22:12. It could be that the contextual incongruity of the phrase, "against them by lot," in Judg 20:9 acts as a marker of literary interrelationship, since עלה בגורל does occur in a military context in Judg 1:3, where it is tied to taking possession of allotted territories.[286] Thus R² may have combined references to two different intertexts in the formulation of Judg 20:9, namely Josh 22:12 and Judg 1:3. This conclusion has significant implications for dating R², since Ronnie Goldstein views the unique phrase in Josh 22:12 (along with other uncharacteristic phraseology) as evidence that Josh 22:9–34 derives from the latest strata of Priestly literature.[287]

Phinehas ben Eleazar the priest (Josh 22:13; Judg 20:28). The mention of Phinehas ben Eleazar is firmly rooted in Josh 22:13, since he is mentioned as the head of the delegation three more times in the story, in verses 30–32. Apparently, it was important to note that a priest led the delegation due to the sacral nature of the accusation leveled against the Transjordanian tribes. Moreover, the delegation compares the present violation with the incident at Peor (Josh 22:17), on which occasion Phinehas ben Eleazar proved himself zealous in the cause of YHWH (Num 25:6–13). Thus the mention of Phinehas ben Eleazar as head of the delegation in Josh 22 heightens the narrative conflict by setting the figure of the zealous priest in opposition to the cultic rebellion attributed to the Transjordanian tribes. As previously noted, the single and sudden appearance of Phinehas in Judg 20:28 is suspicious. The question yet to be resolved is whether R² added mention of Phinehas to the third stage of oracular consultation under the influence of Num 31 or Josh 22, or whether both texts played a decisive influence upon R².

Accompanied by ten chieftains; one chieftain for the paternal houses of each of the tribes of Israel, each was head of his paternal house among the contingents of Israel (Josh 22:14)/*ten men from each hundred of each*

---

285. See Num 26:55; 33:54; 34:13; 36:2; Josh 14:2; 19:51; 21:4–8; Judg 1:3; Mic 2:5; 1 Chr 6:46–50; 24:5; and discussion in ch. 1.
286. See discussion below.
287. Goldstein 2002, 47–49.

of the tribes of Israel, and one hundred from a thousand, and a thousand from each ten thousand* (Judg 20:10). A complex interrelation is evident between these verses and Num 31:4.

Judg 20:10: ולקחנו עשרה אנשים למאה ומאה לכל שבטי ישראל לאלף ואלף לרבבה

Josh 22:14: וְעֲשָׂרָה נְשִׂאִים עִמּוֹ נָשִׂיא אֶחָד נָשִׂיא אֶחָד לְבֵית אָב לְכֹל מַטּוֹת יִשְׂרָאֵל

Num 31:4: אֶלֶף לַמַּטֶּה אֶלֶף לַמַּטֶּה לְכֹל מַטּוֹת יִשְׂרָאֵל

Judges 20:10 notes the selection of one-tenth of the Israelite forces to forage for provisions for the remainder of the fighting force. Such a notice pertaining to provisions for the forces is unique to Judg 19–21. However, the notice itself serves no function within the narrative, as no further reference is made to this foraging group. Since the formulation of the notice is similar in several points to other passages, it may have been inserted into the narrative with the purpose of triggering associations with other texts.

Judges 20:10, Num 31:4, and Josh 22:14 all deal with selecting a representative group from *all the tribes of Israel* in a situation of impending war. There are two major points of contact with Josh 22: the selection of "ten men/chiefs" (אנשים/נשיאים עשרה) and the phrase "all the tribes of Israel" (לכל שבטי/מטות ישראל). In Judg 20:10, ten men of every hundred (one-tenth) are chosen to forage for provisions. Since this element is not further realized in the story, the specification of one-tenth of the force for this purpose is arbitrary and may have been influenced by other narrative contexts. In Josh 22:14, the ten chiefs represent the ten Cisjordanian tribes (the half of Manasseh that settled west of the Jordan counting here for a full tribe), and they make up the delegation sent to negotiate with the Transjordanian tribes. Since the number of delegates is calculated in accordance with the narrative context and the delegation itself is mentioned again at the story's conclusion (Josh 22:30, 32), it would appear that the delegation of *ten* chiefs is integral to Josh 22. In Num 31:4, by contrast, the group selected to go to war against Midian represents all twelve tribes. Thus one thousand are called up from each tribe, producing a total of twelve thousand (Num 31:5). As in Josh 22, this number is calculated in accordance with the narrative context.

Surprisingly, the phrase לכל שבטי/מטות ישראל is found only in these three texts (Judg 20:10; Num 31:4; Josh 22:14), which may indicate that they are interrelated. While Num 31:4 and Josh 22:14 employ the Priestly term מטה, Judg 20:10 uses the more common term שבט, which occurs ten times throughout the Gibeah narrative.

There is an evident loose associative tie among all three texts, but this interrelationship may have developed during scribal transmission once a scribe recognized the role Num 31 played in the shaping of Judg 20–21, on the one hand, and Josh 22, on the other hand. However, despite the use of common terms and similarity of formulation in the three texts, neither Josh 22:14 nor Num 31:4 reflects the relation of one-tenth that is central to Judg 20:10. There the relation of one-tenth is expressed in a tripartite ascending structure: ten to one hundred, one hundred to a thousand, and a thousand to ten thousand.

It is possible that an additional text inspired this motif. In Amos 5:3, we find a similar representation of one-tenth expressed in descending order: a thousand, one hundred, ten. While in Judg 20:10 one-tenth of the men are set aside to provide for those sent to combat, in Amos 5:3 all that remains of the whole is one-tenth. Finally, while the subject reduced by one-tenth in Judg 20:10 is the army that was sent against the sinful city of Gibeah, in Amos 5:3 the subject of reduction is the nameless sinful city itself. The inversion in Judg 20:10 of the motif found in Amos 5:3 might indicate intentional motif transformation. If so, the transformed element borrowed from a prophetic setting provides a subtextual commentary on the narrative. By stripping the motif of the reduction by one-tenth from its retributive effect and applying it to the punitive expedition, the author of Judg 20:10 hints at the difference in fate between Amos's sinful city and Gibeah—while one-tenth escape the destruction of Amos's sinful city, none escapes the destruction of Gibeah (Judg 20:42–48). From this, it appears that R^2 drew upon a variety of sources in the formulation of the peculiar remark in 20:10. Accordingly, the purpose of the otherwise superfluous notice about the foragers may be to mark R^2's rereading of the Gibeah story in light of the Priestly narratives in Num 31 and Josh 22, and to allude to a subtextual layer of criticism based upon the transformation of the motif borrowed from Amos 5:3.

What is this treachery/evil that you have committed/that has occurred among you (Josh 22:16; Judg 20:12)—the two phrases are parallel in structure and meaning:

Judg 20:12: מה הרעה הזאת אשר נהיתה בכם
Josh 22:16: מה־המעל הזה אשר מעלתם

TEXT, SUBTEXT, AND INTERTEXTUAL MOSAIC   273

The difference in formulation derives from the preference in Josh 22:16 for the Priestly expression למעול מעל, while Judg 20:12 (N¹) makes use of a unique formulation, נהיתה רעה, that otherwise occurs only in 20:3 (R²).

CONCLUSIONS

Most of the structural elements that parallel those in Josh 22:9–16 are already present in the N¹ strand of Judg 19:30–20:13, while most of the verbal parallels between Judg 19–21 and Josh 22 derive from R². The structural parallels are general and may derive from the common nature of the two incidents described, namely, the breach of the community's normative rules by one of its constituents. However, R² restructured the narrative by advancing the deployment of troops against Gibeah before a delegation was dispatched to negotiate extradition of the guilty parties (20:11), and this restructuring undermines the purpose of the delegation motif. The proceedings in Josh 22 seem to have been designed to demonstrate how armed conflict may be prevented by mending divisions within the congregation. This model, however, is set aside by those who shaped the Gibeah story. N¹'s narrative was fashioned to highlight the intransigence of the Benjaminites in their solidarity with Gibeah, thus placing them belong the pale of YHWH's people, while R² seems to have reworked the narrative so it would reflect a negative image of workings of the congregation, in which zeal and armed force precipitate division of the integral wholeness of the community.

More substantial evidence for literary interrelation between the two stories lies in the verbal parallels, most of which seem to have been introduced into Judg 19–21 by R². All of the common formulations and motifs were well rooted in their context in Josh 22, while three were dysfunctional or disruptive in the context of Judg 19–21, namely, mention of "the land of Gilead" in Judg 20:1; selection of "ten men in a hundred out of all the tribes of Israel" in 20:10; and mention of Phinehas ben Eleazar in 20:28. Such contextual "ungrammaticality" seems to indicate that these parallel elements were borrowed from their original context in Josh 22 and planted in Judg 20 in order to mark R²'s dialogue with Josh 22.

It now remains to consider the purpose of R²'s dialogue with Josh 22. R²'s revisions in Judg 20:1–12 may have been intended to recast the story as a counterpart to the story in Josh 22, just as the Deuteronomist(s) fashioned the Ai story as a complementary counterpart to the conquest of Jericho. Accordingly, while Josh 22:9–34 demonstrates how the עדה might act in a positive fashion to enforce its norms, R²'s revision of the Gibeah story illustrates the negative aspects, since overzealous steps taken by the עדה itself may bring about fragmentation and dissolution of its unity.

The chronological relation between the composition of the R² strand in Judg 19–21 and Josh 22 remains to be considered. On the one hand, it is possible that R² not only revised Judg 19–21 but also composed other materials inserted into the Deuteronomistic History. In this case, R² might be identical with the author of Josh 22. On the other hand, Josh 22 might already have been included in the Joshua scroll that was known to R². In this case, he noted the latent similarity in structure between Josh 22 and N¹ and was motivated by the preexisting verbal analogy between Josh 22:16 and Judg 20:12 to broaden the similarity with additional verbal parallels. This matter should be decided on the basis of additional considerations, tied to the structure and purpose of the different redactional layers responsible for the present shape of the Former Prophets. Intriguing as this question is, it might defy resolution.

4.9. Isolated Parallels

In the previous sections I have discussed texts that interrelate with Judg 19–21 on several points. In these cases, the broad web of connections in structure and phraseology along with the incidence of unique parallels support the argument for literary interrelation. By comparison, the case for literary interrelation between isolated verses in separate contexts is considerably more tenuous. In any case, the analysis has shown that N¹ and R² commanded a large repertoire of texts upon which they could draw for imagery, motifs, and allusions, such as the Sodom story, Deuteronom(ist)ic laws, the narratives of the conquest of Ai, Saul's history, and the story of Tamar; while R²'s literary proficiency included the Priestly strand in the pentateuchal narratives (the Midianite war) and the Priestly edition of Joshua as well (the account of the Transjordan altar). Given the proficiency of these authors, it is reasonable to consider the possibility that they also made isolated reference to other literary materials from the corpora known to them.

"This has not happened or been seen since the day the Israelites came up from the land of Egypt till this very day" (Judg 19:30)

The response of those who viewed the dismembered body of the concubine in Judg 19:30 is composed of two different formula: (1) "This (such

TEXT, SUBTEXT, AND INTERTEXTUAL MOSAIC 275

a thing) has not happened (been seen) since/until" (2) and "since the day the Israelites came up (went out) from the land of Egypt till this very day." Only in Judg 19:30 do these two formulas appear in conjunction with each other.

The formula לא־נהיתה ולא־נראתה כזאת is a variation of a base formula that falls into two major groups, those with the *qal* form [288]לא היה and those with the *niphal* form לא נהיה/נראה.[289] The formula with the *qal* form occurs mostly in relatively early sources (plague narrative in "non-P" and DtrH), while the formula with the *niphal* forms seems to belong to postexilic sources.[290] According to this breakdown, the formula in Judg 19:30 fits in with the group of late texts. However, N[1] did not employ the formula in a mechanical fashion but reworked it in a unique manner. First, the verb is compounded, while elsewhere only one of the verbs occurs (לא הנהיה/נהיתה or לא נראה).[291] Second, the comparative is employed with the demonstrative pronoun (כזאת),[292] rather than a construction with דבר(ים) (as in Deut 4:32; Neh 6:8) or with a personal pronominal suffix (as in Exod 9:18, 24; 11:6; Joel 2:2). Third, the chronological reference of

---

288. Exod 9:18, 24; 10:14; 1 Kgs 3:12 (cf. 3:13); 2 Kgs 18:5; 23:25; 2 Chr 1:12. With the exception of Josh 10:14 all these formulas are preceded by either the relative pronoun אשר (Exod 9:18, 24; 1 Kgs 3:12; 2 Chr 1:12), a temporal לפני (Exod 10:14) or אחרי (2 Kgs 18:5), or a comparative כמוך (2 Kgs 23:25; cf. 1 Kgs 3:12).

289. Exod 11:6; Judg 19:30; 1 Kgs 10:12; Joel 2:2; Neh 6:8; Dan 12:1; see also Deut 4:32.

290. The apparent exception in Exod 11:6 may be the result of scribal intervention due to the strong similarity between the phrasing there and Joel 2:2, where the *niphal* does occur; otherwise, the *niphal* is absent from the other incidences of the formula in the plague narrative. On the relative late dating for Deut 4:32, see, e.g., Rofé 1985, 441–43; Nelson 2002, 61–62; Veijola 2004, 114–15; Otto 2012, 535–38. 1 Kgs 10:12 along with v. 11 are an interpolation that disrupts the continuity within the story of the queen of Sheba (1 Kgs 10:1–13); see, e.g., Montgomery 1950, 218. Lipiński (2010, 265–71) suggests that 1 Kgs 10:11–12 as well as other notices dealing with Solomon's and Hiram's naval ventures derive from the Persian period.

291. נהיה/נהיתה in Exod 11:6; Deut 4:32; Joel 2:2; Neh 6:8; Dan 12:1; לא נראה in 1 Kgs 10:12.

292. Use of the comparative form of the demonstrative pronoun seems mainly characteristic of late texts or strata. Particularly instructive is Isa 66:8, which seems to interact with Deut 4:32–34, but Isa 66:8 exchanges the form כמהו that is found in Deut 4:32 with כזאת. Elsewhere כזאת occurs in Gen 45:23; Judg 8:8; 13:23; 15:7; 1 Sam 4:7; 2 Sam 14:13; 17:15; 1 Kgs 7:37; 2 Kgs 5:4; 9:12; Jer 2:10; Esth 4:14; Ezra 7:27; 9:13; 1 Chr 29:14; 2 Chr 30:26; 31:20; 32:15; 34:22.

comparison למיום serves as a link for anchoring the additional "bringing up from Egypt" formula.

Variations on the formula למיום עלות בני־ישראל מארץ מצרים עד היום הזה occur seven more times, all of which appear in Deuteronomistic contexts (Deut 9:7; 1 Sam 8:8; 2 Sam 7:6; 1 Kgs 8:16; 2 Kgs 21:15; Jer 7:25; 11:7). The variations between the formulas include interchange between the roots עלה/יצא; between *qal* and *hiphil* conjugations; between prefixed and independent constructions (ל)מן היום/(ל)מיום; between "from Egypt" and the construct phrase "from *the land of* Egypt"; and designation of the people brought out of Egypt by a pronoun, by "(sons of) Israel," or by "fathers." Despite attempts to explain the variants as the result of diachronic developments within the "deliverance from Egypt" formula, a thorough comparison shows that the interchanges cut across all the instances of the formula in a random fashion and probably reflect nothing more than stylistic variation.[293]

Given the marked Deuteronomistic provenance of the formula, several scholars saw its occurrence in Judg 19:30 as evidence of Deuteronomistic authorship or editing.[294] However, Deuteronomistic idiom, themes, and ideology were long-lived and can be found in patently late works.[295] Since Deuteronomism continued to influence Judean literary production long after the composition of the Deuteronomistic History, the use of Deuteronomistic idiom and themes does not necessarily indicate that a work was

---

293. Jüngling (1981, 242–44) argued that only the formulas with יצא are Dtr, while those with עלה are pre-Dtr. However, this is controverted by the case in Jer 11:7, which employs עלה. Gross (1974) argued that the formulas with *qal* forms are earlier than those with *hiphil*, but this is controverted by the use of the *qal* in 2 Kgs 21:15 and Jer 7:25, which undoubtedly belong to the same stratum as 1 Kgs 8:16 and Jer 11:7, which employ the *hiphil*. More recently Gross (2009, 847) opined that all instances of the formula are Deuteronom(ist)ic or even later. It should be noted that within the set of variations, only Judg 19:30 employs *qal* עלה, and only 1 Kgs 8:16 employs *hiphil* הוציא; the other instances employ either *hiphil* העלה (1 Sam 8:8; 2 Sam 7:6; Jer 11:7) or *qal* יצא (Deut 9:7; 2 Kgs 21:5; Jer 7:25).

294. See, e.g., Schunck 1963, 64; Veijola 1977, 17–22; Arnold 1990, 64; but see Becker 1990, 264.

295. See, e.g., Neh 1:9 (cf. Deut 12:11; 14:23; 26:2; 30:4); Dan 9:4; Neh 1:5; 9:32 (cf. Deut 7:9; 1 Kgs 8:23); 1 Chr 22:12–13 (cf. Deut 1:21; 4:45; 5:1; 6:1; 7:11; 12:1; 17:19; 31:6–7, 23; Josh 1:6–7, 9; 8:1; 10:25). The long-lasting influence of Deuteronomism also left its mark on the Qumran library, as can be seen in works such as Dibrei Moshe (1Q22), the Temple Scroll (11Q19), and MMT (4Q394–399); see Weissenberg 2008.

authored or edited by any of the authors or editors associated with the circles that produced the Deuteronomistic History. Therefore, it is important to determine whether the idiom is employed in stereotyped fashion, or whether its use here deviates from Deuteronomistic conventions. In the latter case, its use would most likely be derivative, rather than properly Deuteronomistic.[296]

The "deliverance from Egypt" formula regularly occurs in Deuteronomistic expository discourses that mark critical points in the historical narrative, such as the retrospective discourse about receiving the law at Horeb (Deut 9:7), the establishment of monarchy (1 Sam 8:8), the dynastic promise to David (2 Sam 7:6), the consecration of the temple (1 Kgs 8:16), and the announcement of judgment against Judah (2 Kgs 21:15). With the exception of Judg 19:30, the formula always refers to the relations between the people and YHWH.[297] By contrast, the formula in Judg 19:30 makes no reference to YHWH and instead is employed to comment on the breakdown of relations in the social sphere. Furthermore, the incident related neither marks a turning point in history nor reverberates elsewhere in the Deuteronomistic History. Thus its use here appears to be derivative, not properly Deuteronomistic. N^1 may have employed the "deliverance from Egypt" formula in order to draw an ironic analogy between the Outrage at Gibeah and the formative events in the Deuteronomistic History. Why would such a marginal event that left no other imprint upon the historical imagination motivate the comment that nothing like it had been seen since the deliverance from Egypt? At any rate, this comment is voiced by the people, not by the narrator, and it provides the rationale for their gathering at Mizpah. This may have provided the means for N^1 to deride the baseness of the circumstances that led up to the outbreak of civil war. Thus the combination and derivative use of the formulas, along with the modifications in accordance with LBH usage, further supports the surmise that N^1 represents a postexilic composition.

---

296. On these methodological questions problem, see also, e.g., Van Seters 1999, 160–61.

297. The incidence of the formula in Jer 7:25 and MT Jer 11:7 might have been influenced by the use in Deut 9:7; 1 Sam 8:8; 2 Kgs 21:15, where the period from the deliverance from Egypt to "this very day" is characterized by recurrent sin against YHWH; see recently Römer 2011, 66–68.

The Betrothal of Rebekah (Gen 24)

The episode of the concubine at Gibeah in Judg 19 interacts with two different sections dealing with hospitality in the story of the betrothal of Rebekah, Gen 24:25, 54–57. The phrase גם תבן גם מספוא occurs only in Gen 24:25 and Judg 19:19, and in both cases it is found in a similar context when a potential host and a wayfarer meet. Furthermore, the only other mention of תבן ("straw") along with מספוא ("feed") is to be found farther on in the story of Rebekah's betrothal (Gen 24:32). While תבן is a fairly common term, occurring in different literary strata,[298] מספוא is found in only one other literary context.[299] In 24:25, Rebekah offers straw and feed for the visitor's pack animals in response to the question posed by Abraham's servant in verse 23. Rebekah's offer demonstrates her hospitality and indicates that she is the divinely designated wife for Isaac (cf. vv. 12–14). After the guest is brought to the house, the straw and feed are mentioned again, thus showing that the offer was carried out (v. 32). In Judg 19:19, the "Levite" wayfarer hastens to allay the Ephraimite's reluctance to grant him shelter for the night by mentioning that he has both straw and feed, as well as adequate provisions for himself and his party. Since the narrative makes no further mention of the straw and feed afterward, it appears likely that the Levite's words were borrowed from a literary context in which they are deeply embedded, namely Gen 24:25. In this case, N¹ appears to draw an inverse analogy between hospitality scenes and contrasts the Ephraimite's reluctant offer to the Levite with the generous and festive hospitality Abraham's servant enjoyed at Laban's house.

Several points of interaction can also be observed between the section that closes the visit at Laban's house (Gen 24:54–57) and the visit of the Levite at his father-in-law's house (Judg 19:4–8). Only in these two stories do the three verbs occur together: ויאכלו וישתו וילינו ("eat, drink, and stay the night"; Gen 24:54; Judg 19:4). Following this report of hospitality, both stories relate how the host suggests to "go later" in an attempt to delay the guest's departure with the daughter of the household (ואחר תלך/תלכו; Gen 24:55/Judg 19:5).[300] An inverse analogy is found afterward in the guest's reaction. In Gen 24:56, Abraham's servant protests, "don't make me

---

298. See Gen 24:25, 32; Exod 5:7, 10–13, 16, 18; Judg 19:19; 1 Kgs 5:8; Isa 11:7; 65:25; Jer 23:28; Zech 9:3; Job 21:18; 41:19.

299. See Gen 42:27 and 43:24 in the Joseph story.

300. The collocation occurs only once more, in Josh 2:16, when Rahab suggests

delay" (אל תאחרו אתי), in response to the suggestion that he wait several days before departing with Rebekah. By contrast, in Judg 19:8 the Levite's father-in-law suggests that he stay to eat and "tarry" (והתמהמהו) until past noon, and ultimately the Levite fails in his mission to take the concubine back home to Mount Ephraim because he acquiesced to the suggestion to delay his departure. Finally, in Gen 24, Rebekah is appealed to and voices her acquiescence to leave with Abraham's servant (24:57–58), in striking contrast to the Levite's concubine, who is afforded no opportunity to speak her mind and express her willingness to return to her husband.

The number of inverse application of parallels between the hospitality scenes appears to indicate literary interaction between the Gibeah story and the story of Rebekah's betrothal. These inversions create ironic tension at critical junctures in the Gibeah narrative, inviting the reader to compare the disastrous chain of events leading to the concubine's violent death and the felicitous operation of divine providence in uniting Rebekah with Isaac. The ironic aspect of the parallels in the Gibeah story probably indicates the reemployment of borrowed material. Although earlier consensus attributed the story of Rebekah's betrothal to J, Alexander Rofé has convincingly argued for a Persian period composition.[301] Thus N[1]'s familiarity with the narrative in Gen 24 may indicate that he too belongs to this period.

THE BINDING OF ISAAC (GEN 22:10)

The Gibeah story shares a single parallel formulation with the story of the binding of Isaac:[302]

Judg 19:29: ויקח את־המאכלת ויחזק בפילגשו וינתחה לעצמיה
Gen 22:10: וישלח אברהם את־ידו ויקח את־המאכלת לשחט את־בנו

The parallel is striking since the term מאכלת ("knife") is rare.[303] Moreover, in both cases a man takes the knife in order to use it against a

---

that the spies flee Jericho and hide in the mountains, and only *afterward go* on their return trip to the camp at Gilgal.

301. Rofé 1990.

302. The analogy between the stories has been observed previously by Unterman 1980, 161–65; Jüngling 1981, 234; Trible 1984, 80; Rudin 1985, 153–54.

303. See once more in Gen 22:6, and the plural in Prov 30:14, where it parallels חרבות.

member of his family. However, the act is undertaken in opposing circumstances in each story. Abraham raised his knife over his live son, whom he was saved from slaying through last-minute divine intervention. By contrast, the concubine was already dead when the Levite raised his knife over her, and none intervened to prevent him from cutting her body to pieces.

The rarity of the parallel expression, along with the inverse circumstances, seems to indicate that the two texts are literarily related. However, these two texts by themselves do not provide evidence for the direction of dependence. It is tempting to surmise that the author of the story of the concubine at Gibeah was familiar with the story of the binding of Isaac, since an allusion to Abraham's sacrifice imbues the Levite's act with ironic significance. Abraham bound his beloved son in obedience to divine commandment and was spared his son in reward for his blind obedience. Conversely, the Levite acts on his own behalf and sacrifices his concubine, whom he does not appear to love, as implied by his four-month wait before taking steps to bring her home. He further seems to sacrifice her twice: first, when he handed her over alive to the mob for them to abuse, and again, after her death, when he dismembered her with the knife. The inverse analogy reinforces the brutal characterization of the Levite by marking the contrast between his acts and those of Abraham.

Nevertheless, recent diachronic studies might challenge this reading. On the one hand, classical source criticism viewed the Binding of Isaac as a continuation of the E narrative in Gen 20–21.[304] On the other hand, more and more scholars now suggest a late origin for the story in Gen 22, since it engages the Deuteronomistic themes of divine testing and polemic against child sacrifice and since it seems to be tacked on to the main thread of the Abraham narrative.[305] Since it is difficult to dispel the possibility that Gen 22 began to be regarded as authoritative Scripture at a time subsequent to the composition of Judg 19, it seems preferable to regard the parallel between the stories as either fortuitous or as the result of a late learned scribal intervention designed to evoke the image of Abraham's sacrifice.

---

304. For a recent defense of this position, see, e.g., Schorn 2006; Yoreh 2010, 65–70.

305. See, e.g., Van Seters 1992, 261–64; Levin 1993, 175–77; Schmid 2008, 268–76; Ska 2013, 266–27, with reference to further literature there.

The Counsel of Ahitophel (2 Sam 16:20–21)

The Levite's words to the assembly at Mizpah in Judg 20:7, "deliberate and consider here," are paralleled by those spoken by Absalom to Ahitophel:

Judg 20:7: הבו לכם דבר ועצה הלם
2 Sam 16:20: הבו לכם עצה מה נעשה

These two texts represent the only occurrence of the phrase הבו (לכם) עצה, and both deal with counsel regarding concubines (see Ahitophel's counsel in 2 Sam 16:21: "Have sex with your father's concubines"). Absalom's application for advice is firmly rooted in the context of 2 Sam 15:12–17:23, which relates how Hushai gained faith with Absalom and engineered the dismissal of Ahitophel. In this section the root יעץ ("to counsel") is employed sixteen times and operates as a *Leitwort*.[306] Ahitophel's advice regarding David's concubines is also rooted in the narrative context, since after acting upon this advice, Absalom would unwittingly fulfill Nathan's prophecy and shame David by lying with his wives (2 Sam 12:11). The Levite's appeal to take counsel, by comparison, is unnecessary in its context. The root יעץ occurs only one additional time in the Gibeah story (Judg 19:30), and despite the Levite's appeal, the narrative does not report any deliberations before the spontaneous decision to make war on Benjamin.[307] The interrelation between the texts invites the reader to draw an analogy between the Levite and Absalom, since both brought on a bitter civil war. In this case, the likelihood of intentional literary allusion by R² is supported by the fact that the narrative has utilized other materials borrowed from the Succession Narrative, particularly from the story of Tamar.

The Gibeonites' Vengeance (2 Sam 21:2–5)

A subtle intertextual relation exists between the story of the Outrage at Gibeah and the story of the Gibeonites' vengeance in 2 Sam 21.[308] According to 2 Sam 21, the bloodguilt incurred when Saul massacred the Gibeon-

---

306. See 2 Sam 15:12, 31, 34; 16:20, 23 (three times); 17:7 (twice), 11, 14 (three times), 15 (twice), 21.
307. By contrast, cf. the deliberations how to rehabilitate Benjamin after the war (Judg 21:7–10, 16–20).
308. Edenburg 2014, 162–63.

ites brought about a lengthy drought in the days of David, and the drought came to an end only after expiating the bloodguilt by impaling Saul's offspring. Thus, like the Gibeah story, the account of the Gibeonites' vengeance has an anti-Saulide tendency. Further, both texts show familiarity with the tradition of the special relationship between Jabesh-gilead and the tribe of Benjamin. According to Judg 21:7–12, the virgins from Jabesh provided continuity for the remnant of Benjamin following the war, while 2 Sam 21:12 is familiar with the tradition regarding the daring raid of the men of Jabesh on Beth-shean and the internment of Saul's and his sons' remains in Jabesh (cf. 1 Sam 31:8–13). Both narratives conclude similarly: in 2 Sam 21 with the near decimation of the house of Saul and in Judg 20–21 with the destruction of Gibeah, Saul's town, and the near annihilation of his tribe, Benjamin. There is also a web of cross-connections between a short section in 2 Sam 21 and the Gibeah story in Judges. First, 2 Sam 21:2–3 and Judg 21:7 exhibit an inverse parallel formation (2 Sam 21:2–3, ובני ישראל מה נעשה להם ... מה אעשה לכם; Judg 21:7, ואנחנו נשבענו ... נשבעו להם בה') and also deal with opposite situations: the Israelites in Judg 21 had decimated Benjamin according to the oath they swore before YHWH and now *seek to circumvent* the oath, while the Gibeonites had been decimated *in violation* of an oath, and David seeks to rectify the oath violation. This converse analogy builds upon the final form of both stories.

Another set of cross-connections radiates out from 2 Sam 21:5 to different parts of the Gibeah story. Here the phrases נשמדנו, -מ דמה לנו, התיצב ב-, and בכל גבול ישראל are echoed in Judg 19:29; 20:2, 5; 21:16. However, none of these links represents a unique parallel.[309]

2 Sam 21	Judg 19–21
² The Israelites **swore** to them [ובני ישראל נשבעו להם], but Saul sought to wipe them out.	21 ⁷ "*What shall we do for them* [מה נעשה להם], (to provide) wives for the survivors?
³ David asked the Gibeonites, "*What shall I do for you* [מה אעשה לכם]?"	For we **swore** ... [ואנחנו נשבענו בה'] not to give our daughters to them."

---

309. *Piel* דמה occurs thirteen more times, all seemingly late: Num 33:56; Judg 20:5; Isa 10:7; 14:24; 40:18, 25; 46:5; Hos 12:11; Pss 48:10; 50:21; Cant 1:9; Lam 2:13; Esth 4:13. The *hithpael* התיצב occurs more than forty times (for התיצב ב-, see Exod 19:17; Deut 31:14; 1 Sam 10:23; 2 Sam 23:12). בכל גבול ישראל occurs also in 1 Sam 11:3, 7; 1 Kgs 1:3; 2 Kgs 10:32; 1 Chr 21:12. However, נשמד מ- (*niphal*) is rare and occurs only once more outside 1 Sam 21 and Judg 21; see Jer 48:42.

5 "The man who exterminated us and who thought [דמה לנו] to eradicate us [נשמדנו מ-] so we should not remain [התיצב] within the borders of Israel [בכל גבול ישראל]...."

20 5 "They thought [דמו] to kill me."
21 16 "What shall we do (to provide) wives for the remainder, since all women were eradicated [נשמדה מ-] from Benjamin?"
20 2 The leaders of all the people (from) all the tribes of Israel presented themselves before the assembly of [התיצבו בקהל] God's people.
19 29 He sent her throughout all the borders of Israel [בכל גבול ישראל].

Admittedly, the case for intentional literary echoing is tenuous and supported mainly by the thematic analogies between the stories and by the fact that a single sentence in the one text seems to have influenced formulations throughout the text of the other. It should further be noted that the different points of contact with 2 Sam 21:2–5 are distributed throughout both N¹ and R² in Judg 19–21 (N¹: בכל גבול ישראל, 19:29; התיצב, 20:2; -ב, 20:5; ואנחנו נשבענו בה' מה נעשה להם, 21:7; R¹: דמו, 20:5; נשמד מ-, 21:16). Since the elements shared with 2 Sam 21 in N˙ are not unusual and one element probably derived from a different intertext (בכל גבול ישראל, 19:29; cf. 1 Sam 11:3, 7), there are not sufficient grounds to conclude that N¹ deliberately reused formulations picked up from 2 Sam 21. Given that additional vocabulary is also shared by the Gibeah story and 2 Sam 21 (TN + בעלי, 2 Sam 21:12; Judg 20:5; רחוב, 2 Sam 21:12; Judg 19:15, 17), we should consider the possibility that both compositions derive from the same milieu. R² might have noticed the similarity in expressions and tendency between the two stories and added more intertextual links referring back to 2 Sam 21:5.

It is also significant that both stories are placed along with other unconnected material at the end of their respective book scrolls. Although it was once thought that the story of the Gibeonite vengeance was displaced from an earlier context before 2 Sam 9,[310] more recent research shows it to be a very late addition to the Samuel scroll.[311] This might imply that materials in appendices like Judg 17–21 and 2 Sam 21–24 were com-

---

310. See Budde 1890, 256; 1902, 304–13; Smith 1898, xxvi-vii, 374; Carlson 1964, 196–226; McCarter 1984, 18, 516–17; Na'aman 2009a, 105.
311. Edenburg 2014.

posed and attached to the end of scrolls as a means for revising the outlook of the books in their earlier form. I will pursue these implications further in the conclusions of this study.

4.10. The Prologue and Appendix of Judges

Ancient interpreters already took note of the peculiar relationship between the appendix and the prologue of the book of Judges. For example, Judg 17–18 and 19–21 do not appear to follow the chronological progression of the savior stories but instead presume the chronological framework of 1:1–2:5. Both 18:30 and 20:28 mention priests belonging to the third generation following Aaron and Moses, which supposedly places the narrated events in the period immediately following the demise of Joshua and Eleazar (Josh 24:29, 33; Judg 1:1). For this reason, Josephus—as befits a historian who seeks to write a chronologically coherent narrative—placed the accounts of the Danite migration and the Outrage at Gibeah before the stories of the judges.[312]

At the same time, the repeated notice of Joshua's death, burial, and successors (Josh 24:28–31; Judg 2:6–10) brackets the material in Judg 1:1–2:5, marking it as a digression from the main narrative of the Deuteronomistic History. As has long been noted, there is smooth narrative transition running directly from the notice of Joshua's death in Josh 24:29–30 to Judg 2:7, 10–11, which serves as an exposition to the programmatic introduction to the period of the judges. This digression constitutes an alternate version of the conquest in Judg 1 that revises or supersedes the Deuteronomistic conquest account in Joshua, followed by a theological interpretation of the settlement failures in Judg 2:1–5.[313] Once this digression was appended before the introduction to the period of the Judges, it disrupted the continuity of the Deuteronomistic historical narrative and provided a new prologue to the period of the judges.

So too the narratives in Judg 17–21 disrupt the thematic and chronological scheme that connects Jephthah and Samson with Samuel. Judges 17–18 and 19–21 lack all the hallmarks of the Deuteronomistic savior sto-

---

312. See Josephus, *Ant.* 5.2.1–5.3.2 §§120–181; and see Rashi (Judg 17:1), Gersonides (17:1; 19:10), Isaiah di Trani (20:28), Kimchi (17:6); and in recent times Auberlin 1860, 539; Budde 1897, xv; Talmon 1986, 45–47.

313. See, e.g., Auld 1975; Younger 1995; Smend 2000, 107–10; Kratz 2005, 197–98; Edenburg 2012b, 251–53.

ries, namely, the themes of apostasy and return to YHWH, oppression by foreign nations and deliverance, as well as the figure of the savior (מוֹשִׁיעַ) or inspired leader and the typical chronological framework, in which periods of servitude alternate with years of peace under the leadership of the savior. Accordingly, they are thought to constitute an intrusive appendix that was tacked on to the end of the Deuteronomistic book of Judges.[314]

However, since the 1960s, the editorial unity postulated by Noth for the Deuteronomistic History has been challenged by scholars who subscribe to double- or multiple-redaction theories. Various scholars belonging to this group have argued that the differences in outlook and literary structure between the framing chapters (Judg 1:1–2:5, 17:1–21:25) and the continuous narrative in Josh 1:1–13:33 and Judg 2:6–16:31 result from the work of different Deuteronomistic revisions.[315]

Other scholars have taken a holistic approach to the question of the relationship between Judg 1:1–2:5, 17:1–21:25, and the body of the book of Judges, arguing that a concentric structural unifies the parts of the book into a tight-knit thematic whole.[316] However, concentric structures may serve as an editorial tool for imparting a semblance of unified structure to material of disparate nature and origin, and thus do not necessarily indicate unity of composition, as is evident in the case of the Samuel appendix (2 Sam 21–24).

The evaluation of the motifs and verbal analogies shared by Judg 1:1–2:5, 17:1–18:31, and 19:1–21:25 may aid in determining whether these

---

314. E.g., Auberlen 1860; Budde 1888; Frankenberg 1895, 168; Noth 1966, 121 n. 29, 168; more recently, Gray 1967, 242; O'Brien 1989, 98; Becker 1990, 295–96; Römer and de Pury 2000, 122–23. For a short period, a complex cut-and-paste scenario held sway, according to which the narratives were included in the JE edition of Judges, then excised by Dtr, but independently preserved and later reinserted into the DtrH by a post-Dtr redactor; see, e.g., Moore 1895, xxiv–xxxi; Budde 1897, xi–xvi; Burney 1970, xxxvii, 443–58. Eissfeldt (1925, 105–16) rejected this scenario as implausible, and claimed that Dtr made only minor additions of typical phraseology. According to him, Judg 18–17 and 19–21 are not an appendix to the story of the judges but an introduction to the story of the monarchy; see also Schulte 1972, 78.

315. See, e.g., Schunck 1963, 60–68; Boling 1975, 36–37; Veijola 1977, 16–29; Peckham 1985, 35–38; Soggin 1987, 280–303; Smend 2000, 107–10; Mayes 2001, 256–58.

316. See, e.g., Gooding 1982; Dumbrell 1983, 25; Peckham 1985, 35–37; Exum 1990, 213; O'Connell 1996, 10–13, 260–61.

materials stem from a common source,[317] were assembled from diverse sources and appended to Judges by a common editor,[318] or were added by different authors or editors at different stages in the growth of Judges in order to impose a semblance of unity upon the materials.[319] The resolution of this issue has direct bearing upon how we define the structure and purpose of the Deuteronomistic History, as well as the techniques employed in its composition and revision. Thus in the following sections I not only discuss the textual interrelations but also reexamine whether these materials derive from Deuteronomistic composition or redaction.

THE STORY OF MICAH'S IMAGE (JUDG 17–18)

Until recently, most scholars tended to ascribe the story of Micah's image to a pre-Deuteronomistic author[320] and thought that the narrative was already included in a pre-Deuteronomistic edition of Judges[321] or was transmitted independently until appended to a late edition of Judges.[322] However, in the second half of the twentieth century several scholars argued that the narratives in Judg 17–18 and 19–21 display marks of Deuteronomistic composition or editing and that they play a central role in introducing the Deuteronomistic account of the establishment of the monarchy.[323] These scholars interpret the purpose of the narratives in

---

317. See, e.g., Bertheau 1845, 192–94; Moore 1895, xxx–xxxv; Budde 1897, ix–xv; Eissfeldt 1925, 107–10; Gurewicz 1959, 37–40; Kaufmann 1961, 21; Cundall 1969–70; Schulte 1972, 77–80, 94–98, 102–5; Crüsemann 1978, 155–67; Mayes 1983, 79; Bauer 1998, 133–52, 440–47.

318. See, e.g., Bleek 1878, 198–99, 203; Frankenberg 1895, 73–74; Auld 1976, 45; Veijola 1977, 15–29; Peckham 1985, 35–37; Gray 1986, 194–234; Soggin 1987, 31, 269, 279–81; Stone 1988, 397, 406–8.

319. See, e.g., Noth 1966, 168; 1962, 79; 1991, 8; Boling 1975, 29–38; Becker 1990, 296–306. Noteworthy is Amit's view that Judg 1:1–2:5 and 17:1–18:31 belong to the body of Judges, while 19:1–21:25 is a late appendix; see Amit 1999, 127–60, 313–16, 335–50.

320. See, e.g., Moore 1895, xxx–xxxi (J); Burney 1970, xlix, 408–16 (JE); Crüsemann 1978, 160–62 (Solomon's reign); Noth 1962, 81–82 (period of Jeroboam I); Gray 1986, 223–24 (734–22 BCE); Soggin 1987, 269; and Amit 1990, 18–19 (732–622 BCE); cf. also Mayes 2001, 269.

321. See. e.g., Moore 1895, xxx; Burney 1970, xlix; Amit 1999, 63–75, 317–36.

322. E.g., Noth 1966, 168; 1962, 79; 1991, 8; Gray 1986, 224; O'Brien 1989, 98.

323. See, e.g., Schunck 1963, 67; Boling 1975, 29–38 ("Deuteronomic"); Veijola 1977, 15–29 (DtrG); Peckham 1985, 35–37 (Dtr²); Mayes 2001, 256–58; see Becker

light of the recurring formulas "In those days there was no king in Israel; every man did as he thought right" (17:6; 21:25; cf. 18:1; 19:1), which, they argue, serve to justify the institution of kingship and the need for central government.[324] Their approach is grounded on the assumption that both Judg 17–18 and 19–21 depict a state of anarchy; but this assumption is questionable and requires reexamination.[325] It is also methodologically questionable whether the purpose of the narratives should be interpreted on the basis of these formulas, since the formulas are actually editorial comments and their original relation to the narratives is not self-evident.[326] Finally, those who accord Judg 17–21 a place within the Deuteronomistic History tend to overlook that these stories disrupt the continuity between the narrative blocks dealing with Samson, Eli, and Samuel, the judges related to the Philistine menace (Judg 14–16; 1 Sam 1–7).

Since Veijola's work held particular sway in late-twentieth-century discussion of the relationship between Judg 17–18, 19–21, and the Deuteronomistic History, it is appropriate to examine his arguments in some detail.[327] Veijola attempted explain the Deuteronomist's motivation in breaking the continuity between Samson and the last two judges. According to his view, the Deuteronomist (DtrG) fit the narratives of Judg 17–21 into place in order to illustrate the significance of "doing wrong in the eyes of YHWH," thus justifying the Philistine domination of Israel after the death of Samson.[328]

However, Veijola's arguments are problematic. First, he does not adequately account for the inconsistency he seems to attribute to his first Deuteronomistic historian in departing from the tight structure he imposed upon his materials. The "wrongdoing" formula adequately served this Deuteronomist's purposes throughout the savior stories, since it could easily be amplified to specify the foreign gods worshiped (Judg 3:7; 10:6) or complemented by an anonymous prophetic rebuke (6:8–10).[329]

1990, 296–306, who restricts traces of Dtr redaction to Judg 17–18 (DtrN). Others, e.g., Eissfeldt 1925, 96 n. 4, 109; Kaufmann 1961, 56–57; and Schulte 1972, 78, accept this explanation of the purpose of Judg 17–21, but attribute the composition and redaction of the material to pre-Dtr scribes.

324. See, e.g., Veijola 1977, 15–16; Crüsemann 1978, 162.
325. See, e.g., Wellhausen 1957, 237; Amit 1999, 345–48.
326. Stone 1988, 408.
327. E.g., Soggin 1987, 265, 280–81, 300–301; Mayes 2001.
328. Veijola 1977, 28–29.
329. Otherwise the formula occurs alone in Judg 3:12; 4:1; 6:1; 13:1.

Why, then, should he suddenly depart from his scheme and illustrate the wrongdoing in two lengthy narratives? Second, "doing wrong in the eyes of YHWH" nearly always refers to violation of cultic stipulations of Deuteronomy.[330] Thus according to the Deuteronomistic conception of the period of the judges, the primary cause of wrongdoing appears to be cultic transgression, and the worship of foreign gods triggers the cycle of punishment, crying to YHWH, and deliverance (e.g., Judg 2:11–13; 3:7; 10:6). Even though the story of Micah's image may illustrate the Deuteronomistic idea of "doing wrong in the eyes of YHWH,"[331] this hardly holds true for the narrative in Judg 19–21, which is devoid of cultic wrongdoing. If the two narratives were intended to illustrate the wrongdoing that sparked the cycle, we should expect them to come right before or right after the Deuteronomistic introduction to the period of the judges (e.g., following 2:11 or 3:6).[332] Finally, it is not clear why it should be necessary to fully illustrate the wrongdoing that led to Philistine domination of Israel, when 13:1 already noted that YHWH delivered the Israelites over to the Philistines for forty years since "they did what was wrong in the eyes of YHWH." Indeed, no illustration is necessary to explain why the Philistines still menace Israel in 1 Sam 4, since Samson, unlike the other saviors, is not

---

330. In Deuteronomy and Kings the "wrongdoing" formula ("to do wrong in YHWH's eyes," 'ה בעיני הרע עשה) is applied only to worship of other gods, the making of cultic images, or sacrifice at illegitimate altars, while in Judges and Samuel it applies to less specific infringements; see Deut 4:25; 9:18; 17:2; 31:29; Judg 2:11; 3:7, 12; 4:1; 6:1; 10:6; 13:1; 1 Sam 15:19; 1 Kgs 11:6; 14:22; 15:26, 34; 16:19, 25, 30; 21:20, 25; 22:53; 2 Kgs 3:2; 8:18, 27; 13:2, 11; 14:24; 15:9, 18, 24, 28; 17:2, 17; 21:2, 6, 15, 20; 23:32, 37; 24:9, 19. See similar use of the inverse formula, "doing right in the eyes of YHWH" ('ה בעיני הישר עשה) in Deut 12:25, 28; 13:19; 1 Kgs 11:33, 38; 15:5, 11; 22:43; 2 Kgs 10:30; 12:3; 14:3; 15:3, 34; 16:2; 18:3; 22:2. Only in two instances, Deut 21:9 and 2 Sam 12:9, does either formula indicate social, not cultic, wrongdoing, while in 2 Kgs 21:16 bloodshed is mentioned in addition to doing wrong in the eyes of YHWH.

331. Micah's image (ומסכה פסל, Judg 17:3–4; 18:14, 17–18, 20, 30–31) is a direct violation of the stipulations of Deut 4:16, 23, 25; 9:12; 27:15; cf. 2 Kgs 17:16. Micah's ad hoc appointment of priests certainly echoes Jeroboam's innovations (Judg 17:5, 12; cf. 1 Kgs 12:31; 13:33), but does not necessarily reflect a Dtr view of "wrongdoing." Deuteronomy is markedly unconcerned with the appointment of priests, and only sporadically remarks that the priests are Levites (17:9, 18; 18:1; 21:5; 24:8; 27:9; 31:9), while Kings makes no further mention of Jeroboam's appointment of priests after 1 Kgs 13:33.

332. See also the similar critique of Stone 1988, 37–38.

credited with delivering Israel. Although Veijola's conclusions have been adopted by several scholars, any one of the difficulties outlined above seriously challenges Veijola's claim that Judg 17–21 are original to the design of the Deuteronomistic History.

With regard to the composition of Judg 17–18, we should consider several additional points. First and foremost, Judg 17–18 does not display a critical mass of Deuteronomistic idioms or motifs.[333] At the same time, the purpose of the story is open to varying interpretations, fitting a broad time frame.[334] Nevertheless, the implied polemic aimed against the sanctuaries of Dan and Bethel (and the priestly line who served there) presumes an anti-Samarian orientation that is possibly coupled with a Judean ideology of cult centralization. Even though the themes of the story of Micah's cult image were of particular relevance to the Deuteronomistic program, the lack of Deuteronomistic idiom points to the likelihood that the story was produced outside the circle of the Deuteronomistic scribes.[335] Moreover, since the language of the composition is SBH, without observ-

---

333. See O'Brien 1989, 97–98; contra Veijola 1977, 15–29; and more recently Mueller 2001, 85–86. Nonetheless, Guillaume (2004, 138) thinks that "in spite of the lack of typically Deuteronomistic expressions, the whole narrative coheres with the Josianic period." Veijola argued for Dtr influence in four elements, but only one is a specific Dtr collocation; see Edenburg 2012b, 446.

334. Crüsemann (1978, 160–62) and Noth (1962, 81–82) viewed the story as a Judean polemic dating from the time of Solomon or Jeroboam that targeted the *premonarchic* cult at Dan; see further Niemann 1985, 143–47. However, most think that the polemic is directed against the northern *royal* shrines established by Jeroboam. Gray (1986, 223–24) and Amit (1990, 18–19; 1999, 378–79) both date the polemic to the time of Hezekiah, while Veijola (1977, 15–29) attributes the polemic to the preexilic composition of the DtrH (DtrG), and Becker (1990, 296–306) and Mueller (2001, 125–28) relate it to an exilic nomistic redaction (DtrN). However, this polemic could also have risen at the beginning of the Persian period, among circles that supported the restoration of Jerusalem temple, since during the interim period of Babylonian rule alternate cult sites, such as Shechem and Bethel, seem to have enjoyed a renaissance. Most recently, Bauer (1998, 429–47) and Na'aman (2005a, 52–55) have argued for postexilic composition of the story, and Guillaume (2014) proposed a Hellenistic dating.

335. See also Na'aman 2005a, 52–53; Edenburg 2012b, 445–47.

able traces of LBH,[336] it seems unlikely that the story was composed later than the early fifth century.[337]

The polemic inherent to the story of Micah's image might have been relevant to audiences both before and after the composition of the Deuteronomistic History. Thus determining when the narrative was placed in its context depends, ultimately, upon the view we take of the Deuteronomistic History. Noth's theory for a Deuteronomistic History was based on the reconstruction of an integral composition characterized by structural, thematic, and chronological unity. Noth's Deuteronomist gathered, selected, and occasionally reworked his sources. He assembled them in a continuous narrative, with a cohesive chronological framework, and he marked the transitions from era to era with programmatic evaluations framed as speeches or summations of the course of events. If we seriously consider the proposition of a Deuteronomistic work of history, then we must admit that both Judg 17–18 and 19–21 disrupt the chronological framework and narrative continuity of narration for the so-called period of "judges," which extends from the death of Joshua to the establishment of the monarchy.[338] This, in my opinion, is a decisive factor against attributing either the composition or placement of Judg 17–18 to any phase of Deuteronomistic editing. Thus I find Noth's view preferable: "It is recognized that Judg. 17–21 was not part of Dtr's work but was added later."[339]

Shared Motifs

Covert reference to Bethel. Even though the story of Micah makes no mention of Bethel in Judg 17–18, there is good cause to surmise that Micah's home is supposed to be located there.[340] The story's overt polemic is aimed against the sanctuary and cult at Dan (18:27–31);[341] thus it is also reason-

---

336. Priestly idiom does occur in 18:1, namely, נחלה לשבת (cf. Num 35:2) and נפל לו (ב)נחלה (cf. Num 24:2; Josh 13:6; 17:5; 23:4; Ezek 42:1; 47:14, 22; 48:29). However, 18:1 is a compositional link between sections of the narrative and may have been influenced by late redaction.

337. Na'aman (2005a, 54–55) suggested that the lack clear anti-Samaritan polemic in the story indicates that it was composed "no later than the late fifth century BCE, when the Samaritan temple on Mount Gerizim was built."

338. See Römer and de Pury 2000, 122–23; see also Becker 1990, 296–306.

339. Noth 1991, 77 n. 2.

340. See Amit 1990, 12–19; 2000, 111–18.

341. See, e.g., Noth 1962. Guillaume (2004, 141) thinks that Bethel is not men-

able to expect the narrative to attack the sanctuary of Bethel, particularly since it is depicted as the primary royal sanctuary of the kingdom of Israel.[342] Moreover, Micah's private sanctuary in Mount Ephraim is termed a "house of God" (בית אלהים), a transparent pun on the name of Bethel (cf. also Gen 28:17). Finally, Micah's actions, whereby he set a molten image in his sanctuary and personally appointed a priest to preside there, all reflect the measures attributed to Jeroboam with regard to the Bethel cult (1 Kgs 12:28–33). Thus the covert reference to Bethel seems firmly rooted in the Micah story.

Judges 19:18 might also imply that the Levite's home was at Bethel. The reading of the MT, בית יהוה, might be a tendentious designation for בית־אל, and the double reading ביתי preserved by the LXX might accurately represent the text's intention. In any case, in the subsequent sections of the story, the narrators mention Bethel by name and feel no need to mask their references to Bethel (N¹ 20:18, 26; R² 21:2). But while Judg 17–18 employs satire to denigrate the Bethel sanctuary, Judg 19:18, 20:18–28, and 21:2–3 represent it as a legitimate "house of YHWH."[343] Thus the covert reference to Bethel plays no vital role in either the plot or the polemic of the Gibeah story, and the intimation that the Levite dwelt at Bethel is no more than a secondary motif. N¹ may have used this covert reference to Bethel as an associative link between the Gibeah story and the story of Micah.

The opening of the stories. Both stories employ the same opening formula: "There was a man from TN,"[344] and in both cases the protagonist's home is in Mount Ephraim. The identification of Micah as an Ephraimite

---

tioned in the story because it already assumes its annexation by Josiah, and instead addresses the second phase of the Josianic program: uniting all Israel under the rule of a single king.

342. See Jer 48:13; Hos 10:5; Amos 3:14; 7:13. In DtrH Bethel overshadows the Dan sanctuary. For example, Jeroboam offers sacrifice at Bethel, rather than Dan (1 Kgs 12:32–33); 2 Kgs 17:27–28 implies that the Dtr scribe considered Bethel to have continued as the main cult site after the demise of the northern kingdom. Furthermore, apart from Judg 18 and 1 Kgs 12, the sanctuary at Dan figures only three more times, 2 Kgs 10:29; Jer 4:15; Amos 8:14.

343. See Blenkinsopp 1998, 30–34; Gross 2009, 857.

344. See also Judg 13:2; 17:7; 1 Sam 1:1; 9:1; cf. also Job 1:1. Stipp (2006, 136–37), Levin (2011, 136), and Müller (2013, 211–15) suggest that this formulaic opening was the hallmark of a collection of stories dealing with the premonarchic period. However, I think it more feasible that the formula was employed as an editorial device to mask seams between blocks of material by means of imitative association.

is certainly essential for detecting the covert polemic directed against Bethel and Jeroboam in Judg 17–18.[345] This, however, is not true in the case of the Levite's affiliation with Ephraim in Judg 19–21, since the story there revolves around Gibeah.[346] In the Gibeah story, it was important to locate the Levite's home sufficiently distant from the father-in-law's town so that if he departed in the afternoon, he would have to interrupt his journey and stop for the night at Gibeah. Since Benjamin is targeted by the story's polemic, the narrator could hardly place the Levite's home in Benjamin; but there was no reason not to locate his home in a town north of Benjamin. That both protagonists hail from Mount Ephraim is probably neither coincidental nor an independent element in the narratives, since it has been applied to create an inverse relation to Bethlehem; in 17:8 an Ephraimite (Micah) has a Levite from Bethlehem stay in his home in Mount Ephraim, while in 19:1–9 a Levite from Mount Ephraim pays a visit to Bethlehem. Since the origin of the protagonist in Mount Ephraim is essential to the story of Micah, but not to the Gibeah story, it is reasonable to conclude that N^1 borrowed this element from Judg 17–18 and patterned the opening of 19:1 upon the opening in 17:1.

The role of Levites in the stories. That the young man from Bethlehem is a Levite plays a crucial role in the development of the narrative in Judg 17–18. He is designated as a Levite eight times throughout the narrative (17:7, 9, 10, 11, 12, 13; 18:3, 15). Since he was a Levite, he had no inheritance of his own but dwelt in Bethlehem as a resident alien (17:7). For that reason, he left Bethlehem to "take up residence wherever he could find a place" (17:8–9). Since he was a Levite, Micah also preferred him as priest at his private sanctuary, in place of his own son (17:5, 10–13). In addition, as a Levite he was familiar with the procedure for consulting the oracle, and for this reason the Danite spies asked him to verify whether YHWH would grant them success on their mission (18:5–6). Finally, the Danites bribed him to defect from Micah's service and join their ranks because, as a Levite, he could establish a priestly dynasty in their new territory (18:19–20, 27, 30).

By contrast, Judg 19–21 refers to the concubine's husband only twice as a Levite (19:1; 20:4), and nowhere is he shown to fill any of the roles associated with Levites. Thus it is reasonable to conclude that his char-

---

345. See Amit 1990, 13–14; Na'aman 2005a, 48–51; cf. the introduction of Jeroboam in 1 Kgs 11:26: "Jeroboam son of Nabat was an Ephraimite from Zeredah."
346. Amit 2000, 127.

acterization as a Levite is a secondary attribute that was inserted into the story in order to create an associative link with Judg 17–18.[347] It seems that the narrator also tightened this link by reworking the traditional opening formula, "There was a man from TN," in order to echo the status of the young Levite in 17:7 as a resident alien; and thus began the Gibeah story with, "there was a man, a Levite, who resided at the far end of Mount Ephraim."

The route of the two Levites. In Judg 17:7–9, the young Levite from Bethlehem travels as far as Mount Ephraim, where he is received with hospitality, while in Judg 19 the Levite from Mount Ephraim travels to visit in Bethlehem and then returns to his home in Ephraim.[348] That Bethlehem was the Levite's destination in Judg 19 is significant, for the hospitable welcome afforded there helps represent Bethlehem as the antithesis of Gibeah. Since Bethlehem and Gibeah were David's and Saul's respective hometowns, the contrasting characterizations of the two cities in Judg 19 could mask a covert polemic directed against Saul, who stands in an antithetic relation to David's ideal kingship.[349] Accordingly, N¹ might have located the destination of the Levite's journey in Bethlehem in order to further the purpose of his story. By contrast, the story of Micah in Judg 17 attaches no special significance to the fact that the young Levite came from Bethlehem. Indeed, readers might find his Bethlehemite origin to stand in his favor, but such a reading runs against the current of the narrative's general tendency, which represents him in an equivocal light.[350] In this case, the mention of Bethlehem is a dysfunctional element in 17:7–9, and it may have been inserted into in order to create a mirror image of the other Levite's journey in Judg 19, from Mount Ephraim to Bethlehem.

---

347. See also Budde 1897, 127; Eissfeldt 1925, 52; Schunck 1963, 66; Jüngling 1981, 254; Amit 1999, 353; Stipp 2006, 132–33; Gross 2009, 813; cf. Abravanel on Judg 19:1. However, others have followed Josephus (*Ant.* 5.2.8 §144) and found it significant that he is characterized as a Levite; see, e.g., Trible 1984, 66; Arnold 1990, 66; Becker 1990, 270–72, 297. Indeed, if the narrative does hint that he dwelt at Bethel, then we might expect that his figure is intended to parody the Bethel priesthood. However, the negative aspects of his character are not related to any role he might be expected to play as a Levite, but rather to his crass behavior toward the concubine along with his unreliable testimony at the pantribal assembly.

348. The inversion was already pointed out by Budde 1897, 127.

349. See, e.g., Güdemann 1869, 363–68; Crüsemann 1978, 164; Jüngling 1981, 293; O'Connell 1996, 299–302; Amit 2000, 181.

350. See Amit 1999, 327.

Ephraimites grant hospitality to Levites. The invitation Micah extended to the young Levite to stay with him in Mount Ephraim provided an occasion to appoint him priest at the shrine erected for Micah's molten image (Judg 17:8–10). That Micah should reside in Mount Ephraim is, of course, necessary in order to intimate that his shrine is a parodic representation of the Bethel sanctuary. Similarly, in 19:16–21 a Levite is invited to stay for the night at the house of an Ephraimite, but this Ephraimite resides in Gibeah of Benjamin. The "visit in a hostile town" plot required that the host be a resident alien (cf. Gen 19:9), but it was not necessary to identify him as an Ephraimite, since any other non-Benjaminite affiliation would have sufficed as well. It is possible, then, that the identification of the host at Gibeah as an Ephraimite was influenced by the adjacent story about Micah.

Priests as grandsons of Moses and Aaron. Judges 18:30 reveals that the anonymous young Levite is none other than Jonathan son of Gershom son of Moses (משה). Ancient Near Eastern literary convention customarily placed the point of a text at its conclusion; thus many have concluded that the purpose of the Micah story is to relate a tendentious version of the foundation of the sanctuary at Dan, at which officiated a Mushite, rather than Aaronide, priestly dynasty.[351] If so, then the young Levite's lineage is essential to the purpose of the Micah story. In the Gibeah story, by contrast, the sudden mention of Phinehas ben Eleazar ben Aaron is problematic and may have been introduced into the narrative in order to align it chronologically with Judg 17–18.[352]

The role of Shiloh in both stories. According to Judg 18:31, Micah's image stood at the new shrine the Danites prepared for it, "all the time that the house of God stood at Shiloh," but this statement is at odds with verse 30, which states that the cult site and Mushite priesthood functioned "until the land went into exile."[353] Various proposals have been advanced to resolve the contradiction by means of emendation,[354] but it is more likely that one of the statements is a secondary accretion. In my opinion, 18:30 provides the appropriate conclusion for the anti-Ephraimite narrative by explaining how Micah's image and his Levite founded the sanctuary that supposedly stood at Dan "until the land went into exile." By contrast,

---

351. See, e.g., Bertheau 1845, xiv; Cross 1973, 195–215; Soggin 1987, 268–69; Becker 1990, 253; Amit 1999, 332–33.
352. See above, ch. 1.
353. See, e.g., Soggin 1987, 276.
354. See, e.g., *BHS* on 18:31; and O'Connell 1996, 481–83, on 18:30.

18:31 seems a foreign appendage that was devised in order to add a temporal reference to the time the sanctuary existed at Shiloh—information that first comes to the fore in 1 Sam 1. Hence the statement regarding the house of God at Shiloh might have been added to the end of the story in order to create an associative link with Samuel's birth narrative.[355] Examination of the references to Shiloh in Judg 21 also indicated that they may have been integrated into the narrative for the same purpose.[356] This may imply that Judg 17–18 was first appended and linked with Samuel's birth narrative, and then at a later stage Judg 19–21 was interpolated, necessitating additional links between Judg 21 and 1 Sam 1.[357]

VERBAL ANALOGIES

In those days there was no king in Israel; every man did as he thought right (17:6; 21:25; cf. 18:1; 19:1). The editorial character of this refrain is evident in both narratives,[358] but it remains to be seen whether it was added to both at the same stage of redaction. In my opinion, this possibility should be rejected on grounds of style and content.[359] If the same redactor added the formulas to both narratives, we might expect he would utilize them in the same fashion. For example, he could have employed them to frame the Micah story in 17:1 and 18:31, similar to their placement in 19:1 and 21:25. Alternatively, he could have inserted them between the major stages of the Gibeah narrative (e.g., before 20:1 and 21:1), where they would serve as running commentary on events related, just as he did in 17:6 and 18:1. The different fashion in which they were added to each narrative seems to imply that they were added at separate stages of redaction.

Since the judgment formula occurs in conjunction with the chronological designation, "In those days there was no king in Israel," the refrain is thought to characterize the premonarchic period as a time of anarchy in which "every man did as he thought right." The refrain thus reflects an ideal

---

355. Zakovitch 1983, 179.
356. See above, ch. 1.
357. Zakovitch 1983, 179.
358. See above, ch. 1.
359. See Bertheau 1845, 215; Güdemann 1869, 361–62; Bleek 1878, 203; Noth 1962, 79; Boling 1975, 293–94; Crüsemann 1978, 157; Gray 1986, 348; Soggin 1987, 280–81; Amit 1999, 345–47; contra Burney 1970, 410–11; Veijola 1977, 15–17; Becker 1990, 292–93; Mayes 2001, 253–56.

view of the monarchy as a means of maintaining social order and serves to justify the establishment of monarchic rule. The censure of the refrain in Judg 17–18 is certainly aimed at the foundation of the shrines at Bethel and Dan, along with their priesthood and cult images. The refrain implies that such offenses could occur only in the absence of a central authority and that a king would take measures for proper governance of the cult.[360] Moreover, it has been noted that the judgment formula: איש הישר בעיניו יעשה seems to interact with Deuteronomistic idiom and ideology,[361] since for the Deuteronomistic scribes, to do right in one's *own* eyes is the inverse of doing right in the *eyes of YHWH* (cf. Deut 12:8, 25, 28). Indeed, within the Deuteronomistic History the expression "to do right [or wrong] in the eyes of YHWH" nearly always refers to adherence to (or violation of) the Deuteronomistic cultic stipulations.[362] Thus the chronological refrain and judgment formula are entirely appropriate to the story of Micah's image.[363]

In Judg 19–21, however, the theme of apostasy and idolatry is absent. There Gibeah and Benjamin are censured for social offenses, specifically, abrogation of hospitality, sexual assault, and refusal to hand over offenders for administration of justice. While these offenses do indicate a breakdown of social norms, it is questionable whether the overall narrative presents a picture of anarchy, since the tribes act promptly and spontaneously to enforce social norms and punish their abrogation.[364] In addition, it is unlikely that a king could have averted the assault at Gibeah or avenged the death of the concubine more effectively than the concerted

---

360. See, e.g., Güdemann 1869, 361; Veijola 1977, 15–16; Crüsemann 1978, 162; Jüngling 1981, 278. By contrast, Mueller (2001, 105–17) argues that the formula does not promote an ideal view of the monarchy so much as censure kings who did not uphold covenant strictures. Moreover, he claims that the formula is specifically directed against a particular king who "did not act as a king" (105), possibly Jehoiakim or Zedekiah (117). Mueller thinks the king is implicitly included in the criticism directed against "each man" doing as he saw fit (105). However, the preceding clause specifically excludes the king from judgment, since "in those days, there was no king in Israel." More likely, a king—Jeroboam—is indeed targeted by the story, as persuasively demonstrated by Na'aman 2005a, 48–51. However, this conclusion is based upon the characterization of Micah in the story, not upon the judgment formula itself.

361. See, e.g., Veijola 1977, 15–16; Mayes 2001, 255–58; Mueller 2001, 112–16.

362. See n. 330 above.

363. However, this does not necessarily imply Dtr authorship; see Na'aman 2005a, 52.

364. See, e.g., Güdemann 1869, 361; Amit 1999, 337–39.

action taken by the tribes in the narrative.[365] Indeed, it is doubtful whether the offenses represented in the Gibeah story were ever under the jurisdiction of monarchic authorities.[366] Thus even if the chronological designation and judgment formula further the purpose of the story of Micah's image, they are not appropriate to the context of the Gibeah story. Therefore, I conclude that the formulas were borrowed from the Micah story and affixed to frame the Gibeah story, with the purpose of creating a semblance of continuity between the adjacent narratives.

בית לחם יהודה (Judg 17:7, 8, 9; 19:1, 2, 18). The apposition of "Bethlehem" and "Judah" occurs three times each in Judg 17 and in Judg 19 but is encountered elsewhere in only two other texts (1 Sam 17:12; Ruth 1:1–2). Since the action in both stories moves from south to north, it should be evident that Bethlehem refers to the well-known southern town, even without the additional designation of "Judah."[367] However, in Judg 19, the designation בית לחם יהודה counters גבעה אשר לבנימין (19:14). The tribal designations added to the town names might signal to the reader of Judg 19 that the story does not deal with a local incident of limited significance but with events affecting intertribal relations. By contrast, the location of the young Levite's origins in Bethlehem of *Judah* is at odds with the implied criticism of the Bethel and Danite priesthoods, which he supposedly founded. Since the expanded geographical designation is at home in Judg 19 but not in Judg 17, it seems likely that in this case an associative link was taken up from the Gibeah narrative and planted within the Micah story.

מאין תבוא (Judg 17:9; 19:17). Although this formulation occurs elsewhere,[368] only in these two cases is the question addressed to a wayfarer by a potential host. Since the answers of both wayfarers are identical, namely, that they left Bethlehem, it seems evident that the similarity derives from literary interdependency.

אין (שם) מחסור כל דבר (Judg 18:10; 19:19). The expression occurs solely in these two narratives. In 19:19, the Levite lists his provisions and then states that "nothing is lacking" (אין מחסור כל דבר). After this, the

---

365. See, e.g., Güdemann 1869, 361; Trible 1984, 84; Amit 1999, 338–39.
366. See Gen 34; Deut 19:12; 21:1–7, 22:22–27; 2 Sam 14:5–7, where jurisdiction of rape and homicide is relegated to the family or the local authorities. See also RS 17.230; 17.146; 17.42 for a similar situation at Ugarit in the Late Bronze Age.
367. For the northern town of Bethlehem in Zebulon, see Josh 19:15; Judg 12:8–10.
368. See Josh 9:8; Jonah 1:8; Job 1:7; see also Gen 29:4; 42:7.

old Ephraimite answers him with a double reply: "Anything you lack is on me [כל מחסורך עלי]; just don't sleep in the square." The doubling in both men's speech may imitate polite discourse. However, the Levite's statement, אין מחסור כל דבר, lacks a dative object and therefore seems elliptic.[369] By contrast, the syntax in 18:10 is not deficient (אין שם מחסור כל דבר אשר בארץ), and the statement adds pertinent information about the area of Laish: not only is it spacious and inhabited by a peaceful, unsuspicious people, but it can also supply all the needs of the Danites. Thus it seems to me that the shared phrase is more at home in its context in Judg 18 than in Judg 19.

They built [ויבנו] *the city/cities and dwelt in it/them* [וישבו בה/בהם] (Judg 18:28; 21:23). This exact collocation is paralleled only once more, in Josh 19:50, which notes that Joshua "built the town [Timnath-serah] and settled there."[370] While all three notices occur at the end of narrative blocks, Judg 18:28 and Josh 19:50 are the most clearly related. In these two passages, towns are (re)built and settled by groups who dispossessed the previous inhabitants. Judges 18:28 signals the successful solution of the problem facing the Danites at the opening of the last section of the narrative: "In those days the tribe of Danites sought an inheritance [נחלה] to settle, because until that day no inheritance had fallen to their lot [נפלה בנחלה] among the tribes of Israel" (18:1). Similarly, the building and settlement of Timnath-serah marks the completion of the division of the land into tribal inheritances: "When they finished allotting [לנחל] the land by its boundaries, the Israelites gave an inheritance [נחלה] to Joshua son of Nun" (Josh 19:49). Moreover, the notice in Josh 19:49–50 about granting Timnath-serah to Joshua immediately follows the alternate version of the Danites' conquest of Laish/Leshem (Josh 19:47). These interrelations might indicate that Judg 18:1b, 28 and Josh 19:49–50 were formulated by the same author-redactor.

In contrast to Josh 19:50 and Judg 18:28, Judg 21:23 relates the restoration of destroyed cities by their previous inhabitants upon returning to their territory. This statement is not necessary to the narrative, and the report of Benjamin's rehabilitation could have satisfactorily concluded in verse 23a–bα, which notes that they returned to their territory with the wives found for them. The additional mention of rebuilding Benjamin's

---

369. See Ps 34:10, אין מחסור ליראיו; 1 Kgs 11:22, מה אתה חסר עמי.
370. See 24:13; Amos 9:14; Ps 69:36; 2 Chr 8:2.

TEXT, SUBTEXT, AND INTERTEXTUAL MOSAIC 299

cities may have been introduced into the narrative in order to evoke an association with the conclusion of the adjacent story of the conquest of Laish by the Danites (18:28).

IMPLICATIONS REGARDING THE REDACTION HISTORY OF JUDG 17–18, 19–21

Intertextual links with Judg 17–18 are distributed throughout the chapters of the Gibeah story, but the bulk of them are concentrated in the opening chapter (Judg 19), which stems entirely from N¹.[371] The parallels include unique language (אין מחסור כל דבר) as well as shared motifs, which were well integrated into one context but dysfunctional in the other. Thus there is sufficient evidence to conclude that the parallels indicate deliberate literary interrelation. For the most part, Judg 17–18 proved to supply the original context for the shared material. Nonetheless, Judg 17–18 also appears to have absorbed some elements that were lifted from Judg 19–21. In one instance, the shared material seems to derive from a common source, and in another instance, the adjacent contexts of the stories seems to have exerted influence in both directions.[372]

These findings suggest that N¹ composed Judg 19–21 for its present context at the end of the Judges scroll and employed reiteration, parallel motifs, and formulations as devices for creating associative links in order to mask seams between originally disparate material. To this end,

---

371. The material in Judg 19 shared by N¹ and Judg 17–18 includes the short formula: "In those days there was no king in Israel"; the opening formula: "There was a man from Mount Ephraim"; the figure of a Levite; the Mt. Ephraim–Bethlehem route; בית לחם יהודה; מאין תבוא; a covert reference to Bethel; אין מחסור כל דבר; a Levite who stays with an Ephraimite. The shared elements deriving from N¹ in Judg 20 comprise the figures of a Levite and a priest who is grandson of one of the leaders of the exodus from Egypt; and in Judg 21, the role of Shiloh; ויבנו ערים וישבו בהם; the full judgment formula.

372. Elements Judg 19–21 borrowed from chs. 17–18 include the covert reference to Bethel; the opening formula: "There was a man (from) Mount Ephraim"; the figure of a Levite; אין מחסור כל דבר; a Levite who stays with an Ephraimite; priests who are grandsons of leaders of the exodus; ובנו ערים וישבו בהם; "In those days there was no king in Israel; each man did as he saw fit." Elements Judg 17–18 borrowed from chs. 19–21 include the Mt. Ephraim–Bethlehem route, and the apposition בית לחם יהודה. Mutual influence is represented by מאין תבוא, while the mention of Shiloh in both narratives seems to be borrowed from a common source, 1 Sam 1.

N¹ picked up elements from the Judg 17–18 and weaved them into the opening section of his narrative in order to create a semblance of compositional continuity between the now neighboring narratives. It is possible that N¹ also sought to strengthen the link by planting in Judg 17–18 some elements that he lifted from his own composition in Judg 19–21. In addition, the rather forced references to Shiloh at the end of both stories (18:31; 21:12, 19–21) were probably devised to contend with the lack of any chronological or thematic continuity to link the end of the Judges scroll to the beginning of the Samuel scroll, which opens with Samuel's birth narrative in 1 Sam 1.

The links with 1 Sam 1 may derive from different stages of revision. I think that in the first stage, Judg 17–18 was added to the end of the Judges scroll following the Samson cycle in Judg 13–16, thereby disrupting the narrative continuity of the period of Philistine domination, which extends from Judg 13–16 into the first half of the Samuel scroll.³⁷³ The double endings of the story of Micah's image (Judg 18:30–31) are mutually exclusive and hardly derive from the same hand. Since 18:30 provides the appropriate conclusion for the tendentious narrative of the foundation of the royal sanctuaries at Dan and Bethel, 18:31 should be considered a secondary accretion from a later redactor, who added the reference to the sanctuary at Shiloh in order to smooth the transition between the Micah story and 1 Sam 1. At a subsequent stage, N¹ composed the Gibeah story and picked up the reference to the yearly feast at Shiloh from 1 Sam 1:3 and wove it in to his narrative (Judg 21:19) in order to connect the new

---

373. The Samson story and Samuel's birth narrative display various associative links, and these might indicate that a stage in which the Samuel narratives were conceived as the direct continuation of the Samson cycle. These links include the introductory formula ויהי איש, which only in 1 Sam 1:1 and Judg 13:2 is followed by the indefinite term אחד (cf. ויהי איש alone in Judg 17:1; 19:1; 1 Sam 9:1; Job 1:1); the unique expression ומורה לא יעלה על ראשו (Judg 13:5; 16:17; 1 Sam 1:11); 1 Sam 1:22 in 4QSamᵃ where Samuel is to be a nazirite "forever, all the days of his life," which parallels Samson's designation as a nazirite "until his dying day" (Judg 13:7). The nazirite theme is inherent to the framing stories of the Samson cycle but is not taken up elsewhere in the Samuel narratives. This suggests that the Samson story might have concluded the Judges scroll before the addition of the two appendix narratives in Judg 17–21, and that scribe(s) employed similarly formulated introductions to the Samuel and Samson stories, and added the nazirite motif to Samuel's birth narrative in order to create a semblance of continuity running from the end of one scroll to the beginning of the other. See also Zakovitch 1983, 173–74.

end of the Judges scroll to the beginning of the Samuel scroll by means of an associative thread. In the final stage, R² expanded the original Gibeah narrative with additional intertextual links drawn from the sources utilized by N¹, including the reference to the camp at Shiloh in 21:12. Since Judg 17–18 appears to be a post-Deuteronomistic insertion into the Deuteronomistic History, it follows that the Gibeah story, which incorporates links with both Judg 17–18 and 1 Sam 1, is also a post-Deuteronomistic composition. Moreover, the reconstruction above supports the likelihood that Judg 19–21 was fit into place in the stage in which the Judges scroll took its final shape.

As noted above, a few associative links with Judg 19–21 were also planted in Judg 17–18. This minor reworking of Judg 17–18 might derive from either N¹ or R². If so, their purpose would have been to create the impression of reciprocal interrelation between the adjoining narratives. But it is equally possible that a later scribe was responsible for the assimilation in Judg 17–18 of the few elements borrowed from Judg 19–21. On the basis of all these findings, it possible to conclude that Judg 17–18 and 19–21 stem from different sources, were edited separately, and were inserted at separate stages into their contexts, where they disrupt the narrative flow of the Deuteronomistic History. The superficial similarity between the two narratives is due to the fact that the Gibeah story was conceived for its context as the final unit to precede the metanarrative of the establishment of the monarchy. Since the story of Micah's image was already in place, immediately preceding Samuel's birth narrative, N¹ was able to borrow elements from Judg 17–18 and integrate them into the Gibeah story, all with the purpose of facilitating the addition of a new narrative block between Judg 17–18 and 1 Sam 1.

THE PROLOGUE OF JUDGES (JUDG 1:1–2:5)

The prologue in Judg 1:1–2:5 is composed of at least two separate units: 1:1–36, which consists of a collection of conquest and settlement traditions, arranged geographically from south to north; and 2:1–5, which comprises an accusation and judgment speech that is delivered by a divine messenger and followed by an expression of the people's remorse.[374] In the past, many

---

374. On the complexity of Judg 1:1–2:5, see, e.g., Blum 2010, 256–62, 274–76; Rake 2006.

thought that 1:1–36 represented an early, pre-Deuteronomistic version of the conquest and accorded it greater historical reliability than the account given in the book of Joshua.[375] However, this version is no less tendentious than the conquest account of the book of Joshua.[376] Moreover, most of the information related in Judg 1:1–36 is directly related to material in the book of Joshua (particularly Josh 13–19), and in several instances it can be demonstrated that the shared material has been subject to tendentious reworking in Judg 1.[377] Some more recent scholars also hold that Judg 1 is not of one piece, neither with regard to its sources nor to its compositional history.[378] Regardless whether one considers Josh 13–19 to be an integral part of the Deuteronomistic History[379] or a post-Deuteronomistic addition,[380] it seems evident that the dependency of Judg 1:1–36 upon the material in Joshua marks it as a post-Deuteronomistic composition.

The section in Judg 2:1–5 was often attributed to circles connected with J, since it interacts with Exod 23:20–33 and 34:10–16.[381] However, it also interacts with Deut 7:1–6 and is replete with Deuteronomistic formulas. Accordingly, Rudolf Smend proposed that the Bochim passage derives from a "nomistic" Deuteronomistic author (DtrN) who reedited the Deuteronomistic History in the period of the exile.[382] The placement of the Bochim passage immediately after the catalog of settlement failures in Judg 1:21–36 serves to reinterpret the list of failures, by which omitting to

---

375. See, e.g., Moore 1895, 4–7; Burney 1970, xxxix; Weinfeld 1967, 93–97; Gray 1986, 194–95; and a full survey of the history of research in Rake 2006, 1–21.

376. See, e.g., Auld 1975; Brettler 1989a, 402; Weinfeld 1993, 388–400; Rake 2006. Guillaume (2004, 87–105) argued at length that Judg 1:4–18, 27–34 was composed as Judean propaganda at the time of Manasseh.

377. See, e.g., Auld 1975; Mullen 1984; Fishbane 1988, 203; Na'aman 1994, 260–68; Younger 1995; Rake 2006, 34–60.

378. See, e.g., Brettler 2002, 92–93; Blum 2010, 274–76; Rake 2006, 68–90.

379. See, e.g., Smend 2000, 99–102; cf. Weinfeld 1972, 182; Auld 1980, 52–71; Römer and de Pury 2000, 114–15.

380. See, e.g., Noth 1991, 66–68; Van Seters 1983, 331–36; O'Brien 1989, 72–75; Nelson 1997, 8–9; Knauf 2008, 20–21; Blum 2010, 255.

381. See, e.g., Moore 1895, 4–7; Weinfeld 1967, 98; cf. Gray 1986, 195. Others limited J to 2:1, 5; see Wellhausen 1899, 210; Burney 1970, 2. See discussion of these issues by Blum 1990, 365–78; Rake 2006, 9–14.

382. See Smend 2000. His position has been adopted by Veijola 1982, 184–86; Becker 1990, 49–58. Blum (2010, 257–62) attributes the passage to a postexilic "Hexateuch"-oriented context; see also Rake 2006, 105–22. By contrast, Guillaume (2004, 112–14) proposes that the section derives from the time of Josiah.

drive out the "native" inhabitants is equated with entering into voluntary alliance with them.[383] While 2:1–5 builds upon 1:21–36, the opposite does not hold—the catalog of failures in Judg 1 does not presume or anticipate the messenger's accusation in 2:1–3.[384] If it is true that Judg 1 is a late overriding of a Deuteronomistic conquest account,[385] then Judg 2:1–5 must derive from an even later stage of revision.[386] The late origin of 2:1–5 is further indicated by the way it combines formulas that derive from different redactional layers of the Pentateuch. Most of these formulas are also current in postexilic literature.[387] The variety and number of sources

---

383. See Blum 1990, 366–69; 2010, 256–62; Rake 2006, 102. For Blum, this holds true only for the *present* context of the Bochim incident, since he thinks that the passage was originally at home in a messenger and Gilgal tradition complex. According to him, the original target of the messenger's indictment was the Gibeonite treaty, rather than the settlement failures; see Blum 1990, 366–67; 2010, 256–57.

384. See, e.g., Weinfeld 1967, 94–96; Mullen 1984, 40–41; Blum 1990, 366–67; Smend 2000, 108; Becker 1990, 49–51; Amit 2000, 120–23.

385. See, e.g., Edenburg 2012b, 452–53; 2012c, 61.

386. Contra Blum 2010, 256–62; Kratz 2000, 200; Rake 2006, 104–5, 123–24, who hold that Judg 1 was added before 2:1–5 at a latest stage in the development of the book.

387. J: מה זאת עשית(ם) (Gen 3:13; 12:18; 26:10; 29:25; 42:28; Exod 14:5, 11; cf. Jonah 1:10); both J and Dtr: אשר נשבע לאבות (Exod 13:5; Num 11:12; 14:23; Deut 1:8; 4:31; 7:12–13; 13:18; 19:8; 28:11; 29:12; 31:7, and at least ten times more; Josh 5:6; 21:43–44; Jer 32:22); J and post-Dtr: (את האמרי) גרש מפני(ך) (Exod 23:29–30; 34:11; Josh 24:12; Judg 6:9; Ps 78:55; 1 Chr 17:21; wholly lacking in Deuteronomy); היה למוקש (Exod 10:7; 23:33; 34:12; Josh 23:13; Judg 8:27; 1 Sam 18:21; Pss 69:23; 106:36; wholly lacking in Deuteronomy); מלאך ה' ("the angel of YHWH," Gen 16:7–11; 22:11, 15; Exod 3:2; Num 22:22–27, 31–35; Judg 5:23; 6:11–12, 21–22; 13:3, 13–21; 2 Sam 24:16; 1 Kgs 19:7; 2 Kgs 1:3, 15; 19:35; Isa 37:36; Hag 1:13; Zech 1:11–12; 3:1, 5; Mal 2:7; Pss 34:8; 35:5–6; 1 Chr 21:12, 15–18, 30; wholly lacking in Deuteronomy); both Dtr and post-Dtr: ישבי הארץ (e.g., Gen 36:20; Num 33:52, 55; Josh 2:9, 24; 7:9; 9:24; 13:21; Jer 1:14; 6:12; 10:18; 13:13; 25:29–30; Joel 1:2, 14; 2:1; Zeph 1:18; Zech 11:6; Ps 33:14; Neh 9:24; 1 Chr 11:4; 22:18; 2 Chr 20:7; wholly lacking in Deuteronomy); שמע בקול ה' ("obey the voice of YHWH," e.g., Deut 8:20; 13:19; 15:5; 27:10; 28:1–2, 15, 45, 62; 30:8,10; Josh 5:6; 1 Sam 12:15; 15:19–20, 22; 28:18; 1 Kgs 20:36; 2 Kgs 18:12; Jer 3:25; 7:28; 26:13; 38:20; 42:6, 13, 21; 43:7; 44:23; Zech 6:15; Ps 106:25; Dan 9:10; cf. Num 14:22; Josh 22:2; Judg 6:10; 1 Sam 12:14; Zeph 3:2); נתץ מזבחות (Deut 7:5; 12:3; Judg 6:28, 30–32; 2 Kgs 11:18; 23:15; cf. Exod 34:13 and Chronicles' *Sondergut*: 2 Chr 31:1; 33:3; 34:4); P: הפר ברית (Gen 17:14; Lev 26:15, 44; Ezek 17:15–16, 18; Zech 11:10; cf. elsewhere Deut 31:16, 20; 1 Kgs 15:19; Isa 24:5; 33:8); לא הפר ברית לעולם— *hapax*, but cf. ברית עולם (Gen 9:16; 17:7, 13, 19; Exod 31:16; Lev 24:8; see elsewhere 2 Sam 23:5; Isa 24:5; 55:3; 61:8; Jer 32:40; 50:5; Ezek 16:60; 37:26; Ps 105:10 // 1 Chr

that influenced the composition of 1:1–2:5 (including all the redactional strands of the Pentateuch), along with the continued prevalence of most of its formulas into the postexilic period, present weighty evidence in favor of a post-Deuteronomistic origin for 1:1–36 and 2:1–5.[388]

SHARED MOTIFS

Jerusalem as a Jebusite town (Judg 1:21; 19:10–12). According to Judg 1:21, Jerusalem was a Jebusite settlement, while in 19:10–11 Jebus is a place name that the narrator identifies with Jerusalem.[389] These are the only references to Jebusites or Jebus in the book of Judges. Furthermore, in both Judg 1 and 19, the depiction of Jerusalem as a Jebusite town occurs in an anti-Benjaminite context. In 19:10–12, the designation *Jebus* serves to characterize Jerusalem as a non-Israelite town and explains why the Levite adamantly refused to stop there for the night (cf. Gen 20:11). At the same time, this characterization throws into relief the Benjaminites' reception of the Levite and his concubine in Gibeah, since the non-Israelite inhabitants of Jebus/Jerusalem could hardly have afforded them worse treatment than that which they received at the hands of Benjaminites of Gibeah. Similarly, the anti-Benjamite tendency of Judg 1:21 faults Benjamin for not dispossessing the Jebusites of Jerusalem,[390] although previously Judah was already credited with conquering non-Jebusite Jerusalem (v. 8).[391]

16:17). For further discussion, see also Weinfeld 1967, 95; Nelson 1981, 45–52; Veijola 1982, 185 n. 25; Van Seters 1983, 341–43; cf. Becker 1990, 50–55. It should be noted that Veijola's discussion is based upon the disputed assumption of a Dtr redaction of the Tetrateuch.

388. Burney (1970, 2, 37–40) ruled similarly regarding 2:1b–4: "The speech which is put into the mouth of the Angel of Yahweh appears to be a free composition by R^P, based upon reminiscence of passages in the Pentateuch and Josh." (2). See also Blum 1990, 366–67, 377.

389. See Josh 15:63; 18:28; 2 Sam 5:6; 1 Chr 11:4; see Hübner 2007.

390. See Josh 15:63, according to which *Judah* failed to dispossess them.

391. Aharoni (1987, 172) assumed that these statements reflect historical developments during the period of settlement. However, Judg 1 is of dubious historical value, due to its tendentious editing and dependency upon other sources; see, e.g., Auld 1975; Weinfeld 1993, 390–98. By contrast, Wong (2006, 29–31) attributes the statements to the editorial stage of Judges, but fallaciously concludes that Judg 19:10–12 presumes 1:21 and that this implies that both the prologue in Judg 1 and the epilogue in 17–21 derive from the same stage of composition. However, Judg 19:10–12 relays all the information necessary and does not imply prior knowledge of 1:21.

Bethel associated with weeping (Judg 2:1, 4–5; 20:23, 26; 21:2). Bethel is explicitly connected with weeping in Judg 20:26 and 21:2. Although 20:23 does not specify where the Israelites wept "before YHWH," the parallels in verses 18 and 26 imply that here too the Bethel sanctuary was the site of both lament and oracular rites. The weeping motif is undoubtedly at home in the narrative of the double defeat in Judg 20 since weeping frequently figures in lamentation over defeat or national disaster.[392] The motif is also appropriate in its context in Judg 21, where it serves to undermine the outcome of the civil war by representing it as a pyrrhic victory.

The MT of Judg 2:1–5, by contrast, makes no mention of Bethel and refers instead to a place with the singular name of Bochim ("weeping," v. 1). There a divine messenger rebukes the people for failing to dispossess the inhabitants of the land and to destroy their altars.[393] Thereupon the people broke down and wept and then named the place Bochim.[394] The LXX, however, identifies Bochim with Bethel. Although the LXX reading may represent an interpretive gloss rather than a true textual variant, this interpretation has a strong basis in biblical traditions that associate Bethel with weeping (e.g., Gen 35:8; Hos 12:5) and may indeed reflect the intent behind the MT. Amit surmises that the author of 2:1–5 avoided explicit mention of Bethel, since the text was designed as a hidden polemic directed against Bethel.[395] The difficulty with this approach is that the passage in 2:1–5 lacks allusion to any of the cult violations typically associated with Bethel. Furthermore, no condemnation is implied by the Israelites' weeping at Bochim upon hearing the angel's rebuke, nor are

---

392. See weeping in the wake of defeat, Josh 7:6; 1 Sam 4:12; 2 Sam 1:2, 12; and in the wake of general national disaster, Lev 10:6; Num 25:6; 1 Sam 11:4; 30:4; 2 Sam 15:23, 30; 2 Kgs 8:11–12; 20:3; 22:19; Isa 22:4, 12; Jer 41:6; Joel 2:12; Zech 7:3; Pss 78:64; 137:1.

393. The rebuke appears to assume the failures listed in Judg 1, but not vice versa; see, e.g., Weinfeld 1967, 94–96; Mullen 1984, 40–41; Smend 2000, 108; Becker 1990, 49–51; Amit 2000, 120–23.

394. Some have thought that this represents a real local etiological tradition; see, e.g., Gray 1986, 242–43; Soggin 1987, 30–31. But local etiological traditions associate a known place with an event that supposedly occurred there and that purports to explain the origin of the place name; see, e.g., Gen 21:31; 28:19; 31:48; 33:17; Exod 15:23; Josh 5:9. Bochim, by contrast, is not a known place, and the name etiology does not "explain" a known name, but rather explicates the association of weeping with the implied subject, Bethel.

395. Amit 2000, 119–28.

they criticized for offering propitiatory sacrifice to YHWH at "that place" (המקום as a technical term for a cult site).³⁹⁶ Moreover, the immediate context provides no clue that Bochim is a masked reference to Bethel.³⁹⁷ If the allusion was initially dependent upon the traditions preserved in Gen 35:8 and Hos 12:5, then the author pictured an ideal reader of high literary competence. This, in itself, is not unfeasible. However, another possibility should be entertained: that the allusion was devised with another key text in mind, closer in literary proximity, namely, the interludes of crying at Bethel in Judg 20–21. This alternative may be preferable, since it assumes a less exclusive audience. Acceptance of this supposition has important consequences for the redaction history of the book of Judges, since it indicates that the Bochim episode was not composed prior to the Gibeah story. It would appear that Judg 2:1–5 was either composed along with Judg 19–21³⁹⁸ or that the Bochim episode was composed to counter the favorable representation of Bethel in Judg 19–21 and was introduced into its context after the Gibeah story was already in place.

Offer of sacrifice following weeping (Judg 2:5; 21:4; cf. 20:26). In Judg 2:1–5 the people weep in lamentation over the divine messenger's rebuke and then offer sacrifice, undoubtedly in an attempt to appease their God and abate his anger (v. 5, ויזבחו שם לה'). In both 20:26 and 21:4, the Israelites sacrifice burnt and peace offerings "before YWHW" after weeping (ויעלו עלות ושלמים לפני ה'). The people weep over the disastrous defeat in 20:26 not only because of their losses but also because defeat was understood as a sign of divine disfavor. Hence here too the burnt sacrifice is offered to appease their God. In 21:4, by contrast, the people weep, build an altar (מזבח), and sacrifice burnt offerings following *victory*. This sacrifice is hardly a propitiatory offering, since after the victory there was no more need to appease God. Nor can it be understood as a thank offering for the victory, whose consequences the people lament (vv. 3–4). Moreover, the note that the people then erected an altar at Bethel is also suspicious, since they already sacrificed there on the eve of the third battle (20:26). If 20:26 assumes that an altar already existed at Bethel, then why did R² find it necessary to note that an altar was erected on the occasion of

---

396. See also Blum 2010, 260.

397. However, readers familiar with the geographical background might perhaps infer that the route of the messenger from Gilgal to Bochim is identical with the route to Bethel via Wadi Suwienit; cf. Josh 7:2; 2 Kgs 2:18, 23.

398. See, e.g., Wong 2006, 40–42.

the final convocation for lamenting at Bethel? It appears, then, that both the sacrifice and the construction of an altar (מזבח) are out of place in 21:2–4. Possibly, R² introduced them into this context in order to evoke association with the sacrifice (זבחים) following weeping at Bochim.

VERBAL ANALOGIES

They inquired of YHWH/God, saying: "Who of us shall be the first to go up to attack [להלחם]/*to war* [למלחמה]?" *YHWH answered: "Judah"* (Judg 1:3; 20:18). The parallel is unique not only as a whole but also with regard to the structure of the question.[399] The question and answer make sense in the context of Judg 1, which assumes the division of the land by lot as described in Josh 14–19 (cf. Judg 1:3; Josh 14:1–2; 18:1–10), following which each tribe had to take possession of his inheritance by driving out the native inhabitants. However, neither the question nor the answer is appropriate to the story of the battle at Gibeah. There the narrative repeatedly states that all Israel acted together, with the sole exception of Benjamin (e.g., 20:1, 11, 17, 19, 24, 30). Moreover, the narrative neglects to follow up the oracle's designation of Judah to lead the attack; in fact, there is no other reference made to Judah in the entire story. Thus it seems certain that the question and answer were borrowed from Judg 1:1–2 and artificially planted in 20:18.[400]

עליה בגורל/עלה אתי בגורלי (Judg 1:3; 20:9). The collocation עלה + גורל occurs in a military context in Judg 1:3, where Judah proposes that they and the tribe of Simeon work together to take possession of their inheritances. In this case, the narrator makes metonymic use of the term גורל ("lot"), whereby the process (drawing lots) is named to indicate the result (the portion drawn in lot).[401] In 20:9 the tribes declare עליה בגורל, in announcing the decision reached by their consultation ("Now, this is what we shall do with regard to Gibeah," etc.). However, this text is difficult, not

---

399. Nowhere else is the oracle consulted to verify *who* should lead the attack; instead, the question commonly posed is *whether* to attack (see, e.g., 1 Sam 23:2–4; 2 Sam 2:1; 1 Kgs 22:6).

400. See, e.g., Frankenberg 1895, 74–75; Moore 1895, 432; Burney 1970, 448, 454; Noth 1966, 166; Eissfeldt 1963, 70; Mayes 1974, 44, 81; Crüsemann 1978, 159; Veijola 1982, 186–88; Amit 1999, 356; Gross 2009, 823; contra Auld 1975, 268.

401. See Josh 18:6, 8; see also Num 36:3; Josh 17:14, 17; 18:11; 19:10; 21:20; Isa 17:14; 57:6.

only because עליה בגורל is elliptic, but also because בגורל does not signify "by lot" but division of the land into portions.⁴⁰² While the MT seems to have lost the verb of the clause that is preserved in the LXX (נעלה עליה), in both versions בגורל is probably a gloss influenced by 1:3. The question remains whether this gloss derived from R² or was added by a later scribe.

העיר/כל הערים שלחו באש(Judg 1:8; 20:48). The collocation שלח באש occurs with עיר as its object only in these two contexts.⁴⁰³ The preceding discussion of the interrelations with other texts showed that the formulation of Judg 20:48 was influenced by several other texts (Num 31:10; Deut 2:34–35; 13:16; Josh 8:24). Even though R²'s expansion of this verse echoes Deut 13:16–17, he refrained from using the Deuteronomistic expression שרף באש and preferred instead the rare expression שלח באש that occurs also in Judg 1:8. In this case too it seems likely that the parallel derives from borrowing on the part of R².

Two formulas are shared by both Judg 2:1–5 and 20–21, but these formulas are fairly common. Three times Judg 20 designates "going up to ... Bethel" (ויעלו ... בית־אל) for oracular consultation before going to battle and for sacrifice and weeping after defeat (20:18, 23, 26–27a). Here "going up to Bethel" is connected to its status as a cult site, rather than its topographical locale.⁴⁰⁴ On the face of things, 2:1 speaks of going up from Gilgal in the low-lying Jordan valley to Bochim, which is presumed to lie in the central hills. However, since Bochim is immediately connected to an angelophany and the offering of sacrifice, the "going up" here also carries pilgrimage connotations. In any case, this sense of עלה is quite common.⁴⁰⁵ The other shared expression is וישאו קולם ויבכו (2:4; 21:4), which is a well-known narrative formula.⁴⁰⁶ Accordingly, the *verbal* analogies between 2:1–5 and 20–21 do not provide conclusive evidence on their own.

וילכו/ויצאו איש לנחלתו (Judg 2:6; 21:24). The expression איש לנחלתו [verb] occurs only twice more (Josh 24:28; Jer 12:15). Although most agree

---

402. See above, ch. 1.

403. The formula with the *piel* of the verb occurs only twice more, in 2 Kgs 8:12 (object: מבצריהם) and Ps 74:7 (object: מקדשך). The equivalent Dtr idiom is שרף באש; see, e.g., Deut 7:5, 25; 12:3; 13:17; Josh 6:24; 11:6, 9, 11.

404. See Gen 35:1, 3; 1 Sam 10:3; see also 1 Kgs 12:27–29.

405. See additionally Exod 34:24; Isa 2:3; Jer 31:6; Ps 122:4.

406. See, e.g., Gen 27:38; 29:11; Num 14:1; 1 Sam 11:4; 24:17; 30:4; 2 Sam 3:32; 13:36; Job 2:12; Ruth 1:9, 14. The parallel Ugaritic formula, *yšu gh wyṣḥ*, occurs more than thirty times in Ugaritic literature.

TEXT, SUBTEXT, AND INTERTEXTUAL MOSAIC   309

that Judg 2:6 and Josh 24:28 are related, they do not concur which was patterned upon the other.⁴⁰⁷ In any event, Judg 21:24 has a double closing formula, which probably results from redactional expansion: "At that time, the Israelites went away, each to his own tribe and clan; each left there for his own territory." Of these two formulas, verse 24aα, ויתהלכו משם בני־ ישראל בעת ההיא איש לשבטו ולמשפחתו, seems the most appropriate since the narrative revolves around family and tribal concerns. Indeed, the reference to *territory* in the second formula, verse 24aβ, ויצאו משם איש לנחלתו, is incongruous with the narrative, which makes no other mention of נחלה. By contrast, the term נחלה is appropriate to the formula in 2:6 (cf. Josh 24:28), since it concludes Joshua's career with his dismissal of the tribes so they may take possession of the territory he allotted them. From this it follows that the superfluous parallel closing formula in Judg 21:24aβ was probably added to the end of the narrative in order to create an associative link with 2:6.

IMPLICATIONS REGARDING THE REDACTION HISTORY OF JUDGES

The analysis uncovered a degree of mutual interrelation between the Gibeah story and the prologue to the book of Judges, with parallel material distributed throughout both texts (Judg 1:1–2, 8, 21; 2:1–6; 19:10–12; 20:9, 18, 23, 26, 48; 21:2, 4, 24). The bulk of the shared material originally stems from 1:1–2:6 and was reutilized in Judg 19–21 by R² (עליה בגורל, 20:9; "Who of us shall be the first to go up," etc., 20:18; כל הערים שלחו באש, 20:48; altar building and offer of sacrifice after weeping, 21:4; ויצאו משם איש לנחלתו, 21:24). Mutual influence or shared tradition might lie behind some of the other parallels, such as, ויעל/ויעלו בכים/בית־אל, 2:1; 20:18 [N¹]; Jerusalem a Jebusite town, 1:21; 19:10–12 [R²]; וישאו קולם ויבכו, 2:4; 21:4 [R²]. It appears that Judg 19–21 influenced the prologue on only one point: the association of Bethel/Bochim with weeping (2:1–5). However, this single case carries considerable weight since the identification of Bochim with Bethel depends largely upon the reader's familiarity with the role of Bethel in both the N¹ and R² strands in Judg 19–21.

The compositional analysis previously indicated that R² reworked the first Bethel scene (20:18) and added a fourth Bethel scene in 21:2–4, thus

---

407. See Judg 2:6, וישלח יהושע את־העם וילכו בני־ישראל איש לנחלתו; Josh 24:28, וישלח יהושע את־העם איש לנחלתו; see, e.g., Burney 1970, 52–53; Smend 2000, 107–8; Auld 1975, 263–65; O'Brien 1989, 80–81; Brettler 1989b, 433–35.

revising the graduated scheme upon which N[1] patterned the original three scenes (20:18, 23, 26–28).[408] A significant effect of R[2]'s revision of the composition was the creation of an *inclusio* in which the first and final scenes at Bethel in Judg 20–21 echo the opening and closing of 1:1-2 and 2:1-5:

Judg 1:1-2	Judg 20:18
	They *went up to Bethel*
[1] The Israelites inquired of YHWH, saying, "Who of us shall be the first to go up against the Canaanites and fight them?" [2] YHWH replied: *"Judah shall go up."*	and the Israelites inquired of God, saying, "Who of us shall be the first to go up and fight the Benjaminites?" YHWH replied: *Judah shall be first.*
	ויקמו <u>ויעלו בית אל</u>
<u>וישאלו</u> בני ישראל בה' <u>לאמר</u> מי יעלה לנו אל הכנעני <u>בתחלה להלחם</u> בו ויאמר ה' יהודה יעלה	<u>וישאלו</u> באלהים <u>ויאמרו</u> בני ישראל מי יעלה לנו <u>בתחלה למלחמה</u> עם בני בנימן יאמר ה' יהודה בתחלה

Judg 2:1-5	Judg 21:2-4
[1] The messenger of YHWH *went up* from Gilgal *to Bochim*.	[2] The people came *to Bethel*
	and sat there till evening before God
[4] The people *raised their voice and wept*.	and *raised their voice and wept* bitterly.
[5] So they named that place Bochim and offered sacrifice [ויזבחו] there to YHWH.	The people rose early on the next day and built an altar [מזבח] there and sacrificed burnt and peace offerings.
[1] <u>ויעל</u> מלאך ה' מן הגלגל אל <u>הבכים</u>	[2] ויבא העם <u>בית אל</u>
[4] <u>וישאו</u> העם את קולם ויבכו	וישבו שם עד הערב לפני האלהים <u>וישאו</u> קולם ויבכו בכי גדול
ויקראו שם המקום ההוא בכים <u>ויזבחו</u> שם לה'	[4] ויהי ממחרת וישכימו העם ויבנו שם <u>מזבח</u> ויעלו עלות ושלמים

In effect, this *inclusio* brackets the limits of the post-Deuteronomistic scroll of Judges.[409] That N[1] does not interact with Judg 1:1–2:5 may imply that

---

408. See above, ch. 1.
409. See also Brettler 1989a, 399; Blum 2010, 274–76.

N¹ was not yet familiar with this material.[410] If this holds, then the scroll that lay before the author of the Gibeah story (N¹) most likely opened in Judg 2:6–9 with the recapitulation of the ending of the Joshua scroll (Josh 24:28–30).[411] Moreover, the mutual relations between the R² strand of the Gibeah story and the prologue in Judg 1:1–2:5 might indicate that they stem from the same stage in the editing and revision of the Judges scroll.[412] In any case, the scribe who added the Bochim passage did little to integrate the addition into its context following the catalog of settlement failures. Instead, he made do with casting the incident as a proleptic echo of the interludes of weeping at Bethel in Judg 20–21. In this fashion, he created an envelope by means of associative links that connect the introductory additions to the appendices, and thereby set a limit to the growth of the scroll.

Thus the findings from the intertextual analysis of Judg 1:1–2:5, Judg 17–18, and Judg 19–21 present a basis for reconstructing the post-Deuteronomistic redaction that shaped the scroll of Judges and marked it off as a self-contained piece, thus disrupting the continuity of the Deuteronomistic

---

410. For example, the Israelites of N¹'s narrative are ignorant of any divine reproach delivered before them previously at "the place of weeping"/Bochim/Bethel; otherwise, it would be hard to understand why they persist in seeking a favorable oracle there. Neither does Judg 17–18 presume knowledge of the material in 1:1–2:5. To be sure, there are some points of similarity between both texts, e.g., veiled reference to Bethel (2:1–5; 17:1, 5) as well as the difficulties the Danites faced in settlement (1:34–35; 18:1). However, the exposition in 18:1 does not assume the Amorite pressure exerted upon the Danite settlement in the Shephelah, as related in 1:34–35 (cf. Josh 19:41–47). Instead 18:1 states that "no territory had fallen to their lot among the tribes of Israel," which contradicts the picture presented by both Josh 19:40–48 and Judg 1:34–35.

411. Needless to say, the problem of the overlap between Josh 24:28–31 and Judg 2:6–10 is beyond the scope of the present study. Nonetheless, I surmise that the overlapping of ends and beginnings of scrolls served as a means to indicated continuity within the scroll medium; see Haran 1985. In my opinion, the Joshua narrative ended at 24:30. This ending was reduplicated at the beginning of the Dtr account of the judges in Judg 2:6–9, with a transition in 2:10 effected by the programmatic introduction, by means of the generation that did not know YHWH. At a subsequent stage in the transmission of the Joshua scroll, this transitional element was taken up and inserted after Joshua's burial notice in Josh 24:30. In a similar vein, see also Brettler 1989b; 2002, 96–97. For further discussion, references, and views, see Blum 2010, 252–53; Kratz 2005, 197–200.

412. See Blum, 2010, 274–75; Gross 2009, 823–25, 883–85.

History. When N¹ composed the Gibeah story, the story of Micah (Judg 17–18) was already in place, preceding Samuel's birth narrative (1 Sam 1:1–28). N¹ attempted to weave his composition into its context by means of associative links with the adjacent narratives (Judg 17–18; 1 Sam 1:1–28) and tightened the ties by introducing links from Judg 19 into the Micah story. At this point, the metanarrative still moved smoothly from the death of Joshua to the introduction to the period of the judges (Josh 24:28–30/ Judg 2:6–9; 2:10–3:6). Later, the material in Judg 1:1–2:5 was composed, possibly with an eye to supplanting the account of the tribal allotments in Josh 15–19. The compositional history of this material is not entirely clear, and Judg 2:1–5 was probably composed as a later theological reinterpretation of Judg 1. Given the mutual influence between Judg 1:1–2:5 and 19–21, I think it possible that R² not only expanded and revised the Gibeah story but also played an instrumental role in shaping the prologue to Judges. Accordingly, R² appears to be responsible for delineating the book of Judges as a discrete literary entity, disregarding the prior periodization of the Deuteronomistic History.

4.11. Summary and Conclusions

The intertextual analysis of the Gibeah story showed that it interacts with a variety of texts from different strata in the Pentateuch and the Deuteronomistic History. The cases discussed evince common motifs combined with unique verbal parallels and justify the argument for intentional literary interrelation. Moreover, an unusual or dysfunctional application of parallel elements was frequently evident, and in most cases it occurred in Judg 19–21, thus indicating literary borrowing by the authors of the Gibeah story. In a few cases, the resulting similarity between the texts triggered further interaction, in which a source text absorbed elements from the borrower.[413]

Some of the texts contributed plot elements in addition to motifs and wording. For example, Gen 18–19 contributed major elements that shaped the plot of the Gibeah story, including the dual and antithetical hospitality scenes, violation of hospitality and rape as cause for the destruction of a city, concern for future progeny of the survivors, and

---

413. E.g., Josh 7:5, "*about* thirty-six men" (cf. Judg 20:31, 39); Josh 8:15, וינגעו לפני (cf. Judg 20:34, 41); Josh 8:19, "the ambush *rose* quickly from its place" (cf. 20:33, 37); Judg 17:7–9, בית־לחם יהודה (cf. Judg 19:1–2, 18).

the two-stage solution of the survivors' problem. The Ai story also contributed the major elements of the battle narrative, such as defeat followed by victory, lament "until evening" at a cult site following defeat, and victory achieved by the combined tactics of ambush and feigned retreat. Other texts contributed single plot elements, like summoning an assembly by dispatching body parts (1 Sam 11:7), holding a semijudicial hearing before carrying out judgment (Judg 20:3b–6; cf. Deut 13:15; 17:4, 9; 19:16–20), and preserving virgin girls alone from the group targeted in war (Num 31:17–18).

Materials were borrowed and reutilized in different fashions. Some of the texts contributed several elements that were woven together in a specific, parallel context in the Gibeah story, as with Gen 18:1–4 and 19:1–3 // Judg 19:3–10 (hospitality); Gen 19:1–10 // Judg 19:14–24 (breach of hospitality); 2 Sam 13:11–17 // Judg 19:23–28 (rape scenes); Josh 7:2–6, 8:1–29 // Judg 20:14–48 (battle accounts); Num 31:15–18 // Judg 21:10–12 (punitive expeditions). Following the initial creation of an analogy, the authors tended to deepen the intertextual relations by borrowing additional elements from the same sources, and distributing these throughout the Gibeah story (e.g., 2 Sam 13:16 // Judg 20:13; Num 31:4–5, 10, 49 / Judg 20:10, 48; 21:3). The Gibeah story did not provide a parallel context for all the source texts. Nonetheless, the authors distributed throughout the narrative elements they lifted from sources like the Saul narratives (1 Sam 10–14), the laws of Deuteronomy, the prologue to Judges (Judg 1:1–2:5), and the story of Micah (Judg 17–18). R^2's revisions display a familiarity with N^1's sources, yet he did not limit himself to broadening the parallels with the previous sources, but also enlarged the intertextual repertoire by drawing upon additional sources, some of which might not have been known to N^1 (e.g., Num 31; Josh 22:9–32; Judg 1:1–2:5; 2 Sam 21:1–14). In some instances, materials borrowed from different sources were woven together in a single verse.[414]

In the entire lengthy composition, only limited sections display no formal intertextual relations (19:12–13; 20:8, 11, 19–22, 24, 35, 43–44, 46; 21:1, 5–9, 13–18, 20–22). The composition of such a complex intertextual

---

414. For example, N^1 in Judg 19:19 combines references to Gen 24:25 and Judg 18:10; Judg 19:23–24 alludes to both Gen 19:7 and 2 Sam 13:12; Judg 20:40 borrows from Josh 8:20 and Deut 13:17. R^2 in Judg 20:48 has composite references to Josh 8:24; Deut 2:34–35; 3:6–7; 13:16; Num 31:10; and Judg 1:8; and Judg 21:12 borrows from Deut 22:28; Num 31:18; and Gen 19:8.

mosaic assumes that the sources that were drawn upon have attained an authoritative standing among the reading audience. It is not surprising that similar intertextually composite compositions are to be found in late biblical literature, such as the composite hymns in Jonah 2:3–10[415] and 1 Chr 16:8–36 (cf. Pss 105:1–15; 96:1–13; 106:47–48). This composite intertextual style reaches unprecedented heights in extrabiblical compositions from Qumran, such as 4QFlorilegium (4Q174), 1QDibrei Moshe (1Q22), and 4QTestimonia (4Q175), in which unmarked citations from a variety of biblical sources are woven together, resulting in a new text marked by a unique composite style and transmitting a new message. Thus the very depth and breadth of textual interreference inherent in the Gibeah story mark its affinity with the later, rather than earlier, end of the biblical literary spectrum.

Linguistic Findings Crossed with Intertextual References

Verses with no LBH	Corresponding intertexts
19:1	Judg 17:1, 7–9; 18:1
2	Deut 22:21; Judg 17:7–9; 1 Sam 27:7
4	Gen 24:54–55; Deut 22:15
5	Gen 18:5; Deut 22:15
6	Gen 24:54–55; cf. 1 Kgs 21:7; Ruth 3:7
7	Gen 19:3; cf. 24:54–55
8	Gen 19:2; Deut 22:15
13	
18	Judg 17:7–9
19	Gen 24:25; Judg 18:10
20	Gen 19:2–3
26	2 Sam 13:17
27	Deut 22:21; 2 Sam 13:17
30	Deut 4:32; 9:7; 1 Sam 8:8; 2 Sam 7:6; 1 Kgs 8:16; 10:12; 2 Kgs 21:15
20:5	2 Sam 21:5

---

415. See Wolff 1986, 131–38.

7	2 Sam 16:20-21
8	
10	Deut 22:21; Num 31:4; Josh 22:14
11	
12	Josh 22:16
13	Deut 13:6, 14; 22:21; 1 Sam 10:26-27; 11:12-13; 2 Sam 13:16
14	
18	Judg 1:1-2; 2:1
19-22	
23	Josh 7:6
24	
27	1 Sam 14:8
28	Num 31:28; Josh 22:13; Judg 18:30
29	Josh 8:2
30	
31	Josh 7:5; 8:5-6, 14, 24
33	Josh 8:19
36	Josh 8:2
37	Josh 8:19
39	Josh 8:6
40	Deut 13:17; Josh 8:20
41	Josh 8:20
47	Josh 8:15 (20); 1 Sam 14:2
21:1	
2	Josh 7:6; Judg 2:4
6	
14-15	
17-18	
20	
24	Judg 2:6
25	Judg 17:6

It is now possible to evaluate the hypothesis raised earlier, following the linguistic analysis, in which I surmised that the lack of any trace of LBH in various sections of the narrative may be due to conscious evoking of classical texts or formulas. Crossing the linguistic findings with the instances of literary intertextual relations shows that most of the sections lacking traces of LBH indeed evoke corresponding intertexts, thus validating the hypothesis that the classical language in these instances derives from the dependence upon classical sources (see the chart above). It turns out that only in limited sections did the authors achieve independent classical formulation without traces of LBH (19:13; 20:8, 11, 14, 19–22, 24, 30; 21:1, 6, 14–15, 17–18, 20). From this I conclude that the classical flavor of the story's language is mainly due to its heavy literary dependency upon classical texts. Had the authors set out to write a composition free of intertextual borrowing, their style and language might have borne even more of the hallmarks of recognizably late biblical literature.

It is also possible now to examine how N^1 and R^2 each drew upon authoritative texts in order to shape the final form of the narrative. N^1 fashioned the structure of the narrative by means of plot elements borrowed from Gen 18–19, Josh 7–8, and 1 Sam 11:7. It appears, indeed, that the plot was not conceived independently but was largely dictated by the materials at his disposal. In one case, at least, the combination of different plot elements produced an unresolved theological problem, in which the Israelites are twice defeated, even though the oracle repeatedly returned favorable replies. This difficulty may be an unintentional result of the combination of two conflicting plot elements: the defeat-victory scheme borrowed from Josh 7–8, and the conventional model of oracular consultation before taking the field.

The sources utilized by N^1 derived from: (1) the so-called Yahwistic strand of the Pentateuch (Gen 18–19); (2) the Deuteronomistic redaction of the Deuteronomic law corpus (Deut 13:6, 13–18; 17:2–13; 19:9, 16–20; 21:21; 22:13–29; 24:7); (3) the Deuteronomistic History (Deut 2:34; 3:6; 4:32; Josh 7:1–6; 8:1–29; 1 Sam 8:8; 10:26–27; 11:7, 12–13; 14:2; 2 Sam 13:11–17); and (5) postexilic compositions (Gen 24; Judg 17–18). It is reasonable to assume that the variety of sources utilized by N^1 reflects the body of literature that had achieved "classic" status by his time. Thus his use of late Deuteronomistic material does not make him a Deuteronomist or even a contemporary of the circles who produced the classic Deuteronomistic literature, but rather implies that he lived and worked a generation or two later. Since N^1 evinces no familiarity with the classic compositions of the Persian period, he probably belongs to the early stages of this period. This conclusion also helps explain how he succeeded to express himself independently, on occasion, in SBH, without noticeable slips in the direction of LBH.

Intertextual links are distributed throughout nearly the entire N¹ strand in Judg 19-20, with only limited pockets displaying wholly independent formulation (19:11-12; 20:14-22, 24, 28, 43, 45). By contrast, the N¹ material in Judg 21 demonstrates far less verbal interrelation, although the structure of the section may have been influenced by the story of Lot's daughters in Gen 19 (see independent formulation by N¹ in Judg 21:1, 6-9, 13-14, 20-22, 24). It appears that N¹ deliberately utilized sources suitable for his purpose. Thus he chose to pattern the framework of his plot upon the story of Sodom and the conquest of Ai, since they all revolve around the total destruction of a city. Motifs borrowed from the story of Sodom— breach of hospitality and threat of male rape—also supplied the moral sanction for Gibeah's destruction. This sanction was further bolstered by allusions to the law of the apostate town. N¹ also employed elements from the story of Tamar and the laws relating to sexual violations of virgin girls, since they contributed toward establishing rape as the *causus belli* for the war at Gibeah. Deuteronomistic formulas were reworked and utilized in order to comment on the happenings (19:30, "This has not happened or been seen since the day the Israelites came up from the land of Egypt till this very day"; 20:13, "so that the evil may be expunged from Israel"). N¹ also employed motifs and formulations found in the Saul narratives (1 Sam 10:26-27; 11:7, 12; 14:2), and these were usually employed to create an ironic analogy between Saul's actions and the events in the Gibeah story.

How did the use of literary allusion by N¹ help shape the purpose of his narrative? The texts that had the greatest contribution to the structure of the story dealt with the destruction of the city and justification of its fate. As it turns out, the texts borrowed from the Saul narratives had little impact upon the structure of the narrative. The Saul narratives contributed only one plot element (circulating a dismembered body as summons to assembly), and the few intertextual references to the Saul stories were incorporated into isolated verses (19:29; 20:1, 13, 47). If, as many think, Saul is the intended target of the story's polemic,[416] then it is surprising

---

416. See, e.g., Auberlin 1860, 550-56; Güdemann 1869, 365-68; Bleek 1878, 203; Brettler 1989a, 412-15; Amit 2000, 178-84.

that the author incorporated only a limited number of literary borrowings from the Saul stories and that these have limited impact upon the structure of N¹'s narrative. For this reason, I think it more likely that the target of the polemic is implied in the number of allusions to sinful cities that were wiped out along with their allies.

It seems that R² both understood and adopted N¹'s method of intertextual composition. He added further allusions to texts already employed by N¹ (the conquest of Ai, the Saul narratives, laws of Deuteronomy, and Judg 17–18) and created allusions to additional texts, which then became part of the pool of intertextual sources (Num 31; Josh 22:9–34; Judg 1:1–2:5; 2 Sam 21:1–14). That N¹ made no reference to these additional texts may indicate that they either were not known or were not available to him. Likewise, that R² was familiar with Num 31 and Josh 22:9–34 may imply that this revision is "post-Priestly." R² drew upon this augmented pool of sources to add new plot elements to the narrative, such as the quasi-judicial inquiry (Judg 20:3b–6; cf. Deut 13:15; 17:4, 9; 19:16–20) and the selection of virgin girls to be saved from extermination (Judg 21:10–12; cf. Num 31:17–18). The late redactor also expanded the battle description in order to describe the feigned retreat and the action of the ambush on the Gibeah road. R² employed a variety of techniques in incorporating the additional intertextual references: some he interpolated into the prior narrative strand (e.g., the mention of Jebus in Judg 19:10–11), while others he incorporated into reworked material (e.g., 20:29–31) or in expansions of his own composing (e.g., 20:3b–11). R²'s contribution to the purpose of the narrative is evident in the sections he composed freely, without interacting with other sources. Thus he emphasized the ideal unity of Israel as a pantribal entity, acting "as *one man* from Dan to Beer-sheba" (20:1, 8, 11), under the auspices of the sacral congregation of the עדה (20:1; 21:10, 13, 16) and קהל (20:1–2; 21:5, 8). This tendency may reflect the ideal unity inherent in the postexilic concept of the temple state, whether this concept implies an actual political entity of Persian period Yehud or derives from a utopian construct of Priestly circles.[417]

Whatever may have been the compositional history of Judg 1:1–2:5, the mutual relations between the R² strand in Judg 19–21 and the post-Deuteronomistic prologue in 1:1–2:5 suggest that they belong to the same

---

417. On the concept of the temple state, see Weinberg 1992; see critiques of the concept by Williamson 1998; Blenkinsopp 2001; Bedford 2001.

final redaction of the Judges scroll. The two scribes—N^1 and R^2—also exhibit different editorial methods with regard to the relations between the Gibeah narrative and its context in the post-Deuteronomistic editions of Judges and Samuel. N^1 concentrated on masking the lack of chronological continuity between the adjacent narratives and employed associative links to smooth the transition between them. R^2, by contrast, worked to establish a new framework for the narratives of the period between the death of Joshua and the birth of Samuel by means of mutual ties between the Gibeah story and the new prologue to Judges. R^2's efforts, in effect, worked in the opposite direction from those of his predecessor, since his contributions to the final form of the Gibeah story act to intensify the chronological disjunction between the narrative and its context. R^2 does not appear to have been troubled by this, and his aim may have been to restructure the preexisting historiographic metanarrative by marking off Judg 1–21 from the events leading up to the establishment of the monarchy.

5
Context and Purpose of the Story of the Outrage at Gibeah

The results of this study lead to the conclusion that the story of the "Outrage at Gibeah" is a post-Deuteronomistic work that was composed for its present context by an author who was familiar with a large body of biblical literature upon which he drew in constructing his narrative. The full sweep of the plot may be attributed to a single author (N^1, the primary narrative strand), but doublets, inconsistencies, and sudden changes in outlook and style indicate that the main narrative has been reworked by a later hand (R^2, the secondary revision), who added explicatory expansions in 20:3b–11, 31–35, 45–46; 21:2–5, 10–11, 15–18, and introduced language influenced by the Priestly literature. The freedom R^2 employed by adapting Priestly style to his own uses—including unique collocations, which he might have coined himself—might indicate that he read Priestly texts (or heard them performed) but did not himself belong to the Priestly circles. The geographic background and linguistic profile of the primary narrative show that the composition is firmly anchored in the early Persian period. Accordingly, the purpose of the narrative should be understood as reflecting concerns current during the early postexilic period. Behind the bizarre and gruesome narrative cast in the distant past lies a political polemic that deals with the threat of factitiousness and the dissolution of the unity of an ideal postexilic "Israel."

The only section of the narrative that might have had an independent existence is the description of the decisive battle, but even here we can only speak of an independent poetic source, which was thoroughly reworked and integrated into a prose framework based upon the story of the conquest of Ai. The original context and full extent of this verse account are uncertain. Thus the circumstances of the battle commemorated in verse may have been completely different from those related now by Judg 19–21. The circumstances that led to the battle commemorated by the song might be rooted in the border conflicts between Israel and Judah rather than in a forgotten event in the premonarchic period. No evidence was found that Hosea's allusions to a battle at Gibeah (Hos 9:9; 10:9) refer specifically to the story of the Outrage at Gibeah. More likely, Hosea's allusions refer to a now-forgotten tradition, perhaps to the event behind the poetic source utilized by N¹. Thus I conclude that any relationship one might find between the battle scene in Judg 20 and Hosea's references in Hos 9:9 and 10:9 is best explained as deriving from independent reference to a shared source.

The post-Deuteronomistic character of the composition is evident from the paucity of Deuteronomistic idiom. In the few cases when Deuteronomistic idiom does occur in Judg 19–21, it has been employed in an uncharacteristic fashion that points to late derivative use. For example, the idiom עשה (לא) הישר בעיני) nearly always occurs in the Deuteronomistic History in connection with (in)fidelity to YHWH; however, the theme of apostasy is totally missing from Judg 19–21. Similarly, the *Herausführungsformel* is regularly used by the Deuteronomist scribes in expository discourses marking critical points in the historical narrative,¹ and with the exception of Judg 19:30 it always relates to the relations between the people and YHWH. By contrast, the formula in Judg 19 occurs in connection with the breakdown of social relations, and the incident related neither marks a turning point, nor reverberates elsewhere in the historical narrative.

Finally, the Deuteronomistic injunction to eradicate evil (ובערת הרע) is regularly addressed in the second person, while in Judg 20:13 the narrator has changed the address to the first person plural in order to adapt it to its context in the narrative. This change places the Benjaminites ("you") in opposition to "all Israel" ("us"). The ideal "pantribal" body addresses Benjamin in the second person when voicing their demands to hand over the men of Gibeah, while establishing their authority to enforce the demands by voicing the Deuteronomistic injunction in the first person plural. The placement of the injunction at this point in the narrative casts the story as

---

1. E.g., the retrospective discourse on the plains of Moab (Deut 9:7), the institution of monarchy (1 Sam 8:8), the dynastic promise to David (2 Sam 7:6), the consecration of the temple (1 Kgs 8:16), and the announcement of judgment against Judah (2 Kgs 21:15).

CONTEXT AND PURPOSE   323

an illustration of how Deuteronomic legislation should ideally be enforced.[2] Notwithstanding, the story does not really illustrate any specific Deuteronomic law but only certain motifs that have been transformed within the narrative. For example, the offense, which incited the intertribal war—namely, the rape of the concubine—significantly differs from the Deuteronomic laws of sexual assault.[3] Moreover, the only offense in Deuteronomy that is punishable by decimation of an entire population is the incitement of a whole city to worship other gods (Deut 13:13–18). By contrast, the crime committed in Gibeah is neither incitement nor apostasy, but sexual assault and homicide, and these entail individual, rather than corporate, punishment. While the narrator seems aware of Deuteronomic legal motifs, the story does not interact with specific laws and does not illustrate their application. Instead, I think the "extermination of evil" formula serves to justify the far-reaching steps taken in the narrative and to excuse the considerable gap in the plot between the cause (rape of a woman) and the result (decimation of Benjamin). Such use of the formula does not further the themes of the Deuteronomistic History, and accordingly is more derivative, than properly Deuteronomistic. In conclusion, while the authors of the primary narrative and the later revision seem to be familiar with the Deuteronomistic History (N[1] and R[2]) and Priestly literature (only R[2]), their innovative use of Deuteronomistic and Priestly idiom places them at a distance from the mainstream Deuteronomistic and Priestly circles.

Further support for the hypothesis that the narrative was composed in the postexilic period derives from the linguistic analysis of its language. The "classical" flavor permeating the story's language and style is superficial and results from the author's drawing upon the stock of texts that had attained by his time a classic or authoritative standing. At the same time, different characteristics of Late Biblical Hebrew (LBH) are distributed throughout the text, in both main and secondary strata. The incidence of LBH in the narrative cannot be dismissed as the result of intervention by

---

2. See Jüngling 1981, 265–69.
3. The laws of sexual assault (Deut 22:22–29) distinguish between marital status of the victim and place of the attack. The offense in the story should fall under two rubrics: "fornication with a married woman" (בעולת בעל, Deut 22:22), and "assault in the city" (Deut 22:23–24). However, these laws, as formulated, do not envision circumstances embedded in the Gibeah story, namely, nonconsensual fornication with a married woman or the possibility that a victim in the city may cry out without any help forthcoming.

the late redactor, since there is no trace of R² in chapter 19, even though this section also displays LBH usage and innovative expressions. Notwithstanding, the amount of LBH usage is quite limited in relation to compositions like Ezra-Nehemiah and Chronicles. Therefore, the language of the composition should probably be characterized as "transitional LBH." This allows us to further narrow down the time of composition to the early postexilic period.

Both N¹ and R² constructed large sections of the narrative from plots, motifs, and verbal formulations that they extracted from the stock of received literature. The pool of texts upon which N¹ drew included the non-Priestly strand in the Pentateuch (Gen 18–19); the Deuteronomistic redaction of the Deuteronomic law corpus (Deut 13:6, 13–18; 17:2–13; 19:13, 16–20; 21:21; 22:13–29; 24:7); the Deuteronomistic History (Deut 2:34; 3:6; 4:32; Josh 7:1–6; 8:1–29; 1 Sam 8:8; 10:26–27; 11:7, 12–13; 14:2; 2 Sam 13:11–17); as well as postexilic compositions (Gen 24; Judg 17–18). Such a mass of allusions to so many different texts is unparalleled in the Deuteronomistic History. That N¹ was familiar with the later Deuteronomistic strata of Deuteronomy as well as with postexilic compositions gives a tentative context for the initial composition of the narrative.[4] R² not only tightened the existing literary links with additional allusions to the texts referred to by N¹, but added new allusions to texts stemming from the latest layer of the Priestly strand in the Hexateuch, namely, Num 31 and Josh 22:9–34.

The geographical background of the narrative in Judg 19–21 helps evaluate the historical reality behind the narrative. Since the material evidence from the excavations of Gibeah (Tel el-Ful) indicates that the site did not become a town until the late eighth-seventh centuries, the description of a premonarchic town at Gibeah in Judg 19–20 must be either fictional or anachronistic. In light of the fact that the settlement at Gibeah reached its peak in the seventh-sixth centuries and was abandoned after the beginning of the Persian period, the possibility should be considered that the description of the battle leading to the destruction of Gibeah reflects the circumstances related to the times of the story's author. Similarly, the role Bethel and Mizpah play in the narrative best matches the situation prevailing during the Babylonian and early Persian period, when Mizpah served as a major administrative center, and older cult sites, like Bethel, regained

---

4. Similarly, see Gross 2009, 868–69.

their standing until the temple cult in Jerusalem was restored in the at the end of the sixth century.

Most scholars have followed one of three different approaches regarding the purpose of the story of the Outrage at Gibeah and found that it serves either as a justification for the institution of monarchy, an anti-Saulide polemic or an anti-Benjaminite polemic. The first approach views the Gibeah story as an introduction to the story of the foundation of the monarchy, since it is thought to illustrate the lawlessness and anarchy that prevail in a society with no central authority.[5] Thus it is supposed that the story argues for the necessity of kingship as a means to maintain social order. However, the details of the story do not support this view, for the tribes spontaneously act in perfect accord to avenge the wrong committed by the people of Gibeah, and it is doubtful that a king could either prevent the crime or act with greater efficacy to punish the wrongdoers. Indeed, apart from the editorial framing statements, "In those days there was no king in Israel" (Judg 19:1a; 21:25a), nothing in the story implies that it overtly or covertly deals with kingship or the need for monarchic rule. This editorial frame was shown to have been tacked on to the narrative in order to insert it into its context, and therefore it cannot indicate anything about the composition's intent.[6] If anything, the story seems to extol an ideal view of a leaderless society capable of acting to enforce the social norms and values. Thus the placement of the Gibeah story within its context does *not* supply a proper introduction to the story of the founding of the monarchy.

The second approach, which views the story as an anti-Saulide polemic, is based upon the borrowed formulations from the story of Saul. These create a web of analogy between events in the narrative and actions undertaken by Saul. Moreover, the sites at which the events of the story occur led different readers to conclude that Saul is the covert subject of the story, particularly since Gibeah is represented as Saul's hometown, where he later holds court as king (e.g., 1 Sam 10:10; 11:4; 26:1), while Jabesh-gilead is central to the story of Saul's popular acclamation as king (1 Sam 11). In addition, placement of the first hospitality scene in Bethlehem creates an antithetical analogy between this town and Gibeah, site of the concubine's rape and murder. Thus the mention of these two cities,

---

5. See, e.g., Crüsemann 1978, 162; Jüngling 1981, 275–78, 292–93; Veijola 1977, 15–29; Mayes 2001, 256–58.

6. See also Noth 1962, 79; Amit 1999, 351.

Gibeah and Bethlehem, has been thought to allude to the two kings associated with them, Saul and David, and even to "typify" them according to their respective town of origin.[7] This reading seems to be further borne out by the apparently superfluous scene in which the Levite deliberates over spending the night in Jebus/Jerusalem (Judg 19:10–12).[8] The choice to include this scene in the narrative might have been calculated to afford the reader the opportunity to consider how the outcome of the story might have been different if only the Levite had accepted his servant's advice. In other words, the scene invites the reader to compare Benjaminite Gibeah with Jebusite Jerusalem, which the reader knows as the royal city of the house of David. Thus different signs in the story might imply that it covertly deals with rival royal lineages and indirectly supports David's line by directing polemic against Saul's town and tribe.[9]

Nonetheless, it is unlikely that the critical attitude toward Saul provided the impetus for composing this story. Allusions to the Saul narrative are few, sporadic, and unsystematic. The various elements in the composition—depiction of characters, allusions, and opposition between Gibeah and both Bethlehem and Jerusalem—do not work together to denigrate Saul and thereby to indirectly support David's line, for the inner-biblical allusions do not create a consistent analogy in which specific characters in the story may be viewed as Saul's and David's alter egos. While it may be suggested that Saul is represented by the Levite, who dismembers the concubine's corpse, the Levite is related neither to the town of Gibeah nor to the tribe of Benjamin, but comes from Mount Ephraim and suffers at the hands of the people of Gibeah. In addition, if the Levite is supposed

---

7. See, e.g., Auberlen 1860, 550–56; Güdemann 1868, 365–68; Bleek 1878, 203; Brettler 1989a, 412–15; Amit 1994, 35; 2000, 184–88; de Hoop 2004, 25–26; Stipp 2006, 140–59; 2011, 231–34.

8. The superfluity of the scene is apparent upon considering an alternative formulation based upon vv. 10–15: "Since the man did not want to stay, he departed on his way and came as far as **Gibeah**, accompanied by a pair of pack donkeys and his concubine. As they approached **Gibeah**, the day had waned …, so they turned aside there in order to stop over at Gibeah." 10 וְלֹא־אָבָה הָאִישׁ לָלוּן וַיָּקָם וַיֵּלֶךְ וַיָּבֹא עַד־נֹכַח יְבוּס הִיא יְרוּשָׁלִָם [גִּבְעָה] וְעִמּוֹ צֶמֶד חֲמֹרִים חֲבוּשִׁים וּפִילַגְשׁוֹ עִמּוֹ. 11 הֵם עִם־יְבוּס [גִּבְעָה] וְהַיּוֹם רַד מְאֹד וַיֹּאמֶר הַנַּעַר אֶל־אֲדֹנָיו לְכָה־נָּא וְנָסוּרָה אֶל־עִיר־הַיְבוּסִי הַזֹּאת וְנָלִין בָּהּ. 12 וַיֹּאמֶר אֵלָיו אֲדֹנָיו לֹא נָסוּר אֶל־עִיר נָכְרִי אֲשֶׁר לֹא־מִבְּנֵי יִשְׂרָאֵל הֵנָּה וְעָבַרְנוּ עַד־גִּבְעָה. 13 וַיֹּאמֶר לְנַעֲרוֹ לְךָ וְנִקְרְבָה בְּאַחַד הַמְּקֹמוֹת וְלַנּוּ בַגִּבְעָה אוֹ בָרָמָה. 14 וַיַּעַבְרוּ וַיֵּלֵכוּ וַתָּבֹא לָהֶם הַשֶּׁמֶשׁ אֵצֶל הַגִּבְעָה אֲשֶׁר לְבִנְיָמִן.

9. See, e.g., Güdemann 1869, 364–66; Crüsemann 1978, 164; Brettler 1989a, 412–15; Amit 1994; 2000, 184–88; 2006, 656–58; Stipp 2006, 2011.

to represent Saul, we might expect a sharp contrast between his character and that of the concubine's father, whose home in Bethlehem might signal that he represents David. However, the father's figure is not depicted in an ideal fashion, and he may even be viewed as an overbearing host, who pressed his guest to make a late departure and in so doing shares in the responsibility for tragic outcome of the subsequent events. If Saul was the subject of the story's polemic, then it is surprising that the author did not devise a consistent set of analogies or that he incorporated only a limited amount of material drawn from the story of Saul—material that had little impact on the structure of the primary narrative of the Outrage at Gibeah.[10] Thus it is necessary to consider the possibility that the primary target of the story's polemic is not Saul but rather another subject.

The cumulative evidence suggests that the third approach hits closest to the mark by relating the story's purpose with the anti-Benjaminite orientation of the narrator.[11] There can be no doubt that the Gibeah story was conceived as an anti-Benjaminite polemic, given that the explicit comments in 19:16 and 20:4, 12–14 shape the readers' attitude toward Benjamin throughout the rest of the narrative. Although the story concludes with the rehabilitation of Benjamin, this ending was necessitated by the context for which the narrative was intended. The author probably wanted to kill off Benjamin but was constrained by the fact that Benjamin, as both a lineage and a territory, is central to the story of the foundation of the monarchy. Thus, as a compromise, the final act of the story explains that Benjamin survived—although greatly reduced—only thanks to the concern of the other tribes for the ideal wholeness of Israel. Thus the narrative's purpose is best indicated by its avowed subject, namely, the wrongdoings of Benjamin and its unwarranted preservation from annihilation, based solely on the idea that no means be spared to prevent the violation of the wholeness of "all Israel."

The intertextual references that most significantly influenced the shape of the narrative dealt with the theme of the corrupt city, which is completely destroyed due to the evil doings of its inhabitants (Gen 19; Josh 7–8; Deut 13:13–18). The historical circumstances of the period of the composition of the story of the Outrage at Gibeah provide a prism for understanding the analogy between Gibeah, on the one side, and Sodom,

---

10. See also Gross 2009, 821.
11. See, e.g., Eissfeldt 1963, 75–77; Schunck 1963, 67; Roth 1963, 300; Stone 1988, 473.

Ai, and the apostate town, on the other side. Gibeah represents an archetype of a town that thrived, relatively, during the period of the Babylonian conquest, when Jerusalem and its southern environs were badly depleted. At this time, Gibeah appears to have expanded, perhaps with an influx of refugees from the area of Jerusalem, and similar growth is apparent throughout other sites in Benjamin as well.[12] Jeremiah 37:12–16 reflects a negative attitude held by Judahite royalists, for whom those fleeing to Benjamin were not held to be refugees but traitors to the Judean cause and Babylonian collaborators. During the period of Babylonian rule, the towns of Benjamin may have gained in prestige and economic status, as the administrative center was transferred from Jerusalem to Mizpah in Benjamin. Moreover, while the Jerusalem temple lay in ruins, cult sites, like Bethel on the northern border of Benjamin, offered an alternative for conducting propitiatory rites and may have attracted pilgrims from more distant areas. The status of the area of Benjamin and Benjaminite lineage traditions in the postexilic period is further borne out by Benjamin's prominence in the book of Chronicles.[13] That the final form of Chronicles' genealogical prologue includes two lengthy (albeit composite) Benjaminite lineages might indicate that throughout the Persian period a strong family located in the environs of Gibeah or Gibeon cultivated a lineage tradition linking them to the claims of a long-dead king who presumably founded the monarchy without founding a dynasty.[14] However, whether the family not only adhered to the ancient Saulide family burial at Zela (2 Sam 21:14) but also fostered hopes for advancement on the basis of their tradition of a Saulide lineage is a matter for speculation.[15] On the one hand, such a scenario appears plausible, since lineages serve as a means to legitimize claims to rights, holdings, and possessions. But on the other hand, there is no textual documentation that outwardly represents Persian period Saulide claims.

The end of Babylonian rule afforded the opportunity to rebuild Jerusalem and rehabilitate its temple. Whereas Persian imperial policy supported the rehabilitation of the temples in conquered lands, such a

---

12. See, e.g., N. Lapp 1981, 39, 43–44; Blenkinsopp 1998, 2003; Lipschits 1998, 472–82; 1999, 158–59, 179–85; 2005, 195–97, 204–5, 241.

13. See Knoppers 2006.

14. See Brettler 1989a, 413–15; Edelman 2001, 77–83; Knoppers 2006, 206–10.

15. See the extended argument of Edelman (2001) and P. Davies (2007) in favor of a resurgence of Saulide-Davidic rivalry in the Persian period.

CONTEXT AND PURPOSE   329

venture was ultimately dependent upon significant local support.[16] Late sources indicate difficulties in repopulating Jerusalem (Neh 7:4; 11:1-2), while attempts to explain the destruction of the temple as a willed act of abandonment by YHWH undoubtedly led to a decline in its prestige. This theological quandary surely added to the difficulties in recruiting the resources necessary for the temple rebuilding (see Hag 1:2-11).[17] A positive ideological platform for rebuilding the temple has been discerned in postexilic prophetic literature, according to which YHWH chose to renew his residence in his city (see Hag 1:7-8; Zech 8:2-15).[18] It possible that this positive rhetorical stance, in support of the rehabilitation of Jerusalem, was accompanied by negative rhetoric intended to delegitimize "Benjamin" by means of its fictional representation as a factious entity, which goes to war to protect one of its cities from just retribution.[19] Although the depiction of Benjamin as an entity, rather than a region, is anachronistic, the story's author adopted the tribal representation since it was appropriate to the setting in the premonarchic period.

This explanation best accounts for the context and purpose of the composition as well as the choice of intertexts it engages. Admittedly, the author's purpose might have been served better by targeting one of Benjamin's principal cities, such as Mizpah or Bethel. Instead, both these cities receive favorable treatment in the story. The positive attitude toward Mizpah and Bethel in the story might have stemmed from the standing of these towns in the author's time. Indeed, the representation of Bethel as a *legitimate* cult site indicates that no layer of the story is driven by the ideology of cult centralization. This probably is a further indication that comprehensive narrative was composed prior to the restoration of the Jerusalem temple. Gibeah, however, was abandoned about one generation into the Persian period. Furthermore, the choice of Gibeah as the target of the story might have been motivated by the existence of a prior poetic source about a war that took place there. Thus the availability of a prior source dealing with a long-forgotten event may have been a leading factor in choosing Gibeah to represent the Benjaminite "Sodom."

The view presented here regarding the historical context and purpose of the composition of the story of the Outrage at Gibeah casts addi-

---

16. Briant 2002, 43-48.
17. See, e.g., Tadmor 1999; Bedford 2001, 303-4.
18. Bedford 2001, 234-64.
19. See Guillaume 2004, 202-11.

tional light on the tension within the story between separatism and the ideal unity of "all Israel." Although the final chapter of the story revolves around the concern to uphold the completeness of the pantribal framework by means of Benjamin's restoration, the oath against connubium with Benjamin remains in force. Here the narrator employs the story's Israelites to voice his concerns regarding lineage and connubium as a means for preserving and strengthening self-identity. The narrator identifies with a group that refrains from entering into blood alliance with Benjaminites, and those who do so are either allies of Benjamin or were coerced. Notwithstanding the lament that "a tribe has been cut off from Israel" (21:6), the narrator betrays the outlook of an exclusivist in-group vis-à-vis Benjamin and all those allied with them through blood ties. It is tempting to tie this outlook to the attitude adopted by the minority elite of Persian era "returnees" toward connubium and lineage as a means for preserving their self-identity, but it is questionable whether such conclusions are warranted by the evidence of the text.[20] The list of returnees in Ezra-Nehemiah includes a contingent identified by place of origin rather than lineage, and most of these place names are Benjaminite towns (Ezra 2:23–28; Neh 7:27–32). Even if this list originally had a different purpose (such as a census list of those remaining in Benjamin and other environs), it has been appropriated and set within the context of the returnee list.[21] Hence, according to the exclusivist ideology of the returnees in Ezra-Nehemiah, Benjaminite "returnees" are part of "Israel" and included within the scope of connubium. Furthermore, Benjamin was an integral part of the province of Yehud, as it previously had been of Judah.[22] There also are no grounds to view the Benjaminites of the story as a cipher for inhabitants of Samaria, and to view the anti-Benjamin polemic as indicative of a broader anti-Samarian sentiment. Indeed, the only "Samarians" in the story are the two Ephraimites—the Levite and his host in Gibeah. Thus it seems preferable to view the story as a reflection of conflicting interests between rival groups within Yehud—those who advanced the restoration of Jerusalem against those who backed the relatively new preeminence of Benjaminite towns.

---

20. These conclusions, however, are upheld by Guillaume 2004, 210–12.
21. See, e.g., discussion by Williamson 1985, 21–34; Lipschits 2005, 158–68; Knauf 2006, 301–2.
22. Na'aman 2009a.

The placement of the story of the Outrage at Gibeah between the story of Micah's image (Judg 17–18) and Samuel's birth narrative (1 Sam 1) is also indicative of its purpose. On the one hand, the Gibeah story is an independent and self-contained narrative,[23] which could easily have between placed at a number of different junctures, such as following Judg 1 (see Josephus, *Ant.* 5.2.8 §§120–170), after the ark narrative (1 Sam 4:1–7:1), or even between any of the savior stories in Judges. On the other hand, we have seen that recurring catchphrases link the Gibeah story to the two narratives immediately preceding and following, thus indicating that the narrative was composed for its present context. Thus, even though we may be justified in interpreting the aims of the narrative as an independent composition, we can achieve full appreciation of its purpose only by considering how it functions within the context for which it was composed.

This placement of the story stems from a mode of revision that I call "overriding." The author who utilizes this method refrains from reworking or otherwise emending the material he received but "overrides" its message by appending new blocks of narrative that challenge the reader to question the concepts and ideals embodied in the previous metanarrative.[24] The scribes who employed the tactic of "overriding" did not integrate their texts into the narrative strand of the host composition but simply placed them alongside the previous narrative, generally at strategic junctures: preceding introductions, as with the alternate account of the conquest (Judg 1:1–2:5), or following summations, as with the notices tacked on to report of Moses's death (Deut 34:7–9, 10–12), the lists following the summary of the conquest (Josh 13:1–19:48), the account of the covenant at Shechem (Josh 24), and the report about life under Babylonian rule (2 Kgs 25:22–30).[25]

By and large, the overriding purpose of texts such as these has been overlooked. The old approach viewed these blocks as editorial accidents

---

23. The only data in the story that are dependent upon external narratives are the mention of the ark and Phinehas ben Eleazar (20:27b–28a), which severs the continuity between the speech marker (v. 27a) and the speech itself (20:28b). Neither Phinehas nor the ark figures further in the story. Thus the parenthetic comment in vv. 27b–28a undoubtedly is a secondary gloss; see, e.g., Wellhausen 1957, 237; Moore 1895, 434; Burney 1970, 448; Veijola 1977, 22; Becker 1990, 276.

24. This method was already employed by second-millennium cuneiform scribes in the revision of law collections; see Otto 1994.

25. See Edenburg 2012c.

or appendices, which were added in order to update the main narrative or to supplement it with antiquarian information derived from alternate sources for which no proper context was found within the stream of the main narrative.[26] But the view of these materials as incidental leftovers obscures the editorial intentions that might have led to their inclusion in the historiographic narrative. More recently, canonical or final-form critics have despaired of reconstructing the redaction history of the biblical compositions and instead try to make sense of their final form. This approach has led to forced interpretations of unified and surprisingly symmetric structures, which these critics uncover in the final form of Judges and other books of the Former Prophets.[27] Needless to say, this approach is oblivious to the role revision plays in producing the text's final form.

Accordingly, we should examine how the story of the Outrage at Gibeah overrides a previous tendency inherent in the Deuteronomistic History. In my opinion, the placement of an anti-Benjaminite polemic prior to the narrative block dealing with the establishment of the monarchy acts to counterbalance the positive attitude toward Benjamin, which is apparent in the Deuteronomistic History, and predisposes the reader to suspect all things associated with Benjamin and Gibeah. In this context, the story serves to *override* the portrayal of Benjamin as the instrument through which YHWH manifests his favor in providing a divinely ordained king to rule Israel. This editorial tactic leads the reader to question not only the legitimacy of Benjamin, its towns, and populace, but also to view as dubious any institution born on Benjaminite soil.

Finally, the results of this study shed light on the stages that severed the continuity between the scrolls making up the Deuteronomistic History, thereby producing the books of the Former Prophets as we know them. With regard to Judges, the final stage in the process was the work of the scribe I identify as R^2. This scribe not only revised the story of the Outrage at Gibeah but incorporated intertextual references to Judg 1:1–2:5, and thus established the boundaries of Judges as a discrete book. In light of R^2's affinity with Priestly literature, it is possible that he belonged to the same scribal circle that was responsible for the Priestly revision of Joshua. Furthermore, since his contributions to Judg 1:1–2:5 and Judg 19–21 bracketed off Judges from the original narrative continuity of the

---

26. See, e.g., Auberlen 1860, 536–68; Noth 1991, 168; McCarter 1984, 16–19.
27. See, e.g., Peckham 1985; O'Connell 1996; Sweeney 1997; Wong 2006.

Deuteronomistic History, the possibility should also be considered that he might have also been involved in forming the appendices to Samuel. These conjectures help explain the similarities in style, motifs, and tendency that Judg 19-21 shares with Josh 22:9-34 and 2 Sam 21:1-14.

These findings may help reconstruct the process by which a discrete book of Judges emerged out of the continuous historical narrative in the Deuteronomistic History. The first stage saw the development of the account of the period of the Judges within the Deuteronomistic History. In this stage, the narrative of the period of the Judges included Judg 2:7-12:15 and was continued in 1 Sam 1-3.[28] In the second stage, the Micah and Danite narrative (Judg 17-18) was added, breaking the continuity of the account of the Judges. The discontinuity was masked however, by associative ties that link the narrative to its immediate context at that stage. Thus the opening of Judg 17:1, "There was a man from Mount Ephraim," picks up on the burial notice of Abdon who was buried at Pirathon in the land of Ephraim (Judg 12:15), while the conclusion of the story with the extraneous note that Micah's image was kept at Dan "all the days the house of God stood at Shiloh" (Judg 18:31), picks up on the mentions of the house of YHWH at Shiloh in Samuel's birth narrative (1 Sam 1: 7, 24). The third stage was marked by N^1's composition of the Outrage at Gibeah story, which was devised for its context between Judg 17-18 and 1 Sam 1. Here too, N^1 utilized associative links with the adjacent narratives in order to ease the transition between the disparate materials. In addition to the many interconnections with the previous narrative in Judg 17-18, N^1 also attempted to create a tie between the Gibeah story and Samuel's birth narrative by means of the mention of the yearly festival at Shiloh (Judg 21:19), which figures prominently in 1 Sam 1:3-22. In the last stage, the Judges narrative was severed from the account of the conquest in Joshua by the introduction of the prologue Judg 1:1-2:5, and the new compositional concept of the Judges scroll as an independent work was reflected in the revision of Judg 19-21 by R^2, in which he added allusions to various the motifs and formulations from the

---

28. For the view that the collection of savior stories (Judg 3-12) had a prior literary history, see, e.g., Richter 1963, 319-43; Guillaume 2004; Gross 2009, 82-85. For the view that the Samson stories are of a later origin, and tacked on to the end of the savior stories in a post-Dtr stage, see, e.g., Noth 1991, 84-85; Gnuse 2007, 229-13; Gross 2009, 89-90. How late is debatable; therefore I have not attempted to place them within this reconstruction.

prologue. In doing so, R^2 produced a virtual frame for Judges as a separate and inclusive book.

Bibliography

Achenbach, Reinhard. 2003. *Die Vollendung der Tora: Studien zur Redaktionsgeschichte des Numeribuches im Kontext von Hexateuch und Pentateuch.* Beihefte zur Zeitschrift für altorientalische und biblische Rechtsgeschichte 3. Wiesbaden: Harrassowitz.
Adams, William J. 1987. *An Investigation into the Diachronic Distribution of Morphological Forms and Semantic Features of Extra-biblical Hebrew Sources.* PhD diss., University of Utah.
Aharoni, Yohanan. 1979. *The Land of the Bible: A Historical Geography.* Translated and edited by Anson F. Rainey. Rev. ed. Philadelphia: Westminster.
Aḥituv, Shmuel. 1992. *Handbook of Ancient Hebrew Inscriptions.* Biblical Encyclopaedia Library 7. Jerusalem: Bialik Institute.
———. 1995. *Joshua.* Mikra leYisraʾel. Tel Aviv: Am Oved.
Ahlström, Gosta W. 1984. "The Travels of the Ark: A Religio-Political Composition." *JNES* 43:141–49.
Aichele, George, and Gary A. Phillips, eds. 1995. *Intertextuality and the Bible.* Semeia 69/70. Atlanta: Scholars Press.
Albrektson, Bertil. 1981. "Difficilior Lectio Probabilior: A Rule of Textual Criticism and Its Use in Old Testament Studies." *OtSt* 21:5–18.
Albright, William F. 1922. "Gibeah of Saul and Benjamin." *BASOR* 6:8–11.
———. 1924. *Excavations and Results at Tell et-Ful (Gibeah of Saul).* AASOR 4. New Haven: Yale University Press.
———. 1939. "The Israelite Conquest of Canaan in the Light of Archaeology." *BASOR* 74:11–23.
Alt, Albrecht. 1953. "Judas Gaue unter Josia." Pages 276–88 in vol. 2 of *Kleine Schriften zur Geschichte des Volkes Israel.* Munich: Beck.
Alter, Robert. 1978. "Biblical Type-Scenes and the Uses of Convention." *Critical Inquiry* 5:355–68.
———. 1981. *The Art of Biblical Narrative.* New York: Basic Books.

———. 1986. "Sodom as Nexus: The Web of Design in Biblical Narrative." *Tikkun* 1:30–38.
Amit, Yairah. 1987. "The Dual Causality Principle and Its Effects on Biblical Literature." *VT* 37:385–400.
———. 1989. "The Multi-purpose 'Leading Word' and the Problems of Its Usage." Translated by Jeffrey M. Green. *Prooftexts* 9:99–114.
———. 1990. "Hidden Polemic in the Conquest of Dan: Judges XVII–XVIII." *VT* 60:4–20.
———. 1994. "Literature in the Service of Politics: Studies in Judges 19–21." Pages 28–40 in *Politics and Theopolitics in the Bible*. Edited by H. G. Reventlow, Yair Hoffman, and Benjamin Uffenheimer. JSOTSup 171. Sheffield: JSOT Press.
———. 1999. *The Book of Judges: The Art of Editing*. Translated by Jonathan Chipman. BibInt 38. Leiden: Brill.
———. 2000. *Hidden Polemics in Biblical Narrative*. BibInt 25. Translated by Jonathan Chipman. Leiden: Brill.
———. 2001. *Reading Biblical Narratives: Literary Criticism and the Hebrew Bible*. Translated by Yael Lotan. Minneapolis: Augsburg Fortress.
———. 2006. "The Saul Polemic in the Persian Period." Pages 647–61 in *Judah and the Judeans in the Persian Period*. Edited by Oded Lipschits and Manfred Oeming. Winona Lake, IN: Eisenbrauns.
Anbar, Moshe. 1982. "Genesis 15: A Conflation of Two Deuteronomic Narratives." *JBL* 101:39–55.
———. 1985. "The Story about the Building of an Altar on Mount Ebal: The History of Its Composition and the Question of the Centralization of the Cult." Pages 304–9 in *Das Deuteronomium: Entstehung, Gestalt und Botschaft*. Edited by Norbert Lohfink. BETL 67. Leuven: Leuven University Press.
Andersen, Francis I., and David Noel Freedman. 1980. *Hosea*. AB 24. Garden City, NY: Doubleday.
———. 1989. *Amos*. AB 24A. New York: Doubleday.
Arnold, Patrick M. 1989. "Hosea and the Sin of Gibeah." *CBQ* 51:447–60.
———. 1990. *Gibeah: The Search for a Biblical City*. JSOTSup 79. Sheffield: JSOT Press.
Arnold, William Rosenszweig. 1917. *Ephod and Ark*. Cambridge: Harvard University Press.
Assis, Eliyahu. 2004. "'For It Shall Be a Witness between Us': A Literary Reading of Josh 22." *SJOT* 18:208–31.

Auberlen, Carl August. 1860. "Die drei Anhänge des Buchs der Richter in ihrer Bedeutung und Zusammengehörigkeit." *TSK* 33:536–68.
Auld, A. Graeme. 1975. "Judges I and History: A Reconsideration." *VT* 25:261–85.
———. 1976. "Review of Boling's Judges: The Framework of Judges and the Deuteronomists." *JSOT* 1:41–46.
———. 1980. *Joshua, Moses and the Land: Tetrateuch-Pentateuch-Hexateuch in a Generation Since 1938*. Edinburgh: T&T Clark.
———. 1994. *Kings without Privilege*. Edinburgh: T&T Clark.
Avigad, Nahman, and Benjamin Sass. 1997. *Corpus of West Semitic Stamp Seals*. Jerusalem: Israel Academy of Sciences and Humanities.
Avioz, Michael. 2007. "The Role and Significance of Jebus in Judges 19." *BZ* 51:249–56.
Bach, Alice. 1999. "Rereading the Body Politic: Women and Violence in Judges 21." Pages 389–401 in *Women in the Hebrew Bible: A Reader*. Edited by Alice Bach. New York: Routledge.
Bal, Mieke. 1988. *Death and Dissymmetry: The Politics of Coherence in the Book of Judges*. Chicago: University of Chicago Press.
Bar-Efrat, Shimon. 2004. *Narrative Art in the Bible*. Translated by D. Shefer-Vanson. JSOTSup 70. Repr. London: T&T Clark.
Barr, James. 1987. *Comparative Philology and the Text of the Old Testament*. Winona Lake, IN: Eisenbrauns.
Barthes, Roland. 1979. "From Work to Text." Pages 73–81 in *Textual Strategies: Perspectives in Post-Structuralist Criticism*. Edited by Josué V. Harari. Ithaca, NY: Cornell University Press.
Barton, John. 2004. "Dating the 'Succession Narrative.'" Pages 95–106 in *In Search of Pre-exilic Israel: Proceedings of the Oxford Old Testament Seminar*. Edited by John Day. London: T&T Clark.
Bauer, Uwe F. W. 1998. *"Warum nur übertretet ihr SEIN Geheiss!": Eine synchrone Exegese der Antierzählung von Richter 17–18*. BEATJ 45. Frankfurt am Main: Lang.
Bautch, Richard. 2007. "Intertextuality in the Persian Period." Pages 25–35 in *Approaching Yehud: New Approaches to the Study of the Persian Period*. Edited by Jon L. Berquist. SemeiaSt 50. Atlanta: Society of Biblical Literature.
Bechtel, Lynn M. 1994. "What If Dinah Is Not Raped? (Genesis 34)." *JSOT* 62:19–36.
Becker, Uwe. 1990. *Richterzeit und Königtum: Redaktionsgeschichtliche Studien zum Richterbuch*. BZAW 192. Berlin: de Gruyter.

Bedford, Peter Ross. 2001. *Temple Restoration in Early Achaemenid Judah.* JSJSup 65. Leiden: Brill.

Beentjes, Pancratius C. 1996. "Discovering a New Path of Intertextuality: Inverted Quotations and Their Dynamics." Pages 31–50 in *Literary Structure and Rhetorical Strategies in the Hebrew Bible.* Edited by L. J. de Regt, Jan de Waard, and J. P. Fokkelman. Assen: Van Gorcum.

Begg, Christopher. 1986. "The Function of Josh 7:1–8:29 in the Deuteronomistic History." *Bib* 67:320–34.

Bendavid, Abba. 1951. *Biblical Hebrew and Mishnaic Hebrew* [Hebrew]. 2nd ed. Tel Aviv: Devir.

———. 1967. *Biblical Hebrew and Mishnaic Hebrew* [Hebrew]. 2nd ed. Tel Aviv: Devir.

Ben-Porat, Ziva. 1976. "The Poetics of Literary Allusion." *PTL* 1:105–28.

———. 1978. "The Reader, the Text, and Literary Allusion" [Hebrew]. *HaSifrut* 26:1–25.

———. 1985. "Intertextuality" [Hebrew]. *HaSifrut* 34:170–78.

Ben Zvi, Ehud. 1992. Review of *Biblical Hebrew in Transition: The Language of Ezekiel,* by M. F. Rooker. *CBQ* 54:540–42.

———. 1997. "The Urban Center of Jerusalem and the Development of the Literature of the Hebrew Bible." Pages 194–209 in *Urbanism in Antiquity: From Mesopotamia to Crete.* Edited by Walter E. Aufrecht, Steven W. Gauley, and Neil A. Mirau. JSOTSup 244. Sheffield: Sheffield Academic.

———. 2009. "The Communicative Message of Some Linguistic Choices." Pages 260–90 in *A Palimpsest: Rhetoric, Ideology, Stylistics, and Language Relating to Persian Israel.* Edited by Ehud Ben Zvi, Diana V. Edelman, and Frank Polak. PHSC5. Piscataway, NJ: Gorgias.

Bergey, Ronald. 2003. "The Song of Moses (Deuteronomy 32.1–43) and Isaianic Prophecies: A Case of Early Intertextuality?" *JSOT* 28:33–54.

Berlin, Adele. 1984. "Jeremiah 29:5–7: A Deuteronomic Allusion." *HAR* 8:3–11.

Bertheau, Ernst. 1845. *Das Buch der Richter und Rut.* KHAT. Leipzig: Weidmann.

———. 1883. *Das Buch der Richter und Rut.* 2nd ed. KHAT. Leipzig: Hirzel.

Besters, André. 1965. "Le sanctuaire central dans Jud., XIX–XXI." *ETL* 41:20–41.

Beuken, Wim A. M. 1967. *Haggai–Sacharja 1–8: Studien zur Überlieferungsgeschichte der frühnachexilischen Prophetie.* Assen: Van Gorcum.

Biddle, Mark E. 2002. "Ancestral Motifs in 1 Samuel 25: Intertextuality and Characterization." *JBL* 121:617–38.
Bleek, Friedrich. 1878. *Einleitung in des Alte Testament*. Edited by Julius Wellhausen. 4th ed. Berlin: Reimer.
Blenkinsopp, Joseph. 1964. "Jonathan's Sacrilege; 1 Sam 14, 1–46: A Study in Literary History." *CBQ* 26:421–49.
———. 1972. *Gibeon and Israel: The Role of Gibeon and the Gibeonites in the Political and Religious History of Early Israel*. Cambridge: Cambridge University Press.
———. 1995. *Sage, Priest, Prophet: Intellectual and Religious Leadership in Ancient Israel*. Louisville: Westminster John Knox.
———. 1996. "An Assessment of the Alleged Pre-Exilic Date of the Priestly Material in the Pentateuch." *ZAW* 108:495–518.
———. 1998. "The Judaean Priesthood during the Neo-Babylonian and Achaemenid Periods: A Hypothetical Reconstruction." *CBQ* 60:25–43.
———. 2000. *Isaiah 1–39*. AB 19. New York: Doubleday.
———. 2001. "Did the Second Jerusalemite Temple Possess Land?" *Transeuphratene* 21:61–68.
———. 2003. "Bethel in the Neo-Babylonian Period." Pages 93–107 in *Judah and the Judeans in the Neo-Babylonian Period*. Edited by Oded Lipschits and Joseph Blenkinsopp. Winona Lake, IN: Eisenbrauns.
———. 2006 "Benjamin Traditions Read in the Early Persian Period." Pages 629–45 in *Judah and the Judeans in the Persian Period*. Edited by Oded Lipschits and Manfred Oeming. Winona Lake, IN: Eisenbrauns.
———. 2013. "Another Contribution to the Succession Narrative Debate (2 Samuel 11–20; 1 Kings 1–2)." *JSOT* 38:35–58.
Blum, Erhard. 1990. *Studien zur Komposition des Pentateuch*. BZAW 189. Berlin: de Gruyter.
———. 2010. "Der kompositionelle Knoten am Übergang von Josua zu Richter: Ein Entflechtungsvorschlag." Pages 249–80 in *Textgestalt und Komposition: Exegetische Beiträge zu Tora und Vordere Propheten*. Edited by Wolfgang Oswalt. FAT 69. Tübingen: Mohr Siebeck.
Bodi, Daniel. 2013. "The Numerical Sequence x/x + 1 in Aramaic Aḥiqar Proverbs and in Ancient Near Eastern Literature." Pages 13–25 in *Aliento: Énoncés sapientiels brefs, traductions, traducteurs et contextes culturels et historiques*. Edited by Marie-Christine Bornes-Varol and Marie-Sol Ortola. Échanges sapientiels en Méditerranée 4. Nancy: Presses Universitaires de Nancy.

Boecker, Hans Jochen. 1970. *Redeformen des Rechtslebens im Alten Testament.* 2nd ed. WMANT 14. Neukirchen-Vluyn: Neukirchener Verlag.
Bohmbach, Karla G. 1999. "Conventions/Contraventions: The Meanings of Public and Private for the Judges 19 Concubine." *JSOT* 83:83–98.
Böhme, W. 1885. "Richter c. 21." *ZAW* 5:30–36.
Boling, Robert Gordon. 1975. *Judges.* AB 6A. Garden City, NY: Doubleday.
———. 1982. *Joshua.* AB 6. Garden City, NY: Doubleday.
Born, Adrianus van den. 1954. "Etude sur quelques toponymes bibliques." *OtSt* 10:197–214.
Brettler, Marc Zvi. 1989a. "The Book of Judges: Literature as Politics." *JBL* 108:395–418.
———. 1989b. "Jud 1,1–2,10: From Appendix to Prologue." *ZAW* 101:433–35.
———. 1997. 'The Composition of 1 Samuel 1–2." *JBL* 116:601–12.
———. 2002. *The Book of Judges.* London: Routledge.
Briant, Pierre. 2002. *From Cyrus to Alexander: A History of the Persian Empire.* Translated by Peter T. Daniels. Winona Lake, IN: Eisenbrauns.
Brown, Ken. 2015. "Vengeance and Vindication in Numbers 31." *JBL* 134:65–84.
Buber, Martin. 1967. *Kingship of God.* Translated by Richard Scheimann. 3rd ed. New York: Harper & Row.
Budd, Philip J. 1984. *Numbers.* WBC 5. Waco, TX: Word.
Budde, Karl. 1888. "Die Anhänge des Richterbuches." *ZAW* 8:285–300.
———. 1890. *Die Bücher Richter und Samuel: Ihre Quellen und ihr Aufbau.* Giessen: Ricker.
———. 1897. *Das Buch der Richter.* KHAT 7. Freiburg: Mohr Siebeck.
———. 1902. *Die Bücher Samuel.* KHAT 8. Tübingen: Mohr Siebeck.
Burney, Charles Fox. 1970. *The Book of Judges with Introduction and Notes on the Hebrew Text of the Books of Kings.* New York: Ktav.
Butler, Trent C. 1983. *Joshua.* WBC 7. Waco, TX: Word.
Callaway, Joseph A. 1968. "New Evidence on the Conquest of Ai." *JBL* 87:312–20.
Campbell, Antony F. 1975. *The Ark Narrative (1 Sam 4–6; 2 Sam 6): A Form-Critical and Traditio-Historical Study.* SBLDS 16. Missoula, MT: Scholars Press.
Carlson, Rolf August. 1964. *David, the Chosen King: A Traditio-Historical Approach to the Second Book of Samuel.* Stockholm: Almqvist & Wiksell.

Carr, David McLain. 2005. *Writing on the Tablet of the Heart: Origins of Scripture and Literature*. Oxford: Oxford University Press.

———. 2011. *The Formation of the Hebrew Bible: A New Reconstruction*. Oxford: Oxford University Press.

Carroll, Robert P. 1986. *Jeremiah: A Commentary*. OTL. London: SCM.

Caspari, Wilhelm. 1911. "Der Stil des Eingangs der israelitischen Novelle." *ZWT* 53:218–53.

Cassuto, Umberto. 1973. "The Israelite Epic." Pages 69–109 in *Bible and Ancient Oriental Texts*. Vol. 2 of *Biblical and Oriental Studies*. Translated by Israel Abrahams. Jerusalem: Magnes.

Chapman, Cynthia R. 2004. *The Gendered Language of Warfare in the Israelite-Assyrian Encounter*. HSM 62. Winona Lake, IN: Eisenbrauns.

Charlesworth, James Hamilton. 2006. "Towards a Taxonomy of Discerning Influence(s) between Two Texts." Pages 41–54 in *Gesetz im frühen Judentum und im Neuen Testament: Festschrift für Christoph Burchard*. Edited by Dieter Sänger and Mathias Konradt. Fribourg: Academic Press; Göttingen: Vandenhoeck & Ruprecht.

Childs, Brevard S. 2003. "Critique of Recent Intertextual Canonical Interpretation." *ZAW* 115:173–84.

Christensen, Duane L. 1976. "The March of Conquest in Isaiah X 27 c–34." *VT* 26:385–99.

Cody, Aelred. 1969. *A History of Old Testament Priesthood*. AnBib 35. Rome: Pontifical Biblical Institute.

Cross, Frank Moore. 1953. "The Council of Yahweh in Second Isaiah." *JNES* 12:274–77.

———. 1973. *Canaanite Myth and Hebrew Epic*. Cambridge: Harvard University Press.

Cross, Frank Moore, and David Noel Freedman. 1997. *Studies in Ancient Yahwistic Poetry*. Grand Rapids: Eerdmans.

Crouch, Carly L. 2014. *Israel and the Assyrians: Deuteronomy, the Succession Treaty of Esarhaddon, and the Nature of Subversion*. ANEM 8. Atlanta: SBL Press.

Crüsemann, Frank. 1978. *Der Widerstand gegen das Königtum: Die antiköniglichen Texte des Alten Testamentes und der Kampf um den frühen israelitischen Staat*. WMANT 49. Neukirchen-Vluyn: Neukirchener Verlag.

———. 1996. *The Torah: Theology and Social History of Old Testament Law*. Translated by A. W. Mahnke. Minneapolis: Fortress.

Culler, Jonathan. 1981. *The Pursuit of Signs*. London: Routledge & Kegan Paul.
———. 2002. *Structuralist Poetics: Structuralism, Linguistics and the Study of Literature*. London and New York: Routledge.
Culley, Robert C. 1976. *Studies in the Structure of Hebrew Narrative*. Philadelphia: Fortress.
Cundall, Arthur Ernest. 1969–1970. "Judges: An Apology for the Monarchy?" *ExpTim* 81:178–81.
Davidson, Robert. 1964. "Orthodoxy and the Prophetic Word: A Study in the Relationship between Jeremiah and Deuteronomy." *VT* 14:407–16.
Davies, Graham I. 1992. *Hosea*. NCB. Grand Rapids: Eerdmans.
Davies, Philip R. 1977. "The History of the Ark in the Books of Samuel." *JNSL* 5:9–18.
———. 1992. *In Search of "Ancient Israel."* JSOTSup 148. Sheffield: JSOT Press.
———. 2007. "The Trouble with Benjamin." Pages 93–111 in *Reflection and Refraction: Studies in Biblical Historiography in Honour of A. Graeme Auld*. Edited by Robert Rezetko, Timothy Henry Lim, and W. Brian Aucker. VTSup 113. Leiden and Boston: Brill.
Day, John. 1979. "The Destruction of the Shiloh Sanctuary and Jeremiah VII 12, 14." Pages 87–94 in *Studies in the Historical Books of the Old Testament*. Edited by J. A. Emerton. VTSup 30. Leiden: Brill.
———. 1985. *God's Conflict with the Dragon and the Sea: Echoes of a Canaanite Myth in the Old Testament*. Cambridge: Cambridge University Press.
De Vries, Simon J. 1975. "Temporal Terms as Structural Elements in the Holy-War Tradition." *VT* 25:80–105.
Demsky, Aaron. 1973. "Geba, Gibeah, and Gibeon: An Historico-Geographic Riddle." *BASOR* 212:26–31.
Derrida, Jacques. 1979. "Living On / Border Lines." Translated by James Hulbert. Pages 75–176 in *Deconstruction and Criticism*. Edited by Harold Bloom. New York: Continuum.
Dietrich, Walter. 2007. "Achans Diebstahl (Jos 7): Eine Kriminalgeschichte aus frühpersischer Zeit." Pages 57–67 in *"Sieben Augen auf einem Stein" (Sach 3,9)—Studien zur Literatur des Zweiten Tempels: Festschrift für Ina Willi-Plein zum 65. Geburtstag*. Edited by Friedhelm Hartenstein and Michael Pietsch. Neukirchen-Vluyn: Neukirchener Verlag.
———. 2013. "The Layer Model of the Deuteronomistic History and the Book of Samuel." Pages 39–65 in *Is Samuel among the Deuteronomists?*

Current Views on the Place of Samuel in a Deuteronomistic History. Edited by Cynthia Edenburg and Juha Pakkala. AIL 16. Atlanta: Society of Biblical Literature.

Dijk-Hemmes, Fokkelien van. 1989. "Tamar and the Limits of Patriarchy: Between Rape and Seduction (2 Samuel 13 and Genesis 38)." Pages 135–56 in *Anti-covenant: Counter-Reading Women's Lives in the Hebrew Bible*. Edited by Mieke Bal. JSOTSup 91. Sheffield: Almond.

Dion, Paul-Eugene. 1980. "'Tu feras disparaître le mal du milieu de toi.'" *RB* 87:321–49.

———. 1991. "Deuteronomy 13: The Suppression of Alien Religious Propaganda in Israel during the Late Monarchical Era." Pages 147–216 in *Law and Ideology in Monarchic Israel*. Edited by Baruch Halpern and Deborah W. Hobson. JSOTSup 124. Sheffield: JSOT Press.

Dorsey, David A. 1991. *The Roads and Highways of Ancient Israel*. Baltimore: Johns Hopkins University Press.

Doyle, Brian. 2004. "'Knock, Knock, Knockin' on Sodom's Door': The Function of פתח/דלת in Genesis 18–19." *JSOT* 28:431–48.

Driver, Godfrey Rolles. 1947. "Mistranlations in the Old Testament." *Die Welt des Orients* 1:29–30.

———. 1951. "Hebrew Notes." *VT* 1:241–50.

Driver, Samuel Rolles. 1913. *Notes on the Hebrew Text and the Topography of the Books of Samuel*. 2nd ed. Oxford: Clarendon.

———. 1972. *An Introduction to the Literature of the Old Testament*. Gloucester, MA: Peter Smith.

Dumbrell, William J. 1983. "'In Those Days There Was No King in Israel; Every Man Did What Was Right in His Own Eyes': The Purpose of the Book of Judges Reconsidered." *JSOT* 25:23–33.

Dus, Jan. 1964. "Bethel und Mispa in Jdc. 19–21 und Jdc. 10–12." *OrAnt* 3:227–43.

Edelman, Diana Vikander. 1992. "Jabesh-Gilead." Pages 594–95 in vol. 3 of *Anchor Bible Dictionary*. Edited by David Noel Freedman. 6 vols. New York: Doubleday.

———. 2001. "Did Saulide-Davidic Rivalry Resurface in Early Persian Yehud?" Pages 69–91 in *The Land That I Will Show You: Essays on the History and Archeology of the Ancient Near East in Honor of J. Maxwell Miller*. Edited by J. Andrew Dearman and M. Patrick Graham. JSOTSup 343. Sheffield: Sheffield Academic.

Edenburg, Cynthia. 1998. "How (Not) to Murder a King: Variations on a Theme in I Sam. 24; 26." *SJOT* 12:64–85.

———. 2003. "The Story of the Outrage at Gibeah (Jdg. 19–21): Composition, Sources and Historical Context" [Hebrew]. PhD diss., Tel Aviv University.

———. 2009. "Ideology and Social Context of the Deuteronomic Women's Sex Laws (Deuteronomy 22:13–29)." *JBL* 128:43–60.

———. 2012a. "Joshua 9 and Deuteronomy, an Intertextual Conundrum: The Chicken or the Egg?" Pages 115–32 in *Deuteronomy in the Pentateuch, Hexateuch, and the Deuteronomistic History*. Edited by Raymond Person and Konrad Schmid. FAT 2/56. Tübingen: Mohr Siebeck.

———. 2012b. "'Overwriting and Overriding,' or What Is *Not* Deuteronomistic." Pages 443–60 in *Congress Volume: Helsinki, 2010*. 20th Congress of the International Organization for the Study of the Old Testament. Edited by Martti Nissinen. VTSup 148. Leiden: Brill.

———. 2012c. "Rewriting, Overwriting, and Overriding: Techniques of Editorial Revision in the Deuteronomistic History." Pages 54–69 in *Words, Ideas, Worlds: Essays in Honour of Yairah Amit*. Edited by Athalya Brenner and Frank Polak. Sheffield: Sheffield Phoenix.

———. 2014. "II Sam 21,1–14 and II Sam 23,1–7 as Post-Chr Additions to the Samuel Scroll." Pages 167–82 in *Rereading the Relecture? The Question of (Post)chronistic Influence in the Latest Redactions of the Books of Samuel*. Edited by Uwe Becker and Hannes Bezzel. FAT 2/66. Tübingen: Mohr Siebeck.

———. 2015. "Paradigm, Illustrative Narrative or Midrash: The Case of Josh 7–8 and Deuteromic/istic Law." Pages 123–37 in *The Reception of Biblical War Legislation in Narrative Contexts: Studies in Law and Narrative*. Edited by Christoph Berner and Harald Samuel. BZAW 460. Berlin: de Gruyter.

———. forthcoming a. "2 Sam 21–24: Haphazard Miscellany or Deliberate Revision?" In *Insights into Editing*. Edited by Reinhard Müller and Juha Pakkala. Contributions to Biblical Exegesis and Theology. Leuven: Peeters.

———. forthcoming b. "'David Reproached Himself': Revisiting 1 Sam 24 and 26 in Light of 2 Sam 21–24." In *The Books of Samuel: Stories-History-Reception History*. Edited by Walter Dietrich. BETL. Leuven: Peeters.

Ehrensvärd, Martin. 1997. "Once Again: The Problem of Dating Biblical Hebrew." *SJOT* 11:29–40.

———. 2006. "Why Biblical Texts Cannot Be Dated Linguistically." *HS* 47:177–89.
Ehrlich, Arnold Bogumil. 1968. *Randglossen zur hebräischen Bibel.* Vol. 3. Hildesheim: Olms.
Eissfeldt, Otto. 1925. *Die Quellen des Richterbuches.* Leipzig: Hinrichs.
———. 1963. "Der geschichtliche Hintergrund der Erzählung von Gibeas Schandtat (Richter 19–21)." Pages 54–80 in vol. 2 of *Kleine Schriften.* Edited by Rudolf Sellheim and Fritz Maass. Tübingen: Mohr Siebeck.
Elliger, Karl. 1966. *Leviticus.* HAT 4. Tübingen: Mohr Siebeck.
Elwolde, John F. 1997. "Developments in Hebrew Vocabulary between Bible and Mishnah." Pages 17–55 in *The Hebrew of the Dead Sea Scrolls and Ben Sira: Proceedings of a Symposium Held at Leiden University, 11–14 December 1995.* Edited by T. Muraoka and J. F. Elwolde. STDJ 26. Leiden: Brill.
Emmerson, Grace I. 1984. *Hosea: An Israelite Prophet in Judean Perspective.* JSOTSup 28. Sheffield: JSOT Press.
Engelkern, Karen. 1989. "פילגש *pilegeš*." *TDOT* 11:549–51.
Eskhult, Mats. 1990. *Studies in Verbal Aspect and Narrative Technique in Biblical Hebrew Prose.* Studia Semitica Upsaliensia 12. Uppsala: Almqvist & Wiksell.
———. 2003. "The Importance of Loanwords for the Dating of Biblical Hebrew Texts." Pages 8–23 in *Biblical Hebrew: Studies in Chronology and Typology.* Edited by Ian Young. JSOTSup 369. London: T&T Clark.
Exum, J. Cheryl. 1990. "The Centre Cannot Hold: Thematic and Textual Instabilities in Judges." *CBQ* 52:410–31.
Exum, J. Cheryl, and David J. A. Clines, eds. 1993. *The New Literary Criticism and the Hebrew Bible.* JSOTSup 143. Sheffield: JSOT Press.
Fales, Frederick Mario. 2012. "After Taʿyinat: The New Status of Esarhaddon's *Adê* for Assyrian Political History." *RA* 106:133–58.
Faust, Avraham. 2003. "Judah in the Sixth Century B.C.E." *PEQ* 135:37–53.
Fewell, Danna Nolan, ed. 1992. *Reading between Texts: Intertextuality and the Hebrew Bible.* Louisville: Westminster John Knox.
Finkelstein, Israel. 1988. *The Archaeology of the Israelite Settlement.* Jerusalem: Israel Exploration Society.
———, ed. 1993. *Shiloh: The Archaeology of a Biblical Site.* Tel Aviv University Institute of Archaeology Monograph Series 10. Tel Aviv: Institute of Archaeology, Tel Aviv University.

———. 2010. "Archaeology as a High Court in Ancient Israelite History." *JHS* 10. http://www.jhsonline.org/Articles/article_147.pdf.
———. 2011a. "Saul, Benjamin and the Emergence of 'Biblical Israel': An Alternative View." *ZAW* 123:348–67.
———. 2011b. "Tell el-Ful Revisited: The Assyrian and Hellenistic Periods (with a New Identification)." *PEQ* 143:106–18.
———. 2012. "The Great Wall of Tell en-Nasbeh (Mizpah), the First Fortifications in Judah, and 1 Kings 15:16–22." *VT* 62:14–28.
Finkelstein, Israel, and Thomas Römer. 2014. "Comments on the Historical Background of the Abraham Narrative: Between 'Realia' and 'Exegetica.'" *HBAI* 3:3–23.
Finkelstein, Israel, and Lily Singer-Avitz. 2009. "Reevaluating Bethel." *ZDPV* 125:33–48.
Fishbane, Michael. 1988. *Biblical Interpretation in Ancient Israel*. 2nd ed. Oxford: Clarendon.
Fitzmyer, Joseph A. 1995. *The Aramaic Inscriptions of Sefire*. 2nd ed. BibOr 19A. Rome: Pontifical Biblical Institute.
Floyd, Michael H. 2003. "Deutero-Zechariah and Types of Intertextuality." Pages 225–44 in *Bringing Out the Treasure: Inner Biblical Allusion in Zechariah 9–14*. Edited by Mark J. Boda and Michael H. Floyd. JSOTSup 370. London: Sheffield Academic.
Fokkelman, Jan P. 1992. "Structural Remarks on Judges 9 and 19." Pages 33–45 in *"Sha'arei Talmon": Studies in the Bible, Qumran, and the Ancient Near East Presented to Shemaryahu Talmon*. Edited by Michael Fishbane and Emanuel Tov. Winona Lake, IN: Eisenbrauns.
Fowler, Mervyn D. 1987. "The Meaning of *lipnê* YHWH in the Old Testament." *ZAW* 99:384–90.
Fox, Michael V. 1980. "The Identification of Quotations in Biblical Literature." *ZAW* 92:416–41.
Frankenberg, Wilhelm. 1895. *Die Composition des deuteronomischen Richterbuches*. Marburg: Elwert.
Fritz, Volkmar. 1994. *Das Buch Josua*. HAT 7. Tübingen: Mohr Siebeck.
———. 1995. *The City in Ancient Israel*. BibSem 29. Sheffield: Sheffield Academic.
Frow, John. 1990. "Intertextuality and Ontology." Pages 45–55 in *Intertextuality: Theories and Practices*. Edited by Michael Worton and Judith Still. Manchester: Manchester University Press.
Frymer-Kensky, Tikva S. 1998. "Virginity in the Bible." Pages 79–96 in *Gender and Law in the Hebrew Bible and the Ancient Near East*. Edited

by Victor H. Matthews, Bernard M. Levinson, and Tikva S. Frymer-Kensky. JSOTSup 262. Sheffield: Sheffield Academic.
Garrett, Duane A. 1997. *Hosea, Joel*. NAC. Nashville: Broadman & Holman.
Gass, Erasmus. 2005. *Die Ortsnamen des Richterbuchs in historischer und redaktioneller Perspektive*. ADPV 35. Wiesbaden: Harrassowitz.
Genette, Gérard. 1982. *Palimpsestes: La littérature au second degré*. Paris: Seuil.
Gertz, Jan Christian. 2012. *T&T Clark Handbook of the Old Testament: An Introduction to the Literature, Religion and History of the Old Testament*. London: T&T Clark.
Gesenius, Wilhelm. 1910. *Gesenius' Hebrew Grammar*. Edited by E. Kautzsch. Translated by A. E. Cowley. 2nd ed. Oxford: Clarendon.
Geus, Cornelis H. J. de. 1976. *The Tribes of Israel*. SSN 18. Assen: Van Gorcum.
Gibson, John C. L. 1975. *Aramaic Inscriptions*. Vol. 2 of *Textbook of Syrian Semitic Inscriptions*. Oxford: Clarendon.
———. 1982. *Phoenician Inscriptions*. Vol. 3 of *Textbook of Syrian Semitic Inscriptions*. Oxford: Clarendon.
Gibson, Shimon, and Gershon Edelstein. 1985. "Investigating Jerusalem's Rural Landscape." *Levant* 18:139–56.
Gitin, Seymour, Trude Dothan, and Joseph Naveh. 1997. "A Royal Dedicatory Inscription from Ekron." *IEJ* 47:1–16.
Gnuse, Robert. 2007. "Abducted Wives: A Hellenistic Narrative in Judges 21?" *SJOT* 22:228–40.
Gogel, Sandra Landis. 1998. *A Grammar of Epigraphic Hebrew*. RBS 23. Atlanta: Scholars Press.
Goldstein, Ronnie. 2002. "Joshua 22:9–34: A Priestly Narrative from the Second Temple Period." *Shnaton* 13:43–81.
Gooding, David W. 1982. "The Composition of the Book of Judges." *ErIsr* 16:70*–79*.
Gordis, Robert. 1949. "Quotations as a Literary Usage in Biblical, Oriental and Rabbinic Literature." *HUCA* 22:157–219.
———. 1950. "Democratic Origins in Ancient Israel: The Biblical 'EDAH.'" Pages 369–88 in *Alexander Marx Jubilee Volume*. New York: Jewish Theological Seminary of America.
Gordon, Pamela, and Harold C. Washington. 1995. "Rape as a Military Metaphor in the Hebrew Bible." Pages 308–25 in *A Feminist Companion to the Latter Prophets*. Edited by Athalya Brenner. FCB 8. Sheffield: Sheffield Academic.

Graham, John Allen. 1981. "Previous Excavations at Tell el-Ful." Pages l 1–17 in *The Third Campaign at Tell el-Ful: The Excavations of 1964*. Edited by Nancy Lapp. AASOR 45. Cambridge: American Schools of Oriental Research.

Gravett, Sandra Lynne. 2004. "Reading 'Rape' in the Hebrew Bible: A Consideration of Language." *JSOT* 28:280–89.

Gray, John. 1967. *Joshua, Judges and Ruth*. NCB. London: Oliphants.

———. 1976. *I and II Kings: A Commentary*. Rev. ed. OTL. Philadelphia: Westminster.

———. 1986. *Joshua, Judges and Ruth*. Rev. ed. NCB. Grand Rapids: Eerdmans.

Greenfield, Jonas C. 1999. "Hadad." *DDD* 377–82.

Grintz, Jehoshua M. 1961. "'Ai Which Is beside Beth-Aven': A Re-examination of the Identity of 'Ai." *Bib* 42:201–16.

Gross, Walter. 1974. "Die Herausführungsformel—Zum Verhältnis von Formel und Syntax." *ZAW* 86:425–53.

———. 1996. *Die Satzteilfolge im Verbalsatz alttestamentlicher Prosa*. FAT 17. Tübingen: Mohr Siebeck.

———. 2009. *Richter*. HThK. Freiburg: Herder.

Güdemann, Moritz G. 1869. "Tendenz und Abfassungszeit der letzten Capitel des Buches der Richter." *MGWJ* 18:357–68.

Guenther, Allen R. 2005. "A Typology of Israelite Marriage: Kinship, Socio-economic, and Religious Factors." *JSOT* 29:387–407.

Guillaume, Philippe. 2004. *Waiting for Josiah: The Judges*. JSOTSup 385. London: T&T Clark.

———. 2014. "Hesiod's Heroic Age and the Biblical Period of the Judges." Pages 146–64 in *The Bible and Hellenism: Greek Influence on Jewish and Early Christian Literature*. Edited by Thomas L. Thompson and Philippe Wajdenbaum. Durham: Acumen.

Gunkel, Herman. 1910. *Genesis*. 3rd ed. HKAT. Göttingen: Vandenhoeck & Ruprecht.

Gunn, David M. 1974a. "The 'Battle Report': Oral or Scribal Convention?" *JBL* 93:513–18.

———. 1974b. "Narrative Patterns and Oral Tradition in Judges and Samuel." *VT* 24:286–317.

———. 2005. *Judges*. Blackwell Bible Commentaries. Malden, MA: Blackwell.

Gurewicz, S. B. 1959. "The Bearing of Judges i–ii. 5 on the Authorship of the Book of Judges." *ABR* 7:37–40.

Halpern, Baruch. 1983. "Doctrine by Misadventure: Between the Israelite Source and the Biblical Historian." Pages 41–73 in *The Poet and the Historian: Essays in Literary and Historical Biblical Criticism*. Edited by Richard E. Friedman. HSS 26. Chico, CA: Scholars Press.
Haran, Menahem. 1978. *Temples and Temple-Service in Ancient Israel: An Inquiry into the Character of Cult Phenomena and the Historical Setting of the Priestly School*. Oxford: Clarendon.
———. 1981. "Behind the Scenes of History: Determining the Date of the Priestly Source." *JBL* 100:321–33.
———. 1985. "Book-Size and the Device of Catch-Lines in the Biblical Canon." *JJS* 36:1–11.
Harper, William Rainey. 1905. *A Critical and Exegetical Commentary on Amos and Hosea*. ICC. Edinburgh: T&T Clark.
Harrison, Timothy P., and James F. Osborne. 2012. "Building XVI and the Neo-Assyrian Sacred Precint at Tell Tayinat." *JCS* 64:125–43.
Hebel, Udo J. 1989. *Intertextuality, Allusion, and Quotation: An International Bibliography of Critical Studies*. New York: Greenwood.
Hentschel, Georg, and Christina Niessen. 2008. "Der Bruderkrieg zwischen Israel und Benjamin (Ri 20)." *Bib* 89:17–38.
Hertzberg, Hans Wilhelm. 1964. *I and II Samuel: A Commentary*. Translated by John Bowden. OTL. London: SCM.
———. 1965. *Die Bücher Josua, Richter, Ruth*. 3rd ed. ATD 9. Göttingen: Vandenhoeck & Ruprecht.
Hoffman, Yair. 1988. "The Technique of Quotation and Citation as an Interpretive Device." Pages 71–79 in *Creative Biblical Exegesis: Christian and Jewish Hermeneutics through the Centuries*. Edited by Benjamin Uffenheimer and Henning Graf Revenlow. JSOTSup 59. Sheffield: JSOT Press.
Hoffmann, David Z. 1913. *Das Buch Deuteronomium*. Berlin: Poppelauer.
Hölscher, Gustav. 1922. "Komposition und Ursprung des Deuteronomiums." *ZAW* 40:161–255.
Honeyman, Alexander Mackie. 1952. "Merismus in Biblical Hebrew." *JBL* 71:11–18.
Hoop, Raymond de. 2004. "Saul the Sodomite: Genesis 18–19 as the Opening Panel of a Polemic Triptych on King Saul." Pages 17–26 in *Sodom's Sin: Genesis 18–19 and Its Interpretations*. Edited by Ed Noort and Eibert Tigchelaar. Leiden: Brill.

Horst, Friedrich. 1930. *Das Privilegrecht Jahves: Rechtsgeschichtliche Untersuchungen zum Deuteronomium*. FRLANT 28. Göttingen: Vandenhoeck & Ruprecht.

Houston, Walter J. 1997. "Misunderstanding or Midrash? The Prose Appropriation of Poetic Material in the Hebrew Bible." *ZAW* 109:342–55, 534–48.

Hübner, Ulrich. 1992. *Die Ammoniter: Untersuchungen zur Geschichte, Kultur und Religion eines transjordanischen Volkes im 1. Jahrtausend v. Chr.* Abhandlungen des Deutschen Palätinavereins 18. Wiesbaden: Harrassowitz.

———. 2007. "Jerusalem and the Jebusites." Pages 17–22 in *Jerusalem before Islam*. Edited by Zeidan Kafafi and Robert Schick. Oxford: Archaeopress.

Hurvitz, Avi. 1967. "The Language and Date of Psalm 151 from Qumran" [Hebrew]. *ErIsr* 8:82–87.

———. 1971. "Linguistic Observations on the Biblical Usage of the Priestly Term עדה" [Hebrew]. *Tarbiz* 40:261–67.

———. 1972. *The Transition Period in Biblical Hebrew* [Hebrew]. Jerusalem: Bialik Institute.

———. 1974. "The Evidence of Language in Dating the Priestly Code." *RB* 81:24–56.

———. 1982. *A Linguistic Study of the Relationship between the Priestly Source and the Book of Ezekiel: A New Approach to an Old Problem*. CahRB 20. Paris: Gabalda.

———. 2000. "Can Biblical Texts Be Dated Linguistically? Chronological Perspectives in the Historical Study of Biblical Hebrew." Pages 143–60 in *Congress Volume: Oslo, 1998*. Edited by André Lemaire and Magne Sæbø. VTSup 80. Leiden: Brill.

———. 2003. "Hebrew and Aramaic in the Biblical Period: The Problem of 'Aramaisms' in Linguistic Research on the Hebrew Bible." Pages 24–37 in *Biblical Hebrew: Studies in Chronology and Typology*. Edited by Ian Young. JSOTSup 369. London: T&T Clark.

———. 2006. "The Recent Debate on Late Biblical Hebrew: Solid Data, Experts' Opinions, and Inconclusive Arguments." *HS* 47:191–210.

Hutzli, Jürg. 2010. "The Literary Relationship between I–II Samuel and I–II Kings: Considerations Concerning the Formation of the Two Books." *ZAW* 122:505–19.

Hyatt, J. Philip. 1937. "A Neo-Babylonian Parallel to *Bethel-Sar-Eṣer*, Zech 7:2." *JBL* 56:387–94.

Irvine, Stuart A. 1998. "Enmity in the House of God (Hosea 9:7–9)." *JBL* 117:645–53.
Jacobsen, Thorkild. 1970. "Primitive Democracy in Ancient Mesopotamia." Pages 157–70 in *Toward the Image of Tammuz and Other Essays on Mesopotamian History and Culture*. Cambridge: Harvard University Press.
Japhet, Sara. 1993. *I and II Chronicles: A Commentary*. OTL. Louisville: Westminster John Knox.
Jastrow, Marcus. 1903. *A Dictionary of the Targumim, the Talmud Babli and Yerusahalmi, and the Midrashic Literature*. 2nd ed. New York: Putnam.
Jeremias, Jörg. 1983. *Der Prophet Hosea*. ATD 24.1. Göttingen: Vandenhoeck & Ruprecht.
Joosten, Jan. 1996. *People and Land in the Holiness Code: An Exegetical Study of the Ideational Framework of the Law in Leviticus 17–26*. VTSup 67. Leiden: Brill.
Joshel, Sandra Rae. 1992. "The Body Female and the Body Politic: Livy's Lucretia and Verginia." Pages 112–30 in *Pornography and Representation in Greece and Rome*. Edited by Amy Richlin. Oxford: Oxford University Press.
Jüngling, Hans-Winfried. 1981. *Richter 19—Ein Plädoyer für das Königtum: Stilistische Analyse der Tendenzerzählung Ri 19,1–30a; 21,25*. AnBib 84. Rome: Biblical Institute Press.
Kaufmann, Yehezkel. 1959. *Joshua* [Hebrew]. Jerusalem: Kiryat Sefer.
———. 1960. *The Religion of Israel: From Its Beginnings to the Babylonian Exile*. Translated and abridged by Moshe Greenberg. Chicago: University of Chicago Press.
———. 1961. *Judges* [Hebrew]. Jerusalem: Kiryat Sefer.
Keefe, Alice A. 1993. "Rapes of Women/Wars of Men." *Semeia* 60:79–97.
Kelso, James Leon. 1968. *The Excavation of Bethel (1934–1960)*. AASOR 39. Cambridge: American Schools of Oriental Research.
Kim, Dong-Hyuk. 2013. *Early Biblical Hebrew, Late Biblical Hebrew, and Linguistic Variability: A Sociolinguistic Evaluation of the Linguistic Dating of Biblical Texts*. VTSup 156. Leiden: Brill.
Klein, Lillian R. 1988. *The Triumph of Irony in the Book of Judges*. BLS 14. Sheffield: Almond.
Klein, Ralph W. 1983. *1 Samuel*. WBC 10. Waco, TX: Word.
Kloppenborg, John S. 1981. "Joshua 22: The Priestly Editing of an Ancient Tradition." *Bib* 62:347–71.

Knauf, Ernst Axel. 1988. *Midian: Untersuchungen zur Geschichte Palästinas und Nordarabiens am Ende des 2 Jahrtausends v. Chr.* Wiesbaden: Harrassowitz.

———. 1990. "War 'Biblisch-Hebräisch' eine Sprache? Empirische Gesichtspunkte zur linguistischen Annäherung an die Sprache der althebräischen Literatur." *ZAH* 3:11–23.

———. 2006. "Bethel: The Israelite Impact on Judean Language and Literature." Pages 291–349 in *Judah and the Judeans in the Persian Period*. Edited by Oded Lipschits and Manfred Oeming. Winona Lake, IN: Eisenbrauns.

———. 2008. *Josua*. ZBK 6. Zurich: Theologischer Verlag.

Knierim, Rolf P., and George W. Coats. 2005. *Numbers*. FOTL. Grand Rapids: Eerdmans.

Knoppers, Gary Neil. 2006. "Israel's First King and 'the Kingdom of Yhwh in the Hands of the Sons of David': The Place of the Saulide Monarchy in the Chronicler's Historiography." Pages 187–213 in *Saul in Story and Tradition*. Edited by Carl S. Ehrlich. FAT 47. Tübingen: Mohr Siebeck.

———. 2012. "The Relationship of the Deuteronomistic History to Chronicles: Was the Chronicler a Deuteronomist?" Pages 307–42 in *Congress Volume: Helsinki, 2010*. Edited by Martti Nissinen. VTSup 148. Leiden: Brill.

Koch, Christoph. 2008. *Vertrag, Treueid und Bund: Studien zur Rezeption des altorientalischen Vertragsrechts im Deuteronomium und zur Ausbildung der Bundestheologie im Alten Testament*. BZAW 383. Berlin: de Gruyter.

Koehler, Ludwig, Walter Baumgartner, and Johann J. Stamm. 2001. *The Hebrew and Aramaic Lexicon of the Old Testament*. Translated and edited under the supervision of M. E. J. Richardson. Study edition. 2 vols. Leiden: Brill.

Köhlmoos, Melanie. 2006. *Bet-El—Erinnerungen an eine Stadt: Perspektiven der alttestamentlichen Bet-El Überlieferung*. FAT 49. Tübingen: Mohr Siebeck.

Kottsieper, Ingo. 2004. "שבע *šāḇaʿ*; שבעה *šeḇuʿâ*." *TDOT* 14:311–36.

Kratz, Reinhard Gregor. 2005. *The Composition of the Narrative Books of the Old Testament*. Translated by John Bowden. London: T&T Clark.

Kristeva, Julia. 1986a. "Word, Dialogue and Novel." Pages 35–61 in *The Kristeva Reader*. Edited by Toril Moi. Oxford: Blackwell.

———. 1986b. "Revolution in Poetic Language." Pages 90–113 in *The Kristeva Reader*. Edited by Toril Moi. Oxford: Blackwell.
Kropat, Arno. 1909. *Die Syntax des Autors der Chronik verglichen mit der seiner Quellen: Ein Beitrag zur historischen Syntax des Hebräischen*. BZAW 16. Giessen: Töpelmann.
Kugel, James Lewis. 1981. "On the Bible and Literary Criticism." *Prooftexts* 1:217–36.
———. 1987. "The Bible's Earliest Interpreters." Review of *Biblical Interpretation in Ancient Israel*, by Michael Fishbane. *Prooftexts* 7:269–83.
Kutscher, Eduard Yehezkel. 1982. *A History of the Hebrew Language*. Edited by Raphael Kutscher. Jerusalem: Magnes.
Labahn, Antje. 2003. "Metaphor and Intertextuality: 'Daughter of Zion' as a Test Case; Response to Kirsten Nielsen 'From Oracles to Canon'—and the Role of Metaphor." *SJOT* 17:49–67.
Landsberger, Benno. 1968. "Jungfräulichkeit: Ein Beitrag zum Thema 'Beilager und Eheschliessung.'" Pages 41–105 in *Symbolae iuridicae et historicae Martino David dedicatae*. Edited by J. A. Ankum, R. Feenstra, and W. F. Leemans. Leiden: Brill.
Lauinger, Jacob. 2011. "Some Preliminary Thoughts on the Tablet Collection in Building XVI from Tell Tayinat." *Canadian Society for Mesopotamian Studies Journal* 6:5–14.
Lapp, Nancy L., ed. 1981. *The Third Campaign at Tell el-Fûl: The Excavations of 1964*. AASOR 45. Ann Arbor: American Schools of Oriental Research.
Lapp, Paul W. 1965. "Tell el-Fûl." *BA* 28:2–10.
Lasine, Stuart. 1984. "Guest and Host in Judges 19: Lot's Hospitality in an Inverted World." *JSOT* 29:37–59.
Lemaire, André. 2006. "Hebrew and Aramaic in the First Millennium B.C.E. in the Light of Epigraphic Evidence (Socio-Historical Aspects)." Pages 177–96 in *Biblical Hebrew in Its Northwest Semitic Setting: Typological and Historical Perspectives*. Edited by Steven E. Fassberg and Avi Hurvitz. Jerusalem: Magnes.
Lemche, Niels Peter. 1985. *Early Israel: Anthropological and Historical Studies on the Israelite Society before the Monarchy*. VTSup 37. Leiden: Brill.
Levin, Christoph. 1993. *Der Jahwist*. FRLANT 157. Göttingen: Vandenhoeck & Ruprecht.

———. 2006. Review of *Linguistic Evidence for the Pre-Exilic Date of the Yahwistic Source*, by Richard M. Wright. *RBL*. http://www.bookreviews.org/pdf/4860_5055.pdf.

———. 2011. "On the Cohesion and Separation of Books within the Enneateuch." Pages 127–54 in *Pentateuch, Hexateuch, or Enneateuch? Identifying Literary Works in Genesis through Kings*. Edited by Thomas Dozeman, Thomas Römer, and Konrad Schmid. AIL 8. Atlanta: Society of Biblical Literature.

Levine, Baruch A. 1993. *Numbers 1–20*. AB 4. New York: Doubleday.

———. 1994. "'The Lord Your God Accept You' (2 Samuel 24:23): The Altar Erected by David on the Threshing Floor of Araunah." *ErIsr* 24:122–29.

———. 2000. *Numbers 21–36*. AB 4A. New York: Doubleday.

Levinson, Bernard Malcolm, and Jeffrey Stackert. 2012. "Between the Covenant Code and Esarhaddon's Succession Treaty: Deuteronomy 13 and the Composition of Deuteronomy." *JAJ* 3:123–40.

L'Hour, Jean. 1963. "Une législation criminelle dans le Deutéronome." *Bib* 44:1–28.

Licht, Jacob. 1995. *A Commentary on the Book of Numbers, XXII–XXXVI* [Hebrew]. Edited by S. Aḥituv. Jerusalem: Magnes.

Lipiński, Edward. 2010. "Hiram of Tyre and Solomon." Pages 251–72 in *The Books of Kings: Sources, Composition, Historiography and Reception*. Edited by Baruch Halpern and André Lemaire. VTSup 129. Leiden: Brill.

Lipschits, Oded. 1998. "Nebuchadrezzar's Policy in 'Hattu-Land' and the Fate of the Kingdom of Judah." *UF* 30:467–87.

———. 1999. "The History of the Benjamin Region under Babylonian Rule." *TA* 26:155–90.

———. 2005. *The Rise and Fall of Jerusalem: Judah under Babylonian Rule*. Winona Lake, IN: Eisenbrauns.

Lipschits, Oded, and Oren Tal. 2007. "The Settlement Archaeology of the Province of Judah: A Case Study." Pages 33–52 in *Judah and the Judeans in the Fourth Century B.C.E.* Edited by Oded Lipschits, Gary N. Knoppers, and Rainer Albertz. Winona Lake, IN: Eisenbrauns.

Lipschits, Oded, Omer Sergi, and Ido Koch. 2010. "Royal Judahite Jar Handles: Reconsidering the Chronology of the LMLK Stamp Impressions." *TA* 37:3–32.

Lissovsky, Nurit, and Nadav Na'aman. 2003. "A New Outlook at the Boundary System of the Twelve Tribes." *UF* 35:291–332.

BIBLIOGRAPHY 355

Liverani, Mario. 2004. "Messages, Women, and Hospitality: Inter-tribal Communication in Judges 19–21." Pages 160–92 in *Myth and Politics in Ancient Near Eastern Historiography*. Edited by Zainab Bahrani and Marc Van De Mieroop. London: Equinox.

Loader, J. A. 1990. *A Tale of Two Cities: Sodom and Gomorrah in the Old Testament, Early Jewish and Early Christian Traditions*. Contributions to Biblical Exegesis and Theology 1. Kampen: Kok.

Locher, Clemens. 1986. *Die Ehre einer Frau in Israel: Exegetische und rechtsvergleichende Studien zu Deuteronomium 22,12–21*. OBO 70. Fribourg: Universitätsverlag; Göttingen: Vandenhoeck & Ruprecht.

Lohfink, Norbert. 1999. "Was There a Deuteronomistic Movement?" Pages 36–66 in *Those Elusive Deuteronomists: The Phenomenon of Pan-Deuteronomism*. Edited by Linda S. Schearing and Steven L. McKenzie. JSOTSup 268. Sheffield: Sheffield Academic.

Lundbom, Jack R. 1996. "The Inclusio and Other Framing Devices in Deuteronomy I–XXVIII." *VT* 46:296–315.

———. 2013. *Deuteronomy: A Commentary*. Grand Rapids: Eerdmans.

Macchi, Jean-Daniel. 1999. *Israël et ses tribus selon Genèse 49*. OBO 171. Fribourg: Editions universitaires; Göttingen: Vandenhoeck & Ruprecht.

MacDonald, Burton. 2000. *"East of the Jordan": Territories and Sites of the Hebrew Scriptures*. ASOR books 6. Boston: American Schools of Oriental Research.

Macintosh, A. A. 1997. *A Critical and Exegetical Commentary on Hosea*. ICC. Edinburgh: T&T Clark.

Magen, Yitzhak, and Michael Dadon. 1999. "Nebi Samwil (Shmuel Hanavi–Har Hasimha)" [Hebrew]. *Qadmoniot* 32:62–77.

Magen, Yitzhak, and Israel Finkelstein. 1993. *Archaeological Survey of the Hill Country of Benjamin*. Jerusalem: Israel Antiquities Authority.

Mai, Hans-Peter. 1991. "Bypassing Intertextuality: Hermeneutics, Textual Practice, Hypertext." Pages 30–59 in *Intertextuality*. Edited by Heinrich F. Plett. Berlin: de Gruyter.

Magonet, Jonathan. 1983. *Form and Meaning: Studies in Literary Techniques in the Book of Jonah*. Sheffield: Almond.

Matthews, Victor H. 1992. "Hospitality and Hostility in Genesis 19 and Judges 19." *BTB* 22:3–11.

Mayes, Andrew D. H. 1974. *Israel in the Period of the Judges*. SBT 2/29. London: SCM.

———. 1981. *Deuteronomy*. 2nd ed. NCB. Grand Rapids: Eerdmans.

———. 1983. *The Story of Israel between Settlement and Exile: A Redactional Study of the Deuteronomistic History*. London: SCM.
———. 1985. *Judges*. Old Testament Guides 3. Sheffield: JSOT Press.
———. 2001. "Deuteronomisitic Royal Ideology in Judges 17–21." *BibInt* 9:241–58.
Mays, James L. 1969. *Hosea: A Commentary*. OTL. London: SCM.
Mazar, Amihai. 1990. *Archaeology of the Land of the Bible: 10,000–586 B.C.E.* New York: Doubleday.
———. 1994. "Jerusalem and Its Vicinity in Iron Age I." Pages 70–91 in *From Nomadism to Monarchy: Archaeological and Historical Aspects of Early Israel*. Edited by Israel Finkelstein and Nadav Na'aman. Jerusalem: Yad Ben-Zvi.
Mazar, Amihai, David Amit, and Zvi Ilan. 1984. "The 'Border Road' between Michmash and Jericho and Excavations at Ḥorvat Shilḥah" [Hebrew]. *ErIsr* 17:236–40.
Mazor, Lea. 1994. "A Textual and Literary Study of the Fall of Ai in Joshua 8" [Hebrew]. Pages 73–108 in *The Bible in the Light of Its Interpreters*. Edited by Sara Japhet. Jerusalem: Magnes.
McCarter, Peter Kyle. 1980. *I Samuel*. AB 8. Garden City, NY: Doubleday.
———. 1984. *II Samuel*. AB 9. Garden City, NY: Doubleday.
———. 1994. "The Books of Samuel." Pages 260–80 in *The History of Israel's Traditions: The Heritage of Martin Noth*. Edited by Steven L. McKenzie and M. Patrick Graham. JSOTSup 182. Sheffield: Sheffield Academic.
McCown, Chester Charlton, ed. 1947a. *Archaeological and Historical Results*. Vol. 1 of *Tell En-Naṣbeh*. Berkeley: Palestine Institute of Pacific School of Religion; New Haven: American Schools of Oriental Research.
———. 1947b. "Conclusions as to the Identification of the Site." Pages 57–59 in *Archaeological and Historical Results*. Vol. 1 of *Tell En-Naṣbeh*. Edited by Chester Charlton McCown. Berkeley: Palestine Institute of Pacific School of Religion; New Haven: American Schools of Oriental Research.
McKenzie, John L. 1959. "The Elders in the Old Testament." *Bib* 40:522–40.
McKenzie, Steven L. 1991. *The Trouble with Kings*. VTSup 42. Leiden: Brill.
———. 1998. "Mizpah of Benjamin and the Date of the Deuteronomistic History." Pages 149–55 in *"Lasset uns Brücken bauen ..."*: *Collected Communications to the XV Congress of the International Organziation for the Study of the Old Testament, Cambridge 1995*. Edited by Klaus-

Dietrich Schunck and Matthias Augustin. BEATAJ 42. Frankfurt am Main: Lang.
———. 2000. "The So-Called Succession Narrative in the Deuteronomistic History." Pages 123–35 in *Die sogenannte Thronfolgegeschichte Davids: Neue Einsichten und Anfragen*. Edited by Albert de Pury and Thomas Römer. OBO 176. Fribourg: Universitätsverlag; Göttingen: Vandenhoeck & Ruprecht.
———. 2010. "Elaborated Evidence for the Priority of 1 Samuel 26." *JBL* 129:437–44.
Meek, Russell L. 2014. "Intertextuality, Inner-Biblical Exegesis, and Inner-Biblical Allusion: The Ethics of a Methodology." *Bib* 95:280–91.
Meer, Michael N. van der. 2004. *Formation and Reformulation: The Redaction of the Book of Joshua in the Light of the Oldest Textual Witnesses*. VTSup 102. Leiden: Brill.
Merendino, Rosario Pius. 1969. *Das deuteronomische Gesetz*. BBB 31. Bonn: Hanstein.
Mettinger, Tryggve N. D. 1993. "Intertextuality: Allusion and Vertical Context Systems in Some Job Passages." Pages 257–80 in *Of Prophets' Visions and the Wisdom of Sages: Essays in Honour of R. Norman Whybray on His Seventieth Birthday*. Edited by Heather A. McKay and David J. A. Clines. JSOTSup 162. Sheffield: JSOT Press.
Milevski, Ianir. 1996–97. "Settlement Patterns in Northern Judah during the Achaemenid Period, According to the Hill Country of Benjamin and Jerusalem Surveys." *BAIAS* 15:7–29.
Milgrom, Jacob. 1976. "Profane Slaughter and a Formulaic Key to the Composition of Deuteronomy." *HUCA* 47:1–17.
———. 1979. "Priestly Terminology and the Political and Social Structure of Pre-Monarchic Israel." *JQR* 69:65–77.
Miller, J. Maxwell. 1974a. "Jebus and Jerusalem: A Case of Mistaken Identity." *ZDPV* 90:115–27.
———. 1974b. "Saul's Rise to Power: Some Observations Concerning 1 Sam 9:1–10:16; 10:26–11:15 and 13:2–14:46." *CBQ* 36:157–75.
———. 1975. "Geba/Gibeah of Benjamin." *VT* 25:145–66.
Miner, Earl Roy. 1993. "Allusion." Pages 38–39 in *The New Princeton Encyclopedia of Poetry and Poetics*. Edited by Alex Preminger and T. V. F. Brogan. Princeton: Princeton University Press.
Möhlenbrink, Kurt. 1938. "Die Landnahmesagen des Buches Joshua." *ZAW* 56:238–68.

Montgomery, James A., and Henry Snyder Gehman. 1951. *A Critical and Exegetical Commentary on the Books of Kings*. ICC. Edinburgh: T&T Clark.
Moore, George Foot. 1895. *A Critical and Exegetical Commentary on Judges*. ICC. Edinburgh: T&T Clark.
Mueller, E. Aydeet. 2001. *The Micah Story: A Morality Tale in the Book of Judges*. New York: Lang.
Muilenburg, James. 1947a. "The History of Mizpah of Benjamin." Pages 45–49 in *Archaeological and Historical Results*. Vol. 1 of *Tell En-Naṣbeh*. Edited by Chester Charlton McCown. Berkeley: Palestine Institute of Pacific School of Religion; New Haven: American Schools of Oriental Research.

———. 1947b. "The Literary Sources Bearing on the Question of Identification." Pages 23–44 in *Archaeological and Historical Results*. Vol. 1 of *Tell En-Naṣbeh*. Edited by Chester Charlton McCown. Berkeley: Palestine Institute of Pacific School of Religion; New Haven: American Schools of Oriental Research.

Mullen, E. Theodore. 1984. "Judges 1:1–36: The Deuteronomisitic Reintroduction of the Book of Judges." *HTR* 77:33–54.
Müller, Reinhard. 2013. "1 Samuel 1 As the Opening Chapter of the Deuteronomistic History?" Pages 207–23 in *Is Samuel among the Deuteronomists? Current Views on the Place of Samuel in a Deuteronomistic History*. Edited by Cynthia Edenburg and Juha Pakkala. AIL 16. Atlanta: Society of Biblical Literature.
Müllner, Ilse. 1999. "Lethal Differences: Sexual Violence as Violence against Others in Judges 19." Pages 126–42 in *A Feminist Companion to Judges*. Edited by Athalya Brenner. FCB 2/4. Sheffield: Sheffield Academic.
Na'aman, Nadav. 1977. "Campaigns of the Assyrian Kings to Judah in the Light of a New Assyrian Document" [Hebrew]. *Shnaton* 2:164–80.

———. 1979. "Sennacherib's Campaign to Judah and the Date of the *LMLK* Stamps." *VT* 29:23–86.

———. 1984. "Ephraim, Ephrath, and the Settlement in the Judean Hill Country" [Hebrew]. *Zion* 49:325–31.

———. 1986a. "Hezekiah's Fortified Cities and the *LMLK* Stamps." *BASOR* 261:5–21.

———. 1986b. "The Inheritance of Dan and the Boundary System of the Twelve Tribes." Pages 75–117 in *Borders and Districts in Biblical Historiography*. JBS 4. Jerusalem: Simor.

———. 1987. "Beth-Aven, Bethel and Early Israelite Sanctuaries." *ZDPV* 103:13–21.

———. 1992. "The Pre-Deuteronomisitic Story of King Saul and Its Historical Significance." *CBQ* 54:638–58.

———. 1994. "The 'Conquest of Canaan' in the Book of Joshua and in History." Pages 218–81 in *From Nomadism to Monarchy: Archaeological and Historical Aspects of Early Israel*. Edited by Israel Finkelstein and Nadav Na'aman. Jerusalem: Yad Ben-Zvi.

———. 1995. Review of *Gibeah: The Search for a Biblical City*, by Patrick M. Arnold. *JNES* 54:150–51.

———. 1996. "Sources and Composition in the History of David." Pages 170–86 in *The Origins of the Ancient Israelite States*. Edited by Volkmar Fritz and Philip R. Davies. JSOTSup 228. Sheffield: Sheffield Academic Press.

———. 1999. "The Fire Signals of Lachish Revisted." *PEQ* 131:65–67.

———. 2005a. "The Danite Campaign Northward (Judges XVII–XVIII) and the Migration of the Phocaeans to Massalia (Strabo IV 1,4)." *VT* 55:47–60.

———. 2005b. "The Kingdom of Judah under Josiah." Pages 329–98 in *Ancient Israel and Its Neighbors: Interaction and Counteraction*. Vol. 1 of *Collected Essays*. Winona Lake, IN: Eisenbrauns.

———. 2006. "The Law of the Altar in Deuteronomy and the Cultic Site near Shechem." Pages 339–58 in *Ancient Israel's History and Historiography: The First Temple Period*. Vol. 3 of *Collected Essays*. Winona Lake, IN: Eisenbrauns.

———. 2009a. "The Sanctuary of the Gibeonites Revisited." *JANER* 9:101–24.

———. 2009b. "Saul, Benjamin and the Emergence of 'Biblical Israel.'" *ZAW* 121:211–24, 335–49.

———. 2014a. "Jebusites and Jabeshites in the Saul and David Story-Cycles." *Bib* 95:481–97.

———. 2014b. "The Settlement of the Ephrathites in Bethlehem and the Location of Rachel's Tomb." *RB* 121:516–29.

Nahkola, Aulikki. 2001. *Double Narratives in the Old Testament: The Foundations of Method in Biblical Criticism*. BZAW 290. Berlin: de Gruyter.

Neef, Heinz-Dieter. 1987. *Die Heilstraditionen Israels in der Verkündigung des Propheten Hosea*. BZAW 169. Berlin: de Gruyter.

Nelson, Richard David. 1981. *The Double Redaction of the Deuteronomistic History*. JSOTSup 18. Sheffield: JSOT Press.

———. 1993. *Raising Up a Faithful Priest: Community and Priesthood in Biblical Theology*. Louisville: Westminster John Knox.
———. 1997. *Joshua: A Commentary*. OTL. Louisville: Westminster John Knox.
———. 2002. *Deuteronomy: A Commentary*. OTL. Louisville: Westminster John Knox.
Niccacci, Alviero. 1997. "Basic Facts and Theory of the Biblical Hebrew Verb System in Prose." Pages 167–202 in *Narrative Syntax and the Hebrew Bible*. Edited by Ellen van Wolde. BibInt 29. Leiden: Brill.
Niditch, Susan. 1982. "The 'Sodomite' Theme in Judges 19–20: Family, Community, and Social Disintegration." *CBQ* 44:365–78.
———. 1993. *War in the Hebrew Bible: A Study in the Ethics of Violence*. New York: Oxford University Press.
———. 2008. *Judges: A Commentary*. OTL. Louisville: Westminster John Knox.
Nielsen, Eduard. 1995. *Deuteronomium*. HAT 6. Tübingen: Mohr Siebeck.
Niemann, Hermann Michael. 1985. *Die Daniten: Studien zur Geschichte eines altisraelitischen Stammes*. FRLANT 135. Göttingen: Vandenhoeck & Ruprecht.
Nihan, Christophe L. 2007. *From Priestly Torah to Pentateuch: A Study in the Composition of the Book of Leviticus*. FAT 2/25. Tübingen: Mohr Siebeck.
———. 2013. "1 Samuel 8 and 12 and the Deuteronomistic Edition of Samuel." Pages 225–73 in *Is Samuel among the Deuteronomists? Current Views on the Place of Samuel in a Deuteronomistic History*. Edited by Cynthia Edenburg and Juha Pakkala. AIL 16. Atlanta: Society of Biblical Literature.
Nobel, Paul R. 2002. "Esau, Tamar, and Joseph: Criteria for Identifying Inner-Biblical Allusions." *VT* 52:219–52.
Nogalski, James D. 1996. "Intertextuality and the Twelve." Pages 102–24 in *Forming Prophetic Literature: Essays on Isaiah and the Twelve in Honor of John D. W. Watts*. Edited by J. W. Watts and P. R. House. JSOTSup 235. Sheffield: Sheffield Academic Press.
North, Francis S. 1954. "Aaron's Rise in Prestige." *ZAW* 66:191–99.
Noth, Martin. 1935. "Bethel und Ai." *Palästinasjahrbuch* 31:7–29.
———. 1962. "The Background of Judges 17–18." Pages 68–85 in *Israel's Prophetic Heritage: Essays in Honor of James Muilenburg*. Edited by B. W. Anderson and W. Harrelson. London: SCM.

―――. 1965. *Leviticus: A Commentary*. Translated by J. E. Anderson. OTL. Philadelphia: Westminster.
―――. 1966. *Das System der zwölf Stämme Israels*. 2nd ed. Darmstadt: Wissenschaftliche Buchgesellschaft.
―――. 1968. *Numbers: A Commentary*. Translated by James D. Martin. OTL. London: SCM.
―――. 1971. *Das Buch Josua*. 3rd ed. HAT 7. Tübingen: Mohr Siebeck.
―――. 1991. *The Deuteronomistic History*. 2nd ed. JSOTSup 15. Sheffield: Sheffield Academic Press.
Nowack, Wilhelm. 1902. *Richter, Ruth und Bücher Samuelis*. HKAT. Göttingen: Vandenhoeck & Ruprecht.
O'Brien, Mark. 1989. *The Deuteronomistic History Hypothesis: A Reassessment*. OBO 92. Fribourg: Universitätsverlag; Göttingen: Vandenhoeck & Ruprecht.
―――. 1995. "The Book of Deuteronomy." *CurBS* 3:95–128.
O'Connell, Robert H. 1996. *The Rhetoric of the Book of Judges*. VTSup 63. Leiden: Brill.
O'Connor, Michael Patrick. 1991. "Cardinal-Direction Terms in Biblical Hebrew." Pages 1140–57 in vol. 2 of *Semitic Studies in Honor of Wolf Leslau*. Edited by Alan S. Kaye. 2 vols. Wiesbaden: Harrassowitz.
Ofer, Avi. 1994. "'All the Hill Country of Judah': From a Settlement Fringe to a Prosperous Monarchy." Pages 92–121 in *From Nomadism to Monarchy: Archaeological and Historical Aspects of Early Israel*. Edited by Israel Finkelstein and Nadav Na'aman. Jerusalem: Yad Ben-Zvi.
Olyan, Saul M. 1994. "'And with a Male You Shall Not Lie the Lying Down of a Woman': On the Meaning and Significance of Leviticus 18:22 and 20:13." *Journal of the History of Sexuality* 5:179–206.
Oswalt, John. 1986. *The Book of Isaiah: Chapters 1–39*. NICOT. Grand Rapids: Eerdmans.
Otto, Eckart. 1993. "Das Eherecht im mittelassyrischen Kodex und im Deuteronomium." Pages 259–81 in *Mesopotamica—Ugaritica—Biblica: Festschrift für Kurt Bergerhof*. Edited by Manfried Dietrich and Oswald Loretz. AOAT 232. Kevelaer: Butzon & Bercker; Neukrichen-Vluyn: Neukirchener Verlag.
―――. 1994. "Aspects of Legal Reforms and Reformulations in Ancient Cuneiform and Israelite Law." Pages 163–82 in *Theory and Method in Biblical and Cuneiform Law: Revision, Interpolation and Development*. Edited by B. M. Levinson. JSOTSup 181. Sheffield: Sheffield Academic Press.

———. 1996. "Treueid und Gesetz: Die Ursprünge des Deuteronomiums in Horizont neuassyrischen Vertragsrechts." *ZABR* 2:1–52.

———. 1997. "Das Deuteronomium als Archimedischer Punkt der Pentateuchkritik: Auf dem Wege zu einer Neubegründung der de Wette'schen Hypothese." Pages 321–39 in *Deuteronomy and Deuteronomic Literature*. Edited by C. H. W. Brekelmans. BETL 133. Leuven: Leuven University Press; Peeters.

———. 1998. "False Weights in the Scales of Biblical Justice? Different Views of Women from Patriarchal Hierarchy to Religious Equality in the Book of Deuteronomy." Pages 128–46 in *Gender and Law in the Hebrew Bible and the Ancient Near East*. Edited by Bernard M. Levinson, Tikva Frymer-Kensky, and Victor H. Matthews. JSOTSup 262. Sheffield: Sheffield Academic Press.

———. 1999. *Das Deuteronomium: Politische Theologie und Rechtsreform in Juda und Assyrien*. BZAW 284. Berlin: de Gruyter.

———. 2012. *Deuteronomium 1–11*. Part 1: *1, 1–4, 43*. HTKAT. Freiburg im Breisgau: Herder.

Otzen, Benedikt. 1975. "בְּלִיַּעַל *beliyyʿal*." *TDOT* 2:131–36.

Pakkala, Juha. 1999. *Intolerant Monolatry in the Deuteronomistic History*. Publications of the Finnish Exegetical Society 76. Helsinki: Finnish Exegetical Society.

———. 2006. "Der literar- und religionsgeschichtliche Ort von Deuteronomium 13." Pages 125–37 in *Die deuteronomistischen Geschichtswerke: Redaktions- und religionsgeschichtliche Perspektiven zur "Deuteronomismus"-Diskussion in Tora und Vorderen Propheten*. Edited by Markus Witte, Konrad Schmid, Doris Prechel, and Jan Christian Gertz. BZAW 365. Berlin: de Gruyter.

Peckham, Brian. 1985. *The Composition of the Deuteronomistic History*. HSM 35. Atlanta: Scholars Press.

Penchansky, David. 1992. "Staying the Night: Intertextuality in Genesis and Judges." Pages 77–88 in *Reading between Texts: Intertextuality and the Hebrew Bible*. Edited by D. N. Fewell. Louisville: Westminster John Knox.

Phillips, Anthony. 1973. "Some Aspects of Family Law in Pre-Exilic Israel." *VT* 23:349–61.

———. 1975. "*Nebalah*—A Term for Serious Disorderly and Unruly Conduct." *VT* 25:237–42.

Polak, Frank. 1994. *Biblical Narrative: Aspects of Art and Design* [Hebrew]. Biblical Encyclopaedia Library 11. Bialik Institute: Jerusalem.

———. 1996. "Prose and Poetry in the Book of Job." *JANES* 24:61–97.
———. 1997. "Development and Periodization of Biblical Prose Narrative" [Hebrew]. *Beth Miqra* 43:30–52, 143–60.
———. 1998. "The Oral and the Written: Syntax, Stylistics and the Development of the Biblical Prose Narrative." *JANES* 26:59–105.
———. 2002. "Parameters for Stylistic Analysis of Biblical Hebrew Prose Texts." Pages 254–81 in *Bible and Computer*. Proceedings of the Association Internationale Bible et Informatique, "Form Alpha to Byte," University of Stellenbosch, 17–21 July, 2000. Edited by J. Cook. Leiden: Brill.
———. 2003. "Style Is More Than the Person: Sociolinguistics, Literary Culture, and the Distinction between Written and Oral Narrative." Pages 38–103 in *Biblical Hebrew: Studies in Chronology and Typology*. Edited by Ian Young. JSOTSup 369. London: T&T Clark.
———. 2006. "Sociolinguistics: A Key to the Typology and the Social Background of Biblical Hebrew." *HS* 47:115–62. http://www.jtsa.edu/Documents/pagedocs/JANES/1998 26/Polak26.pdf.
———. 2012. "Language Variation, Discourse Typology, and the Sociocultural Background of Biblical Narrative." Pages 301–38 in *Diachrony in Biblical Hebrew*. Edited by Cynthia L. Miller-Naudé and Ziony Zevit. LSAWS 8. Winona Lake, IN: Eisenbrauns.
Polzin, Robert. 1969. "*HWQY'* and Covenantal Institutions in Early Israel." *HTR* 62:227–40.
———. 1976. *Late Biblical Hebrew: Toward an Historical Typology of Biblical Hebrew Prose*. HSM 12. Missoula, MT: Scholars Press.
———. 1980. *Moses and the Deuteronomist*. New York: Seabury.
Porten, Bezalel, and Ada Yardeni, eds. 1986–1999. *Textbook of Aramaic Documents from Ancient Egypt*. Jerusalem: Hebrew University in Jerusalem.
Prag, Kay. 2002. "Bethlehem: A Site Assessment." *PEQ* 132:169–84.
Pressler, Carolyn. 1993. *The View of Women Found in the Deuteronomic Family Laws*. BZAW 216. Berlin: de Gruyter.
Propp, William Henry. 1993. "Kinship in 2 Samuel 13." *CBQ* 55:39–53.
Qimron, Elisha. 1986. *The Hebrew of the Dead Sea Scrolls*. HSS 29. Atlanta: Scholars Press.
———. 1992. "Observations on the History of Early Hebrew (1000 B.C.E.– 200 C.E.) in the Light of the Dead Sea Documents." Pages 349–61

in *The Dead Sea Scrolls: Forty Years of Research*. Edited by Devorah Dimant and Uriel Rappaport. STDJ 10. Jerusalem: Yad Ben-Zvi.

Rad, Gerhard von. 1966. "The Beginnings of Historical Writing in Ancient Israel." Pages 166–204 in *The Problem of the Hexateuch and Other Essays*. Translated by E. W. Trueman Dicken. Edinburgh: Oliver & Boyd.

———. 1972. *Genesis: A Commentary*. OTL. Translated by John H. Marks. London: SCM.

Rake, Mareike. 2006. *"Juda wird aufsteigen!": Untersuchungen zum ersten Kapitel des Richterbuches*. BZAW 367. Berlin: de Gruyter.

Redford, Donald B. 1970. *A Study of the Biblical Story of Joseph (Gen 37–50)*. VTSup 20. Leiden: Brill.

Rendsburg, Gary. 1980. "Late Biblical Hebrew and the Date of 'P.'" *JANES* 12:65–80.

———. 1990. *Linguistic Evidence for the Northern Origin of Selected Psalms*. SBLMS 43. Atlanta: Scholars Press.

Revell, Ernest John. 1985. "The Battle with Benjamin (Judges XX 29–48) and Hebrew Narrative Techniques." *VT* 35:417–33.

———. 1996. *The Designation of the Individual: Expressive Usage in Biblical Narrative*. Kampen: Kok Pharos.

Reviv, Hanoch. 1985. "The *'Edah* between History and Historiography" [Hebrew]. *Shnaton* 9:145–55.

———. 1989. *The Elders in Ancient Israel*. Jerusalem: Magnes.

Rezetko, Robert. 2003. "Dating Biblical Hebrew: Evidence from Samuel-Kings and Chronicles." Pages 215–50 in *Biblical Hebrew: Studies in Chronology and Typology*. Edited by Ian Young. JSOTSup 369. London: T&T Clark.

———. 2009. "What Happened to the Book of Samuel in the Persian Period and Beyond?" Pages 237–52 in *A Palimpsest: Rhetoric, Ideology, Stylistics, and Language Relating to Persian Israel*. Edited by Ehud Ben Zvi, Diana Vikander Edelman, and Frank Polak. Piscataway, NJ: Gorgias.

———. 2013. "The Qumran Scrolls of the Book of Judges: Literary Formation, Textual Criticism, and Historical Linguistics." *JHS* 13. http://www.jhsonline.org/Articles/article_182.pdf.

Ribichini, Sergio. 1999. "Baetyl." *DDD* 157–59.

Richter, Wolfgang. 1963. *Traditionsgeschichtliche Untersuchungen zum Richterbuch*. BBB 18. Bonn: Hanstein.

Riffaterre, Michael. 1978. *Semiotics of Poetry*. Bloomington: Indiana University Press.

———. 1990. "Compulsory Reader Response: The Intertextual Drive." Pages 56–78 in *Intertextuality: Theories and Practices*. Edited by Michael Worton and Judith Still. Manchester: Manchester University Press.
Ringgren, Helmer. 1977. "בער *bʿr*." *TDOT* 2:201–5.
Rofé, Alexander. 1985. "The Monotheistic Argumentation in Deuteronomy 4:32–40: Contents, Composition and Text." *VT* 35:434–45.
———. 1987. "Family and Sex Laws in Deuteronomy and the Book of the Covenant." *Henoch* 9:131–59.
———. 1988a. *Introduction to Deuteronomy: Part I and Further Chapters* [Hebrew]. Jerusalem: Akademon.
———. 1988b. "The Vineyard of Naboth: The Origin and Message of the Story." *VT* 38:89–104.
———. 1990. "An Enquiry into the Betrothal of Rebekah." Pages 27–39 in *Die Hebräische Bibel und ihre zweifache Nachgeschichte: Festschrift fürRolf Rendtorff zum 65. Geburtstag*. Edited by Erhard Blum, Christian Macholz, and Ekkehard W. Stegemann. Neukirchen-Vluyn: Neukirchener Verlag.
———. 2003. "The History of Israelite Religion and the Biblical Text: Corrections Due to the Unification of Worship." Pages 759–93 in *Emanuel: Studies in Hebrew Bible, Septuagint and Dead Sea Scrolls in Honor of Emanuel Tov*. Edited by Shalom M. Paul, Robert A. Kraft, Lawrence H. Schiffman, and Weston W. Fields. VTSup 94. Leiden: Brill.
———. 2005. "Defilement of Virgins in Biblical Law and the Case of Dinah (Genesis 34)." *Bib* 86:369–75.
Röllig, Wolfgang. 1999. "Bethel." *DDD* 173–75.
Rollston, Christopher A. 2010. *Writing and Literacy in the World of Ancient Israel: Epigraphic Evidence from the Iron Age*. ABS 11. Atlanta: Society of Biblical Literature.
Römer, Thomas. 1994. "The Book of Deuteronomy." Pages 178–212 in *The History of Israel's Traditions: The Heritage of Martin Noth*. Edited by Steven L. McKenzie and M. Patrick Graham. JSOTSup 182. Sheffield: Sheffield Academic Press.
———. 2001. "Recherches actuelles sur le cycle d'Abraham." Pages 179–211 in *Studies in the Book of Genesis*. Edited by André Wénin. BETL 155. Leuven: Leuven University Press.
———. 2005. *The So-Called Deuteronomistic History: A Sociological, Historical and Literary Introduction*. London: T&T Clark.

———. 2011. "Das deuteronomistische Geschichtswerk und die Wüstentraditionen der Hebräischen Bibel." Pages 55–88 in *Das deuteronomistische Geschichtswerk*. Edited by Hermann-Josef Stipp. ÖBS 39. Frankfurt am Main: Lang.
Römer, Thomas Christian, and Marc Zvi Brettler. 2000. "Deuteronomy 34 and the Case for a Persian Hexateuch." *JBL* 119:401–19.
Römer, Thomas, and Albert de Pury. 2000. "Deuteronomistic Historiography (DH): History of Research and Debated Issues." Pages 24–141 in *Israel Constructs Its History: Deuteronomistic Historiography in Recent Research*. Edited by Albert de Pury, Thomas Römer, and Jean-Daniel Macchi. JSOTSup 306. Sheffield: Sheffield Academic.
Rooker, Mark F. 1990. *Biblical Hebrew in Transition: The Language of the Book of Ezekiel*. JSOTSup 90. Sheffield: Sheffield Academic.
Rose, Margaret A. 1979. *Parody/Meta-fiction*. London: Croom Helm.
Rösel, Hartmut Nahum. 1976. "Studien zur Topographie der Kriege in den Büchern Josua und Richter." *ZDPV* 92:10–46.
Rost, Leonhard. 1982. *The Succession to the Throne of David*. Translated by M. D. Rutter and D. M. Gunn. Sheffield: Almond.
Roth, Wolfgang M. W. 1963. "Hinterhalt und Scheinflucht: Der stammespolemische Hintergrund von Jos 8." *ZAW* 75:296–303.
Rothenbusch, Ralf. 2003. "Die eherechtlichen Rechtssätze in Deuteronomium 22,13–29 im Kontext der altorientalischen Rechtsgeschichte." Pages 153–212 in *Das Deuteronomium*. Edited by Georg Braulik. ÖBS 23. Frankfurt: Lang.
Rudin-O'Brasky, Talia. 1982. *The Patriarchs in Hebron and Sodom (Genesis 18–19): A Study of the Structure and Composition of a Biblical Story* [Hebrew]. Jerusalem Biblical Studies 2. Jerusalem: Simor.
———. 1985. "The Appendices to the Book of Judges (Judges 17–21)" [Hebrew]. *Beer-Sheva* 2:141–65.
Rudolph, Wilhelm R. 1966. *Hosea*. KAT 13.1. Gütersloh: Mohn.
Rüterswörden, Udo. 1996. "Das Böse in der deuteronomischen Schultheologie." Pages 223–41 in *Das Deuteronomium und seine Querbeziehungen*. Edited by Timo Veijola. Schriften der Finnischen Exegetischen Gesellschaft 62. Göttingen: Vandenhoeck & Ruprecht.
———. 2002. "Dtn 13 in der neueren Deuteronomiumforschung." Pages 185–203 in *Congress Volume: Basel, 2001*. Edited by André Lemaire. VTSup 92. Leiden: Brill.
Salvesen, Alison. 1998. "*keter*." Pages 67–73 in *Semantics of Ancient Hebrew*. Edited by T. Muraoka. AbrNSup 6. Leuven: Peeters.

Sandmel, Samuel. 1961. "The Haggada within Scripture." *JBL* 80:105–22.
Sarna, Nahum. 1963. "Psalm 89: A Study in Inner Biblical Exegesis." Pages 29–46 in *Biblical and Other Studies*. Edited by A. Altmann. Cambridge: Harvard University Press.
Satterthwaite, Philip E. 1992. "Narrative Artistry in the Composition of Judges XX 29ff." *VT* 42:80–89.
Schley, Donald Gilmer. 1989. *Shiloh: A Biblical City in Tradition and History*. JSOTSup 63. Sheffield: JSOT Press.
Schmid, Konrad. 2006. "The So-Called Yahwist and the Literary Gap between Genesis and Exodus." Pages 29–50 in *A Farewell to the Yahwist? The Composition of the Pentateuch in Recent European Interpretation*. Edited by Thomas B. Dozeman and Konrad Schmid. SymS 34. Atlanta: Society of Biblical Literature.
———. 2008. "Abraham's Sacrifice: Gerhard von Rad's Interpretation of Genesis 22." *Int* 62:268–76.
———. 2010. *Genesis and the Moses Story: Israel's Dual Origins in the Hebrew Bible*. Translated by James D. Nogalski. Siphrut 3. Winona Lake, IN: Eisenbrauns.
———. "The Deuteronomistic Image of History as Interpretive Device in the Second Temple Period: Towards a Long-Term Interpretation of 'Deuteronomism.'" Pages 369–88 in *Congress Volume: Helsinki, 2010*. Edited by Martti Nissinen. VTSup 148. Leiden: Brill.
Schmidt, Ludwig. 2004. *Das vierte Buch Mose: Numeri Kapitel 10,11–36,13*. ATD 7.2. Göttingen: Vandenhoeck & Ruprecht.
Schniedewind, William M. 1999. "Qumran Hebrew as an Antilanguage." *JBL* 118:235–52.
Schniedewind, William M., and Daniel Sivan. 1997. "The Elijah-Elisha Narratives: A Test Case for the Northern Dialect of Hebrew." *JQR* 87:303–37.
Schulte, Hannelis. 1972. *Die Entstehung der Geschichtsschreibung im Alten Israel*. BZAW 128. Berlin: de Gruyter.
Schunck, Klaus-Dietrich. 1963. *Benjamin: Untersuchungen zur Entstehung und Geschichte eines israelitischen Stammes*. BZAW 86. Berlin: Töpelmann.
Seeligmann, Isac Leo. 1962. "Hebräische Erzählung und biblische Geschichtsschrieibung." *TZ* 18:305–25.
———. 1963. "Menschliches Heldentum und göttliche Hilfe." *TZ* 19:385–411.

Segal, Moses Hirsch. 1958. *A Grammar of Mishnaic Hebrew*. Oxford: Clarendon.
Seidel, Moshe. 1956. "Parallels in the Book of Isaiah and the Book of Psalms" [Hebrew]. *Sinai* 38:149–72, 229–42, 272–80.
Seitz, Gottfried. 1971. *Redaktionsgeschichtliche Studien zum Deuteronomium*. BWANT 5.3. Stuttgart: Kohlhammer.
Shemesh, Yael. 2007. "Rape Is Rape Is Rape: The Story of Dinah and Shechem (Genesis 34)." *ZAW* 119:2–21.
Ska, Jean-Louis. 2013. "Genesis 22: What Question Should We Ask the Text?" *Bib* 94:257–67.
Skinner, John. 1930. *A Critical and Exegetical Commentary on Genesis*. 2nd ed. ICC. Edinburgh: T&T Clark.
Smend, Rudolf. 2000. "The Law and the Nations: A Contribution to Deuteronomistic Tradition History." Pages 95–110 in *Reconsidering Israel and Judah: Recent Studies on the Deuteronomistic History*. Edited by Gary N. Knoppers and J. G. McConville. Winona Lake, IN: Eisenbrauns.
Smith, Henry Preserved. 1898. *A Critical and Exegetical Commentary on the Books of Samuel*. ICC. Edinburgh: T&T Clark.
Smith, Mark S. 1997. "How to Write a Poem: The Case of Psalm 151A (11QPs^a 28.3–12)." Pages 182–208 in *The Hebrew of the Dead Sea Scrolls and Ben Sira: Proceedings of a Symposium Held at Leiden University 11–14 December 1995*. Edited by T. Muraoka and J. F. Elwolde. STDJ 26. Leiden: Brill.
Snaith, Norman Henry. 1967. *Leviticus and Numbers*. Century Bible. New edition. London: Nelson.
———. 1978. "The Altar at Gilgal: Joshua 22:23–29." *VT* 28:330–35.
Soggin, J. Alberto. 1972. *Joshua: A Commentary*. Translated by R. A. Wilson. OTL. London: SCM.
———. 1987. *Judges: A Commentary*. Translated by John Bowden. 2nd ed. OTL. London: SCM.
Sommer, Benjamin D. 1998. *A Prophet Reads Scripture: Allusion in Isaiah 40–66*. Stanford: Stanford University Press.
Stadler-Sutskover, Talia. 2002. "The Leading Word and Its Roles in Judges 19–21." Pages 295–307 in *Bible and Computer*. Proceedings of the Association Internationale Bible et Informatique "From Alpha to Byte." Edited by Johann Cook. Leiden: Brill.
Stern, Ephraim. 1982. *The Material Culture of the Land of the Bible in the Persian Period 538–332 B.C.* Warminster: Aris & Phillips.

———. 2001. *The Assyrian, Babylonian, and Persian Periods 732–332 B.C.E.* Vol. 2 of *Archaeology of the Land of the Bible*. ABRL. New York: Doubleday.
Sternberg, Meir. 1987. *The Poetics of Biblical Narrative: Ideological Literature and the Drama of Reading*. Bloomington: Indiana University Press.
Steymans, Hans Ulrich. 2006. "Die literarische und historische Bedeutung der Thronfolgevereidigungen Asarhaddons." Pages 331–49 in *Die deuteronomistischen Geschichtswerke: Redaktions- und religionsgeschichtliche Perspektiven zur "Deuteronomismus"-Diskussion in Tora und Vorderen Propheten*. Edited by Markus Witte, Konrad Schmid, Doris Prechel, and Jan Christian Gertz. BZAW 365. Berlin: de Gruyter.
Stipp, Hermann-Josef. 2006. "Richter 19: Ein frühes Beispiel schriftgestützter politischer Propaganda in Israel." Pages 127–64 in *Ein Herz so weit wie der Sand am Ufer des Meeres: Festschrift für Georg Hentschel*. Edited by Susanne Gillmayr-Bucher, Annett Giercke, and Christiana Niessen. Würzburg: Echter.
———. 2011. "Beobachtungen zur ehemaligen literarischen Selbstständigkeit von Ri 19." Pages 221–42 in *"Ruft nicht die Weisheit...?" (Spr 8,1): Alttestamentliche und epigraphische Textinterpretationen*. Edited by Kristinn Ólason. ATSAT 91. St. Ottilien: Eos.
Stoebe, Hans-Joachim. 1973. *Das erste Buch Samuelis*. KAT 8.1. Gütersloh: Mohn.
Stone, Ken. 1995. "Gender and Homosexuality in Judges 19: Subject-Honor, Object-Shame?" *JSOT* 67:87–107.
Stone, Lawson Grant. 1988. *From Tribal Confederation to Monarchic State: The Editorial Perspective of the Book of Judges*. PhD diss., Yale University. Ann Arbor: UMI.
Stuart, Douglas K. 1987. *Hosea–Jonah*. WBC 31. Waco, TX: Word.
Stulman, Louis. 1992. "Sex and Familial Crimes in the D Code: A Witness to Mores in Transition." *JSOT* 53:47–63.
Sweeney, Marvin A. 1997. "Davidic Polemics in the Book of Judges." *VT* 47:517–29.
———. 2001. *King Josiah of Judah: The Lost Messiah of Israel*. Oxford: Oxford University Press.
Tadmor, Haim. 1987. "The Aramaization of Assyria: Aspects of Western Impact. Pages 449–70 in *Mesopotamien und seine Nachbarn: Politische und kulturelle Wechselbeziehungen im alten Vorderasien vom 4. bis 1.*

Jt. v. Chr. Edited by Hans Jörg Nissen and Johannes Renger. Berlin: Reimer.

———. 1999. "'The Appointed Time Has Not Yet Arrived': The Historical Background of Haggai 1:2." Pages 401–8 in *Ki Baruch Hu: Ancient Near Eastern, Biblical, and Judaic Studies in Honor of Baruch A. Levine.* Edited by Robert Chazan, William W. Hallo, and Lawrence H. Schiffman. Winona Lake, IN: Eisenbrauns.

———. 2006. "Treaty and Oath in the Ancient Near East" [Hebrew]. Pages 183–213 in *Assyria, Babylonia and Judah: Studies in the History of the Ancient Near East.* Edited by Mordechai Cogan. Jerusalem: Bialik Institute and the Israel Exploration Society.

Talmon, Shemaryahu. 1978. "The Presentation of Synchroneity and Simultaneity in Biblical Narrative." Pages 9–26 in *Studies in Hebrew Narrative Art throughout the Ages.* Edited by Joseph Heinemann and Shmuel Werses. ScrHier 27. Jerusalem: Magnes.

———. 1986. "'In Those Days There Was No מלך in Israel'—Judges 18–21." Pages 39–52 in *King, Cult and Calendar in Ancient Israel.* Jerusalem: Magnes.

Tidwell, N. L. 1995. "No Highway! The Outline of a Semantic Description of *Mesillâ*." *VT* 45:251–69.

Toorn, Karel van der. 2007. *Scribal Culture and the Making of the Hebrew Bible.* Cambridge: Harvard University Press.

Toorn, Karel van der, Bob Becking, and Pieter W. van der Horst, eds. 1999. *Dictionary of Deities and Demons in the Bible.* 2nd ed. Leiden: Brill; Grand Rapids: Eerdmans.

Tov, Emmanuel. 1986. "The Nature of the Differences between MT and the LXX." Pages 19–46 in *The Story of David and Goliath: Textual and Literary Criticism: Papers of a Joint Research Venture.* By Dominique Barthélemy, David W. Gooding, Johan Lust, and Emanuel Tov. OBO 73. Fribourg: Editions universitaires.

———. 1992. *Textual Criticism of the Hebrew Bible.* Minneapolis: Fortress; Assen and Maastricht: Van Gorcum.

Trebolle Barrera, Julio. 2008. "A Combined Textual and Literary Criticism Analysis: Editorial Traces in Joshua and Judges." Pages 437–63 in *Florilegium Lovaniense: Studies in Septuagint and Textual Criticism in Honour of Florentino García Martínez.* Edited by Hans Ausloos, Bénédicte Lemmelijn, and Marc Vervenne. BETL 224. Leuven, Paris, and Dudley, MA: Peeters.

Trible, Phyllis. 1984. *Texts of Terror: Literary-Feminist Readings of Biblical Narratives*. Overtures to Biblical Theology. Philadelphia: Fortress.
Tull, Patricia Kathleen. 2000. "Intertextuality and the Hebrew Scriptures." *CurBS* 8:59–90.
Unterman, Jeremiah. 1980. "The Literary Influence of 'the Binding of Isaac' (Genesis 22) on 'the Outrage at Gibeah' (Judges 19)." *HAR* 4:161–65.
Utzschneider, Helmut. 2002. "Situation und Szene: Überlegungen zum Verhältnis historischer und literarischer Deutung prophetischer Texte am Beispiel von Hos 5,8–6,6." *ZAW* 114:80–105.
Van Seters, John. 1975. *Abraham in History and Tradition*. New Haven: Yale University Press.
——— . 1983. *In Search of History*. New Haven: Yale University Press.
——— . 1992. *Prologue to History: The Yahwist as Historian in Genesis*. Louisville: Westminster John Knox.
——— . 1994. *The Life of Moses: The Yahwist as Historian in Exodus–Numbers*. Louisville: Westminster John Knox.
——— . 1999. "Is There Evidence of a Dtr Redaction in the Sinai Pericope (Exodus 19–24, 32–34)?" Pages 160–70 in *Those Elusive Deuteronomists: The Phenomenon of Pan-Deuteronomism*. Edited by Linda S. Schearing and Steven L. McKenzie. JSOTSup 268. Sheffield: Sheffield Academic Press.
——— . 2000. "The Court History and DtrH: Conflicting Perspectives on the House of David." Pages 70–93 in *Die sogenannte Thronfolgegeschichte Davids*. Edited by Albert de Pury and Thomas Römer. OBO 176. Fribourg: Universitätsverlag; Göttingen: Vandenhoeck & Ruprecht.
Vaux, Roland de. 1965. *Ancient Israel*. Translated by John McHugh. New York: McGraw-Hill.
——— . 1978. *The Early History of Israel*. Translated by David Smith. London: Darton, Longman & Todd.
Veijola, Timo. 1977. *Das Königtum in der Beurteilung der deuteronomistischen Historiographie*. Helsinki: Suomalainen Tiedeakatemia.
——— . 1982. *Verheissung in der Krise: Studien zur Literatur und Theologie der Exilszeit anhand des 89. Psalms*. Annales Academiae Scientairum Fennicae B/220. Helsinki: Suomalainen Tiedeakatemia.
——— . 1995. "Wahrheit und Intoleranz nach Deuteronomium 13." *ZTK* 92:287–314.
——— . 1996. "Bundestheologische Redaktion im Deuteronomium." Pages 242–76 in *Das Deuteronomium und seine Querbeziehungen*. Edited by

Timo Veijola. Schriften der Finnischen Exegetischen Gesellschaft 62. Göttingen: Vandenhoeck & Ruprecht.

———. 2004. *Das 5. Buch Mose: Deuteronomium, Kapitel 1, 1–16, 17.* ATD 8.1. Göttingen: Vandenhoeck & Ruprecht.

Verheij, Arian J. C. 1990. *Verbs and Numbers: A Study of the Frequencies of the Hebrew Verbal Tense Forms in the Books of Samuel, Kings, and Chronicles.* SSN 28. Assen: Van Gorcum.

Wallis, Gerhard. 1952. "Eine Parallele zu Richter 19 29ff. und 1. Sam. 11 5 ff. aus dem Briefarchiv von Mari." *ZAW* 23:57–61.

Waltke, Bruce K., and Michael Patrick O'Connor. 1990. *An Introduction to Biblical Hebrew Syntax.* Winona Lake, IN: Eisenbrauns.

Watson, Wilfred G. E. 1984. *Classical Hebrew Poetry: A Guide to Its Techniques.* JSOTSup 26. Sheffield: JSOT Press.

Wazana, Nili. 2013. *All the Boundaries of the Land: The Promised Land in Biblical Thought in Light of the Ancient Near East.* Winona Lake, IN: Eisenbrauns.

Webb, Barry G. 1987. *The Book of the Judges: An Integrated Reading.* JSOTSup 46. Sheffield: JSOT Press.

Weinberg, Joel. 1992. *The Citizen-Temple Community.* Translated by Daniel L. Smith-Christopher. JSOTSup 151. Sheffield: JSOT Press.

Weinfeld, Moshe. 1967. "The Period of the Conquest and of the Judges as Seen by the Earlier and the Later Sources." *VT* 17:93–113.

———. 1972. *Deuteronomy and the Deuteronomistic School.* Oxford: Clarendon.

———. 1983. "Zion and Jerusalem as Religious and Political Capital: Ideology and Utopia." Pages 75–115 in *The Poet and the Historian: Essays in Literary and Historical Biblical Criticism.* Edited by Richard Elliott Friedman. HSS 26. Chico, CA: Scholars Press.

———. 1993. "Judges 1.1–2:5: The Conquest under the Leadership of the House of Judah." Pages 388–400 in *Understanding Poets and Prophets: Essays in Honour of George Wishart Anderson.* Edited by A. Graeme Auld. Sheffield: JSOT Press.

———. 1997. "The Transition from Tribal Republic to Monarchy in Ancient Israel and Its Impression on Jewish Political History." Pages 215–32 in *Kinship and Consent: The Jewish Political Tradition and Its Contemporary Uses.* Edited by Daniel J. Elazar. 2nd ed. New Brunswick, NJ: Transaction.

Weiser, Artur. 1962. *Samuel: Seine geschichtliche Aufgabe und religiöse*

Bedeutung. Traditionsgeschichtliche Untersuchungen zu 1. Samuel 7–12. FRLANT 81. Göttingen: Vandenhoeck & Ruprecht.
Weisman, Ze'ev. 1992. "Ethnology, Etiology, Genealogy, and Historiography in the Tale of Lot and His Daughters (Genesis 19:30–38)" [Hebrew]. Pages 43*–52* in *Sha'arei Talmon: Studies in the Bible, Qumran, and the Ancient Near East Presented to Shemaryahu Talmon*. Edited by Michael Fishbane and Emanuel Tov. Winona Lake, IN: Eisenbrauns.
Weiss, Meir. 1963. "Einiges über die Bauformen des Erzählens in der Bibel." *VT* 13:456–75.
———. 1965. "Weiteres über die Bauformen des Erzählens in der Bibel." *Bib* 40:181–206.
Weissenberg, Hanne von. 2008. "Deuteronomy at Qumran and in MMT." Pages 520–37 in *Houses Full of All Good Things: Essays in Memory of Timo Veijola*. Edited by Juha Pakkala and Martti Nissinen. Publications of the Finnish Exegetical Society 95. Helsinki: Suomen eksegeettinen seura.
Wellhausen, Julius. 1899. *Die Composition des Hexateuchs und der historischen Bücher des Alten Testaments*. 3rd ed. Berlin: Reimer.
———. 1957. *Prolegomena to the History of Ancient Israel*. New York: Meridian.
———. 1963. *Die Kleinen Propheten*. 4th ed. Berlin: de Gruyter.
Welten, Peter. 1969. *Die Königs-Stempel: Ein Beitrag zur Militärpolitk Judas unter Hiskia und Josia*. Wiesbaden: Harrassowitz.
Wenham, Gordon J. 1972. "Betûlāh 'A Girl of Marriageable Age.'" *VT* 22:326–48.
———. 1994. *Genesis 16–50*. WBC 2. Waco, TX: Word.
Westermann, Claus. 1985. *Genesis 12–36: A Commentary*. Translated by John J. Scullion. CC. Minneapolis: Augsburg.
———. 1986. *Genesis 37–50: A Commentary*. Translated by John J. Scullion. CC. Minneapolis: Augsburg.
Whybray, Roger N. 1987. *The Making of the Pentateuch*. JSOTSup 53. Sheffield: JSOT Press.
Williamson, Hugh G. M. 1982. *1 and 2 Chronicles*. NCB. Grand Rapids: Eerdmans.
———. 1985. *Ezra-Nehemiah*. WBC 16. Waco, TX: Word.
———. 1998. "Judah and the Jews." Pages 145–63 in *Studies in Persian History: Essays in Memory of David M. Lewis*. Edited by Maria Bro-

sius and Amelie Kurhrt. Achaemenid History 11. Leiden: Nederlands Instituut voor het Nabije Oosten.
Willis, Timothy M. 2001. *The Elders of the City: A Study of the Elders-Laws in Deuteronomy*. SBLMS 55. Atlanta: Society of Biblical Literature.
Wilson, John Albert. 1945. "The Assembly of a Phoenician City." *JNES* 4:245.
Wilson, Robert R. 1999. "Who Was the Deuteronomist? (Who Was Not the Deuteronomist?): Reflections on Pan-Deuteronomism." Pages 67–82 in *Those Elusive Deuteronomists: The Phenomenon of Pan-Deuteronomism*. Edited by Linda S. Schearing and Steven L. McKenzie. JSOTSup 268. Sheffield: Sheffield Academic Press.
Wolde, Ellen van. 1997. "Texts in Dialogue with Texts: Intertextuality in the Ruth and Tamar Narratives." *BibInt* 5:1–28.
———. 2002. "Does ʿinnâ Denote Rape? A Semantic Analysis of a Controversial Word." *VT* 52:528–44.
Wolff, Hans Walter. 1974. *Hosea*. Translated by Gary Stansell. Hermeneia. Philadelphia: Fortress.
———. 1986. *Obadiah and Jonah: A Commentary*. Translated by Margaret Kohl. CC. Minneapolis: Augsburg.
Wong, Gregory T. K. 2006. *Compositional Strategy of the Book of Judges: An Inductive, Rhetorical Study*. VTSup 111. Leiden: Brill.
Worton, Michael, and Judith Still, eds. 1990. *Intertextuality: Theories and Practices*. Manchester: Manchester University Press.
Wright, Addison G. 1966. "The Literary Genre Midrash." *CBQ* 28:105–38, 417–57.
Wright, David P. 2003. "The Laws of Hammurabi as a Source for the Covenant Collection (Exodus 20:23–23:19)." *Maarav* 10:11–87.
Wright, Richard M. 2003. "Further Evidence for North Israelite Contributions to Late Biblical Hebrew." Pages 129–48 in *Biblical Hebrew: Studies in Chronology and Typology*. Edited by Ian Young. JSOTSup 369. London: T&T Clark.
Yoreh, Tzemah. 2010. *The First Book of God*. BZAW 402. Berlin: de Gruyter.
Young, Ian. 1993. *Diversity in Pre-Exilic Hebrew*. FAT 5. Tübingen: Mohr.
———. 1997. "Evidence of Diversity in Pre-Exilic Judahite Hebrew." *HS* 38:7–20.
———. 1999. "עַם Construed as Singular and Plural in Hebrew Biblical Texts: Diachronic and Textual Perspectives." *ZAH* 12:48–82.
———. 2001. "*ʿEdah* and *Qahal* as Collective Nouns in Hebrew Biblical Texts." *ZAH* 14:68–78.

———. 2003. "Late Biblical Hebrew and Hebrew Inscriptions." Pages 276–311 in *Biblical Hebrew: Studies in Chronology and Typology*. Edited by Ian Young. JSOTSup 369. London: T&T Clark.

———. 2009. "What Is 'Late Biblical Hebrew'?" Pages 253–68 in *A Palimpsest: Rhetoric, Ideology, Stylistics, and Language Relating to Persian Israel*. Edited by Ehud Ben Zvi, Diana Edelman, and Frank Polak. PHSC 5. Piscataway, NJ: Gorgias.

Young, Ian, Robert Rezetko, and Martin Ehrensvärd. 2008a. *An Introduction to Approaches and Problems*. Vol. 1 of *Linguistic Dating of Biblical Texts*. Bible World. London: Equinox.

———. 2008b. *A Survey of Scholarship, a New Synthesis and a Comprehensive Bibliography*. Vol. 2 of *Linguistic Dating of Biblical Texts*. Bible World. London: Equinox.

Younger, K. Lawson. 1990. *Ancient Conquest Accounts: A Study in Ancient Near East and Biblical History Writing*. JSOTSup 98. Sheffield: JSOT Press.

———. 1995. "The Configuring of Judicial Preliminaries: Judges 1.1–2.5 and Its Dependencies on the Book of Joshua." *JSOT* 68:75–92.

Zakovitch, Yair. 1979. *"For Three ... and for Four": The Pattern of the Numerical Sequence Three-Four in the Bible* [Hebrew]. Jerusalem: Makor.

———. 1983. "The Associative Arrangement of the Book of Judges and Its Use for the Recognition of Stages in the Formation of the Book" [Hebrew]. Pages 161–83 in *Isac Leo Seeligmann Volume: Essays on the Bible and the Ancient World*. Edited by Alexander Rofé and Yair Zakovitch. Jerusalem: Rubinstein.

———. 1985. "Reflection Stories—Another Dimension of the Evaluation of Characters in Biblical Narrative" [Hebrew]. *Tarbiz* 54:165–76.

———. 1993. "Through the Looking Glass: Reflections/Inversions of Genesis Stories in the Bible." *BibInt* 1:139–52.

Zehnder, Markus. 2009. "Building on Stone? Deuteronomy and Esarhaddon's Loyalty Oaths." *BBR* 19:341–74, 511–35.

Zenger, Erich. 2008. *Einleitung in das Alte Testament*. 7th ed. Kohlhammer Studienbücher Theologie 1.1. Stuttgart: Kohlhammer.

Zevit, Ziony. 1982. "Converging Lines of Evidence Bearing on the Date of P." *ZAW* 94:481–511.

———. 1983. "Archaeological and Literary Stratigraphy in Joshua 7–8." *BASOR* 251:23–35.

Zimmerli, Walter. 1979. *Ezekiel 1: A Commentary on the Book of the Prophet Ezekiel, Chapters 1–24*. Translatedy by R. E. Clements. Hermeneia. Philadelphia: Fortress.

Zorn, Jeffrey R. 1993. "Tell en-Nasbeh: A Re-evaluation of the Architecture and Stratigraphy of the Early Bronze Age, Iron Age and Later Periods." PhD diss., University of California, Berkeley.

———. 1997. "Mizpah: Newly Recovered Stratum Reveals Judah's Other Capital." *BAR* 23.5:28–38, 66.

———. 2003. "Tell en-Naṣbeh and the Problem of the Material Culture of the Sixth Century." Pages 413–47 in *Judah and the Judeans in the Neo-Babylonian Period*. Edited by Oded Lipschits and Joseph Blenkinsopp. Winona Lake, IN: Eisenbrauns.

Zorn, Jeffrey, Joseph Yellin, and John Hayes. 1994. "The $m(w)ṣh$ Stamp Impressions and the Neo-Babylonian Period." *IEJ* 44:161–83.

Index of Ancient Sources

Hebrew Bible

Genesis

Ref	Page
1:11	124
1:12	124
1:17	120
1:21	124
1:25	124
1:27	47, 120
1:28	120
2:10	146
2:11	132
2:23	47
3:8	149
3:13	303
3:13–14	266
4:1–5	166
4:19	138
5:22	149
5:24	149
5:29	149
6:2	138
6:9	149
6:15	25
6:17	137
8:9	149
8:11	138
9:16	303
10:29	140–41
11:29	
12:6	152
12:6–7	102
12:8	100–101
12:18	303
13	185
13:4	209
13:8	182
13:14	132
13:13	19, 150
13:17	149
13:18	102
14:3	140–41
14:7	86
14:23	237
15:10	141
16	167
16:7–11	303
16:10–12	188
17:1	149
17:4	146
17:7	303
17:13	303
17:14	261, 303
17:18–21	166
17:19	303
18–19	174–95, 312, 316, 324
18:1–4	313
18:1–5	190
18:1–8	186
18:2	190
18:3–8	15
18:4–8	187
18:5	190–91, 314
18:10	153
18:13	126
18:14	43, 153
18:15	195
18:25	61, 126
19	129, 134, 161–62, 175–95, 317, 324

Genesis (cont.)

19:1	190
19:1–2	176
19:1–3	313
19:1–10	179, 186, 313
19:1–13	174–86
19:1–38	133
19:2	142, 180, 190–91
19:2–3	314
19:2–7	15
19:3	176, 187, 190
19:4	127, 130, 133, 150, 181, 184, 225, 237, 239
19:5	125
19:5–8	178
19:6	247
19:7	182, 253, 313
19:8	123, 156, 161, 177–78, 180–84, 188–89, 248, 258, 313
19:9	161, 190, 294
19:9–13	177
19:11	247
19:12	237
19:13	175
19:14	133
19:15	195
19:15–16	193
19:16	193–95
19:18	182
19:19	48, 148, 177, 195
19:23	142
19:26	195
19:30	187, 189
19:30–35	188
19:30–38	187, 190, 194
19:31	187–88
19:31–35	187
19:32	187, 189
19:33	188
19:35	188
20–21	280
20:9–12	266
20:11	304
21	167
21:12–13	166
21:31	305
22	280
22:6	279
22:10	279
22:11	303
22:14	92
22:15	303
22:19	14
22:20–24	188
22:24	124
23:2	66, 268
23:19	268
24	278–79, 316, 324
24:11	138
24:12–14	278
24:16	246, 258
24:23	278
24:25	143, 278, 313–14
24:28–29	246
24:31–33	15
24:32	143, 278
24:32–33	176
24:40	149
24:50–51	246
24:54	278
24:54–55	314
24:55	278
24:56	278
24:63	138
25:1	245
25:1–4	188
25:4	140–41
25:6	245
25:11	145
25:16	86
25:19–34	167
25:21–26	188
25:27–34	167
26:10	303
26:11	148
27:8	133
27:35	167
27:38	308
28:1–9	166
28:11	145

INDEX OF ANCIENT SOURCES 379

28:17	291	37:3	166
28:19	101, 305	37:7	46, 141
29:4	15, 297	38:9	147
29:11	308	38:11	247
29:25	303	38:16	214
29:25–26	266	38:29	149
29:31–30:23	188	39:12	251
31:1	12	40:10	46
31:13	101	40:15	138
31:23	48, 137	41:3	144
31:24	137	41:39	140
31:26	266	41:56	237
31:31	266	42:7	15, 294
31:42	69, 153	42:23	214
31:48	305	42:27	143, 278
32:4	150	42:28	303
32:9	65	43:10	69, 153, 193
32:25	145	43:19	247
32:25–31	102	43:24	143, 278
33:10	182	43:24–25	15, 176
33:11	190	43:32	15
33:17	305	43:34	151
33:18	66, 268	44:7	61
34	241–42, 269, 297	45:1	177
34:1	20	45:3	48
34:2	19, 250–51	45:23	275
34:3	246	47:21	137
34:7	18, 241–42, 250	48:7	103
34:12	245–46	48:13–19	166
34:14	126	48:15	149
34:15	137	49:8	43
34:22	137	49:27	138
34:24–25	137	49:28	140–41, 143
34:29	237	49:30	108, 268
34:31	14		
35:1–3	308	Exodus	
35:3–7	101	1:18	126
35:4	102, 145	2:11	12
35:6	66, 268	2:20	15, 126
35:8	102, 305–6	2:23	12
35:19	103	3:2	303
35:22	245	3:16	136, 261
36:20	303	3:18	136, 261
36:35	150	4:29	261
37:2	245	5:4	124

Exodus (cont.)

Reference	Pages
5:7	278
5:10–13	278
5:11	261
5:16	278
5:18	278
6:25	261
8:25	181
9:18	152, 275
9:20–21	45
9:24	146, 275
9:26	132
10:5	130
10:6	52
10:7	303
10:14	275
11:6	146, 275
11:7	152
12:6	137
12:10	130
12:13	132
12:21	136, 261
12:22–23	248
12:39	193
12:47	128
13:5	303
13:12	137
13:15	137
14:5	303
14:11	303
14:11–13	266
14:12	25, 144
14:15–31	47
14:21–16	166
15:1–18	47
15:3–10	166
15:5–10	47
15:8–15	46
15:15	48
15:23	305
16:1–2	128
16:16	25, 133, 144
16:22	136, 261
16:32	144
17:1	128
17:5–6	136, 261
18:12	136, 261
18:25	206
19:2	213
19:7	261
19:17	282
19:18	214
19:22	149
19:24	83
20:11	237
20:21	132
20:24	140
21:13	45
21:16	138
21:19	149
22:7	150
22:15–16	245
23:20–33	302
23:27	43
23:29–30	303
23:33	303
24:1	261
24:1–2	83
24:5	140
24:9	136, 261
24:14	143, 261
25:2	143
27:21	52
28:1	36
28:8	124
28:10	130
28:31	151
29:1	25–26, 144
29:17	222
29:34	130
30:33	143, 261
31:1	137
31:16	303
32	36
32:6	140
32:11	126
32:19	19
32:30	83
32:33	63, 143
33:11	178, 303

34:10–16	302	11:15–16	124
34:12	303	11:22	124
34:13	303	14:8	65
34:24	308	14:18	130
34:29	214	14:29	130
35:4	25, 144	14:36	237
35:20	128	14:38	247
35:21–23	143	15:2	143
35:23–24	130	15:5	143
39:5	124	16:9–10	26
39:22	151	16:17	150
		16:26	65
Leviticus		16:28	65
1:6	222	16:34	126
1:12	222	17:2	25, 144
2:3	130	17:3	143
2:10	130	17:4	261, 264
3:7	93	17:8	143
4:13	128, 137	18:6	143
4:13–14	261	18:17	137
4:15	136, 261	18:18	138
4:22	136	18:22	241, 258
5:4	139	18:24	140
5:15–26	198	18:26	241
5:21–22	198	19:6	130
5:22	123	19:10	148
6:2	145	19:11	198
6:9	130	19:29	137
6:15–16	151, 238	20:2	62, 143, 198
7:16–17	130	20:9–10	62, 143
8:3–4	137	20:13	258
8:4	128	20:15	62
8:5	25, 144	20:20	62
8:10	237	20:23	140
8:20	222	20:27	198
8:32	130	21:7	138
9:1	136, 261	21:13	138
9:2	261	21:18	143
9:3	261	21:21	143
9:5	128	22:3	143
9:6	25, 144	22:4	143
9:22	140	22:18	143
10:6	305	22:24	209
10:12	130	22:25	140
10:16	130	24:8	303

Leviticus (cont.)		11:16	136, 261
24:14	128, 137, 198, 269	11:20	126
24:15	143	11:22	149
24:16	128, 198	11:24–25	261
24:23	198	11:30	65, 136
26:12	149	12:1	138
26:15	303	14:1	128, 308
26:40	198	14:2	128
26:44	303	14:5	137
27:18	130	14:10	128, 198
27:24	133	14:15	222
27:28–29	198	14:22	303
27:29	62	14:23	303
		14:36	128
Numbers		14:41	126
1:18	137	15:11	133
1:44	136	15:24	128
1:51	145	15:35	269
2:2	213	15:35–36	198
2:3	136	15:36	128
3:32	136	16:2	162
4:6	151	16:3	128, 137, 150
4:18	261	16:19	137
4:19	143	16:25	136
4:34	136, 261	17:5	36
4:46	136	17:6	128
4:49	143	17:7	137
5:3	52	17:11	213
5:6–7	198	17:16–24	36
5:7	133	17:21	136
5:12	143	19:14	237
5:21	139	20:2	137
7:2	136	20:4	150
7:11	136	20:8	137
7:18	136	20:11	128
7:84	136	20:29	128
8:6–20	155	21:1	22, 47
8:7	144	21:11	142
8:9	137	21:20	150
8:26	133	21:27–30	47
10:3	128	21:32	132
10:8–9	257	22:22–27	303
10:10	140	22:29	19, 153
10:33	92	22:31–35	303
11:12	303	22:34	214

23:11–12	266	31:49	260
23:23	153	31:53	120
24:2	290	31:54	125
24:25	12	32:2	136, 261
25	255	32:8	144
25:1–5	98	32:28	261, 315
25:6	305	33:19–20	104
25:6–13	257, 270	33:40	108, 268
25:8	154	33:52	303
25:13	36	33:54	26, 270
26:55	26, 270	33:55	303
27:2	136	33:56	282
27:4	261	34:13	26, 270
27:7	151	34:18	136
27:11	146	35:2	290
27:17	128	35:24–25	128, 269
27:19–21	228	36:1	261
27:20	128	36:1–13	155
29:39	32	36:2	26, 270
30:2	25, 144	36:3	261, 307
30:3	139	36:3–4	151
30:11	139	36:6	25, 144
30:14	139	36:7–8	151
30:17	246		
31	120, 129, 255–63, 313, 318, 324	Deuteronomy	
31:4	271–72, 315	1:8	303
31:4–5	256, 313	1:12	152
31:6	120, 257	1:15	206
31:8	147	1:17	146
31:10	308, 131	1:21	276
31:12	65	1:22	146
31:13	136, 261	1:36	46, 148
31:13–18	260	2:10	168
31:14	132	2:12	168
31:14–16	260	2:14	132
31:15–18	313	2:20	168
31:16	225	2:21–22	149
31:17	137, 259	2:23	85
31:17–18	257–60, 262, 313, 318	2:26	142
31:18	259, 313	2:34	52, 308, 316, 324
31:19	264	2:34–35	237, 313
31:26	261–62	3:5	32, 141
31:27	132	3:6	52, 316, 324
31:35	137, 258	3:6–7	237, 313
31:47	120	3:17	142

Deuteronomy (cont.)

Reference	Pages
3:18	132
3:27	142
4:7	146
4:16	137, 288
4:20	146
4:16	288
4:23	288
4:25	288
4:31	303
4:32	146, 152, 275, 314, 324
4:32–34	275
4:41	142
4:47	142
4:49	142
5:1	276
5:22	136
5:23	146
6:1	276
6:15	149
7:1–6	302
7:5	148, 303, 308
7:8	139
7:9	276
7:11	276
7:12–13	303
7:17	152
7:25	148, 308
7:25–26	198
8:20	303
9:7	152, 276–77, 314, 322
9:10	136
9:12	288
9:18	288
9:20	36
9:21	148
10:4	136
10:6	36
10:14	237
11:3	124
11:17	213
11:24–25	46, 148
11:30	108, 142, 144
12:1	276
12:3	148, 303, 308
12:8	296
12:11	276
12:25	288, 296
12:28	288, 296
12:30	149, 152
13:1	232
13:1–19	234, 248
13:2–6	231–32
13:3	232
13:3–4	306
13:4	232
13:6	232, 242, 315–16, 324
13:7	232
13:7–12	231–32, 242
13:8	146
13:9	232
13:11	232
13:13	157, 232, 241
13:13–18	198, 231–40, 242–43, 316, 323–24, 327
13:14	133, 181, 232, 239, 315
13:15	241, 313, 318
13:16	236–40, 308
13:16–17	308
13:17	92, 142, 148, 151, 215, 218, 236, 238, 308, 313
13:17–18	235
13:18	232, 236, 303
13:19	232, 288, 303
14:3	241
14:14–15	124
14:23	276
15:3	45
15:5	303
15:19	137
16:21	144
17:2	288
17:2–7	241, 243
17:2–13	316, 324
17:4	241, 131, 318
17:7	242
17:9	36, 241, 131, 318
17:12	242
17:18	36
17:19	276

18:1	36	22:21	18, 241–42, 247–48, 250, 314–15
18:9–12	241		
18:16	136	22:22	242, 244, 323
18:21	152	22:22–27	297
18:21–22	168	22:22–29	269, 323
19:8	303	22:23	75, 247, 259
19:9	316	22:23–24	244, 323
19:12	261, 297	22:23–27	244
19:16–20	241, 313, 316, 318, 324	22:23–29	244
19:17–19	242	22:24	19, 242, 244, 248
19:18	241	22:25	251
19:19	242	22:25–27	244–45
20:2	146	22:28	75, 247, 251, 259, 313
20:5–7	143	22:28–29	244–45
20:7	138	22:29	19, 246
20:10	146	23:2–9	136, 250
20:10–11	197	23:6	252
20:10–14	196	23:12	138
20:11	146	23:15	149
20:12–14	196	24:3–5	138
20:13–14	260	24:4	241
20:14	197, 237	24:7	138, 242, 316, 324
21:1–7	297	24:8	36
21:3	146	24:21	148
21:6	146	25:9	144
21:9	288	26:2	276
21:10–13	247	26:19	206
21:11–14	260	27:1	136, 261
21:13	146	27:10	303
21:14	19	27:13	141
21:17	149	27:14	154
21:19	193	27:15	288
21:21	198, 242, 316, 324	28:1	206
22:2	146	28:1–2	303
22:13–14	138	28:11	303
22:13–21	244	28:15	303
22:13–22	244	28:25	92, 146
22:13–29	244–48, 316, 324	28:45	303
22:14	146, 149	28:48	206
22:14–15	244	28:62	303
22:15	193, 314	29:9	154, 261
22:15–16	246	29:11	139
22:19	246	29:12	303
22:20	61, 126	29:13	139
		29:18–20	139

Deuteronomy (cont.)		2:16	278
29:21–24	185	2:17	139
30:4	276	2:19	237
30:7	139	2:20	139
30:8	303	2:24	303
30:10	303	3:8	228
30:14	146	3:12	154
31:7	303	3:13–17	166
31:6–7	276	3:17	228
31:9	136, 261	4:2	154
31:14	282	4:5	143
31:16	303	4:8	143
31:17	148	4:10	228
31:20	303	4:13	132
31:21	148	4:16	228
31:23	276	4:18	209
31:28	261	4:19	108
31:29	148, 288	5:4	25, 137, 144
31:30	136, 150	5:6	303
32:2	47	5:9	305
32:7a	47	6–8	235
32:8	47, 143	6–10	196
32:10b	47	6–11	131, 199
32:11b	47	6:3	46, 141, 144
32:20–21	47	6:6	228
32:23	47	6:14	144
32:26	47	6:15	46, 141, 145
32:27	140	6:16	209
32:30	152	6:21	52, 237
32:35	148	6:24	148, 237, 308
32:50	36	6:27	197
33:10	151	7–8	120, 129, 133, 161, 195–221, 316, 327
33:29	45, 198		
34:7–12	331	7:1	198
		7:1–6	316, 324
Joshua		7:1–26	197
1:1–13:33	285	7:2	44, 100, 108, 142, 145, 306
1:3	46, 148	7:2–5	199
1:4	142, 234	7:2–6	313
1:6–7	276	7:3	127
1:9	276	7:4–5	131, 150, 200
1:15	142	7:5	51, 146, 212, 218–19, 312, 315
1:18	143	7:6	136, 199, 206, 305
2	121	7:7–9	60, 199
2:9	303	7:8	43

7:9	303	8:24–25	197
7:10	126	8:25	52, 131, 147, 257
7:11	198	8:25–26	197
7:12	43	8:26	131
7:13	61	8:26–28	215
7:14	154	8:27	197, 237
7:15	148, 241, 250	8:27–28	219
7:19–20	61	8:27–29	197
7:25	148, 198	8:28	221
8	162, 196, 202	8:30	61
8:1	199, 276	8:31	140
8:1–2	211	8:33	209, 228
8:1–29	313, 316, 324	8:35	136, 150
8:2	197, 206–7, 215, 218, 237, 315	9	
8:2–24	157	9:1–2	22, 197
8:3–9	211	9:3	131
8:4	217	9:6	65
8:4–8	207	9:6–7	154
8:5	146, 209, 218	9:8	15, 297
8:5–6	203, 207, 210–11, 217, 219, 315	9:9	170
		9:15	135–36, 261
8:6	125, 127, 200, 207–10, 217–18, 315	9:16	146
		9:18	61, 128, 135–36, 261
8:7–8	217	9:19	61, 148
8:9	100	9:20	139
8:10	136, 197	9:21	135
8:10–14	211	9:24	303
8:10–29	197	9:27	135
8:11	212, 214, 217–19	10:1	131, 197
8:12	206, 218	10:1–5	22
8:14	215, 218–19, 315	10:6	65, 131, 150, 213
8:14–15	203, 214, 217, 219	10:11b	47
8:15	44, 215, 218–19, 315	10:14	275
8:16	99, 209, 217	10:24	132, 154
8:17	217	10:25	144
8:19	145, 203, 212–13, 218–20, 312, 315	10:25	276
		10:28	216
8:19–22	216	10:29–39	80
8:20	214–15, 217–18, 238, 313, 315	10:30	216
8:20–21	131, 203	10:40	61
8:21	203	10:42	61
8:22	216, 218	11:1–4	22
8:23	146	11:1–5	197
8:24	131, 203, 211, 215–16, 218–19, 308, 313, 315	11:3	142
		11:6	148, 153, 308

Joshua (cont.)

11:8	51, 142	17:16	133, 149
11:9	148, 308	17:17	307
11:11	148, 308	18:1	70, 107, 128, 135, 137, 264
11:12	216	18:1–10	307
11:14	237	18:2	154
11:19	131	18:4	149
12:1	141–42, 147	18:6	307
12:3	142	18:8	149, 307
12:7	141, 147	18:8–10	70, 107
13–19	131, 302, 331	18:9	66
13:5	142	18:11	307
13:6	290	18:12	100
13:7	154	18:12–13	101
13:8	142	18:16	139
13:14	61	18:20	151
13:21	303	18:21–28	91, 102
13:23	151	18:22	102
13:28	151	18:25–28	22
13:33	61	18:28	89, 91, 138, 151, 304
14–24	36	19:1	151
14:1	141, 261	19:4	100
14:1–2	307	19:7	104
14:2	26, 270	19:8	151
14:9	46, 148	19:9	151
14:14	61	19:10	307
14:15	168	19:12	142
15–19	312	19:13	104
15:8	139	19:15	103–104, 297
15:15	131, 168	19:16	151
15:20	151	19:27	142
15:32	104	19:34	142
15:59b	103	19:40–48	311
15:63	131, 138, 304	19:45	104
16:1–2	101	19:46	145
16:3	152	19:47	298
16:8	151	19:49	298
16:9	151	19:50	298
17:2	130, 137	19:51	26, 70, 107, 270
17:3	141	20:6	135
17:5	290	20:9	135
17:6	130	21:1	261
17:7	131	21:2	70, 267
17:11	131	21:4–8	26, 270
17:14	307	21:5	130
		21:16	154

21:20	130, 307	24:1	136, 154
21:24–25	104	24:2	61
21:26	130	24:8	125, 149
21:34	130	24:11	86, 150
21:40	130	24:12	303
21:43–44	303	24:23	61
22	129–30	24:26	102
22:2	303	24:27	135, 198
22:6	149	24:28	69, 308–9
22:7	154	24:28–30	311–12
22:9	66, 70, 264, 267–68	24:28–31	311
22:9–10	66	24:28–33	284
22:9–16	273		
22:9–32	313	Judges	
22:9–34	263–74, 318, 324, 333	1	131, 284, 303–5, 307, 312, 331
22:10	264, 268	1–18	155
22:10–11	264	1–21	319
22:11	264–65	1:1	282, 284,
22:12	26, 66, 70, 128, 135, 137, 265, 268–70	1:1–2	157, 307, 309–10
		1:1–36	301–2, 304
22:13	268, 270, 315	1:1–2:5	284–86, 301–12, 310–13, 315, 318, 331–33
22:13–14	263		
22:13–15	265	1:3	26, 270, 307–8
22:14	261, 270–72, 315	1:4–18	302
22:15	268	1:8	148, 237, 304, 308, 309, 313
22:16	128, 266, 269, 272–74, 315	1:10	168
22:16–18	135	1:11	131, 168
22:17	263, 269–70	1:19	131
22:18	135, 269	1:21	138, 304, 309
22:19	264, 266	1:21–36	302–3
22:20	135, 263, 269	1:22	127
22:21–29	266	1:23	168
22:24	61	1:25	216, 237
22:24–25	264	1:27	131
22:27	140	1:27–34	302
22:30	135, 261, 269, 271	1:30–31	131
22:30–32	263, 270	1:33	131
22:32	268, 271	1:34–35	311
22:33	147, 269	2:1	302, 305, 308–9, 315, 318
22:34	264	2:1–3	303
23:4	142, 290	2:1–5	102, 284, 301–6, 308–12
23:13	146, 303	2:1–6	309
23:15	149	2:3	146
23:16	213	2:4	309, 315
24	331	2:4–5	305

Judges (cont.)

Ref	Pages
2:5	102, 302, 306
2:6	69, 308–9, 315
2:6–9	311–12
2:6–10	284, 311
2:6–16:31	2, 285
2:7	284
2:7–12:15	333
2:10–11	284
2:10–3:6	312
2:11	288
2:11–13	288
2:18	149
2:22	127
3–12	131, 333
3:1	141
3:6	138
3:7	287–88
3:12	133, 287–88
3:14	133
3:15	133
3:17	133
3:18	133
3:26	193
3:29	132, 147
4	47
4:1	287–88
4:5	39
4:10	99
4:12–13	22
4:13	99
4:14–15	83
4:16	61, 147, 152
5	47
5:4	150
5:8	46
5:14	154
5:19	46
5:23	303
5:24	46
5:26	46
5:31	142
6:1	287–88
6:5	127, 255
6:9	303
6:10	303
6:11–12	303
6:13	140
6:16	222
6:21–22	303
6:28	303
6:30–32	303
6:34–35	99
6:36–40	82
7:2	1
7:3	140
7:6	130
7:8	154
7:9	83
7:14	154
7:15	65
7:16	40
7:22	61
7:23	154
7:23–24	99
7:25	147
8	127
8:1–3	199, 266
8:2	148
8:5	127, 131, 150
8:8	131, 150, 275
8:9	131, 150
8:10	130, 147, 132–33
8:14–16	131
8:16	86
8:19	127
8:22	154
8:24	127, 218
8:26	32
8:27	303
8:31	124
9	86, 150, 154
9:6	145
9:25	206
9:27	46, 148
9:40	147
9:43	40
9:44	237
9:49	131
9:52	148

9:54	213	17-21	4, 283-84, 287
9:55	154	17:1	3, 23, 80-81, 284, 292, 295, 300, 311, 314, 333
9:57	131, 150		
10:6	287-88	17:1-18:31	285-86
10:14	127	17:1-21:25	285
10:17	99	17:3-4	288
10:18	246, 131	17:3-5	3
11		17:5	288, 292, 311
11:8	131	17:6	3, 5, 12-13, 284, 287, 295, 315-16
11:11	206		
11:39	258	17:7	12-13, 291-93, 297
12		17:7-9	103, 133, 293, 312, 314
12:1	99, 148	17:7-10	3
12:4	131, 150	17:8	80-81, 292, 297
12:5	131, 150	17:8-9	3, 292
12:6	147	17:8-10	294
12:8-10	103, 297	17:8-11	15
12:15	333	17:9	15, 292, 297
13-16	154, 300	17:10	146, 292
13:1	287-88	17:10-13	292
13:2	12, 291, 300	17:11	292
13:3	303	17:12	288, 292
13:5	300	17:13	292
13:7	300	18:1	3, 5, 12-13, 74, 154, 287, 290, 295, 298, 311, 314
13:12	124		
13:13-21	303	18:1-10	307
13:15-20	15	18:2	80-81, 132
13:16	214	18:3	127, 145, 292
13:18	126	18:5-6	292
13:23	141, 153, 275	18:7	127
14-16	287	18:10	297-98, 313-14
14:2-3	138	18:12	139
14:10	124	18:13	80-81
14:19	124	18:14	288
15:7	275	18:14-20	3
15:11	266	18:15	292
16:2	46, 141, 145	18:17-18	288
16:9	209	18:19	154
16:12	209	18:19-20	292
16:17	300	18:19-26	3
16:20	37, 214	18:20	288
16:31	124	18:22	48, 127, 137, 145
17-18	3, 12-13, 37, 127, 154, 284, 286-301, 311-13, 316, 318, 324, 331, 333	18:22-23	99
		18:24	138
		18:26	127

Judges (cont.)

18:27	127, 148, 237, 292
18:27–31	290
18:28	298–99
18:29	139
18:30	3, 37, 85, 154, 284, 288, 292, 294, 300, 315
18:30–31	3, 288, 300
18:31	70, 107–8, 285, 294–95, 299–300, 333
19–21	9–77, 284, 286, 312
19:1	12–14, 24, 79, 128, 133, 138, 293, 295, 297, 300, 325
19:1–2	12, 14, 103–4, 133, 158, 176, 246, 312
19:1–9	292
19:1–30	13–20, 28
19:1–20:13	45
19:1–21:24	79
19:1–21:25	285–86
19:2	14, 79, 124, 133, 145, 247–48, 297
19:3	15, 17, 19, 125, 129, 145–46, 156
19:3–6	246, 248
19:3–9	75, 186, 190–93
19:3–10	15, 194, 313, 314
19:4	14–15, 79, 145–46, 190, 278
19:4–8	278
19:4–9	81
19:5	14, 79, 129, 190–91, 278
19:6	190–91
19:7	129, 146, 190
19:8	14, 79, 129, 145, 193, 195, 279
19:8–9	79, 190, 246, 248
19:8–14	85
19:9	14, 17, 28, 124, 129, 138, 145–46, 190–91
19:9–10	191, 246
19:9–11	155
19:9–12	156
19:10	14, 28, 124, 129, 133, 139, 152, 214, 284
19:10–11	138–39, 304, 318
19:10–12	304, 309, 326
19:10–13	81, 85
19:10–25	179
19:11	14, 17, 22, 79, 126–27, 139, 145, 317
19:11–13	178
19:12	18, 28, 112, 123, 133, 154–56, 248, 317
19:12–13	313
19:12–16	14, 82
19:13	14, 17, 146, 175, 316
19:14	14, 22, 44, 79, 82, 144–45, 297
19:14–15	15
19:14–17	156
19:14–24	313
19:14–28	81
19:15	14, 22, 27, 85, 125, 128–29, 142, 176, 283
19:15–25	174–86
19:15–28	14–15
19:16	14, 44–45, 79, 82, 124, 128, 130, 156, 327
19:16–17	16, 82, 176
19:16–21	294
19:17	14–15, 22, 27, 33, 128, 133, 142, 283, 297
19:18	16–17, 81, 103–4, 128, 133, 291, 297, 312
19:18–19	16
19:19	17, 143, 178–79, 278, 297, 313
19:20	14, 16, 18, 85, 142, 176, 180–81
19:21	125
19:21–22	14, 156
19:22	2, 18–19, 22, 27–28, 44–45, 82, 125–28, 130, 133, 150, 177–78, 181–82, 184, 225, 239
19:23	28–29, 82, 133, 178, 182–83, 193, 241, 250
19:23–24	183–84, 250–51, 253, 313
19:23–28	314
19:24	28, 123–125, 133, 155–56, 178–79, 183–84, 241, 250, 252
19:24–25	246
19:25	14, 19, 28–29, 44–45, 79, 124–25, 129, 145–46, 156, 177, 193, 195, 251–52
19:26	14, 79, 129, 145–46

INDEX OF ANCIENT SOURCES 393

19:26–27   14, 79, 129, 132, 158
19:27   124, 128–29, 246
19:28   14, 17, 125, 128, 156, 247–48, 251, 253
19:29   4, 14–15, 124–25, 156, 223–24, 246, 279, 282–83, 317
19:29–30   30, 223
19:29–20:1   221–22, 224
19:29–20:2   20
19:29–20:13   22
19:30   13, 15, 24, 28, 128–29, 146, 152, 154, 158, 222
19:30–20:7   265
19:30–20:13   273–77, 281, 317, 322
20–21   308
20:1   23–25, 27–29, 66, 75–76, 83–84, 99, 128, 135–36, 152, 154, 268–69, 273, 295, 307, 317–18
20:1–2   4, 21, 23, 25, 27, 76, 261, 265, 318
20:1–3a   24–25
20:1–6   155
20:1–10   27
20:1–11   37
20:1–12   273
20:1–13   22–31, 75
20:1–17   30–31
20:1–18   22
20:1–28   55
20:1–48   13
20:2   23–25, 27–29, 64, 68, 74, 76, 82–83, 128, 132–33, 150, 153, 155–56, 222, 226, 229, 282–83
20:2–3   22–23
20:3   28, 76, 82, 99, 136, 146, 152, 154, 261, 273
20:3–5   157–58
20:3–6   265
20:4   28, 76, 82, 128–29, 133–34, 147, 292, 327
20:4–6   28, 242, 246
20:4–7   16, 18, 21, 26, 241, 269
20:4–10   22
20:5   85, 129, 150, 282–83, 314
20:5b–7   134

20:6   21, 25, 28–29, 76, 82, 85, 125, 133, 137, 150, 153, 156, 207, 241, 250
20:7   28, 155, 157, 281
20:8   25–29, 63, 129, 145, 155, 157, 222, 261, 313, 316, 318
20:8–10   26, 134
20:8–11   4, 26
20:9   25, 27, 29, 66, 75, 144, 156, 269–70, 307, 309
20:10   21, 27–29, 66, 74, 85, 128–29, 153, 157, 271–73, 313
20:11   21–22, 23, 27–28, 76, 154, 157, 210, 266, 261, 273, 307, 313, 316, 318
20:11–13   27
20:12   24, 74, 129, 146, 153, 158, 261, 266, 272–74
20:12–13   21–24, 26, 29, 76, 82–83, 92, 134, 157, 241
20:12–14   327
20:12–16   82
20:12–17   25
20:13   1, 19, 21, 23, 28–29, 44–45, 77, 92, 129, 133, 144, 181, 224–26, 239, 242–43, 251–52, 266, 273, 313, 317, 322
20:13–14   82, 154
20:14   22, 24–25, 28, 83, 129, 316
20:14–16   23
20:14–17   24, 31, 76
20:14–22   317
20:14–48   28, 45, 92, 313
20:15   45, 44, 51, 75, 128–33, 156
20:15–16   32, 51, 55
20:16   25, 28, 51, 76, 128–29, 132–33, 140, 147, 155–56
20:17   24–25, 28, 75, 83, 128–29, 132, 140, 154–56, 212, 261, 307
20:18   31–33, 60–61, 75–76, 82–83, 101, 134, 157, 261, 291, 305, 307–10
20:18–19   154
20:18–25   21
20:18–28   32–37, 76, 291

Judges (cont.)
20:19   83, 154, 307
20:19–20   31, 34
20:19–21   230
20:19–22   313, 316
20:19–24   157
20:20   83, 154, 217
20:21   10, 23, 31, 34, 85, 147, 158, 212, 217
20:22   31, 34, 44–45, 79, 129, 154, 217
20:22–23   32
20:22–24   34
20:23   29, 31, 33–34, 60–61, 75, 77, 79, 82–83, 129, 134, 206, 305, 308–10
20:23–27   154
20:23–48   203–221
20:24   31, 34, 79, 217, 307, 313, 316–17
20:25   10, 23, 28, 31, 54, 79, 85, 128–29, 132, 140–41, 147, 155–56, 212, 217–18, 256
20:26   25, 28, 31, 60, 79, 82, 101, 140, 155, 206, 291, 305–6, 308–9
20:26–28   61, 75, 83, 310
20:26–48   21
20:27   79, 206, 218–19, 227–229, 308
20:27–28   31, 35, 126, 227
20:28   3, 21, 29, 36, 77, 83, 125, 128–29, 134, 257, 262, 270, 273, 284, 317
20:29   37–42, 53–55, 75, 128–29, 206–7, 218
20:29–30   31, 34
20:29–31   53–54, 56, 76, 200, 318
20:29–35   38–41, 51
20:29–42   157
20:29–48   37–58, 95, 196, 201, 217
20:30   31, 37, 39, 76, 79, 154, 217, 307, 316
20:30–31   37, 42, 53, 208, 210
20:30–32   207, 211
20:30–35   48, 201
20:31   10, 22–23, 27, 31, 39, 42, 44, 48, 52, 54–55, 76, 85, 128–29, 147, 157–58, 200, 207–9, 211–12, 218–19, 312
20:31–32   27, 38, 55, 203, 209, 216–19
20:31–34   40, 48, 54
20:32   22, 27, 39, 42, 44, 54, 101, 125–29, 134, 156, 200, 208–10, 218
20:32–33   56, 76
20:32–34   45
20:32–45   48, 94
20:33   27, 38–40, 42, 44, 48, 54, 75, 85, 128–29, 147, 151, 157, 213, 217–20, 312
20:33–34   40–41, 54, 212, 218–20
20:34   39–40, 44, 54, 126–27, 129, 132, 148, 202, 213–14, 217–19, 256, 312
20:35   10, 28, 31, 38, 40–41, 50–52, 54–55, 128–29, 132, 140, 147, 155–56, 210, 217, 313
20:36   10, 41, 44, 55, 128, 154, 201–2, 206–7, 218
20:36–38   38, 41, 53, 128
20:36–44   41–50, 54, 201
20:36–45   76
20:36–46   210
20:37   22, 27, 44, 48, 75, 92, 148, 158, 212–13, 216, 218–20, 236–37, 312
20:37–38   27, 42–42, 54, 203, 218
20:38   22, 27, 44, 125, 128–29, 151, 154, 156, 158, 201, 214, 217–19
20:38–43   158
20:39   38, 41–44, 48, 129, 147, 154, 200, 203, 209–10, 212, 218–19, 312
20:39–41   158, 201
20:40   22, 27, 42–44, 54, 92, 129, 151, 195, 203, 214–15, 218, 236, 238–39, 313
20:40–42   217
20:41   41, 44, 48, 54, 148, 154, 195, 214, 218–19, 312
20:41–43   44
20:42   44, 45, 48, 50, 54–55, 85, 125, 128, 132, 147, 149, 154, 200, 215–16, 218

INDEX OF ANCIENT SOURCES 395

20:42–43	44, 156, 201	21:5–9	313
20:42–48	272	21:5–14	59
20:43	45–48, 55, 75, 125, 141–42, 148, 152, 156, 214, 216–17, 317	21:6	10, 29, 52, 58–59, 63–64, 74–77, 93, 153–55, 188, 330
20:43–44	313	21:6–7	4, 60, 64, 67–68, 76, 188, 261
20:44	31, 50–52, 55, 140–41, 217	21:6–14	62–63
20:44–45	38	21:6–22	187
20:44–46	38, 155	21:7	58–59, 62–64, 67–68, 128–30, 156, 187, 282–83
20:44–48	31		
20:45	48, 50, 52, 56, 75, 85, 125, 137, 148, 156, 158, 187, 203, 215, 218–19, 317	21:7–9	263
		21:7–10	281
		21:7–12	282
20:45–46	50–51, 215	21:8	25, 27, 44–45, 63–64, 74–76, 82–83, 99, 153, 155, 318
20:45–48	50–53		
20:46	28, 38, 50, 52, 128, 132, 140–41, 156, 217, 313	21:8–9	64
		21:8–10	105, 261
20:47	48, 51–53, 55, 75, 187, 203, 215, 218, 227, 229, 317	21:8–12	59
		21:8–14	69–71, 188
20:47–48	56, 76	21:9	64–65, 75, 129–30, 156
20:48	10, 44–45, 52–53, 55, 75–76, 128, 130, 148, 154, 156, 188, 195, 203, 216, 218–19, 236–40, 262, 308–9, 313	21:9–10	129, 131–32
		21:9–12	75
		21:9–14	65
		21:10	25, 29, 125, 128–30, 135, 156, 256–57, 318
21:1	44–45, 59–60, 62–64, 68, 75–76, 83, 99, 129, 154, 187, 295, 305, 313, 315–17		
		21:10–11	65–66, 69, 76, 259–60, 321
		21:10–12	255, 257, 259, 262, 313, 318
21:1–3	261		
21:1–5	75	21:10–13	76, 155
21:1–23	45	21:10–14	187
21:1–24	28, 71	21:11	29, 66, 75, 129, 144, 156, 257, 259–60
21:1–25	58		
21:2	79, 82, 101, 291, 305, 309	21:11–12	137, 258, 262
21:2–4	59–61, 75, 307, 309–10	21:12	44–45, 64, 66, 75, 105, 107–8, 123, 125, 129–32, 155–56, 188, 247–48, 257–59, 263, 267–68, 282, 300–301, 313
21:2–5	76, 82, 321		
21:3	4, 52, 58, 61, 63, 74, 77, 93, 126, 129, 153, 155, 188, 261–62, 291, 313		
		21:12–13	76
21:4	60, 140, 306, 308–309	21:12–14	65
21:4–5	63, 154–55	21:13	29, 44, 75, 128, 135, 318
21:4–8	26	21:13–14	59
21:5	25, 27, 29, 59–60, 62–63, 65, 74–75, 82–83, 99, 129, 132–33, 136, 139, 143, 153, 155–56, 158, 261, 318	21:13–18	313
		21:14	44, 68, 105, 129, 149, 158
		21:14–15	59, 158
		21:15	44–45, 58, 67, 68, 74, 77, 93, 129, 149, 153, 158
21:5–8	4		

396 DISMEMBERING THE WHOLE

Judges (cont.)	
21:15–17	4
21:15–18	67–68, 75–76, 188, 321
21:15–23	59
21:16	28–29, 52, 58–59, 67–68, 76, 128, 130, 135–36, 149, 155–56, 158, 187–88, 261–63, 282–83
21:16–18	67
21:16–20	281
21:16–23	63
21:17	52, 58, 67–68, 74, 77, 93, 153
21:18	10, 16, 58, 62–63, 68, 129
21:19	70–71, 75, 101, 107–9, 142, 156, 300, 333
21:19–21	300, 107
21:19–22	70, 76
21:19–23	68–71, 187
21:20	71, 75, 129
21:20–22	313
21:21	70, 108, 129, 138, 155, 247
21:21–22	123
21:21–23	123
21:22	68, 70, 125, 129, 153, 155, 158
21:23	44–45, 69–71, 123, 129, 138, 143, 155–56, 298
21:23–24	76
21:24	12, 26, 29, 69, 74, 79, 149, 153, 155, 158, 308–9
21:25	3, 5, 12–13, 126, 285, 287, 295

1 Samuel	
1	17, 295, 299–301, 312, 331, 333
1–2	118
1–3	81, 333
1–4	70
1–7	287
1–11	71
1:1	12, 291, 300
1:3	70, 107–9, 300
1:3–22	333
1:3–28	70
1:7	81, 333
1:9	107–8
1:11	300
1:22	300
1:24	81, 107–8, 333
2:13	178
2:14	107
2:15	178
2:28	228
2:30	61, 149
2:35	36, 149
3:3	132
3:10	37
3:15	81
3:17	144
3:20	152, 237, 268
3:21	107–108
4	113, 288
4–7	331
4:3	60, 108, 126, 136
4:3–4	107
4:4	35, 107
4:9	34, 146
4:12	305
4:20	153
5:2	144
5:5	46, 148
5:7	150
6:15	150
6:17	141
6:18	52
7–10	99
7:1	150
7:1–2	228
7:7	22
7:9	151, 238
7:9–11	83
7:16	101
8–12	4
8:4	136
8:8	276–77, 314, 316, 322, 324
9:1	12, 291, 300
9:9	168
9:10	132
9:16	153
9:20–21	166
9:26	145
10:2–5	85
10:2	145

INDEX OF ANCIENT SOURCES

10:3	101, 308	13:15	85
10:5	85, 91, 95, 132, 221	13:16	85
10:5–7	92	13:16–18	44
10:8	140	13:17	40
10:10	85, 91, 95, 325	13:17–18	215
10:10–11	92	13:22	149
10:10–16	13	13:23	39
10:11	146	14	226–29
10:17	83–84, 99	14:2	85, 87, 221, 227, 229, 315–17, 324
10:17–25	98, 226	14:3	107, 228
10:18	61	14:4	39
10:23	282	14:6	1
10:25–26	149	14:8	315
10:26	85, 96, 221	14:8–10	82
10:26–27	157, 224–26, 315–17, 324	14:16	85, 87, 178
10:27	19, 229	14:18	35, 227–29
11	106, 161, 262, 325	14:18–19	228
11:1	105, 150	14:20	99, 227
11:1–11	224, 229	14:22	48, 137, 156
11:1–13	133	14:23	100, 228
11:3	105, 222, 282–83	14:24	156
11:3–4	106	14:26	139
11:4	85, 91, 106, 221, 305, 308, 325	14:26–28	83
11:4–7	95	14:30	69, 153
11:5	105	14:36	145–46
11:7	125, 144, 221–24, 282–83, 313, 316–17, 324	14:36–37	82, 228
11:9–10	105	14:37	228
11:11	40	14:38	25, 226, 229
11:12	139, 317	14:38–40	227
11:12–13	157, 224–26, 229, 315–16, 324	14:40	226
12:1–25	226	14:41	61, 228
12:2	149	14:44	144
12:14	303	14:46	228
12:15	303	15:3	52, 237
13:2	85, 130	15:19	288
13:3	85, 91, 95	15:19–20	303
13:3–5	22	15:22	303
13:4	99	15:34	12, 85, 91, 95, 149, 221
13:5	100	16:4	86, 103
13:6	156	16:8–12	166
13:8	43	17:2	156
13:9	140	17:4	167
13:13	69, 153	17:12	12, 103–4, 133, 297
		17:12–15	103

1 Samuel (cont.)

17:16	138	24:5–8	173
17:19	156	24:23	12, 83
17:23	167	25:2	124
17:24–25	156	25:12	43
17:27	126, 144	25:13	212
17:38	206	25:14–15	215
17:40–51	167	25:17	19, 308
17:41	146	25:21	260
17:47	125, 136	25:22	144
17:52	51	25:25	19, 182, 225
18:5	132	25:27	149
18:21	303	25:32	61
19:3	132	25:34	61, 145
19:4	124	25:36	145
19:6	83	25:39–40	138
20:6	103	26:1	85, 91, 95, 221
20:8	126	26:18	126
20:12	153	27:1	222, 325
20:13	144	27:7	133, 145, 314
20:14	137	27:11	144
20:18	260	28:1	12
20:19	144	28:10	83
20:25	37, 260	28:14	133
20:27	260	28:18	303
20:28	103	28:21	48
20:38	48, 148, 213	30:1	148
20:41	144	30:3	148
20:42	83	30:4	305, 308
21:4	130	30:7–8	82, 228
21:4–7	130	30:7–10	83
22:2	143, 212	30:9	130
22:6	85, 91, 95, 221	30:14	148
22:15	140	30:27	100
22:19	216, 237	30:27–31	133
23:2	82	30:31	149
23:2–4	307	31:1	147, 154
23:6	82, 228	31:2	48, 137
23:9–11	228	31:4	19
23:10–11	61	31:8–13	282
23:11–12	86	31:11	132
23:13	149, 212	31:11–13	105–6, 262
23:19	85, 91, 95, 221	31:12	132
23:27	213	31:13	107
24:3	132		

INDEX OF ANCIENT SOURCES 399

2 Samuel		10:9	216
1:2	305	10:10	130
1:5	152	10:12	34
1:6	48	10:14	127
1:12	305	10:18	147
1:14	147, 152	11:1	147
1:19	152	11:2	138, 149
1:20	142	11:9	247
1:19	152	11:16	132
1:25	152	12:9	138, 288
1:27	152	12:11	281
2:4–5	105, 131–32	12:18	152
2:4–7	106	12:21–23	266
2:5–7	263	12:23	126
2:22	152	12:28	130
2:24	145	13	134
2:30	260	13:2	133
2:32	103	13:4	133
3:9	144	13:6–8	133
3:10	152, 268	13:7	247
3:17	136	13:10	133
3:24	126	13:11	251
3:32	308	13:11–17	248–55, 313, 316, 324
3:34	225	13:12	18–19, 182–83, 241, 250–51, 253, 313
3:35	144		
4:1	48	13:14	19, 251–52
4:5	258	13:16	251–52, 313, 315
5:3	136	13:17	133, 252, 314
5:6	139, 304	13:20	133
5:14	141	13:22	19, 133, 152
5:17–18	22	13:25	182
6:8	149	13:27	253
6:9	152	13:32	19
6:17	140	13:36	308
6:18	140	14:2	39
6:19	152, 154	14:5–7	297
7:6	149, 152, 276–77, 314, 322	14:10	148
7:7	149	14:11	83
7:10	209, 225	14:13	150, 275
7:11	152	14:19	140
9	283	15:4	143
9:9	178	15:6	61
10:2	149	15:12	281
10:7	22	15:12–17:23	281
10:6	257	15:13	154

2 Samuel (cont.)

15:14	237	20:19–20	261
15:23	305	20:21	80–81
15:24	228	20:22	12
15:28	193	21	281–83
15:30	305	21–24	13, 283, 285
15:31	281	21:1–14	313, 318, 313, 318, 333
15:34	281	21:2	124, 156
16:1	133	21:2–3	282
16:7	181, 225	21:2–5	281–84
16:15	154	21:3	151
16:18	154	21:5	149, 222, 282–83, 314
16:20	281	21:6	84, 91, 221
16:20–21	281, 315	21:7	139
16:23	281	21:9	91
17:1	257	21:12	105–6, 138, 142, 150, 263, 282
17:4	136	21:14	328
17:7	281	21:17	83
17:11	152, 268, 281	22:17–20	47
17:12	130	23:5	303
17:14	154, 281	23:9	154
17:15	136, 275, 281	23:12	282
17:16	213	23:24	103
17:18	213	23:29	85
17:21	213, 281	24	134
17:22	145	24:2	152, 268
17:24	154	24:9	132
18:15	46, 141	24:12	123
18:22	126	24:15	152, 268
19:14	144	24:16	149, 303
19:15	222	24:16–17	147
19:24	83	24:25	140
19:25	152		
19:42	138	1 Kings	
19:42–44	154	1:2	75, 247, 259
19:43	146	1:3	222, 282
20:1	12, 181	1:6	144
20:2	154	1:9	144–45
20:4–5	99	1:11	214
20:6	149	1:17	83
20:8	145	1:25	145
20:11	63, 143	1:27	126, 146
20:14	137	1:29	83
20:17	146	2:7	146
20:19	151	2:23	144
		2:26	228

INDEX OF ANCIENT SOURCES 401

2:26–27	36	9:21	130
2:27	107	9:22	132
2:29	144	9:25	140
2:35	36	10:1–13	275
2:43	139	10:9	206
3:12	275	10:11	275
3:15	140	10:12	127, 275, 314
4:2	141	10:15	32
4:8	141	10:19	144
4:11	146	11:6	288
4:12	144	11:9	61
5:3	32	11:11	61
5:5	152, 268	11:15–16	137
5:6	257	11:26	12, 292
5:7	146	11:27	144
5:8	278	11:29	108
5:15	124	11:33	288
5:21	206	11:38	288
6:24	237	12:3	136, 150
7:9	140	12:15	108
7:16	206	12:16	149
7:16–42	46, 141	12:18	198
7:31	124	12:20	135–36
7:37	275	12:21	137
8:1	136–37	12:23	130
8:1–3	154	12:24	146
8:2	137, 154	12:27–29	308
8:3	136	12:28–29	37
8:5	135–36	12:28–32	36
8:14	136, 150	12:28–33	291
8:15	61	12:29–33	101
8:16	276–77, 314, 322	12:31	36, 288
8:17	61	12:32–33	291
8:20	61	13:1	64, 101
8:21	132	13:4	101
8:22	136, 150, 213	13:6	209
8:23	61, 276	13:10–11	101
8:25	61, 276	13:18	198
8:31	139	13:24–25	144
8:41–42	170	13:28	144
8:55	136, 150	13:31	144
8:59	146	13:32	101
8:65	136	13:33	288
9:16	149	13:34	149
9:20	124, 156	14:3–4	108

1 Kings (cont.)		22:20	2
14:3–4	108	21:1–2	144
14:6	126	21:3	83, 213
14:7	61, 206	21:3–4	151
14:12	251	21:7	314
14:13	61	21:10	181
14:22	288	21:13	181, 225
15:2	89	21:20	288
15:5	288	21:25	288
15:10	89	22:17	123
15:11	288	22:43	288
15:17–22	98	22:53	288
15:18	104, 130		
15:19	303	*2 Kings*	
15:22	85, 91, 94	1:3	303
15:26	288	1:15	303
15:29	108	2:2–3	101
15:30	61	2:17	190
15:34	288	2:18	306
16:2	206	2:23	101, 306
16:13	61	3:2	288
16:19	288	3:10	125
16:25	288	3:13	125
16:26	61	3:21	22, 99
16:30	288	3:25	46, 141
16:31	138	3:26	132–33
16:33	61	4:7	130
17:17	150	4:16	182
18:23	222	4:16–17	153
18:31	143	5:2	246
18:33	222	5:4	275
19:2	153	5:16	190
19:7	303	5:18	104
20:6	153	5:20	178
20:9	209	5:22	64, 80
20:29	147	6:14	46, 141
20:30	130	6:15	46, 141, 152
20:34	142	6:31	144
20:36	303	7:1	153
20:39	260	7:9	145
21:10	19, 133, 239	7:13	130
21:13	19, 133, 239	7:18	153
21:21	242	7:19	61
22:6	33, 307	8:1	251
22:9	213–14	8:11–12	305

INDEX OF ANCIENT SOURCES 403

8:12	148, 308	17:30	131, 150
8:18	288	17:31	149
8:27	288	18:3	288
9:12	275	18:5	45, 275
10:4	152	18:8	52
10:6	153	18:12	303
10:9	141	18:14	80
10:19	260–61	18:24	152
10:29	101, 291	19:21	144
10:30	288	19:35	303
10:32	222, 282	20:3	149, 305,
10:33	142	20:13	130
11:2	138	20:15	137, 237
11:5	25–26, 144	20:20	45
11:8	46, 141	20:39	260
11:15	132	21:2	288
11:18	303	21:3	69
12:3	288	21:5	276
12:10	144	21:6	288
13:2	288	21:9	149
13:11	288	21:12	61
14:3	288	21:14	146
14:7	147	21:15	275, 277, 288, 314, 322
14:13	149	21:16	288
14:24	288	21:20	288
15:3	288	22:2	288
15:9	288	22:19	305
15:10–14	105	23:2	152
15:16	237	23:4	101
15:18	288	23:11	149
15:24	288	23:15	110, 303
15:28	288	23:15–19	101
15:29	80	23:16	132
15:34	288	23:20	132
16:2	288	23:25	275
16:5–9	90	23:32	288
16:10	124	23:37	288
16:17	206	24:7	237
17:2	288	24:9	288
17:7–23	143	24:16	132
17:13	223	24:19	288
17:16	288	25:1	40
17:17	288	25:4	40
17:27–28	291	25:9	149
17:28	101, 152	25:11	130

2 Kings (cont.)

Reference	Pages
25:17	46, 141
25:19	130
25:22–25	98
25:22–30	331

Isaiah

Reference	Pages
1:4	47
1:4–9	185
1:10	47
1:16–17	47
1:21	146, 153
1:24	149
1:26	209
2:3	92, 308
2:8	133
2:18	151
3:9	184
5:19	124, 148
5:25	140, 142
5:27	209
7	90
7:17	152
8:1	148
8:3	148
8:23	153
10:6	142
10:7	282
10:12	124
10:27	90
10:27–32	90
10:28–29	85
10:29	39, 84, 89
11:7	278
11:15	46, 148
13	130
13:8	48
13:9	185
13:10	124, 142
13:15	130
13:19	184–85
14:17	247
14:24	282
15:3	142
15:8	46, 141
16:13	144
17:6	148
17:8	45, 138
17:14	26, 307
19:13	226
19:14	124
19:19	144
21:3	48
22:3	130
22:4	305
22:12	305
23:8	141
24:5	303
24:11	138, 142
24:13	148
27:1	166
28:1	142
28:21	124
29:9	193
30:29	92
31:2	225
32:7	137
32:9–11a	47
33:8	303
34:14	139
37:22	144
37:36	303
39:2	130
39:4	236
39:6	236
40:18	282
40:25	282
41:25	142
42:16	46, 148
42:17	43
43:20	215
44:7	45
45:6	142
45:7	140
46:5	282
48:17	46, 148
48:19	149
50:8	143
50:11	61
51:9–10	166

INDEX OF ANCIENT SOURCES 405

54:16		124	9:7		206
55:1		45	9:11		45
55:3		303	9:20		142
55:7		225	10:18		303
57:6		26, 397	11:2		131
58:6		209	11:5		139
58:14		151	11:7		276–77
59:14		142	11:9		131
59:19		142	11:12		131
60:22		148	11:19		261
61:8		303	11:21		131, 150
62:3		142	11:23		131
66:2		140	12:2		146
65:15		139	12:14		148
65:25		278	12:15		308
66:7		137	13:13		131, 303
66:8		275	13:18		141
			13:27		137
Jeremiah			14:22		141
1:14		303	15:16		146
2:10		275	16:2		138
2:34		141	17:20		131
3:7		141	17:25		131
3:18		64	17:26		98
3:25		303	18:8		149
4:4		131	18:10		149
4:15		81, 291	18:11		131
5:1		142	19:3		131
5:13		144	19:5		145
5:19		141	20:15		137
5:30		146	20:18		126
6:1		151	21:10		145
6:3		40	23:10		139
6:9		48, 148	23:14		184
6:12		303	23:28		278
7:7		152	25:2		131
7:12		107–8, 113, 209	25:5		152
7:12–14		107	25:29–30		303
7:14		107, 113	26:1		126
7:25		152, 276–77	26:2		27
7:28		261, 303	26:3		149
8:1		131	26:6–9		107
8:6		149	26:13		149, 303
8:8		152	26:19		149
9:2		46, 148	27:1		126

Jeremiah (cont.)

Ref	Pages	Ref	Pages
27:3	223	41:5	108
27:5	133	41:6	305
27:16	213	41:17	103, 144
27:18	130	42:6	303
27:19	130	42:8	152
27:21	130	42:10	149
28:7–9	168	42:13	303
28:9	177	42:16	137
29:14	149	42:18	131, 139
29:18	139	42:21	303
29:23	18, 241, 250	43:7	303
30:6	137	43:13	145
31:6	83, 308	44:12	139
31:34	152	44:14	27
32:22	303	44:23	148, 303
32:31	152	44:28	27
32:32	131	46:9	132
32:40	303	48:13	100, 291
32:44	98	48:17	152–53
33:7	209	48:19	146
33:11	209	48:28	131
33:13	98	48:31	131, 150
34:2	145	48:36	131
34:3	124	48:38	142
34:22	145	48:42	282
35:4	144	49:8	131
35:13	131	49:9	148
35:17	131	49:18	184–85
36:1	126	49:20	131
36:31	131	49:26	142
37:8	145	49:30	131
37:12–15	110	50:5	303
38:17	145	50:14–15	40
38:18	145	50:20	133
38:19	19	50:30	142
38:20	303	50:34–35	131
38:21	25, 144	50:40	184–85
38:22	130	51:4	147
38:23	145	51:12	131
39:8	145	51:24	131
39:9	130	51:32	48, 145
40–41	98	51:33	46, 148
40:5	151	51:35	131
41:3	130	51:47	147
		51:62	152

INDEX OF ANCIENT SOURCES 407

52:7	40	16:60	303
52:13	145	17:9	209
52:15	130	17:15–16	303
52:22	46, 141	17:18	140, 303
52:25	130	18:2	169
		18:3	170
Ezekiel		18:11	140
1:13	149	18:12	241
1:15	144	18:17–18	45
3:7	252	19:1	136
3:15	45	19:6	149
4:2	40, 206	19:8	40
4:5	143	20:1	136
6:7	147	20:3	136
6:13	140	20:8	252
7:27	48	20:40	151
8:1	136	21:12	146
8:3	132	21:17	136
8:11–12	136	21:28	139
8:16	212	21:30	136
9:2	144	22:6	136
9:5–6	147	22:9	137
9:6	143	22:10–11	19
9:8	147	22:11	137, 241
10:6	144	23:7–8	145
10:9	144	23:17	258
11:15	131	23:21	137
11:18	241	23:24	40
12:19	131	23:27	137
14:1	136	23:29	137
14:4	147	23:34	209
14:7	147	23:35	137
15:6	131	23:39	144
16:12	141	23:44	137
16:15–16	145	23:47	198
16:17	137	23:48–49	137
16:24	142	24:4	222
16:27	137	24:6	26
16:30	140	24:13	137
16:31	142	26:18	48
16:36	146	27:3	151
16:40	198	27:8	131
16:43	137, 140	27:9	86
16:44–58	184–86	27:11	40
16:58	137, 140	28:12	151

Ezekiel (cont.)		6:9	137
28:14	149	7:10	140
29:6	131	8:8	261
30:4	147	8:14	148
32:2	147	9:1	17
32:7	124	9:7–8	93
33:21	64	9:9	93, 95, 322
32:22–24	147	9:15	98
33:30	144	10:5	36, 98, 101, 291
35:15	151	10:9	93–95, 112, 322
37:19	154	10:15	144
37:26	303	11:1–2	94
38:4	132	12:4–5	94
39:6	148	12:5	101–2, 305–6
39:8	146	12:9	149
40–48	135	12:11	282
40:7	144	12:12	98
42:1	290		
43:8	144	Joel	
43:17	124	1:2	61, 303
43:27	140	1:14	303
45:8	154	1:19–20	215
45:9	136	2:1	303
45:15	140	2:2	146, 275
45:17	140	2:12	305
46:2	140		
47:13	154	Amos	
47:14	290	1:4	148
47:20	152	1:7	148
47:22	290	1:10	148
48:1	154	1:12	148
48:29	290	2:2	148
		2:5	148
Hosea		2:8	144
1:2	17	2:9	149
4:12	17	3:14	101, 291
4:13	98	4:4	101
4:15	98, 100–101	4:11	184–85
5:1–2	98	5:3	272
5:8	89, 91, 98, 101	5:5–6	101
5:8–14	90	5:11	151
5:8–6:6	91	5:16	142
5:10	90	6:10	133
5:13	90	7:10	101
6:8	225	7:13	291

INDEX OF ANCIENT SOURCES 409

8:12	237	Habakkuk	
8:14	291	1:4	46, 141
9:8	149	1:8	148
9:10	148	2:3	148
9:14	298	3:6	46
		3:10	124
Obadiah		3:13	46
1–9	11	3:14	46
5	148	3:15	46
11	213	3:16	46
19	151	3:19	46, 148
Jonah		Zephaniah	
1	129	1:15	152
1:7	26	1:18	48, 303
1:8	297	2:9	184–85
1:10	303	3:2	303
3:5	150		
4:7	145	Haggai	
4:11	14	1:2–11	329
		1:7–8	329
Micah		1:13	303
1:5	140	2:13	140
2:5	26, 150, 270	2:18	152
2:13	149		
3:2–3	45	Zechariah	
3:5	45	1–8	118
4:2	92	1:10–11	149
4:6	45	1:11–12	303
4:10	147	2:12	148
4:14	206	3:1	303
5:1	103–104	3:5	303
6:14	45	6:11	141
7:1	148	6:15	303
7:2	124	7:2	100, 102
7:6	181	7:3	305
7:10	142	7:12	223
7:12	152	8:2–15	329
7:13	146	8:3	92
		8:4–5	142
Nahum		8:7	142
2:4	124	8:10	146
2:5	142	8:12	140
		8:17	139
		9:1	154

Zechariah (cont.)

9:3	278	34:8	303
10:10	149	34:10	298
10:12	149	34:22	148
11:6	303	35:5–6	303
11:10	303	37:28	261
12:11	104	37:38	261
13:3	124	38:23	148
14:2	130	40:14	148
14:7	138	44:18	140
14:10	89, 104, 152	48:6	48
14:16	130	48:10	282
		50:1	52, 142
		50:21	282
Malachi		51:21	151
1:4	69	55:9	148
1:9	61	55:12	142
1:11	142	58:8	149
1:14	137	59:7	138
2:6	124	59:15	138
2:7	124, 303	60:2	147, 257
2:16	61	62:13	124
		63:9	137
Psalms		64:10	124
5:6	213	65:12	141
5:10	124	69:23	303
5:13	141	69:36	298
6:3–4	48	70:2	148
6:11	48	70:6	148
8:6	141	71:12	148
10:7	124	74:7	148, 308
10:9	138	74:13–17	166
13:21	303	77:4–7	47
17:9	46, 141	78:12	151
18:9	214	78:43	151
18:17–20	47	78:55	303
21:4	141	78:64	305
22:13	46, 141	80:13	149
22:20	148	83:18	48
24:3	92	89:10–11	166
25:5	46, 148	90:6	138
25:9	46, 148	90:7	48
26:3	149	90:10	148
26:10	137	91:10	146
30:8	48	96:1–13	314
33:4	124	103:4	141

INDEX OF ANCIENT SOURCES 411

103:22	124	6:22	148
104:2	93	6:24	123
104:3–10	166	7:8	143–44
104:17	132	7:12	142, 144
104:29	48	9:4	143
104:31	124	10:23	137
105:1–15	314	13:19	146
105:9	139	14:7	217
105:10	303	14:18	46, 141
105:15	148	16:11	124
106:13	124	16:23	124
106:25	303	16:26	124
106:36	303	16:27	181
106:47–48	314	19:14	151
107:7	46, 148	19:24	124
107:22	124	20:7	149
111:6	124, 151	20:17	124
113:3	142	21:27	241
118:23	61	22:13	142, 147
119:35	46, 148	24:7	124
119:60	148, 193	24:9	137, 241
119:150	137	28:22	48
122:4	308	30:14	279
124	118		
127:3	151	Job	
132:5	149	1:1	12, 291, 300
137	118	1:5	144
137:1	305	1:7	149, 297
141:1	148	1:12	181
141:2	151	1:17	40
142:8	46, 141	2:2	149
144	118	2:7	52
144:14	142	2:12	308
145:9	124	3:1	124
145:17	124	3:25	45
151	118	4:5	48
		4:17	124
Proverbs		4:20	138
1:20	142	5:19	48, 148
4:9	141	8:6	153
4:11	46, 148	8:18	261
5:8	247	12:9	140
5:10	123	16:14	149
5:20	123	18:8	149
6:12	225	19:9	141

Job (cont.)		2:4	103
20:2	148	2:5	246
21:6	48	3:3	177
21:18	138, 278	3:7	314
23:15	48	4:2	86
24:12	52	4:7	168
25:3	124	4:11	103
26:8–13	156		
28:8	46, 148	Lamentations	
29:3	124	1:1	153
29:7	85, 142	1:13	148
31:11	137	1:18	124
33:29	140	2:1	153
35:16	124	2:11–12	142
36:2	46, 141	2:13	282
36:30	124	2:15	151
37:3	124	3:29	124
37:7	124	4:1–2	153
37:11	124	4:6	184–85
38:8	147	5:11	19
38:8–11	156	5:16	141
39:18	153		
40:23	124, 147	Qoheleth	
41:9	124	3:11	237
41:19	278	3:15	45
		3:22	124
Canticles		4:12	209
1:2	124	6:7	124
1:7	152	7:23	140
1:9	282	7:28	140
2:10	251	8:2	139
2:13	251	8:3	48
3:2	142–43	8:9	140
3:6	214	9:1	140
		9:2	139
Ruth		9:4	63, 143
1:1–2	103, 133, 297	10:13	124
1:2	103	10:14	45
1:4	138	11:6	138
1:6	150	11:9	140
1:9	308	12:4–5	143
1:14	308		
1:17	138	Esther	
1:19	103	1:5	152
1:22	103	1:11	46

INDEX OF ANCIENT SOURCES 413

1:20	152	2:28	102, 150
2:2–3	75, 247	2:61	138
2:3	259	3:1	222
2:5	12	3:3	138
2:7	246	4:1	61
2:17	46	4:3	61
2:18	151	4:6	131
4:6	85, 142	6:17	154
4:13	282	6:21	61
4:14	275	7:5	36
5:1	247	7:6	61
5:13	140	7:27	275
6:8	46	8:3–14	137
6:9	85, 142, 144	9:13	275
6:11	85, 142, 144	9:15	61
7:8	45	10:5	61
8:15	141	10:8	136
		10:9	61, 142
Daniel		10:14	136, 237
2:1	146	10:44	138, 140–41
5:12	143		
8:7	144	Nehemiah	
8:17	144	1:2–3	130
8:27	146	1:5	276
9:4	276	1:9	296
9:10	303	3:2	131, 150
9:11	139	3:7	89, 98, 131, 150
9:14	124	3:7–17	98
9:21	153	3:13	131
9:25	142	3:20	247
10:13	144	3:23	144
11:26	147	3:35	149
12:1	130, 146, 275	4:8	130
12:7	140	4:13	130
		4:15	145
Ezra		5:12–13	61
1:3	61	6:8	146, 275
2:21	104	6:14	104
2:22	150	6:17	45
2:22–23	131	6:18	139
2:23	150	7:3	131
2:23–28	330	7:4	329
2:26	89	7:25	89
2:27	150	7:26	104, 150
2:27–28	131	7:26–33	131

Nehemiah (cont.)		6:54	104		
7:27–32	330	6:55	130		
7:28	150	6:62	130		
7:29	150	7:7	261		
7:30	89, 150	7:8	140		
7:32	102	7:11	140		
7:33	150	7:40	140		
7:70–71	45	8:2	47		
8:1	85, 142, 222	8:6	261		
8:3	85, 142, 145	8:10	261		
8:16	85, 142	8:28	261		
9:24	303	8:38	140		
9:32	276	8:40	46, 140		
10:1	140	9:9	140, 261		
10:30	139	9:33	140, 261		
10:35	26	10:1	154		
11:1	26	10:2	137		
11:1–2	329	11:4	303		
11:29	104	10:7	154		
11:30	152	10:11–12	105		
11:31	89, 102	11:4	139, 304		
12:22	261	11:4–5	138–39		
12:29	89	11:31	85		
13:1	150	12:1–2	133		
13:6	140	12:1–41	133		
13:15	46, 148	12:2	132, 147		
13:18	144	12:9	133		
		12:24–25	132		
1 Chronicles		12:25–26	133		
1:23	140	12:29–31	133		
1:32	245	12:31	181		
1:33	140	12:33–34	133		
1:46	151	12:38	154		
2:23	140	12:39	133, 140		
2:51	104	12:41	140		
2:54	104	13:2	150		
4:4	103	13:14	145		
4:30	100	15:25	136		
4:32	104	16:1	140		
4:41	130	16:2	140		
5:18	46, 154	16:12	124		
5:30	36	16:16	139		
5:30–31	36	16:17	303–304		
6:46	130	16:40	138		
6:46–50	26	17:9	209		

17:21	303	2 Chronicles	
19:2	149	1:11	61, 126
19:10	216	1:12	175
19:11	130	2:3	138
19:15	127	3:1	124
20:5	167	4:12–13	141
21:4	149	5:3	154
21:5	132	6:46	137
21:10	123	7:7	140
21:12	147, 282, 303	8:2	298
21:15	145, 149	8:8	130
21:15–18	303	9:11	127
21:16	136	9:12	43
21:26	140	9:18	144
21:30	303	9:29	108
22:6	61	10:15	108
22:12–13	276	11:4	146
22:18	303	11:16	61, 154
23:14	154	11:18	138
23:25	61	11:21	138
23:30	138	13:2	89, 95
24:3	36	13:3	132
24:5	26	13:5	61
24:6	261	13:14	216
24:19	61	13:17	132, 147
24:20	130	13:21	138
25:5–6	140	14:7	46, 132, 140–41, 148
26:8	140	15:2	149
26:10	124	15:4	61
26:16	145	15:13	152
26:32	154	15:15	139
27:1	143	16:1–6	98
27:16	154	17:13	181
27:25	85	17:17	132
27:31	140	17:18	132
28:1	154	18:16	123
28:4	61	19:4	152
28:8	150	20:1–30	134
28:9	149	20:7	303
29:6	154	20:15	131
29:8	130	21:18	131, 140
29:10	61	20:19	61
29:17	140	20:20	131
		20:22	206
		20:23	131

2 Chronicles (cont.)

20:24	147
21:2	140–41
21:11	131
21:13	131
21:19	153
22:1	131
23:4	25–26, 144
23:14	132
24:3	138
24:6	151
24:9	151
24:11	144
26:11	32, 132
28:15	144
29:4	85, 142
29:29	130
29:32	140–41
30:1	61
30:5	61, 152, 268
30:26	275
31:1	140, 303
31:2	140
31:4	131
31:10	130
31:16	137
31:19	137
31:20	275
32:6	142
32:15	275
32:22	131
32:26	131
32:30	124
32:33	131
33:3	69, 303
33:9	131, 149
34:4	303
34:9	131
34:21	130
34:22	275
34:30	131
34:32	131
34:32–33	130
35:7	130, 143
35:18	131
35:20	140
36:15	223

Dead Sea Scrolls

Community Rule	136
Damascus Document	136
Dibrei Moshe	5, 276
Miqṣat Haʿaśê ha-Torah	276
Pesher Habbakkuk	136
Temple Scroll	5, 276

West Semitic Inscriptions

Amman Citadel	121
Arad	
16	121
17	121
24	121
40	121, 145
Deir ʿAlla	121
Ekron	121
Eshmunazer (KAI 14)	143
Ḥorvat ʿUza	121
Kilamuwa (KAI 24)	143
Kuntillet ʿAjrud	121
Lachish	
3	121
4	121, 151
Mesha (KAI 181)	121

INDEX OF ANCIENT SOURCES 417

Nerab (*KAI* 225, 226)	143	Pseudo-Philo, *Biblical Antiquities*	2, 34, 161
Panammu (*KAI* 214)	150		

MISHAH AND TALMUDS

Sefire (*KAI* 222–224)
  iA   150, 223, 233
  iii   150

Mishnah
Bekorot	138
Berakot	146
Bikkurim	138
Ketubbot	138
Peʾah	150
Qiddushin	138
Roš Haššanah	152
Sanhedrin	140
Šabbat	150
Soṭah	138
Taʿanit	70
Yebamot	138

ANCIENT NEAR EASTERN TEXTS

Babylonian Chronicles	234
Esarhaddon treaty (VTE)	233
Gilgamesh	13
Hammurabi's Laws (CH)	17, 189, 258
Hittite Laws	189
Mati'ilu and Assurnirari treaty	233
Middle Assyrian Laws (MAL)	17, 244
Sinuhe	13
Ugaritic texts	135
Wenamun	135

Babylonian Talmud
Baba Batra	138
Baba Meṣiʿa	138
Baba Qamma	150
Berakot	140, 150
Beṣah	138
Ketubbot	150
Megillah	140
Pesaḥim	150, 152
Qiddushin	138
Roš Haššanah	140
Sanhedrin	2, 146
Šabbat	140
Temurah	140
Yomah	140

GREEK AND LATIN AUTHORS

Eusebius, *Onomasticon*	39, 105
Jerome, *Letters*	85
Josephus, *Jewish Antiquities*	3, 32, 35, 59, 62, 103–4, 161, 214, 223, 284, 293, 331
Josephus, *Jewish War*	85
Livy, *History*	178

Jerusalem Talmud
Ketubbot	138

MIDRASH

Esther Rabbah	146
Exodus Rabbah	140, 146
Genesis Rabbah	138, 146, 150, 188

Lamentations Rabbah	140
Leviticus Rabbah	140
Mekilta R. Shimon	140
Mekilta R. Yishmael	140
Numbers Rabbah	140
Qoheleth Rabbah	146
Sifre Deuteronomy	20
Sifre Numbers	138
Tanḥuma	138

Medieval Jewish Commentators

Abravanel	45, 50, 81, 223, 293
Gersonides	59, 284
Ibn Ezra	93, 188
Isaiah di Trani	3, 284
Kimchi	43, 52, 81, 93, 108, 177, 212, 284
Nachmanides	161, 177
Rashi	20, 81, 93, 177, 188, 284

Index of Modern Authors

Achenbach, Reinhard 262
Adams, William J. 120
Aharoni, Yohanan 86, 91, 103, 215, 304
Aḥituv, Shmuel 121, 196, 212, 264–65
Ahlström, Gosta W. 228
Aichele, George 160
Albrektson, Bertil 173
Albright, William F. 39, 84–87, 96, 105, 196
Alt, Albrecht 91
Alter, Robert 15, 165, 179
Amit, Yairah 10, 13, 15, 29, 34, 37, 55, 70, 80–82, 102, 104, 108, 112, 186, 198, 222, 224, 227, 242, 260, 262–63, 286–87, 289–90, 292–97, 303, 305, 307, 317, 325–26
Anbar, Moshe 136, 141
Andersen, Francis I. 91, 93, 148
Arnold, Patrick M. 85, 90, 93–94, 105, 175, 196, 276, 293
Arnold, William Rosensweig 34, 228
Assis, Eliyahu 264–65, 268
Auberlen, Carl August 3, 104, 285, 326, 332
Auld, A. Graeme 117, 284, 286, 302, 304, 307, 309
Avigad, Nahman 104
Avioz, Michael 81, 88, 139,
Bach, Alice 1
Bal, Mieke 1
Bar-Efrat, Shimon 29
Barr, James 122
Barthes, Roland 163
Barton, John 254
Bauer, Uwe F. W. 286, 289

Bautch, Richard 162
Bechtel, Lynn M. 19
Becker, Uwe 3, 6, 9, 12, 16, 21, 23, 25–26, 32–34, 36, 51, 53, 59–60, 63–67, 69, 81, 83–84, 94, 153, 156, 209–10, 223–24, 276, 285–86, 289–90, 293–95
Bedford, Peter Ross 318, 329
Beentjes, Pancratius C 142
Begg, Christopher 198
Bendavid, Abba 116, 118, 128
Ben-Porat, Ziva 168–69
Ben Zvi, Ehud 99, 118, 120
Bergey, Ronald 164
Berlin, Adele 168
Bertheau, Ernst 9, 32, 44, 51–52, 59, 63, 66, 108, 153, 222, 255, 286, 294–95
Besters, Andre 9, 50, 53, 66, 81, 83, 153, 155
Beuken, Wim A. M. 102
Biddle, Mark E. 162, 164
Bleek, Friedrich 16, 34, 104, 108, 222, 224, 286, 295, 317, 326
Blenkinsopp, Joseph 36, 83–84, 90, 92, 94, 99, 101–3, 110–11, 117, 119, 130, 135, 228, 255, 291, 318, 328
Blum, Erhard 301–4, 306, 310–11
Bodi, Daniel 15
Boecker, Hans Jochen 241, 265–66
Bohmbach, Karla G. 19
Böhme, W. 59, 65, 69, 108, 225, 260, 262
Boling, Robert Gordon 4, 59, 175, 177, 181, 197, 211–12, 264–65, 285, 295
Born, Adrianus van den 85, 175

-419-

Brettler, Marc Zvi   104, 112, 118, 135, 174, 179, 183, 224, 302, 309–11, 317, 326, 328
Briant, Pierre   329
Brown, Ken   260, 262
Buber, Martin   5
Budd, Philip J.   66, 129, 256, 262
Budde, Karl   3, 6, 9, 14, 23–24, 39, 46, 53, 59, 63, 65–67, 70, 83, 138, 141, 175, 178–79, 213, 222, 226, 283–86, 293
Burney, Charles Fox   3, 6, 9, 14, 17, 21, 23–26, 33–34, 36, 39, 43, 45–47, 50–51, 53, 59, 63, 65, 134, 141, 148, 161, 175, 193, 195–96, 213, 222, 255, 260, 285–86, 295, 302, 304, 307, 309, 331
Butler, Trent C.   264
Callaway, Joseph A.   197
Campbell, Antony F.   21
Carlson, Rolf August   249, 283
Carr, David McLain   135, 254
Carroll, Robert P.   168
Cassuto, Umberto   166
Chapman, Cynthia R   178
Charlesworth, James Hamilton   165–66
Childs, Brevard S.   163, 166
Christensen, Duane L.   90
Coats, George W.   262
Cody, Aelred   36
Cross, Frank Moore   36, 46, 135, 294
Crouch, Carly L.   233
Crüsemann, Frank   5, 9, 12, 32–33, 83, 135, 210, 286–87, 289, 293, 295–96, 307, 325–26
Culler, Jonathan   163, 165, 169
Culley, Robert C.   162
Cundall, Arthur Ernest   186
Dadon, Michael   96
Davidson, Robert   168
Davies, Graham I.   94
Davies, Philip R.   93, 228, 328
Day, John   107, 166
De Vries, Simon J.   83
Demsky, Aaron   85
Derrida, Jacques   162

Dietrich, Walter   197–98, 226
Dijk-Hemmes, Fokkelien van   249
Dion, Paul-Eugene   233–35, 240–41, 243
Dorsey, David A.   39, 44, 85, 215
Doyle, Brian   177, 248
Driver, Godfrey Rolles   45, 146
Driver, Samuel Rolles   70, 166, 134–35, 138, 228
Dumbrell, William J.   285
Dus, Jan   53, 64–65, 83, 99
Edelman, Diana Vikander   105, 328
Edelstein, Gershon   140
Edenburg, Cynthia   92, 118, 132, 134, 150, 163, 166–67, 170, 173, 197, 211, 235, 244–45, 281, 283–84, 289, 303, 331
Ehrensvärd, Martin   116, 118
Ehrlich, Arnold Bogumil   45, 52, 64, 67, 213
Eissfeldt, Otto   9, 16, 24, 34, 45, 63, 66, 69, 178, 285, 286–87, 293, 307, 327
Elliger, Karl   136, 261
Elwolde, John F.   117–20
Emmerson, Grace I.   93–94
Engelkern, Karen   245
Eskhult, Mats   117, 120, 126, 128
Exum, J. Cheryl   9, 14, 163, 285
Fales, Frederick Mario   233
Faust, Avraham   89
Fewell, Danna Nolan   163
Finkelstein, Israel   85–89, 93–94, 96, 98, 100–101, 107, 110–11, 185
Fishbane, Michael   108, 139, 168, 171, 302
Fitzmyer, Joseph A.   233
Floyd, Michael H.   169, 172
Fokkelman, Jan P.   13
Fowler, Mervyn D.   82
Fox, Michael V.   170
Frankenberg, Wilhelm   210, 285–86, 307
Freedman, David Noel   46, 91, 93, 148
Fritz, Volkmar   85, 210, 264–65
Frow, John   162
Frymer-Kensky, Tikva S.   19, 244
Garrett, Duane A.   91

INDEX OF MODERN AUTHORS

Gass, Erasmus 47, 52, 85, 88, 96, 104–5, 108
Genette, Gerard 10
Gertz, Jan Christian 135
Geus, Cornelis H. J. de 86, 111
Gibson, John C. L. 142, 150
Gibson, Shimon 140
Gitin, Seymour 121
Gnuse, Robert 70, 333
Gogel, Sandra Landis 120–21
Goldstein, Ronnie. 129, 265, 269–70
Gooding, David W. 285
Gordis, Robert 135, 170
Gordon, Pamela 19, 178
Graham, John Allen 84, 86–88
Gravett, Sandra Lynne 19
Gray, John 3, 6, 9, 21, 24, 26, 32, 45–47, 50–51, 59, 70, 81, 83, 94, 99, 102, 108, 135, 141, 148, 151, 175, 177, 179, 196–97, 210, 222, 260, 285–86, 289, 295, 302, 305
Greenfield, Jonas C. 104
Grintz, Jehoshua M. 196
Gross, Walter 9, 13, 19, 21–22, 25, 27, 33, 37, 46, 60, 64, 66, 76, 82, 111, 151, 153, 177, 179, 222–23, 225, 239, 249, 276, 291, 293, 307, 311, 324, 327, 333
Güdemann, Moritz G. 15, 81, 104, 112, 293, 295–97, 317, 326
Guenther, Allen R. 138
Guillaume, Philippe 84, 91, 111, 178, 289–90, 302, 329–30, 333
Gunkel, Herman 175, 181, 185, 188–89
Gunn, David M. 2, 165
Gurewicz, S. B. 286
Halpern, Baruch 47
Haran, Menahem 82, 99, 135, 311
Harper, William Rainey 94
Harrison, Timothy P. 233
Hebel, Udo J. 1989 169–70
Hentschel, Georg, 2, 9, 22, 53, 83
Hertzberg, Hans Wilhelm 92, 99, 106, 108, 197
Hoffman, Yair 170
Hoffmann, David Z. 241
Holscher, Gustav 135, 240
Honeyman, Alexander Mackie 52, 237
Hoop, Raymond de 104, 222, 326
Horst, Friedrich 232, 235, 240–41
Houston, Walter J. 47, 50
Hübner, Ulrich 105, 139, 304
Hurvitz, Avi 116–18, 120, 122, 135, 144, 151, 171
Hutzli, Jürg 117
Hyatt, J. Philip 102
Irvine, Stuart A. 94
Jacobsen, Thorkild 135
Japhet, Sara 90
Jastrow, Marcus 138, 143
Jeremias, Jörg 90–91, 98
Joosten, Jan 9
Joshel, Sandra Rae. 178
Jüngling, Hans-Winfried 9, 12–14, 16, 21, 24, 81, 94, 153, 156, 161, 175, 177–79, 183, 223, 230, 241, 143, 145, 176, 179, 293, 296, 323, 325
Kaufmann, Yehezkel 66, 81, 135, 177–78, 181, 213, 155, 260, 264, 286–87
Keefe, Alice A. 134, 249
Kelso, James Leon 100–101
Kim, Dong-Hyuk 121
Klein, Lillian R. 9, 179
Klein, Ralph W. 226, 228
Kloppenborg, John S. 66, 129, 265
Knauf, Ernst Axel 91, 101–2, 117, 120–22, 197, 256, 302, 330
Knierim, Rolf P. 262
Knoppers, Gary Neil 328
Koch, Christoph 233–35
Koch, Ido 86
Köhlmoos, Melanie 101–11
Kottsieper, Ingo 62
Kratz, Reinhard Gregor 185, 284, 303, 311
Kristeva, Julia 162–64
Kropat, Arno 116
Kugel, James Lewis 168
Kutscher, Eduard Yehezkel 116, 138
Labahn, Antje 163
Landsberger, Benno 158

Lauinger, Jacob 233
Lapp, Paul W. 86–89
Lapp, Nancy L. 86–89, 110, 328
Lasine, Stuart 1, 9, 20, 134, 161, 172, 174–75, 179, 187, 224
Lemaire, Andre 120, 163
Lemche, Niels Peter 111
Levin, Christoph 12, 117–18, 185, 280, 291
Levine, Baruch A. 129, 132–35, 255–56, 258, 260, 262, 264–65
Levinson, Bernard Malcolm 233
L'Hour, Jean 243
Licht, Jacob 257
Lipiński, Edward 275
Lipschits, Oded 86, 89, 97, 99, 101, 104, 108, 110, 112, 328, 330
Lissovsky, Nurit 101
Liverani, Mario 16–17, 21, 66, 75, 146, 187, 223
Loader, J. A. 181, 187
Locher, Clemens 242–45
Lohfink, Norbert 4
Lundbom, Jack R. 231
Macchi, Jean-Daniel 141
MacDonald, Burton 105
Macintosh, A. A. 90, 93–94
Magen, Yitzhak 96, 100, 110
Mai, Hans-Peter 163
Magonet, Jonathan 172–74
Matthews, Victor H. 176, 180
Mayes, Andrew D. H. 4, 9, 83, 156, 159, 231, 243, 285–87, 295–96, 307, 325
Mays, James L. 93
Mazar, Amihai 44, 88
Mazor, Lea 162, 196, 203, 206, 219
McCarter, Peter Kyle 91–92, 99, 130, 136, 154, 224, 226, 228, 283, 332
McCown, Chester Charlton 93
McKenzie, John L. 86
McKenzie, Steven L. 99, 130, 132, 173, 255
Meer, Michael N. van der 196, 203, 219
Merendino, Rosario Pius 230, 235, 243, 245

Mettinger, Tryggve N. D. 162
Milevski, Ianir 89, 101, 110
Milgrom, Jacob 135
Miller, J. Maxwell 85, 139, 223, 226
Miner, Earl Roy 165, 169
Möhlenbrink, Kurt 264–65
Montgomery, James A. 105, 275
Moore, George Foot 3, 9, 14, 16, 21, 24–26, 32–34, 37–39, 41, 43, 45–47, 50–52, 59, 63, 65–67, 69–70, 81, 85, 93–94, 102–3, 105, 130, 132, 141, 148, 151, 153–54, 175, 177, 181, 193, 196, 203, 206, 209, 213, 222, 226, 255, 260, 262, 285–86, 302, 307, 331
Mueller, E. Aydeet 13, 289, 296
Muilenburg, James 82, 96, 99
Mullen, E. Theodore 302–3, 305
Müller, Reinhard 12, 291
Na'aman, Nadav 26, 36, 80, 84–86, 90–91, 93–95, 98, 100–103, 105–6, 108, 139, 220, 224, 226–28, 242, 254, 283, 289–90, 292, 296, 330
Nahkola, Aulikki 166
Neef, Heinz-Dieter 98
Nelson, Richard David 36, 70, 91, 103, 162, 196–98, 203, 210, 233, 241, 244, 264–65, 302, 304
Niccacci, Alviero 46
Niditch, Susan 12, 18, 32, 59, 161, 175, 177, 181, 194, 235, 262, 265
Nielsen, Eduard 198, 235, 243–44, 247
Niessen, Christina 2, 9, 22, 53, 83
Nihan, Christophe L. 135, 226
Nobel, Paul R. 165
Nogalski, James D. 164, 166, 168, 171–72
North, Francis S. 101–2
Noth, Martin 3, 12, 14, 33–34, 53, 59, 63, 84, 99, 106, 136, 197, 210, 212, 256, 261–62, 285–86, 289–90, 295, 302, 307, 325, 332, 333
Nowack, Wilhelm 70
O'Brien, Mark 3, 226, 231, 285–86, 289, 302, 309
O'Connell, Robert H. 9, 223, 235, 285, 293–94, 332

O'Connor, Michael Patrick	142	Roth, Wolfgang M. W.	93, 196, 327
Ofer, Avi	103	Rothenbusch, Ralf	244
Olyan, Saul M.	18, 258	Rudin-O'Brasky, Talia	47, 62, 162, 175, 179, 181, 186-87, 189, 196, 263, 279
Osborne, James F.	233		
Oswalt, John	90	Rudolph, Wilhelm R.	93-94
Otto, Eckart	142, 198, 231-35, 240, 243-45, 275, 331	Rütersworden, Udo	234-35, 242-43
		Sæbø, Magne	163
Otzen, Benedikt	19, 182, 225	Salvesen, Alison	46, 141
Pakkala, Juha	198, 234, 240	Sandmel, Samuel	166
Peckham, Brian	4-5, 285-86, 332	Sarna, Nahum	168
Penchansky, David	176	Sass, Benjamin	104
Phillips, Anthony	18, 245	Satterthwaite, Philip E.	9, 37
Phillips, Gary A.	163	Schley, Donald Gilmer	108
Polak, Frank	10-11, 15, 20, 34, 46-47, 74, 118, 122, 128-30, 133, 144, 167, 189	Schmid, Konrad	117, 135, 185, 280
		Schmidt, Ludwig	262
		Schniedewind, William M.	119-20
Polzin, Robert	14, 41, 116, 120, 123, 138, 213, 223	Schulte, Hannelis	84, 162, 175, 285-87
		Schunck, Klaus-Dietrich	4-5, 9, 33, 53, 63, 65-66, 83, 99, 153, 155, 159, 196, 222, 224, 276, 285-86, 293, 327
Pressler, Carolyn	244, 259		
Propp, William Henry	249		
Pury, Albert de	3, 285, 290, 302	Seeligmann, Isac Leo	12, 41, 47, 198
Qimron, Elisha	116, 119-26, 128	Segal, Moses Hirsch	123, 128
Rad, Gerhard von	175, 189, 254	Seidel, Moshe	172
Rake, Mareike	301-3	Seitz, Gottfried	230-33, 235, 238, 241-43
Redford, Donald B.	143		
Rendsburg, Gary	119-20	Sergi, Omer	86
Revell, Ernest John	9, 34, 37, 41	Shemesh, Yael	19
Reviv, Hanoch	27, 86, 189	Singer-Avitz, Lily	100-101, 111
Rezetko, Robert	117-21	Ska, Jean-Louis	280
Ribichini, Sergio	100	Skinner, John	188-89
Richter, Wolfgang	21, 333	Smend, Rudolf	284-85, 302-3, 305, 309
Riffaterre, Michael	163, 168-69	Smith, Henry Preserved	92, 100, 283
Ringgren, Helmer	243	Smith, Mark S.	119
Rochberg, Francesca	166	Snaith, Norman Henry	255, 262, 264
Rofé, Alexander	36, 143, 232, 239, 241-45, 249, 275, 279	Soggin, J. Alberto	16, 38-39, 41, 45-45, 51-52, 70, 81, 83-84, 103, 108, 141, 153-54, 156, 159, 161, 175, 178, 181, 193, 197, 223, 264, 285, 286-87, 294-95, 305
Röllig, Wolfgang	100		
Römer, Thomas	3, 135, 185, 197, 220, 231, 235, 277, 285, 290, 302		
Rooker, Mark F.	41, 116, 118-20, 123, 213	Sommer, Benjamin D.	164, 168-70
		Stackert, Jeffrey	233
Rose, Margaret A.	170, 172	Stadler-Sutskover, Talia	29, 134
Rösel, Hartmut Nahum	33, 39, 53, 105, 155, 162, 171, 196, 210	Stern, Ephraim	89, 97
		Sternberg, Meir	11
Rost, Leonhard	254	Steymans, Hans Ulrich	233

Stipp, Hermann-Josef 6, 12–13, 16–18, 21, 139, 146, 156, 179, 186, 190, 249, 254, 291, 193, 326
Stoebe, Hans-Joachim 226, 228
Stone, Ken 177
Stone, Lawson Grant 286–88, 327
Stuart, Douglas K. 90, 93
Sweeney, Marvin A. 12, 255, 332
Tadmor, Haim 105, 120, 234, 329
Tal, Oren 112
Talmon, Shemaryahu 3, 11, 42, 284
Tidwell, N. L. 39
Toorn, Karel van der 254
Tov, Emmanuel 17, 81, 136, 173, 206
Trebolle Barrera, Julio 27
Trible, Phyllis 1, 9, 14, 248, 279, 293, 297
Tull, Patricia Kathleen 162–64, 169
Unterman, Jeremiah 279
Utzschneider, Helmut 91
Van Seters, John 117, 140, 166, 174, 185–86, 189, 255, 277, 280, 303–4
Vaux, Roland de 99, 196
Veijola, Timo 4–5, 33–34, 59, 63, 66, 82–84, 99, 102, 142, 159, 224, 226, 230–31, 234–35, 240, 243, 275–76, 285–87, 289, 295–96, 302, 304, 307, 325, 331
Verheij, Arian J. C. 118, 128–29
Wallis, Gerhard 21, 223
Washington, Harold C. 19, 178
Watson, Wilfred G. E. 46
Wazana, Nili 47
Webb, Barry G. 9
Weinberg, Joel 318
Weinfeld, Moshe 27, 231, 233, 235, 265, 302–5
Weiser, Artur 99
Weisman, Ze'ev 289
Weiss, Meir 65, 207
Weissenberg, Hanne von 276
Wellhausen, Julius 34, 39, 94, 98, 102, 134, 161, 174, 195–96, 287, 302, 331
Welten, Peter 87
Wenham, Gordon J. 177, 186–87, 189, 244, 259

Westermann, Claus 66, 161, 175, 177, 181, 189
Whybray, Roger N. 11, 134–35, 167
Williamson, Hugh G. M. 90, 98, 102, 104, 318, 330
Willis, Timothy M. 269
Wilson, John Albert 135
Wilson, Robert R. 4
Wolde, Ellen van 19, 163–64
Wolff, Hans Walter 90, 93–94, 98, 129, 314
Wong, Gregory T. K. 4, 265, 304, 306, 332
Wright, Addison G. 170
Wright, David P. 258
Wright, Richard M. 151
Yoreh, Tzemah 280
Young, Ian 118–21, 128–29, 136, 145, 147
Younger, K. Lawson 22, 284, 302
Zakovitch, Yair 15, 70, 172, 295, 300
Zehnder, Markus 234
Zenger, Erich 185
Zevit, Ziony 135, 196–97
Zimmerli, Walter 212
Zorn, Jeffrey R. 96–100

www.ingramcontent.com/pod-product-compliance
Lightning Source LLC
Chambersburg PA
CBHW021351290426
44108CB00010B/189